Leonard H. Clark
JERSEY CITY STATE COLLEGE

Raymond L. Klein
UNIVERSITY OF ARIZONA

John B. Burks
JERSEY CITY STATE COLLEGE

THE AMERICAN
SECONDARY
SCHOOL
CURRICULUM

The Macmillan Company, New York
Collier-Macmillan Limited, London

First Printing

Library of Congress catalog card number: 65-10244

THE MACMILLAN COMPANY, NEW YORK
COLLIER-MACMILLAN CANADA, LTD., TORONTO, ONTARIO

Printed in the United States of America

Preface

In the past most teachers and parents alike have uncritically accepted the secondary-school curriculum as good. Consequently, except for some minor changes, the secondary-school curriculum has remained about the same for many years.

Now, however, there is no longer a passive acceptance of the *status quo* in secondary schools. Day after day both scholarly journals and the popular press hold the secondary-school curriculum up for criticism and propose schemes for improving it. Even so, neither the American people nor the educational profession know exactly what it is they expect of the high school. Even people who are experts in the field of secondary education do not know. For example, Fred Wilhelm says:

> If some community were to come to the leaders in secondary education and, "We'll give you the money and the freedom to develop the right high school program," is there any one of us who could give them a clear image of what we would aim at? Could we genuinely resolve the conflicting needs and demands upon secondary education, and properly serve all the amazingly diverse youth? I'm not so sure. I think we've been kidding ourselves a good bit, while we mentally derogate the principals and teachers because they haven't found the solutions.[1]

Under the circumstances it is small wonder that many Americans believe the time has come to take a good, hard look at the secondary-school curriculum and reappraise it. This book should help the student make such an examination and appraisal, for it is designed to describe the theory and substance of the secondary-school curricula in American senior and junior high schools. To this end it tries to present the background of secondary-school curricula, the present situation, and even some possible courses of action, in the hope that the reader may find clues that will help him to understand, if not solve, some of the many problems connected with these curricula. Specifically the introductory chapters explain the foundation of curriculum theory and present different points of view, some

[1] Fred T. Wilhelm, "The Importance of People," *Educational Leadership,* 16: 43, October, 1958.

typical European solutions to secondary-school curriculum problems, and a statement of our own position.

The major portion of the book examines the curriculum subjects, the cocurriculum, curriculum organization, and the processes of curriculum evaluation and development. The chapters on the various curriculum subjects attempt to show the present situation in the disciplines and to spot trends. This approach holds also for the other chapters. In all of them there is considerable reference to specific school programs and special notice of new developments within the field, even though an entire chapter centers exclusively on recent advances.

At times we point out the directions in which we think school programs should develop. In those cases where we have done this, the recommendations represent the opinions and beliefs of the individual writers, for all three authors insist on retaining their rights, as scholars and individualists, to their own points of view. On the whole however, in spite of minor disagreements, the position presented has in every case come from an eclectic, middle-of-the-road, somewhat conservative philosophy.

Nevertheless, the book is descriptive rather than prescriptive. Except for the chapter "The Role of the Secondary School," which is a frank attempt to advocate a position, we have tried to present different points of view objectively and to describe the situation as it exists rather than as we wished it existed. It is for this reason that the book is organized according to the traditional subjects—not because we necessarily think that the curriculum should be so organized.

We hope to give the reader a good understanding of what the American secondary-school curriculum is like, how it got to be that way, and where it seems to be going. We believe the book will be useful in both graduate and undergraduate courses in the secondary-school curriculum and to curriculum workers, administrators, teachers, and others interested in American secondary education.

We wish to acknowledge our indebtedness to the many persons— students, teachers, and friends—who have helped us write this book. Grateful thanks are due to the students, teachers, school districts, state departments of education, and publishing houses who have allowed us to reproduce their materials. We are particularly grateful to the teachers and administrators at local, state, and federal levels who have taken time to answer our questions and to furnish us with materials, to William R. McCoy for his help with the bibliographies, and to Maria A. Clark who not only typed the manuscript innumerable times, but also read and proofread the copy and suggested many improvements.

LEONARD H. CLARK
RAYMOND L. KLEIN
JOHN B. BURKS

Contents

Chapter 1

Some Lessons
from the History
of Education

The modern secondary-school curriculum is a product of its past. Although our philosophies of education, the needs of our communities, the desires and goals of our pupils and their parents, and the social climate all influence what we teach, when all is said and done it is the past that has made our secondary-school curricula what they are today.

EDUCATION IN ANCIENT TIMES

EDUCATION OF PRIMITIVE MAN

We do not, of course, have much direct knowledge of the education of prehistoric man, but we can infer a lot from the archeological evidence and from what we see in present-day "primitive" cultures.

In those early days education was a family matter. Hunting and food gathering were taught largely through imitation and games and actual experiences. This education was realistic and practical. Mothers and fathers, and sometimes other members of the tribe, did the teaching. In addition the curriculum for adolescents was largely concerned with preserving the traditions of the tribe. Children learned the traditions through stories told about the campfire, but for adolescents learning the tribal lore and religious secrets was much more rigorous. The men taught these things to the boys in a strenuous training period shortly before the boys were to be initiated into manhood. In similar fashion girls were taught

1

the tribal lore by the women of their tribe. Vestiges of these ancient practices may be seen in our modern commencement activities and in the coming-out parties of society debutantes.

As soon as specialized vocations, artists, and shamans for instance, began to appear, it became necessary to teach certain youths these professions. Thus specialized vocational education began. In earliest times the teaching was most likely done through some sort of apprenticeship system in which the young person assisted the artist or shaman, who, in turn, taught the youth the secrets of his craft. In some instances these ancient specialists seem to have conducted vocational schools.

> At Limeuil in the Dordogne a number of trial pieces executed on pebbles have been collected. They may be the copybooks of an art school; on some pieces corrections, as if by a master's hand, have been noticed. The artist-magicians were experts, specially trained for their task.[1]

SCHOOLS IN THE EARLIEST CIVILIZATIONS

Early in the history of both the Fertile Crescent and the Nile Valley the temples gained control of vast amounts of property. To administer such great estates required a system for accounting, measuring, and record keeping. Because of this need, the priests invented reading, writing, and arithmetic. Soon thereafter these new inventions forced them to create temple schools in which to teach young aspirants for the priesthood how to read, write, and figure and to carry out the duties of priesthood. Thus we see that the first secondary schools were both utilitarian and vocational.

Although these early secondary schools were functional at first, after a time they became formalized, ivory-towered, old-fashioned, and bookish. Long after Sumerian had ceased to be a living language, schools in the Fertile Crescent continued to give it an honored place in the curriculum. In Egypt too scholarship tended to point to the past.

> Instead of demanding that a book should be up to date and embody the latest discoveries, the Egyptian or Babylonian student valued it for its antiquity. A publisher would then advertise his wares not as a "new and revised edition," but as a faithful copy of a fabulously old text. And so the "jacket" of the Rhind Mathematical Papyrus runs: "Rules for enquiring into nature and for knowing all that exists. The role was written in the thirty-third year of King Aauserre in the likeness of a writing of antiquity made in the time of King Nemare (1880–1850 B.C.). It was the scribe Ahmose who made this copy".[2]

Probably this inclination of men in our earliest civilizations to orient their scholarship and curriculum toward the past came from their tend-

[1] V. Gordon Childe, *Man Makes Himself* (New York: New American Library of World Literature, 1951), p. 56.
[2] *Ibid.*, pp. 150–151.

ency to venerate the written word. For in ancient days writing was magic.
As Childe[3] says,

> . . . The immortalization of a word in writing must have seemed a
> supernatural process; it was surely magical that a man long vanished
> from the land of the living could still speak from a clay tablet or a
> papyrus roll. Words thus spoken must possess a kind of *mana*. Thus
> learned men in the East, like schoolmen in our own Middle Ages, were
> apt to turn to books in preference to Nature.

At any rate, the early curriculum did not take long to become bookish
and out of touch with the realities of contemporary life.

That the first secondary schools were utilitarian and vocational is true;
it is also true that they were aristocratic. The young men trained in the
priestly schools were destined to be leaders and rulers. Not for them was
the common man's lot. As an ancient Egyptian document puts it,

> Put writing in your heart that you may protect yourself from hard labor
> of any kind and be a magistrate of high repute. The scribe is released
> from manual tasks; it is he who commands. . . . Do you not hold the
> scribe's palette? That is what makes the difference between you and the
> man who handles an oar.
>
> I have seen the metal worker at his task at the mouth of his furnace
> with fingers like a crocodile's; he stank worse than fish-spawn. Every
> workman who holds a chisel suffers more than the men who hack the
> ground; wood is his field and the chisel his mattock. At night when he
> is free, he toils more than his arms can do (at overtime work); even at
> nights he lights (his lamp to work by). The stone cutter seeks work in
> every hard stone; when he has done the great part of his labor his arms
> are exhausted, he is tired out. . . . The weaver in a workshop is worse
> off than a woman; (he squats) with his knees to his belly and does not
> taste (fresh) air. He must give loaves to the porters to see the light.[4]

GREEK AND ROMAN SCHOOLS

Our modern secondary school's earliest ancestors in the direct line are
the Greek secondary schools. Many of our modern institutions are largely
an outgrowth of Greek thought, and our secondary schools are no exception. Several prototypes of our modern secondary schools can be found
in Greece and in the Roman adaptations of the Hellenistic schools.

Education in Sparta and Athens. Spartan schools were created to serve
the purposes of an authoritarian state. The curriculum was eminently
functional. In the words of a Spartan king, it taught boys "what they
ought to do when they grow to be men." Because Sparta was a military
state, the Spartan curriculum was a military one. Its main purpose was
to imbue the youths with warlike virtues. To carry out this aim effec-

[3] *Ibid.*, p. 150.
[4] *Ibid.*, p. 149.

tively the state took the youths from their homes and educated them in military camps where they would be free from softening home influences. Gymnastics and military experiences were stressed and intellectual subjects minimized. "Theirs was not to reason why; theirs was but to do or die," so academic subjects were of little value.

For a warlike dictatorship Spartan education was supremely successful. Modern totalitarian governments have attested to their faith in the Spartan system of developing unthinking loyalty and obedience by imitating parts of the Spartan system.

Athenian education has been more directly influential on the American secondary-school curriculum than Spartan education has been. From it we get the concept of the liberal arts—the arts of free man—and the idea of a well-rounded education. Although the Athenians antedate by centuries the whole-child cliché, they tried to educate the whole child by combining intellectual, physical, aesthetic, and moral education. At least one educational historian feels that they accomplished their purpose "with a success rare indeed in later history."[5]

In ancient Athens secondary education consisted largely of athletics. By the fifth century B.C. this old education could not cope with the complexities of the changing times. Athens had become a world power. Its people were sophisticated, intelligent, and skeptical. Democracy had become the order of the day, and so men needed the skills and knowledges useful in a democracy. In the democracy of Athens the most important of these was the ability to speak in the assembly. The old educational system made no provisions for teaching these practical skills and knowledges.

The New Education. As so often happens when there is an educational void, private venture tried to meet the demand. In this instance, the breech was filled by the Sophists, itinerant professional teachers who had come to Athens to seek their fortunes. Many of them were excellent teachers. Among the most famous were Socrates, the great philosopher,[6] and Protagoras, the inventor of grammar. Others were opportunists and quacks who were willing to teach anything at the drop of a drachma. Still, they served a purpose: they provided instruction in the practical subjects that the young men needed—such things as rhetoric, grammar, and dialectic, which were essential if a young man was to distinguish himself in the community.

With the new education two new types of Greek secondary schools arose. The first of these was the Platonic philosophical school, which attempted to provide a background for philosophical studies by pursuing such subjects as music, number, geometry, and astronomy. The

---

[5] John S. Brubacher, *A History of the Problems of Education* (New York: McGraw-Hill Book Company, Inc., 1947), p. 250.

[6] Some will object to classifying Socrates as a Sophist, but certainly he was one of the moving forces of the new education.

other was the school of rhetoric advocated by Isocrates. This school included such subjects as geography, history, law, political science, art, ethics, and logic as a preparation for public affairs. Soon these schools too became formalized. Seneca, Nero's teacher, speaking of the rhetorical schools of Rome, said, *"Non vitae sed scholae discimus";* "We do not teach for life, we teach for school."

As one might expect, the introduction of the new studies caused a tremendous uproar. Advocates of the traditional education blamed the new education for causing delinquency, lack of respect for elders, and immorality. Aristophanes pilloried Socrates for conducting a "thinking school" in which boys learned how to turn black into white by means of dialectic legerdemain.[7] In fact, alarm concerning the effects of the new education on youth was the ostensible cause of Socrates' being tried and executed for misguiding youth. The perennial argument between the advocates of the new and the old education has a long, if not honorable, history.

Liberal vs. Vocational Education. These schools were the forerunners of the liberal arts and grammar schools. In Roman times the schools of rhetoric swallowed up the philosophical schools. As a result the Romans preserved the philosophical studies—arithmetic, geometry, astronomy, and music—as well as grammar, rhetoric, and logic in their training of orators. Thus the seven liberal arts of medieval times were born. In addition the Romans added the study of the Greek language, thus giving impetus to the emphasis on foreign language so common to Western education.

The seven liberal arts early picked up an aristocratic tinge. To the Greeks vocational education was unworthy and degrading. Aristotle said that although children should be taught useful things, young children should be taught "only such kinds of knowledge which will be useful to them without vulgarizing them." He goes on to define what he means in this fashion:

> And any occupation, art, or science, which makes the body or soul or mind of the freeman less fit for the practice or exercise of virture, is vulgar; wherefore we call those arts vulgar which tend to deform the body, and likewise *all paid employment, for they absorb and degrade the mind.* There are also some liberal arts quite proper for a freeman to acquire, but only in a certain degree, and if he attends to them too closely, in order to attain perfection in them, the same evil effects will follow. The object also which a man sets before him makes a great difference; if he does or learns anything for his own sake or for the sake of his friends, or with a view of excellence, the action will not appear illiberal; but if done for the sake of others, the very same action will be thought menial and servile.[8]

[7] Aristophanes, *The Clouds.*
[8] Aristotle, *Politics,* Book VII, Jowett's translation.

No concept of liberal education could be more snobbish. This attitude still continues as part of our liberal arts tradition. Vocational education is considered inferior education simply because it is vocational and consequently illiberal, vulgar, "menial and servile."

Although the schools of the Sophists were utilitarian, they were class schools. Here the Sophists tried to teach upper-class boys the skills that would help them become successful men. By Roman times this utilitarian ideal had fallen by the wayside in at least some of the schools. Quintillian accused teachers of oratory of teaching useless subjects simply for their disciplinary value. So he tried to combat this practice. He thought the education of an orator should combine the professional skills and knowledges necessary for an orator with the attitudes of thought and breeding that result from a broad, truly liberal education. He did not believe in education that had no use, except possible disciplinary value. In the long run Quintillian lost the battle. In the late Roman Empire the grammar schools lost all contact with reality and specialized in teaching a florid Latin style which seems to have been the epitome of poor taste.

MEDIEVAL SECONDARY EDUCATION

THE MEDIEVAL LATIN SCHOOL

The traditions of the classical secondary schools were carried along into medieval times, even though in extremely corrupt forms. Fixed by the work of Martianus, Capella, Boethius, and Cassidorius, the last of the Roman scholars, the seven liberal arts became the heart of the medieval secondary-school curriculum.

By this time, these studies had become a sorry remnant of the once glorious learning of Greece and Rome. The Christian fear that pagan learning might corrupt the faithful had squeezed the *trivium* subjects until they were quite empty. The *Ars Minor* of Donatus, the famous elementary grammar text used for more than eight hundred years, was only 14 pages long. Rhetoric had degenerated to a study of rules for letter writing and record keeping, and logic was used only for heresy hunting. Of the *quadrivium* only arithmetic remained in any strength. For a time about all that was left of classical scholarship could be included in a short book of excerpts like Capella's *Marriage of Philosophy and Mercury*. The entire curriculum of the early medieval school consisted of little more than the rudiments of Latin.

Still, these medieval Latin schools were somewhat functional because they served as training grounds for the Latin clerks who conducted much of the business of Church and state and had to know Latin in order to do their work. At first these men were educated only in the monasteries, cathedrals, or collegiate churches. Later the cities provided burgher schools for the children of the "City Fathers," and the rich and powerful guilds established guild schools for the crabbed medieval Latin that was used as a lingua franca in the world of church, business, and the state.

Latin medieval times also brought the great revival of learning which we call scholasticism. Men were no longer completely satisfied with the dried bones of Latin scholarship served up by the medieval schools. In addition new knowledge was beginning to seep into Europe from other lands to challenge the minds of scholars. The dissatisfaction and the new knowledge were both the cause and result of an unrest that led men to seek rational justification and confirmation of beliefs which they had previously accepted on faith alone. Consequently the revival of learning was accompanied by a revival of philosophy and a resurgence in the study of logic and rhetoric. The disputation and arguing of theses became a major sport. All over Europe scholars gathered to form universities where they could learn from each other and argue their theories. The secondary schools of the period, as is usual with secondary schools, followed the example of the universities, even to the extent of carrying on interscholastic disputations.[9] So we find that in a sense the schools in medieval times tended to develop from the top down.

THE APPRENTICESHIP SYSTEM

During the middle ages education for the nonscholarly occupations was a matter of apprenticeship. The prospective merchant or tradesman first served a master craftsman as an apprentice. Upon completing his apprenticeship he became a journeyman and worked for his master by the day. When the journeyman had acquired sufficient funds and had demonstrated his competence by completing a masterpiece to the satisfaction of the guild members, he was made a master in his own right and could set up shop for himself. The training of knights followed the same apprenticeship pattern. First, the boy served his lady as a page, learning court etiquette, reading, writing, and the polite diversions of society. Then he was promoted to squire and served his lord, who in turn taught him the arts of war. Later, upon proving his prowess in the knightly arts, he was dubbed knight. This instruction was entirely functional, at least at first. There was nothing academic about it, although jousting was continued long after it had lost any value in battle.

In general, much of medieval education centered around the practical. Even the lectures and disputations were a type of apprenticeship, and extremely functional and vocational, because they gave the young scholar a chance to practice his profession under the watchful eye of a master. To this day the university has remained a vocational institution. Even the colleges of liberal arts are largely vocational schools for the training of professional scholars.

---

[9] I. L. Kandel, *History of Secondary Education* (Boston: Houghton Mifflin Company, 1930), p. 58.

THE RENAISSANCE AND MODERN TIMES

THE REBIRTH OF LEARNING

Although the Dark Ages were probably not nearly as dark as many people think they were, they were dark enough. It was not until the end of the fourteenth century that the great Renaissance began to be felt in secondary education. This rebirth, unlike the twelfth-century revival of learning, was a resurgence of the classical spirit. Instead of the formalized medieval schools with their crabbed medieval Latin curriculum, the Renaissance stressed functional learning. The ideal was to create well-rounded, well-informed, polished ladies and gentlemen of the world.

The Ideal Renaissance School. The court school Vittorino da Feltre established in Mantua in 1423 typifies the ideal Renaissance school. He called this school, which was formed for the children of the Gonzaga family and other carefully selected boys, *La Giocassa,* or The Pleasant House, because he thought education should be a joyous experience, not an ordeal. Primarily Vittorino's aim was to teach his pupils to become men of action who would serve the state well. Therefore he tried to develop the pupils' minds, bodies, and morals into a harmonious whole by supervising their entire development—not only intellectual activities, but also their food, clothing, recreation, health, and interests. As one would expect from a great classical scholar, Vittorino taught Latin throughout the entire curriculum, from the beginning to the end. But he did not teach it as empty exercises; he taught it as the key to the great glories of the past and to a fuller life today.

Thus in the ideal Renaissance school the humanities replaced the seven liberal arts. In addition to becoming fluent in both oral and written Latin, and becoming familiar with the works of the Latin and Greek classical writers and the writings of the Church Fathers, the Renaissance youth studied considerable mathematics, especially as it applied to drawing, mensuration, and surveying. Physical education also played a large part in the program; so did such functional subjects as fencing, etiquette, and military science. That the program was quite comprehensive is shown by the following list of courses from a typical court school:

Latin	Geography
Greek	Law
Vernacular Language	Jurisprudence
Military Science	Music
Mathematics	Drawing
Science	Painting
History	Physical Accomplishment.[10]

[10] Kandel, *op. cit.,* p. 136.

The Renaissance humanistic school with its emphasis on classical learning long remained the pattern for schools throughout the Western world. Although the Protestant Reformation wrought great changes in elementary education, its founders continued the emphasis on the humanistic studies as the proper type of education for youth. This was only natural, because Luther, Melanchthon, Calvin, and others influential in education were themselves classical scholars. Similarly the new Roman Catholic secondary schools of the period, for example, those founded by the Jesuits, continued the humanistic tradition.

The Decline of Ciceronianism. As long as the schools taught the humanities as a source of functional learning, they remained a vital force. Unfortunately the humanistic schools soon became formalized shadows of themselves. Instead of teaching how to live by means of the classics, the curriculum degenerated to the mere drill on Latin style commonly called Ciceronianism. Pupils memorized such works as Lily's Latin grammar, even though they barely understood its content, and conversed by the use of phrase books.

Of course, when Latin was a lingua franca, this curriculum had some merit, in spite of the atrocious teaching method, because a man well-versed in Latin could make himself understood anywhere in Western Christendom. But when Latin was replaced by the modern tongues, the curriculum lost much of its validity. Unfortunately for many boys and girls, both the curriculum and the method hung on until quite modern times. To justify their teaching, teachers claimed that it was not the content which was valuable, but the mental discipline afforded by dreary exacting drill. Typical of the formalized schools were the *gymnasien* and grammar schools that still exist in modified form in Europe and carry on, to a considerable extent, the old tradition.

For some families the fact that the Ciceronian schools and the Latin grammar education were completely out of touch with contemporary life seemed to be an advantage. For one thing they thought any schooling so difficult and tedious must be beneficial in developing strength of character in the young. Moreover, such education gave each youth unmistakable caste marks that should assure him a place in society. As Brubacher puts it when speaking of the Latin curriculum:

> From the seventeenth to the nineteenth centuries, there were yet others who, though they had little or no regard for the formalized Humanistic curriculum, nevertheless laid great social store on having the imprint of the stereotyped curriculum stamped upon the boy. Relatively few families could afford this sort of education for their boys; therefore, worthless as they thought it was in content, they valued its rarity as a badge of class distinction.[11]

[11] Brubacher, *op. cit.*, p. 425. From *History of the Problems of Education*, by J. S. Brubacher, Copyright McGraw-Hill Book Company, Inc. Used by permission.

The formalized Ciceronian Latin Grammar School was the secondary school that the Puritans brought with them from England. From its very inception this school, like all the other humanist schools, was essentially aristocratic. Its sole purpose was to prepare boys for college entrance. Because the college entrance requirements, to take those of Harvard for an example, were the ability to read Cicero extempore, to make and speak true Latin in prose and verse, and to decline paradigms of Greek nouns and verbs, the masters of the Latin grammar schools tended to limit themselves to these studies.

HUMANISTIC, SOCIAL, AND SENSE REALISTS

Of course, not everyone was willing to put up with a dry, formalized program of worthless Ciceronianism. Humanistic realists like François Rabelais and John Milton argued for a return to the vitality of the humanistic school. They recommended that the classical schools teach such down-to-earth subjects as agriculture, natural history, and geography by reading the works of the ancient authors in those fields.

The social realists also viewed the curriculum of the Ciceronian school with alarm. The best known of these, Michel de Montaigne, like the Renaissance courtiers, would give the priorities in education to those subjects that would help a young person to get along in the world. High on his list are such studies as etiquette, dancing, horsemanship, modern languages, and travel.[12]

Many people agreed with Montaigne. During the seventeenth and eighteenth centuries wealthy families frequently hired tutors to give their children the type of education the social realists advocated in preference to sending them to the grammar schools. In France and Germany social realist academies (*Ritterakademien*) were formed to teach the knightly graces. Another indication of the spirit of the times was a rash of dancing masters, fencing masters, and other private-venture establishments that sprang up all over Europe and the colonies.

An even greater break from the Ciceronian tradition was that of the sense realists, foremost among whom were J. A. Comenius and Francis Bacon, forerunners of our modern scientific movement in education, who placed new emphasis on the vernacular and science. In Europe the movement toward a realistic curriculum gained impetus with the *Pedagogium* of August Francke, which broke from the classical tradition by providing *Realien*—specimen, gardens, scientific apparatus, laboratories, and workshops—and culminated in the *Realschule*, which was designed to meet the needs of the children of the middle classes. The curriculum of the *Realschule* included such divergent subjects as geography, history, writing, arithmetic, economics, drawing, geometry, religion, Latin,

[12] Michel de Montaigne, *Selected Essays* (New York: The Modern Library, Random House, Inc., 1949), p. 47.

French, German, and manufactures. In its turning toward the scientific and utilitarian, this type of school reflects the spirit of the age. In America this spirit resulted in the founding of the academy.

The American Academy. In spite of being the typical secondary school in the colonies, the Latin grammar school never was able to get a good foothold in the United States. Clearly it was not designed to meet the needs of a new nation growing up on a new continent, and so the colonists began to look elsewhere for a curriculum valuable to their children. As in Europe, they soon turned to private-venture schools, which gave instruction in foreign languages, mathematics, bookkeeping, surveying, and other subjects needed by men of business in a new country.

Where there was so much demand, someone was bound to start a school designed to meet the need. In America it was the great utilitarian, Benjamin Franklin, who provided the answer. In 1749 he proposed that "some persons of Leisure and public Spirit apply for a CHARTER, by which they may be incorporated with Power to erect an ACADEMY for the Education of Youth."[13] It was Franklin's hope that this academy would provide youth with a functional curriculum containing, as he says, "those things which are likely to be most useful and most ornamental. Regard being had for the several Professions for which they are intended."

The curriculum included such things as writing in a fair hand, drawing, arithmetic, accounting, geometry, astronomy, the English language, history (including the Greek and Roman historians *in translation*), natural history, mechanics, commerce, and the preservation of health. Not all students were expected to take the same course, but rather each was to select those courses most useful to him. The classical languages were no longer considered the heart of the curriculum. In Franklin's thinking they were very nearly frills.

Unfortunately the practical curriculum that Franklin set so much store on did not develop in the Philadelphia Academy as he had hoped, but the idea was not totally lost. During the Revolutionary War, in 1778, the Phillips brothers founded an academy in Andover, Massachusetts, which provided instruction in both an English and a Latin department. From this time on, until about 1850, academies became increasingly more popular, probably because they tried to teach what the people wanted.

Because the academy was usually a private school dependent in part upon tuitions for its very existence, one can imagine that its administrators were quite sensitive to public demand. Like some of our adult centers today, it seemed to follow the principle that if enough people wished a course to support it, the school should try to offer it. As a result it offered a wide variety of courses. For instance, at Wesleyan Seminary in Michigan, the pupil could select his own curricula from the following:

[13] Benjamin Franklin, *Proposals Relating to the Education of Youth in Pennsylvania,* 1749. Cited in Edgar W. Knight and Clifton L. Hall, Readings in American Educational History (New York: Appleton-Century-Crofts, Inc., 1951), p. 77.

FIRST TERM: Mental Arithmetic; Elocution; Rhetoric; Geomerty, begun; Geography of the Heavens; Bookkeeping; Botany; Political Economy; Astronomy; Governmental Instructor [probably a civics manual].

SECOND TERM: English Composition; Analysis of Words; Ancient Geography; Universal History; Geometry, completed; Trigonometry; Mental Philosophy; Elements of Criticism; Evidences of Christianity; Natural Theology.

THIRD TERM: Modern Geography; History of the United States; Surveying and Navigation; Mental Philosophy; Logic; Agricultural Chemistry; Animal Chemistry; Analogy of Religion; Geology; Mineralogy.

EVERY TERM: English Grammar; Analysis of Language; Written Arithmetic; Higher Arithmetic; Elementary Algebra; Higher Algebra; Anatomy and Physiology; Natural Philosophy; Chemistry; Drawing; Painting; Music; Greek; Latin; French; and German.[14]

Soon, however, like so many schools, the academy forgot its original purpose and became formalized and academic. Many academies, designed primarily to give utilitarian terminal education to boys and girls, turned themselves into college preparatory schools. This spelled the beginning of the end of the academy as a live institution. So in the latter half of the nineteenth century the academy began to die.

The Birth of the High School. The academy's early success led to the creation of the high school. The academy had filled the need of the middle class admirably. But it was a private institution, and it was expensive. In the words of the School Committee of Boston:

> . . . The mode of education now adapted, and the branches of knowledge that are taught at our English Grammar schools, are not sufficient, extensive nor otherwise, to bring the powers of the mind into operation, nor to qualify a youth to fill usefully and respectably many of those stations, both public and private, in which he may be placed. A parent who wishes to give a child an education that shall fit him for active life, and shall serve as a foundation for eminence in his profession, whether Mercantile or Mechanical, is under the necessity of giving him a different education from any which our public schools can now furnish. Hence, many children are separated from their parents and sent to private academies in this vicinity, to acquire that instruction which cannot be obtained at public seminaries. Thus many parents, who contribute largely to the support of these institutions, are subject to heavy expense for the object, in other towns.[15]

To correct this situation the school committee created the Boston English Classical High School. Immediately it was a great success, and soon was imitated throughout the country. High schools became particularly popular on the frontier because they provided an educational ladder and a

14 Kandel, *op. cit.*, p. 415.

15 Kandel, *op. cit.*, pp. 426–427. Quoting from the subcommittee's report on the basis of which the School Committee voted to establish the English Classical School November 9, 1820.

logical extension of the common school. Most high schools followed a curriculum pattern similar to those of the academies with their English and Latin departments and wide variety of courses.

The Decadence of the High School. Soon the high school, like the academy, started to go to seed academically. Even though many of its pupils were terminal pupils who had no intention of going to college, the high school curriculum concentrated on the formalized academic college preparatory subjects, which sapped its vitality. The famous report of the Committee of Ten typifies the thinking behind this trend. The committee, in spite of the fact that it specifically recognized the terminal role of the high school, recommended that all pupils study the college preparatory subjects for their disciplinary value and that "every subject which is taught at all in the secondary school should be taught in the same way and to the same extent to every pupil so long as he pursues it, no matter what the probable destination of the pupil may be, or at what point his education may cease." Naturally the program they recommended was dominated by humanistic and mental disciplinary ideals and the college preparatory function.

The college preparatory subjects also received reinforcement from the many attempts made near the turn of the century to reform and standardize collegiate education. The formation of accrediting associations, the Carnegie unit, the College Entrance Examination Board, the National Education Association Committee on College Entrance Requirements, all tended to cut the secondary-school curriculum in a college preparatory pattern. The result was that the high schools found themselves pretty much under the thumb of the colleges in the early part of the twentieth century.

THE QUEST OF THE FUNCTIONAL

Other forces were seeking to direct the high school curriculum toward the functional. As the nation developed, an increasing demand for vocational education—industrial, commercial, and agricultural—arose. To meet these demands, some cities established special schools for vocational training, but specialized secondary schools never became as popular in this country as they did in Europe. Most high schools tried to meet the new demand by adding vocational courses, such as stenography, vocational agriculture, and mechanical arts, and by revising old courses to make them more practical and useful.

The Seven Cardinal Principles. Accompanying the demand for the practical in the early part of the twentieth century was a tremendous upsurge in high school enrollment, which doubled each decade. Increasingly it became evident that it was time for a reexamination of the high school curriculum. In 1918 the Commission on Reorganization of Secondary Education attempted to redefine the role of the secondary school.

Their concept of secondary education, as expressed in their report *Cardinal Principles of Education,* was much broader than the narrow college preparatory program advocated by the Committee of Ten. In fact, the academic aspects of the secondary-school program took on a relatively minor role. According to the Commission, each of the following areas should be included in the major objectives of education:

1. Health
2. Command of fundamental processes
3. Worthy home membership
4. Vocation
5. Citizenship
6. Worthy use of leisure time
7. Ethical character[16]

Inadequacy of the High School Curriculum. Thus the secondary school found itself committed, in theory at least, to providing a broad education to a large segment of the population. The pattern of academic and vocational courses that had grown up between the Civil War and World War I was not adequate for the task. The tremendous growth in school population, which continued through the depression, brought into the school many boys and girls who, in former years, would not have been admitted and who could not cope with the courses intellectually. A major reconstruction of the entire program was needed.

Unfortunately, with few exceptions, little except minor tinkering with the old curriculum was done. Courses and methods designed to teach the academically minded and the vocationally eager were used to teach the dull and the uninterested. The result has been, all too often, watered down courses, too easy to challenge the bright, but so hard that they frustrated the dull.

As one can imagine the result was less than satisfactory. In 1945 a conference on vocational education, sponsored by the United States Office of Education pointed out that, although the boys and girls who were preparing to go to college and the boys and girls who were engaged in definite vocational preparation were well served by our secondary-school curricula, the schools provided little for boys and girls who were not preparing for college or a specific vocation. As a result of this conference, a concerted attempt was made in certain circles to relate high school curricula more closely with the life goals of the pupils. This movement has received considerable notoriety as education for life adjustment. Although it has been the subject of much discussion and no little confusion, and although critics of modern education have used it as a whipping boy on which to blame many of the inadequacies of modern

[16] Commission on the Reorganization of Secondary Education, *Cardinal Principles of Education,* U.S. Office of Education, Bulletin 1918, No. 35 (Washington, D.C.: Government Printing Office, 1918), pp. 10–11.

education, in actuality, education for life adjustment has had very little impact on either the public or private secondary schools in this country.

The Progressive Education Movement. Education for life adjustment has been closely linked to the progressive education movement. All during the twentieth century the philosophy of pragmatism has had considerable vogue among schoolmen and educationists. As far as education is concerned the main tenets of the philosophy are that education is part of living and that subject matter is only a means to an end and so should be subordinated to the learner and learning. Some progressive educators seemed to wish to do away with subject matter altogether.

Progressivism has been partially responsible for a movement to integrate and fuse courses in order to make them more meaningful and useful. Thus elementary courses in the sciences were combined into general science and history, geography, government, and economics into the social studies. It was also hoped that these fused courses would more closely meet the needs of all youth. This trend led to the "core curriculum," in which subject matter lines were disregarded entirely. Although relatively few core curricula have been inaugurated, frequently they have been associated with life-adjustment programs. In other instances, they merely represent the combination of two or more courses or subjects to form an interdisciplinary double-period course.

THE PRESENT UNREST

Except for the fusion or integration in English and the social and natural sciences, these new movements have had little effect on our secondary-school curriculum. If anything is sure about our secondary schools, it is that they are not, and never have been, progressive. Still, the schools have changed. Because of their reputation for being useless as well as being difficult, dull, dry, and dreary, the traditional academic subjects have become proportionally much less popular than they had been. This condition has caused considerable alarm among intellectuals who were already disturbed by what they had heard and read about modern "progressive education." This alarm turned to hysteria when it became evident that Russian learning was powerful and energetic. Frenzied articles in the popular press accused the schools of incompetence and malpractice. Many writers laid the "failure of the secondary schools" to the "new education" and demanded a return to the solid traditional subjects and discipline. The furor caused many to lose confidence in the public secondary schools and has made a reappraisal of the secondary-school curriculum necessary.

At present, just what the secondary-school curriculum of the future will be is not apparent. Some indices point toward a return to the theory of mental discipline and training the mind. Other indices point toward a more functional vital curriculum. The new programs in mathematics and foreign languages are examples of such indices. In any case the battle is joined. There is no turning back.

SOME LESSONS FROM HISTORY

What lessons does the history of the secondary-school curriculum have to teach us? They are many, of course, but one of the most striking is how often certain surprising phenomena recur in the secondary schools of every country and every era of Western civilization. From the résumé of educational history in the preceding sections it should be evident that among these recurring phenomena are five general tendencies that are worthy of further discussion. The following paragraphs will attempt to summarize the chapter by pointing up these five tendencies.

1. TO VENERATE THE WRITTEN WORD

The first of these tendencies is a tendency to venerate the written word. In ancient days writing must have seemed like magic. Its magic persists to this very day. In spite of the efforts of such men as Montaigne, Rousseau, Franklin, Dewey, and Kilpatrick, our secondary-school curricula are singularly bookish. As a result textbooks determine the curriculum and dominate the instruction in almost every American secondary school —an anomaly in the Age of Atomic Science. Attempts to reduce the bookishness of the curriculum in favor of a more functional approach designed to teach boys and girls how to act and think have been branded anti-intellectualism, for the *mana* of the written word is so great that often intellect seems to be equated with verbalizing in the minds of both educators and laymen.

Not only has the curriculum been bookish, but during most of the history of Western civilization it has been monopolized by the study of languages. The curriculum of the eighteenth-century grammar schools, for instance, was almost entirely language—preferably foreign and dead. Even in twentieth-century America language study made up three quarters of some high school curricula. For instance, consider the following college-preparatory curriculum of a Connecticut high school three decades ago.

Grade IX	*Grade XI*
Algebra I	Plane Geometry
Latin I	Latin III
English I	English III
History I	French II
Grade X	*Grade XII*
Latin II	Latin IV
English II	English IV
French I	French III
Algebra II	Solid Geometry and
	Trigonometry

2. TO WORSHIP THE PAST AND CLING TO SUBJECT AND METHODS
LONG AFTER THEY HAVE OUTLIVED THEIR USEFULNESS AND TO
RESIST THE ADVENT OF NEW SUBJECTS AND CURRICULA

Perhaps the magic in the written word is also responsible for our almost slavish respect and reverence for the past. In any case, throughout history our secondary schools have been oriented toward the past. We have seen this to be true in the earliest times in the Fertile Crescent and Ancient Egypt, and we can see it today in our modern high schools with their emphasis on the English "classics" of the past century. The schools of the Sophists and the private-venture schools and academies in eighteenth-century America were all attempts to shake loose from curricula long since gone to seed.

3. TO FORMALIZE VITAL CURRICULA, SUBJECTS, AND METHODS
SO THAT THEY BECOME MEANINGLESS ENDS IN THEMSELVES AND
TO INVENT SPURIOUS REASONS FOR HANGING ON TO THESE PET-
RIFIED CURRICULA AND METHODS RATHER THAN TO FACE UP TO
THEIR DEFICIENCIES

Almost every new subject, curriculum, or method of teaching was introduced into the schools in order to make the school more vital and functional. But soon the teachers lost sight of the functional purposes of the innovation. Instead of being a means of teaching boys and girls something important to them the subject matter became an end in itself and so the vitality slowly seeped out to be replaced by dull dry formalism. Ciceronianism is the prize example of this phenomenon. More recently, similar crimes have been committed by "Deweyites," who hardened his five steps in problem solving into "five formal steps" just as rigid as those of any Herbartian.

The net result of this formalism and veneration of the past and the written word is that for a large part of its history the secondary-school curriculum has been almost completely out of touch with real life. Probably at least one third, more likely one half, of the secondary-school curriculum today could be eliminated without any student's missing out on any learning of real importance to him. Because so much of the curriculum has had so little value, educators have had to invent false reasons for including their subjects. "Why does one need to learn trigonometry?" "Because it will teach pupils to think logically." "Why does one have to learn French?" "Because it will help pupils improve their English." These are false evasive answers that teachers have invented because the real reasons have escaped them or no longer exist. Undoubtedly studying can have a disciplinary value, but when one *has* to justify a subject, or course, by its disciplinary value, one can be fairly sure that, *as taught*, this subject or course no longer has much value for the pupils.

Even worse, these evasions often hide the fact that subjects like trigonometry and French have real places in the modern curriculum for real functional reasons and that these real reasons require some changes in the content and method of teaching to make them live and function in the second half of the twentieth century.

4. TO AIM THE CURRICULUM AT SNOBBISH UPPER AND UPPER-MIDDLE-CLASS GOALS AND NEEDS AND TO NEGLECT THE GOALS AND NEEDS OF COMMON PEOPLE

One reason that the secondary-school curriculum has been out of touch with life is that for the major portion of its career it has been a curriculum for the upper classes. Even today completion of the grammar school in Europe or the college-preparatory curricula in our high schools carries a certain amount of status. Pupils and parents cling to these curricula for their prestige value.

The aristocratic tinge of our secondary schools is also indicated by the historic college domination of the secondary-school curriculum. Because the schools have been aristocratically inclined, they have taken it as their first mission to prepare boys and girls for higher education. Thus the secondary school, throughout its long history, has been the creature of the institution of higher learning. Not only have the colleges dictated to the secondary schools what courses they should teach and how they should teach them, but also they have presented an example the secondary schools have been only too eager to follow, even though the pupils concerned may have had no use for this sort of curriculum.

5. TO MAINTAIN A RUNNING BATTLE BETWEEN THE OLD AND NEW EDUCATIONAL THEORIES SO THAT EDUCATIONAL HISTORY BECOMES A SERIES OF ACTIONS AND REACTIONS IN WHICH SUCCESSIVE MOVEMENTS OR FACTIONS REBEL AGAINST THEIR PREDECESSORS

In every age there is a battle between the old and the new education. The progressive elements feel that the conservatives are impeding progress. This has always been so and probably always will be so. The schools of the Sophists were accused of weakening the moral fiber of the country, the scholastics were accused of leading youth into heresy, and the academies were accused of degrading academic standards because of their English curriculum. The battles to introduce the sciences and the modern languages into the curriculum were long, hard, and bitter. In the long run, however, the battles turned out to be merely delaying actions. Slowly the curriculum has moved forward in spite of protests. The present status of the curriculum is the result of a continuous development over thousands of years. It will continue to move forward for years to come.

Although the curriculum continues to develop, the history of the secondary-school curriculum has been a serious succession of ups and downs. Time and again, new, dynamic, functional movements with vital missions have rocked the educational scene. Yet each in turn has fallen by the wayside, struck by the dead hand of tradition or suffocated by empty formalism. Thus we find that the history of education has consisted of short bursts of youthful vitality followed by periods of empty sterility or reaction.

These shifts are caused by at least two reasons. One is that new movements lose their vitality as they get older and become formalized and decadent and so cause people to become impatient with them. The other is that new movements in education are almost always reactions against the *status quo.* Today we are in the midst of a revolt against much of the progressive movement's teachings. Part of the revolt seems to be an attempt to return to the *status quo ante,* but much of it is an attempt to put a new and different vitality into the curriculum. What direction it will take finally still remains to be seen.

SUGGESTED READINGS

BENJAMIN, HAROLD. *The Saber-Toothed Curriculum.* New York: McGraw-Hill Book Company, Inc., 1936.

A satire ridiculing the marked propensity for continuing obsolete curricula.

BRUBACHER, JOHN S. *A History of the Problems of Education.* New York: McGraw-Hill Book Company, Inc., 1947.

See Chapters 9, 10, and 14. A standard text in the history of education. An excellent discussion of the history of secondary education and curriculum.

CHILDE, V. GORDON. *Man Makes Himself.* New York: The New American Library of World Literature, Inc., 1951.

An exciting account of the development of knowledge during the early beginnings of history.

COMMAGER, HENRY. "A Historian Looks at the American High School," in *The High School in a New Era,* Francis S. Chase and Harold A. Anderson (eds.). Chicago: University of Chicago Press, 1958.

A discussion of the place of the high school in contemporary America in light of the history of American schools and the nation.

EBY, FREDERICK. *The Development of Modern Education.* Second edition. Englewood Cliffs, New Jersey: Prentice-Hall, Inc., 1952.

A standard text in the history of education since the Renaissance.

EBY, FREDERICK, and CHARLES FLINN ARROWOOD. *The History and Philosophy of Education.* New York: Prentice-Hall, Inc., 1940.

A standard text of the history of education from early times to the Renaissance. This text and the preceding one give detailed accounts of the various movements in educational history.

GOOD, HARRY G. *A History of American Education.* Second edition. New York: The Macmillan Company, 1962.

A popular text in the history of American education which gives a particularly good account of the rise of modern American secondary-school system.

——. *A History of Western Education.* Second edition. New York: The Macmillan Company, 1960.

An extremely good textbook in the history of education from prehistoric to contemporary times.

KANDEL, I. L. *History of Secondary Education.* Boston: Houghton Mifflin Company, 1930.

Probably the best available reference on the development of secondary education.

KNIGHT, EDGAR W., and CLIFTON L. HALL. *Readings in American Educational History.* New York: Appleton-Century-Crofts, Inc., 1951.

A book of readings that contains numerous documents pertaining to the development of the American secondary-school system.

LATIMER, JOHN FRANCIS. *What's Happened to Our High Schools?* Washington: Public Affairs Press, 1958.

A study by a classical scholar of the changes in the high school curriculum from the 1890's to the 1950's, based largely on government statistical data.

MARROU, H. I. *A History of Education in Antiquity.* New York: Sheed and Ward, 1956. Also New American Library of World Literature, Inc., 1964.

A detailed study of curriculum, methods and organization of schools in classical times.

MULHERN, JAMES. *A History of Education.* New York: The Ronald Press Company, 1959.

A social interpretation of the history of education. Interesting chapters on primitive education and education in the ancient world. Chapters 13 and 14 deal with the rise of the modern educational systems in Europe and the United States.

POWER, EDWARD. "Persistent Myths in the History of Education," *History of Education Quarterly*, 2: 140–151, September, 1962.

An argument that certain modern educational beliefs and practices stem from misunderstandings of what has happened in the past.

SACK, SAUL. "Liberal Education: What Was It? What Is It?" *History of Education Quarterly*, 2: 210–224, December, 1962.

A discussion of different concepts of liberal education and their development, particularly in the liberal arts college curricula in the United States.

VAN TIL, WILLIAM, GORDON F. VARS, and JOHN L. LOUNSBERRY. *Modern Education for the Junior High School Years.* Indianapolis: The Bobbs Merrill Company, Inc., 1961. Unit 1.

Unit 1 contains a good description of the development of the junior high school.

WESLEY, EDGAR B. *N.E.A.: The First Hundred Years.* New York: Harper and Row, Inc., 1957.

Chapter 6 gives a short account of the development of the high school from the middle of the past century to the present.

Chapter 2

Philosophical
Considerations

Differences in life views and educational philosophies are responsible for many of the controversies concerning the secondary-school curriculum.

In general, there seem to be two basic categories of viewpoints concerning education—the traditionalist and the progressivist. Among the traditionalists we may include the perennialists who wish to return to the curricula of the past, for example, the advocates of the Great Books program, and the essentialists who would prefer to see the curriculum and the world remain pretty much as they are. Among the progressivists we number the innovators who feel that because this is a world of change we need to prepare boys and girls now to cope with whatever the world becomes tomorrow, and the reconstructionists who wish to make the world over according to their new, and presumably better, pattern. These classifications are no doubt arbitrary and overly simplified, but they should serve as convenient vehicles for pointing out some philosophical points of view and their implications for the secondary-school curriculum.

THE AIMS OF THE SECONDARY-SCHOOL CURRICULUM

THE OTHERWORLDLY AIM OF EDUCATION

When Socrates introduced the concept of the divine soul he also introduced at least one educational corollary, the belief that the chief aim of education must be *to cultivate the soul.* The assumption here is that man is essentially a spiritual creature, the possessor of an immortal soul. Because the soul is the essential quality in man and because it lives on forever, long after one's mundane corporeal existence has ended, it seems obvious that the curriculum should emphasize spiritual values. Frequently, but not always, educators of this persuasion are inclined to believe that the proper method for cultivating spirituality is to indoctrinate boys and girls with the beliefs of a certain faith. Because one of the tenets of persons who believe in the spirituality of the individual is that no matter how base and gross our bodies are, we can approach godliness and that the chief end of man is to do so, it is only natural that they should emphasize moral and religious training and give a secondary role to everything else.

These beliefs are reflected in the curricula of the church-supported schools, which almost always emphasize religion, the humanistic tradition, and the otherworldly goals of education. In such educational systems spiritual values come first, and all other values come later.

EDUCATION FOR INTELLECTUAL DEVELOPMENT

Closely allied with the concept of education as a medium for cultivating the soul is the notion that the major purpose of education is to develop the intellect.

The Disciplined Mind. Just how one goes about developing the intellect depends upon one's concept of the mind. The most common conception of the mind is that it is a *thing* which exists inside of one and which has some connection or other with the soul. Because they think of the mind as a thing, lay people often give it the properties of a thing; so do some philosophers. Both Platonic and Aristotelian theory tend to liken mind to muscle, for instance.

From these ancient theories, and more modern ones of similar nature, has come the belief, very current today, that the mind can be trained and that certain subjects will train it better than others. Consequently, according to these theories, the curriculum builders should select the studies that will provide the most rigorous training of the mind. The practical value of the subject matter is not important. Education is not for knowledge; it is for power. It is the discipline, not the content, that counts.[1]

The Mind As a Receptacle. Another theory pictures the mind as a receptacle in which to store knowledge. According to this theory the child is born without any ideas at all. Rather his mind is like an empty box that could be filled with knowledge. Consequently, by controlling

[1] See I. N. Thut, *The Story of Education* (New York: McGraw-Hill Book Company, Inc., 1957), Part II.

a child's experiences, one could make the child's mind whatever he wished.)

The best-known exposition of the mind as a receptable is Locke's *tabula rasa* theory, in which he compared the mind to a blank tablet on which experience writes. Herbart's theory of apperception was quite similar. In this theory he posited that one's mind was built up by its power of assimilating new knowledge through the senses by means of the process of apperception. In apperception the apperceptive mass (mind) not only adds new experiences to its store of knowledge, it also interacts with each new experience so that one's mind and the experience are both changed in the process. In this way one's past experiences determine one's understanding of new experiences and one's new experiences change one's attitudes, beliefs, and behavior.

Modern theories of the behaviorists, connectionists, and similarly oriented psychologists and philosophers follow the same general tenor. These theories suggest that mental circuits or connections are established in the central nervous system by conditioning or some similar process. Once these circuits are established, the body, like an electronic brain, hums away making decisions, emoting, and performing all the other functions of the mind according to the patterns imprinted on it. Changes in mental behavior result from further conditioning, which stamps in new mental circuits and stamps out old ones.

(These theories of mind put considerable stress on the necessity of storing up essential knowledge so that one can use it later. They also imply the need for emphasis upon drill and habit formation in order to form the mental circuits that determine how the mind behaves. Machine teaching was introduced and developed by psychologists of this persuasion.)We should also point out that such points of view usually require that there be an authoritarian selection of the curriculum. Because the mind is primarily a storehouse of knowledge, according to this theory, the teacher should put into the pupils' minds the knowledges, skills, and attitudes that are essential. Here it is not the form but the subject matter that is most imporant.[2]

The Dynamic Mind of the Progressives. (Progressivists have been rather partial to the theory that although the mind is a function of the body and chiefly involves the nervous system, it is not exclusively the function of the nervous system. The whole organism is involved. Not only do the pupils learn with their heads, but they also learn with their hands and their hearts. Therefore they are inclined to look with favor on learning activities that require physical activity as well as what is ordinarily considered mental activity.

[2] For discussion of modern behavioristic theories see Winfred F. Hill, *Learning: A Survey of Psychological Interpretations* (San Francisco: Chandler Publishing Company, 1963).

These theorists believe that the mind evolves evolutionarily. To them mind is more than just the ingesting of experience, it is the process of giving meaning to experience and thereby creating new intelligence or problem-solving ability. In other words, they believe that each person creates his own mind through thinking and problem solving, which Dewey calls the method of intelligence.

This type of mind is not a storehouse of knowledge. Rather it depends upon learning through the solving of problems—real problems that require real solutions, not canned problems whose solutions are already known. To implement their theories the progressivists recommend a curriculum made up largely of practical problem-solving activities in those areas most likely to be useful to the pupil whether they be academic or not.[3]

Three Methods of Intellectual Development. The preceding discussion should have made evident to the reader that there are at least three conceptions of how the school should develop the intellect: (1) through disciplining the mind; (2) through filling the mind with essential content; and (3) through creating mind via the method of intelligence. Traditionalists in education usually favor the first two of these methods; progressivists almost invariably favor the third. Both traditionalists and progressivists, almost without exception, insist that intellectual development is an essential goal of secondary education. The quarrel between them mainly concerns how the intellectual powers should be developed.[4]

Instruction vs. Creative Learning. Nevertheless, a basic split between traditionalists and progressivists centers around whether education should consist of instruction or of creative self-learning at the secondary level. The first of these views pictures learning as a relatively passive process in which the mind is disciplined and filled with knowledge by a teacher or some other outside agent. The other viewpoint portrays it as an active process in which the learner, by using his brain and also his hands, legs, and the rest of the body, actually constructs knowledge as he goes along. The first of these theories lends itself to curricula and methods that present preprepared material to the pupil for ingestion via lecture, demonstration, television, teaching machines, or some other method that feeds the knowledge to the pupil in a more or less static process. The second concept of learning implies the need for a flexible curriculum that emphasizes student activity and knowing how rather than knowing what.

On the whole, traditionalists tends to lean toward education as instruction while progressivists are more likely to believe in education as creative self-learning. As we learn more about teaching and learning

[3] See Theodore Brameld, *Philosophies of Education in Cultural Perspective* (New York: Holt, Rinehart and Winston, Inc., 1955), Part II; and John L. Childs, *American Pragmatism and Education* (New York: Holt, Rinehart and Winston, Inc., 1956).

[4] See Thut, *op. cit.*, for extensive development of three positions similar to the above.

both traditionalists and progressivists seem to be becoming more and more convinced of the need for dynamic teaching situations and active learners, however.[5]

EDUCATION FOR CITIZENSHIP?

The third important aim that we shall discuss is education for citizenship. All educational theoreticians, progressivists and traditionalists alike, wish the schools to foster good citizenship. Their disagreements concern method and priority. In general, traditionalists tend to give priority to intellectual rather than moral development on the general theory that intellectual development leads to good citizenship. This belief stems from the Socratic premise that no man would do evil if he knew what was good. Traditionalists also place great faith in discipline as a builder of moral character and good citizenship.

Progressivists usually place great emphasis on education for citizenship. Because of their insistence that the intellectual and the practical are not different, the progressivists' approach to citizenship education emphasizes practical experience rather than academic learning to the extent that their citizenship programs may seem anti-intellectual to the traditional-minded.[6]

Education for Freedom and Democracy. Associated with education for citizenship are two other goals about which there is much confusion and disagreement. They are *education for freedom* and *education for democracy.* Again the differences between traditionalists' and progressivists' positions are mostly a matter of method. Traditionalists tend to believe that the schools should prepare boys and girls for freedom primarily by providing them with the knowledges and discipline. Accordingly many traditionalists would subject pupils to strong doses of authoritative discipline and instruction. Otherwise, they say, how will boys and girls know how to handle freedom well?[7]

Progressivists disagree. To them the only way to learn to handle freedom and to live democratically is to have many experiences in democratic living. Consequently progressivists would free boys and girls from authoritative instruction and discipline and give them much practice in democratic living and self-discipline.

To Build an Elite? In *The Republic* Plato describes three categories of men: the philosophers and rulers, whom he called men of gold; the warriors, whom he called men of silver; and the artisans and tradesmen, whom he called men of clay. In setting up these categories, the aristo-

[5] See Brameld, *op. cit.,* p. 236.

[6] William H. Kilpatrick, *Philosophy of Education* (New York: The Macmillan Company, 1951), p. 430 f; Roy O. Billett, *Fundamentals of Secondary School Teaching* (Boston: Houghton Mifflin Company, 1940), Ch. 2.

[7] See Jacques Maritain, *Education at the Crossroads* (New Haven, Conn.: Yale University Press, 1943), pp. 25–28 *et passim.*

cratic Plato ran true to one of the major tenets of his class: namely, that some people are by nature better than others, and so positions of leadership and responsibility should be given to the most capable. In other words, Plato believed that good government depended upon the establishment of an intellectual elite.

Since Plato's day, and before, persons who shared his views in the need for an intellectual elite have seen to it that the creation of an intellectual elite has been one of the major purposes of education in the Western world. From this purpose has come the selective school system so typical of European secondary education. In the United States the fostering of an intellectual elite has also been an important objective of American secondary schools. Thomas Jefferson's[8] famous plan for establishing a selective secondary-school system illustrates the importance he placed on educating the *best* students. When Jefferson wrote that "all men are created equal," seemingly he did not mean absolutely equal.

Jacksonian democracy rejects the need for an elite—intellectual or otherwise. In their reaction against European autocracies and east coast priggishness, the pioneers became convinced that one man was as good as another, and so one man's opinion was as good as another's. To this day many modern Americans remain certain that we have no need for experts or an elite group.[9] Additionally they suppose any method or curriculum that fosters the building of an intellectual elite or points to certain individuals as better intellectually than their fellows is undemocratic and un-American. This belief is the cause of many objections to homogeneous grouping, tracking, and other devices designed to provide for individual differences.[10]

EDUCATION FOR THE INDIVIDUAL OR THE GROUP?

For many centuries men commonly believed that the earth was the center of the universe and that man was the most important thing on earth. This principle of the value of the individual has remained all-important in modern times. Although some churches place more importance upon the earthly individual than do others, all of them agree on the all-importance of each single immortal soul. Modern progressivists have also preached the dignity of each single individual regardless of color, race, religion, or political persuasion. They have insisted that each person always be considered as an end, never as a means. That is why

[8] Thomas Jefferson, Bill "For the More General Diffusion of Knowledge" introduced into the Legislature of Virginia, 1779. Cited in Edgar W. Knight and Clifton L. Hall, *Readings in American Educational History* (New York: Appleton-Century-Crofts, Inc., 1951), pp. 299–306.

[9] Thut, *op. cit.*, p. 353 ff.

[10] See also Ephraim Vern Sayers and Ward Madden, *Education and the Democratic Faith* (New York: Appleton-Century-Crofts, Inc., 1959), pp. 262–287, for a discussion of quality in education.

Kilpatrick[11] holds that educational systems that attempt to mold children to fit adult patterns are violating the pupils' rights as persons by using them as means to an end. A similar emphasis on individuality has become a central theme in modern existentialist philosophy.

The implication for the curriculum is self-evident: the major aim of education should be to ensure that each youth can make the most of his life and fulfills his potentialities; a curriculum that subordinates any child to the crowd is absolutely unbearable. Accordingly, the best curriculum is pupil-centered.

With the exploding of the Ptolemaic theory and the discovery that the earth was a relatively small planet circling a comparatively small star in one of a vast number of galaxies, to believe that man was a special creation and the special concern of the Creator became rather difficult. It seemed more likely that man was a tiny speck who could not possibly be of any significance whatsoever in a universe of such dimensions. Furthermore, the formulation of the modern theories of evolution and the many scientific discoveries of the modern era made the idea of a personal God seem rather farfetched to many hard-headed thinkers. Of course, such notions were not wholly new. For ages some thinkers have held that man was not of much consequence. Ancient Greeks pictured him as a plaything of the gods. Oriental philosophy has often pictured man as an insignificant creature, a slave to the wheel of life, which turns on and on carrying man through an interminable life of woe.

Such thinking fosters the idea that the group should always come before the individual. According to this belief, the purpose of education should be to promote the welfare of the group. In societies that place the group before the individual great stress is placed upon accepting one's role in society and in cooperating. Boys and girls are taught to subordinate their personal desires in order to cooperate, as in the "Hopi way," and to sacrifice themselves to the state in case of necessity, as did the Spartan boys and the many who died for their native lands during the recent World Wars. The ends justify the means, they say, and the ends are greater than the individual.

Theories that emphasize the unimportance of man lend themselves to mass learning techniques, the overriding of individual differences, and to curricula that accentuate the acceptance of one's fate, conformity, and compliance with the wishes of the powers that be. Creativeness, individual expression, individuality, nonconformity, and the seeking for personal fulfillment are discouraged by such philosophies.

THE VOCATIONAL AIMS

In the minds of most parents and students, the major purpose of education is to prepare boys and girls for a vocation. Vocational preparation has

[11] William H. Kilpatrick, *Philosophy of Education* (New York: The Macmillan Company, 1951), p. 325.

always been an important educational aim at all school levels and is accepted without question by great numbers of educators, both traditionalist and progressive. Nevertheless, in some circles teaching practical and vocational subjects is in bad repute.

The rift between the liberal and practical studies was made quite clear by Aristotle in his *Politics*, as we have seen in Chapter I. Aristotle's reason for dividing the studies into liberal and illiberal ones seems to come from his theory that man is part spirit and part matter. The liberal studies were associated with the intellectual, that is, spiritual, side of man. The practical arts, on the other hand, were associated with the vulgar body and its vulgar appetites. Particularly was this true of the vocational studies, which had the additional stigma of being associated with the working classes.

In addition to the aura of being "spiritual studies," the liberal arts have had certain other advantages that have made them socially superior to the practical and vocational arts. Since the time of Plato, who introduced the disciplinary concept of education, teachers have thought that the liberal studies trained the mind better. Mathematics and language study have been particularly favored as mind trainers. Moreover, because they were thought to deal with universal truths, their advocates believed that the study of liberal arts could prepare students for any future situation.

A more reasonable argument for liberal studies is that when taught well, they give pupils an opportunity for hard study and close thinking and so are wonderful media by which to teach pupils good habits of thinking and working. Probably this last argument, plus the fact that certain of the liberal studies have very practical uses in the modern world, is the most common reason for teaching the liberal studies today.[12]

Progressivists tend to view the traditional awe for the liberal studies with horror. They reject the hylomorphic theory of man. To them man is all one piece. Neither the body nor the soul can be better than the other because they are both one. Therefore the practical and the liberal studies can no longer be separated on the basis of the spiritual and the bodily. In fact, they cannot even be separated on the basis of abstractness, because many vocational subjects are very abstract indeed and require closer thinking than the so-called liberal studies do.

As a matter of fact, progressivists are inclined to think that, in the final analysis, it is not the subject matter but the way it is taught that counts. In their opinion, if the teaching emphasizes learning how to think, probably the pupil will learn to think. If the teaching does not, then probably the pupil will not learn it, no matter what the content is.[13]

---

[12] See Mark Van Doren, *Liberal Education* (Boston: Beacon Press, 1959), for an eloquent defense of the liberal tradition.

[13] Thut, *op. cit.*, gives an excellent account of the development of these theories.

WHAT SUBJECT MATTER?

THE VALUE OF SUBJECT MATTER

Both traditionalists and progressivists recognize the value of subject matter. Progressivists are likely to put considerably more stress on the child than the traditionalists do, but in spite of much invective to the contrary, progressivists, even in child-centered schools, believe that boys and girls must be taught something. That something is subject matter. However, progressivists and traditionalists disagree on many points, such as:

> What knowledge is most worth?
> Should we emphasize process or information?
> Should a curriculum be fixed or flexible, constant or differentiated, practical or liberal?

To a large extent one's answers to these questions depend upon one's system of values.

Beliefs Concerning Values. The educators who hold to essentialist and perennialist beliefs are inclined to look upon values as absolute, fixed, objective qualities inherent or intrinsic in the thing being valued. According to their theories a pound of gold has worth because it is a pound of gold. It makes no difference at all where the gold is, what use one has for the gold, what role gold has in the culture, or what the market value for gold is today. Its real value is always the same. Any fluctuation in the market value merely indicates that we do not appreciate the gold's real value.

Thus, according to this way of looking at value, a thing is right or it is wrong, it is good or it is bad, it is up to standard or it is not. If it is wrong to kill, then to kill is wrong—no matter whether one kills in self-defense or as a soldier on the field of battle or as an executioner carrying out the sentence of the court. Value is value, without exception. Circumstances do not alter cases.

The progressives, as a rule, look askance at any value held to be absolute. Rather they are inclined to believe that values are relative, changeable, subjective, and instrumental. According to them, the value of our pound of gold depends upon the situation. If I wanted a pound of gold, if gold is valued in my country, if the market value for gold is up, then the value of the gold is greater to me than it would be if these conditions did not obtain. Value, according to this theory, is not intrinsic but determined by outside influences.

Value is also instrumental. Things are not just good, they are good for something. The worth of something is determined by the use one can put it to. In a bank, a loaf of bread may not be as valuable as the pound of gold, but it is worth much more than the gold on a desert isle. Whatever is useless is worthless. Handsome is as handsome does. Instead of being absolute, value is conditional and fluctuates with the situation.

The two arguments presented have been extremes. In actual practice, both camps tend to compromise their positions. The philosopher who defines values as want satisfaction may also point out the considerable difference between what one desires and what one should desire. Likewise the absolutist may point out that some values are quite obviously instrumental. Still one can say that, in general, educational perennialists and essentialists are inclined to believe in fixed, absolute, intrinsic, objective values, and that progressivists and reconstructionists tend to favor relative, changeable, subjective, instrumental values.

THREE THEORIES CONCERNING SUBJECT MATTER

In line with the above are three viewpoints concerning the worth of subject matter. They are: (1) Subject matter should be taught for its own sake; (2) subject matter should be taught for use; (3) subject matter is merely a medium for the teaching of intellectual processes, skills, attitudes, ideals, and appreciations.[14]

The first of these positions derives from the belief that everything has intrinsic value. Holders of this position believe that each subject has value in and of itself. Naturally then, some subjects are more valuable than others, not because they are more useful than others but because they have greater intrinsic value. According to this position, whether or not the pupil will ever make use of Latin, algebra, or physical education, does not matter. The important thing is that he study the subjects that have the greatest intrinsic value.

The second position holds that the value of a subject depends upon the use that is made of it. This position derives from the philosophical belief that value is operational. Basically this is an essentialist position. According to it, in planning curricula, priority should be given to those studies that the boys and girls most likely will need to know. In this sense these subjects are essential. The doctrine of contingent value discussed in Chapter VI comes from this belief.

The third position is that favored by the progressives. In this changing world of changing values, no subject matter is essential for its intrinsic value, and it is very difficult to tell which subject matter is really likely to be most functional. Therefore the progressives say it is not the subject matter but the process of education that matters. In their view subject matter is only a medium by which to teach pupils the skills they need to become independent individuals. Consequently they favor flexible curricula, teacher–pupil planning, and courses in which plans evolve as the class goes along.

[14] See J. Paul Leonard, *Developing the Secondary School Curriculum*, rev. ed. (New York: Holt, Rinehart and Winston, Inc., 1955), Ch. 9, for a more extended explanation of those three positions.

Education for Immediate or Deferred Use. Traditionally, secondary-school curricula have been based on the second of the theoretical positions concerning subject matter described above. Its purpose has been to prepare pupils for adult life. Nowadays the skills and knowledges taught in traditional schools are largely the ones that presumably the students will need when they grow up. Moral virtues are taught authoritatively now so that the pupils will know how to discipline themselves as adults. The progressivists, on the contrary, are inclined to believe that if the youth learns how to cope with his adolescent life, his adulthood will take care of itself. Therefore progressivists concentrate on subject matter that is important to the problems of youthful living and tend to slough over much of the knowledge that traditionalists feel youths should store up for possible use in adult life. After all, they imply, what is subject matter anyway but a vehicle for teaching pupils how to meet whatever situation comes along.

A FIXED OR A FLEXIBLE CURRICULUM

By and large, traditionalists seem to think that the curriculum should consist of subject matter that has permanent value. On this point generally they are divided into two camps, one of which, the perennialists, insists that we should turn our curriculum back to reinstate the values and subject matter that have proved themselves in the past and the other of which, the essentialists, hopes to include the essential subjects of today. In effect, both of these positions advocate about the same curriculum, although the essentialists are more favorable to the sciences than the perennialists are.[15]

Essentialists and perennialists tend to believe in the need for constant fixed curricula because they believe that this is a world of permanence. Of course, they recognize that the world is full of surface changes, but they discount most of these as mere surface variations that in no way affect the essence of anything. So they remain convinced of the permanence of all basic things and their values.

Belief in immutable essences or universals comes from ancient Platonic and Aristotelian hypotheses. In Plato's scheme reality consisted of immaterial ideas; material things are only poor imitations of reality, which exists only in spirit universally, eternally, and perfectly—everywhere the same, always. Aristotle did not accept Plato's ideas, but he did believe in universals. His theory was that although reality was both material and spiritual, the essence of every object or being was its form—another perfect universal spiritual abstraction.

The rise of science and the discovery of the so-called scientific laws strengthened the belief in universals. The startling discoveries of Copernicus, Galileo, Newton, and other great scientists seemed to indicate that

15 See Brameld, *op. cit.*

the universe ran precisely and accurately according to laws that were irrevocable, eternal, and universal. In essence, the scientific laws of Newton and the first principles of Aristotle seem to have much in common.

To the eyes of those who believe in universals truth also seems to be universal and unchanging, for, because the essence of things cannot change, then truth cannot change. Furthermore, neither can value. Studies that were true and valuable in ancient Greece are just as true and valuable today. Therefore once we get hold of a good curriculum we should keep it, for, if it is really good, it will always be good, and if it is the best, it will always be best. There is no need to change. That is why some scholars place so much faith in the "Great Books Curriculum"[16] and why a visiting Britisher can take pride in the fact that their mathematics curriculum had not changed in "the last five hundred years."[17]

Progressivists usually believe that this is a world of flux. They are quite skeptical of the existence of essence, universals, and universal truths. About the only universal law to which they subscribe is this: *And this too shall change.*

This attitude is quite common to the man in the street. He cannot see much sense in the theory of universals, and many philosophers, including the ancient Greeks mentioned above, have agreed with him. Among these have been the twentieth-century progressivists and the medieval nominalists.

Modern scientific research has also questioned the theory of absolutes and universals. The results of modern observation and experimentation have shaken scientists' faith in the immutable laws of nature postulated by early scientists. Evidently the laws of nature are not always obeyed. There seems to be an exception to every rule. Instead of moving steadily in their courses as they ought to, the planets seem to jiggle a little. And matter seems to be made up of little bits of something or other that keep flying about bumping into each other helter-skelter so that we cannot measure them accurately, but must resort to statistical approximations—means, medians, standard deviations, probable errors, and so on, in describing their actions. Apparently the truth is not so certain after all.

Progressivists are likely to believe that truth is also in a state of flux. Truth, they are inclined to believe, depends upon the circumstances. According to their operational truth, nothing is true in or of itself alone but because of its consequences. In other words, if a theory works, then it is true; if it does not work, it is not. The same criterion holds for other data also. If they work, we can consider them true; if they do not, we must conclude that they are false.

---

[16] See Mortimer Adler, "In Defense of the Philosophy of Education," in Nelson B. Henry (ed.), *Philosophies of Education*, Forty-first Yearbook, National Society for the Study of Education (Chicago: University of Chicago Press, 1942).

[17] He was wrong, of course. Their mathematics curriculum has changed.

This concept conceives of truth as much more flexible than the essential belief. Under the essential belief truth is definite and unalterable; there can be no hedging or shilly-shallying; either something is true or it is not true. But the progressive pragmatic view of truth is not definite at all. One cannot really tell whether something is true until one sees the consequences. Moreover, the truth varies from time to time, from occasion to occasion, and from place to place. And so one cannot mark out any subject matter as essential to the curriculum. As a result of this belief they see no reason why we should cling to any particular curriculum or subject unless it has a practical, that is, operational, value. Consequently they are inclined to think that the best curriculum is one that is continually revised. If there is one thing that progressivists are sure of, it is that the curriculum best suited for today will not be the best suited for tomorrow.

DIFFERENTIATED VS. COMMON CURRICULUM

Implicit in the argument that the curriculum should be fixed and unchanging is the notion that the same curriculum should serve all pupils. Modern progressivists and some traditionalists feel that, on the contrary, curricula should be differentiated so that they can best serve the needs of individual boys and girls.

Providing for Individual Differences. As we have noted in an earlier section, many persons believe that one aim of education should be to provide an elite, and therefore there should be one type of curriculum provided for the selected few and another for the run-of-the-mill students. Even when they did not favor the establishing of an elite, those who believe that persons differ from each other have often favored differentiated curricula. Some of them have gone so far as to advocate a separate individual curriculum for each pupil. More frequently school people develop curricula for different purposes, such as for college preparation, for general education, and for vocational preparation. In order to build curricula suited to the differences in individuals, curriculum builders have introduced multiple tracks, parallel curricula, ability and homogeneous grouping, accelerated programs, and a host of other devices designed to differentiate the curriculum so that the individual pupil may make the most of his peculiar potentialities.

A Common Curriculum for All. On the other hand, some educationists and educators are suspicious of attempts to provide for individual differences. Quite understandably, but perhaps wrongly, they bristle at anything that smacks of creating an elite or granting special privileges to any group. Besides, they fear that differentiated curricula and other provisions for individual differences may deprive boys and girls of the equality of opportunity which is their right in a democracy.

At this point it should be emphasized that many educators feel that democracy does not imply a need for curricular sameness. Equality, they say, may imply equality in the sight of God, but that does not necessarily mean that each of us is equally worthy. One can, according to this belief, provide for each according to his worth (or his abilities) without in any way violating his right to equal treatment. In a similar vein some speak of equality of opportunity and of equal rights and freedom. According to this view, each person has a right to try, and no one should say him nay, but it is assumed that the combined influence of native ability and effort will separate the wheat from the chaff. Jefferson's idea of a natural aristocracy is sympathetic to this view.

The Neo-Scholastic Argument. Because of a quite different theory, some modern scholastics favor a common curriculum in preference to a differentiated one. In brief, their theory holds that because in essence all people are much the same, all persons should have much the same curriculum. Adler supports this belief with syllogisms such as the following:

> *Major.* All individuals having the same specific nature have the same natural powers or capacities.
> *Minor.* All individual men have the same specific human nature.
> *Conclusion.* All individual men have the same natural powers or capacities.[18]

and

> *Major.* Good habits (virtues) are the same for all men.
> *Minor.* Education should aim at the formation of good habits.
> *Conclusion.* Education should aim at the same objectives for all man (or, what is equivalent, the aim of education should be the same for all men).[19]

To them it seems only logical that all pupils should be given an opportunity to study the same intellectual material. Keeping this material from pupils debars them from an opportunity to train their minds and from any chance of becoming familiar with the great works that all men should know. To the objection that all pupils cannot cope with this material, the scholastic replies "that all individual men have the same natural powers or capacities" and so anyone can master anything anyone else can if he tries long and hard enough. Besides, no one has the right to deny any youth the opportunity to come in contact with the great truths whether he succeeds in profiting from them or not.

Who's To Judge? A serious problem that causes some educators to favor common curricula when they might otherwise favor differentiated curricula is this: How does one separate the superior from the inferior? If one does provide special curricula, how does one know which pupils will benefit from them? How can one be sure that one is not dooming a potential leader to mediocrity by placing him in an environment that will never waken his potential or give him a chance to waken himself?

[18] Adler, *op. cit.,* p. 244.
[19] *Ibid.,* p. 239.

Our schools are notorious for branding geniuses, such as Sir Winston Churchill and Thomas Edison, nincompoops and fostering nameless nincompoops as geniuses. According to this point of view, to separate the geniuses from the nincompoops at 11 plus, as in the British system, requires an omniscience not frequently found in mere mortals.

Because human judgment has proven to be so frail, many teachers, who otherwise are concerned about individual differences, feel that all boys and girls should have a chance at the most demanding curricula. If they belong to the traditionalist school, teachers usually advocate that the curricula for all should consist of the traditional academic courses. In practice, however, the modern high schools have had to maintain differentiated curricula in order to meet the demands of the parents.

AUTHORITY, DEMOCRACY, AND FREEDOM

THE CASE FOR AUTHORITY

Throughout the entire course of recorded history, men have generally believed that there was more to the world than meets the eye. This is why we have created authorities to direct us, to inform us, to correct us, and to watch over us. We have created churches to teach, explain, and interpret the absolute truths and to see to it that we behave in accordance with these truths. We have created governments that enact laws and regulations that explain to us how we should behave and that try to see to it that we behave as we should. We have created schools in which school officials decide what should be taught, and how it should be taught, and those officials try to see to it that teachers carry out the curricula presented. Likewise, teachers determine what pupils should learn and how they should learn it and try to see to it that the pupils learn as they are supposed to. All our history is permeated by the idea of an authority that knows best and should direct and control our behavior.

Almost all the educational systems that have been tried have been more or less authoritarian. The age, knowledge, and experience of the adult teacher puts him in a position where he is clearly superior to the pupil—particularly at the elementary and secondary-school levels. Therefore almost every educational theorist has thought it necessary for teachers to give pupils the benefit of their superior knowledge. R. B. Perry, for instance, insists that education must use the method of authority because, of necessity, education involves restraint, redirection, and control by those who know better.[20] This is generally the position taken by many idealists and realists, and, in spite of their protestations to the contrary, reconstructionists.

Belief in the necessity for at least some authoritarianism is a natural

[20] R. B. Perry, as quoted in Israel Scheffler, *Philosophy and Education* (Boston: Allyn and Bacon, Inc., 1958), pp. 17 and 23.

sequence to beliefs in absolute knowledge that exist apart from the individual and become known to man by revelation or by discovery. In either case the knowledge comes from an authoritative source and is passed on to the learner, who himself can become an authority. Moreover, in order to become an authority, the learner must submit himself, to some extent at least, to the authority which is his source of learning. Thus learning is always in some degree imposed upon the learner. Lectures, demonstrations, recitations, pseudo problems with predetermined solutions, drill, and other teacher-centered types of teaching are often means used for the authoritative imposition of knowledge.

Faith in authority is also closely tied to the concept that education should create an elite. Members of the elite presumably have greater ability and better knowledge than other people do. Therefore, the argument goes, because the elite are better informed and more talented, they should force their will on the common people whether the common people like it or not.

THE DEMOCRATIC SCHOOL

Even though educators usually have a high regard for authority, many thinkers, particularly pragmatists and reconstructionists, have become very suspicious of authoritarian education. Evidently they fear with Lord Acton that "power tends to corrupt, absolute power corrupts absolutely." The history of education, particularly in totalitarian lands, is replete with incidents that seem to confirm their fears.[21]

Whether authority corrupts or not, in recent years authority has become suspect. One reason for this is that so often it has been proved to be wrong. The discoveries of a host of modern scientists have overthrown many dogmas formerly held by authority to be incontestable, absolute truths. These discoveries, coupled with the experience of many Americans that poor boys do make good and that ordinary men can and do conduct their affairs extraordinarily well when the occasion arises, have led to disenchantment with authority and a rising faith in the common man. This reaction was particularly characteristic of the small pioneer communities where the common man ruled himself quite satisfactorily without the benefit of a ruling or expert elite. Such experiences have given ordinary Americans faith in their own capabilities and made them suspicious of authority.

In a reaction against the dreary schools of the nineteenth century John Dewey and others similarly oriented tried to create democratic schools. In these schools pupils were to be freed from imposed knowledge and from the domination of authoritarian teachers. Here the pupil would be free to investigate areas of genuine interest to him and to unleash his mind so as to cope creatively with actual problems whose as yet unknown answers were worth trying to find out. Instead of school policy,

---

[21] Kilpatrick, *op. cit.,* Ch. 1 *et passim,* cites numerous examples.

rules, curriculum, teaching methods, and so on, being imposed, the young people were to share in governing the school and planning its activities.[22]

TO INDOCTRINATE OR NOT TO INDOCTRINATE

Men convinced that truth is outside somewhere waiting to be received or discovered frequently insist that the youth of the nation must be indoctrinated so that they can become good Americans. They believe, as did Herbart, that emotions are learned from knowledge. Therefore they take it for granted that pupils must be indoctrinated with the right knowledge so that they will behave properly and have the right beliefs, attitudes, ideals, appreciations, and skills.

The progressivist fears indoctrination as he fears all authoritative methods. He has faith only in the method of intelligent thinking. In his estimation no pupil should ever be asked to accept any belief without an opportunity to examine all the data and put the belief to the test. Furthermore, because he believes all truth to be temporary, the progressivist presumes that the pupil must learn to determine his own beliefs for himself. Consequently, under no condition should we use the method of authority to force any doctrine, belief, or attitude on an immature human. To do so is immoral. It prevents him from becoming himself and also prevents him from reaching the truth. Because the truth always changes, indoctrination may fix hard beliefs in the youth that will make it impossible to face facts objectively in the future and to make the proper decisions when the truth changes.[23]

This type of thinking upsets many traditionalists. Kandel says that because of fear of indoctrination, democracies often fail to teach the democratic "ideals upon which the common will must be founded."[24] Brameld and other constructionists are afraid that the progressivist views of Kilpatrick will lead to a loss of direction and aimless wandering and even to the following of false gods. In spite of Kilpatrick's warning that indoctrination leads to running in the ruts and inability to cope with new situations, most educators still continue to teach authoritatively, in at least some aspects, and most teachers try to indoctrinate old beliefs into the pupils because they think that these are the right beliefs.

TO ACCEPT OR TO CREATE

As we have noted earlier some philosophers have thought of the world as a machine that grinds on inexorably for no particular reason and to no particular end. Another group of thinkers have contended that the world is progressing purposefully toward some definite end. Among

---

[22] Thut, *op. cit.*, Ch. 21.

[23] See Kilpatrick, *op. cit.*, particularly Ch. 9 and p. 307 ff.

[24] I. L. Kandel, *Conflicting Theories of Education* (New York: The Macmillan Company, 1938), p. 65.

them was Hegel, who thought that God had a plan for the universe and that change is God thinking and tinkering with his plan.

The upshot of both of these theories is a conviction that the world is just about as good as one can expect and that there is very little one can do to improve it. Therefore the wise man will not "kick against the pricks" but will submit to the world as it is and learn to get along with it and be content with his lot.

The common belief that human nature is fixed and unchangeable also supports the position that one should accept the world passively. This belief is common to both those who profess to believe that man is a special creation and those who believe that he is just another animal. The arguments for it seem to be, on the one hand, that God made man as a finished product and so he cannot be changed and, on the other hand, that if man is only an animal, to expect better behavior from him is merely pipe dreaming. Believers in the biological concept are especially pessimistic because they are inclined to be convinced that this is a dog-eat-dog world in which only the fittest survive. Educationally their beliefs can lead to an emphasis on the practical, the vocational, and the materialistic aspects of education.

Akin to the problem of mutability of human nature is another basic philosophical problem: whether or not people are free to determine their own lives or whether in the long run all is determined for us by an outside power. Traditionalists consider man to be relatively helpless. Even though individuals may have a modicum of choice, final decisions are made by the outside power. In any case the mere mortal can do little but to submit to the will of the Almighty. In fact, one of the world's great religions has incorporated this idea of submission into its name, *Islam*.[25] The necessity for submission is also supported by the determinists, who feel that present events are all determined by what happens before. Consequently we humans can only make superficial decisions, which are forced on us by the events that lead up to the decision.

Submission as a way of life is not acceptable to everyone. Tragedy is full of stories of men who have defied the Gods and have been destroyed by their temerity. Other poets have proclaimed with Henley that

> I am the master of my fate;
> I am the captain of my soul.

Much of Christianity takes this point of view. If one really tries, one can overcome all one's difficulties and make one's way to the Promised Land, and in the long run, one can shape one's own destiny and that of the world in which one lives. Progressivists also believe that man is not entirely a creature of environmental influence. True, the environment influences the person, but the person also influences the environment.

---

[25] Defined according to the *Oxford English Dictionary* as "resignation, surrendering (to God)."

In this interaction the individual has considerable influence on his own fate because he can, at least to a degree, adjust the environment to suit himself. Furthermore, if this environment does not suit him, by using his intelligence he can create a new environment. Man was not made to submit but rather to make his impress on the world. When he is not satisfied with his fate, he attempts to create a better one. Whether this is because of a creative force, or because of his immortal soul, or because of his own creative intelligence, makes little difference. Man is not fate's plaything. He cannot be written off as unimportant, for he can, if he tries hard enough, change the world.

This very optimistic view of life implies the need of a dynamic education that will give the young people the power to determine the proper direction of human destiny. In contrast, the concept that we can only submit ourselves to the will of fate leads to a passive educational system designed to preserve the *status quo*. In short, those who believe that man must make his own way favor creative learning, whereas those who believe that we must accept the world as it is are more likely to favor instruction.

TRADITION AND THE MODERN CURRICULUM

Essentialists and perennialists as a rule feel the need to glorify our cultural heritage. Conservatives, like Russel Kirk, assert that the modern world needs a reaffirmation of the truths that lie in tradition. They contend that in the United States preoccupation with the immediate has led to a "tendency to minimize the lessons of tradition and to stress the importance of change."[26] While they do not object to change, they object to change for the sake of change. Change, they feel, should be slow and orderly and should progress toward well-recognized goals. These critics usually are not the kind who are enthusiastic about things just because they are old, but because they think that the standards, values, ideas, and beliefs of the past have proved themselves. By preserving the tradition we can give life continuity, stability, and direction. If we forget the values of tradition, they believe, we shall flounder aimlessly from change to change.

WHICH TRADITION?

The progressivists believe that this is a world of change. Nothing can be preserved forever, and if it could be, it would change anyway. Venus de Milo once had arms! Consequently progressivists believe that by holding to the past we distort the future. They believe, as so many laymen do, that if one does not move forward, one falls backward. Nevertheless, most of the thoughtful progressives do not gainsay the values of the past and of tradition. Their position is that nothing is good just because

---

[26] Kandel, *op. cit.*, p. 57.

it is old and that tradition does not guarantee worth. Past values, standards, practices, and beliefs need to be evaluated just as modern ones do. The valid ones can help us today and in the future, but the false ones will hinder us.

The past includes many traditions and many lessons. We must pick and choose from them. As we have seen, what is commonly called the traditional education is associated with perennialism and essentialism, but progressivist education too has a long and honorable tradition. It includes Socrates and the Sophists of ancient Greece, the Renaissance schoolmaster Vittorino, the seventeenth-century Comenius, the eighteenth-century Rousseau, the nineteenth-century Pestalozzi and Parker, as well as the modern progressivists who made themselves felt with great force in the *early* twentieth century. As Weisberg says:

> If what I have been arguing is correct, the issue of "traditionalism" vs. "experimentalism" in education is to be construed in a radically different light. No traditionalist can appeal to tradition *qua* tradition, for, as I have tried to show, he is appealing only to some value which must be defined on valued grounds. Moreover, "tradition" is no longer the exclusive province of "traditionalists." The questions which should concern educators are the specific ones, and include a variety of traditions. We move now from general appeals to tradition to concern for specific issues and values. And this is where the great debates in educational theory should take place.[27]

In short, the problems of pedagogy should be decided on their merits in view of past experience, present knowledge, and future possibilities.

SUMMARY

Much of the controversy in secondary education results from differences in philosophical background. In general, educators and educationists are divided into two main camps—the traditionalists and the progressivists. Basically both groups want the same thing of education, that is, they want education to improve pupils' minds and to make them better citizens. But because of their different orientations they find it difficult to agree on how to achieve these *desiderata*, or even on what "improving the mind" and "better citizenship" are. To a traditionalist, improving the mind is primarily filling the mind with good things from an outside source; the contrary-minded progressivists believe that mind developing is essentially a do-it-yourself project. For these reasons traditionalists favor instruction, whereas progressivists favor creative self-learning. Similarly traditionalists hope to teach good citizenship by means of instruction in what is right, but progressivists would have the pupil do it by living democratically. This same division also can be seen in the traditionalists' emphasis on education as preparation for the future, the

[27] Harold Weisberg, "Tradition and the Traditionalists," in Sheffler, *op. cit.*, p. 243.

need for developing elites, and holding group values over those of the individual, as against the progressivists' insistence on education for now, individual values, and "democratic" education.

The ancient dichotomy of body and spirit has caused a split between the liberal and practical arts and the downgrading of the vocational aim of education. Traditionalists continue to uphold the classic belief in superiority of the liberal subjects, but progressivists have, by and large, rejected the dichotomy of body and soul and with it the superiority of either the liberal or the practical arts over the other. They suspect that it is not subject matter itself but how one uses the subject matter that really makes the difference.

All teaching must contain subject matter. But what subject matter? Traditionalists are inclined toward accepting permanent curricula based on the innate or operational value of subject matter; progressivists lean toward flexible curricula whose values change according to use, but which are primarily valuable as media for teaching processes.

Both traditionalists and progressivists believe in differentiated curricula, and both traditionalists and progressivists believe in common curricula. Traditionalists base their support of differentiated curricula on society's need for developing an elite of the specially talented; the progressivists, on the need for developing each individual's potential to the utmost. Some demands for common curricula seem to stem from misunderstanding of the nature of boys and girls and of democracy by members of both camps.

What type of curriculum best serves a democratic nation? Is it a curriculum that features authoritarian classes, imposed discipline, and indoctrinated beliefs? The traditionalists think so, for how else can inexperienced children learn to become right thinking, well-disciplined adults? But in progressive theory only through creative learning by means of the method of intelligence, self-discipline, and practicing democratic living in schools can the child become the father of a democratic man. Probably one reason for this difference in viewpoint comes from the traditionalists' basically pessimistic belief that one has to accept the world as it is and make the best of it, as opposed to the progressivists' optimisim which holds that through his own efforts man can remake this battered old earth into paradise. "Man is the measure of all things," and so he should not submit to authority, power, and order, but should continually strive for progress.

SUGGESTED READINGS

ARISTOTLE. *Politics.* Book VIII.
    A description of Aristotle's basic position concerning the curriculum and its purposes.
BAYLES, ERNEST E. *Democratic Educational Theory.* New York: Harper and Row, Inc., 1960.

An excellent analysis of democratic education from a pragmatic, relativist point of view.

BECK, CARLTON E. *Philosophical Foundations of Guidance.* Englewood Cliffs, New Jersey: Prentice-Hall, Inc., 1963.

The author traces historically what he considers to be the philosophical foundations of the guidance movements and offers propositions and a framework for the philosophy of guidance in the future.

BODE, BOYD H. *Modern Educational Theories.* New York: The Macmillan Company, 1927.

An analysis and evaluation of varying educational approaches by one of America's greatest educational philosophers, a leader in the progressive movement.

BRACKENBURY, ROBERT L. *Getting Down to Cases.* New York: G. P. Putnam and Sons, 1959.

An elementary text in the philosophy of education which presents important educational problems. These problems are analyzed from different points of view.

BRAMELD, THEODORE. *Philosophies of Education in Cultural Perspective.* New York: Holt, Rinehart and Winston, Inc., 1955.

An educational point of view giving analyses and criticisms of progressivism, essentialism, and perennialism which seeks to acquaint the secondary schoolteacher with the kinds of concepts and problems that are central to philosophy, education, and culture in their interrelations in today's world. This book is written from the viewpoint of a reconstructionist.

———. *Toward a Reconstructed Philosophy of Education.* New York: Holt, Rinehart and Winston, Inc., 1956.

The reconstructionist position presented by one of its leading proponents.

BROUDY, HARRY S. *Building a Philosophy of Education.* Second edition. Englewood Cliffs, New Jersey: Prentice-Hall, Inc., 1961.

A popular textbook on the philosophy of education. Chapters 12–15 deal specifically with problems of curriculum and method.

BUTLER, J. DONALD. *Four Philosophies.* Revised edition. New York: Harper and Row, Inc., 1957.

One of the very best textbooks on philosophies of education and their practices in education and religion.

CHILDS, JOHN L. *American Progressivism and Education.* New York: Holt, Rinehart and Winston, Inc., 1956.

An important study by one of the leading pragmatists on the past and future of pragmatism as an educational movement.

DEWEY, JOHN. *Democracy and Education.* New York: The Macmillan Company, 1916. Reprinted as a Macmillan Paperback book, 1961.

An educational classic in which Dewey presents most of his basic educational positions.

HANSEN, KENNETH. *Philosophy of American Education.* Englewood Cliffs, New Jersey: Prentice-Hall, Inc., 1960.

An attempt by the author to select and synthesize notions from various philosophies into a practical, workable educational philosophy for modern times.

HENRY, NELSON B. (ed.). *Modern Philosophies and Education.* Fifty-fourth Yearbook of the National Society for the Study of Education, Part I. Chicago: University of Chicago Press, 1955.

An important symposium of articles by scholars of various schools of philosophy in which they explain and justify their individual positions.

———. *Philosophies of Education.* Forty-first Yearbook of the National Society for the Study of Education, Part I. Chicago: University of Chicago Press, 1942.

Description of five major philosophical positions—pragmatism, realism, idealism, Aristotelianism, and scholasticism—by their leading representatives. This is one of the best references for a beginner in the field of educational philosophy.

KANDEL, I. L. *Conflicting Theories of Education.* New York: The Macmillan Company, 1938.

An examination of various problems and theories of education by a foremost essentialist who objects to much in both traditional and progressive theory.

KILPATRICK, WILLIAM HEARD. *The Foundation of Method.* New York: The Macmillan Company, 1925.

One of the clearest expositions of the progressive theory.

———. *Remaking the Curriculum.* New York: Newson and Company, 1936.

A series of articles originally published in the N.E.A. Journal, in which Kilpatrick explains and justifies some of his educational theory. Chapter 7 deals specifically with the secondary-school curriculum.

KNELLER, GEORGE F. *Existentialism and Education.* New York: Philosophical Library, Inc., 1958.

One of the few good references on the relationship of existentialism to educational theory.

LEONARD, J. PAUL. *Developing the Secondary School Curriculum.* Revised edition. New York: Holt, Rinehart and Winston, Inc., 1953.

Contains excellent chapters on the theoretical bases of various beliefs concerning the secondary-school curriculum.

LOCKE, JOHN. "Some Thoughts Concerning Education" and an "Essay on Human Understanding." Excerpts from these works are contained in Sterling P. Lamprecht, *Locke Selections.* New York: Charles Scribner's Sons, 1928.

Locke's theories concerning the nature of the mind and education, including his *tabula rasa* and *disciplinary* beliefs.

MARITAIN, JACQUES. *Education at the Crossroads.* New Haven: Yale University Press, 1943.

A discussion of the purposes and practices of education by a leading Thomist philosopher and critic of progressive education.

PARK, JOE (ed.). *Selected Readings in the Philosophy of Education.* Second edition. New York: The Macmillan Company, 1963.

A book of readings in the philosophy of education selected to explain and illustrate various schools of educational thought: pragmatism, idealism, realism, catholicism, protestantism, Judaism, and contemporary movements.

PHENIX, PHILIP H. *Philosophy of Education.* New York: Holt, Rinehart and Winston, Inc., 1958.

An excellent, standard introductory text in educational philosophy.

PLATO. *Meno.*

A dialogue in which Plato presents his theory of ideas and the nature of learning and teaching.

———. *The Republic.* (Particularly Book VII).

Plato's description of Utopia. One of the great books on education and educational theory. Book VII presents the theory of ideas, but comments concerning education are interspersed throughout the entire work.

———. *Protagoras.*

A report of a discussion between Protagoras and Socrates concerning the teaching of the moral virtues and whether moral virtues can, in fact, be taught at all.

RYLE, GILBERT. *The Concept of Mind.* London and New York: Hutchinson's University Library, 1949.

An attempt to explode traditional "myths" concerning the nature of the mind as something different from the body.

SCHEFFLER, ISRAEL. *Philosophy and Education.* Boston: Allyn and Bacon, Inc., 1958.

A book of readings representing various viewpoints concerning certain problems of education. The author attempts to establish a closer relationship between general and educational philosophy.

SKINNER, B. F. *Science and Human Behavior.* New York: The Macmillan Company, 1953.

This book presents a theory of learning which is the basis of much of the present theory behind teaching machines.

SMITH, B. OTHANEL, WILLIAM O. STANLEY, and J. HARLAND SHORES. *Fundamentals of Curriculum Development.* Revised edition. New York: Harcourt, Brace and World, 1957. Part V.

A careful study of educational and other theories in direct relationship to their implications for the curriculum.

THUT, I. N. *The Story of Education.* New York: McGraw-Hill Book Company, Inc., 1957.

An excellent, readable history of the philosophy of education which attempts to show the development of three basic positions in educational theory from the earliest times to the present.

ULICH, ROBERT. *History of Educational Thought.* New York: American Book Company, 1950.

Excellent presentation of the educational theories and beliefs of the most famous and influential thinkers from Plato to Dewey.

VAN DOREN, MARK. *Liberal Education.* Boston: Beacon Press, 1959. First published by Henry Holt and Company, New York, 1943.

An extremely interesting discussion of liberal education by a famous author and teacher in the humanistic tradition.

WHITEHEAD, ALFRED NORTH. *The Aims of Education.* New York: The Macmillan Company, 1929. Also published as a paperback by The New American Library, New York, 1953.

An essay on the aims of education by the great mathematician and philosopher.

Chapter 3

Psychological
Backgrounds

Psychology is a relatively new science and a particularly difficult one. Because of its newness and difficulty it contains a great number of unsubstantiated theories concerning the nature of man and how he learns. Presumably many of these theories will be eliminated as more and more psychological facts are discovered. In the meantime various schools of psychology hold conflicting theories. Still, the various schools of psychology are not so far apart as one might believe. All of them accept as true such a large common body of facts that for educators to foster curricula incompatible with the nature of the learner and the nature of learning seems to be unnecessary.

THE NATURE OF THE LEARNER

THE SELF

Each pupil is an individual. He is duplicated nowhere in the world, never has been and never will be. He comes to our doors with his own peculiar abilities, talent, interests, knowledges, attitudes, ideals, appreciations, skills, and understandings. These characteristics and potentials are the result of both the genetic make-up he has inherited from his parents and the impact of the social and physical environment in which he has lived. The sum total of all these makes up his individual personality or self. Differences in personality affect our understanding, appreciation, interests, emotions, ideals, and the like. To a great extent they determine what we perceive. A common error of teachers is to think that boys and girls see and hear the same things in a classroom. They do not, because that which one perceives is dependent on his attention, his visual or audial acuity, his past experiences, his previous understandings, his attitudes, his interests, and a myriad other things. In other words, each person's perception is dependent upon his personality. So also are his understandings and attitudes.

Consequently we err when we read into other people's acts implications based upon our own personalities or when we think that because such and such is important and interesting to us, it must be important and interesting to others. People are different, and so each one requires a different curriculum if he is to receive maximum benefit from schooling. On the other hand, although no two people are exactly alike, most people are more alike than they are different. This makes it possible, and even necessary, to provide "common experiences" in the curriculum.

EACH INDIVIDUAL AS SEVERAL SELVES

Not only is each person a unique self, he is a multiplicity of selves, for each one of us has at least four selves: his real self, the self he thinks he is, the self others think he is, and the self he would like to be. Each of these selves holds implications for curriculum building.

The real self is somewhat hard to identify. Theoretically it should be the sum of one's traits, but this definition does not suffice because our traits are not constant. Like the young hero of *She Stoops to Conquer*, who was a devil with barmaids but a poltroon with ladies, each of us has a protean quality. Circumstances alter persons and personalities, and one's real self wears many guises. From these various guises we piece together our real selves. The better the parts fit together, the healthier we shall be, but few of us are able to completely integrate all the parts of our personalities.

Quite different from what we are is what we think we are. Some persons undervalue themselves and are unhappy; others overvalue themselves and live in a "fool's paradise." Each of us is inclined to gloss over his foibles and rationalize his actions. If it were not so, many of us would lead pretty desperate lives, for our well-being requires that our self-concepts be favorable. Also desirable for our mental health is the ability to look at one's self objectively and to accept one's self for what he is.

One's self-concept is largely dependent on others' opinion of him. Even so, other pupils' evaluation of anyone differs as a result of interpersonal relationships and differences in taste, values, understandings, and other facets of their life styles. The young husband's concept of his new wife may be quite different from that of the rejected suitor.[1]

[1] Lawrence E. Cole and William F. Bruce, *Educational Psychology* (New York: Harcourt, Brace and World, Inc., 1950), pp. 324–345.

In addition to his concept of himself as he is, each of us has a concept of himself as he would like to be. Maybe he is trying to achieve this ideal, or maybe it is little more than a fantasy. In any case, this is the self that leads us on to greater heights. It makes us struggle for the good life and keeps us from degrading ourselves. It is our conscience, our goal, and our dream. Without it we would be little indeed. But when it is too far removed from our concept of what we actually are, or think we are, the effect on the ego may be shattering.

IMPLICATION FOR THE CURRICULUM

These psychological facts of life have serious implications for the curriculum maker. If the curriculum is to be adequate for all pupils, it must provide many different experiences and content so arranged that each pupil can select the experiences best suited for his particular needs. At the same time it must also provide common experiences and content so as to meet the needs youths have in common. But because people are so different in so many different ways, the curriculum must allow pupils to gain the common learnings in different ways and different amounts. Furthermore, the curriculum maker must consider the effect of the curriculum on pupils' self-concepts. A curriculum that gives pupils incorrect views of themselves is a bad curriculum. Unfortunately some school curricula do give pupils wrong impressions of their merits. By emphasizing false values, school curricula may give boys and girls bloated opinions of themselves. Witness the football hero who finds his fame to be only transitory or the supposed scholar whose school's low standards have not prepared him for college competition. Other curricula so emphasize rigor and academic excellence that they destroy pupils' self-esteem. A good curriculum will help boys and girls develop selves that are adequate for their roles in society and establish reasonable concepts of their own worth.

DEVELOPMENTAL TASKS AND NEEDS

THE DEVELOPMENTAL TASKS

The secondary-school pupil is neither a child nor an adult; he is a child becoming an adult. His basic life concern is to grow from childhood to adulthood. To do so he must successfully carry out such developmental tasks as:

1. To learn to understand oneself, to live with and compensate for one's inadequacies, and to make the most of one's assets.
2. To learn what it is to be a young man or young woman and to learn to act accordingly.
3. To develop a suitable moral code.
4. To learn how to act one's part in a heterosexual society.

5. To determine, prepare for, and become placed in his vocation.
6. To acquire a suitable philosophy of life.
7. To build a system of values.
8. To establish himself as an independent individual free from his mother's apron strings.
9. To learn how to make reasonable decisions in serious matters on his own responsibility without undue reliance on an older person.
10. To master the social and intellectual skills and knowledges necessary for adult life.
11. To learn the skills of courtship and to establish close friendships with persons of the opposite sex as preparation for finding a suitable mate.
12. To break away from his childhood home.
13. To learn what kind of person he is himself and to learn to live with himself.[2]

Differences in Accomplishing Tasks. To expect everyone to fully complete every one of his developmental tasks is too much. No one ever achieves perfection in these tasks. Rather each person achieves in some areas at the expense of other areas and makes progress in different areas at different times. Nevertheless, each person who does not successfully complete a particular developmental task remains stunted in this respect, even though he may have attained adulthood in other ways.

Most young people complete most of their developmental tasks during adolescence, but few complete them exactly on schedule. In this matter, as in other aspects of growth and development, pupils behave differently. Some pupils mature early, and others are late bloomers. Furthermore, progress in the achievement of the various goals differs within individuals: many do not complete their developmental tasks in the expected order. Yet in spite of the many differences in individuals, most of us do complete our developmental tasks according to the general pattern. This is fortunate because it seems to be difficult to complete a developmental task after the propitious moment has passed. The young man who does not succeed in freeing himself from his mother's apron strings in his youth may find it doubly hard to do so in later life.

Unevenness of Growth. The unevenness with which pupils complete their developmental tasks is typical of all aspects of human growth and development. Intellectual ability provides another example of uneven development. Intelligence tests indicate that intelligence develops in fits and starts. At times it seems to spurt ahead rapidly; at other times, to rest quietly on a plateau. Some boys and girls are late bloomers, whose

---

[2] Robert J. Havighurst, *Human Development and Education* (New York: Longmans, Green and Company, 1953), Ch. 1, pp. 9–15, 19–20; *Developmental Tasks and Education*, 2nd ed. (New York: Longmans, Green and Company, 1952).

abilities and aptitudes do not appear until after those of their peers. Consequently, although intelligence quotients tend to be fairly constant and brilliant youths usually grow up to be brilliant adults, any program that separates pupils into different curricula on the basis of intellectual ability early in life may be unjust to some children.

THE NEEDS OF YOUTH

Closely associated with the developmental tasks are the needs of youth. A need is just what the name implies—something that one requires in order to function well. These needs do not affect each individual in the same way nor do they always exert the same pressure on the same individual. Nevertheless they determine to a large extent what we are and what we do. Paramount among the needs of youth is the necessity of successfully completing as many developmental tasks as possible.

Maslow has attempted to arrange our needs into a hierarchy to show their relative importance and power. In order of strength they are:

1. Physiological needs
2. Safety
3. Love and affection
4. Self-esteem and independence
5. Prestige (approval of others)
6. Self-actualization.[3]

The point of this hierarchy is that the stronger needs must be satisfied before the higher needs become important to us. True, many poets may have starved in garrets in order to satisfy their needs for self-expression, but most of us find that when we are very hungry, somehow self-realization does not seem quite so necessary. Although individual differences in this respect are tremendous, in general, the needs in the higher categories are not insistent until the more basic needs are satisfied.

Whether Maslow's categories hold for all pupils or for any pupil at all times is doubtful, but the hierarchy does point out that youth has many kinds of important needs and that intellectual needs are not always the most urgent ones.

IMPLICATION FOR THE CURRICULUM

Both the developmental tasks and needs of youth hold forth many implications for curriculum building.

Importance of Developmental Tasks. The importance of completing one's developmental tasks can hardly be exaggerated. Presumably finishing them is more important than learning any list of French irregular

[3] A. H. Maslow, "A Theory of Human Motivation," *Psychological Review*, 50: 370–396, 1943.

verbs or geometric propositions. To what extent the school should accept the responsibility for seeing to it that boys and girls accomplish these developmental tasks is probably moot, but it seems obvious that the school should do nothing to make the completing of these tasks unnecessarily difficult. In any case curriculum makers must also understand that boys and girls will spend much of their time trying to complete their developmental tasks whether the school provides for them or not, for these matters are really important to the boys and girls. The curriculum worker needs to bear this fact in mind when building a curriculum.

Needs: A Source of Curriculum. In building the curriculum one should consider the needs of youth. First, the needs are the bases for human action. They are basic motives and influence in some way or other whatever we do. The skills, understandings, appreciations, ideals, and attitudes necessary to these needs become the material from which one builds the curriculum. If one of our needs is to maintain a healthy body, then probably part of the curriculum should be given over to teaching boys and girls how to keep healthy. If one of the needs is to eat, perhaps part of the curriculum should be given over to how to earn one's bread and butter. If the social needs are important, perhaps the curriculum should give some time to developing social skills. The mere fact that a need exists may not be sufficient reason for providing for it specifically in the curriculum; other agencies may do the job better, but the existence of a need makes it imperative that the curriculum builder consider carefully whether or not curricular provisions for the need should be made. It is for this reason that the Educational Policies Commission based its 1944 proposals for revision of the secondary-school curriculum on the "Ten Imperative Needs of Youth."[4]

The hierarchy of needs has important implications for curriculum building. If the curriculum fails to allow for the more basic needs or threatens these needs, the chances for attaining such goals as self-realization will be close to nil. Therefore a school that threatens a child's need for love and affection, self-esteem and independence, or prestige will probably not be as successful in teaching understanding and the academic and creative skills as one that provides for and supports these basic needs. Evidently the school that operates as a "pleasant house" will be a more successful place for learning than a strict, rigorous, discipline-centered institution.

The hierarchy of needs has another possible implication for the curriculum builder. The fact that some needs seem to be more basic than others may indicate that some learnings are more essential than others. Consequently the curriculum builder should consider whether the needs at the various levels are properly provided for and whether or not the

[4] See Ch. VI.

school should be giving more time to the more essential learnings instead of aiming its program almost exclusively toward "higher things," as has been the custom in the past, or whether these needs should be attended to in other ways by other institutions.

Need for Differentiation. In any class both developmental tasks and needs of the pupils differ from youth to youth. It follows then that identical curriculum experiences cannot fully satisfy each member of any class or grade, and so curricula must be differentiated so as to meet the various needs of individual boys and girls.

On the other hand, the fact that growth, including intellectual growth, is uneven, makes suspect any curriculum that puts boys and girls into tracks or streams too early. Some boys and girls are late bloomers, as we have pointed out, and the curriculum should help them to bloom when their time comes. Rigid tracks often place unnecessary hurdles in the paths of the late bloomers. To be adequate for all, the curriculum must be flexible. It must provide experiences for all pupils at their own levels and opportunities for pupils to change from level to level and track to track as they progress.

THE NATURE OF INTELLIGENCE

In spite of the many books written about intelligence, no one seems to know exactly what intelligence is. It has been described as the ability to adjust, the ability to think critically, and the ability to learn. The *Oxford English Dictionary* defines it as the ability to understand. In his *Educational Psychology* Stephens[5] says that in discussions of psychological investigations intelligence usually means whatever it is that intelligence tests measure. The truth of the matter is that we do not know exactly what intelligence is nor exactly how it works.

GENERAL INTELLIGENCE OR SPECIFIC INTELLIGENCE

Some theorists have argued that intelligence is a general all-purpose potential. According to this theory intelligence consists of a general factor that can handle all types of problems equally well. The theory denies the existence of special kinds of intelligence, such as spatial intelligence or verbal intelligence. Rather one's abilities in these areas are determined by the way one develops his general over-all potentialities. Other theorists believe that intelligence is made up of separate talents, bound together just as a bundle of wires is bound together to make a cable. Typical of these supposed talents, or group factors as they are sometimes called, are verbal ability, spatial ability, number ability, and the ability to reason

[5] J. M. Stephens, *Educational Psychology,* rev. ed. (New York: Holt, Rinehart and Winston, Inc., 1956), Ch. 5.

inductively. Consequently, according to this theory, a person with little potential verbal ability may have great potential talent for numbers. Recent studies seem to indicate the existence of both group factors and a general factor in intelligence.

A NUMBER OF THINGS

Frequently teachers equate intelligence with verbal ability. By and large, intelligence tests are verbal tests. However, evidence indicates that verbal skill is not all of intelligence and that boys and girls who do not have academic aptitude may be highly intelligent in other respects. Cole and Bruce[6] make much of what they call effective intelligence. They point out, what all of us have observed, that boys and girls who do not seem to have much academic aptitude are sometimes more effective in life than persons who have much of this aptitude. Their argument is strengthened by the amazing fact that frequently after a lobotomy a patient's intelligence quotient remains at the same high level even though he has become a markedly less effective person.

Many men who have not done well in school are superbly adept at fixing complicated machinery—an occupation which, Gladwin[7] tells us, calls for a high degree of abstract thinking. Quite frequently these highly skilled mechanics cannot verbalize about what they do. In fact, Gladwin continues, even a highly verbal person finds it difficult to explain in words exactly what he did when he repaired a broken-down car.

Recent studies of creativity also cast doubt on the infallibility of the intelligence quotient as an indicator of intelligence. Getzels and Jackson,[8] for instance, have found that highly creative pupils with middling high I.Q.'s scored just as well on achievement tests as less creative pupils with extremely high I.Q.'s did. Studies such as this have led some experiments to conjecture that the I.Q. is not a good indicator of all aspects of intellectual vigor or even of verbal intelligence.

The implication is that at least two quite different kinds of intelligence are involved and that both of these call for high-level learning and thinking. In other words, we have good evidence to believe that people have intelligences rather than intelligence. Evidently intelligence consists of "such a number of things."

NATURE VS. NURTURE

One of the oldest unsolved problems of psychology is whether intelligence is an innate capacity or whether intelligence is developed by the

---

[6] Cole and Bruce, op. cit., Ch. 5.

[7] Thomas Gladwin, "The Need: Better Ways of Teaching Children To Think," *Freeing Capacity To Learn* (Washington, D.C.: Association for Supervision and Curriculum Development, 1960), pp. 23–31.

[8] Jacob E. Getzels and Phillip W. Jackson, *Creativity and Intelligence* (New York: John Wiley and Sons, Inc., 1961).

interaction of the individual and the environment. As yet the returns are not all in, but seemingly the truth of the matter is that it takes a little of both.

Studies of twins and of people reared under primitive conditions seem to indicate that the environment may play a strong role in developing capacity to learn. Gladwin[9] points out that Truckee men find it virtually impossible to learn the skills necessary for one to repair an automobile engine, but readily learn how to navigate far over the open ocean with only the scantiest of charts. Children brought up in complete deprivation, such as a little girl who was starved in an attic for her first five years of life, seem to develop stunted intellects.

Similarly recent studies in creativity and perception seem to show that a pupil's environment plays a large part in determining one's creativity and perception. Evidently the environment plays a considerable role in determining the quality of one's intelligence.

IMPLICATION FOR THE CURRICULUM

If the theories concerning intelligence expanded in the preceding chapters are right, secondary-school courses probably should not be limited to purely academic bookish content. Instead they should be organized so that pupils can express themselves in a number of ways and learn through different kinds of experiences. Furthermore, they seem to indicate the need for a permissive class atmosphere that will allow pupils to make the most of their potentials. Because the environment seems to play a considerable part in the development of intellectual ability, the courses should be designed to encourage original creative thinking rather than repressive memorization and manipulation.

LEARNING

Efficient teaching results from teaching the proper subject matter at the proper time by the proper method. To reach this point teaching must be based on sound principles of learning. Curricula that violate the principles of learning are wasteful. In the following paragraphs we shall examine a few of the principles of learning.

WHAT IS LEARNING?

In the first place, what is learning? According to *Webster's*, to learn means to "acquire knowledge of, or skill in." The implication is that the person who has learned now knows something he did not know, or can do something he could not do, at least not with the same proficiency, before the learning took place. In addition we know that learning can also change one's values, emotions, attitudes, ideals, and appreciations.

[9] Gladwin, *op. cit.*

The burnt child who fears the fire has learned a new emotional response. Learning, then, is a process that results in changed behavior or a changed tendency toward behavior on the part of the learner. This statement implies that the test of a person's knowledge on a topic is whether or not he can use the knowledge. On the other hand one can know something that one cannot explain verbally. Who can adequately describe a toothache? Many a person can perform skillfully highly complicated tasks that he cannot possibly explain intelligently. Evidently at least two different types of knowing are involved; one, verbal; the other, non-verbal.

Many people confuse knowledge with the ability to verbalize, but repetition of words is not necessarily a sign of knowledge. As we have seen, a speaker may be glib about democracy without having much understanding of what democracy means nor even having considered seriously its meaning or its implications. In order to avoid meaningless verbalization, curriculum planners must guard against the temptation to overemphasize vicarious learning and bookish curricula.

HOW WE LEARN

Activity and Learning. How do we learn? We learn through our experiences. Each experience is an interaction with the environment. We learn from what we do to the environment and what the environment does to us. Our burnt child who learned to fear the fire learned from the effect of the environment on him, but a boy who solves a puzzle learns largely from his effect on the environment.

Not all experiences result in learning, of course. After constant repetition an experience seldom produces much learning; neither do experiences that lack meaning or in which the learner is not attending well. In order for learning to be efficient the experience should be novel, vivid, and meaningful, but without experience there can be no learning.

The Whole-Child Concept. Whatever the experience, it involves the whole person. One cannot teach the learner's head alone. The teacher who feels his job is only to fill the youngsters' heads with his subject matter misunderstands his task. His problem is much more difficult. Whenever the youngster brings his head into the algebra class, the rest of his body comes along too. The teacher must deal with the entire personality.

Because one must teach the whole individual, one must expect that the pupil will learn more than subject matter in the classroom. During any class the pupil may be learning habits of industry or of slothfulness, of honesty or dishonesty, of independence or servility. He may be learning how to make himself pleasing to girls, how to influence his friends, how to think critically, or any one of a multitude of other things. These concomitant learnings are real learnings, and they may make the difference between a youngster's successfully assuming his role in life and failure. Often they are more important than the subject matter of the courses.

Learning Is Individual. Earlier we noted that pupils learn in their own individual fashions. What one learns depends on two things: the environment and one's self. In earlier days educators tended to make much of the role of the environment—particularly the teacher—and to minimize the role of the self. Locke, for instance, described the learner "only as a white paper, or wax, to be moulded or fashioned as one pleases."[10] The emphasis was on changing the learner by means of outside influence.

Today we realize that the learner has a large role in his own learning. One's perception makes a great difference in what one learns, for instance. Evidently what the learner does with environmental stimuli has as much bearing on what he learns as the stimuli do. Learning is not solely a matter of outside influence shaping an individual.

Readiness and Learning. School learning is usually a relatively slow process because it is, or should be, developmental. One learning builds on another. Consequently it follows that learning should follow an orderly sequence. A child who does not understand simple division or multiplication should not be expected to succeed with long divisions. He must learn the prerequisite skills before he is ready for the new one. That is to say, boys and girls learn best when they are ready, when they have become sufficiently mature, have acquired the prerequisite understandings and abilities and are sufficiently motivated to learn. Obviously a child who has not yet learned to walk is not yet ready to learn to dance. Neither is the person who does not *want* to learn to dance! Many school behavior problems and "scholastic difficulties" are the direct result of pupils' not being ready.

To attempt to teach a pupil understandings and skills for which he is not ready may be a waste of time. Sometimes one should wait until the pupil is more mature. In other instances it is better to see to it that the pupils acquire the prerequisites at once. At other times one should adjust the level of the material or its presentation to the level of the pupils.[11]

The readiness picture is complicated by other factors. One is that pupils, once ready, do not always stay ready. If, for instance, one wishes to learn to speak a foreign language accent-free, it is best to start it before one's speech-making organs become muscle-bound. Another is that boys and

[10] John Locke, "Some Thoughts Concerning Education," cited in Stirling E. Lamprecht, *Locke Selections* (New York: Charles Scribner's Sons, 1928), p. 15.

[11] In some circles it has become fashionable to derogate readiness. Bruner, for instance, speaks of the "cloying concept of readiness" (*On Knowing*, Cambridge: Harvard University Press, 1962, p. 115). Usually, however, these critics advocate at least a form of readiness. When Bruner (*On Knowing*, p. 123) states that "it is essential that before being exposed to a wide range of material on a topic the child first have a general idea of how and where things fit," he is of course advocating readiness in the sense we speak of in this book.

girls do not all become ready at the same time. There may be a spread of several years between the time that classmates become ready for a certain learning experience. Incidentally, the completion of prerequisite courses is no proof that the youngster has the background necessary to make him ready to learn a particular skill, concept, or even a subject. Many pupils fail because they lack necessary skills or concepts prerequisite to their present work, even though they have sat through prerequisite courses. The curriculum that makes the most of the principle of readiness must indeed be a flexible one.

THINKING AND PROBLEM SOLVING

Thinking is largely problem solving. In general, people of all ages go through the same steps in solving problems. That is to say:

1. They realize that a problem exists.
2. They define what the problem is.
3. They look for clues that will help them solve the problem.
4. On the strength of the clues found, they hypothesize a tentative solution.
5. They test the tentative solution to see whether it is satisfactory.
6. If the solution is not satisfactory, they revert to step three, gather new data, make new hypotheses, and test them until they find a solution or give up.

These steps, which are those expounded by Dewey, are usually associated with the scientific method and inductive reasoning. That they are essential to scientific thought is probably true, but they are not limited to inductive reasoning. They are the steps in a "complete act of thought," and apply equally as well to deductive reasoning.

In ordinary thinking one seldom follows the steps of formal logic to reach conclusions. Logic seems to be more useful to test conclusions than to arrive at them. As a matter of fact, one seldom follows the five steps of thinking in order, "by the numbers"; thinking is more likely to consist of shuffling back and forth from one step to another. Nevertheless, the steps are all intensely important in the complete thinking process. If he is to learn to think well, the pupil must develop skills in carrying out each step. Particularly necessary is the ability to develop new hypotheses.

Developing Skills in Problem Solving. Skill in thinking does not come naturally; it is learned through experience in thinking. Therefore skill in thinking is not a function of subject matter but of method. While it may be easier to utilize thought procedures in some courses than in others, curriculum builders who feel that providing subject matter in certain areas will make boys and girls learn to think are working under a false premise.

Creative Thinking. Creative thinking demands a mind free to range among the data, selecting, reorganizing, and testing. It requires a mind of rich experience, not a mind that is hobbled by memorized facts, but rather a mind that can draw meanings and generalizations from facts. The pupil must learn to avoid stereotypes in his thinking. His mind should be free to find new relationships and new ideas. Instruction that emphasizes fact and drill tends to foster stereotyped thinking. Threat and anxiety also seem to force pupils' thinking into the same old ruts and to make it difficult for them to see new paths that might lead to the solutions they seek.

Of course, knowledge is necessary for creative thinking. The greater the workable knowledge one has, the better his chances of finding the right hypotheses. Without such workable knowledge the creative thinker or artist would have no tools. But this knowledge must not consist merely of unassimilated facts. It must be made up of meaningful concepts that the thinker can arrange and rearrange in his mind until he strikes a promising new hypothesis. Thinkers have been pointing this out ever since the days of ancient Greece, when Heraclitus said that learning a lot of things did not teach the mind, to the modern psychologists who tell us that ". . . dependence of pupils on *memorized* formulas, methods, concepts, and skills without understanding is an enemy to learning not only in mathematics but in all education."[12] Perhaps Xenophon was right when he made one of his characters say, "A question, then, is education."

CONCEPT BUILDING

Our concepts result from our experiences. The more and varied our experiences are, the clearer our concepts become. Of course, an adult or an adolescent can learn a great deal from a lecture, an explanation, or a book, but, if he is limited to these media alone, he cannot develop concepts as full and clear as those resulting from more varied experiences. Therefore if curriculum builders wish pupils to develop clear concepts, they should provide many experiences with the materials and ideas they wish the pupils to learn. Pupils need to manipulate both materials and ideas, to see them in different contexts, to watch them work, and to work with them. To develop good concepts one must guide pupils rather than tell them. Curriculum based on telling and memorizing may result in shallow concepts and empty verbalization rather than true understanding.

THE CASE FOR PRACTICE

In spite of all the evils that may result from improper use of drill, drill and practice do have a place in the curriculum. They are both essential

[12] George G. Thompson, Eric F. Gardner, Francis J. Di Vesta, *Educational Psychology* (New York: Appleton-Century-Crofts, Inc., 1959), pp. 309–310.

in the learning of skills and in learning for retention. Only frequent repetition can make responses automatic and habitual. This is as true of attitudes as it is of skills.

Ordinarily one learns material that is meaningful to him better than material that is not meaningful. Subject matter that lacks meaning also lacks interest. It is difficult to keep motivation high when one is learning such material. Moreover, its lack of meaning makes it difficult for the learner to build relationships and to find clues. As a rule of thumb, if there are two possible ways of learning something, the more meaningful one is the better.

In spite of this rule, some subject matter must be learned by rote. French idiomatic expressions are an example of this type of subject matter. The meanings of these words are purely arbitrary, and if one is ever going to know them, one must just plain learn them, and this takes practice and plenty of it. Even so, meanings and relationships can be utilized to make even such subject matter easier to learn.

ATTITUDES, IDEALS, AND VALUES

Attitudes are emotionalized sets or predispositions that influence our behavior with reference to all situations or objects to which they are related. Ideals are generalized goals, also emotionalized, to which we aspire and which we use as genuine guides to behavior. Values are judgments of worth that result from our attitudes, ideals, and concepts.

Our attitudes are, at least in part, determined by our concepts. In a large measure what we believe about something will decide what our attitude toward it will be. Thus it is that changes in beliefs also change attitudes. Hence one can use direct teaching of facts to teach attitudes.

However, direct teaching of facts does not always change attitudes. Concepts alone do not determine attitudes. Emotions are also involved. A strong attitude may continue to influence a person even though intellectually his beliefs have changed. Does it not sometimes happen that a person does not like another even though he knows the other to be good, kindly, and pleasant? An English professor is known to the modern world almost solely because someone did not like him.

> I do not love thee, Doctor Fell,
> The reason why I cannot tell;
> But this alone I know full well,
> I do not love thee, Doctor Fell.

Even though lectures can be very effective, as a rule, to change another person's attitudes by lecturing him or lecturing to him is extremely difficult. Attitudes are more often caught than taught. To change attitudes one must provide many favorable associations. Because young people tend to imitate the attitudes of persons whom they can admire and identify with, good examples should be provided. For this reason group discussions are effective. Group opinions exert great pressures on the attitudes of individuals, for no adolescent wishes to be a complete outsider. In addition, group discussions seem to give one an opportunity to convince oneself. Because attitudes are emotionalized sets, methods that involve dramatic and emotional appeal are also useful for swaying attitudes. In short, although direct teaching has some value in the building of attitudes, to be most effective the teacher must revert to more devious methods. The curriculum maker must bear this in mind if he wishes to bring about real changes in behavior rather than lip service.

CURRICULUM IMPLICATIONS

Learning theory, although still somewhat indeterminate, has certain very definite lessons for the curriculum builder.

A Curriculum for the Whole Child. One of the lessons in learning theory is that because one deals with the whole child, the curriculum maker must consider concomitant learning as well as the subject matter in the curriculum. Because these learnings are so important, perhaps in curriculum building we should not emphasize particular subject matter so much as we should emphasize such things as the skills of thinking and learning, which now are taught only incidentally in so many classes. In any case the curriculum planner must remember that he is planning curricula for human beings, not disembodied intellects.

On the other hand, the fact that one must deal with the whole child does not necessarily imply that the curriculum should contain all learning in all fields of knowledge. Other agencies are available and should assume their share of the load. The most obvious example is the church, which undoubtedly should be charged with the major responsibility for the religious education of its children.

Curricula for Individuals. The fact that learning is an individual matter also holds implications for the curriculum. Because pupils participate so greatly in their own learning, education can no longer be considered a matter of filling a pupil with subject matter. This being so, curricula should depend less upon telling, drill, and practice and turn to emphasizing creative learning and self-realization. Course content then should be more concerned with process and methods than with information. Psychological findings about thinking, creativity, and concept building all support this conclusion. Similarly what we know about attitude formation also favors the notion of process-centered courses. Evidently, then, there can no longer be any justification for offering courses in which pupils merely cover content by learning and memorizing the information contained in a textbook. This conclusion does not preclude the necessity for repetition, review, and the thorough learning of facts, but it definitely does reject the thesis that such learning should be all of learning in the secondary-school grades.

Evidently the way to teach boys and girls to think creatively is not to emphasize memorizing and drill on facts, but to emphasize the learning of understandings, problem solving, and critical attitudes. Such teaching would probably consist of guiding boys and girls through creative problem-solving activities rather than drill and lecture type of activities.

The fact that learning is individual again points to the need for individualization and differentiation of courses and curricula. Theories of readiness also support this need. Learning is developmental; each learning depends upon and should be based upon previous learning. Therefore curriculum builders should take great care in developing effective learning sequences. Seemingly pupils vary so much that the ideal curriculum would require an individual sequence for each pupil.

TRANSFER OF LEARNING

No learning is worth much unless it can be transferred. Simply stated, transfer of learning is the act of using in one situation something learned in another situation. Manifestly transfer of learning is the principal reason for teaching anything.

FORMAL DISCIPLINE

For many years educators thought that transfer was best brought about by training the faculties of the mind. According to this theory if one practiced reasoning in the study of geometry, he would be able to reason better when he invested in the stock market, or if one memorized the *Allegro* or Gray's *Elegy in a Country Churchyard,* one would be able to remember one's shopping list better, or if one were able to force oneself to translate some frightfully difficult, boring, and meaningless Latin speeches, one would develop the will power to resist the temptations of the market place.

From these beliefs educators derived the doctrine of formal discipline, which taught that it was not so important what boys and girls learned as it was important that the teaching should exercise the "muscles of the mind." The phrase *a disciplined mind* owes its birth to this concept. Because of the nature of their subject matter some theorists conjectured that certain subjects were more disciplinary than others.

RECENT CONCEPTS OF TRANSFER

Alas for our theorists, transfer of learning turned out to be not so simple. Practice in willing does not seem to result in stronger will power, nor does practice in memorizing give one a better memory. Rather learning transfers because of common components in the learning and using situations and the learner's ability to make generalizations and see relationships. Thus a pupil who achieves insight into the structure and processes of a discipline in one course may be able to utilize these insights in another course or in his out-of-school life. Facts, concepts, skills, principles, methods, ideals, and attitudes, all can transfer under proper conditions, but it is the method of study rather than the subject matter that sharpens pupils' abilities to reason, memorize, and concentrate.

MEMORY AND REMEMBERING

Memory serves as a case in point. Remembering is essential to transfer; one cannot very well use again what he cannot bring back to mind, but memory can not be strengthened simply by memorizing. On the contrary, remembering is made up of many skills. Because pupils tend to remember best those things that are meaningful, important, and vivid, teachers can enhance pupils' remembrance of subject matter by emphasizing meanings, principles, generalizations, and processes and by providing plenty of opportunities for review. But the only way one can strengthen memory is to sharpen techniques of remembering.

IMPLICATIONS FOR THE CURRICULUM

Theory concerning transfer of learning has several important implications for the secondary-school curriculum. Because pupils can transfer what they learn from one situation to another, to attempt to build a curriculum that covers every aspect of every subject is unnecessary and unwise. Instead it is preferable to skip judiciously so as to allow a thorough study of a relatively few topics, for thorough study facilitates transfer and an appreciation of the structure of the subject. Courses overcrowded with content in order to cover the subject are archaic and have no place in a modern curriculum.

A second implication is that the inclusion of any subject in the curriculum simply because of its disciplinary value cannot be justified. Unless a course has some functional or operational value for the pupils, it should be dropped.

A third implication is that secondary-school courses should be designed to induce the maximum amount of transfer and so should emphasize generalization, applications, thorough meaningful learning, processes, and attitudes. Ivory-towered courses deserve no place in the curriculum. In addition, so that the content can actually function, there should be plenty of opportunity for review and practice.

MOTIVATION

PUPIL GOALS AND THE CURRICULUM BUILDER

Everything a man does consciously he does in relation to some goal. These goals or purposes determine not only what we do but what we perceive and what we understand and how we react to situations. This is why the pupils who want to learn are likely to do well in our classes.

A person's goals are part of him. No one can establish goals in an individual except the person himself, but he is able to shape them only after he has been subjected to many influences. Because this is so, teachers can influence the goals pupils select and can cause them to change their goals and to discard less desirable goals in favor of better ones. When he builds the curriculum, the curriculum builder is not handcuffed to the fleeting desires of boys and girls. To some extent the goals of boys and girls can be made to fit the curriculum.

Intrinsic and Extrinsic Goals. Goals come in different sizes and shapes. There are intrinsic and extrinsic goals, immediate and deferred goals, and major and minor goals. Intrinsic goals are the goals implicit in the learning itself. When a child works for an intrinsic goal, he works because he wants to work or because the product of the work is valuable to him. The boy who practices long, hard hours on the skating rink because he wants to learn how to skate well is working for an intrinsic goal. An extrinsic goal is an artificial reward that it is hoped will entice a child to do something he does not want to do or sees no value in doing for itself alone.

Everything else being equal, intrinsic goals seem to be more desirable for classroom motivation than extrinsic goals are. Subject matter that has intrinsic value to pupils has longer staying powers than that learned because of extrinsic values. Perhaps one reason for this is that intrinsic goals seem to generate a greater amount of real effort on the part of the learner. Therefore good curricula keep the need for incentives to a minimum. Unfortunately to persuade boys and girls that all schoolwork has intrinsic value is well nigh impossible. Not all our needs are felt needs, and boys and girls must learn some things whether they like it or not. In such cases one must turn to extrinsic goals.

Immediate and Deferred Goals. Similarly immediate goals seem to be more effective motives than deferred goals are. This is quite natural because the goals that are the most immediate are also the most pressing. One should make the most of pupils' immediate goals in teaching, but to build curricula for immediate goals only is not necessary. The interest and attention of adolescents can be sustained by long-range, deferred goals. Still, the teacher in the classroom must depend upon immediate goals as motivation for the pupils' daily class work. Doing so should not be difficult, because most long-range or deferred goals can be broken down into intermediate goals that have immediate value to the learner.

LEVEL OF CHALLENGE

Nothing succeeds like success; failure on the other hand is likely to be debilitating. Of course, a few failures will not make a great difference in one's total life, especially if one has had a large number of successes. But repeated failures are liable to cause emotional problems, which may lead to unfortunate results. To be able to take failures with equanimity one needs to have had enough successes to build up a good opinion of one's self. Otherwise failures may be unbearable and cause complete breakdown.

Setting goals that are beyond one's capabilities tends to discourage and frustrate pupils because they cause failures. Frequently pupils try to escape the pressures of overly high goals by giving up or by misbehaving. If the pupils do continue to try their best, excessive pressure may cause them to learn less efficiently. Like the athlete who presses when the going gets rough, pupils under too much pressure are liable to be less efficient in solving problems and developing clear understandings.

On the other hand, goals that are set too low provide no challenge and may cause slothful habits and discontent. In their own way, low goals can be as frustrating and unsatisfying as ones that are too high. They prevent pupils from having the thrill of worth-while achievement and encourage laziness. Moreover, they may give pupils false notions of their own abilities and instill in them false feelings of self-satisfaction. Worst of all, low goals may prevent pupils from making the most of their potential and realizing their full selves.

Complicating this problem is the fact that pupils' abilities are very different. To set rigid standards or goals for all the pupils of a class would result in goals too high for some pupils and too low for others. Curriculum builders must make allowances for these differences. Presumably curriculum standards should be neither too high nor too low for any child and so should vary from individual to individual.

REWARD, PUNISHMENT, THREAT, AND MOTIVATION

Rewards, threats, and punishment are among the incentives used to promote learning. They are also used to reinforce learning. Rewards on the whole seem to be particularly effective for these purposes. They do tend to motivate pupils to learn and to make learning stronger so that the pupil can more readily retain it and use it in future situations. Knowledge of one's success is a particularly powerful reward. So also is the sheer enjoyment of a fresh, novel, stimulating experience.

The effect of punishment and threats is not so predictable. At times they seem to motivate and reinforce learning rather well. At other times they seem to have quite the opposite effect and may actually bring about and reinforce the very behavior they were supposed to prevent. In threatening situations pupils tend to concentrate on the threat rather than on the problem at hand, and so threatening pupils with punishment may make it impossible for them to solve problems and see relationships as well as they would be able to do ordinarily. In classes where error is regarded as sin pupils do not try out new ideas or venture new thoughts. In schools where teachers criticize pupils overmuch, pupils' self-images may be impaired. Such pupils usually do not learn much because they do not aspire much.

IMPLICATIONS FOR THE CURRICULUM

What implications for curriculum building do we find in the principles of motivation described above? There are several, of course. One is that motivational theory does not limit the curriculum to any particular format. True, immediate intrinsic goals seem to have the most force, and so curriculum builders should attempt to harness these forces by utilizing content that has immediate value for its own sake. Obviously ivory-towered curricula that do not relate at all to pupils' immediate intrinsic goals are suspect. Nevertheless, curricula do not have to be limited to pupils' immediate intrinsic goals. Pupils' goals can be changed, and sometimes must be changed, to meet goals set by adults, and properly encouraged pupils can work toward long-range goals that have relatively little immediate value to them. Consequently, curricula need not be tied to pupils' transitory interests. If to prepare pupils for the future is desirable, the principles of motivation can be utilized for this purpose.

Again psychological principles point to the need for a flexible curriculum. No single curriculum can suffice. Like the other psychological considerations, motivation demands differentiated curricula and courses. Ideally each course and each curriculum should be so differentiated that each pupil, no matter what his abilities and interests, will be challenged to put forth his greatest effort.

Although courses should be challenging, they should not be oppressive. The most effective curricula accentuate the positive and give pupils plenty of opportunity to let their minds range far and wide without fear of reprisals or unreasonable restrictions.

SUMMARY OF IMPLICATIONS

The principal assumption in this chapter is that to be a good curriculum, any curriculum must run in accord with the nature of learning and the nature of the learner.

A review of the psychologies of learning and of adolescence shows that the secondary-school curriculum must be flexible in order to cope with the many differences in pupils. It must be rigorous enough to challenge the most capable, but still not so difficult as to discourage the less able. In it each pupil should find opportunities to capitalize on his capabilities, whatever they may be. Even in the mass education of our great comprehensive high schools, somehow we must find a way to design the curriculum for individuals and for the nature and needs of society.

Not only should the curriculum be designed for individuals, it should also be designed to free individual minds. Rather than to attempt to teach all virtue and all knowledge to each child in every course, the curriculum must be selective so that pupils may be free to "dig deep." To insure the benefits of transfer the curriculum should emphasize methods, structure, principles, and generalizations, as well as usable content. Pupils should be given ample opportunity to solve problems, to investigate independently, to think originally, and in other ways learn the skills of the self-reliant, careful, critical thinker. In the long run, to achieve this purpose, the method of learning is probably more important than the content learned.

Of course, the academic subjects must play a central role in the curriculum. But they cannot be the entire curriculum. Boys and girls have many different talents and many different aspirations, so the curriculum must help boys and girls to develop in many ways. The curriculum that concentrates only on the academic is doing only part of the job. To allow boys and girls to develop the many aspects of their personalities, the curriculum must keep a balance between the academic and the non-academic subjects.

Whether academic or nonacademic, the content of the curriculum needs to be meaningful to the pupils and valuable to them both now and in the future. The fact that boys and girls learn most readily those things that have immediate value does not rule out teaching those things which have deferred value. Everyone acts in relation to long-range goals as well as immediate ones. But whatever the goals, the curriculum should follow an orderly sequence increasing in difficulty and complexity as the child becomes ready.

Above all, the curriculum should free the child so that he can realize his full potential. In the sense that permissiveness means freedom to try even though one makes mistakes, the curriculum should be permissive. Repression and authoritarianism have little place in the secondary-school curriculum. Boys and girls should be free to learn. The curriculum should open new doors so that they can venture forth into independent learning and original creative thinking.

SUGGESTED READINGS

ASSOCIATION FOR SUPERVISION AND CURRICULUM DEVELOPMENT. *Freeing Capacity to Learn*. Washington, D.C.: The Association, 1960.
   Report of the Fourth ASCD Research Institute in which scholars addressed themselves to the problem of how schools can help pupils to learn more effectively and efficiently.
————. *Human Variability and Learning*. Washington, D.C.: The Association, 1961.

A report of a research institute addressed to the problem of individual differences and learning.

——. *Learning and the Teacher.* 1959 Yearbook. Washington, D.C.: The Association, 1959.

An excellent yearbook on the teaching-learning process. Contains two good annotated bibliographies.

——. *Learning More About Learning.* Washington, D.C.: The Association, 1959.

The reports and papers on the Third ASCD Research Institute in which scholars of related fields attempted to focus research findings in their fields on the problems of learning in schools.

——. *New Dimensions in Learning.* Washington, D.C.: The Association, 1962.

A report of an ASCD Research Institute in which scholars from various disciplines comment on the learning, the learner, and the learning process.

BIGGE, MORRIS L., and MAURICE P. HUNT. *Psychological Foundations of Education.* New York: Harper and Row, Inc., 1962.

An excellent introduction to human learning and development showing application to teaching and curriculum.

BRUNER, JEROME S. *The Process of Education.* Cambridge, Massachusetts: Harvard University Press, 1960.

A report of an interdisciplinary seminar that has had considerable impact on contemporary educational thinking. It stresses process and the structure of the disciplines.

COLE, LAWRENCE E., and WILLIAM F. BRUCE. *Educational Psychology.* New York: Harcourt, Brace and World, Inc., 1950.

A basic educational psychology text. In Chapter 3, the authors stress the concept of effective intelligence.

COLEMAN, JAMES C. *Personality Dynamics and Effective Behavior.* Chicago: Scott, Foresman and Company, 1960.

A textbook concerning the problems of human adjustment. Part 3 deals with different kinds of human effectiveness.

COMBS, ARTHUR W. (ed.). *Perceiving, Behaving, Becoming.* 1962 Yearbook, Association for Supervision and Curriculum Development. Washington, D.C.: The Association, 1962.

A yearbook of the ASCD concerning new concepts on human potentiality and their implications for society, education, and the schools.

COMBS, ARTHUR W., and DONALD SNYGG. *Individual Behavior: A Perceptual Approach to Behavior.* Revised edition. New York: Harper and Row, Inc., 1959.

A basic reference presenting modern perceptual approaches for understanding behavior.

ESTES, WILLIAM K. *Modern Learning Theory.* New York: Appleton-Century-Crofts, Inc., 1954.

A critical analysis of five different theories of learning.

GETZELS, JACOB H., and PHILIP W. JACKSON. *Creativity and Intelligence.* New York: John Wiley and Sons, Inc., 1961.

A report of an experiment comparing high creative and high-I.Q. youth which concludes that I.Q. measures only a small aspect of intelligence.

GHISELIN, BREWSTER. *The Creative Process.* Berkeley: University of California Press, 1952. Also a Mentor book. New York: The American Library, 1955.

A study of creative geniuses of the past in an attempt to try to find out the cause of the creative spark.

GWYNN, J. MINOR. *Curriculum Principles and Social Trends.* Third edition. New York: The Macmillan Company, 1960.

Chapters 3 and 9 deal with the psychological backgrounds discussed in this chapter.

HAVIGHURST, ROBERT J. *Developmental Tasks and Education.* Chicago: University of Chicago Press, 1953.

———. *Human Development and Education.* New York: Longmans, Green and Company, 1953.

Exposition of the concept of the "developmental tasks." Contains chapters on the developmental tasks of adolescents and includes consideration of the adolescent peer group.

HENRY, NELSON B. (ed.). *Individualizing Instruction.* Sixty-first Yearbook, National Society for the Study of Education, Part I. Chicago: University of Chicago Press, 1962.

An excellent guide for use in adapting instruction to meet individual needs.

———. *The Integration of Educational Experiences.* Fifty-seventh Yearbook, National Society for the Study of Education. Chicago: University of Chicago Press, 1958.

An explanation of the role of experience in the learning process showing that the kind of learning which takes place is a result of the kinds of experiences which the learner has.

———. *Learning and Instruction.* Forty-ninth Yearbook, National Society for the Study of Education, Part I. Chicago: University of Chicago Press, 1950.

A functional explanation of the close relationship between the basic principles of instruction and learning.

HILL, WINFRED F. *Learning: A Survey of Psychological Interpretations.* San Francisco: Chandler Publishing Company, 1963.

Explains the psychological interpretations of the more common learning theories.

HOLLAND, JAMES G., and B. F. SKINNER. *The Analysis of Behavior.* New York: McGraw-Hill Book Company, Inc., 1961.

A programed text delineating Skinner's theories of learning and conditioning.

HULLFISH, H. GORDON, and PHILLIP G. SMITH. *Reflective Thinking: The Method of Education.* New York: Dodd, Mead and Company, 1961.

A philosophical examination of how we think and its implications for teaching.

HUNT, JOSEPH M. V. *Intelligence and Experience.* New York: The Ronald Press Company, 1961.

An exhaustive study of the influence of experience on intelligence which concludes that the level of a person's adult intelligence can be raised by controlling his experiences as a child.

JERSILD, ARTHUR T. *The Psychology of Adolescence,* Second edition. New York: The Macmillan Company, 1963.

A thoroughgoing discussion of the adolescent and what he is like. Chapter 2 pays particular attention to the "self."

KLAUSMEIER, HERBERT J. *Learning and Human Abilities.* New York: Harper and Row, Inc., 1961.

A thorough educational psychology text that ties psychological principles to classroom learning.

KUBIE, LAWRENCE S. *Neurotic Distortion of the Creative Process.* Lawrence: University of Kansas Press, 1958.

A presentation of Kubie's theories of thinking and the role of the preconscious and his hypothesis that "drill and grill" teaching techniques distort the creative process.

RYLE, GILBERT. *The Concept of Mind.* New York: Barnes and Noble, 1949.

A philosophical examination and refutation of older theories of mind and an explanation of mind on a functional basis.

STATON, THOMAS F. *Dynamics of Adolescent Adjustment.* New York: The Macmillan Company, 1963.

A text describing adolescents—"what is happening to them, how they think and feel, why they act as they do"—from the point of view of a clinical psychologist.

THORPE, LOUIS P., and ALLEN M. SCHMULLER. *Contemporary Theories of Learning.* New York: The Ronald Press Company, 1954.

A discussion of several theoretical positions concerning learning with attempts to show their implication for education.

TORRANCE, E. PAUL. *Creativity.* Washington, D.C. The National Education Association, 1963.

A summary of the present knowledge concerning creativity on a popularized level by one of the leading authorities in the field.

TOWNSEND, EDWARD ARTHUR, and PAUL J. BURKE. *Learning for Teachers.* New York: The Macmillan Company, 1962.

An excellent text on learning. Good chapter on reinforcement and programing.

TRAVERS, ROBERT M. *Essentials of Learning.* New York: The Macmillan Company, 1963.

A research-oriented overview of the principles of learning. Good theoretical background material.

Chapter 4

Society and
the School

Education is a creature of the culture, and so, in the long run, it is the culture that determines what the secondary-school curriculum is to be in any particular country or society.

OUR CHANGING CULTURE

THE FORCE OF CULTURE

Every living person is what his culture has made him. Even our bodies are shaped by our culture. As every American knows, fashion can alter figures. Rubens' then stylishly buxom models would slim down considerably if they were to live in modern diet-conscious America.

If culture can change our physical beings, it can shape our personalities even more. The child who was born and reared in Illinois is quite a different person from what he would be if he had been born and reared a Hindu.

If man is a creature of his culture, culture is also a creation of man. Man creates and maintains his culture by means of education. From the day a child is born to the day he dies, his relatives, friends, and acquaintances pressure him to act according to cultural patterns. Even in the most nonconformist of families, the adults indoctrinate their children in the folkways of their group, just as their parents indoctrinated them when they themselves were young. And when these children grow up they, in turn, teach these same folkways, slightly altered to fit the times, to their children. In this fashion men pass on the culture from generation to generation.

Implications of Education's Role in Building Culture. The role of education in shaping culture leads to some frightening implications. The first of these is that man is not primarily a child of nature but a creature of culture. Doing what comes naturally is not necessarily natural at all; it is more likely learned, and learned at the hands of one's culture. If people are competitive, it may not be because of something innate in their genetic composition, but because society has taught them to be competitive.[1] Perhaps they might just as easily have been brought up to be cooperative. Much of what the layman considers to be human nature turns out to be simply the familiar pattern of behavior of his own culture— patterns that may be abhorrent to people of other cultures. *Human nature is largely a product of culture. Therefore men can change human nature.*

A second implication is that *because man creates his culture he can also change it.* This is not easy to do. To make drastic changes in a culture requires drastic action and may cause great discord, as recent events in Africa and Asia show. To change the tangible aspects of a culture is exceedingly difficult, for many men find it astonishingly difficult to give up old, inefficient, but familiar, tools for new, efficient ones. But to change customs, beliefs, values, institutions, and other intangible aspects of a culture is excruciatingly more difficult. It can seldom be done overnight, but it can be done—by using the power of education.

CULTURAL LAG AND THE SCHOOL

Cultures change slowly, for in every land and in all peoples there runs a strong conservative element. Even in times of rapid changes and in cultures that make a fetish of being up to date, resistance to change is likely to be the rule rather than the exception. It is this conservatism that causes us to try to fight twentieth-century crime with nineteenth-century law-enforcement systems. This phenomenon is sometimes called social lag or cultural lag. Cultural lag is one reason why it is so difficult to change school curricula. Note how few schools ever adopted really progressive methods and curricula and how in an era of stress the populace returns to the "tried and true" methods and the content of traditional secondary education. Of all the problems of the secondary curriculum building, the problem of social lag is one of the most acute. Because of social lag, the secondary-school curriculum has been woefully out of date throughout most of its entire history in the United States.

The Impact of Culture on Education. The kind of educational system

[1] See Ashley Montagu *On Being Human* (New York: Henry Schuman, Inc., 1951) for an interesting development of this thesis.

a society provides depends upon its culture. Is education to be centered in the school, or should it be shared with the home or the church? Which of the various institutions should be responsible for what education? Shall education be extended into adulthood, or shall it be limited to children? What shall the children study? These questions are all decided by the people of a group on the basis of their cultural values. In particular, cultural values determine the curriculum. If the classics are valued by the society, then the classics will be taught, but if business is what the society values, then business will be taught. If the society values competition, boys and girls will be taught to be competitive; if it values cooperation, boys and girls will be taught to cooperate. So we Americans have a secondary-school curriculum that reflects our values. If it differs from curricula in other lands, it is largely because our values are different.

THE SOCIOECONOMIC–CULTURAL REVOLUTION

Undoubtedly the most striking characteristic of modern life is change. Almost every day, it seems, someone discovers, develops, or invents something that makes what we knew obsolete. Even the very shape of the world seems to be changing. New nations appear overnight. The vast distances and dreadful geographical barriers that made continent fortresses impregnable in 1940 can no longer protect anyone from instant ballistic and air-borne nuclear fire.

THE CHANGING ECONOMIC SITUATION

Our economy is no longer a laissez-faire capitalism, but is now a combination of corporation and state capitalism, plus state socialism, small business, and cooperatives. Most of the business conducted in this country is done by big corporations and by big government. Small, independent businesses have become relatively rare. Even in the retail grocery business the great majority of outlets in the nation are operated by large organizations—chain stores or cooperative associations.

The large organizations have tended to make relations between customer and seller, labor and management, lawmaker and citizen, in fact all concerned, more impersonal. Employees, even important employees, have become cogs in the wheel, and personal values are lost in the vastness of gigantic organizations or are sacrificed on the twin altars of efficiency and system.

We in the United States live in an economy of abundance. The American nation has a higher standard of living than any nation has had before. As a matter of course the ordinary American provides himself and his family with luxuries that in other times and other countries even the well-to-do could not afford. And yet, although a land of plenty, the United States is no longer a land of unlimited resources, but a land forced to import both raw and manufactured materials because of shortages in the local economy. We have become a consuming economy rather than a producing economy. A great percentage of our citizens are employed in providing services rather than in producing goods. Government employment has grown to unprecedented proportions. Today's situation contrasts sharply with the early history of our nation when almost everyone who worked was a producer of goods.

In a period of unprecedented prosperity we are in debt. Our entire economy of abundance seemingly is built upon the willingness of people to buy whether "they need it or not." By buying we create profits so that others can buy and create profits so we can buy more and create more profits, and so on. Credit, and what appears to be almost a mania for acquiring the newest, fanciest, biggest, and best, seem to be the prime movers that keep the American economic system rolling. The demand for the latest, which keeps people buying, is sustained by the continual, inescapable, insistent exhortations of the advertisers and the planned obsolescence the manufacturers build into their products to cause us to replace the old while it is still new. To support the economy by spending well, even beyond one's means, is almost one's patriotic duty.

The Changing Employment Pattern. Already urbanization, technicalization, and population shifts have caused many changes in the country's employment pattern. The United States is no longer a primarily agricultural community; only about one tenth of our labor force works at farming. Neither is ours a country of laborers. Because of the great increase in productivity resulting from technological advances in industries of all sorts, white-collar workers now outnumber blue-collar workers. The smaller American home, high labor cost, and the invention of innumerable labor-saving devices have also reduced the demand for domestic labor. The vocations that require the least education are rapidly becoming less important in our economy.

The inventions of the past century have created great demands for clerical, technical, managerial, and professional workers so that now workers in these fields account for more than one third of the workers under 40 years of age. Each year the number of workers in these fields increases 6 to 7 per cent. Evidently industry depends upon strong brains rather than strong backs. With the coming of automation brain power will become even more important.

The impact of automation upon modern society can hardly be underestimated. From 1957 to 1962, according to the president of International Business Machines Corporation, largely because of automation and other technological improvements, the automobile industry has been able to increase its production by 13 per cent while reducing the number of its employees by 6 per cent.[2] The experience in other industries is

---

[2] Thomas J. Watson, "Le Chômage," *Realités*, 213: 51, October, 1963.

much the same. At first it was thought that such changes would affect only production of consumer goods, but automation is also revolutionizing other industries, such as banking and retailing. So much so that in the not too distant future only 20 per cent of the present work force would suffice to keep American industry going at its present level.[3]

Because it makes possible increased production with fewer employees working a shorter work week, automation faces the nation with serious social dilemmas similar to those of the industrial revolution of the last century. Most of these problems stem from technological unemployment. Men who were formerly securely employed are being superseded by machines. Most severely hurt are the skilled workers and technicians who suddenly find that their hard-won skills are no longer necessary. As a result of such derangements automation will mean the upgrading of jobs of a few and the downgrading of the jobs of the majority of the workers.[4] Such dislocations face the nation with the necessity of finding new ways of securing the fullest utilization of our labor force.

The many changes in the employment pattern have several implications for education in the United States. In the first place the United States must provide itself with technicians and professional workers. As Drucker says:

> It used to be an axiom that no society could afford more than a mere handful of educated people. Increasingly, we will have to learn that no society can afford more than the merest handful of uneducated people and that strength, economic growth, and perhaps even the sheer survival of a nation will more and more depend upon its ability to educate everybody up to, and probably well beyond, the limits of his abilities.[5]

The need for professional and technical workers was so great in the 1950's that the schools of the country were unable to meet the demand. The shortage of trained workers was most noticeable in the mathematical and scientific fields because of the emphasis on the technological race with the Soviet Bloc, but it was just as real in other fields—teaching among them. Today the shortage continues to exist and may be with us for some time, probably until the mid-seventies. However, in the near future, we can expect college graduates to become a glut on the employment market. As a result the boys and girls who seek professional and technical positions may need more and better preparation. When the institutions of higher learning find it more necessary to be highly selective because of

---

[3] James L. Henderson, speech to New Education Fellowship, New York, September 14, 1963.

[4] *Automation and the Challenge of Education* (Washington, D.C.: The National Education Association, 1962), p. 5.

[5] Peter F. Drucker, in Franklin Patterson (ed.), *Citizenship and a Free Society*, National Council for the Social Studies, Thirteenth Yearbook (Washington, D.C.: National Education Association, 1960), p. 115.

the increase in applicants caused by the population explosion, the caliber of boys' and girls' preparation will become even more important. At the present time more than half our labor force is made up of high school graduates. If, as Drucker implies, in the future the nation is going to need more highly educated workers, a larger percentage of the future labor force will be graduates of postsecondary schools. In view of this prospect it seems that secondary educators should take another hard look at the role of college preparation, preprofessional education, technical education, general education, and specialized education in the secondary schools of our country.

Leisure Time. Changes in the employment pattern, machinery, and automation have brought the American people face to face with a new phenomenon in the history of the world. We have made the common man a member of the moneyed leisure class. Never before has the ordinary worker and his family had so much time to spend enjoying himself and so much money to enjoy himself with. No longer does the average person work from dawn to dusk six or seven days a week; automation and labor-saving machinery have brought us to the point where we can expect the 30-hour week shortly.

As a result many Americans have time on their hands. This unprecedented amount of leisure time has led American men and women to spend more and more time in recreation. Frequently these emancipated adults do not know what to do with themselves, because they do not have the skills and interests that would help them put their leisure time to good use. Consequently many of them fritter away their time in useless and sometimes downright harmful activities.

Critics of education scoff at education for leisure time. But leisure time is one of the facts of American life. Probably the secondary-school curriculum should provide more opportunities for boys and girls to learn how to use their leisure time well and to instill the desire for developing wholesome hobbies and interests.

Implications for the Curriculum. The realities of the economic situation argue for vigorous emphasis on economic education, particularly consumer education and conservation education. Boys and girls should learn the realities of economic life and how to handle their own affairs properly. Curriculum developers must guard against preparing boys and girls for an economic world that does not exist.

Curriculum developers should also reevaluate the curriculum in relation to man's position in society. Particularly important, because of the growth of big business and big government, is the need to reexamine the roles of individuals and competition. Perhaps in our society schools should place more emphasis on teaching cooperation and developing each pupil's individuality even though these goals may seem antithetical.

THE COMMUNITY AND THE CURRICULUM

Changes in Population. Since World War II the population of the entire world has been growing so fast that we commonly speak of "the population explosion." The United States is sharing this huge growth. From 1800 to 1920 our nation doubled during each decade. During the 1930's the rate of increase slowed somewhat, but it picked up again in the 1940's, until it reached 151 million in the 1950 census. This number was increased to 179,323,175 in the 1960 census. By 1980, according to a census bureau forecast, the population will reach 230 million—an increase of approximately one third in twenty years. Providing for such an enormous increase in population will place a gigantic load on the country's resources.

Another population change is the drastic geographic rearrangement of the people that is now going on. Like the pioneers of old, Americans still pick up their belongings to search for new homes where the grass is greener. In the decade between 1940 and 1950 the West Coast increased its population by 49 per cent. Many southern farmers, particularly from the mountains, have flocked to the great cities of the North. These migrations have been fraught with problems of readjustment—particularly when the migrants have moved to an area whose ways of life are very different from those to which they have been accustomed.

The constant shifting of the population causes many difficulties. It prevents many upper- and middle-class families from achieving the stability that once was the mark of the bourgeoisie. It also deprives communities of the support of many middle-class adults who would otherwise be community leaders. It causes much maladjustment in the lives of both adults and children in all classes of American society. Of particular importance to curriculum builders is the fact that boys and girls move from school to school. School transfers are often accompanied by adjustment problems. Not the least of these is the difficulty of providing these mobile children with a reasonable degree of curriculum continuity.

The Changing Community. More and more this land is becoming a land of city dwellers. Soon, if the experts are right, 90 per cent of Americans will live in huge strip or cluster cities created by the moving of both city and rural dwellers to the suburban fringes surrounding our cities. Already the eastern seaboard is virtually one great megalopolis stretched from "north of Boston" well into "Dixie."

Such population changes have brought many community problems. Often families uprooted from their former homes find themselves "without a country." Many of them never really become participants in the life of any community. Moreover, the movement of people in and out of the community sometimes brings clashes of interests and mores between the old residents and their new neighbors. In addition rapid growth in population brings perplexing new problems, such as the need for new schools, fire protection, roads, sidewalks, sewerage, police protection, and recreational facilities that communities can ill afford. Also because in periods of rapid changes communities find it very difficult to forecast future needs and to make adequate provisions for these needs, many growing or changing communities are faced with inadequate facilities and pressing needs with which they cannot cope.

The Family in a Changing Culture. Family life is also changing. Not so very long ago the family was the center of community life. Families were large because children were an economic asset, and many homes were shared by grandparents, and sometimes aunts, uncles, and other relatives, in addition to the immediate family. It was in the home that children were taught the social skills and moral virtues under the watchful eye and frequently stern discipline of Father, the omnipresent, omniscient, omnipotent, and undisputed head of the family, who ruled with the benevolent despotism that is expressed by the word *paternalism.*

The home was the center of family life. Not infrequently it was Father's place of business. If Father did not work at home, his work was usually close enough so that he could walk to work and come home for lunch. Women and children could find enough work in the home to keep them busy, and they were supposed to stay home and tend to it. Home was also the family recreation center. Here the family members amused each other with games, parties, sports, and other pleasurable occupations. Swains interested in the young ladies of the family called at the home and courted them in the family parlor or on the porch swing. All in all, the home was a tight unit in which the family worked and played together. It was secure and cohesive and made a firm basis for young people starting off in life.

No longer is this picture of home and family life a true one. The family has lost its place as the center of community life. Neither is it a tight unit any more. One marriage out of every four breaks up in divorce, and one of every sixteen in desertion. The family has become much smaller; instead of grandparents, maiden aunts, and other relatives adding to the family group, the average family is limited to the parents and two or three children. Because in many families both parents work outside the home, frequently no adult is at home much of the day, and sometimes quite young children are left on their own with no one at home for them to turn to for support or guidance. Because of the complexity of urban or suburban living, the members of the family may not have friends and associates in common. Instead each member of the family may go his own way with his own group. Such lack of family cohesion, coupled with the anonymity of urban living, often leads to delinquency, both juvenile and adult.

Families moving from their old neighborhoods to new urban areas often find it hard to fit in. Urban areas are notoriously callous. Each incoming family must make its place in the new community with little help from its new neighbors. Frequently both parents and children find it lonesome and strange in their new communities. These problems may be aggravated by the modern commuting habits that keep so many adults away from their homes from early morning until late in the evening and make it difficult for commuters to participate in family and community affairs. In some families the father is away so much that the children are almost as deprived as though they were living in broken homes.

Many of the family functions have been turned over to, or usurped by, other institutions. Now families depend upon the school, the young people's societies, the church, the community center, the Boy Scouts, the Boys' Clubs, the Park Department, and other agencies to do many of the things the family used to do itself. Perhaps this is necessary; experts seriously question whether the home and family can cope with the many serious problems of modern society.

Nevertheless the family is still the strongest socializing influence in American society. Perhaps the secondary-school curriculum should give more attention than it has in the past to the problems of home and family living for all pupils.

Youth in American Society. In spite of the fact that Americans seem to make youth a fetish, young people occupy a rather unenviable position in American society. Children are no longer an economic asset; rather they are a great expense. Because of the abundance of conflicting information and misinformation supplied by the mass media, and because of the prevalance of new attitudes and beliefs concerning child rearing, many modern parents are perplexed about how to raise their children. As a result some children are deprived of the security in the home that they so urgently need.

Secondary-school and college boys and girls are mature, or nearly mature, in many ways. Physically many of them are at the height of their powers. A large number of them have attained intellectual, social, and moral levels at least as high, and frequently higher, than those attained by many adults. In more primitive cultures these youths would be ready to play an adult role in society, but in modern American society they are given little or no responsibility. Boys and girls who are ready and eager to make a contribution to society are not allowed to do so. Although emancipated socially, American youths are not wanted in affairs of significance or importance except as hewers of wood and drawers of water. Of course, menial tasks may be excellent training for future participation, but youth needs more than that. Each adolescent boy and girl needs to have an opportunity to become a real member of society, to carry his share of the load, and to know that he is making some contributions, but we forbid him the opportunity. It is small wonder that often American youth feel neglected, insignificant, unwanted, and in the way.

Implications for the Curriculum. If some modern community life brings perplexing problems to the curriculum builder, it seems reasonable to believe that the type of curriculum to be offered by the school should be determined largely by the kind of community the school serves. Yet, with a population as mobile as ours, educational programs designed for a single community may be too parochial. Possibly the time has come when curriculum builders must place curriculum emphasis on national needs rather than local or regional concerns. It may even be that schools should turn to national and state curricula to help solve the problems of curriculum continuity for mobile pupils. The curriculum builder must weigh these possibilities. When communities are disorganized and many people are strangers in their own home towns, probably the school should cooperate in civic programs designed to provide means whereby the community can become more unified and better organized and do all in its power to develop skills, attitudes, and understandings that will help boys and girls to cope with such problems. The changed position of the family requires that other agencies share in what were once considered solely family responsibilities. In spite of the fact that critics tend to scoff at courses in home and family living and life adjustment, the realities of community and family life cry out for someone to assume responsibility for this type of education. Surely curriculum builders should consider the need for such education and to determine how best it can be taught to boys and girls. Perhaps home and family living and life adjustment should have a larger share in the formal education of every secondary-school pupil. Certainly education in these areas should not be left to pure chance, as is so often the case nowadays.

Somehow the secondary school should make better use of the potentialities of its boys and girls; possibly one method for doing this would be to give pupils more real responsibilities in school affairs and in curriculum activities. Curriculum builders should consider the possibilities of developing curricula that give pupils opportunities to cope with real problems of real significance in the school and community. Curricula that feature life situations rather than lifelike situations may well be the answer to one of the trying "problems of youth."

VALUES AND THE CURRICULUM

Values in the Changing American Culture. As a general rule each culture has a hierarchy of values that indicate what that society holds dear. The American people are no exception to this rule. However, one of the striking things about American society is the difference in the values various Americans hold and in the recent rapid changes in American values.

When the immigrants settled in this country, they brought many different cultural patterns with them. To a greater or lesser degree the cultural patterns of the immigrants have stuck to their descendants, and so we find that the diverse ethnic backgrounds of the American people have created a diversity of value patterns in American society. In addition changes in values have been hurried by the rapid technological advances of the last century and the rapid shifting in other aspects of our society, such as employment, the advent of suburban living, and the distribution of wealth. Changes in values have also been encouraged by the utilitarian and pragmatic philosophies of life held by many Americans.

The diversity of value patterns in American culture seems to cause confusion and uncertainty about values for many Americans. This uncertainty seems to be magnified by an emphasis on the pragmatic test and by changing values and a turning away from belief in innate and permanent values. As a result many Americans are not sure of what is good and what is bad, what is right and what is wrong. Therefore, some observers feel, the American people drift aimlessly, without any purpose in their lives or in their society.

If Americans are confused and lack purpose, perhaps the curricula of our schools have helped create the confusion. Oftentimes, because of fear of impinging on the prerogatives of the churches, the schools have studiously avoided teaching moral and spiritual values. In fact, except in a very general way, like being in favor of virtue and against sin, the schools have neglected the teaching of values altogether.

Partly this neglect has been the result of an attempt to be objective and to let pupils arrive at their own decisions. More frequently it has resulted from school teachers' and school administrators' being afraid to take a stand and to deal with controversial issues. Such neglect makes it difficult for boys and girls to establish bases from which to set up their own pattern of values.

Changing Controls in American Society. The American people have long been noted for being an independent, individualistic group free from government domination. Although our forefathers may have believed that the best government was the government that governed least, modern Americans do not seem to think so. At least they submit to much more government than ever before. Evidence of increased government regulation can be seen in such things as zoning laws, building codes, fair practice laws, fair trade laws, Federal Communications Commission regulations, wage-hour laws, child-labor laws, motor vehicle laws, Sunday closing laws, and hundreds of other laws and regulations by which government controls the activities of its citizens. Undoubtedly most of these laws and regulations are necessary and good, but they represent a turning away from the rugged individualism that was the idea of another generation.

Other agencies, such as trade and labor unions, large corporations, professional associations, veterans' associations, and pressure groups, increasingly control the behavior of many people. Although many individualists resist the pressures of these groups, each year social controls increase. Thus, for instance, one's pay and work week are no longer a matter of the employer and employee, but are controlled by negotiations between management and labor; the individuals' hands are tied by collective agreement.

Among the most powerful pressures upon the modern American is that of his peer group. According to Riesman, Whyte, Coleman, and other observers, the peer group has much more influence now than it used to have. The type of house in which one lives, the type of clothes that one wears, the recreation one seeks, in fact all one's activities are at least somewhat influenced by the pressures of the group in which one lives. Sheer propinquity makes it necessary to limit individual freedom in order to provide for the rights of one's neighbors. As a result rugged individualism is difficult to pursue in modern American society.

Mass Media in American Culture. During prime time a top television program on a major network plays to literally millions of viewers. According to a *New York Times* estimate[6] based on a Nielsen Rating, 2,251,000 television sets were tuned to the first Nixon–Kennedy debate of the 1960 presidential campaign in the New York City area alone. When a medium reaches such a gigantic audience, it follows that it must have a tremendous impact upon the people of the nation. Frequently this influence shapes the tastes, values, and customs of millions of American people. Certainly television must have a great effect on the impressionable minds of the young people who watch it for long hours each day. What is true of television must also be true of radio programs, comic books, magazines, books, and newspapers.

The mass media can, and often do, have a very desirable effect upon people. Periodicals are one of the best sources of information about science, natural history, and music. Radio, television, and the press sometimes try hard to eliminate community sores, such as prejudice and intolerance, and to promote good citizenship, even to the point of sometimes supporting unpopular causes. Paperback books have moved much classical and scientific literature from the semioblivion of the university library to the living rooms of American homes, where, at last, people are reading them for fun and profit, instead of merely for college credit.

Unfortunately mass media do not always present their "best profiles"

6 *The New York Times,* September 27, 1960, p. 29.

for public view. Usually they are not taste setters but followers of the public taste. All too often they seem to aim at presenting the very worst material that one dares to exhibit publicly. In particular much of the material designed for children and youth is in very poor taste and sometimes downright immoral and obscene. Fighting, killing, burglary, and other crimes of all sorts are their bill of fare for American children. In spite of an effort to clean them up, comic books still feature violence and immorality. In 1953,[7] children's comedy television programs averaged 36.6 acts of violence per hour. There is little reason to think they are less violent today. What effect can we expect such material to have on young people?

Implications for the Curriculum. Changes in value of the American people and the general American pattern of values should be of much concern to the curriculum makers. It would seem that the school must take its rightful place as a builder of values, but what values the schools should foster, and by what means it should foster them, is a grave problem.

The pressures of environmental controls and mass media on individuals point up a curriculum dilemma, mentioned earlier in this chapter, with which the American school must contend. In order to exist in modern society, boys and girls must learn to conform; at the same time, if they are going to live full lives, each must learn to realize his own individuality. The dilemma presents a difficult problem to which as yet educators have not found an adequate solution.

Whether for good or for ill, there seems to be no doubt that the mass media have tremendous influence in shaping the ideas and attitudes of both the children and adults of our nation. Because they are educational tools of incomparable influence, the curriculum builder must consider how they can best be used and how the pupils can be taught to best use them. Probably the schools should increase their efforst to teach boys and girls how to discriminate and to help them establish high standards of value in the use of current literary and dramatic productions. Certainly when pupils are subjected to so much material on every side, the curriculum that limits itself solely to the classics is inexcusably out of touch with reality.

PROBLEMS OF AMERICAN DEMOCRACY

PROBLEMS OF SOCIAL CLASS

Frequently we Americans claim that we live in a classless society. But there are social classes in the United States, and Americans are well

[7] National Society for the Study of Education, *Mass Media and Education*, Fifty-third Yearbook, Part II (Chicago: University of Chicago Press, 1954), p. 203.

aware of class distinctions. Although they may not ever use the words *social class,* Americans show the true state of affairs when they point out that someone "is one of that East Malaria gang" or "She is one of that snooty Indian Hill Country Club set."

Differences in Values. Each social class has its own way of life, which is, to a greater or lesser extent, different from the way of life of all other classes. In effect each class is a culture of its own. Values prized by one class are not necessarily those prized by another class, for the customs, habits, beliefs, ideals, and attitudes of one's class are born and bred in us just as are other cultural things.

The differences in values of the various social classes present several problems to the secondary-school curriculum builder. Teachers are usually either members of the middle classes or upper-lower-class persons who are trying to move up into the middle class. Quite frequently middle-class teachers find it difficult to understand the values of their lower-class pupils. Often a teacher's background is so different from his pupils that he cannot communicate with his pupils at all. Reports of "Blackboard Jungles" or "Retreats from Learning" sometimes stem from such situations. In such instances teachers are likely to condemn behavior that the boys and girls and their parents consider normal and proper.

Another problem is that the vocal people of the community, as far as public schools are concerned, are the middle-class parents. These middle-class citizens demand that the public schools provide the curricula valued most highly by the middle class and ignore the needs of pupils from other classes.

Curriculum Inequalities. Lower-class pupils are frequently short-changed. The curriculum does not provide for their needs and sometimes places obstacles in their paths. Because intelligence tests presuppose common experiences and opportunities to learn, the test scores of lower-class boys and girls are liable to be lower than their abilities and aptitudes warrant. Similarly the halo effect caused by their dress, manners, and speech makes it difficult for them to get good marks in school. Moreover, middle-class teachers often discourage lower-class youths from attempting to do well. Frequently the lower-class pupils' difficulties are further magnified by the fact that among some lower-class families and adolescent groups learning, studying, "correct English," and "proper manners," are not highly valued, and success in school may be accompanied by loss of friends and the creation of family discord.

In addition the social life of the school and the school extracurricular activities are almost entirely the property of the middle-class pupils. This exclusiveness extends to parents as well. Membership in the parents' organizations is almost universally middle class. Parents from the upper classes do not come, and lower-class parents are made to feel unwelcome.

Public secondary school is truly a middle-class institution. The lower-class youth who attempts to meet the standards of the middle-class school may find many roadblocks in his way, and so also may the middle-class teacher who attempts to instill middle-class ways into children from other classes. The problem of the relation of the curriculum to the various classes has never been squarely faced by the curriculum builders.

Social Mobility and the Curriculum. The classes in American society are not rigid, nor are they set by any firm rules of birth, breeding, or background. These characteristics make possible much moving from class to class. This social mobility has been a characteristic of American society from the very beginning of the colonial period. By means of it many Americans have escaped from the less favored classes to positions of prominence.

Social advancement is achieved in many ways. One of the major tools to use in the climb from class to class is education, for education opens to the lower-class person many of the middle-class and upper-class vocations and gives him opportunities to meet and associate with members of these classes and to learn their class customs. Therefore the secondary-school curriculum maker would do well to consider the implications of social mobility when building a new curriculum.

Present signs seem to indicate that to move upward on the social ladder is becoming more difficult. The increase in educational and living standards of the general populace has raised the floor level of the various classes so that persons aspiring to new levels must attain higher standards than in the past. For a time the closing off of opportunities for lower- and lower-middle-class youth to rise socially may be mitigated by the growth of the technical and service vocations and professions, but even this escape route may be closing. If the prediction that by 1975 the supply of technical and professional workers will exceed the demand proves to be correct, the competition for middle-class position will become severe and upward social mobility extremely difficult.

INTERGROUP RELATIONS

The United States is a nation of many groups. We have ethnic groups, racial groups, religious groups, social groups, special interest groups, and many more. These groups account for much of the great diversity in American culture. They are both a strength and a weakness.

Highly diverse groups find it difficult to coexist amiably. Prejudice, intolerance, bigotry, unfair employment practices, ghettos, and multitudes of other inequities result. In recent years intergroup relations have been fraught with hatred, fear, cruelty, persecution, and violence.

The most spectacular intergroup clashes have had to do with racial relations. Attempts to desegregate in the South have raised racial strife to fever heat, but racial problems are almost as virulent in other parts of the country. Incidents of racial discrimination against the dark-skinned representatives of the United Nations in New York City are a continual source of embarrassment to the United States government, and have evidently done considerable harm to American prestige abroad. The nation must face up to these problems at once. If we do not solve them, soon the results both at home and abroad may be dire indeed.

Religious discrimination still runs rife in the land. During the 1960 presidential campaign Mr. Kennedy's Roman Catholicism was a primary issue in spite of public attempts by both candidates to allay bigotry. Lately anti-Semitism, anti-Catholicism, and anti-Protestantism are reported to have been on the increase. The United States has a long way to go before intergroup rivalries and tensions will give way to the spirit of sportsmanship that T. V. Smith says is democracy.

Historically, intergroup tensions have been relieved in four ways: (1) the disintegration of one or more of the groups; (2) the development of a caste system; (3) the integration of the groups, and (4) pluralism. In our country the first two of these solutions hold little promise. To solve its intergroup problems, the United States must turn either to integration or to pluralism.

Earlier in the present century much was made of the claim that the United States was a melting pot. Nowadays this claim seems less convincing. Instead of integrating, groups of all types continue to cling to their own identities and to the customs and beliefs that give each its identity. Probably some of these groups will never lose themselves into the mass of Americans.

Maybe it is better that they never should do so. Pluralism may be America's strength. For many purposes a cable is superior to a rod. But before pluralism can be successful, much must be done to eliminate the inequities in American society and, through education, eliminate the ignorance, naïveté and fear that is the food of prejudice, intolerance, and group strife. The school curriculum can do much to help solve this problem.

GOVERNMENTAL PROBLEMS

Governmental problems are increasing in the United States. Government has become so big, complex, and impersonal that frequently citizens see no use in participating in it in any way. "You can't fight City Hall" represents all-too-common attitudes and beliefs of city dwellers and towns people alike. And in some of our communities one cannot blame the citizens: their government is corrupt and the dishonest political leaders virtually unassailable. Is it any wonder that in this democratic land citizens increasingly think of the government as "they" rather than "we"?

Crime and Delinquency. The yearly crime bill in the United States is staggering. Estimates differ, but a conservative guess would put the figure well above $15 billion. And crime and delinquency continue to grow. Much crime is organized crime, centered in the gambling industry, but organized crime has crept into many otherwise legitimate businesses as well and forced their costs to be much higher than they would be otherwise. White-collar crime is common. The 1959 scandals concerning "payola," which rocked the television industry, and the 1961 scandals concerning price fixings, are examples of the kinds of practices that occur and are winked at more frequently than we like to realize. With our youth, delinquency seems to be becoming more widely spread every day.

Why have crime and delinquency grown so? As a general rule one can say that crime and delinquency are the product of a culture. If crime and delinquency rise, one may take it as symptomatic of something sick in the culture. Nevertheless, we do have reason to believe that some delinquency must be charged to inadequate and inappropriate curricula and poor methods of teaching in our schools, as the following account of warfare between juvenile gangs shows.

> Gang warfare of the sort can be traced to many factors: the schools' program may not appeal to the young people involved; the home situation may be so difficult that the city streets seem preferable; of even greater importance, however, is that the school in its capacity as family surrogate too often fails to transform the group into a constructive unit. School authorities persistently fall back on negative solutions, such as repressive discipline. A more positive approach, which has long been used by group workers and others who deal with potential delinquency, is to utilize gang leadership and develop worthwhile activities that are characterized by cooperation. When gangs become properly supervised clubs, under their own leadership, they loose many of their conflict attributes and emerge as respectable units in the school.[8]

Certainly if a curriculum revision can do anything to prevent juvenile delinquency, it should be made to do so.[9]

The Urgent International Situation. The problems having to do with international affairs are probably the most serious problems the nation has to face today. The twentieth century has seen the United States emerge as one of the two most powerful nations on the globe. For better or for worse the exigencies of trade, and the struggle for security in a world divided by threat of war, make the United States' role as the leader of the Free World mandatory.

[8] Myles W. Rodehaven, William B. Axtell, and Richard E. Gross, *The Sociology of the School* (New York: Thomas Y. Crowell Company, 1957), p. 120.

[9] See William R. Carriker (ed.), *Role of the School in Prevention of Juvenile Delinquency*, Cooperative Research Monograph No. 10, OE–25034 (Washington, D.C.: Government Printing Office, 1963).

Because the role of world leader is relatively new to us, Americans are not always atune to the responsibilities and duties that go along with leadership. Many Americans still remain isolationists; some are jingoistic and provincial. Frequently we are inclined to be naïve in our international dealings. Consequently our behavior toward other people, both as individuals and as nations, has sometimes been awkward, and may have made our role in international affairs more difficult than it would otherwise have been.

The United States has had to assume world leadership in one of the most difficult periods of our history. With the discovery of nuclear weapons man has put himself in a position in which war is unthinkable and yet ever-threatening. Under these conditions the only hope for civilization is for the nations to cooperate. The evidence of the times indicates that international competition is obsolete, for competition between nations, cold wars, and arms races can lead only to hot wars. To provide a vehicle for international cooperation world leaders worked together to form the United Nations Organization. So far the United Nations has not been as successful as its founders may have hoped. Yet in spite of its inadequacies, the United Nations has served as a forum for world opinion and as a medium for debate between great and small powers. Even with sharply limited authority it exerted much influence to keep the cold war cold in the difficult years following World War II. It well deserves the understanding and support of American citizens.

In addition to the tensions resulting from the struggles between the great powers, population and economic pressures have caused great unrest in the smaller nations. The submerged peoples of the world have become tired of being little people and so are making their bids for "places in the sun." Since the end of World War II many countries have left colonyhood and become nations. Most of these new nations have had great difficulty in launching their ships of state, because the colonial powers had done so little to prepare them for nationhood when they were colonies. The debacle of the Congo is the prime example of such failure. Consequently, in most of these new nations, much must be done to develop their intellectual, social, political, and economic resources. They need help if they are to survive as free nations—especially in the areas of health, economics, and education.

The appearance of these new nations has particular implications in the battle between the democracies of the West and the communist bloc. Because the new countries are liable to associate the Western democratic nations with the exploitation and racial persecution so common in their colonial experiences, they are frequently suspicious of American policies. Being poor and desperately in need of help, they are liable to turn for aid to the communist nations, whose doctrines and promises seem so tempting and with whom they have had no bad dealings. Thus the United States' position with respect to the new nations is a difficult one.

DEMOCRACY AND THE CURRICULUM

Most Americans would agree that, in theory, and to a certain extent in practice, the United States is a democracy. What do they mean when they say *democracy?* This is a difficult question to answer because the term *democracy* has been used so loosely that it no longer has any precise meaning to most men. Moreover, democracy is a relatively new concept in history, and so its meaning has not fully developed in the minds of the people. Most democratic ideas are no older than the European Renaissance.

Our own country was not created as a democracy. Because they had little faith in the common man, the founding fathers created a *republic* in which the *best* people would rule. According to their plan the electorate, which was limited to male property holders, was to elect representatives who were not to represent the will of the people, but to make decisions based on their superior knowledge and ability.

Such lack of faith in the common man is still current in the United States. Many sincere, intelligent, and capable students of mankind and government believe that the people are not fit to govern. They are strongly convinced, as Plato was before them, that government should rest in the hands of an elite.

Representative Democracy. Although the nation was founded as a republic, more and more the representatives have been turning to the people for their decisions. This democratic trend can be seen in the increase of the number of primary elections and referenda during late years. However, because "sheer size" makes direct participation in government impractical, we have turned to representative democracy. In this form of government the citizens select representatives, not to decide as they think best, but to carry out the will of their constituents.

Although the majority can usually have what it wants, representative democracy, as practiced in the United States, provides for the protection of the rights and interests of the minorities also. The presence of the opposition party helps to keep the majority honest and fair. In addition the Constitution provides checks and balances designed to prevent the majority from injuring the minorities. Nevertheless, within the limits set up by the opposition parties and the Constitution, the government reflects the desire of the majority.

A State of Mind. Democracy is more than just a kind of government. T. V. Smith has called it a state of mind. He, and many others, speak of it as a way of life. It is not an easy way of life, as Roy O. Billett points out. It is full of pullings and tuggings by various individuals and groups, and it places great responsibilities on its citizens. To use Billett's own words:

> Democracy presumes, first, that all such conflicts of opinion will be conducted in the spirit of tolerance and fair play, with intelligent consideration of available evidence, with equal opportunity, freedom, and justice to all; and, second, that the conflict will be temporarily resolved by the expressed will of the majority. It also presumes that the judgment of the majority will be a free and honest expression of what it deems best for the group, and that this judgment will be subject to later revision or reversal by the same procedure. It still further assumes enough sportsmanship on the part of the minority to insure a fair trial for the plans and purposes of the majority; and such sportsmanship on the part of the majority that the rights of the minority are guaranteed and protected. In times past, the minority has often been forced by a ruthless majority to surrender its rights or to move on to new territory. Now that America has "grown up," the problems of the minority can find no such easy and undemocratic solution. Individuals and groups who won't play unless they can always have their way are about to discover that they do not approve of democracy—and that democracy does not approve of them.
>   If the conditions suggested above cannot exist, democracy is visionary and unattainable, and the sooner the fact is admitted the better for all concerned.[10]

Judging from the above it would seem that in order to make democracy work, we need a peculiar type of citizen—one who is honest, fair, cooperative, and willing to put the welfare of the group above selfish personal interests. In addition he must be capable of finding out the facts and making reasonable decisions on the basis of the facts, for, as Billett indicates, democracy cannot exist unless citizens who are well informed arrive at reasonably good and similar decisions. Finally they must be able to select capable leaders and to follow their leadership intelligently.

IMPLICATIONS FOR THE CURRICULUM

Obviously the problems of our American democracy are many. It is the wise citizen who can carry out his responsibilities in our country today. How to build a curriculum that will develop citizens who can fulfill their duties as citizens is a problem the curriculum maker must face.

The curriculum builder should note that the curriculum may contribute to delinquency and take care to see to it that instead of being a breeder of delinquency, the school is instrumental in preventing and counterattacking delinquent behavior.

[10] Roy O. Billett, *Fundamentals of Secondary-School Teaching* (Boston: Houghton Mifflin Company, 1940), p. 29.

The international problems our nation faces are great and many. We are handicapped in our attempts to solve these problems because our people have been, and still are, somewhat naïve concerning international relations. The curriculum maker must face up to the responsibility of providing a curriculum that will help develop an intelligent citizenry able to cope with the international problems of a great nation.

In order to develop the type of citizen we need the schools must provide boys and girls with many experiences in problem solving and in democratic living, so that they will learn to think well and live sportsmanlike lives. To learn skills in decision making boys and girls must have plenty of practice in actual thinking. The best kind of practice in thinking is to try to solve actual problems in real situations. The secondary-school curriculum should provide many opportunities for pupils to solve such problems.

SUMMARY OF IMPLICATIONS

Since culture is a creation of man and every man is a creature of culture, both human nature and culture can be changed by education. However, changing them is a slow process. Social influences, such as customs, folk values, pressure groups, batter the curriculum from all sides and ultimately shape it into a form acceptable to the culture.

Our American cultural scene is changing rapidly, so rapidly that much of the curriculum soon becomes out of date unless it is continually revised. Changing employment practices make it necessary to reevaluate our provisions for general and vocational education. The new technical and service industries continually call for increased numbers of highly trained workers. Even so, because of the number of people eager for advanced education, we soon may have a surplus of college-educated technicians, executives, and other white-collar workers. At the same time, technical advances in industry are providing more time for blue-collar workers. Therefore there will be increasing need for instruction in how to use leisure time profitably.

There have also been great changes in the population pattern in the community and in the home. These changes make it mandatory for curriculum builders to reappraise the role of instruction in home and family living, community responsibilities, and other areas of life adjustment. The increasing preponderance of women in the population and in the labor force makes it desirable to reexamine the provisions for education for girls. Our mobile population causes acute problems of continuity and casts considerable doubt on the validity of the old curriculum-building principle that the curriculum should be developed for the needs of a particular community. On the other hand, because of the growth of community problems, the need for community-oriented curricula seems to be greater than ever. A particularly pressing community need is to find a more adequate place for youth in community life. The school could contribute much in this area.

These many changes, plus the changes in both formal and informal societal controls, have caused much confusion about values. Mass media and sheer propinquity are forcing boys and girls to conformist behavior. Schoolmen should examine their programs to check tendencies to crush individuality and originality. At the same time, the school should take the lead in setting standards of values.

American society is faced with many problems. Among them are problems having to do with social class, intergroup relations, crime and delinquency, and problems of government. In building the curriculum we as curriculum builders should take care that we do not aggravate old problems and create new ones. Life in a democratic state is not easy. Its citizens have to learn to be fair, tolerant, and self-sacrificing. They must learn to make judgments honestly and wisely. The skills of democratic citizenship come only from such practice in democratic living. The secondary-school curriculum can, and probably should, provide much of this practice.

SUGGESTED READINGS

ASSOCIATION FOR SUPERVISION AND CURRICULUM DEVELOPMENT. *Forces Affecting American Education.* Washington, D.C.: The Association, 1953.

An important yearbook which depicts the impact of various parts of the culture on the education.

BROOKOVER, WILBUR B. *A Sociology of Education.* New York: American Book Company, 1955.

An excellent elementary textbook in the sociology of education.

CHANDLER, B. J., LINDLEY J. STILES, and JOHN I. KITZUSE. *Education in Urban Society.* New York: Dodd, Mead, and Company, 1962.

A symposium of articles which portrays the forces influencing schools in the modern megalopolis, their implications for education, and new conceptions of education to cope with the realistics of urban living.

CLARK, BURTON R. *Educating the Expert Society.* San Francisco: Chandler Publishing Company, 1962.

A study of the sociology of education which attempts to show the relationships between education and society and the nature of the contemporary educational institution.

COLEMAN, JAMES S. *The Adolescent Society.* New York: The Free Press of Glencoe, 1961.

A study of the adolescent culture, its source, its impact, and its implications for modern secondary education.

CONANT, JAMES B. *Slums and Suburbs.* New York: McGraw-Hill Book Company, Inc., 1961.

A study of school problems caused by social conditions in slum and suburban areas and some recommendations for facing and solving the problems.

COOK, LLOYD ALLEN, and ELAINE FORSYTHE COOK. *A Sociological Approach to Education.* Third edition. New York: McGraw-Hill Book Company, Inc., 1960.

An excellent introductory textbook in educational sociology.

DRUCKER, PETER F. *America's Next Twenty Years.* Reprinted from the March, April, May, and June, 1955, issues of *Harper's Magazine.* New York: *Harper's Magazine.*

A series of articles discussing the issues and problems of contemporary American society and their implications for American life and institutions.

EDUCATIONAL POLICIES COMMISSION. *Education and the Disadvantaged American.* Washington, D.C.: The Commission, N.E.A. and A.A.S.A., 1962.

Tells who the disadvantaged are, and outlines programs to meet their needs.

GINZBERG, ELI (ed.). *Values and Ideals of American Youth.* New York: Columbia University Press, 1961.

Papers given at the Golden Anniversary White House Conference on Children and Youth. Deals with many social problems and resulting problems of values and ideals.

GORDON, C. WAYNE. *The Social System of the High School.* New York: The Free Press of Glencoe, 1957.

A report of a doctoral dissertation in which the author attempted to analyze adolescent behavior in the high school and to explore the relationship between the social studies and the behavior of adolescents.

GROSS, RICHARD E., RAYMOND H. MUESSIG, and GEORGE L. FERSH. *The Problem Approach and the Social Studies.* Washington, D.C.: The National Council for the Social Studies, 1960.

Rationale for teaching social studies through problem-solving techniques with examples of how to do it.

GWYNN, J. MINOR. *Curriculum Principles and Social Trends.* Third edition. New York: The Macmillan Company, 1960.

Chapters 4, 5, 7, 16, and 21 deal with the society and the school discussed in this chapter.

HAVIGHURST, ROBERT J., et al. *Growing Up in River City.* New York: John Wiley and Sons, Inc., 1962.

A longitudinal study of youth during the junior and senior high school years. Concludes that the city does not adequately provide for youth; suggests substitute programs in lieu of the present secondary-school curriculum for pupils for whom the present curriculum has little value.

HENRY, NELSON B. (ed.). *Social Forces Influencing American Education.* Sixtieth Yearbook of the National Society for the Study of Education, Part II. Chicago: University of Chicago Press, 1961.

An N.S.S.E. yearbook depicting the educational implications of cultural factors. One of the best basic references.

HOLLINGSHEAD, A. B. *Elmtown's Youth: The Impact of Social Classes on Adolescents.* New York: John Wiley and Sons, Inc., 1949.

A pioneer study picturing youth in the setting of a midwest community. This book helps to make clear some of the implications of social class on the secondary school.

MACIVER, ROBERT M. *Dilemma of Youth: In America Today.* New York: Harper and Row, Inc., 1961.

A group of excellent speeches on the social problems of youth and their causes by foremost observers of youth and the modern scene.

PACKARD, VANCE. *The Hidden Persuaders.* New York: David McKay Company, Inc., 1957.

A popular analysis of aspects of contemporary society which influences and hems in modern man.

PASSOW, A. HARRY (ed.). *Education in Depressed Areas.* New York: Bureau of Publications, Teachers College, Columbia University, 1963.

Fifteen specialists explore the question "Have the public schools a responsibility for educating culturally disadvantaged children in depressed areas?" Primary concern is given to urban problems, but also considers conditions of cultural deprivation of rural and small town areas.

POUNDS, RALPH L., and JAMES R. BRYNER. *The School in American Society.* New York: The Macmillan Company, 1959.

A very thorough textbook in educational sociology from which much of the thinking for the present chapter was originally derived.

RIESMAN, DAVID, NATHAN GLAZER, and REUEL DENNY. *The Lonely Crowd.* New Haven, Connecticut: The Yale University Press, 1950.

Famous study in which Riesman develops his theory about outer directed and inner directed people.

RODEHAVER, MYLES W., WILLIAM B. AXTELL, and RICHARD E. GROSS. *The Sociology of the School.* New York: Thomas Y. Crowell Company, 1957.

One of the better standard texts in the sociology of education.

SALISBURY, HARRISON E. *The Shook-up Generation.* New York: Harper and Row, Inc., 1958.

A report on youth by one of the nation's foremost reporters.

SCHRAMM, WILBUR. "Television in the Life of the Child—Implications for the School," U.S. Department of Health, Education, and Welfare, Office of Education. *New Teaching Aids for the American Classroom,* OE–34020. Washington, D.C.: Government Printing Office, 1962.

Summary of research on television and young viewers and its implication for education and further research.

SMITH, B. OTHANEL, WILLIAM O. STANLEY, and J. HARLAND SHORES. *Fundamentals of Curriculum Development.* Revised edition. New York: Harcourt, Brace and World, 1957. Chapters 1–4.

A very astute analysis of the modern world and its implications for the desirable curriculum of the future.

WHYTE, WILLIAM H. *The Organization Man.* New York: Simon and Schuster, 1956.

A popularized study of the pressures toward conformity in modern American society.

WITTY, PAUL A., and PAUL J. KINSELLA. "A Report on Television in 1961," *Elementary English,* 39: 26, January, 1962.

A report of a study of televiewing in Chicago. Indicates among other things, that high school pupils spend 13 hours per week looking at television.

Chapter 5

Secondary-School Curricula in Europe

Traditionally the secondary schools in Europe have been highly selective. In their highly class-conscious social structure, that Europeans should have developed a selective system of education is only natural. European educational systems were designed to place boys and girls in the proper niches early. In order to reserve the advantage of a superior education for the best boys and girls only, European educators have utilized systems of examination designed to cull out the academically inferior and prevent any mediocre pupil's occupying school space that might more profitably be used by another.

Recently both Russia and the West have seen a demand for the equalization of educational opportunities for all adolescents. The result has been that most youths are now guaranteed some sort of secondary education until their mid-teens. In general, however, the type of schooling a European youth receives depends upon his supposed merit, for different schools are provided for academically talented, technically inclined, and ordinary pupils.

SECONDARY EDUCATION IN ENGLAND

The Education Act of 1944, which gave England its first really national system of education, also provided for England's first attempt at universal secondary education. In theory, at least, secondary education was no longer for the privileged few; it was the right of all youth, for the act made full-time secondary education free and compulsory for all boys and girls to age 15 and made part-time secondary schooling mandatory for all working youth from 15 to 18 years of age.

THE TRIPARTITE PLAN

To implement their program of universal secondary education the English created a tripartite system of secondary education. The three types of secondary schools established in this system are the grammar school for the university-bound youngster, the secondary technical school for those interested in the skilled trades and technical fields, and the secondary modern schools for the ordinary boy or girl who does not plan to specialize. A few education authorities have established comprehensive secondary schools somewhat similar to the American high schools, but these are not yet very common. All of these secondary schools draw their pupils from the common British primary system, so that now England has an educational ladder that extends through the primary school to the secondary grades.

Proponents of the tripartite plan argue that in the separate schools the needs of the youngsters can be met more efficiently. This system, they point out, provides for the education of an intellectual elite, yet prevents the college-preparatory and technical functions from overshadowing the general education as it has in the American comprehensive high school. In spite of these alleged advantages, a movement for comprehensive secondary schools may be gaining momentum. Considerable opposition to the tripartite system has developed. As someone has said, the grammar school gets the cream; the technical secondary school, the milk; and the secondary modern school, the skimmed milk. Parents resent the implication that their children are skimmed milk and so resent the modern school program. Critics of the plan also point out that 11 is pretty early for making decisions that will affect the course of a person's entire life. They fear that such a system makes little allowance for development of late bloomers or any other change in the circumstances and so may prove disastrous to many lives.[1]

THE ENGLISH SECONDARY GRAMMAR SCHOOL

The English secondary grammar schools have a long and honorable tradition of preparing youth for the university. Undoubtedly they will continue this tradition for some time.

Admission Requirements. As in the other English secondary schools, the pupil comes to the grammar school after completing the primary

[1] A. Harry Passow, *Secondary Education for All* (Columbus, Ohio: Ohio State University Press, 1961), pp. 44–76.

school, usually when he is 11 or 12, or as the English put it, 11 plus. Admission to the grammar school is dependent on an examination, the pupil's primary school marks, and other considerations. Boys and girls who do not meet the requirements for the grammar school are forced to attend either a secondary technical school or a secondary modern school. The result is that parents place great importance on their children's being admitted to the grammar school. This pressure also reflects itself in the lower schools. In the primary schools the practice of coaching pupils for the examination leading toward admittance to the grammar school is not entirely unknown.

The Grammar School Curriculum. The grammar school curriculum reflects its classical past. Its main purpose is college preparatory and, in many respects, it resembles the college-preparatory curricula of secondary schools in the United States. In general, the curriculum covers six or seven years, although many pupils drop out before completing the entire curriculum. Presumably this high rate of dropout is in part caused by the relatively high academic standards and a tendency toward stiff academic teaching methods.

In the first years the grammar school curriculum is much the same as those in other English secondary schools. The difference is in the method of teaching and the difficulty of the material, which is aimed at bright pupils. Subjects include history, geography, English, French, algebra, Spanish, Latin, Greek, arithmetic, chemistry, physics, biology, art, music, handicrafts, domestic science, physical education, and religion. Foreign languages, classical or modern, are started early in the school and pursued to greater lengths than is usually true in the United States.

Specialization and the Sixth Form. After five, sometimes six, years the grammar school pupil has completed his general education and may elect to take the General Certificate of education examination. At this point many youths leave the school. The pupils who continue specialize in three or four subjects for one to three years in what the English call the sixth form. During this period the youth achieve standards seldom reached in American secondary schools. The areas of specialization include such fields as classics, Latin, and modern languages, sciences, mathematics, engineering, commerce, arts and crafts, and domestic science, although opportunities to specialize in the last of these are quite rare.

The sixth form is something peculiar to the English grammar schools. One reason the English shy away from introducing the comprehensive schools is because they find it difficult to fit the sixth form program into them. The main feature of the sixth form is not its emphasis on specialization, although it does give pupils an opportunity to do scholarly work of high caliber and to become thoroughly familiar with an area of specialization, but its emphasis on character building and training in leadership.

Character Building. Character building is an important aim in British secondary schools. The curriculum, the extracurriculum, and the religious instruction—all are used to reach this goal. In this respect the public school has set the pattern for British education. Although the term *public schools* may be used to refer to many sorts of independent secondary schools in England, ordinarily one uses it to refer to the independent, aristocratic, tuition-charging boarding schools that have dominated British secondary education for hundreds of years and have served as the pattern when the government-maintained day grammar schools were established by the Education Act of 1902. From the days of the early nineteenth century the public schools have maintained a policy of pupil participation in the school government through the medium of the sixth form and the prefect system, which owes its strength to the work of Arnold of Rugby and to Thring of Uppingham. Both the sixth form and the prefect system have been continued by present-day "public schools" and have been adapted by modern grammar schools. In the sixth form students hold a position in the grammar school roughly equivalent to that of first classmen in our American service academies with their great responsibilities as leaders in both the academic and social life of the school.[2]

E. B. Castle, a former Head Master now turned professor of education, describes the prefect system this way:

> The unexamined assumption is that character is a product of a type of leadership that tests an individual's moral capacity in several directions: to control his temper; to encourage loyalty within the group for which he is responsible; to control groups, for example a dormitory or classes in prep[3] without the assistance of a master; to see justice done among recalcitrant younger boys to ensure the regularity of life in a community of the immature, and to preserve, and maybe improve, the tone of the school. The exercise of such responsibilities involves a subtle process of devolution from the headmaster downwards. The general pattern is usually as follows: there is a group of school prefects under the leadership of a head boy whose responsibilities extend over the whole school; within each boarding house of about fifty boys, there is a group of house prefects whose main duties are tied up with the welfare of the house; but the head of the house and possibly one or two other prefects in the house group will also be school prefects. Thus prefectorial authority cuts across the division of house and school; the house is, in fact, the training base for school prefecture, for here domestic responsibilities in study houseroom, and dormitory are the testing grounds of ability to lead and control in a wider sphere. . . . Half a dozen senior boys may be responsi-

---

[2] *Ibid.*, pp. 127–139.

[3] I.e., the preparation of lessons or study hall.

ble for organizing the entry of five hundred into school chapel, or morning assembly, without a master in sight. This is no light duty. Success depends not only on a prefect's personal influence but on the total acceptance by the school of his authority, but it nevertheless involves much self confidence, acquired through trial and error in managing smaller but similar situations, such as getting twenty boys to bed by lights out.[4]

This system places a great deal of responsibility on some of the pupils. Sir John Wolfenden describes the responsibility of the head boy as follows:

> He must manage to put across new ideas without putting up the backs of people who are affected by them. He must be his head master's chief advisor and confidant in matters which affect the boys and at the same time he must be able to act as defender of the rights of the people if at any moment he thinks they are in danger. He must move with assurance inside his own hierarchy, and avoid giving offense to any who are quick to take it. And in his hands, for the length of his tenure of office, is that precious, indefinable, enduring possession called the tone of the school.[5]

It is small wonder that the head master is described as "governing the school through the sixth form and the prefect system."

The Extracurriculum. The British also use sports and games to develop character and leadership. Wellington's statement that Britain's wars were "won on the playing fields of Eton" probably contains a great deal of truth. Considerable emphasis is placed upon intramural, competitive sports; British educators have so far successfully resisted the blandishment of interscholastic competition.

The schools also support rather full programs of other extracurricular activities. Like the prefect system and sports program, these activities are thought to promote leadership and build character as well as to broaden the interests of the pupils. Among these activities are such things as debating, dramatics, orchestra, school publications, hobby clubs, and special interest clubs. In many respects the best extracurricular programs in the British schools appear much like the best of those in the schools in the United States.

THE SECONDARY TECHNICAL SCHOOL

In spite of the fact that the secondary technical school was designed to prepare boys and girls to be skilled workers and technicians, its cur-

---

[4] E. B. Castle, *The English Public Schools; Character and Responsibility, The Secondary School Curriculum,* The Yearbook of Education, 1958 (New York: World Book Company, 1958), pp. 210–211.

[5] J. I. Wolfenden, The Public Schools Today, London, 1948, p. 66, quoted by Castle, *ibid.,* p. 211.

riculum is not merely vocational. On the contrary, vocational specialization is usually limited to the last two years of the five-year program, the earlier years consisting largely of general education courses quite similar to the offering in the other secondary schools. During these years the principal differences in curriculum between secondary technical and other secondary schools are largely differences in method of teaching and relative curricular emphasis.

As a matter of fact, because of the apprenticeship laws, relatively few pupils studying for skills receive much vocational training. A shortage of classrooms and facilities forces most pupils to defer entering secondary technical schools until they are about 13 years of age. Because apprenticeship in England lasts five years and must be completed by the time one is 21, many pupils drop out of the secondary technical school to begin their apprenticeship before completing much vocational training at school.

As a rule the technical secondary schools do not have sixth forms. Probably these will be added later. In the meantime graduates of the secondary technical schools may take the examination for the ordinary General Certificate of Education. In some cases pupils may transfer to a grammar school to participate in the sixth form program and so prepare for the university. It is also possible for pupils to go on to higher technical schools and to take advanced technical work in the secondary technical school. Insofar as it can, the secondary technical school attempts to carry on the training in character development typical of the English grammar school curricula, in spite of the lack of sixth form.

THE SECONDARY MODERN SCHOOL

The secondary modern school is for boys and girls who do not attend either a grammar or a technical school. As originally conceived, its graduates were not to be allowed to take the General Certificate of Education examination. This, plus the fact that it was created from higher elementary schools and other nonsecondary-school arrangements, has caused people to look down their noses at it.

By far the largest number of secondary-school youth attend the modern secondary schools. In many cases these pupils are boys and girls who would not have been allowed secondary schooling before World War II. According to the Ministry of Education the purpose of the school is to provide these children with a "good, well-rounded secondary education, not focused primarily on the traditional subjects of the school curriculum, but developing out of the interests of the children." The curriculum was not to be vocational. It was to stimulate their ability to learn, to pursue quality in thought, expression, and craftsmanship, to interpret the modern world to them and to prepare them for life in its widest sense, including a full use of leisure. Of high importance was the aim of creating attitudes of precision and adaptability of careful, thorough workmanship.[6]

The local school authorities have been given considerable latitude in determining their own secondary-modern-school curricula. In general, they give courses similar to those in the general or noncollege curricula of the comprehensive high schools in the United States. Although there seems to be a trend toward adding both secondary grammar school and secondary technical school courses to the curriculum, usually the offerings are limited to such subjects as English, history, geography, mathematics, art and crafts, music, industrial arts, domestic science, physical education and religion. In some situations secondary-modern-school pupils can prepare themselves to sit for the examination leading to the ordinary General Certificate of Education.[7]

COMPREHENSIVE SECONDARY SCHOOLS

So far the comprehensive high school has made little headway in England. It has been rejected because of the fear that one school cannot do the many educational jobs that must be done if all youth are to be educated. On the other hand, many parents resent their children's being barred from the grammar school and so have espoused the comprehensive secondary school as a backdoor approach to getting at least a quasi-grammar-school education for their children. Because it appeals to many parents, that the comprehensive secondary school may be the British secondary school of the future is quite possible. The Labor Party favors its adoption, and certain economic considerations make it seem desirable.

Because both grammar schools and modern schools have added technical courses in order to meet pupil demand, already a large number of British Secondary schools are really either technical-grammar schools or technical-modern schools.[8] If the trend should continue, the result will be either an increase of comprehensive schools or a multilateral system of secondary education. However, the British carry their tendency to stratify secondary schools into their comprehensive schools. In some schools the curriculum is divided into three broad streams that correspond generally to the curricula of the grammar, technical, and modern

---

[6] The Ministry of Education, *The New Secondary Education* (London: His Majesty's Stationery Office, 1947), p. 29, quoted in I. L. Kandel, *The New Era In Education* (Boston: Houghton Mifflin Company, 1951), p. 276.

[7] Ministry of Education report, in *Preparation of General Secondary School Curricula* (Paris: UNESCO, 1960), p. 309.

[8] J. A. M. Davis, "Technical Courses in Modern Schools in England," *The Secondary School Curriculum*, Yearbook of Education, *op. cit.*, p. 173.

schools. Other schools are divided into narrow *A B C D E* "streams" or "tracks" whose curricula lead to more specific goals.[9]

THE GENERAL CERTIFICATE OF EDUCATION

For British grammar school youth the capstone of their secondary-school careers is the examination for the General Certificate of Education. In some respects the General Certificate of Education and its examinations are similar to the College Board examinations in the United States. In addition to being a requirement for entrance to the university the General Certificate of Education is also required by youths entering many of the professions and semiprofessions—even though these vocations do not require university training.

The General Certificate of Education is given at three levels—ordinary, advanced, and scholarship. In order to qualify for university entrance the student must pass examinations in five subjects, at least two of which must be at the advanced level. To meet this requirement the student usually takes the examination for the ordinary certificate before he enters the sixth form and then spends two or three years of specialization in the sixth form preparing for the advanced examinations.

Most Englishmen, and many Americans, praise the General Certificate of Education examinations because they believe these examinations are responsible for bringing about and maintaining high academic standards in English secondary schools. But critics of the English educational system are not all so sure that the examination system is desirable. In general, they deplore the examination on two grounds. In the first place, they believe that the examinations lead to overspecialization. They imply that passing the examinations becomes the sole object of the secondary-school education. Consequently boys and girls begin to specialize early in the grammar school so as to be sure to do well in the ordinary examinations. In the sixth form the temptation to overspecialize is even greater, because scholarships depend upon passing the examination at the highest level.

A second criticism of the General Certificate of Education system is that the necessity for preparing students for the examinations has prevented English schoolmasters from experimenting with new curricula and methods of teaching in the secondary schools, and so, it is claimed, these examinations have stifled desirable changes in English secondary education.

---

[9] Edmund King, "Comprehensive Schools in England: Their Context," *Comparative Education Review*, 3: 13–19, October, 1959; and "Comprehensive Schools in England: Their Prospects," *Comparative Education Review*, 3: 16–21, February, 1960.

LESSONS FROM THE BRITISH SECONDARY EDUCATION SYSTEM

A review of the British secondary-school system seems to indicate the following points, which Americans might do well to ponder.

1. There seems to be a need for an intellectual elite in every society, and the schools should attempt to provide such an elite.
2. In order to maintain an excellent school system one must strive to maintain high standards of excellence.
3. In comprehensive high schools there is a danger of attempting too much and so doing nothing well. One way to avoid this diffusion may be to adopt some sort of "tracking" system.
4. The building of character is extremely important and probably should be a primary purpose of the school.
5. Tracking and tripartite systems may have their advantages, but they also have disadvantages. Systems in which boys and girls must make important vocational decisions at 11 plus are liable to force them to make these decisions before they are ready and so penalize youths for life unnecessarily.
6. The sixth form plan allows students to reach great depths in certain academic areas, but it also tends to become so narrow that students miss the broad general background that presumably they should acquire in the secondary school.
7. The importance of social status takes precedence over the desire for appropriate education. Both pupils and parents take unkindly to the tripartite system of education because of the prestige of the grammar school. Also because no one wants to be skimmed milk, tripartite systems and homogeneous groupings of all sorts may fail.

SECONDARY EDUCATION IN FRANCE

Traditionally three basic principles have undergirded French secondary education. They are:

1. That the schools should concentrate on general education rather than specialized education;
2. That the principal aim of secondary education should be to cultivate reason and logical thinking;
3. That secondary education should be selective.

THE CLASSICAL LYCÉE

The three basic principles can all be seen in the program of the *lycée*, the traditional French prestige secondary school, which was introduced by Napoleon I and which traces its ancestry back to the schools of the medieval age. The purpose of these schools was to provide top-flight classical education to the best youth of the land. In spite of the numerous changes in education, and the introduction and growth of other types of secondary schools in the past century and a half, most Frenchmen continue to think of the *lycée* and its classical curriculum as the epitome of secondary education.

Culture Générale. The purpose of the *lycée* was to impart general culture to its students by means of a classical curriculum. By *general culture* the French meant literary culture. In their eyes science did not appear to be cultural, and technical education seemed almost degrading. Recently the sciences have gained considerable academic respectability, but French educators continue to put great value on long, arduous study of classical literature and the ancient classical languages.

The purpose of general cultural education was to develop thinking men and women. By this type of training French educators hoped to prepare boys and girls for any and all professions, vocations, or other situations they might face. The argument was that because the pupil has presumably learned to think well, he should be able to face any new situation calmly and solve its problems logically, and so does not need more technical training nor instruction in citizenship, morality, home and family living, or social skills.

One undoubted result of the accent on general culture has been the neglect of technical education. Because of its comparative lack of status, technical education never had a real place in the *lycées, collèges,* and the *collèges modernes.* Recent reforms and the upsurge of science notwithstanding, a large number of Frenchmen still view technical and vocational education with scorn.

Developing the Reason. To achieve logical thinking, French secondary education has depended largely on literary analysis. The purpose was not to create literary pedants, but to teach pupils how to think *via* the study of literature. Typical of the exercises used to develop thinking power is the *explication de texte.* According to Marcel Hignette the *explication de texte,*[10] which he believes to be the key to French secondary education, consists of

> . . . bringing to a short text as much data, elucidation, and commentary as is needed to explain it and to make clear its interest and import. To do it in a satisfying way one must be extremely well informed on the subject, and know all that is required about the author, his work and ties; one must also analyze the text, show its plan, and how it holds together, and estimate its intellectual value and the cogency of its argument; but above all one must have a very delicate sensitivity so as to be

[10] Marcel Hignette, "Primacy of the Rationale," *The Secondary School Curriculum,* Yearbook of Education, *op. cit.,* p. 240.

capable of seizing every overtone and the most subtle evocations of a text that must sometimes be read between the lines.

Obviously Hignette feels that this sort of exercise brings out the pupil's powers of musical and poetic sensitivity as well as his powers of reasoning. Perhaps he is right when he says that "such exercises, whilst conspicuously giving an essential place to reason, none-the-less do not forget the other components in human nature.[11] Others feel that they lead to a dry sterility completely out of touch with life.

Principle of Selection. The third undergirding principle of French education has been and continues to be the principle of selective education. The French aim has always been to match each pupil's school curriculum with his abilities and his potential adult role in society. To carry out this purpose before the recent reforms the French maintained an almost bewildering number of different types of schools and curricula and an extensive examination system.

Before the reforms of 1959 French education seemed to be just one examination after another. To enter a secondary school or a *cours complimentaire,* one had to pass an examination; to qualify for a trade, one had to pass another; to graduate, still another; and so on. The number of *brevets,* certificates, and licenses that the French ministry of education issued seems fantastic to an American.

The culmination of the national examination system and French academic secondary education was the *baccalauréat* examination, which, like the British General Certificate of Education, was given in two parts. Most of the time of the first and second classes was spent in preparation for the first part of the *baccalauréat,* after which the student spent a terminal year in a philosophy-centered course supposed to integrate all the learning of previous classes and to prepare him for the second *baccalauréat.*

Reactions of American observers seem to indicate that by and large the national examination system has had a stultifying effect on French education. Seemingly one result of these examinations and certificates was to hold French education to the *status quo* and to discourage educational experimentation, innovation, and local leadership. Under this system academic pressures on the student became intense sometimes to the point that some authorities questioned their effect on pupils' health and personality development.

THE REFORMS OF 1959

On January 7, 1959, a new revolutionary education act, incorporating many far-reaching reforms, became the law in France. These reforms were initiated in the sixth (that is, beginning) classes of the *lycées* and

[11] *Ibid.*

collèges d'enseignement general and in a number of *unités dispersées* that were created in the elementary schools in September, 1960. Although several of the new provisions have yet to be completely fulfilled, considering the immensity of some of the reforms, the change-over is proceeding swiftly and orderly.[12]

In the eyes of the French these reforms represent a "profound transformation of the spirit of teaching, whose repercussions will be felt in the very structure of French society." Their purpose is "to assure each individual the unfettered development of his talents and to make possible the full use of everyone in the life of the nation."[13] They were instituted because it was felt that the traditional system of French education had failed. In the language of the *Institut Pédagogique National:*

> French education, as it was conceived until now, actually created an antagonism between the pursuit of learning and the need for certain young people to enter a profession rapidly. Moreover, it encouraged too many young people on the secondary level to choose literary or legal careers to the detriment of technical or scientific ones. The shortage in France of high level technicians, researchers and science and mathematics professors, proves this point rather convincingly.
>
> While opening up broader educational possibilities to children of the working classes, French education also had to fight certain social and cultural traditions which no longer corresponded to the needs of the country.
>
> The solution lay in part in *expansion* and *modernization* of a widely differentiated system of technical education; it lay no less precisely in *orientation* of young people toward scientific careers, with the condition, however, that scientific education become less theoretical, less exclusively centered on pure mathematics, with a shift in emphasis toward applied science (physics, chemistry, biology).
>
> Such were the objectives of reform.
>
> The reform affirms the equal dignity of technical training and classical culture. And while maintaining the pre-eminence of French intellectuals and scholars, it establishes a new scale of practical values in keeping with the spirit of modern civilization.[14]

In other words, the French have decided that it is no longer wise to put all their eggs in the basket of general literary culture. However, the principle of general culture has not been rejected, and the French emphasis on the importance of the rational and the need for selection still

---

[12] For further information on the new educational reforms see "French System of Education," *Education in France*, Special Issue, The Cultural Services of the French Embassy, undated; and C. H. Dobinson, "French Education Reform," *Comparative Education Review*, 3: 5–13, June, 1959; both have been used as the basis for this discussion.

[13] *Education in France, op. cit.,* p. 27.

[14] *Ibid.*

remain preeminent. Although reduced considerably, the stress of examinations is still great.

The Five Cycles. Under the new law French education is divided into five cycles. These are:

1. Preschool education in voluntary classes attached to primary schools for pupils from 2 to 6 years of age.
2. Elementary schooling compulsory for all pupils from 6 to 11, consisting of teaching of French, moral and civic instruction; reading and writing; arithmetic and metric system; history and geography, especially of France; basic science, drawing, sign, and handicrafts and physical education.
3. The *cycle d'observation* compulsory for all pupils from 11 to 13 who have made normal progress in the primary school. This is the beginning of the pupils' secondary-school experience.
4. Five divisions of more advanced secondary education varying in length and content according to the ability of the child. The age range is from 13 to 18 years, but education is compulsory only until age 16.
5. Higher education that consists entirely of professional training in the universities, institutes, and great professional schools.

The Cycle d'Observation. One of the basic purposes of the reform plan is to carry out the principle of selective education with the utmost efficiency—in their own words, "to assure selection of the best through the advancement of all."[15] Like the English system, it is calculated to distribute boys and girls into schools and curricula according to their talents or merits and to eliminate the influence of tradition and social standing in school placement.

The *cycle d'observation* was established to carry out this selection process efficiently. According to French theory there are three basic types of pupils: those who will benefit from a long secondary education; those who will benefit from a short secondary education; and those who will be best off in a terminal curriculum of practical preparation for working in agriculture, the trades, commerce, or industry. The purpose of the *cycle d'observation* is to give teachers an opportunity to study, evaluate, and guide each pupil into his proper niche in the next educational cycle and his future vocational life, in accordance with his aptitudes, abilities, interests, and other pertinent considerations.

Briefly this is how the *cycle d'observation* works: At the age of 11 the French child who has completed the common elementary school program satisfactorily is placed into the *cycle d'observation* of the type of institution for which he is presumably best suited. At the end of the quarter his

[15] *Ibid.*, p. 8.

case is reviewed and he may be transferred to a different type of school curriculum, if it seems advisable. Twice more, at the end of the first and second years, his case is reconsidered. Finally, at the end of the cycle, he is recommended for one of the five programs of the next cycle. At this point, and at other points, the family is consulted. If the parents do not accept the faculty recommendation, they may request a change. However, this request can not be honored until the pupil has satisfactorily negotiated an obligatory aptitude test in the new curriculum.

The Five Upper Divisions. Upon completing the second year of the *cycle d'observation* a pupil can enroll in one of five upper divisions of the secondary school. These subdivisions, which are really begun during the first year of the *cycle d'observation,* are:

1. Terminal education (*l'Enseignement Terminal*). This comprises three years of elementary schooling in addition to the *cycle d'observation* and which features primarily experience in industry or agriculture as well as a continuation of basic general education.

2. The short general education curriculum (*l'Enseignement Général Court*). The cycle of observation plus three years in the *collèges d'enseignement général* is for fairly able boys and girls who are not technically inclined and who do not have the ability or desire for university preparation.

3. The long general education curriculum (*l'Enseignement Général Long*). The topmost secondary-school curriculum leading toward the baccalaureate degree. In the new broadened curriculum pupils may elect from seven streams leading to the first baccalaureate examination and five seventh-year streams leading to the second baccalaureate examination.

4. The short professional educational curriculum (*l'Enseignement Professionel Court*). This is a three-year curriculum for pupils who have finished the cycle of observation in another school and is designed to train them as craftsmen.

5. The long professional curriculum (*l'Enseignement Professionel Long*). Under this heading are included several curricula for the bright or brilliant pupil who is technically inclined. From these curricula come the highly skilled technicians and technical specialists. In these schools it is possible for students to win the degree of *technicien supérieur breveté,* which is equivalent of the upper baccaleaureate.

The Baccalaureate Examinations. The purpose of long general education in France is to prepare students for the baccalaureate examination, the passing of which admits the student into the *baccalauréat,* the first university degree.

In practice a student must have the *baccalauréat* to be admitted to the degree program at a French university, although provisions have been made for underprivileged youth to gain admittance on the passing of a special examination. To enter the *grands écoles* students usually need two or three years of additional study after the *baccalauréat* in order to prepare for the very difficult entrance examination, the *concours*. For youth not planning to go on to institutions of higher learning the *baccalauréat* is a key to admission into the good positions in business or government. It is the most prestigious of all French secondary-school diplomas.

The Reforms Evaluated. Although far-reaching to the French, the new reforms may not seem quite so exciting to the Americans. The basic principles of selective education, general education, and emphasis on logical thinking still persists to be the bases of the educational system. Still, the French have found it necessary to modify their curriculum in all three counts. General education has not proved sufficient for the training of practical men in the twentieth century. The French have found it necessary to expand their curriculum to teach logical thinking by means of the scientific and practical arts and practical experience. While the examination system continues as a part of the system of selectivity, guidance techniques and aptitude testing have to some extent replaced the rigid achievement testing of the former system. In general, the French reforms have reflected a desire to have a more human, flexible, practical educational system based upon sound psychological and social principles.

THE CLASSES NOUVELLES

In an attempt to get away from the formalism of the usual French teaching method, new methods of teaching were introduced experimentally in 1945. In trial classes, called *classes nouvelles,* the teachers tried to put the principles of child psychology to work. Particular stress was placed upon providing for individual differences, the elimination of competition between individuals in favor of group competition and group cooperation, and giving the pupils opportunities to share in the responsibilities of student life. All in all the *classes nouvelles* were eminently successful. Not only are they being continued in pilot schools, but their less costly practices have been incorporated in the lower classes of all French secondary schools. Unfortunately, because of the influence of the baccalaureate examination, *lycées professeurs* have been slow to adopt new techniques in the upper classes. Thus we see again that national examinations can hinder educational experimentation and innovation.

LESSONS FROM THE FRENCH

The French seem to want selective secondary education; their traditional school system has always been highly selective, and their new educational plans call again for a highly selective secondary-school organization. Seemingly the French take kindly to a plan that removes the pupils with limited academic ability from the academic curriculum, so their system seems to fit their purposes very well. Whether Americans would accept such a plan of school organization so readily is moot. Even in France with its enthusiasm for selective secondary education, the reforms of 1959 indicate that specialized education should not start too early in life and needs to be based on a strong guidance program.

Critics of American education frequently state that American high schools are not rigorous enough, but French experience with the *lycée* seems to point up a fact that these critics sometimes forget, namely that extremely rigorous schooling in the academic subjects may prevent the full development of the pupil. Some of the reforms in the French schools were designed to reduce the amount of homework because the *lycée* seemed to be too rigorous for the pupils' good.

French schools have prided themselves on the excellence of their academic program, and many critics find the intellectual attainments of the academic secondary school admirable. On the other hand, some French critics are disturbed because they feel that the emphasis on academic learning by means of the old "tried and true" methods have sacrificed the development of character and social training. To counteract an overemphasis on the academic, they have introduced experimental progressive *classes nouvelles* and reduced the amount of homework. It seems that all academic work and no play makes Jacques a dull boy.

Another frequent claim made by some critics of American secondary education is that there should be a national or state examination system in order to standardize the curriculum and to secure and maintain high academic standards. To standardize our curriculum more than we do might be advantageous, but the French experience seems to indicate that national examinations hamstring experimentation and innovation and so make educational progress much more difficult. French experience also seems to indicate that strong central control of the schools also impedes experimentation and innovation. In an age of change and progress probably any organization or procedure that discourages experimentation should be treated very cautiously.

RUSSIAN SECONDARY EDUCATION

THE TEN-YEAR SCHOOL

During the 1950's the cold war and the Russian advances in science and technology turned the attention of Americans to Russian education. Many critics of American education at this time pointed to the Russian ten-year school system as the acme of academic success. How these people must have sighed in relief when Comrade Khrushchev sounded the death knell of the ten-year school in 1957.

Provisions for Differences. Soviet theory does not allow for individual differences in pupils. In Russia it is nurture rather than nature that makes the differences that we all know. Therefore the Russians, so fanatically committed to the monolithic state, were also committed to the monolithic school system. To carry out their theories they set up a single-curriculum school for their boys and girls consisting of four years of the elementary school and three years of secondary school, plus an additional three years to make up the complete secondary school. Even though some children might attend different schools for one reason or another, supposedly all pupils were to study the same materials as outlined by government syllabi and government textbooks, although in practice there seems to have been considerable difference in the content of courses from school to school. However, lack of clear, accurate data makes it difficult to determine just what Soviet practice really is.

The Ten-Year Curriculum. The curriculum of the old ten-year school was rigorous and academic but with a utilitarian slant. Considerable emphasis was placed on the sciences, although the Russian version of the humanities was not neglected. In accordance with Soviet doctrine all subjects were taught from a purposely biased point of view in order to foster Soviet attitudes and beliefs. Facts, particularly historical facts, were often changed so as to support current political policy. The purpose of the ten-year school was to make boys and girls into suitable tools of the state. This the school seemed to be accomplishing with terrifying success.

In the Soviet Union schools placed great emphasis on "quality education." Great stress was placed on examinations, high selection standards, and long, stringent homework assignments. Their efforts seemed to be quite successful. According to an analysis by the Educational Testing Service, the examinations given to pupils at the end of their tenth year indicated that Russian education in mathematics and science compared favorably with that of the American college-preparatory program.[16]

Polytechnic Education. An unusual feature of the Russian secondary-school curriculum is its stress on polytechnic education. In theory polytechnic education is an attempt to correlate the practical and theoretical aspects of the sciences. Thus, under this plan, not only the study of practical applications, but actual experiences with the uses of science in industry would be coordinated with instruction in the theoretical sciences. Usually, carrying out the polytechnic program was to be done by intro-

[16] See George S. Counts, *The Challenge of Soviet Education* (New York: McGraw-Hill Book Company, Inc., 1951) for an excellent account of the ten-year school and its curriculum.

ducing machine shops, industrial arts, and similar practical experiences into the science curriculum proper.

In practice, however, in the ten-year school, polytechnic education was neglected. The law of December 24, 1958, seeks to vitalize the polytechnic aspects of the curriculum. Even before the new law had been decreed, schools were introducing more of this type of schooling.[17]

In spite of polytechnical education, the ten-year school was not a vocational school. Polytechnic education was part of Soviet general education. Vocational education was provided by a variety of technical and labor reserve schools. Under the 1958 reforms these schools have been retained. They ranged from schools which were little more than labor camps, through labor reserve schools with excellent trade school curricula, to technical schools featuring such studies as metallurgy, radio engineering, agriculture, education, and law.

EDUCATIONAL REFORM

Dissatisfaction with Ten-Year School. In spite of the supposed emphasis on polytechnic and practical education, Soviet education had been singularly academic. Then ten-year school program prepared pupils for university entrance and for little else. The teaching methods, influenced by a rigid examination system in which the teachers were rated by the success of their students, were far from imaginative. Emphasis was on memory, lecture, and textbook learning. Laboratory and creative experiences were neglected. In the eyes of Premier Khrushchev such schools were too much like the *gymnasium* of the bourgeoisie.

Russian dissatisfaction with the ten-year school came to a head in 1958. On April 15 of that year Premier Khrushchev told the Komsomol Congress, "Our ten-year school prepares young people only to enter higher educational establishments. Life has long ago shown that this conception of the secondary school is incorrect."[18] He amplified his position later when he said: "In spite of the attainment of the Soviet schooling, there are great deficiencies in the functioning of our schools which cannot be tolerated any longer. The chief defect, marking both our secondary and higher schools, is their isolation from life."[19] In his report of

---

[17] See Richard V. Rapacz, "Polytechnic Education and the New Soviet School Reforms," in George Z. Bereday and Jaan Pennar, *The Politics of Soviet Education* (New York: Frederick A. Praeger, Publishers, 1960), pp. 28–44; also William K. Medlin, Clarence B. Lindquist, and Marshall L. Schmitt, *Soviet Education Programs,* O.E.–14037, Bulletin, 1960, No. 17 (Washington, D.C.: Government Printing Office, 1960), Ch. 3.

[18] N. S. Khrushchev, speech to the 13th Komsomol Congress, April, 1958, reported in Pravda, translated by Ina Schlesinger in *School and Society,* 86: 63, February 14, 1959.

[19] N. S. Khrushchev, "School and Life," reported in *School and Society,* 87: 72, February 14, 1959; translation by Ivan D. London.

the Central Committee to the Twentieth Party Congress he was even more explicit on this point.

Provisions of the New Law. As a result of these complaints the Supreme Soviet of the U.S.S.R. made sweeping changes in its educational system in a law enacted on December 24, 1958. This law was based on a statement issued by the Central Committee of the Communist Party and the Council of Ministers of the U.S.S.R. on November 12, 1958.

> The Soviet school is called upon to prepare all-around educated people, well-grounded in the foundations of science, but at the same time capable of systematic physical work. The Soviet school is called upon to cultivate in the youth a desire to be useful to society and to participate actively in the production of values necessary for society.[20]

To this end, the statement continues:

> The point of departure for a correct resolution of the task of the reconstruction of the school is the recognition that at a certain age all young people should be included in socially useful work and that their instruction in the foundations of science should be related to productive work in industry or agriculture. Hence the necessity of a correct correlation in the secondary school of general, polytechnical, and a vocational education based on a wise combination of work and study with leisure and normal physical development of children and youth.
>
> Thus an intimate relationship of instruction with life, with production, and with practical Communist construction should be the guiding principle in the study of the foundations of science in the school. And this principle should determine the content, the organization, and the methods of teaching. From the very first years of instruction children should be psychologically prepared for subsequent participation in socially useful activity, in labor.[21]

Under the new law, compulsory education was increased to eight years rather than the seven years formerly compulsory. The eight-year school is to be "an incomplete secondary-general-educational labor polytechnical school which:

> . . . will graduate young people with a greater fund of general knowledge. They will be psychologically and practically better prepared to participate in socially useful activity. A school of this type will resolve more successfully the tasks of Communist education and of labor and polytechnical instruction. It will offer the students a wider range of knowledge, will eliminate the overloading of studies now present in

[20] "On the Strengthening of the Relationship of the School with Life and on the Further Development of the System of Public Education in the Country," Thesis of the Central Committee of the Communist Party and the Council of Ministers of the U.S.S.R. (Moscow, 1958), translated in George S. Counts, *Khrushchev and the Central Committee Speak of Education* (Pittsburgh: The University of Pittsburgh Press, 1959), pp. 39–40.

[21] *Ibid.,* p. 41.

the seven-year school, will make possible a more serious treatment of the physical education of the children, and will develop in them good artistic taste.[22]

After completing the eight-year school the pupils must go out to work in industry, agriculture, or some other form of productive labor. Pupils gifted in mathematics, art, or music, may be excused from this work requirement. (Soviet society places great value on the talented artist or performer.) After a year or two of working, boys and girls may go on to finish their secondary-school work, but most pupils who are interested in preparing for the university will have to do so in part-time schools while continuing to work. To provide for the completion of secondary education, the law calls for the establishment of the following three types of secondary schools:

1. *Schools for working youth and rural youth.* These are part-time schools that offer after-working-hours classes in general education similar to the curriculum in the eighth, ninth, and tenth grades of the old ten-year school. Working youth who have completed the eighth grade may study in these schools in the evening, or by correspondence courses, or, after meeting certain requirements, two or three days a week. Normally these schools will provide the main road for youths striving for entrance to the institutions for higher learning.

2. *Secondary general education, labor, and polytechnical schools with production training.* These are a new type of institution. The three-year curriculum combines the academic curriculum with polytechnical training and with factory or agricultural apprenticeship and prepares its students directly for enrollment in an institution of higher learning. These schools, which may or may not be associated with the eight-year schools, provide the most direct route to higher education for ambitious talented youth.

3. *Secondary specialized schools.* These schools include the *technicum,* whose main purpose is to train technicians and semiprofessional and managerial workers. Under the new law students wishing to enter these schools must be graduates of the eight-year school. Special accelerated curricula are also offered for graduates of the complete secondary-school program as described earlier. For most pupils these vocational schools will be terminal institutions. However, 5 per cent of the topmost students become eligible to apply for admission to the higher technical institutions that prepare engineers.

EXTRACURRICULAR EDUCATION

In Russia the formal school is only a part of the youth's education. The state seeks to dominate the youth through governing his social life.

[22] *Ibid.*

Much of the boys' and girls' instruction comes through the many extra-curricular circles and clubs. Examples of these are the English Circles in which boys and girls practice their English and the Young Communist League. Organizations of this sort are connected with youth centers as well as the school. Usually these are conducted or supervised by trained personnel—often teachers earning extra compensation. These organizations are used to influence the life of the pupils and to train them to be good Soviet citizens and workers. Through them education pervades the entire life of the pupils.

LESSONS FROM THE RUSSIANS

Although the excellence of the Russian ten-year school was extolled by many American observers, the Russians themselves did not seem to be highly satisfied with it, as the summary reformations in the late 1950's prove. Khrushchev's objections to the ten-year school seem to have been that it was too academic, and so the recent reforms have been aimed at making the classwork more practical and to correlate it with the work-aday world. No matter what the culture, ivory-towered secondary-school curricula and the formalizing of teaching methods seem to be a continual threat. Russia has taken drastic steps to eliminate them.

Another reason for the Russian switch from the ten-year school may have been a need to recognize more fully the differences among individuals. Theoretically the Russians do not accept the concept of individual differences, and so the ten-year school was supposed to teach all the boys and girls the same subject matter in the same way. Visitors to Russian schools indicate that, in spite of Russian protests to the contrary, the attempts to teach all the boys and girls the same thing in the same way, were not successful. At least the new plan calls for culling out the boys and girls after the eighth year. Whether a school system that does not recognize individual differences can succeed is problematic. The Russian experience seems to indicate that more than one curriculum is necessary, particularly at the secondary and collegiate levels. Academic high school or college education may not be good for everyone.

One of the marvels of Russian education reported in the press is the high motivation of Russian pupils. In Russia the motivation is kept up by the high status of education plus the use of strong incentives to keep effort high. One of the strongest of these is the power of group opinion, which the Russians exploit to the hilt. Evidently it is possible to keep pupils striving even when classes are dull and stodgy if the society values learning enough and truly tries.

All aspects of Russian life permeate Russian education, and Russian education permeates all aspects of Russian life. Although the purpose of the Russian school system is to train Soviet citizens who will serve the state well, the Russians do not expect their schools to do the entire job, and so they supplement it with circles, youth organizations, and other educational activities not associated with the school directly. In Russian education the big push is on, but the school does not have to make the effort alone. Americans might do well to consider whether in the United States we are making a total effort to raise up strong citizens for a strong America and whether or not the country is placing too much burden for the total educational program on the school.

SUMMARY OF IMPLICATIONS

Other nations faced with the problem of educating their youth have tried solutions different from those attempted in the United States. Evidently none of them have been any too well pleased with their results.

In general, European school systems have been committed to some form of selective education. Evidently the experience in foreign countries indicates that the successful operation of secondary schools necessitates differentiating curricula in order to provide adequately for the differences in pupils. To maintain a good school requires high standards, but not necessarily the same standards for everyone. "To each his own" might very well be our motto. Tracking may be one way of providing for differences, but European experience shows us that one must guard against too early decisions.

The experience of both the French and the Russians show that emphasis on the intellectual can be overdone and cause neglect of the practical aspects of the curriculum. Intellectual values are important, but so are practical values, and character values are even more important. French and Russian insistence on high academic standards seems to have led to a dry sterility and to a one-sidedness that has made drastic educational reforms imperative. On the other hand, through its sixth form and sports programs, British education has managed to place much emphasis on the building of character, which, in the final analysis, is probably where the emphasis should go.

Many critics of American education call for more and more testing and national examination systems. In Europe experience with examinations has not proved so prepossessing that we should follow them headlong. Emphasis on examinations has resulted in "prepping" for the examinations rather than educating children. Where it exists, the examination system has caused the hardening of the *status quo* and teacher fear of innovation and experimentation.

Russian education has proved that if a people really values education and wants a good educational system, it can have it. Their experience makes one wonder if Americans really want first-rate secondary schools enough to exert an all-out effort to get them. Soviet experience also shows that for the maximum educational results a nation must bolster the school's educational efforts with support from other agencies. Is it fair, or wise, to expect any school system to take on the entire job of educating a nation alone and unassisted?

SUGGESTED READINGS

ALEXANDER, WILLIAM M., and J. GALEN SAYLOR. *Modern Secondary Education.* New York: Holt, Rinehart and Winston, Inc., 1959.

Good readable summaries of education in European countries in Chapters 7 and 8.

BEREDAY, GEORGE Z. F., and JOSEPH A. LAUWERYS (eds.). *The Secondary School Curriculum.* The Yearbook of Education, 1958. New York: Harcourt, Brace and World, 1958.

A collection of authoritative articles about secondary education in various countries. (by native experts)

BEREDAY, GEORGE Z. F., and JAAN PENNAR. *The Politics of Soviet Education.* New York: Frederich A. Praeger, 1960.

A series of papers read at a seminar on Soviet education held at the Institute for the Study of the Union of Soviet Socialist Republics in Munich, Germany, in 1958. Excellent articles on certain aspects of Soviet education and its rationales.

BEREDAY, GEORGE Z. F., WILLIAM W. BRICKMAN, and GERALD H. READ (eds.). *The Changing Soviet School.* Boston: Houghton Mifflin Company, 1960.

An analysis of Soviet education by members of the Comparative Education Association who visited the Soviet Union in 1958.

BOITER, ALBERT. "The Khrushchev School Reforms," *Comparative Education Review*, 2: 8–13, February, 1959.

A presentation of the 1958 reforms in Soviet education.

COUNTS, GEORGE S. *The Challenge of Soviet Education.* New York: McGraw-Hill Book Company, Inc., 1957.

An exhaustive study of the Soviet school system, its aims, purposes, and implications. Does not include new reforms.

DENT, H. C. *The Education Act, 1944.* London: University of London Press, Ltd., 1957.

A guide to the education act and its provisions.

——. *The Educational System of England and Wales.* London: University of London Press, Ltd., 1961.

An account of the entire British school system by one of the foremost English authorities.

DOBINSON, C. H. "French Educational Reform," *Comparative Education Review*, 3: 5–13, June, 1959.

An excellent presentation of the recent changes in the French educational system.

Documentation Number 5, Secondary Education. French Cultural Services of the French Embassy. New York: French Embassy, undated (Mimeographed).

A brief explanation of the French secondary-school system, including its curriculum and organization.

"French System of Education," *Education in France*. Special issue. French Cultural Services of the French Embassy. New York: French Embassy, 972 Fifth Avenue (undated).

An English translation of a brochure published by the *Institut Pédagogique National*, which outlines clearly and succinctly the recent reforms in French education.

HECHINGER, FRED M. *The Big Red Schoolhouse*. New revised edition. Garden City, New York: Doubleday and Company, Inc., 1962.

A rather opinionated popularized account of Soviet education and its implications for American schools. Good bibliography.

KANDEL, I. L. *The New Era in Education*. Boston: Houghton Mifflin Company, 1955.

A significant analysis of educational trends, their causes and implications. Although written before many of the recent reforms, the book remains an important reference.

KERR, ANTHONY. *Schools of Europe*. London: Bowes and Bowes Publishers, Ltd., 1960.

Interesting accounts of education in the various countries of Europe— nation by nation.

———. *Schools of Scotland*. Glasgow: William MacLellan, 1962.

An authoritative account of Scottish education, which differs somewhat from that in England and Wales.

KING, EDMUND J. *Other Schools and Ours*. New York: Holt, Rinehart and Winston, Inc., 1958.

One of the better standard textbooks in comparative education.

KLINE, G. L. (ed.). *Soviet Education*. New York: Columbia University Press, 1957.

A series of essays on aspects of Soviet education written by former Soviet citizens who lived and studied in Soviet educational institutions.

KOROL, ALEXANDER G. *Soviet Education for Science and Technology*. New York: John Wiley and Sons, Inc., 1957.

An exhaustive study of Soviet education including the ten-year school. Written before the Khrushchev reforms but still important.

LOWNDES, G. A. N. *The English Educational System*. Revised edition. London: Hutchinson and Company Publishers, Ltd., 1960.

An excellent little book which attempts to put the various parts of the English educational system in the proper perspective for the intelligent English layman, and hence a good introduction for the interested American.

MAYER, MARTIN. *The Schools*. New York: Harper and Row, Inc., 1961. Also Anchor Books Edition, New York: Doubleday and Company, Inc., 1963.

An excellent study of education for the general reader. Contains many illustrations of practice in European school systems.

MEDLIN, WILLIAM K., CLARENCE B. LINDQUIST, and MARSHALL L. SCHMITT. *Soviet Education Programs*. U.S. Department of Health, Education, and Welfare, Office of Education, Bulletin 1960, Number 17. Washington, D.C.: Government Printing Office, 1960.

The report of an American research team's on-the-spot study of Soviet education. Particular attention is paid to the science and mathematics programs, polytechnic education, and the foundations of Soviet education.

MOOS, ELIZABETH. *Soviet Schools Revisited.* New York: National Council of American–Soviet Friendship, 1960.

An excellent brief description of the Soviet school system.

PASSOW, A. HARRY. *Secondary Education for All: The English Approach.* Columbus, Ohio: Ohio State University Press, 1961.

An excellent account of British secondary education. The result of a year's study of British schools by a visiting American educationist.

PEDLEY, ROBIN. *The Comprehensive School.* Baltimore: Penguin Books, Inc., 3300 Clipper Mill Road, 1963.

Many British educators have not been satisfied with the "11+" examination and what it means in terms of the English social and educational systems. New emphasis upon ability rather than birth has created considerable interest in the comprehensive school. The positive advantages of the comprehensive schools are forcefully pointed out.

STUART, BYRON D. "Education in the Soviet Union," *The Bulletin of the National Association of Secondary School Principals,* 43: 175–192, March, 1959.

Observations on secondary education in Russia by a junior high school principal turned college professor who spent five weeks visiting Soviet schools.

UNITED STATES DEPARTMENT OF HEALTH, EDUCATION, AND WELFARE, OFFICE OF EDUCATION. *Soviet Commitment to Education.* Bulletin 1959, Number 16. Washington, D.C.: Government Printing Office, 1959.

The report of the first official United States Education Mission to the Union of Soviet Socialist Republics with an analysis of recent educational reforms.

VAIZEY, JOHN. "Britain in the Sixties?" *Education for Tomorrow.* Harmondsworth, Middlesex: Penguin Books, Ltd., 1962.

A description of the present situation in British education and an indication of current trends including a trend toward comprehensive secondary schools.

YOUNG, MICHAEL. *The Rise of the Meritocracy.* New York: Random House, 1959.

A biting satire of " '11+' and all that."

Chapter 6

The Role of the Secondary School

That education should be regulated by law and should be an affair of state is not to be denied, but what should be the character of this public education, and how young persons should be educated, are questions which remain to be considered. For mankind are by no means agreed about the things to be taught, whether we look to virtue or the best life. Neither is it clear whether education is more concerned with intellectual or with moral virtue. The existing practice is perplexing; no one knows on what principle we should proceed—should be useful in life, or should virtue, or should the higher knowledge be the aim of our training; all three opinions have been entertained.[1]

Aristotle was right. Mankind is by no means agreed about the things to be taught. Today we are still perplexed about what we should teach and what the purposes of secondary education are. This chapter will discuss these questions and take certain definite positions concerning their solution.

THE SECONDARY SCHOOL TODAY

The United States does not have a national school system. Because of constitutional provisions the responsibility for educating youth falls on the various states, which have in part passed on their responsibility to the different school districts in the state. As a result of this decentraliza-

---

[1] Aristotle, *Politics*, VIII.

tion, we find a wide divergence in educational organization and practice from school district to school district. Still, in spite of the lack of central control and resulting differences, the secondary schools and their curricula are much alike in essentials throughout the country.

CHARACTERISTICS OF THE SECONDARY SCHOOLS

American secondary schools ordinarily comprise the junior high schools, senior high schools, and junior colleges of the public school systems and corresponding private institutions maintained by church and lay groups. In general, they include grades 7–14, although in many school systems grades 7–8 are included in the elementary schools and the junior college grades 13–14 are considered to be part of higher education. In the following pages we shall be concerned primarily with the curriculum of the junior and senior high school grades (7–12) of the public school systems. Except in passing, no attempt will be made to discuss junior college curricula nor private school curricula. However, the discussion of public secondary-school curricula will ordinarily apply equally well to private secondary-school curricula of the same type.

Universality of American Secondary Education. If there is such a thing as a typical public secondary school in the United States, it is a school that earnestly attempts to give the best possible education to all adolescent boys and girls in the area it serves. That is to say, its educational program is both universal and comprehensive. When we speak of universal secondary education, we mean that the secondary school is open to all youth of the proper age group who have completed the elementary school curriculum without regard to class, wealth, social standing, intelligence, or other prescriptions.

The United States was the first nation to attempt universal education at the secondary level, and many people, both here and abroad, look on it as a highly extravagant experiment. Previously, Western countries had limited secondary schooling to a few boys and girls selected on the basis of their talents and their social standing. A curriculum designed for all of American youth requires different approaches from those designed for the upper 10 per cent. When the American secondary school has failed, it has usually been because it has failed to shift its curriculum and methods to meet the changed situation.

The Comprehensive Secondary School. As a rule American secondary schools are comprehensive, that is, they try to provide for all pupils—talented or otherwise—whatever their academic goals—underneath the same roof.[2] This too is a source of curriculum problems peculiar to

---

[2] Most comprehensive high schools are not truly comprehensive in the sense that they offer the full range of courses and curricula. Most of them are really academic high schools with some other curricula added.

American schools. In the comprehensive secondary school the curriculum must make provisions for youth preparing for entrance to institutions of higher learning, for youth who are preparing for certain vocations (for example, stenography), for youth who will terminate their schooling as soon as they finish the high school curriculum, or even before, and for those pupils who do not know in which direction they want to go. Because they are specialized, European schools are not faced with these situations. Under the European system the college-preparatory functions, the vocational functions, and the terminal education functions are each portioned out to separate schools. Here specialized schools are usually found only among the private schools, certain state and county schools, and in large cities, such as New York, which provide high schools for performing arts, needle trades, science, and other academic and vocational specialties.

CHARACTERISTICS OF SECONDARY-SCHOOL CURRICULA

Progressive vs. Traditional. As a rule American public secondary schools are conservative. This conservatism is particularly true of the high schools, less so of the junior high schools. Because of the long controversy between the so-called traditionalists and the so-called progressivists, much misunderstanding about this fact has arisen. In this popular quarrel the terms *progressive* and *traditional* have been used so loosely that they have become almost meaningless. Frequently newspaper stories attribute the failings of the most traditional schools to progressivism. Because of this loose handling of the technical term, many lay persons have become convinced that the secondary schools are all "progressive schools." In actuality most secondary schools are neither traditional nor progressive, but a mixture of both, with a leaning toward the conservative. Almost all our public secondary schools, however, have adopted some of the new theories and practices advocated by members of the progressive movement. Movements like the core curriculum, the activity movement, life adjustment education, the problem approach, and so on, have had relatively little impact on the secondary schools. The truly traditional and truly progressive secondary schools in the United States have been almost all private institutions.

The Subject-centered Curriculum. In general, the curriculum in American secondary schools is subject-centered. Pupils have little voice in determining what their curricula will be. Rather it is chosen by the faculty members and administrative officers on the basis of subject matter and presumed adult needs. The nature of the subject, rather than the nature of the pupil, determines the content of the curriculum in most American secondary schools.

In the seventh and eighth grades the subjects offered are usually common to all pupils, although sections may be differentiated according to ability. In the ninth grade and in the senior high school grades the offering is usually differentiated into various types of curricula designed to lead to different specialized goals. At both levels, however, the schools are usually oriented around subject matter courses in which the teacher attempts to teach a certain body of subject matter to the pupils a certain number of periods per week during the course of a year or half year.

THE AIMS OF SECONDARY EDUCATION

THE EXPANDING ROLE OF THE SECONDARY SCHOOL CURRICULUM

By and large, modern secondary schools strive as best as they can to meet the needs of all their pupils, instead of limiting themselves to purely intellectual educational tasks. The 1918 statement of the Commission for Reorganization of Secondary Education, now commonly called the Seven Cardinal Principles of Secondary Education, well illustrates the broad scope of the task set for the schools. In this statement concerning the major aims of secondary education the commission held that the role of secondary education should extend into seven areas:

1. Health
2. Command of the fundamental processes
3. Worthy home membership
4. Vocational efficiency
5. Civic competence
6. Worthy use of leisure time
7. Ethical character[3]

These seven areas truly represent what Brubacher calls "Education for Complete Living." Not one single aspect of human living is omitted from the list.[4] In the eyes of the Commission the role of education was to meet *all of the needs of all of the children of all of the people.* Since 1918 educational writers and educational commissions have issued many other statements describing the purposes of secondary education. In almost every instance the new statements have reaffirmed the "seven cardinal principles" and the theory of "education for complete living."

Nineteenth-Century Beginnings. The movement from narrow classicism to "education for complete living" began during the nineteenth century. Its herald was Herbert Spencer, who in his *Education: Intellectual, Moral,*

---

[3] National Education Association, Commission on Reorganization of Secondary Education, *The Cardinal Principles of Secondary Education*, U.S. Bureau of Education, Bulletin 35, 1918.

[4] See John S. Brubacher, *A History of the Problems of Education* (New York: McGraw-Hill Book Company, Inc., 1947), p. 16. The first chapter of this book is an excellent, interesting account of the history of the development of educational aims, to which the present authors are greatly indebted.

and Physical[5] asks a basic question: "What knowledge is of most worth?" As one might expect of a leading nineteenth-century evolutionary, Spencer's answer to this question is: The knowledge that is of the most worth is *that knowledge which has the most survivor value*. And so he rates the activities of men according to the following order of importance:

1. Those activities which directly minister to self-preservation.
2. Those activities which, by securing the necessaries of life, indirectly minister to self-preservation.
3. Those activities which have for their end the rearing and discipline of offspring.
4. Those activities which are involved in the maintenance of proper social and political relation.
5. Those miscellaneous activities which make up the leisure part of life, devoted to the gratification of the tastes and feelings.

This hierarchy of values broke sharply with tradition. During most of the history of secondary education in Western culture the "miscellaneous activities" that Spencer relegated to last place had had the first, if not the only, priority in secondary schools. They have never completely recovered their old position.

The Ten Imperative Needs of Youth. One of the most authoritative statements of the purposes of secondary education puts the role of secondary education into terms of the needs of youth. The writers of such statements feel that the function of secondary education is to fulfill youth's needs. That the authors of this statement, commonly known as the Ten Imperative Needs of Youth, were imbued with the philosophy of education for complete living is evident from even a quick perusal of the statement which follows:

The Common and Essential Needs That All Youth
Have in a Democratic Society

1. All youth need to develop saleable skills and those understandings and attitudes that make the worker an intelligent and productive participant in economic life. To this end, most youth need supervised work experience as well as education in the skills and knowledge of their occupations.
2. All youth need to develop and maintain physical fitness.
3. All youth need to understand the rights and duties of the citizen of a democratic society, and to be diligent and competent in the performance of their obligations as members of the community and citizens of the state and nation.
4. All youth need to understand the significance of the family for the individual and society and the conditions conducive to successful family life.

[5] Herbert Spencer, *Education: Intellectual, Moral, and Physical* (New York: William L. Allison Company, undated), p. 18.

5. All youth need to know how to purchase and use goods and services intelligently, understanding both the values received by the consumer and the economic consequences of their acts.

6. All youth need to understand the methods of science, the influence of science on human life, and the main scientific facts concerning the nature of the world and of man.

7. All youth need opportunities to develop their capacities to appreciate beauty, in literature, art, music, and nature.

8. All youth need to be able to use their leisure time well and to budget it wisely; balancing activities that yield satisfactions to the individual with those that are socially useful.

9. All youth need to develop respect for other persons, to grow in their insight into ethical values and principles, and to be able to live and work cooperatively with others.

10. All youth need to grow in ability to think rationally, to express their thoughts clearly, and to read and listen with understanding.[6]

The Central Purpose of American Education. In 1961 The Educational Policies Commission of the National Education Association again reemphasized the seven cardinal objectives as set forth in 1918. In a publication called *The Central Purpose of American Education*[7] the Commission said, in substance, that no school fully achieves its goals in the relatively short time pupils spend in the classroom. The school seeks rather to equip each pupil to achieve the goals of education for himself. In other words, the schools must teach its pupils to think independently.

The development of the ability to think is a traditionally accepted educational purpose, which runs through and strengthens all other purposes in statements of educational goals. Sometimes this purpose is called the common thread of education. In its statement, the Educational Policies has sought to identify this aim as the central goal of education around which all other goals must revolve. While still continuing its support for education for complete living, the Commission was trying to emphasize and magnify the intellectual role of the school.

The All-inclusiveness of the Goals. As one can readily see, the objectives for secondary education proposed in these modern statements of educational aims, or needs of youth, are all-inclusive. To fulfill these new objectives the schools have added to their curricula such studies as homemaking for boys; citizenship education; economic education; conservation; driver training; and other new and strange subjects.

The introduction of these new subjects has caused both professional educators and laymen to become alarmed by the possibility that the secondary school is attempting too much. They fear that the schools are

[6] Education Policies Commission, *Education for All American Youth* (Washington, D.C.: National Education Association, 1944), pp. 225–226.

[7] Educational Policies Commission, *The Central Purpose of American Education* (Washington, D.C.: National Education Association, 1961).

trespassing where they have no right. According to their point of view these new subjects are not the business of the schools at all. Rather they should be taught by the home, the church, and other agencies. Many sincere critics believe that if the school attempts to teach all the new subjects it will be forced to neglect the academic subjects that they consider to be the heart of the curriculum.

Truly this danger is a real one. As Benjamin Franklin pointed out in his prospectus for the Philadelphia Academy, there is not time to teach all things "useful and ornamental." "Art is long and life is short"—too short for everyone to learn everything it might be desirable to learn in the secondary schools. The curriculum builders must select for the curriculum those learnings that will be most useful and most ornamental and can be learned most profitably in the time available.

THE ROLE OF THE SECONDARY SCHOOL

Higher Education and the Secondary School. In the minds of many parents and college teachers the primary role of the secondary school is to prepare pupils for entrance to institutions of higher learning—particularly the liberal arts college or university.

Because the baccalaureate degree seems to be becoming the ticket to middle-class status and to many of the "better" jobs, presumably there will be an increase in the percentage of high school boys and girls trying to enter institutions of higher learning. According to a newspaper article by Sylvia Porter in September, 1960, seven out of every ten American families hope to send their children to college. Even now in some communities almost 100 per cent of the boys and girls who graduate from the high school enroll and actually begin to attend classes at a postsecondary education institution of some sort.

On the other hand, many of the boys and girls in our high schools do not have the slightest prospect of attending any sort of higher educational institution when, or if, they complete their high school curriculum. For many of them, postsecondary education is not only beyond their capacities, but has nothing to offer them that will be of real value to them. Even in a wealthy state like New Jersey fewer than half of the high school graduates actually enroll and attend collegiate institutions, as Table I clearly shows. Preparation for college is an important function of the secondary school, but it should not be the dominant one. The schools prepare pupils for life now and for whatever may come in the future.

Should the School Build a New Social Order? Some educators seem to believe that the schools should not only prepare boys and girls for the future, but that they should also prepare the future for the boys and girls. George S. Counts set the tone for such educators when in 1932 he

TABLE I. NEW JERSEY HIGH SCHOOL GRADUATES, CLASS OF 1961

Comparison of Occupations of New Jersey High School Graduates of
1961 With Those of Some Preceding Years*

	I CLASS OF 1947	II CLASS OF 1952	III CLASS OF 1960	IV CLASS OF 1961
NOTE: This table reads as follows: Of the class of 1947, 15 % entered a college of arts, etc.				
TOTAL NUMBER OF GRADUATES	35,221	31,368	51,890	54,246
ADVANCED SCHOOLING	32.3	36.2	45.0	45.4
College of Arts	15.0	16.9	19.0	19.2
State Teachers College	2.2	2.6	5.5	5.3
Engineering College	1.9	3.0	2.9	2.9
Other College or University	4.6	5.6	8.4	8.5
Nursing School	2.3	3.0	2.5	2.2
Technical School	2.6	1.5	1.7	2.3
Business School (not Secondary)	2.6	2.6	3.1	3.2
Others requiring H.S. Diploma for admission	1.1	1.0	1.9	1.8
SECONDARY SCHOOLING	5.9	1.5	2.5	2.5
Post Graduates in Your School	0.9	0.2	0.2	0.2
Other Public and Private Schools	1.5	0.6	0.6	0.6
Vocational School	0.9	0.3	1.2	1.2
Secondary Business School	1.8	0.3	0.3	0.3
Others	0.8	0.1	0.2	0.2
EMPLOYMENT	51.3	51.3	39.3	39.2
Office Positions	23.4	26.7	20.4	19.6
Distributive Occupations	7.1	5.5	5.3	5.8
Trades and Industries	13.6	13.8	8.6	9.2
Farming	0.9	0.7	0.3	0.3
Homemaking	1.2	1.7	1.6	1.7
Miscellaneous	5.1	2.9	3.1	2.6
NATIONAL SERVICE	2.9	7.3	7.7	7.3
Military or Naval	2.6	7.1	7.3	7.0
Merchant Marine	0.2	0.1	0.1	0.1
Other	0.1	0.1	0.3	0.2
MISCELLANEOUS	7.6	3.7	5.5	5.6
Deceased	0.1	0.1	0.0	0.0
Not in School or Employed	4.6	1.5	3.4	3.0
Unaccounted For	2.9	2.1	2.1	2.6

* *Statistical data developed from the Annual Occupations of Graduates Report.*

shook the academic world with his challenge: *Dare the school build a new social order?* The question is really academic. Whether the school dares to or not, to build a new social order is not part of the school's role. Under no circumstances should the school presume to take on this responsibility.

Schoolteachers are not competent to build the social order. Neither is any other particular group in American society. The construction of a new social order in the United States, if there is to be one—and we can be pretty certain that there will be one because history seems to be a succession of one new social order after another—is a responsibility of all the people. No one group, be it school, church, political party, or social caste, should set itself up to be *the* agency to create a new social order. If one does, the resulting social order is liable to turn out to be more like Mr. Huxley's *Brave New World* than like an ideal democracy.

Still, the school does have a part in creating a new social order, if one is to be created. That role is to provide boys and girls with the knowledges and skills with which they can develop the best kind of society possible. The evidence seems to indicate that over the centuries the world has progressed and that, in general, today it is a better place to live in than it used to be. The citizens who graduate from our schools should be equipped to hurry this improvement along. In order to create citizens who can bring about progress, the schools must equip their pupils with the knowledges and skills by which they can determine what the most desirable changes are and the abilities to bring about these changes. In other words, the school has no business trying to create a new social order, but it does have the responsibility for educating a citizenry who can build a new social order, if one is needed.

Obligations of School to Society. The people of a society expect their schools to preserve their way of life. Americans want their schools to turn out good Americans—not good Englishmen or good Russians. They want their children to learn to carry on the American way of life and its institutions and traditions. Therefore they want the school to teach boys and girls their traditions and history and to equip the young people with the understandings, skills, and attitudes necessary for living in that particular society. It is the school's duty to see that this is done.

The people also expect the schools to help improve their way of life. Americans have faith in education. They believe that it can reduce poverty, crime, disease, unhappiness, and most of the other ills of the modern world. Because of this belief American parents sacrifice to save money for their children's education, and the citizens of many American communities tax themselves heavily to maintain good schools. They do so in the hope that their children will be free to enjoy a better life in a better world; the schools should live up to these expectations if they can.

The Reason for Public Education. That the role of education in the United States should be to preserve and to further the democratic way of life seems axiomatic. All nations and societies try to fashion educational systems that will best serve their purposes. The monolithic educational system of the Soviet Union is a striking example of an educational system designed to further the goals of a totalitarian state. Presumably education for democracy should be something quite different from education designed for totalitarianism.

The proof of the pudding is in the eating, and the proof of a curriculum is in the product it produces, not in the subject matter it contains. In a democracy this statement means that the schools must turn out citizens with a democratic state of mind.[8] Such citizens believe in cooperation and fair play. They respect the rights and opinions of others, yet they maintain and defend their own beliefs. They honor the individuality of others and at the same time maintain their own proper self-respect. They are willing and able to share in free and honest debate without recrimination. As members of the majority they accept the responsibility for acting for the welfare of all and for protecting minorities from unfairness. As members of minorities they cooperate with majority decisions without self-effacement, loss of self-respect, toadying, kowtowing, or discontinuing honest support of those things in which they believe. They realize their stake in democracy and the nation and accept their responsibilities and duties willingly. They are capable of intelligent behavior. They face up to reality and decide matters of importance on their merit. They do not allow sentiment, prejudice, and bias to dictate their decisions. They have standards and principles to which they cleave, but their minds are not closed. They are willing and ready to revise their opinions in the light of new evidence. They have the skills and understandings necessary to make good judgments and the physical and mental health and moral strength necessary to carry them out. In short, the citizen with the democratic state of mind is one who puts the general welfare foremost and is ready and capable to work toward the best good for all. T. V. Smith says the essence of democracy is sportsmanship. The ideal education in a democracy will produce true sportsmen. The primary role of the school is to provide such citizens as well as it can. All other roles are subsidiary to this role.

A CURRICULUM FOR DEMOCRACY

DEMOCRACY AND THE CURRICULUM

That the traditional secondary-school program has not been adequate for the preserving and furthering of the democratic way of life seems to be quite obvious. A brief survey of the results of our schools in the past

---

[8] See T. V. Smith and Edward C. Lindeman, *The Democratic Way of Life* (New York: New American Library, 1951), for a discussion of democracy as a state of mind and as sportsmanship.

shows us that we have not produced good sportsmen with the democratic state of mind. Our history is marred by war and strife, injustice and inequities of all sorts—prejudice, bias, self-centered disregard of the common welfare and the rights of individuals, civic irresponsibility in both high places and low, and an almost complete lack of the skills and understandings, not to mention the physical and mental health and moral strength, necessary to promote the democratic way of life of which we dream. So far the traditional curriculum has not produced good democratic citizens. Probably it never can without a change in orientation.

Liberal Arts Not Enough. Several critics of our modern secondary schools have suggested that the reorientation for the American secondary schools should come through a rebirth of the humanities and a reemphasis of the liberal arts. They suggest a curriculum based upon eternal truths and great books. In fact, some humanistic theorists have gone so far as to suppose that the whole of the curriculum, particularly at the upper secondary grade level, might be encompassed in the great books of the past. At first glance such a reorientation looks tempting. Classical scholarship and the "great books" contain much of the supreme thinking of all times. What could be better for our purposes than a curriculum derived from the thoughts and writings of the greatest thinkers and most influential men of history?

Unfortunately further consideration shows us that the humanities have failed to produce the results we need in a democracy. In the first place, the study of the humanities or of the liberal arts does not necessarily provide the attitudes, ideals, skills, and understandings we associate with the democratic state of mind. The liberal studies do not always lead to a love of truth, a thirst for knowledge, an appreciation of the finer values, the power to think objectively, or a passion for fair play. All too often the liberal studies, as taught today, lead only to thoughtless verbalisms. In the second place, throughout history the liberal arts and the humanities have been associated more with the aristocratic than the democratic point of view. They are taught for their cultural value, and "culture," according to Jaeger, the brilliant classical scholar, is simply the aristocratic ideal intellectualized.[9] The fact that so many proponents of the liberal arts advocate a curriculum much too rigorous for slow, or even average, youth and recommend that those who fail it be dropped from school proves aristocratic bias. We shall have to look farther than the liberal studies, *as they are presently conceived and taught,* for imbuing youth with the democratic spirit.

.Education for Today and Tomorrow—Not Yesterday. We cannot afford to limit our secondary-school curriculum to the traditional classical studies because of the tremendous amount of pressing new knowledge that we should make available to our boys and girls. So much knowledge,

---

[9] Werner Jaeger, *Paideia* (New York: Oxford University Press, 1945), Vol. 1, p. 4.

which is commonplace today, has been learned since the turn of the century. Even relatively young adults have seen the century progress from horse and buggy days to the atomic age. In late years changes have occurred so fast that the twentieth century undoubtedly differs more from the nineteenth century than the nineteenth century differs from the first century. Approximately two thirds of modern knowledge has been discovered within the century.

Obviously a curriculum that ignores two thirds of human knowledge is not adequate for the scientific wonder world of the latter half of the twentieth century. The secondary-school curriculum must be oriented to the future. Its purpose is to teach boys and girls those things that are valuable to them now and also those things that will be valuable to them in the future, so that they can function today and tomorrow. Men who ask us to limit our curriculum to the great books of the past are turning their backs on reality and are taking us back to the middle ages.

The past should not, of course, be lightly dismissed. On the contrary, one of the purposes of education is to preserve and maintain the cultural heritage. History and the "classics" have an important part in modern secondary education. The great events and the great books of the past should be studied for their bearing on the present and the future. Men who do not make use of the lessons of the past often find themselves floundering laboriously across rugged terrain in hope of discovering what, had they only known it, other men had already found. We must use and profit from the past, but to turn our faces from the future toward the past is foolish. Knowledge is not power. It is the use of knowledge that is power. By orienting courses toward the past we deprive them of much of the power they might have.

Developing the Tools for Democratic Living. In a democracy the ultimate responsibility for decisions affecting the common good rests with the citizenry. Each individual must accept a share in the responsibility for what the country becomes and what the nation does. His decisions determine the course of history. The individual's role is much more difficult than it would be in an autocracy or a dictatorship. He cannot just sit back and do as he is told. The responsibility for what the nation does and what it becomes is his. He cannot escape it—although he may neglect it.

If citizens are to meet their responsibilities and duties they must be educated up to them. For this reason every pupil needs to learn how to think. He must learn to analyze and interpret data and to make decisions on the merits of the evidence. He should be taught to question and test pronouncements by authorities and pseudo authorities. He needs to learn how to separate fact from rumor, opinion, prejudice, sentiment, and wish. His curriculum must teach him to refrain from ready acceptance of beliefs without putting them to test. Therefore his curriculum should not consist of uncritically swallowing subject matter dictated by a text or by a teacher's lecture. Rather his curriculum should consist largely of investigating, analyzing, discussing, testing, and using subject matter. Uncritical swallowing of subject matter leads to the passive, apathetic citizenry who fall prey to bosses and dictators.

If boys and girls are to have practice in making decisions, they need standards to use in decision making. True, to indoctrinate boys and girls for democracy would be paradoxical, but there is no reason why boys and girls should go out into the world without guidance. Teachers can show the young people what democracy is, what it means, what its ideals are, what it has sought to do, where it has succeeded, where it has failed, and what its dreams are. Giving such guidance and guide-posts to the democratic way of life, and giving boys and girls chances to use these values by testing ideas, attitudes, and courses of action, should help them appreciate and follow the democratic way.

Similarly boys and girls should learn other standards and tests for truth and quality. It is the duty of the school to give them these stand-ards. In a free country the press, television, radio, and other media are virtually uncontrolled. They must not be bridled if we are to remain free, so, because we cannot afford to tolerate censorships, we must tolerate all sorts of productions. But there is no reason why boys and girls need to accept all productions at face value. The schools should provide the boys and girls with criteria by which the taste, moral and intellectual value, and truth of the material presented by the various media can be judged. If the pupils do not learn standards of value and how to develop such criteria for themselves, how can we expect them to make good decisions when faced with new situations and new problems?

Because the democratic way of life is supposed to be based on sports-manship, the educational system should create sportsmanship. The type of education that will achieve the goal must provide many opportunities for pupils to present, debate, and defend opinions. All pupils should have many chances to learn to work and to plan together. They should learn to participate in democratic government by participating in demo-cratic government in school. As Dewey recommended, the school should be a miniature society so that the pupils can have opportunities to live democratically by actively participating in a democratic society. In such schools boys and girls should learn to respect other individuals and their beliefs and opinions in spite of differences in point of view, back-ground, social position, and other considerations.

SUBJECT MATTER AND THE CURRICULUM

The Doctrine of Contingent Value. What subject matter should be in-cluded in a curriculum? In the opinion of the authors it is that subject matter that is most likely to be useful to the individual.

Subject matter has very little value for itself alone. It has value only as a tool. Some subject matter is useful now, and so boys and girls should have a chance to learn it now. Other subject matter will be needed in the future. Just what that subject matter is is difficult to ascertain because no one can predict accurately the future life of any boy or girl, nor the kind of world in which he will live. For this reason the curriculum for an individual should consist of those things that are useful to him now and that appear most likely to be useful to him in the future in view of his goals, his potentials, and his opportunities. In short, the subject matter of an individual should be chosen on the basis of its contingent value to the individual. This is sometimes called the doctrine of contingent value.

Some theorists have felt that one should teach only subject matter that has an immediate value. They imply that if one teaches well those things that are immediately valuable, the future will take care of itself. This may be true in part. By teaching boys and girls the skills of thinking and learning through subject matter having immediate value we can arm pupils with the tools they will need in the future. However, pupils must also learn some skills and knowledges that do not seem to have much immediate value. Boys and girls must learn them because these skills and knowledges presumably will be useful and necessary in the future, whether they are of immediate value or not. The vocational skills are examples of such learnings. Because one can seldom be sure just what skills and knowledges will be needed in the future, the doctrine of contingent values must be used as a guide in selecting these learnings. A curriculum confined to subject matter with immediate value only cannot be adequate.

The subject matter most useful for secondary pupils differs from pupil to pupil. During their secondary education boys and girls should clinch any of the fundamentals they failed to learn in the elementary grades, but secondary education is primarily the period when boys and girls should build upon their academic fundamentals. In this period differentiation begins, because all youth do not, and should not, build in the same way. Every pupil must learn a great amount of academic subject matter during the secondary grades in order to function efficiently, but just what the subject matter is varies from individual to individual. Of course it would be well if all boys and girls had experiences in certain common areas, but there is no reason why every child should have the *same* experiences in these areas or that all children should come out with the same learnings as the result of studying in these areas. Even in the common areas the curriculum of each individual presumably should be different from that of at least some of the other pupils.

To sum up, the first criterion for selecting subject matter is its contingent value, that is, its potential value to the pupil. Subject matter should be usable. We repeat, knowledge is not power; it is the use of knowledge that is power. Therefore the teacher should do his best to include in each pupil's individual curriculum those knowledges, skills, understandings, attitudes, appreciations, and ideas most likely to be useful to him now and in the future. Anything else may be wasteful. There is too much to learn to spend time on the nonfunctional.

The doctrine of contingent value has been criticized for being too utilitarian. The implication is that an educational curriculum, based upon the contingent values, would be grossly vocational and materialistic. This is a misunderstanding. Any knowledge that furthers the good life of an individual is useful knowledge. Any knowledge, skill, understanding, appreciation, ideal, or attitude that makes life richer is functional. Any study that a student wishes to pursue for the fun of it has its place in his curriculum. Equally valuable might be some quite distasteful subject matter that would help to make him more efficient in his chosen vocation or in his personal life. All of these have contingent value.[10]

Teaching More by Teaching Less. Nowadays there is so much subject matter that no one can possibly learn all of it or even all of it in one small field of specialization. Not only is there too much to learn, but subject matter has become elusive. It changes every day. Often what we believe to be a fact today was a dream yesterday and will be a myth tomorrow. Even some of those skills and knowledges whose importance has been repeatedly emphasized in professional writings as the "basic fundamentals" can no longer be considered necessary, fundamental, or even correct.

Therefore the curriculum of today must not consist of merely covering a certain body of content. Boys and girls who merely gobble down facts and information are poorly prepared for a changing world. This statement does not mean that facts and information should be done away with. On the contrary, facts and information are very important. What it does mean is that teachers and curriculum workers should select their subject matter carefully.

Subject matter is valuable for teaching processes, principles, attitudes, ideals, appreciations, and skills. To teach these important learnings does not depend so much on what subject matter one teaches as how one teaches it. One can draw generalizations and processes concerning early civilizations from studying the valley of the Tigris and Euphrates just as well as one can from studying the valley of the Nile. However, one can seldom teach processes and principles in superficial ground-covering courses. Learning of such objectives requires deep, thoughtful study.

In order that pupils may get the most out of what they study, the

---

[10] See Alfred North Whitehead, *The Aims of Education* (New York: New American Library, 1949), pp. 13 ff, for a forceful declaration of this position.

secondary-school curriculum should eliminate much of its subject matter so that pupils can study selected areas more deeply. Would it not be much more desirable to study a few periods carefully than try to give a lick and a promise to every event in world history? By studying fewer topics more deeply pupils could concentrate their learning so that it would really function and so that they could really learn how to use intellectual skills. The modern secondary-school curriculum should be marked by judicious skipping. At present too many teachers attempt to teach too much and so teach nothing well.

The Importance of the Intellectual. To fully realize himself each individual needs to make the most of all of his potentialities. Therefore schools in a democracy must help boys and girls to acquire strong bodies, healthy minds, high moral and ethical standards, and good social attitudes and skills. The good school emphasizes these aspects of development and cooperates with other agencies to secure their optimum development. The curriculum that neglects these aspects is inadequate.

In spite of the importance of fostering the physical, moral, emotional, and social development of its pupils, the peculiar function of the secondary school is to promote their intellectual development. This is the school's major responsibility. Society has assigned the responsibility to the school and counts on the school to develop the intellectual skills and attitudes of its boys and girls to the utmost. No other agency is charged with this responsibility as its major function. Consequently, the school must face up to the fact that, in spite of its many other functions, its primary purpose is, and must always be, the intellectual development of boys and girls. The school neglects this responsibility at its and the nation's peril. *The first responsibility of the school is to teach boys and girls how to think and give them the tools to think with.*

Nevertheless, one must bear in mind that the pupil is a whole child rather than a disembodied mind, and consequently sound intellectual development is tied closely to social, emotional, moral, and physical development. If these aspects are neglected, intellectual development cannot achieve its highest level. Therefore, although the school shares these functions with other institutions, they are essential functions of the school. The answer to the critics who are afraid that the school cannot afford to minister to all of the needs of the boys and girls may well be that the school cannot afford not to do its share for the development of every aspect of the boys' and girls' growth. Because it is the whole child who comes to school, the school must serve all of him. Nevertheless, because the school's peculiar responsibility is to promote the intellectual development of youth, nonacademic areas of the curriculum should be made to be media for intellectual development, and when choices must be made, intellectual matters should ordinarily have priority.

GENERALIZED AND SPECIALIZED EDUCATION

General Education and the Secondary School. In order to perform its role the secondary-school curriculum must include both general and specialized education.

Although it is difficult to demonstrate that studying any particular bit of subject matter is essential for every secondary-school pupil, presumably some learnings are valuable for everyone—no matter what their longings or abilities. These learnings make up general education. Actually general education is not general in nature but really quite specific. It consists of those things that generally would be well to learn but do not prepare one for any particular vocation or avocation.

From his general education one can expect each pupil to receive a reasonably good background in language, science, social studies, the arts, and much of the subject matter important in the business of living, often in business subjects, home and family living, industrial arts and guidance courses. Its principal role is to concentrate on the traits necessary for developing a good citizen in a democracy. Consequently the general education portion of the curriculum should emphasize personal relationships, home management, health, aesthetic values, and concepts concerning democracy and government. Most important of all, it should stress the use of calm judgment and reasonableness in both personal and public affairs.

Frequently general education is equated with liberal education. To do so, however, is probably an error. *General education* is a broader term than liberal education. Liberal education connotes an academic education which, though broad in scope and supposedly designed to be equally beneficial to all, particularly as a background to independent thinking, has primarily to do with the humanities and scientific subjects so commonly found in our liberal arts colleges. In addition to these fields, general education also includes such utilitarian studies as driver training, home and family relations, life adjustment, and industrial arts. Neither general education nor liberal education are designed to prepare anyone for a particular calling. In practice, however, many of the liberal education courses are vocational in that they may prepare one for entrance into an institution of higher learning. Similarly courses designed for general education may actually be an important part of one's preparation for his profession or trade. Seventh grade woodworking may possibly be the first step in the training of a future cabinetmaker, eighth grade general science may be the start of a career in physics, or ninth grade English may be where an embryonic playwright first begins to master the skills of his craft, even though each of these courses would ordinarily be considered as part of one's general education.

Specialized Education. If general education is made up of the subject matter that all boys and girls should have a chance to learn, specialized education is the subject matter that particular boys and girls may want to learn for their own particular reasons. It is *ad hoc* education. Its primary function is to provide for differences in the pupils and to give each pupil a chance to develop in the way that suits him best. It includes vocational, prevocational, and even avocational education. A curriculum designed solely to prepare boys and girls to enter college is really specialized education. Courses meant to prepare one for a business, trade, or profession are specialized education courses.

At times the boundary between specialized and general education becomes exceedingly thin. The rule to follow is this: If the course or curriculum is *ad hoc*, it is specialized education; if not, it is general. A course designed to teach boys and girls to be automobile mechanics is a specialized education course, but a course designed to teach boys and girls how to maintain the family car is a general education course. Sometimes, of course, it is possible for a particular course to be part of a specialized education course for one person and a general education course for another.

For many youths their specialized education will be largely vocational, although some may study specialized education courses for avocational reasons. Sometimes critics of secondary education frown upon vocational courses. They should not do so, because vocational education is an essential role of secondary education. Preparing for a vocation is an essential developmental task of youth. The school should do all it can to help each youth prepare well for this task, and the late years of his high school and college life should be devoted largely to vocational preparation. Persons who object to vocational education in the secondary school would do well to remember that the liberal arts are vocational subjects for scholars, critics, writers, teachers, and the other learned professions. Specialized education's role is to help prepare boys and girls for their individual roles in life. Vocational preparation will make a major contribution to this role.

Relation to Further Education. Earlier it was pointed out that the time has come for Americans to rethink the place of college and vocational preparation in our secondary schools and the attendant problems of general and specialized education and guidance.

Before these problems can be answered satisfactorily, the nation must make some decisions about postsecondary-school education. Should higher education be limited to boys and girls in the upper quarters intellectually; should it be for those in the upper half; or should it be open to all comers? Is the recommendation of the Presidential Advisory Commission of 1948, that one half of the population attend institutions of higher learning two years and that one third of all American youth continue to finish full four years, the answer? If larger numbers of youth go on to institutions of higher learning, are we running the risk of creating a great supply of frustrated college graduates who are unable to find jobs commensurate with their education and so are ripe for the blandishments of communists, fascists, and demagogues of all sorts? If the institutions of higher learning open their doors to greater number of less capable boys and girls, what sort of curricula should be offered? Are thirteenth and fourteenth grades going to become common, and if so, are they to be collegiate or secondary grades? The role of the secondary school and its curriculum depends considerably upon the answers to these problems. If the college takes over the responsibilities for vocational and technical education, then the secondary school can devote more of its curriculum to general education.

Until that time comes the school must provide general education, plus a wide range of specialized education. As far as possible it should provide a wide enough choice of experiences so that each individual pupil can pick those experiences best suited to meet his needs. These experiences must, of course, foster the social, physical, emotional well-being of each pupil, but in spite of these specialized and general missions, primarily the role of the school is to provide each pupil with the intellectual experiences necessary to make him a capable, informed citizen of our democracy. To accomplish this, probably the early secondary years should consist almost entirely of general activities. During the upper grades of the secondary schools, specialized education should take an increasingly important part of the pupil's time until in the final years this specialization becomes almost the entire program. Thus the young person who wishes to prepare for college entrance or the professions will devote almost his entire program to college-preparatory subjects during his last years in the secondary school.

SECONDARY EDUCATION AND THE INDIVIDUAL

Making the Most of Each Individual's Potentialities. If the essence of the democratic way of life is sportsmanship, the foundation of democracy is the integrity of the individual. Because the individual is so important in a democracy, we need to see to it that each individual develops as fully as possible. This need is what is sometimes called the objective of self-realization. Because this need is so great, the curriculum must provide opportunities for boys and girls to make the most of their various talents and to develop their individual personalities to the utmost.

Providing for Individual Differences. If the secondary-school curriculum is to help boys and girls realize themselves, it must provide for individual differences. In some way or other the curriculum must be differentiated so as to allow each individual an opportunity for self-fulfillment. The slow pupil must not be tortured by having to keep up with the brilliant pupils; neither should the brilliant be forced to mark time while the slower pupil tries to catch up; nor should the future engineer be forced to fit a pattern designed for the future classicist. Although some areas of the curriculum should be common to all, no single curriculum pattern can be made that will suit all pupils nor, for that matter, any two pupils exactly. In order to make the most of his individual talents, each boy and girl needs a curriculum made especially for him; one that will suit his individual abilities, goals, and interests. The same curriculum for all boys and girls will not suffice.

The ancient formula for fitting the curriculum to the individual pupil was in effect to provide two education programs; one for the best, another for the rest. Today both schoolteachers and laymen appear to be inclined to follow a similar scheme and to favor the brilliant, academic-minded youth in the planning of secondary-school curricula. Teachers should guard against this inclination, because the secondary schools are now responsible for providing a real education for all youth. As Kandel says:

> . . . a liberal approach to education will refuse to tolerate any longer that distinction which goes back to Aristotle between an education for the masses of an education for the classes. If it is truly liberal such an education will be looked upon as one continuous whole inspired throughout by the spirit of liberty and the ideals of democracy which recognizes the equality of all individuals before God and before man, allowing only for differences to capacity, but seeking to give to each a share in the common purposes of life, moral and religious, material and spiritual, in accordance with his capacities.[11]

To adequately provide for each pupil according to his capacities, the comprehensive American secondary school must provide many curriculum choices from which pupils may choose. In a really good secondary-school curriculum each pupil can follow the pattern of courses best suited for him and will find in each course experiences and subject matter based on his own individual needs. In other words, the curricula, courses, and units should be differentiated so as to give each child his own personal curriculum. Such a school program may seem Utopia, but it is not so very farfetched and is well worth striving for.

Cultivating the Brilliant Mind. One facet of the problem of self-realization is how to utilize the talents of our gifted boys and girls. Because their talents are among our most precious national resources, the school should seek them out and develop them to the utmost.

---

[11] Report of the Committee Appointed to Enquire into the System of Secondary Education in Jamaica, quoted in I. L. Kandel, *The New Era in Education* (Boston: Houghton Mifflin Company, 1955), p. 110.

The brilliant pupils are especially important because they are the raw materials from which future leaders come. It is especially important that they be taught to extend their talents in desirable ways. Too often men and women with capable minds neglect their civic duties. Many are so poorly educated that when they attempt to perform these duties, they are completely inept. They should have experiences in democratic leadership in the secondary schools, such as those provided in the British Grammar Schools, so that the country may profit from their superior intelligence in places of leadership. Some may protest that such a program may establish an intellectual elite. If this accusation is true, then let us establish an intellectual elite at once. To lose good minds is a needless waste.

Not only should the brilliant be groomed for leadership in the community, but they should also be groomed for the scholarly professions that require good minds. Brilliant men are needed in teaching, in science, in medicine, in government, in business, and in all other positions of responsibility and scholarship. Presently many brilliant boys and girls do not make the contributions to society that they should. Of course, not all brilliant people should go into the professions or executive positions. Many an auto owner can think of reasons why some brilliant persons should become garage service managers! Nevertheless, the nation and the world must have the services of many brilliant young people in the learned vocations.

This mission is particularly necessary in these times when the nation's very existence may depend upon the brain power of our scholars. Much has been made of our need for superior scientists. There is an equally great need for scholars in other fields. The nation depends upon the schools to provide the intellectual bases for the scholarship necessary in our leaders in business, scholarship, and government.

The Need for Guidance. A program of studies that provides opportunities for individualized curricula can be satisfactory only in proportion to the excellence of the school's guidance program. Boys and girls should have a chance to make the most of their talents. Comprehensive high schools can help them to do so, but only if pupils are in the proper curricula, courses, and tracks. With the help of a good guidance program boys and girls can select their programs with a much greater chance of success.

Even with good guidance programs the distribution of pupils into curricula and tracks according to their needs and talents is extremely difficult. The problem is complicated by the fact that our methods of measuring interest and ability are quite inaccurate and that youths' interests and abilities are frequently quite unstable. Even intelligence does not always seem to hold steady. Growth spurts and plateaus may cause a boy of relatively good potential to appear to be a poor prospect. Therefore, if one is to find out what boys and girls can do and place them in curricula according to their abilities, one needs expert guidance. In a comprehensive high school the guidance program is the key to success. It is a *sine qua non* in any system of secondary education that attempts to further individual self-realization. Without it, the comprehensive secondary-school curriculum breaks down completely.

CONCLUSIONS

Every nation tries to build an education that will promote its own way of life. In a domocracy the primary goal of secondary education is to develop democratic citizens. The ideal democratic citizen is a mentally and physically healthy individual who handles his own life ably and who also makes a contribution to the welfare of society. The secondary education of such citizens must be well rounded. It will include education for life adjustment, aesthetic education, health and physical education, citizenship education, and moral and spiritual education, but the secondary school's most important role is intellectual. Intellectual development of youth is the task society has specifically assigned to the school. To fulfill this role the secondary school must emphasize democratic attitudes, the critical spirit, and the ability to think. This role is so important that all youth should attend secondary school.

No particular subject matter can be depended upon to fulfill the secondary school's mission. Especially deficient in this respect is the type of education in the past commonly associated with the liberal arts and particularly the humanities, although the deficiency arises from the method of teaching rather than from the subject matter. Modern curricula should emphasize using subject matter as a tool of thinking. Boys and girls should learn to think by actually solving problems by both inductive and deductive reasoning. Similarly the curriculum should provide practice in both democratic action and democratic attitudes through actual practice in the activities of the school functioning as a miniature society.

To fulfill its role each secondary school must provide both general education and specialized education. The general education should consist of those things all pupils should learn. Among these would be such things as home and family living, budgeting, family accounts, personal typing, the three R's, art appreciation, the elements of science, an understanding of government, and an understanding of our past and implications for the future. Specialized education includes studies designed to meet pupils' individual goals. Among these studies are those that prepare boys and girls for institutions of higher learning and for the various vocations. Above all, the school must center its efforts around giving each pupil the intellectual experiences he needs to become an intelligent and successful citizen. Therefore much of the success of a curriculum depends upon an adequate guidance program.

SUGGESTED READINGS

ALCORN, MARVIN D., and JAMES M. LINNEY. *Issues in Curriculum Development.* New York: Harcourt, Brace and World, Inc., 1959.

A book of readings on issues. Chapters 4 and 5 directly concern the role of the secondary-school curriculum.

CONANT, JAMES B. *A Memorandum to School Boards: Education in the Junior High School Years.* Princeton, New Jersey: Educational Testing Service, 1960.

Specific recommendations for the junior high school curriculum.

———. *Slums and Suburbs.* New York: McGraw-Hill Book Company, Inc., 1961.

A report in which Conant makes specific recommendations concerning the task of urban and suburban schools.

———. *The American High School Today.* New York: McGraw-Hill Book Company, Inc., 1959.

The famous Conant report, in which he defends the comprehensive high school and recommends improvement in its academic curriculum.

EDUCATIONAL POLICIES COMMISSION. *Central Purpose in American Education.* Washington, D.C.: National Education Association, 1961.

An influential report of the N.E.A.'s Educational Policies Commission which emphasizes teaching pupils the intellectual skills and the ability to think.

———. *Education and the Disadvantaged American.* Washington, D.C.: The Commission, N.E.A. and A.A.S.A., 1962.

Tells who the disadvantaged are and outlines programs to meet their needs.

FRENCH, WILL. *Behavioral Goals of General Education in High Schools.* New York: Russell Sage Foundation, 1957.

A statement of educational goals in terms of behavior change.

GARDNER, JOHN. *Excellence: Can We Be Equal And Excellent Too?* New York: Harper and Row, Inc., 1961.

A plea for high educational standards in order to preserve democracy.

GREER, EDITH S., and RICHARD M. HARBECK. *What High School Pupils Study.* U.S. Department of Health, Education, and Welfare, Office of Education, Bulletin Number 10, 1962, OE–33025. Washington, D.C.: Government Printing Office, 1962.

A national survey of the scholastic performance of pupils of various abilities.

HENRY, NELSON B. (ed.). *Adapting the Secondary-School Program to the Needs of Youth.* Fifty-second Yearbook of the National Society for the Study of of Education, Part I. Chicago: University of Chicago Press, 1953.

An excellent yearbook presenting many of the school's roles in providing for the needs of youth.

KITZHABER, ALBERT R., ROBERT M. GORRELL, and PAUL ROBERTS. *Education for College.* New York: The Ronald Press Company, 1961.

A report (by a group of college specialists) of how the college preparatory subjects are being taught and observations on how they ought to be taught.

MALLERY, DAVID. *High School Students Speak Out.* New York: Harper and Row, Inc., 1962.

A report of a study of high school pupils' thoughts concerning the school, the curriculum, and teaching. Some of their observations are a devastating commentary on the irrelevance of much of the secondary-school curriculum.

MURPHY, GARDNER. *Freeing Intelligence Through Teaching.* New York: Harper and Row, 1961.

The 1961 John Dewey lecture in which a noted psychologist explains how he believes education can be used to help individuals realize their potentialities.

PASSOW, A. HARRY (ed.). *Curriculum Crossroads.* New York: Bureau of Publications, Columbia University, 1962.

A report of a curriculum conference. Chapter 3 debates the role of the disciplines in the curriculum; Chapter 1 the problem of role and direction.

———. *Education in Depressed Areas.* New York: Bureau of Publications, Teachers College, Columbia University, 1963.

Fifteen specialists explore the question "Have the public schools a responsibility for educating culturally disadvantaged children in depressed areas?" Primary concern is given to urban problems, but the authors consider conditions of cultural deprivation of rural and small town areas.

PRESIDENT'S COMMISSION ON NATIONAL GOALS. *Goals for Americans.* Englewood Cliffs, New Jersey: Prentice-Hall, Inc., 1960.

A good basis for discussion groups which might examine individual and group goals in all areas of life.

SCOTT, C. WINFIELD, CLYDE M. HILL, and HOBERT W. BURNS. *The Great Debate: Our Schools in Crisis.* Englewood Cliffs, New Jersey: Prentice-Hall, Inc., 1959.

A collection of essays pertinent to various issues in American education.

THAYER, V. T. *The Role of the School in American Society.* New York: Dodd, Mead and Company, 1960.

A consideration of the role of the American school in view of its social setting and psychological and philosophical relations. Deals squarely with important issues.

WILES, KIMBALL. *The Changing Curriculum of the American High School.* Englewood Cliffs, New Jersey: Prentice-Hall, Inc., 1963.

The curriculum is presented as a dynamic program, not a fixed abstraction. Teachers, administrators, and parents are helped to see the present and future curriculum needs more realistically, particularly in Chapters 3, 4, and 5.

Chapter 7

The Core
Curriculum and the
Block of Time

The past century has seen a gradual drift from discrete, narrow subjects to broad integrated, interdisciplinary courses that center upon problems of society or problems of youth. The first stage in this shift consists of the correlation of subject matter. At the simplest level correlation consists of teachers pointing out applications of the subject matter to other courses and to the pupils' daily lives. A more sophisticated type of correlation comes when teachers of different courses plan their lessons so that the courses support each other, as in the following far-reaching example.

At Verde Valley the various academic courses are not treated as separate compartments of learning, but are closely related to one another. Students are encouraged to visualize education as a whole and civilization as a great interwoven tapestry in which history, literature, drama, philosophy, religion, the arts and music, and the sciences are the individual parts.

An example of correlation that has been evolved is the following: students who are studying Greek and Roman history may likewise study, in their English classes, the great works of Hellenic literature. In both courses they study the Old Testament, in the one as history, in the other as literature, and they approach an understanding of the philosophy of Socrates and Plato. In art courses as well as in history these same students study the evolution of classical architecture, from Greece through Rome and the Renaissance to the time of Jefferson and the present day. Our large collection of mounted pictures and film strips enable them to compare side by side the great buildings of the past with famous modern buildings in the classical tradition. The same applies to classical sculpture. In music, they study the Greek modes and their influence upon the structure of medieval music. In mathematics and in science courses, the importance of the discoveries of such men as Pythagoras, Euclid and Archimedes is explained and evaluated.[1]

The next stage in the drift toward broad integrated courses is the fusion of courses. Broad field courses are a fusion of courses within a field, for example, general science. Just a short step farther along the drift toward broad integrated courses from the broad field course is the integrated, interdisciplinary course that combines content from two or more fields. The fusion of the English language arts and the social studies courses quite commonly found in junior high school block-of-time courses is an example of this stage of the drift.

The culmination of the drift is the core curriculum in which the subject matter of the course is not taken from any particular field or fields but can be selected from any field that bears on the problem at hand. The reader should note that at this stage the curriculum has made a complete and abrupt shift. Here the courses are problem- or interest-centered. At all the other stages previously described the courses are subject-centered. This shift represents a difference in orientation that many teachers have found difficult to grasp.

THE CORE CURRICULUM

If teachers and laymen alike are confused about any particular area of the secondary-school curriculum, it is about the core curriculum. The confusion probably arises because the word *core* was originally used to denote the "central core of the curriculum," that is, the subjects required of all the boys and girls. In any case the word *core* was quickly applied to many other curriculum devices and designs by which all or part of the general education portion of the curriculum was presented. In 1953 Harold Alberty, in analyzing the current uses of the term, found that programs called core could be fitted into six basic categories.

1. The core consists of a number of logically organized subjects or fields of knowledge each of which is taught independently.
2. The core consists of a number of logically organized subjects or fields of knowledge, some or all of which are correlated.
3. The core consists of broad problems, units of work, or unifying themes which are chosen because they afford the means of teaching effectively the basic content of certain subjects or fields of knowledge. These subjects or fields retain their identity, but the content is selected and taught with special reference to the unit, theme, or problem.

[1] *Verde Valley School* (Sedona, Arizona: The School, undated), p. 7.

4. The core consists of a number of subjects or fields of knowledge which are unified or fused. Usually one subject or field (e.g., history) serves as the unifying center.
5. The core consists of broad, preplanned problem areas, from which are selected learning experiences in terms of the psychobiological and societal needs.
6. The core consists of broad units of work, or activities, planned by the teacher and the students in terms of needs as perceived by the group. No basic curriculum structure is set up.[2]

THE CHARACTERISTICS OF THE "TRUE CORE"

In spite of the confusion and different definitions of core, experts in the field seem to be fairly well agreed that the "true core" is considerably more than a mere rearranging of subject matter. Faunce and Bossing define the core curriculum as a "pattern of the experience curriculum organized into a closely integrated and interrelated whole."[3] Although some writers would differ with Faunce and Bossing concerning the scope of the core curriculum, all agree that any core program that does not hew to the experience curriculum way is not truly a core and is not really worthy of the name.

What then are the characteristics of a true core?

(1) *The core must be common to all pupils.* The true core program is for all pupils, and all pupils are involved in it. It is by definition general education, the core which all pupils must take. A "core program" that does not include all the pupils is an anomaly, not a core.

(2) *The core occupies a large block of time, perhaps as much as one third to one half of the school day.* Almost all authorities agree that a core class needs a large block of time, at the very least a double period each day. Because of the need for greater flexibility and scope in core programs, the double- or triple-period class is probably the most common characteristic of courses called core curriculum.

(3) *The core is guidance-oriented.* Because a true core has to do with the problems and immediate concerns of youth, it is usually considered an excellent medium for guidance activities. Because it gives pupils and teacher an opportunity to get to know each other well, the long block of time lends itself admirably to teacher counseling. Both individual and group guidance services are integrated to the core.

(4) *The true core is problem-oriented.* The content of a true core program consists of the problems of youth and society. Ideally the pupils

---

[2] Harold Alberty, "Designing Programs To Meet the Common Needs of Youth," *Adapting the Secondary-School Program to the Needs of Youth,* Fifty-second Yearbook, Part I, National Society for the Study of Education (Chicago: University of Chicago Press, 1953), Ch. 7, pp. 119–120.

[3] Roland C. Faunce and Nelson L. Bossing, *Developing the Core Curriculum* (Englewood Cliffs: Prentice-Hall, Inc., 1958), p. 58.

and teachers have a great amount of latitude in the choice of problems. The core program of the Hazel Park Junior High School, St. Paul, Minnesota, for instance, has no set course of study.[4] Instead each teacher teaches the units in which he feels his class has an interest or need. The basic philosophy is that each unit will be a theme of interest and need to the student with both language arts and social studies values. Skills (reading, writing, speaking, listening, critical thinking, geographical concepts, and the like) are organized around the context of the theme. Ideas for unit themes come from many sources, for example, unwritten ideas of teachers, units written by local teachers, polling of classes for interests, unit guides from other cities, commercially published units. Examples of typical units taught in Hazel Park's ninth grade have been:

United Nations	Vocations
World Religions	Lives of Great People
Home and Family Living	The Meaning of the United
Our Neighbor Canada	States Constitution
Minnesota	

In order to avoid duplication and gaps in learning, teachers periodically list their units for a file kept in the resource room. This file is open for reference to all teachers. Thus teachers may tell what units have been taught in past years and what units are being taught at the time.

Most core curricula are not quite so unstructured. A more usual technique is to prescribe broad problem areas to be taught in the various grades. In preplanning broad problem areas every effort is made to see to it that the problems selected for study are vital to the pupils. In order to increase flexibility and provide for unforeseen contingencies, teachers are allowed to substitute or add problem areas if the need arises. Typical of the problem areas that might be included are the following, which were among those prescribed for the seventh grade at the Fairmont Heights Junior-Senior High School, Prince George's County, Maryland, in 1955–56.

Problems of School Living
Problems of Personal and Community Health with emphasis on Personal Health
Problems of Intercultural Relations
Problems of Economic Relations[5]

Lurry and Alberty[6] state the case for broad preplanned problem areas in the following cogent argument:

---

[4] The description of the Hazel Park Junior High School program is largely adapted from a letter of Ruth F. Langer, Resource Teacher, at that school.

[5] Lucile L. Lurry and Elsie J. Alberty, *Developing a High School Core Program* (New York: The Macmillan Company, 1957), p. 95.

[6] *Ibid.*, p. 28.

It is the position of the writers that a program lacking a preplanned basic curricular structure is unrealistic in face of existing conditions in teacher shortages, the lack of pre-service education for core teaching, and the dearth of instructional materials suited to the needs of such teaching. Furthermore, to leave the complete choice of areas of study to teachers and pupils with neither total faculty planning nor certain limitations *would seem to invite lack of continuity in the learning experience, and needless repetition and/or severe gaps in the general education experiences of boys and girls.*[7]

(5) *The core ignores subject matter lines but rather considers all knowledge to be its province.* The study of problems can best be attacked by problem-solving techniques. The true core utilizes the method of problem solving throughout. To carry this method out successfully the problems that the pupils investigate must be real, live, open-ended problems. Canned problems and pseudo problems with cut-and-dried, approved solutions are not valid. Advocates of the core support this type of methodology because of the belief that problem solving is the best way to arrive at clear concepts and true understandings, and the philosophical notion that only by learning to solve problems in experience-centered situations can boys and girls learn to face the problems of life efficiently and effectively. Creative learning rather than instruction is the rule for the true core program.

Therefore the subject matter of the core program does not fit into any one subject field or discipline. Usually much of the content comes from the language arts and the social studies, but the scope of the core is not limited by these fields and may well include any other, or all others, of the academic spectrum.

(6) *The core involves pupil–teacher planning.* Problem-centered courses require teacher–pupil planning because an essential element of problem solving is the forming of the problem. Whatever the broad areas prescribed for the particular grade, the pupil and teacher in the program work out together the problems to be solved, the scope and sequence, the methods and procedures to be used in studying them, and criteria for evaluating the success of their study and the conclusions or solutions arrived at.

In order to implement this sort of planning, usually the teacher comes to the class equipped with a resource unit for each of the various problems to be considered. In the resource unit the teacher can find much that will help him guide his pupils as they plan their attack on the unit problem. For example:

Discussion of possible scope and sequence of teaching unit.
Suggested objectives suitable for the unit.
Suggested approaches to the unit.

[7] Italics added.

Suggested experiences and activities.

List of pertinent readings, films, filmstrips, audio-visual aids of all sorts, and similar resources.

Suggestion for evaluative devices, materials, and activities.

(7) *In the core, subject matter and skills are taught as they are needed rather than in any fixed sequence.* Because the problems of youth and society determine the subject matter of core programs, the specific skills and concepts are not taught in any fixed order, but rather are taught as they are needed. To many this seems to be a very dangerous technique. However, authorities on the core, such as Lurry and Alberty, insist that the fundamentals are well taught in core programs.[8] Research indicates that their claims are correct.

(8) *The true core requires considerable teacher preparation.* Core programs must be taught in relation to the other courses in the curriculum. To place the core in a separate compartment, isolated from the other subjects in the curriculum, violates the basic principle on which core theory is founded. Therefore core teachers and the teachers of specialized subjects must plan with each other so that they all can profit optimally from each other's work. In addition the flexibility of the problem approach makes it imperative that the teacher be more than well prepared in order to cope with the many contingencies that may arise.

(9) *In the core individual differences are provided for by method rather than by curricular structure.* Core programs are common to all pupils, but the pupils do not all study identical subject matter. Differentiation to suit the needs, interests, and abilities of the pupils is provided by one variation or another of the unit method.

Ordinarily the unit includes class activities that can be shared by the entire class and a large number of activities that must be done individually or in small groups in laboratory fashion. The laboratory approach gives the pupils plenty of opportunities to plan their own work, to explore facets interesting to themselves, to work at their own speed, and in other ways live up to their own individualities. In addition to providing for individual differences, the laboratory approach gives the teacher plenty of opportunity to confer with individuals and to help them with their problems both academic and otherwise. In this way the unit approach in the core program makes it possible for the teacher to carry out his guidance function much more effectively than the traditional type of teaching does.

RELATIONSHIPS OF THE CORE WITH OTHER COURSES

The core curriculum does not encompass the entire curriculum. Usually it consists of a block of time amounting to two or three periods per day, replacing the social studies and the English language arts in the curricu-

[8] Lurry and Alberty, *op. cit.*, pp. 40–41.

lum, and perhaps also serving as a medium for conducting the guidance program. Less frequently the core program also replaces general education courses in science, mathematics, and art. The more usual practice is to depend on separate courses to teach the subject matter in these fields. Because of their structure and the scope of their content, general education subjects, such as physical education, are probably best taught separately also. Some schools have even found it advisable to teach grammar and other portions of the language arts in additional classes outside the core curriculum structure. However, teachers of art, music, mathematics, science, and other subjects are sometimes called in as consultants by the core teachers whenever the problem areas to be studied in the core curriculum make it seem desirable.

Because the core program deals only with general education, specialized education does not fit into the core program. In order to provide for specialized education, schools ordinarily provide additional courses in the areas concerned. These courses are often called special interest courses. Eliminating special interest courses from the core program does not rule out the use of the core approach in them. On the contrary, Faunce and Bossing insist that the special interest courses should also follow the same type of pattern.

> It is highly important to see the wholeness of the curriculum and to recognize that the learning process applicable to achieving the core competencies apply equally to the development of special interest competencies. There cannot be two opposing theories of learning and of the curriculum successfully in operation at the same time.[9]

Other authorities do not insist on this point. In practice it seems that, more frequently than not, the specialized education portion of the school curriculum consists of traditional, formal courses. Be that as it may, it seems only logical that if the principles of correlation and integration have any value at all, the special interest courses and the core should be planned so that they can support each other as well as possible.

Figure 1 (page 149) indicates how the school day may be arranged when a core program is used.

THE CORE: PRO AND CON

Advantages of the Core. What advantages can be gained from adopting core programs? Many, according to core enthusiasts.

1. One of the most powerful arguments for the core program is that it makes possible the selection of units vital to the general education of the pupils from an overwhelming hodgepodge of subject matter. How better to select the content of the general education courses

---

[9] Faunce and Bossing, *loc. cit.*

FIGURE 1. TYPICAL CORE OR BLOCK-OF-TIME
SCHEDULE

	Name	H.R. 8–1	RM. B–6	Lunch A	
Period	Monday	Tuesday	Wednesday	Thursday	Friday
1.	Core or Block	Core or Block	Core or Block	Core or Block	Core or Block
2.	Core or Block	Core or Block	Core or Block	Core or Block	Core or Block
3.	Core or Block	Core or Block	Core or Block	Core or Block	Core or Block
4.	Math	Math	Math	Math	Math
5.	Home Arts	Science	Science	Science	Science
6.	Home Arts	Music	Typing	Music	Typing
7.	Phys. Ed.	Phys. Ed.	Phys. Ed.	Phys. Ed.	Phys. Ed.

than to center them around the common problems of youth and society?

2. In the core the subject matter relates to life in the home and community and to other school activities. Integrating the subject matter around the real problems of life and society should result in clear concepts and real changes of behavior, rather than the empty verbalism that so frequently results from traditional classes. Therefore a second argument is that the core program, being based on the problems of youth and society, and integrating subject matter from all pertinent fields, yields much more meaningful learning than the traditional separate subject courses do.

3. A third argument for the core is that the methods used in the true core are more in line with what we know about learning[10] than traditional methods are. Because the core provides for active learning by means of problem solving and a variety of other active methods, the teacher is a guide rather than a mentor. Evidently this emphasis on problem solving, pupil–teacher planning, and vital subject matter in core programs has done much to increase the motivation of the pupils. Some principals report that the use of the core approach has reduced discipline problems in their schools.

Although the above argument is cogent and valid, these benefits need not be limited to core. Active methods of the sort described can be used effectively in traditional organizations. The reader should also note that the methods advocated are much more acceptable to persons imbued with the progressive outlook and convinced of the superiority of creative learning over instruction.

[10] See Chapter III for information concerning learning theory and suggested readings in the field.

4. A fourth argument for the core is that it provides an excellent medium for taking care of individual differences within the general education program. That the flexible problem-laboratory approach provides a maximum of opportunity for pupils to capitalize on their individual interests and capabilities is true. Probably, however, this approach needs not be limited to the core program. The proper use of the unit method in the more traditional classes might provide for individual differences equally as well.

5. A fifth argument for the core is that it provides an excellent medium for conducting an essential part of the guidance program. The long blocks of time associated with the core program allow the pupils and teachers to get to know each other well, and the flexible nature of the core program allows ample opportunity for conferences and counseling. More important is the fact that the true core centers around the problems of youth and society. Consequently the subject matter of the core is really practice in solving one's problems, which is the essence of guidance.

6. A sixth purported advantage of the core is that its flexible construction lends itself to teaching pupils how to think and to cope with new situations. The argument is that with this type of program the pupil is not weighted down by a lot of useless dead information, but, rather, is armed with tools for coping with new problems. Because this is a world that changes swiftly and continuously, this emphasis on "know how" rather than "know what" will prepare him to cope with the future, whereas a less flexible subject-centered program would fit him only for the world as it was. Again this seems to be an argument for the method rather than for the core curriculum.

7. Working together to solve real problems should encourage social skills and also attitudes of cooperation and tolerance. Consequently a well-run core program is in effect a laboratory for democratic living in which boys and girls learn the social skills necessary for life in a democracy. Unquestionably, good core programs can encourage democratic skills and values; however, again this argument seems to be an argument for the laboratory approach rather than for the core.

8. A final argument is that the core program encourages intrastaff cooperation and coordination. Of course, staff cooperation is not limited to core programs, but the format of the core seems more congenial to cooperation than the separate subject approach is.

Arguments Against the Core. In spite of the many arguments put forth in its favor, the core has aroused much opposition. Some of the opposition is based upon unthinking reaction against the core simply because the core is new and different. Nevertheless, a good share of it is sincere, reasoned opinion based upon what, to the critic, appear to be sound premises. These objections deserve serious consideration.

1. The first objection to the core is that it leaves out essential subject matter. By essential subject matter the critics usually mean factual information and skills that they believe fundamental to scholarship and to preparation for adult life. The charge is a serious one and one that cannot be easily sloughed off. To date, however, the charge is not proven. The weight of the data available indicates that where the core is taught well, the boys and girls stand up well in examinations on the fundamentals. Still, where there is so much smoke, there may be some fire. Certainly in some core courses, or pseudo courses, the pupils have failed to learn as much as they should have, but the same can be said of academic courses. It may well be that it is not the type of organization but the quality of teaching that makes the difference.

   Be that as it may, the core program, as it is generally conceived, covers a wide gamut of content, and so may make it more difficult for any teacher to insure that the pupils cover particular items adequately. Because both teachers and pupils tend to concentrate on those things they like most, when there is no set plan, some areas may be neglected.

2. The second objection is an extension of the first one, namely, the core includes so much varied subject matter that to expect any teacher to have all the competencies a core teacher should have is unreasonable. A really good core teacher needs a breadth and depth of liberal and specialized education that is hard to find. Dynamic teaching of the type that core demands requires that one know his academic terrain well, because the problem-solving technique may call for him to step out sure-footedly in any number of directions.

3. A third objection is that the pupils in core program lose the values inherent in the content and method of the subject fields because the core program violates the structure of the disciplines. Critics who argue from this point of view fear that in core programs pupils do not have sufficient opportunities to acquire skills in the methods of history, criticism, science, and other disciplines and so will grow up to be intellectual cripples. Probably this argument is spurious, for apparently it is by the method, rather than by the organization, that the skills and structure of the various disciplines are taught.

4. A fourth criticism of the core is that it dilutes the curriculum with content that its critics feel is not worthy of secondary education.

In their estimation real-life problems such as boy-girl relationships, budgeting, and family relationships reek of anti-intellectualism and so should be barred from the secondary school. Proponents of the core tend to brush off this argument as false and unsound psychologically. As the reader can readily see, the differences of opinion on this point stem from differences in philosophy discussed in Chapter 2.

5. Another objection, also based upon a difference in philosophical beliefs, is that the core is soft and leads to undisciplined behavior and to slovenly habits of thinking. Believing, as they do, that the content of the core program lacks rigor, these critics fear that it will sap pupils' intellectual strength. Furthermore, they are afraid that student–teacher planning deprives the pupils of the orderly disciplined academic experience and substitutes in its stead a hodgepodge of miscellaneous confusion.

An Evaluation of the Criticisms. In the opinion of the writers of this book only two of the objections cited are valid ones: (1) the core format makes it possible for teachers and pupils to accidentally skip over important learnings, and (2) the core format makes great demands upon the core teacher. The other faults attributed to core programs are probably not inherent to core, but rather, when they occur, are the result of poor teaching and poor supervision.

Possibly none of the difficulties cited are peculiar to core programs. Whether or not core programs leave pupils with bigger gaps of essential information than traditional courses do is debatable. Of necessity, all curricula leave things out. Whether or not what is left out of any specific curriculum is essential seems to depend on one's definition of essential.

The contention that the load of a core teacher is too great for one teacher to carry effectively is a serious one. Some school systems have found it so difficult to secure teachers capable of handling the job that they have dropped the core program. Of course, it is true that the core program demands excellent teachers, but there is no reason to believe that it demands supermen. Perhaps if our teacher education institutions should provide adequate programs for training good core teachers this problem might fade away.

PREVALENCE OF THE TRUE CORE

The true core program has never been really popular in American secondary schools, and does not seem to be gaining in popularity now. In 1952 a United States Office of Education study of junior and junior-senior high schools indicated that of all the schools reporting core type of programs fewer than one quarter were using true core programs exclusively or "in most classes." A similar study reported in 1958

FIGURE 2. CURRICULUM PROPOSAL FOR
JUNIOR HIGH SCHOOL

Periods	Grade 7	Grade 8	Grade 9
1	Core Curriculum, organized around problems of early adolescent in today's world. Either planned each year by teachers and pupils with complete freedom to select problems of study, or organized around a theme for each year or semester, with resource units to draw on. Within these resource units and themes, teaching and learning units developed by teacher–pupil planning. Replaces such separate subjects as		
2	English, history, civics, geography, health, and science. Basic goals: increased skill in communication, problem solving and critical thinking, developing sound values.		
3			Research carried on by groups and by individuals
4			Mathematics 1
Activity and Luncheon Periods	Two or three shorter periods within which are scheduled luncheon, school clubs, student organizations, remedial programs, research, rest, recreation, social activities, tutoring, study, music appreciation, work on special projects.		
5	Arithmetic	Arithmetic	Electives: Vocal Music Instrumental Music Art Industrial Arts
6	Exploratory Experiences: Art, Music, Industrial Arts, Homemaking	Exploratory Experiences: Art, Music, Industrial Arts, Homemaking	Homemaking Typing General Business General Biology Foreign Language Drafting
7	Physical Education	Physical Education	Journalism or Drama Physical Education

indicated that fewer than 12 per cent of the schools reporting core type of programs were committed to the true core type of program.[11] Percentagewise these studies indicate a "decided slump" in the popularity

[11] Grace S. Wright, *Block-Time Classes and the Core Program in the Junior High School*, Bulletin 1958, No. 6 (Washington, D.C.: U.S. Department of Health, Education, and Welfare, Office of Education, 1958). Our figures cannot be exact, because Wright combined unified studies and true core programs in gathering her information.

of the core program; however, they do not show a decrease in the actual number of schools using the core program because the number of block-of-time or core type of programs had increased greatly.

Schools and school systems that have well-developed core programs seem to be very faithful to them. The truth seems to be that core programs are more difficult to launch than traditional programs, and so poorly designed, hastily built, and inadequately captained core programs are liable to capsize before they are off the ways, but well-designed, carefully built, and strongly led core programs have proved amply seaworthy.

FUTURE DEVELOPMENTS IN THE CORE

The core movement has not been as great a force as its proponents had hoped it would be. Nevertheless, Faunce and Clute seem to be convinced that the core, although still a goal rather than an achievement, is the program of the future in the junior high school. Encouraged by an increase of the block-of-time courses at the seventh and eighth grade level, they have proposed a school organization for the junior high school curriculum centered around a true core program. Their proposal is illustrated as Figure 2 on page 153.

> Perhaps some explanation of Figure 2 is appropriate. In grades seven and eight, four periods are set aside for the core classes whose objectives are increased competence and growth in dealing with the problems of living in a democratic society. Core teachers are also counselors, each with two sections totalling about sixty pupils. The block of time is reduced by one period in grade nine to accommodate the elective program. The activity period is organized around the luncheon hour to provide for all but the team (intramural) games. These are scheduled generally as one phase of the physical education hour. (Figure 2 is not a schedule of classes but a curriculum plan.)
>
> Arithmetic is required as a separate class but it is urged that the teachers of each grade level meet regularly for planning. Thus the mathematics experiences become an integral part of the core experience, but meet an extra period with a special teacher for practice and study of those activities in which special emphasis or skill is desired. Algebra and geometry are not scheduled as such, even in grade nine, but some individuals and groups in "Mathematics 1" are likely to progress into abstract mathematics at least during the ninth year.[12]

What the future of the core curriculum will be is still not yet decided. It appears that in spite of a counter movement toward more traditional organization, the core movement may yet come out on top in the junior high school.

---

[12] Roland C. Faunce and Morrel J. Clute, *Teaching and Learning in the Junior High School* (Belmont, Calif.: Wadsworth Publishing Company, Inc., 1961), p. 95.

THE CORE COURSE

Roy O. Billett has suggested a type of core that may be the key to solving some of the problems associated with core programs. Although proponents of core programs usually hold that a large block of time is necessary for any core program, Billett's plan does not require longer than average daily periods. Rather the core is conceived of as a course that runs concurrently with, and in addition to, the separate subject courses. Such a core course would meet only a single period each day, and possibly only three or four days a week, but nevertheless it would be the heart of the curriculum. Other academic subjects would be correlated with it and their units would be tied to the core units as much as possible. Thus the core courses would stimulate ideas that would be developed in other courses, and experiences in other courses would be pooled in the core course.

Content in a Core Course. As in the core programs previously described, the core course would center around the problems of youth and take its content from any subject field necessary. Its content would include group guidance, occupations, and orientation and real problems of youth. Typical topics might include You and Your Future, Achieving Personal Health and Fitness, Relations with Others, Right and Wrong.[13]

Unlike the core programs previously described, this core course does not attempt to replace any of the courses now taught. The skills and understandings of history and of the language arts would be taught by the history and language arts teachers respectively. In this way one of the most important objections to the core program can be avoided.

Advantages of a Core Course. A core course of this sort has much to offer. As the earlier chapters of this book point out, many of the areas most important to youth are not taught in the ordinary academic curriculum. Among them are home and family living, economic competence, relations with others, and so on. Sometimes such topics are taught in the general education offering of courses in home economics, social studies, business education, general mathematics, industrial arts, music, and art, but frequently they are omitted completely from the curriculum, particularly from the curriculum of the college-preparatory pupils. The core course could remedy this lack without upsetting the academic program in any way.

Such a course could have the additional merit of eliminating some of the repetition sometimes found in general education courses. For instance, sometimes topics like budgeting are taught to boys and girls in general mathematics, general business, and home and family living. The course could bring together units from homemaking, business training, mathe-

---

[13] Roy O. Billett, *Growing Up* (Boston: D. C. Heath and Company, 1958), and accompanying *Teachers Manual* illustrate material suitable for such a core approach.

matics, industrial arts, health, safety, psychology, and other areas to form a sequence that would not only deal with the important common problems of youth, but could present the content from these fields necessary for a complete general education. Elements of mathematics, science, and social science that are not ordinarily taught in the college-preparatory course, but that college-preparatory youths should have a chance to learn if they are going to be adequately educated, for instance, budgeting, could be taught in this course. Certainly the core course is a possibility for developing the core idea in the traditional setting; it deserves careful consideration.

BLOCK-OF-TIME CLASSES

Although true core programs are not very common, block-of-time courses are quite popular, particularly in the junior high school grades. By block-of-time classes we mean classes that meet for double or triple class periods and that combine or replace two or more subjects. Ordinarily the term "block-of-time class" is reserved for general education courses, that is, courses required for all pupils. Nevertheless, there seems to be no reason why the term cannot apply to combinations of other courses, for basically the block of time is simply a scheduling device in which a teacher is assigned the same pupils for two or more consecutive periods in the same room. Its purpose is to provide in the modern secondary school some of the conditions found to be advantageous in the self-contained and semidepartmentalized classrooms of the elementary schools and junior high schools of the past.

Types of Blocks. For our purposes we shall recognize three kinds of block-of-time classes. In the first type the subjects retain their identity, although scheduled together in a multiple period. In this type of block of time the courses taught within the block of time may or may not be correlated. In the second type of block-of-time class the subject matter of the subjects taught has been integrated into a unified course. The third type of block-of-time course is the true core curriculum described in the preceding section. By far the most common type of the block-of-time course is a combination of English language arts and social studies. Other combinations found are science and mathematics, social studies and mathematics, English language arts and mathematics, social studies and science, English language arts and science, and mathematics with English language arts and social studies. Such courses are found most frequently in the seventh grade and decrease rapidly as the grade level rises.

THE BLOCK-OF-TIME COURSE

As a rule the subjects of the block-of-time courses are taught as separate distinct subjects. Thus, in the ordinary double-period, social studies, language arts block of time, one would find that the teacher ordinarily teaches one period of social studies and one period of language arts pretty much as he would have done if he were not teaching a block of time at all. If Wright's 1958 study is any indication, two thirds of the block-of-time classes in this country are of this type. Portions of the seventh grade block-of-time program at the Central Junior High School of Parsipanny, New Jersey, illustrate this type of block-of-time program. As the guide specifically states, the Central Junior High School block of time is neither problem-centered nor fully integrated, but the subject matter in both the language arts and the social studies portions of the block-of-time program is arranged so that teachers can correlate as much as they wish. Therefore some teachers may teach the portions of the block of time as entirely separate courses, whereas others may correlate and integrate if they wish.[14]

Methods in block-of-time courses do not differ from methods used in other good secondary-school courses, except that perhaps the long periods may lend themselves to more variety than the ordinary periods do. The classes are not likely to be problem-centered any more than other academic classes are. When problems are used, they are more likely to center around problems of subject matter than problems of youth, although there is no reason why vital problems of youth cannot be discussed in a block-of-time class—or any other academic class for that matter.

THE UNIFIED STUDIES CORE

A number of schools have integrated the subject matter of the block-of-time program into a completely new course. These fully integrated courses go by many different names and differ from other courses only in that the subject matter is served up in different portions. The shape may be different, but the taste is about the same. More than anything else, they resemble the interdisciplinary courses so common in colleges and universities. For want of a better name we shall call these integrated courses unified studies or unit core programs.

Unit Approach. The teaching method of the unified studies courses is quite likely to be some form of the unit method. Sometimes the teaching is stultified and academic, but frequently it features problem solving and laboratory techniques. Integrated courses are less likely to be taught traditionally than other block-of-time classes are. Usually the sequence of units for unified studies courses follows a subject-centered pattern typical of one of the studies that has been integrated into the unified studies core.

A fine example of such a course is the seventh grade social living course at Royster Junior High School, Chanute, Kansas. Of the 14 topics listed

[14] *Central School Block-Of-Time Study Guide,* Central Junior High School, Parsipanny, New Jersey, p. 10.

for the course all but three are common social studies (World Civilization and Geography) topics. The other three are drawn from the fields
of language arts and guidance. But all the units include both social studies
and language studies experiences.[15]

Interdisciplinary Seminars. An interesting variation of the unified
studies approach that may or may not utilize a block of time is the
interdisciplinary seminar, such as the senior seminar at the Regional High
School in Metuchen, New Jersey. An adaptation of the team teaching
idea, the program in Metuchen consists of a series of lectures on current
topics concerning the humanities and the social sciences given to the
entire senior class by outstanding lecturers and followed up by class
discussions and other assignments in regular class-size sections.

Examples of the topics included in the 1961–62 senior seminars were
Democracy—A Way of Life, What is the Constitution? The Republican
Party in the Twentieth Century, The Democratic Party in the Twentieth
Century, Comparison of the Basic Principles of Communism and Socialism, Shakespeare, and Phoenix Theater presentations of plays by Shaw,
Chekhov, and others. Among the guest speakers scheduled were Norman
Thomas; Harrison Salisbury of *The New York Times*; Norman Madel,
drama critic of the New York *World-Telegram and Sun*; the Republican
and Democratic candidates for Governor; and a series of local dignitaries
and college professors. Filling out the program and tying it together are
student debates, student panels, lectures by local teachers, and small
group meetings.

STATUS OF THE BLOCK OF TIME

Block-of-time classes are common in the junior high schools of the
country but are much less frequent in the high schools. Kalapos' 1958
study of New Jersey schools, in which he found that, although 51 per
cent of the junior and junior-senior high schools he studied had block-
of-time classes in grade 7 or 8, very few (14 per cent) of them continued
the block of time into grade 9, strikingly illustrates the current tendency
to utilize the block of time in grades 7 and 8, but not in the higher
grades.[16] As we pointed out earlier, the great majority of block-of-time
classes consist of two or more distinct courses. Only about a fifth of them
are fused or integrated subject matter courses, and relatively few of
these are true core programs.

Trends in Block of Time. Just what the future of the block-of-time
program is to be is not clear. At present, although the block of time is

[15] Quoted from *Study Guide—Social Living—Seventh Grade,* prepared by Betty
Campbell and Hazel Russell, Royster Junior High School, Chanute, Kansas, 1960.

[16] Stephen A. Kalapos, "Block-of-Time Programs in Junior High Schools in New
Jersey," *Secondary-School Bulletin* (Trenton: New Jersey State Department of Education, March, 1960).

popular in the junior high school, the current pressure on subject matter and the increased stress on the structure of the disciplines may be reversing the movement toward the block of time even at the junior high school level. In New York State the percentage of schools reporting block-of-time programs had fallen from 32.7 in 1956–57 to 22.3 in 1961–62.[17] Still, the block of time has received considerable support from influential sources. The Conant Report on the junior high school and the Association for Supervision and Curriculum Development reports entitled *The Self-Contained Classroom* and *The Junior High School We Need* have supported them.[18]

ADVANTAGES OF THE BLOCK OF TIME

The popularity of block-of-time classes in the junior high school is easily understandable, because the block of time has certain definite advantages in the junior high school grades. In the first place the block of time in grade 7 makes an admirable transition from the self-contained classroom of the elementary school to the departmentalization of the secondary school. Instead of facing the pupil with an entirely new situation, the two-hour or three-hour block allows the pupil to get used to departmentalization and specialization.

Reduction of Pupil–Teacher Ratio. Another aspect of the block of time that makes it particularly helpful in the pupil's transition from the elementary school to the secondary school is that it reduces the number of teachers the pupil must face. This should make the movement from the elementary school easier and should give the child added security.

Similarly the block of time reduces the teacher's pupil load. For instance, a teacher who has two double-period block-of-time classes of 30 students each teaches only 60 pupils, whereas, if he taught four 30-pupil classes of English or social studies he would have 120 pupils. This reduction allows him to learn to know his pupils better and should make it possible for him to teach them more effectively. In addition this more intimate contact makes it possible for the teacher to carry out the guidance function more adequately. In many schools the block-of-time teacher becomes the guidance teacher for his block-of-time class, and the block of time becomes a medium for both group and individual conferences and counseling. Such an arrangement has much in its favor because it provides for counseling by a person who knows the pupil, and it also provides the pupil with a familiar figure to whom to turn for advice. So

[17] Norman Ward Wilson, *Block-Time Programs in Junior High Schools and Six-Year Secondary Schools of New York State,* 1961–62 (Ithaca, N.Y.: School of Education, Cornell University, 1962), p. 2.

[18] James B. Conant, *Education in the Junior High School Years* (Princeton, N.J.: Educational Service, 1960); *The Junior High School We Need* (Washington, D.C.: Association for Supervision and Curriculum Development, 1960).

as to make the most of this advantage of the core, some junior high schools make a practice of having a block-of-time teacher follow a class through three junior high school grades. In this way the school authorities are assured that at least someone knows each child intimately by the end of his junior high school years.

Organization for Effective Teaching. The block of time also lends itself to more effective teaching. Because of the long period one can utilize films, field trips, laboratory work, and other activities too long for single-period classes. For instance, in a two-and-a-half-hour class it might be possible to show a full-length moving picture at one sitting. Short field trips, which might be impossible otherwise, can be conducted in a long block of time without disturbing the rest of the daily schedule. One of the difficulties with certain laboratory periods is that by the time the pupils have got their material ready and started to work, it is time for them to put their things away. The long period gives them time to get some real work done. In short, the block-of-time format gives flexibility to organization for teaching.

By encouraging the integrating and correlating of subject matter, block classes can give additional opportunities for showing relations and application of the material to be studied. For example, the social-studies–language-arts combination gives the pupils social studies content to write their English themes about. An additional benefit is that because the two courses are taught in the same block by the same teacher (usually), teachers of the social-studies–language-arts block should be able to avoid more easily the overlapping of content common in ordinary social studies and language arts courses.

OBJECTIONS TO BLOCK-OF-TIME COURSES

Many teachers and principals look on block-of-time classes with disfavor. Usually their objections are the same as the ones noted earlier for the core—frequently because many teachers confuse block-of-time courses with the core program. This is unfair. Nine tenths of the block-of-time classes are subject-centered courses differing little from ordinary courses. In the minority of cases where the subject matter is fused, the block of time almost always follows a carefully planned sequence of units just as other well-designed academic courses do. Ordinarily block-of-time classes are not experience-centered; they should not be condemned for faults alleged to experience-centered core curricula.

Another criticism is that block-of-time teachers favor one of their subjects over another and consequently neglect one or the other of the subjects included in the block of time. When the courses within the block of time retain their identity, such neglect seems unlikely; when the subjects are fused, well-trained, well-supervised teachers should not find it difficult to give each subject its due.

Like the core curriculum, block-of-time teaching does require exceptionally well-prepared teachers. But providing such teachers is not an insurmountable problem. Hundreds of high school teachers successfully teach combinations of subjects in the ordinary secondary-school program. To teach a correlated block-of-time class should be easier than to try to teach a combination of completely disparate courses in different subjects.

SUMMARY

For the past century there has been a drift from discrete separate subjects to correlation and integration of subject matter. The natural culmination of this drift is the *core curriculum,* a term attended by much confusion. The true core is a multiperiod course, largely pupil-directed, which deals with the important problems of youth and society and draws its subject matter from any discipline that can contribute to understanding the problem under consideration. At present, relatively few schools are using true core curricula, but where they have been carefully worked out they have been successful.

Ordinarily core curriculum courses replace one or more courses, typically English and social studies. Consequently teachers, administrators, and parents fear that the subjects replaced will become diluted. To obviate this difficulty and yet fulfill the very desirable purposes of the core curriculum, Roy O. Billett has suggested the introduction of core courses that would include elements of guidance and problems of youth and society, but would not replace any of the usual subject courses. So far courses of this sort have not become common, but the idea has much merit and should be carefully considered.

Many so-called core courses are a unification of two or more subjects into a single double-period course. Often these courses are called unified studies courses. Frequently the subject matter of the two subjects in these courses is not at all integrated or even correlated. In effect they are simply two courses taught in consecutive periods by the same teacher to the same pupils. A course of this sort is more properly called a block-of-time course. Block-of-time scheduling is common in the junior high school, but uncommon in the senior high school. It has the advantage of giving the teacher considerable time to manipulate his group into desirable teaching arrangements, of giving more time for teacher and pupils to learn to know each other, and to make a more gradual change from the self-contained classroom of the elementary school to the departmentalized organization of the senior high school. Because of its flexibility, its use has proven successful in many junior high school situations even though it requires the teacher to be competent in at least two different subject areas.

Because the secondary-school curriculum is usually subject-centered, the ensuing chapters of this book have been organized around curriculum subjects.

SUGGESTED READINGS

ALBERTY, HAROLD. "Designing Programs to Meet the Common Needs of Youth," in *Adapting the Secondary School Program To Meet the Needs of Youth,* Nelson B. Henry (ed.). Fifty-second Yearbook of the National Society for the Study of Education. Chicago: University of Chicago Press, 1953.

A good analysis and description of core curricula. A basic reference.

ALBERTY, HAROLD, and ELSIE ALBERTY. *Reorganizing the High School Curriculum.* Third edition. New York: The Macmillan Company, 1962.

The latest revision of an outstanding work on secondary-school curriculum. Part II explains and interprets the role of the core curriculum in the total school program.

ASSOCIATION FOR SUPERVISION AND CURRICULUM DEVELOPMENT. *Preparation of Core Teachers for Secondary Schools.* Washington, D.C.: The Association, 1955.

An A.S.C.D. report recommending programs for preparing teachers to teach in core programs. Chapter 1 particularly gives argument for the core program approach.

BEGGE, JEANETTE, and J. T. SANDEFUR. "Social Integration Through a Core Program," *Social Education,* 27: 134–136, March, 1963.

A description of an excellent core program being conducted at Roosevelt High School.

FAUNCE, ROLAND C., and MORREL J. CLUTE. *Teaching and Learning in the Junior High School.* Belmont, California: Wadsworth Publishing Company, Inc., 1960.

A textbook in junior high school education from the core point of view. Chapter 4 contains a proposal for core curricula of the future.

FAUNCE, ROLAND C., and NELSON S. BOSSING. *Developing the Core Curriculum.* Second edition. Englewood Cliffs, New Jersey: Prentice-Hall, Inc., 1958.

A basic reference on all aspects of core curriculum.

GWYNN, J. MINOR. *Curriculum Principles and Social Trends.* Third edition. New York: The Macmillan Company, 1960.

One of the better references dealing with core curriculum.

HENRY, NELSON B. (ed.). *The Integration of Educational Experiences.* Fifty-seventh Yearbook of the National Society for the Study of Education, Part II. Chicago: University of Chicago Press, 1958.

Contains authoritative discussions of the nature of integration and its implications. Chapter 10 deals specifically with the secondary-school curriculum and the use of core curricula in the secondary schools.

HOCK, LOUISE E., and THOMAS J. HILL. *The General Education Class in the Secondary School.* New York: Holt, Rinehart and Winston, Inc., 1960.

An excellent book on core teaching. Part 1 defines, illustrates, and argues for the core approach.

LEONARD, J. PAUL. *Developing the Secondary School Curriculum.* Revised edition. New York: Rinehart and Company, Inc., 1957.

Deals with curriculum through the six-year secondary-school span. Valuable in developing core courses, developing resource units, organizing and using units of work, and developing classroom units.

LURRY, LUCILE L., and ELSIE J. ALBERTY. *Developing a High School Core Program.* New York: The Macmillan Company, 1957.

One of the very best explanations of the core program in action. Illustrates how core programs are developed.

JENNINGS, WAYNE. "The Status of the Core Program," *The Bulletin of the National Association of Secondary School Principals,* 46: 55–57, March, 1962.

A report of a study which indicates that core curriculum programs are continuing to gain strength and acceptance.

MICHELSON, JOHN. "What Does Research Say About the Effectiveness of the Core Curriculum?" *The School Review,* 65: 144–160, Summer, 1957.

Summarizes studies which indicate that core classes teach subject matter as well as traditional classes do.

NOAR, GERTRUDE. *Teaching and Learning the Democratic Way.* Englewood Cliffs, New Jersey: Prentice-Hall, Inc., 1963.

A basic text on junior high school with strong emphases on the core.

SNYDER, EDITH ROACH (ed.). *The Self-Contained Classroom.* Washington, D.C.: The Association for Supervision and Curriculum Development, 1960.

Presents the case for the self-contained classroom, including core and block-of-time classes, and shows how they may be used effectively.

VAN TIL, WILLIAM, GORDON F. VARS, and JOHN H. LOUNSBERRY. *Modern Education for the Junior High School Years.* Indianapolis: The Bobbs-Merrill Company, Inc., 1961. Unit III.

Excellent references on junior high school curriculum by foremost advocates of the core point of view. Unit III is devoted to core per se.

VARS, GORDON F. "Leadership in Core Program Development," *Educational Leadership,* 19: 517–527, May, 1962.

A discussion of the status of the block-of-time and core curriculum, their merits, and reasons for their limited popularity.

WRIGHT, GRACE S. *Block-Time Classes and the Core Program.* Bulletin 1958, Number 6, U.S. Department of Health, Education, and Welfare. Washington, D.C.: Government Printing Office, 1958.

A status study of block-of-time and core classes in American secondary schools.

ZAPF, ROSALIND M. *Democratic Processes in the Secondary Classroom.* Englewood Cliffs, New Jersey: Prentice-Hall, Inc., 1959.

A marvelous methods textbook describing how to organize and conduct a core class democratically.

Chapter 8
The Social Studies

Someone has defined the social studies as a group of studies comprised of such subjects as history, geography, civics, anthropology, sociology, political science, problems of democracy, psychology, psychiatry, and sometimes philosophy and ethics, and called the social studies. Probably this definition is as good as any other, for the term *social studies* has never had a really firm, precise meaning. Nevertheless, in practice, the term is popular for it both distinguishes the social studies—the studies which describe the organization and development of human society and man as a member of social groups—from the social sciences, the studies by which men seek to discover the truth about human behavior and human relations. It also distinguishes elementary and secondary-school courses from college and university courses.

THE OBJECTIVES OF THE SOCIAL STUDIES

The over-all purpose of the social studies curriculum is to promote good citizenship and preserve the American way of life. At least, that seems to be the gist of the published objectives for the social studies, which can be summarized as: (1) to teach boys and girls the skills necessary for good human relationships at home, in the community, in the nation, and in the world at large; (2) to teach boys and girls how to think intelligently and how to face up to the problems of modern society both at home and abroad; (3) to help boys and girls to understand and appreciate the American way of life, its institutions, and their backgrounds; (4) to teach pupils the academic skills necessary for effective, efficient study of the social sciences and history; and (5) to inculcate attitudes and understandings necessary for good citizenship in a harried and changing world.

STATUS OF THE SOCIAL STUDIES CURRICULUM

Largely as a result of the recommendations of the Commission on the Reorganization of the High School in 1916, the social studies curriculum of the average American school system follows a cyclic or spiral system. The rationale behind this plan is that the pupils should be introduced to the various areas of the social studies during the elementary school years, and that the concepts the pupils learn in their early years should be developed and expanded by repeating the subjects in the junior and senior high schools at increasingly deeper and more complex levels.

Most frequently the courses in the cycles are:

First Cycle: Grade 4, Geography; Grade 5, American History; Grade 6, European Backgrounds.

Second Cycle: Grade 7, World Geography, or the Geography of one of the hemispheres; Grade 8, American History; Grade 9, Civics; Grade 10, World History.

Third Cycle: Grade 11, American History; Grade 12, Problems of Democracy.

The pattern, of course, has many variations. Table II will give the reader some notion of the great diversity of practice.

As a rule, junior high school social studies courses are constants, particularly in grades 7 and 8. Constant social studies courses are also the rule in the senior high school. United States History is usually required by state law, and world history and problems of democracy may be required to meet local graduation requirements. In the typical cur-

TABLE II. FREQUENTLY OFFERED SOCIAL STUDIES COURSES BY GRADES
(Most Common Courses Are Italicized)*

JUNIOR HIGH SCHOOL		
7th	8th	9th
World Geography	*American History*	*Civics*
American History–	American History–State	World Geography
Geography	History	World History
American History	American History–Civics	State History–Civics
Geography	American History–	Social Studies
State History–	Geography	
Geography	World Geography	
Social Studies		
State History		

SENIOR HIGH SCHOOL

10th	11th	12th
World History	American History	Problems of Democracy
American History	Economics	American Government
World Geography	Sociology	Sociology
World History—	World History	Economics
Geography	American History—	Psychology
Modern History	Government	American Government
	World Geography	Problems of Democracy
		World History

* Adapted from Willis D. Moreland, "Curriculum Trends in the Social Studies." Social Education, 26: 72–76, 102, February, 1962. This table represents only a sampling of the courses listed by Moreland.

riculum each pupil takes a social studies course in at least five of his six secondary-school years. In addition senior high schools often give electives in such subjects as Latin-American history, the history of the Far East, contemporary affairs, economic education, conservation, and commercial law.

THE INTEGRATED SOCIAL STUDIES COURSES

As a result of the long-range trend toward correlation and integration many courses in a modern program of studies are labeled "social studies" rather than by the name of any specific discipline. Some of these courses are fused courses composed of elements from several social studies; more often they are merely the history, geography, and civics courses of the past under an alias. In spite of changes in nomenclature, except for twelfth grade "problems" courses, few social studies courses represent an amalgamation of the disciplines.

Recently resistance to the trend toward fusion of the social studies has been stiffening. The following statement illustrates the type of thinking that seems to be gathering momentum in social studies circles.

> The premise underlying the core curriculum and various attempts at integrated social studies courses seems to be that a synthesis within history and between the social sciences is in existence. The problem of the teacher in integrated courses is to communicate this synthesis to students. . . . It is clear that synthesis even in the restricted area of American history has not been achieved. It is legitimate to infer that synthesis between the social sciences is even less an accomplished fact.
>
> The validity of courses which assume that junior and senior high school teachers can do what dedicated scholars have been unable to accomplish needs to be evaluated and questioned. Confronted with such a task, teachers can hardly be castigated for falling prey to oversimplification and easy generalization. This is certainly not true of all teach-

ers nor of all core curriculum or integrated courses. But the unvoiced queries of Part One provoke sober thoughts about the current trend toward integration in the social studies curriculum.[1]

This type of argument may have caused a cessation of formal fusion of social studies disciplines, but the trend to integrate and correlate continues, because teachers of history and other social studies remain convinced that one cannot teach history without correlating with other social studies.

CITIZENSHIP EDUCATION

Education for citizenship is a whole-school responsibility. Although this responsibility should be spread throughout the curriculum and extra-curriculum, ordinarily the brunt of the burden for *formal* citizenship education falls on two courses, Civics and Problems of Democracy, whose content most directly concerns political science and government.

THE NINTH GRADE CIVICS COURSE

About half of the secondary schools offer civics in grade 9. Basically the usual civics course is a study of government and the local community, but for most people the role of civics in the secondary-school curriculum has never been clarified. Lacking a specific content and purpose, civics has tended to become something of a catch-all for such extraneous subjects as group guidance, school orientation, and driver training. Possibly such additions may be legitimate, but on the whole they have served to discredit the course in the eyes of scholars and the public. Perhaps because of this reason, the course, never very popular, has been losing support.

PROBLEMS OF AMERICAN DEMOCRACY

Because no pupil could be expected to take courses in all of the social studies, in 1916 the Committee on the Social Studies of the Commission for the Reorganization of the Secondary Education recommended a course that would bring together aspects of sociology, economics, political science, and other pertinent social sciences and apply them to the social problems of the day. The modern twelfth grade course in Problems of American Democracy is the result of this recommendation.

Although they seldom make full use of the problem-solving approach, Problems of American Democracy courses often take their content from the problems and issues of contemporary life. If Liggitt is right, "the problems course for senior-high-school students is developing into an in-

[1] John H. Haefner in *Interpreting and Teaching American History,* Thirty-first Yearbook, National Council for the Social Studies (Washington, D.C.: The Council, 1961), p. 385.

tensive analysis of contemporary issues in which some knowledge of the principle of sociology, economics, and political science is required. In this respect the problems course is moving from a current events discourse to a scientific approach to study of national and world issues."[2]

The plan for the Winchester (Massachusetts) High School's Modern Problems course illustrates the type of course Liggitt had in mind. Instead of textbook learning, the Winchester course features "many special pamphlets, magazines, and books" and a great deal of individual and group research as well as discussion, report, speakers, films, and attendance at several outside meetings and conventions during the year. The topics included in the course all concern vital problems of contemporary society.

A WHOLE-SCHOOL RESPONSIBILITY

Citizenship education should be a major objective in all academic areas and the extra curriculum as well. It cannot be restricted to civics and problems of democracy courses or even to the social studies curriculum. The program of the Verde Valley School, a private college preparatory school in Sedona, Arizona, clearly shows how a school can mass all its resources to promote the development of good citizens. The Verde Valley program of studies[3] places unusually strong emphasis on citizenship, anthropology, ethics, and religion. Cultures and their contributions are stressed in all of the social studies courses and in courses of other fields as well.

Even more impressive than strong emphasis upon citizenship in the academic courses is the extent of pupil involvement in citizenship activities. These activities include a strong student government, club activities, assemblies, "international hours," religious meetings, field trips, work programs, and the assumption of positions of responsibility.

Most outstanding of all is the unusual and exciting field trip program in which, in addition to the familiar type of field trip to nearby places of interest, the pupils visit the Hopi and Navaho Indian Reservations for a week and spend their spring vacation period in Mexico. On these trips not only does the school give pupils opportunities to hear explanation of civic problems by civic leaders and officials, but on the Mexico trips the pupils actually spend a week living in Mexican homes. On both short and

---

[2] William A. Liggitt, *Concepts in History and Social Studies Instruction, Changes in the Past Fifteen Years* (Unpublished manuscript, Jersey City State College, 1961).

[3] The description of the Verde Valley School program is derived from the Verde Valley School Catalog, supplementary material furnished by the school, and a conversation with Mrs. Bret Harte, School Admission Officer and some of the pupils during the summer of 1961. Franklin Patterson has described the school's program in greater detail in *High Schools for a Free Society* (New York: The Free Press of Glencoe, 1960).

long trips the pupils do considerable intensive studying and pursue both individual and group projects and research pertinent to the area being visited.

In order that the pupils may learn to respect work of all kinds and to accept responsibility, each pupil works about the campus. Their jobs include more than the ordinary table-waiting and room cleaning associated with many boarding schools. Pupils actually participate in building construction, painting, repairing, and other necessary jobs.

All in all the program adds up to a most unusual effort to unite all the resources of a school toward civic education. It is in this direction that many educators hope all secondary-school citizenship teaching will go.

THE FUTURE OF CITIZENSHIP EDUCATION

In spite of notable exceptions, like that of Verde Valley School, the ordinary citizenship education program suffers because of several inadequacies:

1. The courses do not have the intellectual or civic depth desired.
2. The teachers and administrators tend to avoid the real issues, and so the citizenship program lacks vitality and validity.
3. The pupils do not have enough opportunity to practice democratic living either in school government or local affairs.
4. The citizenship education is primarily academic and does not have any real contact with community or national affairs.
5. Only history and government are emphasized. The contributions of anthropology, psychology, mental hygiene, and the other behavioral sciences are usually neglected, and the potentialities of extracurriculum as an agency for citizenship training are seldom fully exploited.
6. Citizenship education curricula are diluted by topics and courses dealing with peripheral or extraneous subject matter, such as orientation to school, driver training, safety education, and the evil effects of alcohol and narcotic drugs.

The future of citizenship education may be brighter than its past has been. Institutions and organizations, such as the Tufts Civic Education Center, The Eagleton Foundation, B'nai B'rith, the Commission on American Citizenship of the Roman Catholic Church, and several study groups, have sponsored, and are sponsoring, research and material development for building good citizenship, so that there is now a wealth of material concerning citizenship education available. Also individual high schools are introducing several promising new practices. Among them Franklin Patterson lists:

1. Intensive development of the Modern Problems course in the twelfth grade.

2. Utilization of elements of the newer social and behavioral sciences in the subject matter of high school studies.
3. Schedule and course reorganization, curriculum development, use of new teaching devices and approaches, and in-service study by the high school staff.
4. Using the summer session as a period for a special program of education in responsible citizenship, featuring subject matter in depth, experience in community and school service, and self-government.
5. Tapping, selectively and critically, the many resources outside of the high school which can be used for the improvement of citizenship education.
6. Taking part in a program of special emphasis on a basic aspect of public affairs and citizenship.
7. Creating additional and wider opportunities for youth to participate responsibly in the operation and management of the high school.
8. Using the homeroom as a home base for guidance, student government, and civics activities.
9. Finding ways to conduct field study that will widen horizons and deepen understanding of social, economic and political affairs.
10. Helping to provide practical experience in civic responsibility and community service.[4]

If developing good citizenship is as important as it seems to be, secondary schools should adopt practices of this type for the heart of their curricula.

HISTORY

STATUS AND TRENDS IN HISTORY COURSES

History is ordinarily offered three times in the secondary-school curriculum. American history is usually offered in grades 8 and 11, and world history in grade 10. At present history is the heart of the social studies curriculum.

Trends in the teaching of history parallel the trends in the social studies as a whole. One of the most apparent is the trend to integrate material from other social studies. New history courses are reaching out to include geography, economics, political science, the behavioral sciences, literature, and even the sciences. The movement away from fused courses toward discrete courses in the specific disciplines has not altered this trend toward integration.

Coincident with the trend toward integration and correlation is a trend toward making history more humane. No longer is the average history course merely a history of wars and political campaigns. History now touches the common people and the real problems of living, rather than

[4] Patterson, *op. cit.*, pp. 72–89.

being merely a matter of kings and queens, generals and politicians. The humane tendency is also reflected in the increased emphasis on biography.

Not only is history becoming more human, it is becoming more functional. Emphasis on recent history has increased, and at least lip service is given to the notion that history should be taught so as to illuminate the present. The hectic international situation and the changed role of many underprivileged areas have caused great pressures to make the scope of secondary-school history courses global. For the first time, the American social studies curriculum is recognizing that the Near Eastern history did not end with Cleopatra and that Latin-American history continued after the fall of the Aztecs.

Changes in the content of the history courses are being accompanied by changes of method. Instead of being memory courses, secondary-school courses are beginning to accentuate the methods of history and the use of history as a means for teaching pupils to think reflectively. To effect this change in content and goal, history teachers are increasing their use of problem-solving techniques. Among the specific methods teachers find effective for their new purposes are the use of pupil research, laboratory methods, and the writing of history by the pupils themselves.

If these trends hold true, they promise a dynamic future for history teaching in American secondary schools.

THE WORLD HISTORY COURSE

The world history course characteristic of the tenth grade is an outgrowth of the old two-year sequence of "Ancient History" and "Medieval and Modern European History" recommended by the Committee on the Social Studies in 1916. The sequence had to be shortened to make room for the courses in American history that most state legislatures have made mandatory and broadened to conform with the growing conviction that world history is not commensurate with the history of Western Europe, thus forcing the entire history of the world into a single course. Naturally, on this basis, world history courses have been hard to manage. Of late, they have become less popular.

The Problem of Time. Several attempts have been made to solve the problem of too much world history and too little time. One of these is what Keller calls postholing. Briefly the plan consists of studying certain periods or topics in depth and skipping the material in between. The thinking behind this approach is that because no course can possibly cover the entire subject, to teach a few topics well is better than to teach many topics superficially. Moreover, its proponents think that deep study of a few topics can be effective in teaching the method of historical study and the use of history and historical methodology in thinking. The goal in such courses is not the knowledge of content but the ability to think historically and to use historical content in thinking.

Another approach to the time problem in world history courses has been to make it a two-year course. The 1960 recommendation of the Connecticut State Department of Education illustrates the thinking behind this approach.

> . . . We feel the one-year World History Course is too superficial, and that a knowledge of world developments is essential. In spite of the fact that this is a two-year course, there will be very important delimitations. . . .[5]

Obviously a two-year sequence is none too long to do the job that the Connecticut committee envisages.

Trend to World Civilization Courses. The Watchung Hills (New Jersey) Regional High School World History course illustrates a growing trend to substitute world civilization for world history. This course not only attempts to bring together the social studies into an integrated study of a period, it also exemplifies the common trend toward emphasis on history as a humanity and the current effort to show history as it relates to all of human social activities. According to the course of study:

> . . . The course uses a somewhat conventional chronology of the development of Western Civilization with some attention to the Eastern Civilizations. The course is developed, however, not to teach chronological history, but to begin the development of a theoretical scheme for the analysis of human society. This theoretical scheme emphasizes the mutual relationships existing between the economic, political, and emotive spheres of action. The intention is that this scheme will be used in the later courses for the particular analysis of American Society.[6]

THE HISTORY OF THE UNITED STATES

In accordance with the spiral system, United States History is taught in both the junior high school and senior high school grades. Unfortunately the spiral has not worked very well. In far too many instances the junior high school course is little more than a weaker imitation of the senior high school course, which is itself an imitation of college courses in general American history. The result has often been boredom and disgust among the teachers and pupils.

Recommendations of 1944. In an attempt to eliminate this "outright duplication" in American history courses, the 1944 Committee on American History in Schools and Colleges recommended that in the junior high school American History course two thirds of the time be allotted to the

---

[5] Victor E. Pitkin, *Social Studies for Secondary Schools—Grades 7–12* (revised recommendation) (Hartford: Connecticut State Department of Education, November 7, 1960) pp. 1–5. (Mimeographed.)

[6] Social Studies Department, *New Curriculum,* Partial Revision (Watchung Hills, N.J.: Watchung Hills Regional High School, 1961), pp. 5–6. (Mimeographed.)

one hundred years from 1776 to 1876 and that the senior high school course, although covering the entire chronological period, give about one half of the course to the period since 1865.[7] In general, as a result of these recommendations, junior high school American history courses are oriented toward the events preceding and including the Civil War.

A Longer American History Sequence. Since 1944 several agencies have carried the foregoing recommendations a step further and recommended that American history be a planned two-year sequence. Such is the recommendation of the 1960–61 Committee on Curriculum Planning and Development of the National Association of Secondary-School Principals and the 1961 Yearbook of the National Council for the Social Studies. The sequence suggested by the latter consists of a pre-Civil War history course in grade 8, and a post-Civil War history course in grade 11, or a two-year block of United States History in grades 8–9, followed by elective courses for college-bound pupils in grades 11 and 12. Evidently sentiment for a longer sequence of this type is growing.

Costra County, California, has introduced an interesting course that illustrates not only the movement toward longer American history sequences, but also the trend toward correlating and integrating that is affecting American history courses as well as other social studies courses. This course

> . . . is designed to cover three terms of United States History in place of the usual two. This change was made to give our students a better understanding of the correlation between the history of the United States and the history of the world. The developments in world history are introduced at every point at which they form a pertinent background to the unfolding of the history of the United States. It was assumed that learning world history in relation to the history of the United States would give it more meaning than a separate course in World History.[8]

Despite variants like the Costra County plan, most courses in American history are based on a strictly chronological approach. Other courses are organized around a series of problems, themes, or topics, which are pursued historically. A few courses have been organized on an anti-chronological basis, that is to say, they begin with the present and go backward—counterclockwise, as it were.

In some courses units are centered around the study of a particular area in depth. Usually such a study can best be centered around the locality of the school. In a unit of this sort, boys and girls can actually dig into history in the raw and learn methods of historical research and

[7] Edgar B. Wesley, *American History in Schools and Colleges* (New York: The Macmillan Company, 1944), p. 71.

[8] Elizabeth R. Woodward, "Introduction," *Syllabus United States History with a World History Background, for Grades 9, 10* (Martinez, Calif.: Costra County Schools Office, 1959).

writing through the process of group and individual research. This innovation may also have the desirable outcome of making pupils aware of their own local history and possibly may make them history-conscious.

OTHER HISTORY COURSES

In addition to World History and American History some high schools offer a variety of other history courses. Usually these courses are elective and follow the pattern described in the discussion of World history and American history.

GEOGRAPHY

STATUS AND TRENDS IN GEOGRAPHY COURSES

Curriculum experts have said that history and geography are the heart of the social studies curriculum. If this statement is true, the secondary-school curriculum has heart trouble, for geography has been neglected to the point where it hardly appears at all in many senior high schools and has a firm grip on only one year—usually grade 7—in the junior high school. However, the evidence indicates that interest in geography at the secondary level is growing. There seems to be an increase in world geography courses at the tenth grade level and a trend toward including more geographic content in other social studies courses. The realities of the space age and the increasing need for international understanding have made geographic understanding a necessity.

As a rule, junior high schools require one year of geography. This course is likely to be either world geography or the geography of one of the hemispheres. In many states the tendency seems to lean toward the seventh grade course on the eastern hemisphere. By and large, however, the junior high school geography offerings in at least half of the states are in the words of Wilhelmina Hill "a mishmash."[9]

Recently geography, like history, has been humanized. No longer are geography courses just lists of places and physical characteristics; instead they stress cultural and human geography. Modern geographers think of geography as the history of the future and insist that it should be taught so as to throw light on the passing scene. To accomplish that end the modern geography course is becoming largely an attempt to show the relationships between the environment and man and his economic, political, social, and cultural life. Consequently some educators are finding it advantageous to turn to the regional and areal approaches to geography education.

[9] Wilhelmina Hill, *New Viewpoints in Geography* (speech delivered to New Jersey Council for Geographic Education, Jersey City, 1961).

NEW METHODS IN GEOGRAPHY

Like the history teachers, teachers of geography are changing their methods to include more laboratory and problem-solving methods. In some schools geography classes are taking to the field to actually see the geography and to practice geographic pursuits. More and more frequently boys and girls are learning how to read and understand maps by going out to map a bit of terrain. Depth is being introduced through the use of regional and area approaches and unit assignments, which induce considerable research and concentrated effort from the pupils. Guests from other lands and cultures, moving pictures, television, and firsthand reports by those who have visited the area are bringing the human element into the geography classroom.

If the new developments in geography curriculum and methods continue to gather impetus, geography may some day assume its rightful place in the secondary-school curriculum. But in spite of recent progress much needs to be done before the secondary-school geography offering in the typical American secondary school will be adequate for the need of modern society.

CONTEMPORARY STUDIES

THE NEGLECTED STUDIES

Trends toward modernizing and humanizing the social studies notwithstanding, the contemporary studies do not yet receive the emphasis they deserve. In part this neglect comes from the traditional infatuation with the past and the usual academic resistance to the introduction of new subjects, but mostly it comes from teachers' fears of becoming embroiled in controversy. And so we find that a large number of the areas vital to our boys and girls are closed to them in many schools of the United States. Among these closed areas Hunt and Metcalf[10] list economics, race and minority group relations, social class, sex, courtship and marriage, religion and morality, nationalism, patriotism, and national institutions. It is rather discouraging to note that this list of closed areas is almost identical with the list of neglected areas published by the National Education Association, Department of Superintendents, in its 1936 Yearbook.

It is even more discouraging to realize that many of the neglected areas are areas that earlier chapters point out as essential for the education of youth. Secondary-school social studies curricula will not be adequate until these areas are no longer closed to the pupils.

[10] Maurice P. Hunt and Lawrence C. Metcalf, *Teaching High School Social Studies* (New York: Harper and Row, 1955), pp. 230–231.

Vigorous support for vital teaching of controversial issues in social studies courses is essential. The statement in 1961 of the National Association of Secondary-School Principals is a reassuring step in the right direction.[11]

> Democracy is dependent upon the right of people to study and discuss issues freely. Equally important, it is dependent upon a citizenry which exercises its rights, which keeps well informed, searches actively for divergent points of view, evaluates courses of action in the light of available evidence and basic democratic values, and then acts responsibly on the basis of the decisions made. Such behaviors do not develop by accident; they are learned in the schools within the context of societal problems, many of which are controversial in nature.

TEACHING CURRENT EVENTS

Although current events occupies about one quarter of the social studies time, there are relatively few current events courses. Instead current events are usually taught during special periods in other social studies courses. Usually the current events instruction is completely divorced from the content of the parent course, for most teachers find integrating current events into the course almost impossible. As a result current events instruction frequently lacks structure and purpose. Too often it has deteriorated to meaningless, haphazard parroting of newspaper clippings or thoughtless reciting of the contents of weekly magazines.

SOCIOLOGY AND ANTHROPOLOGY

Sociology and anthropology are not often taught as separate subjects in the secondary schools. Sociology is sometimes found as an elective at the twelfth grade level, but only a small minority of high school pupils take it. Anthropology is seldom taught at all. Some sociology and anthropology is usually included in civics, problems of democracy, and integrated social studies courses, but not to the extent one might desire. Other social studies courses seldom give sociology and anthropology more than a passing reference. In a study in 1950 it was estimated that only 26 per cent of the 1100 schools studied included any sociology of any sort in any of the courses. Possibly this lack of support for sociology can be laid to the fact that much of the content of sociology deals with the controversial closed areas that teachers eliminate in order to avoid criticism. Whatever the cause, the omissions are unfortunate, for frequently what is left out is what really matters most to the individual and to society. In view of the urgency of the sociological problems out-

---

[11] "The Social Studies in the Comprehensive Secondary School," *The Bulletin of the National Association of Secondary-School Principals,* 45: 7–8, September, 1961.

lined in Chapter 4, such flagrant neglect of sociology and anthropology is shocking.

Perhaps the future will not be quite so dark. Elements of sociology and anthropology are being introduced into courses in world civilization and world culture. In a typical unit of the World Culture course recommended for grade 11 by the Pennsylvania Council for the Social Studies, the pupils study not only the geography and history of the country but also the people, their ethnic and racial composition, their language, their values and ideals, their institutions and their contemporary political, social, and economic problems.[12] In addition a certain amount of sociological content has been absorbed by the Problems of Democracy course commonly found in the twelfth grade. For example, one of the four main topics of the Pennsylvania twelfth grade course called Contemporary Problems at Home and Abroad is "sociology."

INTERNATIONAL RELATIONS IN THE SOCIAL STUDIES CURRICULUM

The tensions in the modern world and the growth of the United States from an insular power to the leader of the Western world has brought a greatly increased interest in international affairs into our schools. In some schools international relations is given as a separate elective course, although this practice is exceptional. In many schools considerable effort has been used to add material about international relations to geography, history, and citizenship courses. This movement has been aided by the fact that some civic and patriotic organizations, convinced of the need for international understanding, have sponsored extracurricular activities designed to promote understanding. Among the media used for promoting international understanding are United Nations assemblies, international days, visitors from foreign lands, exchange teachers, exchange students, and even foreign travel. Interschool conferences, such as the United Nations Model Assembly sponsored by Hillyer College of the University of Hartford, and the High School UNESCO Council of New York City, also bring the importance of international affairs home to the pupils. Considerable pamphlet material, such as the Foreign Relations Series of the Foreign Relations Project sponsored by the North Central Association of Secondary Schools and Colleges, has also been made available for social studies classes in international relations.

ECONOMIC EDUCATION

As with sociology, economics courses are rare. When they are offered, they are likely to be half-year elective courses for seniors. Sometimes

[12] Pennsylvania Council for the Social Studies, *A Recommended Curriculum for the Social Studies for the Secondary Schools* (University Park: The Association, 1961), p. 58.

economics courses are offered in the business and commercial curricula. Problems of Democracy and other social studies courses frequently include economics content. So do courses in homemaking and mathematics. On the whole, these economics courses and economics topics in other courses are largely superficial presentations from the consumer point of view. As a result many American adults are economically illiterate.

To remedy the situation, educational groups in recent years have taken strong measures to awaken economic education. Among the groups that have developed curriculum and teaching materials and supported workshops and other curricular development projects are the Joint Council on Economic Education, The National Committee for Education in Family Finance, and the Commission for the Advancement of Secondary Education. In general, these groups have tried to promote the teaching of economics through existing courses rather than by adding further courses in economics.

In the fall of 1961 the National Task Force of Economic Education issued a particularly forceful report on economic education.[13] In the report the committee takes the position that a reasonable understanding of economics is essential for citizenship. Rather than a superficial covering of complex elaborate theories and concepts, the commission emphasizes "the understanding of a few essential concepts and a few major economic institutions, plus an understanding of how these fit together in the functioning of an economy." Above all they emphasize the need for replacing unreasoned judgment by objective rational analysis and "teaching that leads students to examine and think through economic problems for themselves." Their specific proposals for bringing about these understandings follow.[14]

1. That more time be devoted in school curricula to development of economic understanding. In particular:

   (a) That wherever feasible, students take a course in economics or its equivalent under another title, such as Problems of American Democracy, in high school; and that in all high schools of substantial size there be at least an elective senior year course in economics.

   (b) That where economics is not required, courses in problems of American democracy (now taken by approximately half of all high school students) devote a substantial portion of their time to developing economic understanding.

   (c) That more economic analysis be included in history courses, which are taken by nearly all students.

---

[13] Committee on Economic Education, *Economic Education in the Schools*, A Report of the National Task Force on Economic Education (New York: The Committee, 711 Fifth Avenue, 1961).

[14] Committee on Economic Education, *op. cit.*, p. 13.

(d) That business education curricula include a required course in economics.

(e) That development of economic understanding be emphasized at other advantageous points throughout the entire school curriculum, beginning in the lower grades.

2. That major emphasis be placed on an objective, rational way of thinking about economic problems, as well as on knowledge of fundamental economic institutions and concepts for analyzing economic issues.

3. That objective examination of controversial issues be included in the teaching of economics, as an important part of helping students develop the ability to reach their own conclusions on important social problems; and that school boards, administrators and the public support the right of students to this educational experience.

Undoubtedly economics competencies are just as necessary as the three R's. Boys and girls need to learn both societal and personal economics. How the problem of teaching economic literacy can best be tackled is unsettled. At present considerable opinion favors the use of deep research type of economic units in existing social studies courses.

PSYCHOLOGY AND PSYCHIATRY

Someday perhaps psychology and psychiatry may become the queens of the social sciences. So far that time has not come in the secondary schools. Nevertheless, psychology has made an entree into the secondary-school curriculum and seems to be having a slow but steady growth. At present psychology courses can be found in more than 8 per cent of the schools, usually as a twelfth grade elective. Some resistance to psychology has been made on the ground that it represents soft pedagogy, but the objection seems to be misplaced. As the country continues to become more psychology- and psychiatry-conscious, probably psychology courses will become increasingly popular.

NEW MOVEMENTS IN THE SOCIAL STUDIES

THE CONANT REPORT

The social studies has not felt the effect of the various educational reform movements as much as some of the other subject areas have, but they have not been immune to the new unrest and lately have been faced with a rash of new proposals.

Among the most influential reports concerning the secondary schools are the Conant reports on the high school and the junior high school.[15]

[15] James B. Conant, *Education in the Junior High School Years, op. cit.; The American High School Today* (New York: McGraw-Hill Book Company, Inc., 1959).

In these reports Dr. Conant has recommended that social studies be required in both grades 7–8 and three or four years of the grades from 9–12. In grade 7, and perhaps grade 8, Conant seems to favor an English–social-studies block of time,[16] but he very specifically rules out endorsing the unified studies or core approach, which he considers to be controversial. For the grades 9–12 he recommends "two years of history (one of which should be American history) and a senior course in American problems or American government."[17] Each class in the senior course would be a cross section of the school, in which pupils would discuss freely current topics and controversial issues.

Dr. Conant's personal and professional reputation give considerable weight to his recommendations. How much change will result from them is still problematic.

RECENT RECOMMENDATIONS AND PROPOSALS

Since 1959 a spate of new proposals for teaching the social studies have appeared. In general, these proposals advocate five- or six-year sequences of social studies constants in the secondary school carefully articulated with the elementary school social studies sequence. Among the suggested sequences, in spite of recent declarations in favor of the teaching of the disciplines separately, one finds a marked tendency to favor broad courses, such as the *Introduction to the Social Science* recommended by Keller, which includes carefully selected aspects of sociology, anthropology, political science, and economics,[18] and courses in World Cultures. Other characteristics typical of recent proposals are increased emphasis on discovery techniques, a tendency to posthole, and an increased emphasis on geography and the contemporary subjects. The following sequences suggested by a committee of the National Association of Secondary School Principals in 1961 illustrate the kinds of patterns being suggested for the social studies curricula of the future.

Illustration One

Grades 7 and 8:	American history to 1870; local, state, and federal government and United States geography.
Grades 9 and 10:	World geography and world history, both courses organized according to culture areas.
Grades 11 and 12:	United States history (since 1870, with a brief overview of the history prior to 1870) and modern problems.

[16] Conant, *The American High School Today, op. cit.*, p. 22.
[17] *Ibid.*, p. 47.
[18] Charles R. Keller, "Needed: Revolution in the Social Studies," *Saturday Review*, 44: 60–62, September, 1961.

Illustration Two

Grades 7 and 8: (first semester)	Broad field, geographic-centered, socioeconomic units on key and representative regions and nations of the world.
Grade 8: (second semester)	The citizen and his local, state, and national government (functions, relationships, structures, and agencies featured).
Grade 9: (first semester)	Introduction to the understanding of peoples and their institutions (major anthropological and sociological concepts).
Grade 9: (second semester) and Grade 10:	History of selected eras, peoples, areas, and nations of the world with full attention to contemporary aspects and problems.
Grade 11:	United States history and government (with important economic units).
Grade 12:	Contemporary problems that challenge the citizen (limited to 6 to 10 live issues—political, economic, and social, local to international in scope).

Illustration Three

Grade 7:	World vistas—history of the peoples of Eurasia and Africa.
Grade 8:	History of the United States to 1876.
Grade 9:	A. History of a state. B. American government and citizenship—national, state, and local.
Grade 10:	History of the United States since 1876.
Grade 11:	World cultures—Western and non-Western.
Grade 12:	Contemporary problems at home and abroad.[19]

RESEARCH AND DEVELOPMENT PROJECTS

The inauguration of Project Social Studies by the federal government in early 1963, and similar research and development programs by other agencies, will undoubtedly lead to lively experimentation and renovation of the social studies curriculum. Like other government projects, Project Social Studies is designed to help improve curriculum and methods of teaching. It provides funds for three types of activities: (1) basic and applied research projects; (2) curriculum study centers; and (3) research development activities. At the curriculum study centers attempts are being made (a) to redefine the nature and aims of the

[19] *Ad Hoc Committee,* National Association of Secondary-School Principals, "Social Studies in the Comprehensive School," *The Bulletin of the National Association of Secondary-School Principals,* 45: 6–7, September, 1961.

curriculum, (b) to develop instructional methods and materials that will achieve specific aims, (c) to experiment with, evaluate, and revise the newly developed methods and materials, and (d) to disseminate the most promising methods and materials to interested groups.[20] Similar goals are shared by other projects and studies in the separate social studies subjects. Representatives of these are such projects as the *National Task Force on Economic Education, The High School Geography Project, The Anthropology Curriculum Study Project,* and *Improving the Teaching of World Affairs.* Already these and similar projects, which now embrace almost all the social studies areas, have developed and tried out excellent new curriculum guides, texts, pamphlets, and other materials for classroom use.[21]

PROGRAMS FOR THE TALENTED PUPILS

Recent years have brought about an increased interest in programs for the academically gifted boys and girls. In the social studies, as in the other academic fields, one finds both programs of enrichment and of acceleration in homogeneously and heterogeneously grouped classes. Probably because of the emphasis on citizenship education associated with the social studies, pressures to "track and accelerate" the social studies have not been as great as in other subject fields. Nevertheless, some secondary schools make provisions whereby boys and girls may move through social studies more quickly than normally and so qualify either for early entrance or advanced placement in college. By far the more popular of the two is the advanced placement program.

ENRICHMENT PROGRAMS

Provisions for the talented in the social studies usually take some form of enrichment program. Enrichment can be provided in many ways. Some schools provide opportunities for pupils to enrich their programs by conducting research projects or honors papers either in addition to or instead of a portion of the regular curriculum. In some schools, like Evanston Township High School and New York City schools, honors classes are provided for pupils gifted in the social studies. Other schools provide elective and seminar courses that pupils may elect in order to stretch their talents. And of course the brilliant student can also find an outlet for his talents in extracurricular activities. Particularly interest-

[20] Commission on Current Curriculum Developments, *Using Current Curriculum Developments* (Washington, D.C.: Association for Supervision and Curriculum Development, 1963), p. 78; also Gerald R. Smith, "Project Social Studies—A Report," *School Life,* 45: 25–27, July, 1963.

[21] *Ibid.,* pp. 71–85.

ing for the talented social studies students are the interschool conferences and junior historian programs.[22]

RECOMMENDED PROGRAM FOR THE TALENTED

In a joint statement the National Education Association and the
National Council for the Social Studies laid out a list of fundamental
considerations to guide schools in preparing social studies sequences for
the academically talented.[23] Utilizing their own principles, the writers of
the bulletin recommended a revised sequence for grades 9–10 for the
academically talented.[24] Characteristic of the programs designed for the
academically talented are a tendency to feature problem solving and
integration of subject matter. This tendency seems to be true of suggestions coming from educators of both traditional and progressive
persuasion. Evidently social studies courses of the future will combine
stress on the traditional disciplines with the integrated problem-solving
approach advocated by the progressivists. If so, the future of the social
studies curriculum promises to be interesting and exciting.

SUMMARY

Despite recent demands for return to the traditional disciplines, the
various subjects included under the rubric social studies continue in their
trend toward integrating and correlating with each other and with other
subjects. Nevertheless, the subjects are seldom amalgamated into integrated social studies courses. More often the trend is expressed by the
increasing use of problem-solving techniques and the incorporation of
subject matter from other disciplines in discrete courses in history and the
various social sciences.

The major aims of social studies curricula are to promote good citizenship and to preserve the American way of life. While all subjects share
the responsibility for this citizenship goal, the brunt of the load falls on
civics and problems of democracy. On the whole this arrangement has
not been satisfactory, and experts believe that only a total school approach
to citizenship education, like that being pioneered at the Verde Valley
School, can be really effective in creating the attitudes and understandings
needed by American citizens of the future.

History has been the heart of the secondary-school social studies cur-

[22] Milton M. Klein, "High School Programs," *The Social Education of the Academically Talented* (Washington, D.C.: National Council for the Social Studies,
1958), Ch. 7.

[23] Milton M. Klein, *Social Studies for the Academically Talented Student in the
Secondary School* (Washington, D.C.: National Council for the Social Studies, 1960),
pp. 22–25.

[24] *Ibid.*, pp. 27–30.

riculum. Whether it will continue to be so is doubtful, for geography and the contemporary studies are clamoring for a place in the sun. In general, all history courses have been plagued with the problem of too much material and too little time. American history courses have suffered particularly from the cyclic or spiral curriculum introduced in 1916, which has led to much duplication of course work in the junior high school, high school, and collegiate grades. To correct the many deficiencies caused by these problems, authorities have recommended two-year sequential courses in both world and American history, and postholing schemes whereby some topics are studied in depth and others either skimmed or skipped altogether.

Geography, sociology, anthropology, economics, psychology, and other contemporary subjects are neglected in the secondary-school curriculum. Geography is rarely taught more than one year in the junior high school, and the other subjects often receive little more than passing mention in civics, problems of democracy, history, and geography courses. In the future the emphasis on these subjects may change. Numerous groups are taking steps to introduce much more adequate instruction in these areas, particularly in international relations and economics.

Several plans for realigning the social studies curriculum have been put forth. In general, they advocate an expanded social studies curriculum featuring laboratory, problem-solving, research type of activities and increased emphasis on the methods and uses of social science and the contemporary subjects. Similar programs are suggested for the talented, but with more opportunity for enriched experiences through individual effort.

SUGGESTED READINGS

AD HOC COMMITTEE, NATIONAL ASSOCIATION OF SECONDARY-SCHOOL PRINCIPALS. "Social Studies in the Comprehensive School," *The Bulletin of the National Association of Secondary-School Principals,* 45: 1–17, September, 1961.

A statement concerning the role of the social studies in secondary education endorsed by the National Association of Secondary-School Principals.

AMERICAN COUNCIL OF LEARNED SOCIETIES DEVOTED TO HUMANISTIC STUDIES, and THE NATIONAL COUNCIL FOR SOCIAL STUDIES. *The Social Studies and the Social Sciences.* New York: Harcourt, Brace and World, Inc., 1962.

A joint project in which scholars discuss the curricular goals of the various social studies disciplines and area studies. The final chapter discusses the need for revision in the social studies and suggests the direction in which revision should go.

ANDERSON, HOWARD R. (ed.). *Approaches to an Understanding of World Affairs.* Twenty-fifth Yearbook of the National Council for the Social Studies. Washington, D.C.: The Council, 1954.

An important yearbook on the teaching of "International Relations," Chapter 17 has direct reference to the secondary-school curriculum.

ASSOCIATION FOR SUPERVISION AND CURRICULUM DEVELOPMENT. *Educating for Economic Competence.* Washington, D.C.: The Association, 1960.

Proposals for the better teaching of economics in the schools.

ASSOCIATION FOR SUPERVISION AND CURRICULUM DEVELOPMENT. *Using Current Curriculum Developments.* Washington, D.C.: The Association, 1963.

Chapter 8 is especially helpful to the teacher of social studies.

CALIFORNIA STATE CURRICULUM COMMISSION. *Report of the State Central Committee on Social Studies.* Sacramento: California State Department of Education, 1961.

Proposals for developing the social studies around central themes. An important curriculum study.

CARTWRIGHT, WILLIAM H., and RICHARD L. WATSON (eds.). *Interpreting and Teaching American History.* Thirty-first Yearbook of the National Council for the Social Studies. Washington, D.C.: The Council, 1961.

A yearbook primarily concerned with the content of American history. Part II, Chapters 20–24 deal with American history in the modern secondary-school curriculum.

CHIRKIS, CARL, and THERESA HELD. "Translating Social Studies Concepts Into Action," *The Bulletin of the National Association of Secondary-School Principals,* 45: 85–90, September, 1961.

A description of an experiment in citizenship education in a Brooklyn, N.Y., high school.

DEL DUCA, LUANNE, and DANIEL JACOBSON. "The Status of Geography in the Secondary Schools of New Jersey," *The Journal of Geography,* 61: 104–109, March, 1962.

A report of a survey of geography teaching in a "better than average" state which finds it's lacking.

EVERETT, SAMUEL, and CHRISTIAN O. ARNDT (eds.). *Teaching World Affairs in American Schools.* New York: Harper and Row, Inc., 1956.

A study of promising practices in the area of teaching world affairs. Contains accounts of many excellent innovations. Chapters 2 and 3 particularly concern the junior and senior high school curriculum.

FRANZEN, CARL G. F. "Why Geography?" *The Bulletin of the National Association of Secondary-School Principals,* 45: 127–131, February, 1961.

A plea for a course in global geography in the ninth grade and subject-centered study of the various social studies disciplines.

FRASER, DOROTHY MC CLURE, and EDITH WEST. *Social Studies in Secondary-School Curriculum and Method.* New York: The Ronald Press Company, 1961.

A textbook in social studies methods and curriculum. Chapters 21 and 22 describe the development of the present social studies curriculum and present trends and controversies.

GROSS, RICHARD E., LESLIE D. ZELENY, *et al. Educating Citizens for Democracy.* New York: Oxford University Press, 1958.

A book of articles on the social studies curriculum as education for democratic citizenship. Articles cover the curriculum in the various disciplines in the social studies and different approaches toward teaching them.

HANVEY, ROBERT G. "Raising the Standard of Learning in the Social Studies," *Social Education*, 27: 137–140, March, 1963.

A call for a renaissance in the social studies and a suggestion for attaining such a renaissance.

HIGH, JAMES. *Teaching Secondary School Social Studies.* New York: John Wiley and Sons, Inc., 1962.

An excellent basic text in the teaching of the social studies.

HUNT, ERLING M. (ed.). *High School Social Studies Perspective.* Boston: Houghton Mifflin Company, 1962.

A discussion of the role and content of the various social studies disciplines and areas by specialists in the subjects.

HUNT, MAURICE P., and LAWRENCE E. METCALF. *Teaching High School Social Studies.* New York: Harper and Row, Inc., 1955. Part II.

A controversial proposal for making the social studies really meaningful. Part II takes the position that the social studies, not history, should be the heart of the curriculum.

JOHNS, EUNICE (ed.). *Social Studies in the Senior High Schools: Programs for Grades Ten, Eleven and Twelve.* Washington, D.C.: The National Council for Social Studies, 1953.

Discussions of the place of social studies in the secondary school and means for improving them. Includes samples of excellent programs.

JOHNSON, EARL S. *Theory and Practice of the Social Studies.* New York: The Macmillan Company, 1956.

An excellent textbook describing the social studies curriculum and its background.

KLEIN, MILTON M. *Social Studies for the Academically Talented Student in Secondary Schools.* Washington, D.C.: National Education Association, 1960.

A report describing excellent programs designed for talented pupils.

MAAS, HENRY S. "The Role of Members in Clubs of Lower-Class and Middle-Class Adolescents," *Child Development*, 25: 241–251, December, 1954.

A report of data concerning the influence of class on pupils' perception and acceptance of their role in clubs.

NATIONAL COUNCIL FOR THE SOCIAL STUDIES. *A Guide to Contents in the Social Studies.* Washington, D.C.: The Council, 1958. The Association's guidelines and themes for social studies courses.

———. "The Role of the Social Studies," *Social Education*, 26: 315–318, October, 1962.

A statement by a committee of the National Council for the Social Studies setting purposes of teaching the social studies with special emphasis on the systematic development of skills.

NATIONAL TASK FORCE ON ECONOMIC EDUCATION. *Economic Education in the Schools.* New York: Council for Economic Development, 711 Fifth Avenue, 1961.

Proposals for rejuvenating the teaching of economics in the school. An influential report.

PATTERSON, FRANKLIN, *et al. The Adolescent Citizen.* New York: The Free Press of Glencoe, 1960.

A report based on study of citizenship and youth development in secondary education conducted by the Tufts University Civic Education Center. The book discusses citizenship education in the schools as it now exists and examines pertinent social research to deduce ways for building citizenship in the future. Important and scholarly.

—— (ed.). *Citizenship and a Free Society.* Thirtieth Yearbook of the National Council for the Social Studies. Washington, D.C.: The Council, 1960.

A detailed study of the problems of citizenship and citizenship education in the modern world.

——. *High Schools for a Free Society.* New York: The Free Press of Glencoe, 1960.

An important study of citizenship education with suggestions for its improvement.

PAYNE, JOHN C. (ed.). *The Teaching of Contemporary Affairs.* Twenty-first Yearbook of the National Council for the Social Studies. Washington, D.C.: The Council, 1951.

Parts III and VII have particular pertinence to the secondary-school social studies curriculum.

PENNSYLVANIA COUNCIL FOR THE SOCIAL STUDIES. *A Recommended Curriculum in the Social Studies for the Secondary Schools.* University Park: The Council, 1961.

An excellent reworking of the secondary-school social studies curriculum which deserves careful study and consideration.

SIEMERS, ALLAN A. "A National Social Studies Curriculum," *Social Education,* 24: 305–306, November, 1960.

A report of a survey which seems to indicate teacher sentiment in favor of a national social studies curriculum.

VINCENT, WILLIAM S., et al. *Building Better Programs in Citizenship Education.* New York: The Citizenship Education Project, Teachers College, Columbia University, 1958.

A guide for implementing workable programs for citizenship education.

WESLEY, EDGAR B., and STANLEY P. WRONSKI. *Teaching Social Studies in High Schools.* Fourth edition. Boston: D. C. Heath and Company, 1958. Parts I and V.

A standard text on social studies teaching. Chapters deal with each of the social studies.

Chapter 9

The English
Language Arts

The English language arts occupy the central position in the American secondary-school curriculum. In almost every one of our states pupils must take courses in English up through the eleventh or twelfth grade. Thus nine tenths of all high school pupils are enrolled in courses in the English language arts. No other academic subject enjoys such a favored position. The nearest competitor, the social studies, enrolls only about two thirds of the pupils in high schools.

In spite of its favored position in the curriculum, the English language arts curriculum has been the target of criticism from all sides. Not the least of the critics is the National Council of Teachers of English who report that "the teaching of English in this country is far less effective than it should be" and "that too many students are struggling to learn English under greatly inferior conditions." Evidently the English language arts program is due for a major overhauling.[1]

THE SCOPE OF THE ENGLISH LANGUAGE ARTS

Some of the dissatisfaction with the English language arts curriculum stems from its tremendous scope. Basically it consists of four areas, reading, writing, speaking, and listening. Broken down, each of these areas confronts one with a wide list of subareas. A typical English lan-

---

[1] National Council of Teachers of English, *The National Interest and the Teaching of English* (Champaign, Ill.: The Council, 1961), p. 15.

guage arts study guide might include such topics as spelling, punctuation, grammar, diction, semantics, description, narration, play production, expository writing, argumentation, creative writing, vocabulary, reading, listening, poetry, essays, drama, the novel, biographies, autobiographies, literary history, public speaking, corrective speech, oral reading, oral reporting, observation, discussion, voice and articulation, logic, parliamentary procedure, use of the library, radio, television, note taking, study skills, and so on. Truly the modern language arts program reaches into a wide variety of areas.

GOALS FOR THE ENGLISH LANGUAGE ARTS CURRICULUM

The statement of the Goals for Students Attainment prepared by the *Ad Hoc* Committee on English Language Arts in the Comprehensive Secondary School of the National Association of Secondary-School Principals further illustrates the wide range that is expected of the English language arts curriculum. According to this statement the important outcome for students of English should be:

1. Ease, accuracy, and fluency in speaking;
2. Inclination and ability to listen attentively and critically;
3. Growth in reading ability;
4. Growth in interpreting and appreciating literature;
5. Knowledge of the structure of the English language;
6. Habit of using English appropriately;
7. Ability to write clearly, concisely, and honestly;
8. Ability and habit of writing legibly;
9. Knowledge of reference sources and skill in using them effectively.[2]

The expectations of the committee seem hardly moderate, but they are typical of what is demanded of language arts teaching.

TO BE OR NOT TO BE

The scope and range of the language arts curriculum has been so vague that some experts do not believe that separate language arts courses have a place in the curriculum. Rather they recommend that the language arts be fused with other subjects, as in the common English–social-studies block-of-time course. Curriculum experts of this persuasion argue that the English language arts have no content of their own. Hence they believe that it would be more efficient to teach boys and girls to read, write, speak, and listen in social studies and science courses rather than in separate courses in English.

[2] *Ad Hoc* Committee on English Language Arts in the Comprehensive Secondary School, *The Bulletin of the National Association of Secondary-School Principals*, 44: 49, October, 1960.

The argument has much merit. Attempts to teach language skills alone in artificial periods of 45 minutes a day are doomed before they start. Besides, the assignments in English and other courses often overlap, as English teachers try to inject content into their assignments and as the teachers of other courses make greater use of reports, discussion, and other language activities.

On the other hand, everyone's business is no one's business. No matter what the clichés say, all teachers do not teach English. Moreover, English teachers maintain that the English language arts do have a content peculiarly their own. That content is literature, language, and composition. In particular, the National Council of Teachers of English insists that developing the essential skills for reading literature sufficiently justifies separate courses in English.[3]

But these arguments have not fully settled the battle. Much literature, particularly literary history, can be taught effectively in social studies contexts—so also can much of language and composition. Linguistics can quite logically be considered a social science, and, of course, composition is a *sine qua non* in all of the academic disciplines. In spite of the varying pronouncements the verdict in unified studies versus English courses is still Not Proven.

HISTORICAL DEVELOPMENT OF THE ENGLISH LANGUAGE ARTS

The modern English language arts curriculum rates itself among the aristocrats of secondary-school subjects. But in spite of its aristocratic pedigree, English has had a hard time establishing itself among the hierarchy of major subjects. The Latin Grammar School had little place for the vernacular, and even in the academy the English language was not always quite respectable academically.

In the nineteenth century teachers concentrated on separate courses in literature, rhetoric, grammar, and various other language arts. Literature study was primarily linguistic, grammatical, and rhetorical analysis. Most of the composition was devoted to literary topics. Formal grammar was minutely and thoroughly taught, with careful drill on forms, cases, and grammatical laws. Little attention was given to the uses of language in life and living. Evidently the teachers felt that if they could drum the rules of grammar, rhetoric, and logic into pupils' heads they had done all they could be expected to do and that the use of the language in ordinary life situations could take care of itself.

The modern broad field course in the English language arts, combining literature, reading, grammar, composition, and other facets of the subject,

---

[3] Commission on the English Curriculum of the National Council of Teachers of English, *The English Language Arts in the Secondary School* (New York: Appleton-Century-Crofts, Inc., 1956), p. 179.

is a product of the current century and the drift toward integration of subject matter described in earlier chapters.

Studies of the English curricula of Wisconsin and Georgia illustrate the type of courses that have resulted from this shift. In Georgia, for instance, we find that in spite of great differences in curriculum practice the English curriculum typically consists of grammar and usage, 21 per cent; writing, 11 per cent; reading and literature, 21–25 per cent; speaking, 6–10 per cent; spelling and vocabulary, 6–10 per cent; and listening, 1–5 per cent.[4]

PLACEMENT OF LANGUAGE ARTS CONTENT

TWO MAJOR PRINCIPLES

In 1952 a National Council of Teachers of English commission stated flatly that the English curriculum must be developed in the light of two major principles. These principles are:

1. Development of language power is an integral part of the total pattern of the child's growth. [Because the growth is a] continuous process, [and because] each child grows at his own pace . . . a curriculum based on a sound scientific inquiry must therefore recognize that a set level of achievement and mastery of a single prescribed content for all individuals within a given grade are impossible of attainment and do violence to the facts of growth.

2. [Pupils need to develop] language power in the social situation in which it is used. Language power is not something in the back of one's head which he thinks long enough: it is the ability to think and to act in the right way at the right moment, and is developed only through a long series of experiences in trying to act in the appropriate way in a similar situation. . . . skill in a particular way of using language is acquired only through frequent participation in the social activity in which it is involved.[5]

Although these principles suggest a fluid approach to the teaching of language, the exigencies of contemporary curricular organizations seem to require that specific subject matter content be allocated to the various grades in order to insure orderly subject matter sequences.

THE JUNIOR HIGH SCHOOL PROGRAM

Units in the junior high school curriculum may be centered around literature, grammar, composition, or speech or listening activities. Fre-

[4] Paul Farmer and Bernice Freeman, *Teaching of English in Georgia* (Georgia Council of Teachers of English, 1952) cited in Chester W. Harris, editor, Encyclopedia of Educational Research (New York: The Macmillan Company, 1960), p. 459.

[5] National Council of Teachers of English, *The English Language Arts* (New York: Appleton-Century-Crofts, Inc., 1952), pp. 12–14.

quently, but by no means always, junior high school units center around some theme, need, or interest. Usually when units are theme-centered they are also literature-centered, with certain definite content in grammar, usage, composition, and punctuation woven into the unit objectives and procedures. Orientation is an important goal of the junior high school, so that frequently junior high school language arts curricula include units whose purpose is to better acquaint the pupil with his school, its facilities, and their use. Orientation units may include work on study habits, use of the library, school customs and regulations, and other topics that should help pupils make the most of their new school.[6]

The most common procedure in junior high school courses is to include units of several types as in the seventh grade course in Louisville, Kentucky, in which we find the following units:

A Day of Discovery (Orientation)
The Simple Sentence
Write It Well
Growing Up in America
Verbs
Nouns and Pronouns
Boys and Girls of Other Lands
Write That Letter
In Days of Old
Telling How and Why
Enjoying Animals
Modifiers
Laughs, Pranks, and Surprises
Happy Holidays.[7]

Seventh grade units commonly center on animals, sports, adventure, mystery, humor, folklore, and other topics that are exciting to young people and pertinent to the personal problems of growing up. In the eighth grade American life and literature is a typical offering because of the common concern for American history at this level. English language arts units in Grade 9 are more likely to center around the problems of youth and of community and family living. At this grade level also, units centered around literary types become more prevalent.

On the whole, junior high school composition activities are designed to be functional. Among them one finds letter writing; report writing; note taking; taking dictation; completing forms; writing announcements, explanations, minutes, digests, and summaries; and news writing; as well as such literary efforts as writing original stories, sketches, essays, reviews,

[6] Arno Jewett, English Language Arts in American High Schools, U.S. Department of Health, Education, and Welfare, Office of Education, Bulletin 1958, November 13 (Washington, D.C.: Government Printing Office, 1959), Ch. 6, p. 57.

[7] Curriculum Guide, *Language Arts, Junior High School Grades 7–8–9* (Louisville, Kentucky: Office of Curriculum, Louisville Public Schools, October, 1958), pp. 23–29.

diaries, and autobiographical materials. Speech activities hold a prominent place in the junior high school language arts activities, and frequently skills in listening are taught in conjunction with these activities. Typical activities include discussion, conversation, speeches, storytelling, the conducting of meetings, the use of the telephone, dramatics, how to give instructions, making reports, conducting interviews, making announcements, and forming panels.

THE SENIOR HIGH SCHOOL PROGRAM

The senior high school curriculum is much more traditional than that of the junior high school. In grade 10 the literary unit is very common. Some schools devote the grade 10 to world literature, but this movement has not yet become popular. Perhaps the tenth grade course will move toward theme-centered units as the junior high school curriculum has done. In the eleventh grade American literature still remains popular, but English literature no longer dominates the twelfth grade. Where it is offered, English literature is likely to be either an elective or a required course for college-preparatory pupils rather than a course required for all. Other courses found in the twelfth grade include world literature and literature-centered courses based upon either themes of literary types. Because many schools do not require English language arts in grade 12, often the grade 12 English offering is an elective.

Composition in the senior high school seems to be a little less functional than that in the junior high school. Letters, social and business, are commonplace, but so also are writing verse, anecdotes, personal narratives, advertisements, editorials, personal essays, stories, and similar experiences in creative writing. Proofreading is also emphasized frequently. Many high schools place considerable emphasis on the preparation of a research paper, particularly for the college-bound students. As far as oral-aural types of activities are concerned, the senior high school courses seem to be much like those in the junior high school.

TRENDS IN THE ENGLISH LANGUAGE ARTS

Introduction of Reading and Listening. Much of the English language arts curriculum has remained static over the last quarter century and more. Still, several trends and movements can be detected to show that English language arts instruction is not entirely dormant.[8]

The most startling of the changes is the introduction of developmental reading programs into the secondary-school grades. Until recently reading classes were very rare in the secondary schools. Now developmental programs have become common in the junior high school and have been

[8] Jewett, *op. cit.*

introduced into some senior high schools. All appearances indicate that this is a trend that will continue to grow.[9]

During the past quarter century listening also has become part of the English language arts curriculum. Almost as a corollary to the increase in instruction in listening activities is a growth in instruction concerning mass media. That this should be so is only proper and natural when one considers the growth of radio and television, the plethora of magazines and newspapers, and the ubiquitous advertisements that reach out to influence American minds. Partly as a result of these influences, the English language arts curricula are becoming increasingly concerned with critical thinking and propaganda analysis and in some cases elementary semantics and the nature of language.

Increasing Adoption of Unit Methods. Instruction in English language arts seems to be moving toward unit methods. In the units, which seem to be more frequently centered around themes or ideas than around literary types or grammatical topics, teachers weave together reading, writing, speaking, and listening activities into integrated wholes rather than teach them in isolation. Frequently, in keeping with the concerns of modern educational theory, language arts units have taken on a considerable guidance emphasis and a new stress on the rights and duties of citizenship and knowledge and understanding of peoples of other lands and cultures.[10]

Attention to Scope and Sequence. One of the more promising developments in English language arts curricula has been an increased concern by curriculum makers for the scope and sequence of the entire language arts program. This movement has been marked particularly by increased attention to the problem of vertical articulation and the smooth development of the various language arts skills. The scope and sequence chart in the Omaha, Nebraska, curriculum guide illustrates the care with which some English departments are attempting to attain proper articulation and coverage.

> [The chart] indicates that there are appropriate times when certain conventions or principles should be introduced, that these often need emphasis again and again before they become part of the writing skills of pupils, and that there are levels at which most pupils should achieve an acceptable degree of proficiency in respect to their practice. This chart is not inflexible. It suggests what is possible for the majority of academic pupils. Teachers know that there will be some pupils who will progress more slowly than the majority and will not make the achievement that seems to be implied by the chart. Teachers also know that there will be some pupils in a class who are ready for more advanced

---

[9] Henry A. Bamman, Ursula Hogan, and Charles F. Greene, *Reading Instruction in the Secondary School* (New York: Longmans, Greene and Company, Inc., 1961), pp. 4–12.

[10] See Chapter 7.

conventions and principles than are indicated in the chart. Teachers should use the chart as a general guide but should use their own good judgment in interpreting its application to the pupils at either extreme of a class.[11]

GRAMMAR AND LINGUISTICS

THE RULE OF GRAMMAR

In the history of the English language grammar has had a particularly interesting role. The English language is a hybrid and, like many another mixed breed, is blessed (or cursed) with hybrid vigor. This vigor has made the language restless under formal grammatical rules and contemptuous of old-fashioned ways. So throughout its history the English language has been a changing language that has not fit well into rules even though for the last three centuries scholars have fought to make order out of chaos.

THE REVOLT OF THE LINGUISTS

Recently a group of scholars has revolted from the rule of traditional grammar and grammatical rules. In the main this revolt has stemmed from the work of modern linguistic scholars whose careful studies of the language have produced new theories about the nature of the language and how to teach the language arts. In spite of tremendous resistance the new theories and approaches are gaining support and may eventually supplant the traditional approach.

TWO VIEWS COMPARED

Supporters of traditional grammar believe that the study of grammar is the direct way to help boys and girls to learn how to write and speak well. Many of them believe as they do because they are convinced that there is right English and wrong English, and what is right or wrong is determined by grammatical rules. Ergo, if one wishes to teach boys and girls to speak and write correctly, one must teach them the rules.

The position of the new grammar or structural linguistics is quite different. The linguists do not believe in "correct English" per se. Every language is in a constant state of flux, they say. Correct eighteenth-century English is not correct twentieth-century English, nor is correct American English correct British English. Grammar's role is not to prescribe what proper English usage should be, but rather to describe what the language is without judgment as to its merits.

[11] The Curriculum Committee on English, *Tentative Guide For Teachers of English, Grades 7–12* (Omaha, Nebr.: Omaha Public Schools, September, 1961), pp. 23–24.

So far the new grammar has not been widely accepted. A few secondary-school systems, such as Cheltenham Township in Elkins Park, Pennsylvania, have developed thoroughgoing courses utilizing the linguistics approach, but such schools are the exception rather than the rule. One reason, of course, is that teachers are not trained in it and so feel insecure when they leave the familiar traditional courses. Another reason is that most of the textbooks available still stick to conventional grammar.

Summary of "Expert" Opinion. The position of the experts concerning the teaching of grammar can be summed up roughly as follows:

1. Grammar is not a set of rules, but a description of usage. There is no universally accepted system for describing grammar.
2. In the United States grammar should be based upon American English usage. There are different levels of usage in any language. Some usages are more appropriate in some situations than others. Pupils should learn to appreciate this fact and become familiar with the polite usages.
3. Study of grammar is not necessary for learning any language, but the new grammar is probably more effective than conventional grammar. The memorizing of grammatical rules is particularly unrewarding.
4. Grammar is useful for describing and teaching. It gives the pupils a nomenclature and a means for analyzing and so better understanding the English sentence and its parts that can be helpful in learning to write well, if the pupils use it consciously.
5. Individuals differ in their ability to profit from the study of grammar. Seldom can pupils profit from it before the junior high school grades. Many pupils never acquire enough maturity to benefit from grammar and should not be harassed by being forced to study it.
6. The study of grammar of any kind in isolation as a distinct discipline is of little value in helping pupils to learn to speak and write well. Especially the memorization of grammatical rules is not helpful in improving language skills. When grammar is taught it should be functional. Inducing the rules from what one knows of usage is much more effective than trying to learn proper usage from a set of rules.

READING IN SECONDARY SCHOOLS

Recently instruction in reading has begun to move into the secondary school. The urgency of the need for reading instruction for both good and bad readers in secondary schools seems self-evident. Boys and girls who have good academic potential are frequently handicapped by poor reading skills, and many of them drop out of school because of this lack. Other poor readers, who in former days would have been dropped or left behind, now continue into our junior and senior high schools because of the pressure of changing economic, social, and educational patterns.[12]

TYPES OF READING PROGRAMS

Three different types of reading programs can be found in secondary schools. One is the program that provides training for slow boys and girls who are doing as well as can be expected considering their ability and who need continued coaching in reading to develop their limited potential to the utmost. The second type of reading program is the program for boys and girls who for some reason have not learned to read properly, although their potential ability is average or even better than average. As a result of corrective programs some of these pupils make phenomenal gains and soon learn to read at their normal ability level. The third type of reading program is for the already good readers. This program attempts to improve pupils' already adequate skills and to carry each pupil along to higher competencies so that he will be a highly efficient reader who can make the utmost of his potential abilities.

Usually reading instruction has entered the secondary school by means of remedial programs for the retarded readers, but the need for developmental programs has become so obvious that these programs are fast gaining popularity in junior high schools. They are more slowly making a place for themselves in the senior high school.[13]

THE DEVELOPMENTAL PROGRAM

Remedial reading classes are usually taught in special classes or in reading laboratories; developmental reading programs are usually taught by classroom teachers. Probably the most satisfactory arrangement for developmental reading programs is a team approach in which one teacher, be it the reading teacher, the core teacher, or the English teacher, teaches the skills common to reading in all fields; the librarian teaches the library skills, and the various content teachers teach the reading skills necessary for their various subjects. In this connection, one should note that the block-of-time program lends itself well to developmental reading programs, because the block teacher has more time to learn the strengths and weaknesses of his students and teaches in a flexible organization, which lets him group his pupils, differentiate his material, and organize class time for various reading activities.[14]

Marks of a Good Developmental Program. What makes up a good developmental reading program? According to M. Jerry Weiss it is the following:

[12] Bamman, Hogan, and Greene, *op. cit.,* Ch. 1.

[13] *Ibid.,* Ch. 2.

[14] See M. Jerry Weiss, *Reading in the Secondary Schools* (New York: The Odyssey Press, Inc., 1961), for discussions and examples of developmental reading programs.

1. Reading instruction must aim at individual students, taking into account their different backgrounds, abilities, and interests.

2. Flexibility of instruction depends upon the availability of a wide range of reading materials of all kinds and on all sorts of subjects. In an effective program much of the initiative passes to the student and the teacher's role changes to that of a guide, a "listener," a resource person, a critic.

3. Reading instruction means paying attention not only to the basic skills of reading, but also to the general end which education should serve; the widening of the student's intellectual, emotional, and moral horizons.

4. Reading instruction is completely successful only when the student has acquired the habit of active continuous reading and can read with ease in all of the subject areas which, by necessity or choice, he faces.

5. The reading program is not the product of one teacher, but demands the involvement of the entire faculty and administration in a whole-hearted and single-minded concentration on drawing the best possible work out of each student.[15]

Need for Individualization. Weiss's first criterion points out the need for individualization of reading instruction. Without individualization no secondary reading program can be completely successful, for to be truly effective each pupil's lessons should be aimed directly at his own needs. Individualization is imperative even though many different methods for providing for individual differences, for example, differentiation of assignments, ability grouping, grouping within classes, differentiating the purposes for which pupils read the same material, have been devised.[16] No matter what type of grouping or assignments are used, individual differences in children are so great that group methods of teaching reading cannot be really effective.

The years since World War II have seen an accent on speed in reading. This emphasis has invaded some secondary schools as well as the colleges and adult education programs. While boys and girls do need to learn to read efficiently, speed reading is not the essential quality of a reading program. Rather pupils should read for comprehension and understanding and learn to adjust their reading speed to what they are reading. If boys and girls are to learn to read efficiently and effectively, speed in reading must not be overemphasized.

Junior High School Reading Programs. Junior high school developmental reading programs should continue the development of reading skills learned in the elementary grades. These include word attack skills, skills in reading or comprehension, oral reading skills, skills for reading critically, the ability to read more rapidly, and skills in locating informa-

---

[15] *Ibid.*, p. 10.

[16] Guy L. Bond, "Unsolved Problem in Secondary Reading," in J. Allen Figurel (ed.), *Changing Concepts of Reading Instruction*, International Reading Conference Proceedings, Volume 6 (New York: Scholastic Magazine, 1961), p. 202.

tion via proper use of books and reference materials, and study skills. These usually must be taught in three stages:

1. General reading and study skills should be learned in the developmental reading classes.
2. Library skills and the use of reference materials should be taught by the librarian.
3. The reading skills necessary for the studying of the various content fields should be taught by the content teachers, each of whom should be responsible to see that his pupils can (a) "read and study the textbooks used in his course, and (b) develop the special vocabulary in his subject."[17]

Senior High School Reading Programs. The purpose of the senior high school reading program is to develop independent readers who can meet their reading obligations in both their social and vocational lives and who can and will read for personal pleasure and profit. In order to carry out this mission the high school must provide four types of reading instruction:

a. basic instruction in reading;
b. instruction in adjusting skills and abilities to the demands of the content fields;
c. broad and extensive reading of literature so that students can expand their interests and improve their tastes; and
d. corrective or remedial reading instruction.[18]

As in the junior high school, carrying out such a program requires a team approach. Special remedial classes must be provided for boys and girls whose reading is not yet at the high school level, and systematic instruction in reading literature and the other content fields must be provided for normal pupils.

Reading in Content Fields. Reading instruction in the content fields is the responsibility of the content departments concerned. For the sake of efficiency some content departments utilize the services of the reading teachers for teaching reading in their fields while other departments plan and maintain their own programs with their own personnel. In either case the department should see to it that boys and girls are given adequate opportunity to learn the technical vocabulary of the field and the methods of reading attack best suited to the subject, for methods of reading and study do differ from subject to subject, and each field has a vocabulary and language of its own.

Resistance to Developmental Reading Programs. Unfortunately sec-

[17] William D. Sheldon, "Reading Instruction in Junior High School," in Nelson B. Henry, *Development in and Through Reading,* Sixtieth Yearbook of the National Society for the Study of Education, Part I (Chicago: University of Chicago Press, 1961), p. 316.

[18] Guy L. Bond and Stanley B. Kegler, "Reading Instruction in the Senior High School," in Henry, *op. cit.,* p. 328.

ondary-school teachers have resisted the introduction of developmental reading programs in both junior and senior high schools. Content teachers frequently resent the necessity of teaching reading. Even English teachers sometimes feel that teaching of reading is beneath them, as Burton points out.[19] Just the same, developmental reading programs are essential if boys and girls are to avoid the reading and study handicaps that have plagued older generations.

TEACHING LITERATURE

FAILURE IN THE PAST

Everyone seems to agree that the primary purpose for teaching literature is to instill the pupils with love and appreciation for good reading. To judge from the results, much of literature teaching has just the opposite effect from that desired. After years of English courses tremendous numbers of American boys and girls—and men and women—*hate literature*. Why? *Because literature has been taught so as to make it hateful.* Seldom have pupils been allowed to have pleasant experiences with books. Instead literature teaching has consisted of literary history plus cold-blooded dissection of plays, poems, and stories so as to cut out and pickle figures of speech, plot diagrams, and other similar specimens. Or perhaps even worse, literary masterpieces have been taught not as sources of pleasure and beauty, but as media for the "moral edification of the scholars." Under these circumstances, can one wonder why so many American boys and girls have hated, and still hate, literature?

A NEW POINT OF VIEW

Happily English teachers seem to be having a change of heart. The old analysis-centered, didactic, literary history orientation is being superseded by a healthier view of literature teaching, which emphasizes enjoyment and enrichment and the development of human and aesthetic values, not factual content.

This change of viewpoint seems to be bringing about many changes in the teaching of literature. Courses in the history of literature, for example, American literature and English literature, are losing popularity and are being replaced by courses in which pupils read literature for itself alone. Extensive reading of many works is replacing excessive literary analysis, although the study of literary types quite properly continues to find favor in the upper grades of the senior high school. Courses organized around literary types are becoming less common.

Literature for Enjoyment. English teachers are also dropping the

[19] Dwight L. Burton, "Some Trends and Emphases In High School Reading and Literature," in Figurel, *op. cit.*, p. 267.

practice of concentrating literature around a few classics. This trend and its implications warrant further examination. Boys and girls cannot all read with the same ease; neither do they all like the same type of literature. There is no reason why they should. If we wish to convince boys and girls that reading literature can be enjoyable, we must give them reading material they can enjoy and that has some meaning for their own lives. Reading lists should include all sorts of literature—modern books, magazine articles, boys' stories, sports and adventure tales, and any other type of reading that has natural appeal to the pupils. Each pupil should have an opportunity to pick from the lists those works that are congenial to his taste. Reading distasteful literature may develop will power, but it does not create a love for good reading.

Developing Literary Taste. Such a program does not imply that the quality of the readings must be lowered. One can find well-written reading among all types of literature, both ancient and modern. A book does not have to be dull to be good.

If boys and girls are going to develop taste, they need to learn to discriminate. As earlier chapters have pointed out, one cannot learn how to make wise choices without making choices. Boys and girls should be allowed to select what they will read, and, just as you and I do, when they find a work distasteful they should be allowed to put it down.

The foregoing points to the need for an individualized literature program. To share ideas or to introduce a unit, or to provide a basis for discussion or criticism, the pupils should read some works together. But, on the whole, the great differences in levels of reading and taste make an individualized program mandatory. Now that we have so many books in paperback edition, no longer does there seem to be any excuse for the set of books or the anthology approach to literature.

The Multiple Approach. The best approach to the teaching of literature is a multiple approach. Philadelphia's 1960 *Guide to the Teaching of Literature* offers a particularly fine example of a sane approach to the study of literature.

When your purpose is:

To acquaint the class with a classic or a type of literature (for example, fable, fairy tale, tall tale) which is part of their heritage

or

To have the entire class enjoy a reading or listening experience and the discussion which follows

or

To provide an opportunity for group guidance through literature

THEN DO HAVE THE ENTIRE CLASS READ OR LISTEN TO THE SAME STORY OR POEM.

When your purpose is:
   To encourage the development of the reading habit

                              or

   To give opportunity for meeting individual needs, abilities, and
   interests

                              or

   To raise the level of taste in each individual

   THEN GUIDED INDIVIDUAL READING SHOULD BE USED.

When your purpose is:
   To correlate the reading with experiences and activities of interest
   to the pupil

                              or

   To combine general class reading and guided independent reading

                              or

   To provide for individual differences within a common class project

   THEN USE THE UNIT APPROACH.[20]

THE PROBLEM OF CENSORSHIP

A problem accompanying the use of a wider reading list is the problem
of censorship. In the opinion of many teachers and parents some of the
books that deal with the knotty problems of life and the world are not
proper for boys and girls to read. Among the books that have felt the
censor's scissors are Salinger's *Catcher in the Rye*; Huxley's *Brave New
World*; Orwell's *Animal Farm*; Hawthorne's *The Scarlet Letter*; and
Plato's *Republic*.

Naturally children and youth should be protected from evil influences,
but the evidence gives us little reason to believe that boys' and girls' moral
values are affected greatly by what they read. In at least one junior high
school the boys and girls have discussed some of the more lurid portions
of such works as *Brave New World* without the slightest sensationalism.
Probably adult fears are usually excessive, and their attempts to remove
important high-caliber literary works from literature classes misguided.

MASS MEDIA

No modern youth can be considered well educated until he has
learned to use mass media intelligently. Secondary-school curricula must
allow much time for units in the use of newspapers, periodicals, radio,
television, and moving pictures, even at the expense of reducing the
amount of instruction in the classics.

[20] Curriculum Office, Philadelphia Public Schools, *A Guide to the Teaching of
Literature in Grades 7 through 12* (Tentative), (Philadelphia: School District of
Philadelphia, 1960), pp. 9–12.

A Necessary Extension of Literature Teaching. In some circles the offerings of mass media are considered to be tawdry stuff, too insignificant to give class time. This attitude is unfortunate, for instruction in the use of mass media is a necessary extension of the study of literature. Its purpose is to establish standards of taste and to foster critical judgment and mental alertness through the study of the most abundant and available of all literary forms. Boys and girls need to know how to select, interpret, and appreciate these forms just as much as they need to know how to select, interpret, and evaluate novels, poetry, and other literary forms— more so, because the mass media cannot be avoided, and so boys and girls who appreciate them improperly and inaccurately do so at some peril.

The techniques for establishing high standards of taste and critical interpretation and evaluation of any work of art, certainly of any literary art, are basically the same. Although there is no accounting for taste, tastes can be changed and created, and the English teacher's job is to create good taste and to change poor tastes into better ones. To do so is difficult, but it must be done. We cannot hope to raise boys' and girls' critical judgment by retreating to the safety of Scott, Eliot, and Shakespeare. Taste is made in the market place, and boys and girls must learn to make their choices there.

English or Social Studies? The mass media are both literary and social phenomena. Consequently they bring overlap to the social studies and the English language arts curricula. Should the critical study of newspapers really be the job of the social studies or language arts department? Learning how to read critically is a language arts function, but learning how to read social studies materials is a social studies function, and the newspaper is social studies material. Similarly many television and radio programs have as much significance to the social studies teacher as to the English language arts teacher. Therefore the schools are faced with a problem of scope. As it stands in many schools, either the skills of using mass media wisely are taught haphazardly and repetitiously in both English language arts and social studies or, as is more likely to happen, they are completely neglected. The American people cannot afford to let our schools neglect what may be the most pertinent subject matter of our times.

WRITTEN COMPOSITION

Proficiency in writing is the criterion that most laymen use in judging the effectiveness of language instruction. And certainly the need for teaching boys and girls to express themselves well and properly in writing is urgent in modern America.

That the schools have recognized the importance of writing is evident from a perusal of English curriculum guides. The Santa Barbara, California, curriculum guide, for example, outlines a detailed three-track developmental sequence of content, which builds up from grade 7 through grade 14 and from the sentence through to sophisticated analytical college papers. Similar sequences can be found in other curriculum guides, such as those of Omaha, Nebraska, and Louisville, Kentucky. Some of these curriculum guides specify that a considerable portion of the class time be devoted to writing activities. Baltimore County's (Maryland) tenth grade study guide's recommendation that 30 to 40 per cent of teaching time be given to direct instruction in writing is not unusual.

In spite of the attempts of curriculum makers, carrying out successful programs in written composition has not been easy. Logical attempts to teach writing sequentially are defied by the illogicality of the individual differences of the pupils and the complexities of communication. Although logically one should learn to write sentences, then paragraphs, and then themes, psychologically this sequence is not really feasible, for we write sentences and paragraphs only for their contribution to the larger meaning of an entire composition. So it may be that drill in sentence structure and paragraph building may prevent achievement of the larger goal by diverting energies to the parts when the pupil is ready to conquer the whole.

The practical problem of teaching pupils to write well is also complicated by the time and effort it takes to do it. The Baltimore County Curriculum Committee, which states that teachers should provide boys and girls with "some practice in writing each week," is probably right and should be commended for taking that stand. But any teacher who has attempted to read—not to say read carefully—150 papers a week, week after week, knows that this is an enervating, time-consuming operation. As a result many high school English teachers give their pupils very few serious composition assignments. Consequently these pupils do not have anywhere near enough practice in writing and rewriting to realize their potentialities or even to become reasonably proficient.

SOME TRENDS IN THE TEACHING OF COMPOSITION

One of the trends in the English language arts is a movement toward the use of written composition as a means for pupil guidance. This trend is reflected in the National Council of Teachers of English's chapter entitled "Meeting Youth's Needs Through Writing"[21] in which the authors include developing knowledge of one's self and others, respect for the thinking of others, writing about personal concerns, and other kinds of personal writing. Such writing, if used in the way that the commission envisaged, could well be used as a medium for helping boys and girls to understand themselves, their desires, emotions, and potentialities better and thereby to carry out one of the primary functions of the guidance program. In the junior high school years this emphasis on the guidance functions in writing and other areas of the language arts is partly

[21] Commission on the English Curriculum of the National Council of Teachers of English, op. cit., Ch. 9.

responsible for the current popularity for unified studies and English–social studies–guidance block-of-time programs.[22]

Also evident from the data cited above is a trend toward emphasis on critical thinking. Research papers, analyses, reviews, and criticisms are common types of writing activities whose purpose is to help pupils become better thinkers. The ability to use one's mind well is a primary goal of secondary education. There is no place better than the composition class to teach it.

Composition classes tend to place their emphases on clear communication rather than on picayunish matters of grammar and usage. More and more teachers of English composition accent learning how to convey meaning. To them the problem of composition is (1) to determine what one means to say, and then (2) to determine how best to express what one means. Pedantic constructions and prescriptive grammatical rules must give way to clear, idiomatic expression, for, surprisingly, it seems that so-called correct grammatical constructions may obscure meaning, whereas less "correct" grammar may bring the meaning out. Good teachers of composition have always recognized this fact; many modern English teachers are capitalizing on the principle.

SPEAKING AND LISTENING

THE MOST ESSENTIAL PHASE OF THE LANGUAGE ARTS

Speaking and listening are undoubtedly the two most important language activities for the average person. In general, however, the basic skills for these activities are taught at home, and the pupils' listening and speaking habits are pretty well shaped by the time a pupil gets to the secondary school. For that reason teachers have tended to neglect speaking and listening in favor of reading and writing. In past years the National Council of Teachers of English and other organizations have made serious attempts to reduce this neglect. Lately, however, a reaction seems to have set in. Critics of the English curriculum say that one cannot teach everything and therefore English teachers should concentrate on literature, composition, and language only. Other persons seem to feel that speaking and listening are not dignified enough, or not rigorous enough, to be included in a respectable academic curriculum. As a consequence of these criticisms speaking and listening activities may be about to undergo a setback.

The Need to Listen Well. A setback in the teaching of speaking and listening would be disastrous. These activities have never been more necessary. Boys and girls not only need to know how to speak distinctly and how to express themselves effectively, but increasingly they are being thrown into positions that require critical listening as well. Much of what

[22] *Ibid.*

one learns today is learned from an electronic recording or broadcasting device, and so it behooves young scholars to learn to listen well.

The Need for Clear Expression. Even though we are living in a permissive age one is judged by the language he uses. To most of us the ability to express oneself orally is much more necessary than the ability to write well. To learn the skills of speaking and listening is important. Because ones does not ordinarily just learn them naturally, nor can one ordinarily learn them from the study of literature, language, and composition, one must study them directly. That is why speaking and listening activities, such as reading aloud, oral reports, panels and symposiums, and playing records, should make up a large part of the English curriculum.[23]

CHARACTERISTICS OF GOOD PROGRAMS

As in written composition the principal goal in speech and listening is meaningfulness. Speech and listening classes should be communications laboratories in which pupils learn to present their ideas clearly and logically and learn to evaluate ideas presented by others thoughtfully and fairly. Discussions should be a means of attacking problems systematically. The listener should be an active participant who both reacts to the speaker's presentation and analyzes the presentation and the reactions of the listeners.

Speech and listening activities have a definite role in the English language arts program. If English teachers accept their responsibility for teaching the English language arts, and our society continues in the direction it is going, the importance of teaching speaking and listening and its challenge will become more and more insistent. We cannot afford to let it be forced to a minor position by the demands of literature, composition, and language study. After all, mastery of reading, writing, speaking, and listening is essential for competence in using the English language. Without adequate learning in them the study of language, literature, and composition becomes a farce.

PROVISIONS FOR INDIVIDUAL DIFFERENCES

PROGRAMS FOR THE TALENTED STUDENTS

English language arts programs in the secondary schools commonly attempt to make provisions for individual differences in the abilities and goals of their pupils. Tracking is common. If they do nothing else, most high schools provide a college English sequence and a noncollege

[23] See Alexander Frazier, "Making the Most of Speaking-and-Listening Experiences," *English Journal*, 46: 330–338, 65, Speech Leaflet 3, National Council of Teachers of English, 1961, for excellent commentary on the good speaking and listening program.

English sequence. Many schools provide several English tracks, for example, Hartford, Connecticut, High Schools provide four tracks, Santa Barbara, California, three tracks.

In general, programs for the gifted are not so very different from those provided for the dull and the average. Gifted pupils need to develop the same language skills as other children do. The differences come in the fact that they can benefit by deeper, more abstract, subject matter. Academically talented boys and girls can benefit from literary analysis, the pursuit of symbolism, the study of language, and the study of technicalities that would repulse less academically gifted pupils. For them it is quite possible to understand and enjoy "how a poem means," whereas for less academically inclined boys and girls it probably is not.

Advanced and Honors Classes. Some of the advanced courses for academic pupils offer very interesting material and high academic standards. The Manhasset High School, Manhasset, New York, Advanced English IV course gives us an example of a course designed to widen the pupils' cultural background by extensive reading in selected world classics. In this course for which competence in technical English is a prerequisite pupils write twelve or more themes during the year, plus short class writings that emphasize analyses and interpretations. In composition the teachers stress style, organization, tone, and sense of direction. The reading for the course is heavy and varied. During the summer, pupils are required to prepare themselves for the course by reading such works as Wolfe's *Look Homeward Angel*, Fitzgerald's *The Great Gatsby*, and Wharton's *Ethan Frome*. A few of the works specified for classroom discussion are *Tom Jones, Crime and Punishment, Dr. Faustus, Hamlet, Othello, Canterbury Tales, Paradise Lost*, Lecomte du Noüy's *Human Destiny*. As the reader can see, the course demands a high order of intelligence and background on the part of the student.

Enrichment in the Regular Class. Many secondary schools provide for the talented through enrichment programs in the regular classroom. In these heterogeneous classes the enrichment program stresses extensive and intensive reading, creative thinking and writing, effective speech, skills of investigation and research, and unusually high standards of accomplishment.[24] Usually in heterogeneous classes the bright students do much of their work independently. Provisions for brilliant youngsters in the regular classroom can be rather easily made when one uses broad units. With or without utilizing the unit technique, the capable English teacher may find many ways to enrich the heterogeneous class. In their article on "Enriching the English Program for the Academically Talented," Rock and Gard list six of them:

[24] Mildred Rock and Robert R. Gard, "Enriching the English Program for the Academically Talented," in Arno Jewett (ed.), *English for the Academically Talented Student in the Secondary School* (Washington, D.C.: National Education Association, 1960), p. 50.

Enrichment Through Supplementary Activities
Enrichment Through Correlation with Other Subjects
Enrichment Through Reading
Enrichment Through Writing and Speaking
Enrichment Through Extracurricular Activities
Enrichment Through Use of Community Resources[25]

Although the list is impressive, it simply represents good practice in any class and should apply also to the homogeneous class.

PROGRAMS FOR THE SLOW

Many schools provide modified language arts programs for the slow learners. Unhappily many of these programs are simply the normal programs taken at a snail's pace. Other programs attempt to attack the problem of providing suitable courses for slow learners more effectively. Among them is the excellent "modified course in English" for grades 7, 8, 9 in Wilmington, Delaware. In this course the

> Course content for pupils of limited background, ability, or both has been selected to include only the simplest principles of English usage essential to everyday communication. Pupils will vary in their ability to cope with these principles during the junior high school period. Some will reach only minimal proficiency; a few, on the other hand, may achieve a degree of mastery which will permit them to develop further as suggested in programs for more able pupils in grades 7, 8, and 9. Working at his own level, each pupil must progress as he can.[26]

The outline of the course content carries out the statement above. It is eminently practical and concrete. The material to be covered varies from individual to individual, but in every case it is designed to be helpful to the pupil. Plans of this sort represent the highest type of program for slow learners in English.

NEW MOVEMENTS

TO SAVE TIME

To read properly and mark a hundred and fifty 250-word papers and to recheck them after the pupils have corrected their errors requires 28.5 hours per week.[27] When one adds this to the 25 hours teachers normally spend meeting classes, one finds that the English teacher who gives a theme a week has a crushing load. If the National Council of Teachers

[25] *Ibid.*, pp. 52–60.

[26] Dorothy Williams, Chairman, Secondary English Department, *A Guide to the Teaching of a Modified Course in English For Grades 7, 8, and 9* (Tentative), (Wilmington, Del.: Wilmington Public Schools, 1961), p. ix.

[27] William J. Dusel, "Determining an Efficient Teaching Load in English," *Illinois English Bulletin*, March, 1956, p. 4, cited in National Council of Teachers of English, *The National Interest and the Teaching of English, op. cit.*, pp. 92–93.

of English estimate is right, the teacher who does his theme correcting and other duties as they should be done must work more than 70 hours a week.[28] Because modern experts on the teaching of English believe that the way for boys and girls to learn how to write is for them to write and rewrite often, the problem of time has become crucial. To solve this problem curriculum experts have resorted to such schemes as large group instruction and the use of teacher aides and "readers." To date none of these plans seems to be completely satisfactory.[29]

Reducing the Load. Probably the only real solution to the time problem is to reduce the English teachers' load. Conant,[30] the National Council of Teachers of English,[31] the National Commission of Teacher Education and Professional Standards,[32] and others have recommended that English teachers not be responsible for more than 100 pupils in their classes. While such a load would greatly reduce the work of many English teachers and allow them to do their work much more efficiently, it still represents a heavy load for the conscientious English teacher.

THE COMMISSION ON ENGLISH

At the time of writing, in spite of the many complaints about the English curriculum, not much has been done to correct its deficiencies. All that the recommendations of the various commissions and study groups who have pronounced on the teaching of English have done is to recognize the need for English language arts teaching in every high school grade and to hope that all phases of the language arts will be taught well.

One agency, the Commission on English of the College Entrance Examination Board, is attempting to revamp the English curriculum. The commission is also supporting a number of summer school courses in language, literature, and composition, for selected English teachers in the hope that this instruction will raise the level of competence of the teachers who take it and thus serve as the yeast that will cause the standards of all English teachers to rise.

Many experts in the English language arts are upset because the Commission's program is "so narrow." It includes only instruction for college-bound pupils in composition, language, and literature and pointedly

[28] National Council of Teachers of English, *op. cit.*, p. 95.

[29] *Cf.* Lee Frank Lowe, "Theme Correcting via the Tape Recorder," *The English Journal* 52: 212–214, March, 1963; Betty Gittinan, "We Solved the Problem of Size," *The English Journal* 52: 89–93, February, 1963; James R. Squire, "English at the Crossroads," *The English Journal* 51: 381–392, September, 1962; Paul M. Ford, "Lay Readers in the High School Composition Program: Some Statistics," *The English Journal* 50: 522–528, November, 1961.

[30] James B. Conant, *The American High School Today* (New York: McGraw-Hill Book Company, 1959), p. 51.

[31] National Council of Teachers of English, *op. cit.*, p. 96.

[32] Willard E. Givens, *Our Teachers: Annual Report of the Profession to the Public* (Washington, D.C.: National Education Association, 1947), p. 13.

leaves out speaking and listening. Because of this narrowness and an implied emphasis on rather sterile disciplinary goals for the teaching of English, some educators fear that the program will have a regressive influence. Still, if the program serves to strengthen the background of English teachers and to open their eyes to what can be done in the teaching of English literature, composition, and language, the Commission on English may be the force to awaken the long-neglected renaissance in the teaching of all the facets of the English language arts.

PROJECT ENGLISH

In 1961 the United States Office of Education launched a new program to raise the quality of the English curriculum and English instruction. Briefly "Project English" is an attempt to rally the forces of state, local, and national institutions and organizations to determine and study the problems of the English curriculum and to use all the knowledge we have and can attain to solve these problems. To these ends the Office of Education is encouraging research and experimentation and the establishment of centers to plan, develop, and test new educational materials and methods.[33]

SUMMARY

The scope of the four areas of the English language arts curriculum—speaking, listening, reading, and writing—has become so tremendous and indefinite that authorities question whether separate courses in English should be offered at all.

Ideally language development should be continuous and individual, but realistic curriculum workers find it necessary to allocate definite content to specific grade levels. A current trend is to give greater attention to these allocations and to develop scope and sequence charts for the guidance of teachers and supervisors. Other curriculum trends in the language arts are the adding of instruction in reading and listening instruction to secondary curricula and a movement toward increased utilization of the unit approach in English teaching. Also a trend toward replacing traditional prescriptive grammar with descriptive structural grammar seems to be developing.

In spite of resistance, remedial and developmental reading programs are gaining acceptance in both junior and senior high schools. To be most successful such programs should be individualized so that each pupil can learn to read many types of material as efficiently as he can. In this connection, particular attention needs to be paid to reading in the different content fields. Although speed in reading has received much attention in some communities, it should not be the principal objective of reading

[33] "Project English," *School Life*, 44: 25–27, November–December, 1961.

instruction; rather the objective should be for each pupil to learn to read with comprehension as well as he can.

In the past, literature teaching in American schools has failed to bring enjoyment or appreciation of good literature to its pupils. To remedy this glaring defect, literature curricula are dropping the history of literature and detailed analysis approach in favor of methods calculated to increase enjoyment and critical judgment. Fostering enjoyment and critical judgment is also the purpose behind the extension of literature teaching to include mass media. With the influences of these media so omnipresent, the creation and furthering of discriminating taste is one of the most pressing responsibilities of the secondary-school English language arts curriculum.

Composition instruction usually is aimed at the development of clear communications skills—although there seems to be an increased use of composition as a tool for teaching critical thinking and for guidance. Similar objectives are held for oral-aural activities. The increasing importance of oral communication has made the development of efficient listening skills more necessary today than at any time since the invention of movable type.

Tracking is common in language arts curricula. Tracks for slow pupils tend to be watered down versions of college-preparatory classes, although some schools have special courses carefully prepared for this group. In general, the tracks for talented pupils have been more successful; many of them require high levels of criticisms and original thinking of the pupils. Similar demands have also been made of talented pupils in the enrichment activities for the talented given in the regular English classes at some schools.

Several innovations have been introduced into English language arts curricula in order to find ways to give teachers more time to do their work. So far these have not been evaluated well enough to judge their worth fairly, but probably the only way to really benefit both pupils and teachers is to reduce the English teachers' load. At the moment the government and the Commission on English of the College Entrance Examination Board have launched programs designed to rejuvenate the English curriculum. The mere fact that these and other agencies are turning their attention to English language arts curriculum development augurs for more enlightened future for the teaching of English.

SUGGESTED READINGS

ALLISON, ERNEST C. *English Instruction—Rhode Island's Public Junior High Schools.* Barrington, R.I.: The author, 1961.

A report of a survey of junior high school English teaching in Rhode Island.

BAMMAN, HENRY A., URSULA HOGAN, and CHARLES E. GREENE. *Reading Instruction in the Secondary Schools*. New York: Longmans, Green and Company, Inc., 1961.

An excellent recent textbook on the teaching of reading in secondary schools.

BROENIG, ANGELA M. "Development of Taste in Literature in the Senior High School," *The English Journal*, 52: 273–287, April, 1963.

An impressive critical review of literature on the subject. Excellent bibliography.

BURTON, DWIGHT L. "Some Trends and Emphases in High School Reading and Literature," in *Changing Concepts of Reading Instruction*, J. Allen Figurel (ed.). International Reading Association Conference Proceedings. Volume 6. New York: Scholastic Magazines, 1961.

An analysis of the secondary-school reading program and where it is going.

FAY, LEO C. *Reading in the High School*. Washington, D.C.: The National Education Association, 1956.

A leaflet summarizing the field up to the date of publication.

FRIEDERICH, WILLARD J., and RUTH A. WILCOX. *Teaching Speech in High Schools*. Second edition. New York: The Macmillan Company, 1961.

A methods text in speech teaching. Part I describes the scope of the program in speaking and also listening.

FRIES, CHARLES C. *Linguistics and Reading*. New York: Holt, Rinehart and Winston, Inc., 1963.

Brings together a nontechnical descriptive survey of modern linguistic knowledge, an analysis of the reading process in the light of that knowledge, and an examination of the kinds of materials to which the reader must develop high-speed recognition responses.

"Growing Pains in Grammar," *The English Journal*, 47: entire issue, April, 1958.

Issue devoted to the old and new in grammar instruction.

HENRY, NELSON B. (ed.). *Development In and Through Reading*. Sixtieth Yearbook of the National Society for the Study of Education, Part I. Chicago: University of Chicago Press, 1961.

An excellent yearbook presenting authoritative comment and analyses of various aspects of the teaching of reading.

HEYS, FRANK J. "The Theme-a-Week Assumption," *The English Journal*, 51: 320–322, May, 1962.

Report of a study that does not support the theme-a-week assumption.

HOOK, J. N. *The Teaching of High School English*. New York: The Ronald Press Company, 1959.

One of the best standard textbooks on the teaching of English.

"Linguistics," *The English Journal*, 52: 317–370, May, 1963.

An entire issue of the journal devoted to various aspects of linguistics and linguistic teaching. Contains excellent statements on the "new grammars."

MERSAND, JOSEPH. "Individualizing Instruction in English in Large and Small Classes," *The Bulletin of the National Association of Secondary-School Principals*, 44: 111–123, March, 1960.

Proposals for individualizing instruction in English classes. Contains helpful methodological suggestions and examples of curriculum content from New York City's course of study.

MINICLUR, GORDON. "Developing a Reading Program in a Secondary School," *The Bulletin of the National Association of Secondary-School Principals*, 42: 127–129, February, 1958.

A report of the reading program inaugurated at Washington High School, St. Paul.

MOULTON, WILLIAM G. *Linguistics and Language Teaching in the United States, 1940–1960.* Offprint, Trends in Europe and American Linguistics. Utrecht, Netherlands: Spectrum Publishers. Reprinted by Government Printing Office, Washington, 1963.

A brief but comprehensive summary of developments and trends in linguistics during the two decades.

NASSP COMMITTEE ON CURRICULUM PLANNING AND DEVELOPMENT. "English Language Arts in the Comprehensive Secondary School," *The Bulletin of the National Association of Secondary-School Principals*, 44: 46–58, October, 1960.

Position statement endorsed by the National Association of Secondary-School Principals.

NATIONAL COUNCIL OF TEACHERS OF ENGLISH, COMMISSION ON THE ENGLISH CURRICULUM. *The English Language Arts.* New York: Appleton-Century-Crofts, Inc., 1952.

A description of the teaching of the English language arts curriculum representing the viewpoint and recommendations of the NCTE's Commission on English.

——. *The English Language Arts in the Secondary School.* New York: Appleton-Century-Crofts, Inc., 1956.

A textbook on the teaching of the English language arts curriculum in secondary schools prepared by the NCTE Commission on the English Curriculum designed to voice the official line of the commission.

NATIONAL COUNCIL OF TEACHERS OF ENGLISH, COMMITTEE ON ENGLISH PROGRAMS FOR HIGH SCHOOL STUDENTS OF SUPERIOR ABILITY. *English for the Academically Talented Student in the Secondary School,* Arno Jewett, (ed.). Washington, D.C.: The National Education Association, 1960.

A report of the NCTE Committee on English for High School Students of Superior Ability outlining national approaches and programs for the talented in English.

NATIONAL COUNCIL OF TEACHERS OF ENGLISH, COMMITTEE ON NATIONAL INTEREST. *The National Interest and the Teaching of English.* Champaign, Illinois: The Council, 1961.

A report on the state of English teaching which calls for an immediate rejuvenation and revitalization of the English curriculum.

NATIONAL COUNCIL OF TEACHERS OF ENGLISH, NATIONAL CONFERENCE ON RESEARCH IN ENGLISH. *What We Know About High School Reading,* Mary Agnella Gunn (ed.). Champaign, Illinois: The Council, 1958.

A summary of the research on reading in the high school.

OLSON, HELEN F. "Language Arts in the Curriculum," *Educational Leadership.* 19: 302–306, February, 1962.

A look at the organization and approach in language arts curricula. This issue of *Educational Leadership* contains several other interesting articles on the English Language Arts curriculum.

OSTRACH, HERBERT F. "English and the Lower-Class Student," *The English Journal*, 52: 196–199, March, 1963.

An accusation that the present English curriculum has no place for lower-class pupils.

POOLEY, ROBERT C. *Teaching English Usage.* New York: Appleton-Century-Crofts, Inc., 1946.

An analysis of the problems of teaching grammar and usage by one of the nation's leading experts in linguistics.

RINKER, FLOYD. "Priorities in the English Curriculum," *The English Journal*, 51: 309–312, May, 1962.

A declaration for composition, literature, and language as main content of the English language arts curriculum.

ROBERTS, PAUL. *English Sentences* (manual). New York: Harcourt, Brace and World, Inc., 1962.

A manual to a high school text in the "new grammar." This manual clearly and simply explains the theory behind the new program.

ROBINSON, H. ALAN, and ALLAN F. MUSKOPF. "High School Reading—1961," *Journal of Developmental Reading*, Autumn, 1962.

Informative survey of professional literature on junior and senior high school reading.

SQUIRE, JAMES R. "English at the Crossroads," *The English Journal*, 51: 381–392, September, 1962.

A follow-up of the status of the profession eighteen months after the National Interest and the Teaching of English report.

STONE, GEORGE WINCHESTER. *Issues, Problems and Approaches in Teaching English.* New York: Holt, Rinehart and Winston, Inc., 1961.

A collection of essays which presents problems and issues in the teaching of English and suggests a program of action to resolve some of these problems and issues by means of "an articulated English program."

STROM, INGRID M. "Summary of Investigation Relating to the English Language Arts in Secondary Education: 1961–1962," *The English Journal*, 52: 118–136, February, 1963.

A review of research on matters pertaining to the English Language Arts in the secondary schools. Excellent bibliography.

"Unit Teaching," *The English Journal*, 49: entire issue, September, 1960.

An issue devoted to unit teaching in English Language Arts.

WEISS, M. JERRY. *An English Teacher's Reader: Grades Seven Through Twelve.* New York: The Odyssey Press, Inc., 1962.

A collection of articles concerning various phases of English Language Arts curriculum.

———. *Reading in the Secondary School.* New York: The Odyssey Press, Inc., 1961.

A collection of readings concerning secondary-school reading programs. Contains several authoritative and influential statements.

Chapter 10
Foreign
Language Arts

Present Status of Foreign Language Curricula. Although the first American secondary schools were Latin schools, the Latin curriculum has declined until now it is typically a two-year terminal sequence for college-preparatory students only. Similarly, after reaching a high point just prior to the beginning of World War I, instruction in modern foreign languages also declined. At the end of World War II the characteristic modern foreign language curriculum was a two-year sequence of French or Spanish. This lack of interest in the foreign languages was caused by a spirit of isolationism and utilitarianism during the period between the two world wars and by the dropping of foreign languages from college entrance requirements. Pupils and parents could see little practical value in learning a foreign language when it was not required for college admission and one had little expectation of ever visiting a foreign land.

Because of the shortness of the sequence little effort was made to teach anything more than the rudiments of reading in the foreign language. Perhaps it was just as well, for relatively few language teachers were accomplished linguists. The result was that for several generations many Americans grew up to be both tongue-tied and illiterate in any language but their own. This pattern is still characteristic of too many schools.

The mid-1950's saw a renaissance in foreign language teaching, which has since received tremendous extra impetus from the National Defense Education Act of 1958. Foreign language enrollments and curricula have expanded so rapidly that today foreign language courses enroll more pupils than ever before in the history of the country. In order of popularity the foreign languages given in grades 9–12 are Spanish, Latin, French, and German. Enrollments in all other languages, including Russian, are very small. In grades 7 and 8, French and Spanish are the most popular foreign languages, although enrollment in German, Russian, and Latin is increasing at this level.

Trends in Foreign Language Teaching. The rapid changes in foreign language teaching make trends fairly easy to spot. The increasing enrollments have already been mentioned. Other trends that should be noted are:

1. A trend toward placing beginning modern foreign language instruction in the general education portion of the curriculum.
2. A trend toward increasing two-year sequences to sequences of three, four, six or more years in modern foreign languages and of three or four years in Latin.
3. A trend toward beginning modern foreign language instruction in the junior high school or elementary school grades.
4. A trend toward teaching Latin as a second foreign language and moving all Latin instruction into the senior high school grades starting in grade 10 or sometimes grade 9.
5. A trend toward making foreign language sequences really sequential by articulating the foreign language curricula of elementary school, secondary school, and college.
6. A trend toward outlining foreign language sequences by levels rather than by grades so as to gain articulation and flexibility.
7. A trend toward teaching all the aspects of the foreign language thoroughly, but with primary emphasis on speaking and understanding rather than reading.
8. A trend toward utilizing the findings of linguistic research in foreign language teaching.
9. A trend toward teaching foreign languages primarily by the audio-lingual approach.
10. A trend toward utilizing electronic aids, such as language laboratories, in foreign language teaching.
11. A trend toward making foreign language courses more realistic, functional, and interesting.
12. A trend toward using foreign language courses as a medium for study of the geography, culture, and peoples of the lands whose language the pupils are learning.
13. A trend toward eliminating general language and exploratory language courses.

Most of these trends will be discussed specifically later in the chapter.

The National Defense Education Act of 1958. The great upsurge in foreign language teaching is largely the result of the National Defense

Education Act of 1958. Under this act the federal government provided financial assistance to the states in financing the purchase of equipment and materials, and minor remodeling of existing space for the use of such equipment at the local level and adequate supervisory services at the state level.

The provisions of the act have brought about a phenomenal increase in language laboratories and other equipment and greatly improved supervisory services. Newly appointed foreign language supervisors, authorized as a result of this legislation, have been able to upgrade both the number of foreign language curricula and their quality. To this end they have provided much needed supervisory help to local school systems, published curriculum guides and bulletins, and conducted workshops for local teachers.

Similar gains have come from Title VI of this act, which provides for research in foreign language instruction, and most important of all, institutes for the training and retraining of language teachers. The total impact of this title is tremendous. In one summer alone 2,000 foreign language teachers were enrolled in 37 foreign language institutes where they received advanced training focused on the improvement of teaching foreign languages in elementary and secondary schools.

ISSUES IN FOREIGN LANGUAGE TEACHING

Any attempt to change a time-entrenched curriculum is bound to bring problems and controversy. Among the issues raised by the revolutionary changes in foreign language instruction are:

What shall the aims of foreign language teaching be?
Who should study foreign languages?
How long should foreign languages be studied?
When should foreign languages start?
Which foreign languages should be offered?
How many foreign languages should be offered?
By what methods should foreign languages be taught? And what should the content be?

GOALS FOR FOREIGN LANGUAGE TEACHING

The One Primary Purpose. Today there seems to be only one legitimate primary goal for the teaching of any foreign language in a secondary school, that is, to teach boys and girls to communicate in the foreign language. This goal consists of four subgoals:

1. To teach boys and girls to understand the foreign language as it is normally spoken by a native speaker;
2. To teach boys and girls to speak the foreign language easily and idiomatically;

3. To teach boys and girls to read the foreign language with understanding and without dependence upon the dictionary and "translation";
4. To teach boys and girls to write freely and directly in the foreign
language.

Some Subsidiary Goals. Although its principal purpose is to teach the
ability to communicate, the sudy of a language can bring many other
contributions to one's education. Quite properly these potential contributions should become secondary teaching objectives. Among them are:

1. To strengthen pupils' knowledge of language and linguistics and
to help them better understand their native tongue.
2. To strengthen their knowledge and appreciation of foreign cultures.
3. To strengthen understanding of and sympathy for foreign peoples.
4. To promote international understanding and the understanding of
international affairs and relationships.
5. To strengthen aesthetic understandings.
6. To strengthen knowledge of the contribution of foreign peoples and
foreign nations to the United States and to the world.
7. To strengthen pupils' skill in literary analysis and criticism.
8. To familiarize pupils with the literature in the foreign language.

What Foreign Language Teaching Is Not. All of these goals can be
reached through foreign language courses without jeopardizing the major
purpose of foreign language teaching, that is, the communications goal.
Sometimes, however, foreign language enthusiasts oversell the subsidiary
values of foreign language study. To keep the goals in proper perspective
let us examine in the next few paragraphs some of the things foreign
language teaching should not be expected to do.

Learning foreign languages does not necessarily build international
friendships, as the history of Europe amply illustrates. Neither does it
necessarily engender sympathy for, or understanding of, foreigners. English is the most common second language on earth, yet no people are
more often misunderstood than the Americans. International understanding, the study of culture, geography, and the like, can be furthered
through the study of a foreign language, but basically these goals remain
social studies goals. They can best be taught in social studies classes
and should be taught in foreign language classes only incidentally to
the learning of the foreign language. The foreign language class is not a
social studies class.

Neither is it an English class. Any help that foreign language teaching
gives to English improvement is probably incidental and peripheral. The
improvement of pupils' English is not, and should not be, a major goal
for the study of any modern foreign language nor an important reason
for teaching it. Arguments for foreign language instruction based on its
use in English improvement are specious at best.

Neither is foreign language study a medium for disciplining the mind. In the days when foreign language study was losing its hold on the secondary-school population, foreign language teachers made much of the disciplinary value of the foreign languages in order to justify their existence. Some teachers of Latin still fall back on this claim and continue to center their teaching around the disciplinary aim. If they cannot find a more valid reason for teaching it, Latin should be dropped. As an earlier chapter points out, the disciplinary aim is a false aim.

Who Should Study Foreign Languages? Until the early 1950's educators generally believed that only the best pupils could benefit from the study of foreign languages. Almost everyone thought that foreign languages were far too difficult for average pupils to master, and so foreign language courses were ordinarily limited to electives for college-preparatory pupils. Since World War II, however, many educators have come to believe that foreign languages should be part of the general education of all boys and girls. And so in schools like the Edwin O. Smith School, Storrs, Connecticut, foreign language study has been made mandatory for all pupils regardless of their levels of achievement "because the faculty felt that it had value for all pupils and not just a select few."[1]

No pupil who has a real interest in learning a foreign language should be deprived of an opportunity of trying to learn it. Certainly lack of academic genius need not hold him back. Many a pupil with an unenviable academic past has learned a foreign language easily and well. The best way to find out whether a pupil has aptitude for language learning seems to be to let him try. After a reasonable period of trial any pupil who demonstrates that he has little or no aptitude for languages should be excused from further language study.

On the other hand, studying composition and literature in a foreign language requires academic ability just as it does in English. Therefore advanced courses in foreign languages should be reserved for the academically able and interested.

HOW MUCH TIME FOR FOREIGN LANGUAGES?

To learn a language well takes time, for learning a language is a never-ending project. The septagenarian as well as the teen-ager adds new words to his vocabulary and adopts new modes of expressing his thoughts. In language-conscious Europe, educators have long recognized the need for thoroughness in foreign language instruction. Typically European school curricula give seven to nine years to the study of a first foreign language.

In this country almost all experts in foreign language teaching and curriculum agree that the old two-year modern foreign language sequence is inadequate. Instead they recommend continuous developmental se-

---

[1] Alexander Plante, "All Pupils Study Foreign Languages in a Six-Year Sequence," *The Bulletin of the National Association of Secondary-School Principals,* 46: 74–76, February, 1962.

quences extending from the elementary school through the secondary and collegiate grades into adulthood. Many of them think a ten-year sequence from grades 3 through 12 to be ideal. Failing this, the experts believe four years, from 9 through 12, to be the very minimum for a modern foreign language. Anything else, they say, is too short a time to achieve any real purpose.

WHEN TO BEGIN FOREIGN LANGUAGES

At what age children should start to learn foreign languages has long been controversial. Before World War II curriculum builders were convinced that foreign language instruction should be postponed until the high school years. Research studies of the time seemed to show that boys and girls could learn foreign languages most quickly and efficiently during their adolescent years and that learning a second language in childhood injured one's chances of realizing his full potential in his native tongue.

While this position has merit, probably it is more valid when applied to the grammar-translation method than to the audio-lingual method. Still, these arguments are worthy of serious consideration of any person who deals with foreign language curricula. A number of curriculum experts hold that foreign language instruction should be postponed to the secondary grades.

Foreign Languages in Elementary Schools. More recent research indicates that foreign languages can best be learned in childhood between ages four and ten,[2] a finding that seems to confirm common observation over the years. If the findings and observations are correct, at this age the child is neurologically most receptive to language learning. In addition, children from four to ten are not self-conscious, bored by repetition, nor frightened by the bugaboos of grammatical structure. If this evidence is correct, children are readier to learn foreign languages before they are ten than they ever will be again.

Whichever position is correct, foreign languages are spreading into the elementary school curriculum. Where they have entered the elementary curriculum, they have presented the secondary-school curriculum workers with a thorny problem in articulation of the elementary and secondary-school foreign language programs.

The Principle of Continuity. Whether or not foreign language instruction should be included in the elementary schools, theory dictates that once started it should be continued. If only two years of a language are to be given, then instruction should start in grade 11; if three years, grade 10; and so on. Under no circumstances should there be any break

---

[2] Wilder Penfield, "A Consideration of the Neurophysical Mechanisms of Speech and Some Educational Consequences," *Proceedings American Academy of Arts and Sciences*, 82: 201–14, 1953.

in continuity, according to the theory. For this reason no pupil should start a foreign language unless he can continue it through the twelfth grade.

Some school systems have not accepted the supposed need for continuity. In order to carry out the exploratory function of the elementary and junior high school grades, these school systems give the pupils experience in more than one language. Thus in the Washington County, Maryland, schools the pupils begin the study of one language in the elementary schools and switch to another one in the junior high school grades. Later the pupils may elect to continue one or the other of the languages throughout high school. For similar reasons, Washoe County, Nevada, has been experimenting with a general language course in which each pupil takes six weeks, three periods per week, of Latin, French, and Spanish.

The Problem of Vertical Articulation. If boys and girls are to have a continuous sequence of courses in foreign languages open to them, secondary-school offerings must be carefully articulated with those in both elementary schools and colleges. Not only must the secondary school offer the same language as the elementary school does, but also if all the entering pupils do not have the same background it must have some system for giving both beginning and advanced work in several languages. Sometimes this is done by putting entering foreign language pupils into classes with upperclassmen; other schools offer tracked curricula in which two or more levels of a language are given in a single grade. Many school systems try to avoid this problem by limiting all pupils to the same foreign language curriculum in the elementary and junior high school grades.

Native speakers of foreign languages also present an articulation problem. Wherever feasible, such pupils should be given a chance to perfect the language they already know. In schools having only a scattering of foreign-language-speaking pupils they can be absorbed into the normal program by either acceleration or enrichment programs. In schools that have many foreign speaking pupils, a different approach seems desirable. For this reason, Phoenix Union High School in Phoenix, Arizona, has developed a Spanish curriculum for Spanish-speaking youths, which seems to be accepted enthusiastically by parents and students alike. This curriculum centers around "correct grammatical usage in speaking, in terms of remedial work and refinement of expression; and the acquisition of correct reading and writing habits. The text books selected for use in these courses provide this basic presentation through worthwhile cultural content in Spanish. Amplification of cultural subject matter in the texts is achieved by means of individual reports (oral and written), projects and research papers."[3]

[3] Quoted from a letter from Mrs. Louise Arthur, Phoenix Union High School, Phoenix, Arizona, May 2, 1962.

Another problem of articulation comes from the boys and girls who did not enter the sequence at the beginning but wish to get the benefit of studying the foreign language. Among them may be pupils who have had no prior experience or talented pupils who wish to add a second foreign language. Sequences such as those illustrated in the Connecticut bulletin[4] are useful in solving this problem. Some high schools, like Albuquerque, New Mexico, provide tracks so that pupils may start sequences in a particular foreign language at different grade levels.

WHICH LANGUAGE?

Another doctrine almost unanimously accepted by language and curriculum experts states that it is much better for a pupil to learn one foreign language well than to learn two of them superficially. But what foreign language? Under the circumstances of today's world to predict just which language any particular group of pupils is likely to find most useful is an extremely risky venture. Unless it be English, no lingua franca exists, nor can any particular tongue lay claim to a monopoly on commerce or scientific or humanistic scholarship.

Fortunately selecting foreign languages may not be a critical decision. Advocates of foreign language instruction claim that the mastering of a foreign language gives the pupil a psychological set and skills that will enable him to learn other languages more easily. In addition, they say, the mastering of any language brings with it very valuable concomitant learning concerning the nature of language, peoples, and cultures.

Supposedly pupils may gain all these benefits from the study of any language. If the language a person masters in school turns out to be one that he never has occasion to use afterward, all is not lost. The knowledge of method and structure, and the concomitant concepts, attitudes, and skills derived from mastering any language, should stand him in good stead. Consequently each individual can be allowed to choose his language on the basis of his own personal preference from the languages available.

Be this as it may, whenever possible, the doctrine of contingent value should be applied. If it seems that a pupil will have practical use for a particular language, that is the language he should study. For this reason, frequently the historical or geographical setting determines which languages a school should offer. In Maine the State Department of Education recommends French as the most logical language "because this is the first language of a large segment of our population and is the language which represents a major cultural heritage for both the state and the nation."[5] For similar reasons Arizona and New Mexico schools offer

---

[4] See Plan D, Figure 5, below.

[5] Maine State Department of Education, *Guide to Learning in Grades 7, 8, 9* (Augusta, Maine, undated), pp. 2–3. (Mimeographed.)

Spanish, and Hawaiian schools offer Japanese, Hawaiian, Mandarin Chinese, and Hindi.[6] This is as it should be. Under the circumstances obtaining in these states geographical and historical considerations should carry a great deal of weight in determining the foreign language curriculum.

HOW MANY FOREIGN LANGUAGES?

If it is better to learn one foreign language well than two of them superficially, it is also preferable for a school system to offer a full sequence in one language rather than partial sequences in two languages. Specifically, if a school can support only four years of foreign language, it should give all four years to one language rather than offer two years each of two different languages.

Large secondary schools and school systems can support several foreign language sequences. Elkhart, Indiana, offers six-year sequences in both French and Spanish, beginning with grade 7 and supplements them by three-year sequences in Latin and German beginning in grade 10. Smaller schools with limited resources are forced to content themselves with more meager offerings. The Connecticut State Department of Education has suggested four different curriculum patterns to illustrate how foreign language curricula may be adjusted to the resources available.

According to the Connecticut curriculum bulletin, the ideal sequence in a secondary-school foreign language curriculum includes the entire six years from grades 7 through 12. In addition interested, able pupils should be encouraged to start a second foreign language in grade 9. This second language might well be a classical language. This most desirable plan is represented as Plan A, Figure 3.

FIGURE 3. FOREIGN LANGUAGE CURRICULUM,

PLAN A

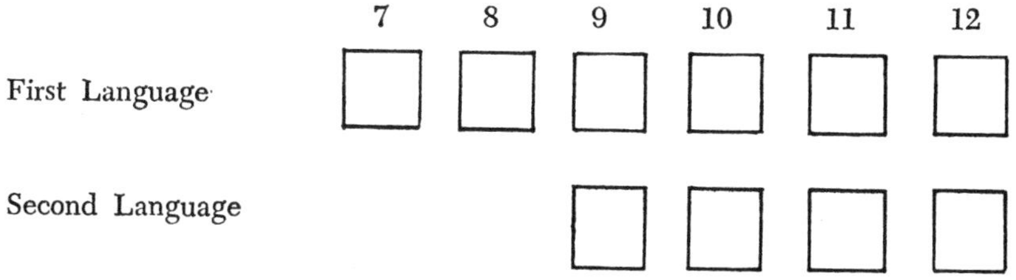

By allowing at least full six years in one language and four years in a second language, this plan gives pupils an opportunity to become proficient in both languages.

[6] At the time of writing, Hindi and most classes in Japanese and Chinese are given only in the elementary schools as part of Hawaii's Frontier Project Asian Languages, Elementary School.

If the full program outlined above is not feasible, the Connecticut bulletin suggests three other alternatives. Plan B (Figure 4) consists of spreading five years of one language over six years, by reducing the amount of time in grades 7 and 8. This plan assures meeting the minimum time allotment in both languages.

FIGURE 4. FOREIGN LANGUAGE CURRICULUM,

PLAN B

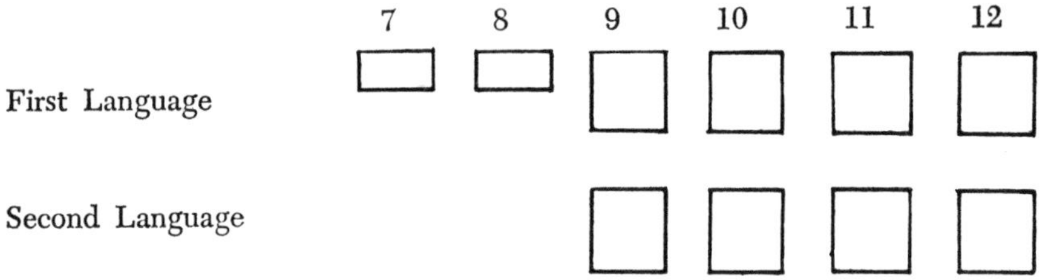

The second alternative, Plan C (Figure 5), spreads four years of the first language over six years and three years of a second language over four years. Plan D (Figure 5), the other alternative, suggests four years of one language in grades 9–12 and three years of a second language in grades 10–12. This plan is particularly useful in school systems organized according to the 8–4 plan.

FIGURE 5. FOREIGN LANGUAGE CURRICULUM,

PLANS C AND D

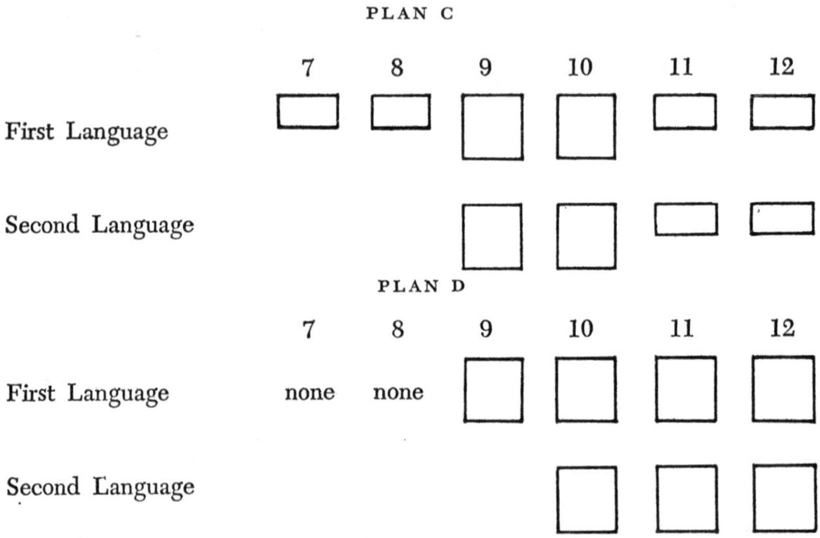

The suggestions offered by the Connecticut Curriculum Bulletin are examples of possible foreign language time sequences. Many other arrangements can be devised. If the recommendations of foreign language experts are carried to their logical conclusions, school systems that are forced to adopt plans similar to Connecticut's Plan C or Plan D probably should drop the second language altogether and add the time gained to the first language.

THE MODERN FOREIGN LANGUAGE CURRICULUM

Basically any language is a set of habits that make up the skills of listening, speaking, reading, and writing. Therefore language teaching is largely a matter of habit formation. To fix habits requires repetition and overlearning to the point where pupil behavior becomes automatic. The basic ingredient in language teaching and learning is practice, practice, practice, and more practice.

The essence of a language is the spoken language. Writing is an attempt to represent speech by symbols; grammar is an attempt to describe and codify the patterns resulting from speaking. Because this is so, to master a language one should first learn to understand it, then to speak it, then to read it, and finally to write it. As John Henry Alsted pointed out in 1630, the old-fashioned grammatical approach is a poor way to learn a language.[7] Modern foreign language curricula try to follow the natural pattern of learning: first an audio-lingual phase in which the pupil learns to understand and speak, and then a phase in which he learns to read and write.

THE AUDIO-LINGUAL PHASE

Audio-lingual training undergirds all modern foreign language instruction because it forms the basis on which to build all the other language skills. Consequently the pupil's first foreign language experiences are all audio-lingual, and only as he becomes adept orally are reading and writing introduced. Even after the pupil has learned to read well, the audio-lingual portion of his studies continues to be most important.

At first audio-lingual activity is confined to eye and ear training without any use of written material. To make it interesting and to give it content the instruction is usually centered upon some theme, such as "My Brother," "My Sister," or "My School." During the prereading period the teacher acts as a model for the pupils to imitate because all language learning at this point is done by direct imitation and practice. Some of the basic activities used in the audio-lingual phase of foreign language study are

---

[7] *"Nulla lingua docetur ex grammatica,"* John Henry Alsted, *Encyclopedia Scientiarum Omnuum,* quoted in Keating, *Comenius Great Didactic,* p. 5.

FIGURE 6. THE TEN-YEAR FOREIGN
LANGUAGE PROGRAM*

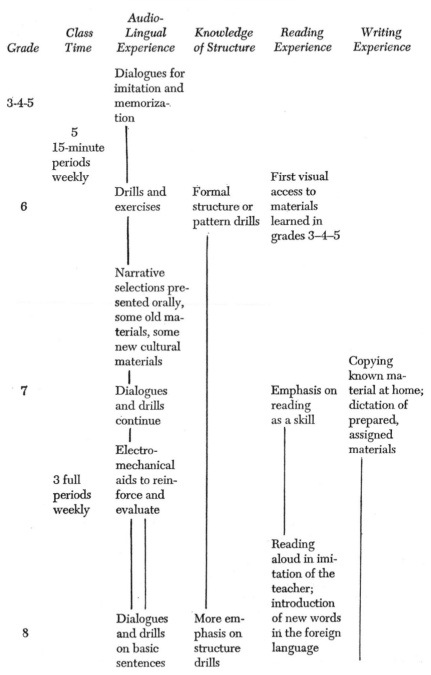

Grade	Class Time	Audio-Lingual Experience	Knowledge of Structure	Reading Experience	Writing Experience
3-4-5		Dialogues for imitation and memorization			
	5 15-minute periods weekly				
6		Drills and exercises	Formal structure or pattern drills	First visual access to materials learned in grades 3–4–5	
		Narrative selections presented orally, some old materials, some new cultural materials			
7		Dialogues and drills continue		Emphasis on reading as a skill	Copying known material at home; dictation of prepared, assigned materials
	3 full periods weekly	Electro-mechanical aids to reinforce and evaluate			
8		Dialogues and drills on basic sentences	More emphasis on structure drills	Reading aloud in imitation of the teacher; introduction of new words in the foreign language	

FIGURE 6.—CONTINUED

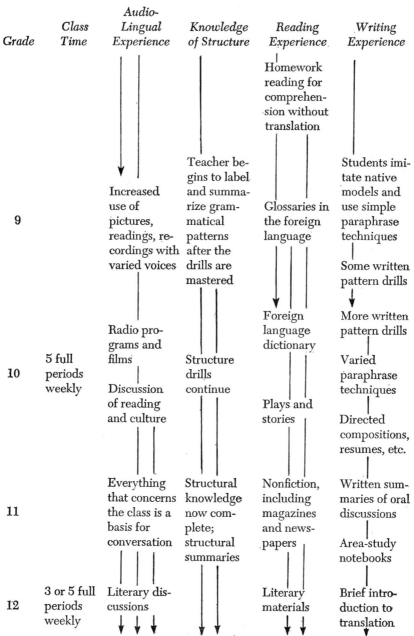

Grade	Class Time	Audio-Lingual Experience	Knowledge of Structure	Reading Experience	Writing Experience
				Homework reading for comprehension without translation	
9		Increased use of pictures, readings, recordings with varied voices	Teacher begins to label and summarize grammatical patterns after the drills are mastered	Glossaries in the foreign language	Students imitate native models and use simple paraphrase techniques
				Foreign language dictionary	Some written pattern drills
		Radio programs and films			More written pattern drills
10	5 full periods weekly	Discussion of reading and culture	Structure drills continue	Plays and stories	Varied paraphrase techniques
					Directed compositions, resumes, etc.
11		Everything that concerns the class is a basis for conversation	Structural knowledge now complete; structural summaries	Nonfiction, including magazines and newspapers	Written summaries of oral discussions
					Area-study notebooks
12	3 or 5 full periods weekly	Literary discussions		Literary materials	Brief introduction to translation

* Wilmarth H. Starr, Mary P. Thompson, and Donald D. Walsh, Modern Foreign Languages and the Academically Talented Student (Washington, D.C.: National Education Association, 1960) pp. 48–49.

dialogue learning, dialogue adaptation, structure (pattern) drill, and practice of dialogue and skills.[8] (See Figure 6.)

The Language Laboratory. Because it seems that the proper use of good recorded material can improve the effectiveness of audio-lingual operations, many secondary schools are investing in language laboratories. These laboratories come in several degrees of complexity. The most sophisticated of them have several channels, so that different lessons can be played at the same time, plus recording and playback features by which pupils may listen to themselves and monitoring devices that allow the teacher to listen to individual pupils and correct them on the spot without interfering with any of the other pupils. Other language laboratories are little more than tape recorders with extra earphones.

How much schools should invest in complicated, expensive laboratories is still problematic. A good teacher can teach well by the audio-lingual method without them. In Lexington, Massachusetts, for several years oral-aural instruction in French was given successfully by the use of texts published in France, supplemented by tapes, records, and other material, but without language laboratories.

What are the advantages of the language laboratory? In the first place, the language laboratory provides model voices that the pupil can listen to and imitate over and over again. Secondly, it allows every pupil in the class to practice speaking aloud and to listen to himself without disturbing anyone else and without fear of embarrassment. Thirdly, many language laboratories are constructed so as to make provision for individual differences easy. If the machine has individual recording and playback features, each pupil can listen to and evaluate himself. Language laboratories also compensate for individual differences by allowing the teacher to listen to individuals without interrupting the group and, in some installations, by permitting different pupils to do different lessons at the same time. Fourthly, not only does the laboratory bring pupils opportunities to hear good renderings of the foreign language, but it also gives them opportunities to hear different speakers and so acquire a listening fluency difficult for a teacher to provide alone. Lastly, in emergencies the language laboratory can fill in for teacher deficiencies. In fact, the language laboratory has been used as a teaching machine to actually teach Spanish without the presence of a Spanish-speaking teacher. Such practice is not desirable however.

In general, language laboratories seem to be sound theoretically and successful practically. Secondary schools are adopting them at an amazingly rapid rate. The increase of from two to thirty language laboratories in Maine during a three-year period is a typical example of

[8] Wilmarth H. Starr, Mary P. Thompson, and Donald D. Walsh, *Modern Foreign Languages and the Academically Talented Student* (Washington, D.C.: National Education Association, 1960), pp. 20–30.

rapid acceptance of these devices throughout the country.[9] The present value and future potential of the laboratory are well summed up in Louis A. Albini's statement concerning the language laboratory experiment at the Pascack Valley (New Jersey) Regional High School:

> We feel that the lab does good; the inhibited youngster will perform in the laboratory whereas he is reticent in class; the students *do* participate more; we can give individual attention more readily because the rest of the class is constructively occupied; students, by comparing their voices with a master voice through audio-active earphones *can* more readily identify their errors.
>
> But whether the amount of good is proportionate to the time that must be spent, the expense that must be accounted for, the effort that must be expended . . . remains to be seen.[10]

DEVELOPING SKILL IN READING A FOREIGN LANGUAGE

Ideally pupils do not attempt to learn to read until they have a fairly firm audio-lingual background in the language, for the goal of reading instruction is to teach pupils to read, not to translate. To facilitate the achievement of this goal, language experts have worked out rather specific recommendations for the teaching of reading a foreign language.

The principal recommendation is that pupils should never be asked to read anything they cannot understand and say, for if a child tries to read what he cannot understand, he soon develops faulty reading habits. To carry out this recommendation reading material in the foreign languages must be graded both to the audio-lingual levels of the pupils and to their age and interest levels as well. Even though a secondary-school pupil may have a childish vocabulary he should not have to read childish material. Neither should he be expected to read material beyond his maturity level. Teachers and curriculum builders must guard against the temptation to force pupils to read masterpieces before the pupils are ready for them.

Some classroom reading should be intensive reading accompanied by drill and analysis, but not all of it. At times pupils should read extensively, both as individuals and in classroom groups. Much classroom reading should consist of the entire group's reading stories and novels rapidly and naturally without being bothered by detailed analysis. Too much drill and analysis leads to poor reading habits and a tendency to translate instead of read.

Of course, pupils should discuss what they read. Except in emergencies, all discussion should be in the foreign language. In the beginning the discussion will have to be limited to repetition: "Where is Suzanne?

[9] Department of Education, State of Maine, Administrative Letter No. 47, September 7, 1961.

[10] Louis A. Albini, "A Commentary on the Pascack Experiment," *Secondary School Bulletin*, New Jersey State Department of Education 17: 9, June, 1961.

Suzanne is in Paris," and so on. Later discussion should become freer, until the pupils arrive at the point at which they can discuss their reading thoughtfully and critically. Usually the pattern of progress goes something like the following: from repetition, to free response questions based on texts, to paraphrasing the text, to resumes, to interpretation, and finally to literary discussion. Obviously, even in the reading phase of modern foreign language study, the accent remains on audio-lingual skills.

FOREIGN LANGUAGE COMPOSITION

Composition is the most difficult of the foreign language skills. Again the principle that one must be able to walk before he can run applies. Consequently experts recommend that the curriculum allow a gradual building up of writing skills. The sequence recommended is very similar to that recommended for the teaching of reading. Because pupils should not be expected to learn to write what they have not previously learned to read (and therefore of course to speak and understand), the pupil's first writing experiences should consist largely of copying what he has read. From mere copying he moves up to more complicated exercises, such as writing from dictation, paraphrasing, summarizing, précis writing, and writing a composition from a prescribed outline, until finally he is writing his own compositions independently.

The Place of Grammar. Teachers of foreign languages now put much less faith in formal grammar than they once did. The audio-lingual technique recommended by foreign language specialists is supposed to teach proper structure by means of oral repetition. In this plan grammatical rules and nomenclature are used only to explain principles, not to prescribe them. However, some authorities believe that learning structure in this way can be overdone, particularly when the students are talented adolescents or adults. Adolescents and adults, who already have some knowledge of language principles and how they work, can learn much through a grammatical approach. They should not be expected to learn in the same way they would if they were babies.

CULTURAL LEARNINGS

In addition to its linguistic role, foreign language instruction should also be a medium whereby pupils learn to understand and appreciate foreign cultures and their contribution to our own way of life.

Foreign language courses are excellently suited for teaching foreign cultures because through the foreign language the students can study a culture directly. Even in the beginning of the sequence the audio-lingual class exercises should be centered around the cultural life of the common people. Early dialogues should deal with the home, school, use of the telephone, shopping, and other topics which, in addition to being functional linguistically, give one a picture of life in the foreign country.

Other class and out-of-class activities should be centered around life abroad. Reading can add much to the pupils' knowledge of a culture. Rather than being limited to "readers" and to works of purely literary merit, pupils should read geography, history, current periodicals, newspapers, and popular magazines. Films, dramas, radio and television programs, recordings, pictures, and visiting lecturers can also be included in class activities. On occasion, pupils may even visit foreign homes and foreign countries. In northern New England trips to French Canada are not unusual, and in some instances pupil exchanges have been arranged across the border. Pupils can also visit abroad through such agencies as the Experiment in Living. Plans for the Davis County School District in Utah call for the members of the Arabic class to "travel to Lebanon for an extensive summer tour." Other similar tours are planned for students of French, Spanish, German, and Chinese.[11]

Foreign language clubs are an interesting source of intercultural understanding. They may sponsor foreign language films, plays, and programs and give foreign language parties. One Latin club even staged a Roman Carnival, albeit a rather staid one, and many clubs have had foreign banquets with foreign language after-dinner speakers. Visitors and immigrants from foreign lands make specially good speakers for such affairs.

Foreign language study can also bring about better understanding of our own culture and its origins. Usually such understandings are achieved by means of correlating with other subjects, but several school systems place great stress on teaching them directly in foreign language courses and foreign language extracurricular activities, such as the skits, projects, and scrapbooks worked up by the French clubs of Alabama high schools to commemorate the 250th anniversary of the first settlement of the state by the French. Activities of this sort should both stimulate interest in foreign languages and bring to the pupils a much fuller awareness of our national debt to foreign cultures.

THE NEW YORK STATE FRENCH SYLLABUS

The New York State French Syllabus is typical of the best attempts to implement the new theories of foreign language teaching. Although it recognizes the desirability of beginning foreign language study in the elementary school grades, the guide is intended to be a practical guide for the teaching of foreign language in secondary schools. To that end it outlines two sequences, a six-year sequence for grades 7–12 and a four-year sequence for grades 9–12. However, the syllabus does not

[11] J. Dale Miller, State Supervisor of Modern Foreign Languages, Utah, in a letter to the writer, June 13, 1962.

prescribe any specific content for the different grades. Instead it describes the curriculum in levels that school systems can move up or down in as seems desirable.

Basically the two sequences are the same except, of course, that the six-year sequence continues the instruction in all skills—understanding, speaking, reading, and writing—to a considerably higher level than the four-year one. Each sequence is designed to give the pupil a strong audio-lingual base and then more gradually to develop skills in reading and writing. Figures 7 and 8[12] show the gradual change in emphasis from level to level.

FIGURE 7. SUGGESTED MODERN LANGUAGE SEQUENCES FOR NEW YORK SCHOOLS. THE SIX-YEAR SEQUENCE

Audio-Lingual	Reading	Writing	Grade 7
Audio-Lingual	Reading	Writing	Grade 8
Audio-Lingual	Reading	Writing	Grade 9
Audio-Lingual	Reading	Writing	Grade 10
Audio-Lingual	Reading	Writing	Grade 11
Audio-Lingual	Reading	Writing	Grade 12

FIGURE 8. THE FOUR-YEAR SEQUENCE FOR MODERN LANGUAGE STUDY

Audio-Lingual	Reading	Writing	Grade 9
Audio-Lingual	Reading	Writing	Grade 10
Audio-Lingual	Reading	Writing	Grade 11
Audio-Lingual	Reading	Writing	Grade 12

The principles underlying both sequences are identical:

1. To utilize the audio-lingual approach.
2. To use the foreign language as much as possible and to minimize the use of English.
3. To teach the foreign language skills in the following sequence: understanding, speaking, reading, writing.

[12] *French for Secondary Schools,* Bureau of Secondary Curriculum Development (Albany, N.Y.: New York State Education Department, 1960), pp. 163–172.

4. To integrate and coordinate skills, knowledges, and attitudes even though the various aspects may be taught separately.
5. To give the pupils opportunities to use the foreign language actively in real or simulated true-to-life situations.
6. To devote beginning instruction to audio-visual experiences without recourse to the textbook. Textbooks will be used later for audio-lingual, reading, and writing instruction. Text material must be chosen so as to promote sequential development of the needed skills.
7. To present and master essential structure patterns through oral drill and meaningful sentences and dialogue with grammatical explanations when necessary.
8. To develop pupil appreciation of the country and people whose language they are studying.
9. To evaluate pupil progress systematically.
10. To correlate with other curriculum areas.
11. To learn a smaller vocabulary well rather than "to have a passing acquaintance with an extensive vocabulary they cannot manipulate."[13]

By and large, the new foreign language curriculum guides that are appearing follow quite closely the example set by the New York syllabus.

THE CLASSICAL LANGUAGES

For centuries the classical languages occupied a central position in the secondary-school curriculum, but that is no longer so. Classical Greek's three-year sequence has disappeared entirely; Latin too has suffered a tremendous decline both in prestige and popularity. Almost everywhere the four-year high-school-Latin-to-be-followed-by-more-college-Latin sequence, so common at the turn of the century, has dwindled to a two-year terminal sequence. In spite of a current revival of interest in the humanities and an upswing in Latin enrollments, long-range trends seem to indicate that Latin is gradually going the way of Greek. The demand of more functional subjects—including the modern foreign languages— leave little space for a subject many Americans believe to be useless.

The fall of the classical languages resulted from several causes. One of these was the disillusionment with the disciplinary aim of the language teaching, which has been described earlier. Another reason was that they really did seem useless. Teachers had no good answer when pupils and parents asked, "What is the use of studying Latin?" and so pupils dropped it. At the same time colleges began to drop their Latin requirements and thus eliminated another reason for studying it. But the most important cause for Latin's loss of customers was the poverty-stricken methods by which it was taught and its youth-shattering curriculum.

Latin teaching was based almost entirely on the grammar-translation

---

[13] *Ibid.*, pp. 11–12 (abridged).

method. For the average pupils most Latin assignments exercised the thumb more than they did the brain. All the pupils did was to look up Latin words in the vocabulary and write down their equivalent in something more or less like English. Undoubtedly uninspired teaching did more than anything else to drive classical languages from their place of honor.

OBJECTIVES OF THE LATIN CURRICULUM

Because Latin is no longer in common vernacular use, the objectives for teaching it are somewhat different from those for teaching a modern foreign language. In general, the cultural goals for the teaching of any language are the same, but the fact that the classical languages are no longer spoken by any national group necessitates a quite different emphasis in linguistic goals. Under these circumstances the reading goal becomes primary. Writing and the audio-lingual aspects of the language serve only as means of promoting the ability to read well. In Latin courses the study of English and its Latin bases also assume an importance not pertinent in modern language courses.

THE LATIN CURRICULUM

The Traditional Curriculum. At the close of the nineteenth century the Latin curriculum had been molded into the pattern that continued until 1926, when the College Entrance Examination Board dropped its prescribed Latin requirements. These courses of the Latin curriculum were:

> *Grade 9:* Intense study of grammar and vocabulary in order to prepare the pupils to read Caesar.
> *Grade 10:* Caesar's *Gallic Wars,* Book I–VI.
> *Grade 11:* Cicero, *Against Cataline.*
> *On Behalf of Pompey.*
> *On Behalf of Archias the Poet.*
> *Grade 12:* Virgil, *Aeneid,* Book I–VI.

This sequence has had an immeasurably strong influence on contemporary Latin curricula. Vestiges of it can still be found in such modern curriculum guides as the Texas standards for Latin courses, which suggest that by the end of the second year the pupils should be reading selections from such prose writers as Caesar and Livy; in the third year, such writings as the six orations of Cicero; and in the fourth year, five books of the Aeneid.[14]

The Present Latin Curriculum. In the 1920's the Classical Investigation

---

[14] Texas Education Agency, *Principles and Standards for Accrediting Elementary and Secondary Schools and Description of Approved Courses, Grades 7–12* (Austin, Texas: October, 1961), pp. 123–124.

set up new goals for the teaching of Latin and overhauled its curriculum. The recommendations called for Latin teachers to widen the reading content of their courses and to supplement their language teaching with background material concerning Roman civilization and culture.

Unfortunately the Classical Investigation assumed a four-year Latin sequence. Almost immediately after their proposals were published the average Latin curriculum became a two-year terminal one, so that the proposals never could be fully implemented. Nevertheless, they did have some influence in opening up the Latin curriculum so that it could better function in the modern school.

Because possessing a good Latin style is no longer the mark of the cultured gentleman, modern Latin courses do not emphasize Latin composition. Instead they concentrate on teaching pupils to read Latin directly and to turn it into good, clean, idiomatic English. Grammar is studied, of course, but functionally, as it is needed, instead of by rule, as it used to be. Some abstruse grammatical constructions are left out altogether. On the other hand, a definite attempt is made to relate instruction in Latin grammar with English grammar, to point out the Latin origins of English, and to utilize the knowledge of Latin derivations in the reading and writing of English.

These changes, of course, represent another instance of the rise of descriptive grammar over prescriptive grammar and the influence of modern studies in linguistics. Some secondary schools have adopted the "linguistics" approach to Latin and teach it audio-lingually as though it were a living language. Teaching in this fashion appears to be quite rewarding, and the movement to an audio-lingual approach to Latin seems to be gathering momentum.

So also has a movement to make Latin more functional by including considerable study of Roman history and institutions. Thus we find that the scope of the modern Latin curriculum, even though restricted by a shortened sequence, has broadened considerably since the turn of the century. For a language presumed dead, Latin is turning out to be a lively corpse. Whether this revival will be more than temporary is yet to be seen. Perhaps it may be Latin's swan song.

SUMMARY

A renaissance in modern foreign languages has brought with it greatly amplified curricula and greatly increased enrollments. Providentially the new curricula are designed to turn out linguists who are proficient in all four of the language skills: listening, speaking, reading, and writing. Although the primary purpose of the foreign language courses is to help pupils acquire fluency in the language, foreign language teachers can make much of their opportunities and give instruction in foreign cultures and their contributions to our own culture. These goals are however subsidiary to the main goal, fluency in the language.

Although not everyone would agree, the general weight of expert opinion seems to favor a ten-year foreign language sequence beginning in the elementary grades. Short periods of instruction in which pupils do not learn language skills firmly are considered wasteful. For that reason it is better for a pupil to study one language well than two languages superficially and better for a school to offer one complete sequence than two incomplete ones. In any event four years of a foreign language is said to be the absolute minimum sequence.

Probably every pupil should have a chance to learn a foreign language no matter what his former academic record. Those who show talent should go on to advanced courses and perhaps a second foreign language in the ninth or tenth grade. Which language one studies does not seem to matter greatly. Therefore pupils should be allowed to choose the language they will study on the basis of personal preference, occupational goals, and availability. But historical and geographical considerations are also important in determining which language a school should offer.

Modern foreign language curricula should be designed to ensure that the pupils acquire strong oral-aural skills before they attempt to read or write. All skills should be developed gradually and sequentially. A basic rule is that no one speaks what he cannot understand, reads what he cannot speak, nor writes what he cannot read. In order to develop the cultural values inherent in language study, audio-lingual exercises, discussions, and readings should include material by which the pupils can learn about the country and way of life of the people whose language is being learned.

The classical languages have been in a decline for the last half century, although Latin seems to have acquired a new lease on life. Culturally the goals of the Latin curriculum are the same as those of modern foreign language curricula, but linguistically the emphasis is on the reading goal and the use of Latin to improve pupils' understanding of English. Latin curricula have become much freer and more interesting since the turn of the century. Reading lists are more extensive and calculated to give pupils insights into classical life and history instead of being limited to Caesar, Cicero, and Virgil. Audio-lingual methods are being introduced successfully and are gaining in popularity. Evidently Latin teachers are trying hard to revive their dead language.

SUGGESTED READINGS

ANDERSON, THEODORE. "The Role of Foreign Language in International Understanding," *The Bulletin of the National Association of Secondary School Principals,* 41: 56–62, December, 1959.

An argument for foreign language as a tool for international understanding.

BRESLEY, LEONARD, *et al.* "Good Teaching Practices," *Report of Surveys and Studies in the Teaching of Modern Foreign Languages.* New York: Modern Language Association, November, 1961.

A report of successful practices in foreign language teaching.

BROOKS, NELSON H. *Language and Language Learning.* New York: Harcourt, Brace and World, Inc., 1960.

One of the most influential books on modern methods of teaching languages.

CONNECTICUT STATE DEPARTMENT OF EDUCATION. *Foreign Languages Grades 7–12.* Curriculum Bulletin, Series Number 5. Hartford: The Department, 1958.

A pioneer bulletin concerning foreign language teaching which has been greatly influential.

FRANZEN, CARL G. J. "Foreign Languages," in *The High School Curriculum,* Harl R. Douglass (ed.). New York: The Ronald Press Company, 1956. Chapter 25.

An excellent presentation of an older point of view concerning foreign language teaching.

French for Secondary Schools. Bureau of Secondary Curriculum Development. Albany, New York: New York State Education Department, 1960.

An excellent guide for the teaching of foreign languages. Many recent state guides have been patterned after it. New York guides in other languages are virtual duplications.

Guide to Learning in Grades 7, 8, and 9, Foreign Languages. Augusta, Maine: State Department of Education, undated (Mimeographed).

An excellent state program for junior high school foreign languages with its rationale.

HUEBENER, THEODORE. *Audio-Visual Techniques in Teaching Foreign Languages.* New York: New York University Press, 1960.

Makes excellent suggestions for the use of audio-visual materials and techniques in the teaching of foreign languages.

HUTCHINSON, JOSEPH C. *The Language Laboratory.* Bulletin 1961, Number 23, U.S. Department of Health, Education, and Welfare, Office of Education. Washington, D.C.: Government Printing Office, 1961.

An authoritative discussion of the use of foreign language laboratories.

JOHNSTON, MARJORIE C. *A Counselor's Guide.* Bulletin 1960, Number 20, U.S. Department of Health, Education, and Welfare, Office of Education. Washington, D.C.: Government Printing Office, 1961.

A presentation of vocational opportunities and careers utilizing foreign language fluency and information concerning opportunities for furthering foreign language in institutions of higher learning.

———. *Modern Foreign Languages in the High School.* U.S. Department of Health, Education, and Welfare, Office of Education. Washington, D.C.: Government Printing Office, 1961.

A report of conference in which the need for foreign language studies was stressed and modes for the implementation discussed.

KETTELKAMP, GILBERT. "Modern Foreign Languages from Where to Where?" *The Bulletin of the National Association of Secondary-School Principals,* 45: 97, September, 1961.

A short discussion of the forces influencing the foreign language curricula in the past and in the present and their implications for the future of foreign language teaching.

O'CONNOR, PATRICIA. *Modern Foreign Languages in High School: Pre-Reading Instruction.* Bulletin 1960, Number 9, U.S. Department of Health, Education, and Welfare, Office of Education. Washington, D.C.: Government Printing Office, 1960.

An account of theory and practice of introducing language instruction via the audio-lingual approach.

PARKER, W. R. *The National Interest and Foreign Languages.* Third edition. Department of State Publication 7324. Washington, D.C.: Government Printing Office, 1962.

Arguments presenting the case for more and better foreign language teaching in the United States.

Reports of Surveys and Studies in the Teaching of Modern Foreign Languages. New York: Modern Language Association, November, 1961.

Facts and figures concerning the teaching of foreign languages in the United States.

SMITH, PHILIP D., JR. *Course of Study for Foreign Languages.* Carson City, Nevada: State Department of Education, 1962.

An excellent example of one of the many state department courses of studies published recently.

STACK, EDWARD M. *The Language Laboratory and Modern Language Teaching.* New York: Oxford University Press, 1960.

A basic reference on language laboratories in foreign language teaching.

STARR, WILMARTH H., MARY P. THOMPSON, and DONALD D. WALSH. *Modern Foreign Languages and the Academically Talented Student.* Washington, D.C.: National Education Association, 1960.

An excellent presentation of the newer modes of teaching foreign language and the foreign language curriculum. Really applies as much to other pupils as to the talented.

"The Teaching of Foreign Languages," *N.E.A. Journal,* 50: 15–27, December, 1961.

A collection of semipopular articles describing various facets of modern approaches to teaching foreign languages in secondary and elementary schools.

Chapter 11

The Sciences

Science is deeply embedded in the life of man; it is concerned with the practical utilitarian activities of man as well as with his quest for knowledge. It helps man communicate with man; it makes it possible for man to be mobile and live in all climates. It also helps man in his striving for the "good life."

Science in a Technological Society. Through science man learns about his environment—the natural world and the social world. Modern objectives of science teaching emphasize ecological aspects of the subjects. Through the study of science the schools attempt to provide the graduate with the understandings, attitudes, and skills that enable him to live constructively and happily with himself and his fellow man.

Because we in the United States are living in a technological society, the schools have an obligation as an instrument of society to disseminate scientific knowledge. Without some of this knowledge the general public will never know what is scientifically true or untrue, nor will they know what it is that makes a person a scientific authority.

Science should be part of the general education program because it helps satisfy the requirements for a basic education. People in a democracy need to understand how and why things react or behave as they do. In a free society science can give the knowledge that keeps the citizen free of the grasp of charlatans, demagogues, and impostors; it is through science that myths, superstitions, and old wives tales may be eliminated. In a very practical way science can help a person be healthier, safer, and happier than he would be without the scientific knowledge.

Science and Leisure. Much has been printed in the past years about the prevalence of poor mental health. Mental health associations advocate the development of various interests so as to maintain emotional stability. The study of science is an excellent medium by which to develop leisure time activities that are both intellectually stimulating and physically satisfying from a tension relieving point of view. Studying science frequently leads to the developing of interests that last long after completion of the secondary-school curriculum. Star watching, bird watching, nature study, photography, and rock hunting are examples of hobbies that may result directly from science classes and clubs. Truly science programs can contribute much recreational as well as academic value.

Learning To Think Scientifically. One reason commonly stated for including science in general education is "to develop one's ability to do scientific thinking." From this statement one might conclude that "scientific thinking" is a special type of thinking peculiar only to scientists. Such reasoning is fallacious. Scientific thinking is nothing more than critical thinking. It is something that in the opinion of the authors of this book should be developed in all courses. Every course, but particularly every science course, can and should teach young people to analyze, to compare, and to check primary sources. Unfortunately not all science courses develop the skills and attitudes necessary for thinking critically. Too many science classes are taught by teachers with closed minds—who not only do not examine, test, arrive at conclusions, and retest ideas and findings themselves, but do not let their pupils think either. Such neglect, and restraint, is inexcusable.

SCIENCE FOR NATIONAL WELFARE

Since 1700 science and its application have made gigantic strides. More progress has been made in the past fifty years than in the preceding hundred, yet we have only begun to ferret out the mysteries of energy and life itself. Yet it is absolutely necessary that our present rate of progress increase. In order to provide a good cultural and intellectual climate favorable to science and to free inquiry, citizens living in a scientific era must achieve a reasonably high degree of understanding of the world of science. General education can contribute to this end by giving all the students the type of background needed to cause them to understand and support the efforts of the scientists.

Need for Scientific Manpower. The application of scientific discoveries has given man the highest degree of comfort and ease of living in the history of civilization. At the same time the products of applied science, for example, the automobile, television, and automation, have created problems yet to be solved. In order to design, build, and maintain the complex products of our intellectual matrix, and to maintain our economy at a high level, we need scientific manpower. So much so that the demand for teachers and scientists is increasing faster than the total labor force. National defense also has created demands upon the scientific manpower. Because the Cold War has developed into a war of science and applied science the federal government must have a continually increasing supply of scientific manpower to maintain a secure position in the world. To meet this demand large numbers of technicians, engineers, and research scientists must be trained by high schools, schools such as the Ward School of Electronics in Hartford, Connecticut (in Russia it would be a technicum), professional engineering schools or colleges, and universities.

Scientific Manpower and the Secondary School. Although it is not the primary function of the high schools to train students to begin work in scientific jobs the day they graduate, the schools must give pupils instruction in the sciences necessary to serve as a base for college and university scientific vocational training.

In order to meet the shortage of scientists predicted for the future pupils having scientific potential should be encouraged to take elective high school science courses. The difficulty for the guidance workers is to determine who has science potential; intelligence alone is not the criterion. Obviously not all scientists are brilliant nor are all brilliant people good scientists. One solution to this quandary is to give all pupils opportunities to "explore" science courses.

THE ROLE OF THE SCIENCE CURRICULUM

This then is what the science curriculum attempts to do:

1. Help the student acquire an understanding and appreciation of science as one of man's great achievements.
2. Help the student acquire a knowledge of man's natural and social world in order to apply this knowledge in attacking problems of everyday living.
3. Help the student acquire a questioning, searching-for-the-truth attitude.
4. Help the pupil explore his own interests and potentials in the field of science.

THE JUNIOR HIGH SCHOOL PROGRAM

ARTICULATION OF ELEMENTARY AND SECONDARY SCHOOL

Good experimental background in the earlier grades is a great help to senior high school science pupils. Pupils who have had a continuous, well-articulated presenior high school program tend to be more successful in senior high schools than pupils whose science instruction in the junior high school grades had been limited to a couple of years of science classes once a week or to a single year of general science. Happily the present vogue is to develop a continuous curriculum in science from the elementary school through the secondary school.

This realization of what 35 years ago was merely a dream has brought with it new problems that have yet to be solved satisfactorily. One of the most serious of these is the problem of articulating the elementary and junior high school science programs, as one can see when one compares the topics included in the junior high school science sequence adopted by the junior high school teachers of Tucson, Arizona, with the 12 content areas contained in a popular elementary school science series.

Tucson Junior High School Science Topics

Unit I	How do scientists think and work?
Unit II	What are the main groups of living things?
Unit III	What is material?
Unit IV	How do heating and cooling change materials?
Unit V	How can one material be changed into another?
Unit VI	How do we use and control fire?
Unit VII	How do magnets work?
Unit VIII	How are all living things alike?
Unit IX	Why do you eat different kinds of food?
Unit X	How do living things depend on each other?
Unit XI	What is energy?
Unit XII	How is gravity useful to us?
Unit XIII	How is the earth related to other heavenly bodies?
Unit XIV	How does the earth's surface change?
Unit XV	How do we control heat?
Unit XVI	What makes the weather change?
Unit XVII	How is electrical energy supplied in our homes?
Unit XVIII	How does your body work?
Unit XIX	How do living things grow and reproduce?
Unit XX	How do we take care of the plants and animals we need?[1]

Elementary School Science Content Areas

1. Plants
2. Animals
3. Conservation
4. Weather and Climate
5. Energy and Physical Changes Around Us
6. Machines
7. Electricity and Magnetism
8. Chemical Changes Around Us
9. Exploring the Sky
10. Exploring the Earth

[1] Tucson Public Schools, *Workshop Report Junior High School Science* (Tucson, Arizona, undated), p. 3.

11. The Human Body, Safety, Health, Foods
12. Science in Industry[2]

In reading these lists the reader should remember that repetition of topics does not necessarily indicate repetition of subject matter. In the spiral plan of curriculum design one may teach the same topics in all grades, but at each grade level the treatment touches different and progressively more difficult aspects of the topics.

Nevertheless the danger of sheer repetition is great. A cursory comparison of the two lists will show their similarities. Let us examine in some detail just one unit common to the two lists, namely astronomy. The Heath program in grades 4–6 covers rotation and revolution of the earth, seasons, angle of sunlight and its effect, movement of heavenly bodies, gravity, facts about the moon, the solar system, instruments for navigation, asteroids, comets, meteors, both artificial and natural satellites, speed of light, solar eclipse, lunar eclipse, types of telescopes, galaxies and escape velocity. The junior high school program for the same unit includes the solar system, orbits, satellites, asteroids, comets, meteors, size of heavenly bodies, facts about the moon, solar eclipse, lunar eclipse, gravitation, gravity, revolution and rotation of the earth, seasons, the universe, galaxies, nebula, speed of light, binoculars, telescopes, space travel. Thus one sees that unless a program is well articulated there could be considerable repetition. To avoid undue repetition science teachers on the secondary level must be familiar with the courses of study used in the elementary grades. The use of pretests at the beginning of the school year can help junior high school science teachers to minimize unnecessary repetition and build courses that are challenging to all students.

SELECTING AND ORGANIZING CONTENT FOR JUNIOR HIGH SCHOOL

One of the fundamental principles of curriculum building is that the curriculum should fit the pupil. By the time the student arrives at the junior high school he may or may not have had as many as six years of science. Furthermore, the science experiences of students during the six elementary school years may differ widely. Some elementary school teachers organize their schoolwork so that science is taught five times a week in 20-minute periods; other teachers teach science only two 15-minute periods a week. One elementary school may encourage extensive field trips to various botanical gardens, zoos, planetariums, and museums, whereas another school "cannot" work out the details. Obviously the pupils in the junior high school teacher's science class may have a considerable range in science knowledge skills, and abilities.

Examination of textbooks and courses of study seems to indicate that

---

[2] Taken from a chart published by the D. C. Heath and Co., *Heath Elementary Science*, 1959.

the following subject matter, which may be stated either as topics or as problems to be solved, is included in the scope of general science: health, living things (plants and animals—all sizes), force, machines, electricity and magnetism, descriptive chemistry, atmosphere, heat, astronomy, rocks, and conservation. The scope encompassed by the topics in this list is extremely broad and presents the curriculum builder with another trying problem. No matter whether the science curriculum is organized on the special plan or its alternative, the one-shot offering in a single grade, there is so much to cover that not much time can be devoted to any one topic. The result is often a "cover the book" approach, in which pupils do not get as much opportunity to study science in depth as they would with fewer topics to explore.

The science curriculum has been patterned in several different ways. They are as follows:

Science Block Patterns. In many junior high schools the basic learnings or general education portion of the curriculum has been organized into some variety of core or block-of-time program. One of these is the center-of-interest plan. In one center-of-interest plan, for instance, science might be incorporated into a core consisting of science, health, physical education, and mathematics in the seventh and eighth grades with no science at all in the ninth grade. Because science center-of-interest plans differ in individual schools however, it is impossible to describe any single plan that would be descriptive of center-of-interest plans in all school systems.

Another plan sometimes used in junior high schools is to include science as one of the studies in unified studies courses. Murray,[3] for example, has suggested the feasibility of a unified course combining geography and science at the eighth grade level because his research shows that geography and both biological and physical science texts at this level have many principles in common.

Science can also be integrated into true core courses at any level. Mikhal[4] analyzed sixteen problem areas, such as family living and critical thinking, to determine possible student activities. In this study he also examined contributions of science and weighed them in terms of adequacy for inclusion in general education. His findings indicated that science should have an important place in core programs. Among the problems that might be considered in grades 7–9 are:

[3] Robert C. Murray, *The Principles of Physical and Biological Science Found in Five Textbooks of Geography for Grade Eight* (unpublished Master's thesis, Boston University, 1959).

[4] Monir K. Mikhal, "Contributions of Science to Selected Problem Areas Proposed for a Program of General Education in the Secondary School," *Science Education,* 39: 300–304, October, 1955.

1. How can we have a healthy body?
2. What are the erroneous beliefs and superstitions common to man, and is there a basis for such beliefs?
3. How does man communicate?
4. How does science affect the way we live?
5. How can man use and yet preserve most of the natural resources?

Science As a Subject. General science courses have a rather anomalous position in the general high school curriculum. While some junior high schools offer science at each grade level, other schools offer it at only one level. At the ninth grade level, although general science may be part of the college-preparatory sequence, frequently it is not considered to be a college-preparatory subject and so may not be accepted for college entrance requirements in science.

When general science was first introduced it was primarily a survey course in which each of the traditional science subjects of the senior high school was organized separately in a logical sequence of its own subject matter. This type of course organization has practically disappeared. In all probability the most common type of organization now is one that avoids science area lines although it may include all divisions of the sciences. In such courses the work goes far beyond a mere accumulation of facts and notions about the environment. Instead the course is more likely to be organized around the problems of living. In it the teachers attempt to have the students study the ways man has controlled his environment to his own purposes as well as the problems that people have to solve in order to live. In this type of a course subject matter is not an end in itself; rather it is a means to understanding and solving problems that are indigenous to the community, the nation, and the world.

Functions of General Science. Unlike much of the pupil-centered work in the elementary school, general science in the junior high school is conceptual, with emphasis not so much on the child as on the child in an environment. During these years it becomes increasingly developmental in structure—a true link between elementary and senior high school science in which junior high school pupils can explore areas preparatory to possible intensive study later. Just as general science touches all children, because most all remain in school through the ninth grade, its breadth touches all ways of life. Well done, it provides an effective medium for creating and maintaining science interest and attracting pupils into senior high school science courses.

Innovations in General Science. Several innovations concerning the placement of general science and the other science courses have been suggested. One common proposal is that one or more of the senior high school sciences be moved downward. Another proposal is to continue general science for six years, beginning with the seventh grade. Experiments with biology in the ninth grade have given mixed results. Generally speaking, it seems that when pupils of average and higher ability in the ninth grade take biology they do not achieve as well as the tenth graders. On the other hand, when they are grouped according to mental age, interests, and motivation, pupils in the ninth and tenth grade accomplish about the same. Some interesting summary statements can be drawn from experimental science curricula described by Brandwein, Watson, and Blackwood.[5]

1. Eighty-five per cent of the pupils taking general science in grade 9 planned to continue science for three more years, but of ninth graders taking discrete science courses only 35 per cent of the earth science class, 30 per cent of the chemistry class, and 40 per cent of the biology class planned to continued science another three years.
2. Tenth grade biology students and eleventh grade chemistry students ranked higher in achievement than ninth grade students taking the same subjects.
3. General science serves the guidance function in that students use the course to plan future course work and vocational preparation.
4. Students taking four years of general science in the senior high school did as well on the New York Regents examinations as students in regular biology, chemistry, and physics courses did.
5. Getting teachers who have the breadth of knowledge and willingness to shake the restrictions of traditional thinking is a difficult task.

JUNIOR HIGH SCHOOL SCIENCE ENROLLMENT

In the past ten years the amount of time and number of classes per week devoted to junior high school general science has increased, especially in grades 7 and 8. The amount of time devoted to science in these grades has increased more than the time for science in the ninth grade. Course enrollments in junior high school science are also increasing. In some of the schools science is required of all eighth and ninth graders. In addition those schools listing general science as an elective report significant increase in student enrollments.

Relative enrollments in ninth grade general science seemed to have decreased somewhat, however. From 1928 to 1956, general science increased steadily until 21.8 per cent of the high school population was enrolled in general science. At that time it enrolled relatively more students than any other science course. Between 1956 and 1958, however,

[5] Paul F. Brandwein, Fletcher G. Watson, and Paul R. Blackwood, *Teaching High School Science, A Book of Methods* (New York: Harcourt, Brace and World, Inc. 1958), pp. 324–326.

the relative enrollment decreased to 21.2 per cent of the high school population, and biology took the lead with 21.3 per cent of the students enrolled.[6] Several reasons have been given for the decrease in general science enrollment. Some educators are of the opinion that the function of exploration formerly fulfilled by general science in the ninth grade is now being done in the seventh and eighth grades. The influence of colleges is also being felt. Some districts now require two years of laboratory sciences for the college-preparatory curriculum and do not recognize general science as one of the sciences meeting college admission requirements. For these and other reasons, in some schools ninth grade general science is being replaced by ninth grade courses in biology or earth science.

THE SENIOR HIGH SCHOOL PROGRAM

ENROLLMENT IN SCIENCE

Since 1955 prominent public figures and other writers and speakers have made attention-getting statements about science education, based upon a rather hasty interpretation of statistics contained in a United States Office of Education report concerning the percentages of pupils taking science in 1954. Unfortunately many people today still believe this erroneous information to be the truth.

When dealing with percentages it is important that one take care to ascertain the base of the statistics being used. In the 1954 study the base was the total four-year high school population. For purposes of illustration let us say that the figure for physics was 4.4 per cent of all the students. What this means is that 4.4 per cent of all pupils enrolled in grades 9–12 were enrolled in physics. It does *not* mean that only 4.4 per cent of high school graduates took physics, as many critics inferred. Rather, because physics is usually a senior subject, it means that more nearly 18 per cent of the graduates had taken physics.

With the preceding comments in mind let us proceed to examine the picture of science enrollments in the United States, shown in Table III. Note that the base in this table is again the total high school population.[7]

Enrollment by Subject. Because statistics about general science were first gathered in 1922, the subject has shown an ever-increasing enrollment. Biology also has been making excellent gains since its introduction to the curriculum in about 1905 and now has more students enrolled in it than the other sciences.

[6] Kenneth Brown and Ellsworth S. Obourn, *Offerings and Enrollments in Science and Mathematics in Public Schools* (Washington, D.C.: U.S. Office of Education, 1961), p. 22.

[7] *Ibid.*, p. 22.

TABLE III. PERCENTAGE OF PUPILS IN THE LAST 4 YEARS
OF PUBLIC HIGH SCHOOLS IN CERTAIN SCIENCE
COURSES: 1890 TO 1956–57

| | PERCENT OF PUPILS | | | |
Year	General Science	Biology	Chemistry	Physics
1890			10.1	22.8
1900			7.7	19.0
1910		1.1	6.9	14.6
1915		6.9	7.4	14.2
1922	18.3	8.8	7.4	8.9
1928	17.5	13.6	7.1	6.8
1934	17.8	14.6	7.6	6.3
1949	20.8	18.4	7.6	5.4
1954–55		19.6	7.3	4.6
1956–57	21.8	20.5	7.5	4.4
1958–59	21.2	21.3	8.9	5.0

When botany and zoology were fused into biology it immediately began to show gains in enrollment over its two parent courses. In 1910 only 1.1 per cent of the pupils enrolled in biology. By 1938 enrollment in biology had increased to 21.3 per cent of the pupils. If schools continue to move biology into the ninth grade, the relatively large number of pupils taking biology will probably continue to increase above the 1958 figure.

The relative enrollment in chemistry has proved to be the most constant of any of the high school science offerings. Ever since 1900 enrollment in chemistry has amounted to approximately 7–9 per cent of the total enrollment.

In considering these figures it must be remembered that the high school enrollment has shown phenomenal gains since 1900. For some time the enrollment doubled every decade. So while the proportion of chemistry students remained constant, the actual number of students increased from approximately 40,000 in 1900 to over 657,000 at the present time. The increase, representing about a 1200-per-cent increase in chemistry enrollment, is considerably greater than the 110-per-cent increase in total population of the United States during the same approximate period.

Proportion-wise physics enrollment decreased between 1900 and 1958. Whereas, in 1900, 19 per cent of the students in high school took physics, by 1958 enrollments in physics had dropped to only 5.0 per cent of all the students. One reason for the drastic change is that in 1900 physics was a tenth grade subject usually required of all students, whereas today it is usually an eleventh or twelfth grade elective. Nevertheless, in spite of the drop in the percentage of enrollment the actual enrollment in physics courses had increased from 98,846 in 1900 to approximately 379,000 in 1958. Thus there is a 284-per-cent increase in enrollment in physics, which again is greater than the population increase of the nation.

Enrollments in sciences other than the traditional sciences in public high schools in the nation amount to about 2.7 per cent of the total high school population in grades 9 to 12.

Increasing Popularity. Several factors indicate that the present interest in science will continue. One factor is the tendency among institutions of higher education to increase college entrance requirements. For example, when Arizona state institutions began to require two years of laboratory science for entrance, some Arizona high schools immediately made the two-year science requirement part of their graduation requirement. Such action enforces high schools to offer advanced courses in biology, chemistry, and physics and also causes increased enrollments.

The Top 15 Per Cent. Interest in science courses seems to be particularly high among "top students." According to a study in 1959 of the top 15 per cent of an Arizona senior class, more than 41 per cent of the 230 cases took science courses three or more years and more than 20 per cent additional two years or more. Because this study was made before the increase in science requirements for college entrance took effect and because most of the top 15 per cent of the school population intend to go to college, one can look for an increase in the number of the academically talented pupils enrolled in science courses.

SUBJECT PLACEMENT IN THE HIGH SCHOOL

The traditional placement of science courses is general science in the ninth, biology in the tenth, chemistry in the eleventh, and physics in the twelfth grade. The few efforts made to offer the subjects earlier have not been wholly successful, probably because of the students' immaturity coupled with a lack of mathematical knowledge. More experiments in this area are needed—it may certainly be that the determining factor might be the better selection of subject matter.

Placement of Specific Courses. As we have seen earlier, general science is a fairly firm fixture in grade 9. Some small schools however in the interest of economy may alternate general science with biology in grades 9 and 10, much as physics and chemistry are alternated in grades 11 and 12. In addition high schools may offer general science as an advanced course in grade 12 or sometimes as a multigrade elective.

Biology has been pretty well stabilized as a tenth grade subject, although a relatively small number of schools have made it a multigrade subject, and some schools have moved it down to grade 9.

Chemistry is offered more often as a multigrade subject than as an eleventh grade offering. In schools that offer advanced biology, chemistry may be offered in grade 12, thus allowing pupils to take advanced biology in grade 11. When such schools offer chemistry and physics in alternate years, both advanced biology and chemistry must be open to eleventh and twelfth graders.

The twelfth grade science course is usually physics, although it may be advanced chemistry or advanced physics. In schools offering advanced physics pupils must, of course, be able to take beginning physics course in the eleventh grade. Eleventh grade physics is offered in only a small number of schools however.

Physical science probably will continue to increase in its attraction to the high school population of the future. At the present time it is often used as the second year of laboratory science required for graduation and as a prerequisite for the regular course in chemistry and physics. Generally it appears to be a multigrade subject offered anywhere from the ninth to twelfth grade levels. Before World War II physical science was offered in more than half of the states, but immediately following the war only a few schools offered the course. Now some schools are offering it as a replacement for general science. In the past, physical science has tended to be a dumping ground, but recently the trend has been to make physical science courses intellectually challenging and stimulating for all pupils.

Science Curriculum Patterns. The following list illustrates one possible placement of various subjects in the science curriculum. In such a curriculum pupils with science aptitude can take six years of challenging work, while at the same time courses are available to the average student who displays interest in scientific matters.

Ninth Grade

Earth Science	Biology
General Science	Physical Science
Chemistry	

Tenth Grade

Biology
Chemistry
Applied Chemistry

Eleventh Grade

Advanced Physical Science	Aviation
Physics	Agriculture
Advanced Chemistry	Advanced Biology
Applied Physics	Meteorology
Astronomy	

Twelfth Grade

Advanced Physical Science	Electronics
Physics	Astronomy
Chemistry	Meteorology
Advanced Physics	Aviation
Advanced Chemistry	Advanced Agriculture
Advanced Biology	Machines and Electricty

SCIENCE FOR THE SLOW LEARNER

All pupils need to understand the methods of science, the influence of science on human life, and the main scientific facts pertaining to the nature of the world and man. Hence science classes must provide for low achievers and slow learners as well as for the brilliant.

By his very nature the slow learner is academically slow; that is why he is called a slow learner. This fact seems obvious, but the hard facts of the matter are that some science teachers seem to be in too great a rush to get these pupils to the last page of the book. A more reasonable pace might well be more profitable.

It is most important, when working with the slow learner, to choose subject matter that he is capable of learning. It is essential that in at least this one instance the curriculum be designed for the learner. We have reason to believe that some of the concepts in science are so abstract that they cannot be learned until the student has matured. The power concept in general science, for example, seemingly cannot be grasped by the average pupil until his mental age is higher than 160 months. Even at 190 months some students find the power concepts too difficult for them. For slow pupils such concepts probably should be omitted.

Such omissions from the course of study should not disturb us. Subject matter in any science course is largely the result of a great deal of selection anyway. Even with omissions the content remaining, if well taught, provides ample material for our courses. In this connection deemphasizing the verbal characteristics of the course will do much to make it worth while to the slow achiever. Of all the subjects offered in high school, science courses are among the best suited for utilization of audio-visual aids. If understanding is emphasized as it should be, there will be much less stress on isolated facts, for example, names of the 104 elements.

The pupil's background also has much to do with his success in the secondary school. If the pupil comes from elementary schools in which science instruction was conspicuous by its absence or its infrequence, he can be expected to do poorer work than someone who has had a rich experience. For such pupils the secondary-school courses may have to be largely repair work. Similarly pupils who do well in biology may just barely get by in physics because the physics course emphasizes mathematical skills. Obviously students who are low in quantitative skills will do poorly if such skills constitute the main part of a course.

LABORATORY VS. DEMONSTRATION

A well-equipped science classroom may cost $135,000 or more. One way to reduce the cost of science classrooms is to substitute teacher demonstrations for pupil laboratory work. If we are to justify its extra cost, it is necessary to show that laboratory work carries with it extra benefits worth the extra costs. To date the evidence is not completely convincing.

As far as general outcomes are concerned, studies seem to favor the demonstration method over the laboratory method. Ordinary written examinations seem to show that pupils learn as much or more with the demonstration method—particularly if the apparatus or the exercise itself is complicated. Because the laboratory method is time-consuming, using the demonstration method enables the instructor to cover the material in a comprehensive manner. Further the demonstration method seems well adapted for developing attentiveness to scientific problems.

Despite the evidence of several studies in favor of the demonstration method in science teaching, it is rather doubtful that pupils should be deprived of science laboratory experiences. As in most things in education, the teaching objectives should determine the methods and content of the courses. If the objective of the course is to develop laboratory skills, certainly the laboratory method seems preferable. Laboratory work should also be useful in developing self-reliance and in developing the individual's powers of critical thinking, independent power of analysis, an open mind, and other skills and attitudes related to problem solving, because as part of his laboratory activities the pupil refines problems, identifies assumptions, interprets data, formulates hypotheses and generalizations, tests hypotheses, and draws conclusions.

In curriculum planning, provision needs to be made for pupils to have the necessary time to do problem-solving activities. Of course, along with the time, the necessary equipment, supplies, and reference material must be provided. One approach that seems to be getting more and more attention is the depth approach, in which teachers forget about covering ground. Instead pupils are allowed to take time to devise experiments, build equipment, and improvise apparatus.

One version of the depth approach is the laboratory block. In this plan during any one semester a six-week period of daily work is devoted to laboratory work, field work, and necessary discussion. Not all students need to be working in the same area, but rather each pupil explores one area of the subject (or discipline) in depth. Work begins with rather simple experiments and proceeds to the complex, with an opportunity for individual research provided for the high ability student. Research that started during the laboratory block may be continued on the student's own time for a year or two if need be.

IMPLEMENTATION OF SCIENCE PROGRAMS

ADVANCED PLACEMENT

In an attempt to take care of the able student educators have developed the advanced placement program. In this program high school pupils may take advanced physics, chemistry, or biology courses after completing the conventional high school program and receive college credit upon satisfactory completion of the examination administered by the Educational Testing Service.[8] The quality of the advanced placement courses in science seems to be quite high. Students who have taken these courses, but received no credit for them, have reported that in some cases their high school courses were superior to their college freshman courses in the same area. Although the danger of using student opinion as evidence is obvious, it is safe to conclude that the advanced placement courses do challenge the superior students.

THE NATIONAL SCIENCE FOUNDATION

The National Science Foundation was formulated in 1950 by the National Science Foundation Act, which directed the foundation to

> . . . develop and encourage the pursuit of a national policy for the promotion of basic research and education in the sciences, to award . . . scholarships and graduate fellowships in the mathematical, physical, medical, biological, engineering, and other sciences. . . .
>
> To maintain a register of scientific and technical personnel and in other ways provide a central clearing-house for information covering all scientific and technical personnel in the United States, including its territories and possessions.[9]

Thus the foundation is a tax-supported federal agency organized into the following sections:

Fellowships: Grants to individual graduate students, teachers, and advanced scholars in science, mathematics, and engineering.

Institutes: Grants to programs of study. Applicants must be science teachers or mathematics teachers. Institutions are given grants to run the institute; participants are given travel allowances, tuition free, of $75.00 per week, plus $15.00 per week per dependent, up to four. Total grants per individual may be as high as $1200 for the summer institute.

Special Projects in Science Education: Grants are given to improve instruction in science, mathematics, and engineering.

Course-Content Improvement Section: Grants are given to produce up-to-date course-content materials and for the development of supplementary training aids to increase the effectiveness of instruction.

BIOLOGY

The subject of biology has for many years been taught as a study of either animal biology or hygiene and organized by chapters of units as

---

[8] This program is described in greater detail in Chapter 18.

[9] Alan T. Waterman and Harry C. Kelly, *National Science Foundations Programs for Education in the Sciences* (Washington, D.C.: National Science Foundation, March, 1959), p. 1.

invertebrate and vertebrate anatomy. Like some of the other subjects in the curriculum, the subject matter has been presented in a noncreative way that implies that all the answers are in the textbook. The teacher has compelled the students to memorize scientific names of animals, plants, and their classifications that are hard to pronounce much less remember.

Launching the Study. In 1958 The American Institute of Biological Sciences took the initiative in reconstructing the curriculum in biology through an effort called the Biological Sciences Curriculum Study (BSCS). Dr. Bentley Glass was named chairman of the study and directed a steering committeee to establish policy for the study. According to its initial proposal the function of the Biological Sciences Curriculum Study is to evaluate present biology offerings, to determine the subject matter in biology that can and should be learned at each school level, and finally to recommend how such learning can best be attained. The Biological Sciences Curriculum Study began operation officially on January 1, 1959, in offices on the University of Colorado campus, in Boulder, where it continues to operate.

The Three Versions. Biology can be taught from many different points of view. Therefore the Biological Sciences Curriculum Study organized three teams of educators to prepare experimental versions of newly organized basic courses in biology. These have been called the Blue Version, the Yellow Version, and the Green Version. Very briefly the versions use the following approaches. Further information can be obtained by examining the texts themselves.

The *Blue Version* stresses physiology and biochemistry. First it considers the basis of life in the properties and organization of matter and then follows up with the study of the activities of these organizations. Genetics is included in terms of conservation and modification of structures along with some study of evolution.

The *Yellow Version* begins with the chemistry and dynamics of the living cell, followed by microbiology. The whole organism is then considered with the traditional major functions treated system by system. Other subject matter includes diversity in the plant and animal kingdoms, genetics, reproduction and development, and, of course, evolution.

The *Green Version* uses the individual organism as the primary unit of study. It is concerned with the organization of individuals into populations, species, and communities and their functioning. Taxonomic diversity of living things is studied along with the history and geography of life and the problem of evolution. The course concludes with the relationships of the parts to the whole and man as part of his biological setting.

The actual process of producing a finished biology course extended over several years. During the summers of 1960 and 1961 writers produced the first texts, then revised the materials on the basis of feedback from schools that were using the different versions. Evaluation of material was done during the school years of 1960–61 and 1961–62. After all possible information had been gathered, three small writing teams revised the Biological Sciences Curriculum Study versions during the summer and fall of 1962, prior to commercial publication in 1963. Biological Sciences Curriculum Study materials include the three versions of the text, laboratory manuals, tests, laboratory blocks, and research prospectuses. Materials for the teachers include laboratory and text guides for each version, a teacher's handbook, a volume on working with the gifted students, a series of films and a volume on laboratory techniques and equipment.[10]

PSSC COURSE IN PHYSICS

Until the Physical Science Study Committee material was produced there had not been any completely new physics textbook written for several decades. The committee began working in November, 1956. Their work was made possible with a grant from the National Science Foundation of $303,000 initially, which has been supplemented generously by further grants and contribution by the National Science Foundation and private agencies—a total of $1,695,000, for instance, being available to cover expenses until September 30, 1958.[11]

The work of the original committee was generally administered by the Massachusetts Institute of Technology. Membership of the committee included professors, high school teachers, educationists, specialists, and technicians. The committee was incorporated in December, 1958, as Educational Services, Incorporated, and since that time the corporation has administered the work of the Physical Science Study Committee. In 1960 the committee's text and equipment were made available commercially by the D. C. Heath Company.

Purposes and Content. The purposes of the course are to give material in depth, emphasizing the intellectual, aesthetic, and historical backgrounds of physical science, and to give a good scientific foundation to the participants. The course is not specifically intended to prepare students for college physics. Its content includes the following:

I. The Universe and Other Things (introduction)
   Sizes and numbers, structure of universe, atomic structures of matter, molecular interpretation of chemistry, size and number of atoms.
II. Light and Waves
   Rectilinear propagation, reflection, refraction, corpuscular and wave models, wave phenomena, mechanical waves, interference, measurement of wave length
III. Mechanics

[10] See W. C. Van Deventer, "BSCS Biology," *School Science and Mathematics,* 63: 89–94, February, 1963, for a discussion of the whole program and the various versions.

[11] Physical Science Study Committee, *First Annual Report of the PSSC Committee* (no date), p. 13.

> Inertia, impulses and momentum, mass, force, kinetic energy gravitation, conservation laws, kinetic theory of gases, Coulomb's Law, forces in electric and magnetic fields, induction on moving conductors.

IV. Atoms
> Discreteness, electron charge, nuclear model of atoms, size, charge, mass of nucleus.[12]

The Physical Science Study Committee course makes intensive use of audio-visual aids. Approximately 70 films have been produced to present experiments that cannot normally be performed in the high school and also to present an explanation of some of the more difficult concepts of physics. There are also more than 30 different laboratory kits that can be obtained by the teacher of the course. Skill in using the laboratory kits and films can be learned by the teacher through attendance at one of the summer institutes. The usual federal subsidy is available to pay the institution, the professors, and the students.

Success or Failure? Naturally any new program runs into difficulties. The Physical Science Study Committee course was not immune. Critics claim the course is too difficult for the physics students in the high school. As part of the evaluation process, the School and College Ability Test was used. It showed that 80 per cent of the Physical Science Study Committee students were above the 75 percentile of the normal twelfth grade. This finding is quite in order because, as previously stated, the course was originally designed for the upper 25 per cent. In terms of achievement, however, a significant fraction of students who were below the 75 percentile on SCAT outperformed higher ability students. In fact, some of the lower-ranked students performed above the median score of some students who ranked above the 90 percentile on SCAT. In general, then, it can be stated that students of different ability attained overlapping distributions of scores on the achievement test.

NEW CHEMISTRY COURSES

There have been several efforts to revise the course in chemistry in the high school. Some of these are still under way; some have received federal money from the National Science Foundation to conduct studies. Two major studies supported by the Foundation are the Chemical Bond Approach (CBA) and the Chemical Educational Material Study (CHEM). Of these the former has been done at Earlham College at Richmond, Indiana, whereas the latter has been conducted at Harvey Mudd College, Claremont, California. In both cases the objective was to make a complete study of the chemistry course, including the subject matter of the course, the laboratory problems, demonstration problems,

[12] *Ibid.,* p. 21.

visual aids, course outlines, textbooks, supplementary readings, and methods of evaluation.

Chemical Bond Approach. The Chemical Bond Approach course is built around the general theme of the chemical bond. Course organization is centered about the topics of atomic structure, chemical bonds, properties, and types of reactions. An experimental edition lists the chapters as follows:

1. The Science of Chemical Change
2. Some Typical Chemical Reactions
3. Electrons, Protons, and Chemicals
4. Structures from Electrons and Protons
5. Disrupture Processes
6. Properties and Chemical Change
7. The Orbital Model of the Atom
8. Energy and Chemical Charges
9. Metals
10. Ionic Bonds
11. Periodic Table
12. Polar Valent Bonds
13. Chemical Equilibrium
14. Acids and Bases
15. Water
16. Chemistry of the OH Group
17. Covalent Halides and Oxyhalides
18. Chemistry of the OH Group: Acids
19. The Nitrogen System of Compounds.[13]

Some authorities have severely criticized the Chemical Bond Approach on the grounds that it is not adequate to cover all the material in chemistry.

The Chemical Education Material Study. The Chemical Education Material Study represents a different approach. Whether or not it is better or worse than the Chemical Bond Approach is still too early to say. It may well be that the final result will be a synthesis of materials of both approaches. As established in 1958 the purpose of the project was to identify the basic fundamentals of chemistry that could and should be taught in the senior high school so as to serve as a foundation for a college level course in chemistry. Chapters for the experimental text of the Chemical Education Material Study are as follows:

1. Chemistry: An Experimental Science
2. Scientific Models and Atomic Theory
3. Atoms Combined in Substances
4. The Gas Phase: Kinetic Theory

[13] Excerpt with permission from *The Science Teacher*, Volume 28, April, 1961, "The New Chemistry" by Alfred B. Garrett.

5. Liquids and Solids
6. Chemistry and the Periodic Table
   Supplementary Reading—Geochemistry
7. Energy
8. Rates
9. Equilibrium
10. Ionic Solutions
11. Acids and Bases
12. Oxidation—Reduction
13. Stoichiometry
14. Believing in Atoms
15. Electrons and Periodic Table
16. Molecules in Gases
17. Bonding in Liquids and Gases
18. Carbon Chemistry
19. The Halogens
20. The Third Row
21. The Second Column
22. The Transition Elements
23. Biochemistry.[14]

During 1960–61 a testing program was conducted to determine the extent to which the course is suited for those students that normally take high school chemistry. The findings show that students enrolled in Chemical Education Material Study courses during that year were considerably above the average of the students that normally take chemistry according to SCAT scores. When the Chemical Education Material Study final achievement test was administered, the results were very similar to those obtained in the Physical Science Study Committee evaluation. A substantial number of students ranking below the 75 percentile on SCAT performed as well as those students who ranked above the 90 percentile on SCAT. Although the high ability of the Chemical Education Material Study group must be taken into consideration, the relative achievement of the various kinds of students seems to suggest that the Chemical Education Material Study type of course can be successfully taught at the senior high school level.

SUMMARY

A certain amount of knowledge and understanding of scientific principles is essential for every American. In addition the school must help provide the nation with the trained scientific manpower needed in a divided atomic world. Basically the goals of the science curriculum are to help pupils acquire understanding and appreciation of science achieve-

---

[14] *Chemical Education Material Study News Letter,* August, 1961, Volume I, Number 4.

ment, knowledge concerning his physical and social environment, and a questioning scientific attitude.

The junior high school science curriculum attempts to articulate the science of the elementary school with the sciences of the senior high school. Sometimes this is done by teaching one or more years of general science, sometimes by core curricula or block-of-time courses. Recently there has been a tendency to bring such courses as biology, physical science, and earth science into the junior high school as part of the general education. Some of the evidence seems to indicate that proportionately more pupils go to advanced science from the general science courses than from discrete courses. The findings seem to be mixed as far as pupil learning in the courses is concerned. Why this should be is not known.

Enrollments in senior high school science courses have increased tremendously in the twentieth century in spite of the fact that a smaller percentage of the student body takes chemistry and physics. The recent stiffening of college admission requirements in science and furor over Sputnik has caused a reassessment of the science program in many schools and a consequent increase in the science requirements for graduation. These same influences have caused numerous private and government groups to investigate the high school science curriculum and to prepare curricula and materials by which to update and generally improve the science offerings. Among the most prominent of these new programs have been PSSC, BSCS, CBA, and CHEM. Although some controversy still remains concerning their effectiveness, evidently most of these programs have been meeting with qualified success.

The usual pattern of senior high school courses includes biology, physics, and chemistry and occasionally electives in other sciences. Rather frequently, nowadays, high schools give advanced work in the sciences in grade 12 as a result of some form of accelerated program. Sometimes the advanced courses are interdisciplinary. Instances in which broad field courses in science have been used to substitute for biology, physics, and chemistry seems to have yielded good academic results. So have courses that substitute teacher demonstration for laboratory work. However, modern thinking in science teaching seems to favor the use of discovery-oriented science courses that emphasize pupil experimentation as a means of learning scientific methods and the attitudes and skills necessary for critical thinking.

SUGGESTED READINGS

ASSOCIATION FOR SUPERVISION AND CURRICULUM DEVELOPMENT. *Using Current Curriculum Developments.* Washington, D. C.: The Association, 1963.

Chapter 7 is especially helpful to the teacher of science in determining the scope and sequence of new science programs.

BRANDWEIN, PAUL F., FLETCHER WATSON, and PAUL BLACKWOOD. *Teaching High-School Science: A Book of Methods.* New York: Harcourt, Brace and World, Inc., 1958.

Chapters include developmental material by subject for the science curriculum.

BROWN, KENNETH E., and ELLSWORTH OBOURN. *Offerings and Enrollments in Science and Mathematics in Public High Schools, 1958.* Bulletin 1961, Number 5. Washington, D.C.: Government Printing Office, 1961.

An up-to-date statistical reference.

BURNETT, R. WILL. *Teaching Science in the Secondary School.* New York: Holt, Rinehart and Winston, Inc., 1957.

Chapter 6 presents good material about the content of science courses.

Curriculum Bulletin Series 1958–59, Number 4, *General Science, Grades 7–8–9.* New York: Board of Education of the City of New York, 1959.

Presents course outlines for science in junior high schools.

GWYNN, J. MINOR. *Curriculum Principles and Social Trends.* Third edition. New York: The Macmillan Company, 1960.

This book is especially good for its bibliographies after each chapter.

NATIONAL SCIENCE TEACHERS ASSOCIATION. *Quality Science for Secondary Schools.* Washington, D.C.: The Association, 1960.

Emphasizes the role of the administrator in improving the science curriculum.

NATIONAL SOCIETY FOR THE STUDY OF EDUCATION. *Science Education in American Schools.* Forty-sixth Yearbook, Part I. Chicago: The University of Chicago Press, 1947.

Chapters 12 and 13 are pertinent.

————. *Rethinking Science Education.* Fifty-ninth Yearbook, Part I. Chicago: The University of Chicago Press, 1960.

Chapters 9, 10, and 11 are good for purposes of curriculum revision.

OBOURN, ELLSWORTH. *Analysis of Research in the Teaching of Science, July 1955–July 1956.* Bulletin 1958, Number 7. Washington, D.C.: Government Printing Office, 1958.

Some material about senior high school—has more material about the junior high school science.

RICHARDSON, JOHN S. *Science Teaching in Secondary Schools.* Englewood Cliffs, New Jersey: Prentice-Hall, Inc., 1957.

Chapter 3 is a general treatment of science in the curriculum.

ROUCEK, JOSEPH S. *The Challenge of Science Education.* New York: Philosophical Library, 1959.

Edited by an eminent educator. Synthesizes writings of science-oriented persons.

Recently, when students were asked to list the most important subjects they had had in high school, mathematics rated right at the top. From the pupils' point of view, mathematics has a high value for its role in preparation for college. Nevertheless, casual examination of programs of studies of American secondary schools will show that mathematics requirements are not proportional to the importance given to mathematics by the pupils, educationists, or mathematicians. Even so, pupils are enrolling in mathematics courses in ever-increasing numbers.

PURPOSES FOR STUDYING MATHEMATICS

High school pupils should study mathematics to give them the tools they need for future work and to learn that mathematics is a creative process by which one can prove an idea—or a hunch—deductively. Teachers should always be prepared to answer the question "Why are we studying this stuff?" The purposes can be explained both in terms of the abstract beauty of the science of mathematics or the use of mathematics to control the time and space in which man is a temporary resident.

INTEREST

That the interests, needs, and abilities of the pupils should be considered in determining the curriculum is a fundamental of curriculum organization. Therefore, if pupils are interested in a particular phase of mathematics, it would seem proper to offer it for them. Of course, pupil interest may derive from many things—an admired friend's work requires mathematics, the pupil's future vocation requires mathematics, his reading and studying have piqued his intellectual curiosity, or his peers have pressured him. In any case, when pupils do show an interest in mathematics, they should be encouraged to pursue it.

KNOWLEDGE

A certain amount of knowledge in the field of mathematics is necessary to operate in one's various roles as a person. Just to fully comprehend the articles in the daily newspaper, one must know the meaning of per cents, graphs, and statistics. Citizenship requires knowledge of fundamental mathematical concepts, so that one can make wise decisions, such as distinguishing between valid and false claims for various financial plans. Thousands of vocations depend on mathematical knowledge—sometimes more, sometimes less; sometimes as part of the training, and sometimes as part of the daily job. All sciences today require an understanding of mathematics. Five to seven hours of mathematics is recommended for prospective biology teachers in some teacher education curricula. Even the defense of the country rests for a large part on persons whose work is mathematics.

JUNIOR HIGH SCHOOL MATHEMATICS

ENROLLMENTS

Examination of the data available shows that mathematics enrollments in the junior high school have increased. In the case of seventh and eighth grade arithmetic, enrollments approach perfection; practically all seventh and eighth graders are taking arithmetic today. Although nine out of ten pupils continue mathematics at the ninth grade level, loyalties here are split between general mathematics and algebra, a college-preparatory subject, with algebra taking the lead. (See Table IV.) Evidently arithmetic is offered almost universally in grades 7 and 8 of the junior high schools, but general mathematics and/or algebra courses are not always available in grade 9.

TWO-TRACK OR MULTITRACK ORGANIZATION

When the junior high school has a two-track mathematics offering, pupils must choose between general mathematics or elementary algebra in the ninth grade. Frequently the criterion is: college-bound, algebra; not college-bound, general mathematics. In some schools this process has resulted in the general mathematics classes' becoming dumping grounds. Accordingly many mathematics teachers consider themselves disfavored

TABLE IV. COMPARISON OF ENROLLMENTS, BY TYPE OF SCHOOL, IN CERTAIN MATHEMATICS COURSES EXPRESSED AS THE PERCENT OF PUPILS IN GRADE WHERE COURSE IS USUALLY OFFERED: FALL 1954, FALL 1956, AND FALL 1958*

YEAR BY COURSE	GRADE	ALL H. S.	REG. 4 YR.	JR. H. S.	SR. H. S.	JR.–SR. H. S.	UNDIVIDED H. S.
General Mathematics	9						
1954		44.5	46.2	42.0		41.3	52.3
1956		43.1	44.6	41.1		41.9	50.1
1958		34.4	NA	NA		NA	NA
Elementary Algebra	9						
1954		64.5	65.9	43.8		66.4	69.1
1956		67.0	69.5	51.7		69.2	68.0
1958		71.6	NA	NA		NA	NA

* *1954 and 1956 figures from Kenneth Brown,* Offerings and Enrollments in Science and Mathematics, *Pamphlet No. 120 (Washington, D.C.: Government Printing Office, 1957). The 1958 figures from Kenneth Brown and Ellsworth Obourn,* Offerings and Enrollments in Science and Mathematics, *Bulletin 1961, No. 5 (Washington, D.C.: Government Printing Office, 1961).*

N.A. means not available.

if they are assigned general mathematics classes. The general opinion seems to be that general mathematics is for pupils of low ability, and therefore teaching it cannot be a joy.

Why General Mathematics? Why then give general mathematics? In most places it is taught for two reasons: (1) to give pupils a year of remedial arithmetic, and (2) to provide a review of arithmetic and exploratory work that prepare for algebra by including informal geometry, arithmetic, and algebra. William David Reeve worked out a placement of content in general mathematics as follows:[1]

7th Grade: Informal Geometry, Arithmetic, Algebra
8th Grade: Algebra, Business Arithmetic, Informal Geometry
9th Grade: Algebra, Numerical Trigonometry, Demonstrative Geometry, and Arithmetic

The Floral Park Program. An integrated sequence in general mathematics has been developed in Floral Park, New York.[2] In this program mathematics is required of all students in grades 7 through 9. Essentially the program is a practical application of the two purposes of general mathematics stated above. In the seventh grade the pupils review the

[1] William David Reeve, "What Should Be the Nature and Content of Junior High School Mathematics?" *Mathematics Teacher,* 48: 415, October, 1955.

[2] Ida A. Ostrander, "A General Mathematics Program for a Large High School," *Bulletin of the National Association of Secondary-School Principals,* 42: 46, May, 1959.

fundamental concepts of arithmetic and are given instruction in geometry. Here the relationship of geometry and algebra is developed by having the students discover the formulas for simple geometric figures. In the eighth grade the pupils continue to reinforce their learning of basic arithmetic fundamentals by learning practical applications, for example, budgets, insurance, taxation, and interest, and to advance their study of geometry by utilizing measurement procedures. In many ways this course seems to be what Reeve calls business arithmetic.

The ninth grade mathematics program in Floral Park introduces what they call a four-track system. Essentially the system consists of a two-track offering in algebra and another two-track offering in general mathematics:

> Track One: Ninth grade Mathematics (Algebra for the superior)
> Track Two: Algebra
> Track Three: General Mathematics
> Track Four: Basic Mathematics

For tracks one and two algebra is the core, track one being for superior pupils who explore various algebraic topics in some detail, and track two being the regular algebra course. Track three appears to be a standard general mathematics course of study, that is, as standard as any general mathematics course of study can be. Track four is a remedial course integrating arithmetic and other mathematical content. Wherever possible, each of the courses makes practical applications, reviews arithmetic processes, and extends the geometric concepts that have been previously developed.

IMPROVING THE JUNIOR HIGH SCHOOL MATHEMATICS PROGRAM

A disadvantage of the common two-track mathematics curriculum is that too often the pupils seem to do more busy work than developmental work in grades 7 and 8. The notion that one must not go too far in grades 7 and 8 because the pupils may be bored when they take algebra in grade 9 seems to be all too prevalent. The result has been overemphasis on mathematics as a series of tricks and a proportionate neglect of the nature of mathematical problems.

This practice is most unfortunate. Mathematics classes at all levels should be concerned with the creative study of mathematics and taught so that pupils become familiar with its structure. When mathematics is taught properly, seventh or eighth grade teachers need no longer worry about preempting the material of the ninth grade course.

The University of Maryland Study. Several organizations and institutions are engaged in studying the mathematics curriculum in the secondary school. Among the projects dealing specifically with the junior high school is a study of junior high school mathematics started at the

University of Maryland in September, 1957. This study represents a cooperative effort on the part of four major school systems in the Washington, D.C. area, the university department of education staff, and the university department of psychology and engineering. Its purpose is to develop experimental courses in the seventh and eighth grades, to find out how seventh and eighth graders think about mathematics, to determine measures of maturity for studying mathematical concepts, and finally to evaluate extensively the entire experimental endeavor.

The National Council of Teachers of Mathematics Plan. In another study the National Council of Teachers of Mathematics has been working for some time to solve the problem of mathematics course content at the seventh and eighth grade level. Their twenty-second Yearbook, entitled *Emerging Practices in Mathematics Education,*[3] would place much modern mathematics at the junior high school level. In the seventh grade the course of study would contain the teaching of the largest possible error, the concept of precision, the whole area of approximate numbers, and the handling of approximate data. Such a course of study would include the use of the fundamental processes to handle approximate data. Readiness for algebra would also be taught by emphasizing the meaning of numbers and by teaching the language of mathematics.

Junior High School Mathematics for Slow Learners. An interesting experiment in teaching mathematics to pupils who might be called slow learners has been conducted in a New York City school located in a rather poor neighborhood having a high rate of delinquency. In this experiment pupils retarded at least two years, with I.Q.'s from 70 to 90, were taught statistical concepts, such as median, mode, average, central tendency, and probability. A follow-up study indicated that these pupils retained these concepts quite well. These same pupils also studied the language of sets. From their study the pupils were able to enter into the abstract world of mathematics and to define such terms as *union* and *intersection*. Their proficiency was amply demonstrated when they proved themselves able to use the symbol U for union satisfactorily and to solve problems such as

$$\{\, 1,\, 2,\, 3\,\} \cap \{\, 3,\, 4,\, 5\,\} = \{\, 3\,\}$$

In addition to learning mathematics the children in this experiment displayed radical changes in attitudes. Pupils became alert where before they had been passive, and class cutting dropped. Probably the pupils' attitudes changed because (a) new material was introduced instead of the old, that they had failed once or twice before; (b) they learned to enjoy mathematics; (c) mathematics was made meaningful to them; and

[3] National Council of Teachers of Mathematics, *Emerging Practices in Mathematics Education,* Twenty-second Yearbook (Washington, D.C.: The Council, 1954).

(d) they learned some mathematics to show off to their less fortunate friends and thus gained some prestige.[4]

Junior High School Mathematics for Gifted Students. Generally speaking, the "able," "talented," or "gifted" students are not segregated into special sections for mathematics instruction in the seventh and eighth grades. (The term *special section* as used herein means a course of study entirely different from that used for most of the student population.) Rather the philosophy of enrichment is prevalent at this level. In some schools able students are members of randomly grouped classes. In such classes enrichment is provided on an individual basis to students who have completed the required assignments; in others homogeneous grouping is used, plus individual enrichment.

A case in point is the program for able students in mathematics that began September, 1958, in the Seattle Public Schools. Although this is a six-year program beginning with grade 7, only the part of the program concerning grades 7–9 will be described at this time.[5]

Grade Seven: Students will have thorough and challenging work in arithmetic from the regular seventh-grade textbook. Enrichment topics will be presented and students will be expected to undertake original study projects. When such a study is complete and the report prepared, it will be presented to the entire class. Some of the enrichment topics include number systems other than our decimal system, topics from the history of mathematics, construction of a slide rule, interesting applications of mathematics.

Grade Eight: Students will finish necessary work in arithmetic in about two months. Elementary algebra will be started and continue throughout the rest of the year. The students are expected to do the most difficult topics of elementary algebra. Discussions in class will emphasize the meanings rather than techniques. Students are expected to work independently on daily assignments and to do original thinking in problem solving. Two or three topics in elementary algebra may be carried over to grade nine.

Grade Nine: Elementary algebra will be completed by the end of the second month. Intermediate algebra will then be introduced and completed by the end of the school year. Students will be expected to do the same fine work in intermediate algebra as in elementary algebra.

The program for the talented in Hillsborough High School is similar in many respects. In this Florida school seventh grade mathematics is "enriched arithmetic 7," grade 8 is "accelerated arithmetic and first-year algebra," and grade 9 is composed of the rest of elementary algebra and

[4] Stephen Krulik, "Experiences with Some Different Topics for Slow Learners," *Bulletin of the National Association of Secondary-School Principals,* 43: 43 ff, May, 1959.

[5] National Association of Secondary-School Principals, "Mathematics in Secondary Schools Today," *Bulletin of the National Association of Secondary-School Principals,* 43: 79, May, 1959.

a beginning of second-year algebra.[6] The two plans differ in that the Seattle plan specifies that intermediate algebra be completed by the end of the ninth grade, whereas in the Hillsborough plan a minimum of a half year of intermediate algebra is specified. The two plans are alike in that algebra is not studied in the tenth grade.

SENIOR HIGH SCHOOL MATHEMATICS

In the late 1950's senior high school mathematics was rather severely criticized. In part this criticism was a result of the same error that caused the unwarranted attack on the sciences, that is, the mistake of not considering the numerical bases used to compute the percentages in tables presenting enrollment data. From the study in 1954 previously cited, for example, hasty critics naïvely assumed that because only 13.5 per cent of the pupils in grades 9–12 were enrolled in geometry, 86 per cent of our high school graduates had never had any plane geometry. Obviously this conclusion was false, because the percentage represents only one year of the graduates' four-year course. Using this same base and assuming plane geometry to be a tenth grade subject, a percentage of 25 per cent for the year would mean that approximately 100 per cent of the graduates had had plane geometry before graduation. The reader is again cautioned to ascertain the base in all tables in which percentages are used to handle numerical data.

TRENDS IN SENIOR HIGH SCHOOL MATHEMATICS

Still much of the criticism was well warranted. In some American school systems one can still complete 12 to 14 years of mathematics without encountering any subject matter developed after the beginning of the nineteenth century. Up until the last few years less curriculum revision has occurred in mathematics than in any other subject offered in the public high school. In spite of the many developments in mathematical theory, statistical records show the subject organization of the mathematics curriculum in many schools had not changed in 160 years.

Plane geometry affords a startling example. For years high school and college teachers and administrators justified geometry because it was thought to be the best vehicle to teach the pupils to think and to express themselves clearly and logically. And so the emphasis remained, year after year, on the same old theorems and formal proofs. Today most mathematicians agree that these objectives would be better attained through the use of new content (for example, the finite geometry) and new approaches (for example, the discovery method).

Fortunately the past few years have brought a new awakening of the

---

[6] Howard Gallant, "A Look at a Multiple Track Mathematics Program," *The Bulletin of the National Association of Secondary-School Principals*, 43: 59, May, 1959.

interest in the field of mathematics. Some plans like the Illinois Plan for teaching mathematics are bringing in modern mathematics. In other attempts at reorganization the subject matter within the traditional subjects of algebra, geometry, solid geometry, and trigonometry has been cut up and reassembled under new course designations. Of course it was never the mathematics that was out of date, but rather the courses of study.

Mathematics Enrollments. Since 1954 high school enrollments in the field of mathematics have been on the increase. (See Table V.)

TABLE V. COMPARISON OF ENROLLMENTS, BY TYPE OF SCHOOL, IN CERTAIN MATHEMATICS COURSES EXPRESSED AS THE PERCENT OF PUPILS IN A GRADE WHERE THE COURSE IS USUALLY OFFERED: FALL 1954, FALL 1956, FALL 1958*

YEAR BY COURSE	GRADE	ALL H. S.	REG. 4 YR.	JR. H. S.	SR. H. S.	JR.–SR. H. S.	UNDI-VIDED H. S.
General Mathematics	9						
1954		44.5	46.2	42.0		41.3	52.3
1956		43.1	44.6	44.1		41.9	50.1
1958		34.4	—	—		—	—
Elementary Algebra	9						
1954		64.5	65.9	43.8		66.4	69.1
1956		67.0	69.5	51.7		69.2	68.0
1958		71.6	—	—		—	—
Plane Geometry	10						
1954		37.4	38.4		33.6	40.0	34.1
1956		41.6	40.3		43.8	41.7	37.8
1958		44.7	—		—	—	—
Intermediate Algebra	11						
1954		28.5	27.6		23.8	29.6	36.4
1956		32.2	29.6		34.5	31.4	35.3
1958		37.0	—		—	—	—
Solid Geometry	12						
1954		6.5	6.5		6.0	7.5	4.4
1956		7.6	7.1		7.6	8.4	6.8
1958		3.9	—		—	—	—
Trigonometry	12						
1954		7.4	6.7		7.7	8.9	4.7
1956		9.2	7.9		9.4	10.9	8.2
1958		11.5	—		—	—	—

* *Kenneth E. Brown,* Offerings and Enrollments in Science and Mathematics in Public High School, *Pamphlet No. 120 (Washington, D.C.: Government Printing Office, 1957), p. 31; and Kenneth E. Brown and Ellsworth Obourn,* Offerings and Enrollments in Science and Mathematics, *Bulletin 1961, No. 5 (Washington, D.C.: Government Printing Office, 1961), p. 62.*

With the exception of general mathematics and solid geometry, enrollments in all of the high school mathematics subjects have increased since 1954. Obviously, in the ninth grade, the increase in algebra enrollment has been at the expense of the enrollment in general mathematics. In plane geometry the enrollment increased from approximately 37 per cent of the students in the tenth grade in 1954 to about 45 per cent in 1958.

TABLE VI. NUMBER AND PERCENT OF PUPILS IN PUBLIC HIGH SCHOOLS *NOT* OFFERING CERTAIN MATHEMATICS COURSES: FALL 1958[*]

COURSE		
General Mathematics (9th grade)	136,897	29.5
Elementary Algebra	7,018	1.5
Plane Geometry	24,105	5.6
Intermediate or Advanced Algebra	35,430	9.7
Trigonometry	97,100	33.2
Solid Geometry	211,875	72.4

[*] *Kenneth Brown and Ellsworth Obourn,* Offerings and Enrollments in Science and Mathematics, *Bulletin 1961, No. 5, 1961 (Washington, D.C.: Government Printing Office) p. 63.*

Most of the pupils are in public schools that offer three years of mathematics in grades 9–12. As Table VI shows, relatively small percentages of students do not have the opportunity to take elementary algebra, plane geometry, or advanced algebra. Still, if educators and the public believe that *all* students in the United States should have an equal opportunity to take mathematics, then the situation needs to be critically examined, for today thousands of students are attending high schools that do not offer advanced mathematics. The exact number cannot be determined from the existing data because of the common practice in small high schools of offering specific mathematics courses in alternate years.

A greater problem shown by comparing Table V with Table VI is that large groups of students could have taken mathematics beyond the one year of elementary algebra but did not do so. Evidently educators are not successful enough in encouraging students to elect more mathematics courses as part of their general education in the senior high school grades.

Subject Matter Trends. Today the college-preparatory sequence still retains essentially the same structure as defined by the Committee of Ten and the Committee on College Entrance Requirements at the beginning of the century. With few variations the program is:

Ninth grade:	Algebra
Tenth grade:	Geometry (Plane)

Eleventh grade: Advanced Algebra
Twelfth grade: Solid Geometry and Trigonometry

In spite of some changes, in the ninth and tenth grades most large city high schools follow a fairly uniform pattern of sequential mathematics courses. In the eleventh and twelfth grades, however, considerable variation occurs. Frequently the pattern is: elementary and intermediate algebra in grades 9 and 10; plane geometry in grade 11; advanced mathematics in grade 12. An increasing trend is to include trigonometry either with algebra or with geometry and to include portions of solid geometry along with the course in plane geometry. This plan eliminates some chaff and permits students who do not pursue mathematics beyond the third year to study some advanced mathematical concepts.

Several criticisms may be leveled at the traditional organization of the mathematics curriculum. Of course, one never really knows what any teacher really includes in a course unless one sits in the class, but speaking in generalizations, the following criticisms do have some validity.

1. The point of view of many mathematics teachers is unsatisfactory. Algebra, for instance, consists largely of manipulation when it should be concerned with mathematical structure, and despite the importance of the study of algebraic sets, inequalities, and deductive reasoning, these receive little or no attention in many algebra courses.

2. Some geometry courses consist almost solely of rote memory work. It is no wonder students drop mathematics after two years if such geometry comprises the second-year course. Moreover, the deductive process is not explained very clearly in spite of the fact that geometry teachers insist that the reason for including geometry in the curriculum is to develop the powers of rational thinking and deductive reasoning.

3. Mathematics courses of study contain much deadwood. Two examples will suffice: extensive solution of triangles by logarithms and the use of Horner's Methods for finding the roots of a polynomial. The time spent upon such topics could well be reduced and spent more profitably on modern topics.

4. Some mathematics teachers, luckily only a few, seem to think that high school mathematics should be the exclusive prerogative of the bright children. That anyone should be so biased is unfortunate, for one of the unusual advantages of Euclidean geometry is that it may include exercises that are teachable to "average" students. It is here that the role of mathematics in general education might well be explored.

MATHEMATICS PROGRAMS

In some areas school system after school system has made two years of mathematics required for high school graduation. Such a requirement confronts the educators with the problem of providing a mathematics program for the pupils who do not go on to college and at the same time furnishing a sound college-preparatory program upon which college mathematics can be based. Pueblo High School in Tucson, Arizona, has attempted to solve this dilemma with what is called the Spiral Mathematics Program.

The Spiral Program. The Spiral Mathematics Program provides an increasingly difficult sequence of interrelated mathematics topics. During the first two years, the pupils study elements of algebra, geometry, and trigonometry, plus logic and consumer concepts, that meet the requirements set for admittance to the physics course. The third year of the spiral continues the interrelated study of algebra, geometry, both plane and solid, trigonometry, and logic at more advanced levels.

Pueblo High School pupils who do not take the spiral mathematics program can substitute one year of Mathematics 1 and 2, which include remedial arithmetic and basic mathematics, and a senior course entitled "Consumer Mathematics," which includes functional mathematics at the individual and consumer levels and meets the requirement for a second year of mathematics for graduation.

The Pueblo High School program also provides for the gifted student. Gifted students who take the third year of the spiral program are part of a Mathematics Seminar. The outline of that course is as follows:

I. Trigonometry
II. College Algebra
   This includes number systems, factoring by inspection and grouping, operations with fractions both simple and complex, and laws of exponents and radicals.
III. Analytic Geometry
   This includes the line, conic sections, and polar coordinates.
IV. The Algebra of Sets—An Introduction
V. Logic: Inductive and Deductive
VI. Probability: An Introduction
VII. Non-Euclidian Geometry
   This includes an introduction to the geometries of Lobachevsky and Riemann.

The emphasis of the course is at all times upon understanding mathematics, not merely upon the acquisition of skills. Special effort is made to have each student become familiar with the logical structure and the scope of mathematics. The latter aim is met by introducing such topics as different number bases, probability, non-Euclidian geometries, and the set theory, as well as the traditional areas of mathematics.

The Floral Park Plan. Organizations in other schools throughout the country contain most or all of the material included in the Pueblo Plan. The Floral Park plan provides tracks in mathematics for three levels of mathematical ability. In its first-year course, for those pupils who cannot profit from a course in algebra, materials from arithmetic, geometry, and algebra are used in units on blueprints, scale drawings, and finding areas. The second-year course for these pupils includes a semester of surveying and a semester of consumer mathematics. Average students can take such courses as intermediate and advanced algebra, geometry, and trigonometry (in which the solution of triangles has been deemphasized). For the superior student, the tenth grade mathematics course includes geometry, algebra, and solid geometry; the eleventh grade course offers more algebra, including the theory and solution of quadratic equations; the extension of the number system to imaginaries, logarithms, and exponents; graphing conic sections and trigonometric functions; the twelfth grade mathematics course, topics from the areas of algebra, analytic geometry, spatial geometry, trigonometry, introductory calculus, statistics, and probability.

SUBSIDIZED EXPERIMENTAL PROJECTS

New ways of teaching and organizing mathematics are being tested with the financial aid of private and public monies. Of the various projects listed below, only a few will be presented in some detail. With one exception all are for senior and junior high school levels or solely for the senior high school level.

Advanced Placement Program of the College Entrance Examination Board— High School.

Boston College Mathematical Series—High School.

Commission on Mathematics of the College Entrance Examination Board— Grades 9–12.

Mathematics Program at Phillips Exeter Academy—High School.

Minnesota National Laboratory—Grades 7–12.

National Council of Teachers of Mathematics, Secondary-School Curriculum Committee—Grades 7–12.

New York State Mathematics Syllabus Committee—Grades 10–12.

School Mathematics Study Group—Grades 7–12 (elementary under development).

University of Illinois Committee on School Mathematics—Grades 7–12.

University of Maryland Mathematics Projects—Grades 7–8.

State Programs:

Commission to Study the Mathematics Curriculum in Texas Elementary and Secondary Schools—K–12.

Illinois Curriculum Program: Study Group on Mathematics—Grades K–14.
Indiana School and College Committee on Mathematics—Grades K–14.
Minnesota School Mathematics Center—Grades 5–9.
Oklahoma State Committee for the Improvement of Mathematics Instruction—Grades K–12.

The Illinois Plan. One of the biggest stumbling blocks to any progress in curriculum reorganization has always been the problem of obtaining properly trained teachers who are ready, willing, and able to teach the proposed courses. Another almost equally difficult problem that often gives the "kiss of death" to curriculum innovations is that of obtaining the proper materials. To avoid ending up with these problems, the creators of the Illinois Plan started out to solve them first before attempting to put the new mathematics curriculum into effect.

The teacher training aspect of the plan has been handled through summer workshops, institutes, and weekend conferences held at the schools as well as at the Project Center. At the conferences, high school teachers were given the help they needed to teach newer concepts of modern mathematics. Without the mathematical institutes to bring the high school teachers up to date, the introduction of new concepts might have been unsuccessful, for the institutes not only refreshed the teachers' mathematical knowledge and skills, but modified their attitudes concerning mathematics and the curriculum as well.

Many traditional courses emphasized only the manipulative side of mathematics and as a result tended to be dull—divorced from common sense, contemporary research, and practical application in the home and in industry. To avoid this pitfall the Illinois curriculum was developed so as to give the conceptual side of mathematics sufficient attention. Needless to say, the development of suitable material could not be accomplished by simply adding and subtracting a little here and there from traditional courses of study. Rather the curriculum builders developed the program from such fundamental questions as "What is a number? What is a function? What is a variable?"[7] It is indeed encouraging to note that the University of Illinois Committee on School Mathematics is also carrying out another sound curriculum procedure, that is, that curriculum study should be a continuing activity. All courses in the program are constantly subject to revision. For this reason communication among the teacher coordinators, the high school teachers, and the project center is kept close.

As this is being written, the syllabi of the courses as derived thus far are as follows:[8]

First Course:
Distinction between numbers and numerals
Real numbers

[7] National Association of Secondary-School Principals, *op. cit.*, p. 12.
[8] National Association of Secondary-School Principals, *op. cit.*, p. 18.

Principles of real numbers (associativity, commutativity, and so on.)
Inverse operations
Relations of inequality
Numerical variable (pronumerals)
Generalization about real numbers
Notation and some concepts of the algebra of sets
Solution of equations, linear and quadratic
Solution of "worded" problems
Ordered pairs of numbers
Graphing equations and inequations
Second Course:
Sets and relations
Linear and quadratic functions
Systems of linear equations
Measures of intervals, areas, angles, and plane regions
Elementary properties of angles, polygons, and circles
Further study of manipulations of algebraic expressions
Third Course:
Mathematical induction (generalizations, hereditary properties, recursive definitions, progressions, Σ–notations)
Exponents and logarithms (continuity and the limit concept)
Complex numbers (field properties, systems of quadratic equations)
Polynomial functions (factor theorem, synthetic division, curve tracing)
Fourth Course:
Circular functions (winding functions, periodicity, evenness and oddness, monotoneity, "analytical trigonometry" rather than "triangle solving," inner circular functions)
Deductive theories (abstraction of postulates from a model, deduction of theorems from these postulates without reference to a model, reinterpretation of the theory to yield information about the models)

School Mathematics Study Group. The School Mathematics Study Group (SMSG) was organized in February, 1958. Work was begun on the revision of the mathematics curriculum with an initial grant of $100,000 from the National Science Foundation. Since that time grants totaling in excess of a million dollars have been given.

The purpose of the School Mathematics Study Group in general is to improve the mathematics offerings in the schools of the country. The group has as its objective the preparation of a curriculum that will stress basic mathematical skills along with understandings of basic concepts and the structure of mathematics. The material is to be presented in such a way as to arouse the interest of the learner and to motivate him to pursue advanced mathematics courses in high school and college. To achieve these purposes the group has prepared textbooks, experimental units, monographs on various mathematical topics, and teacher-training materials. Mathematics institutes have been held to give the teachers training in both techniques and subject matter of the School Mathematics Study Group program.

For grades 7 and 8 the School Mathematics Study Group worked closely with the Maryland project described earlier and developed experimental units that were tried in about 100 classrooms throughout the country. Typical units are:

Why Study Mathematics?
Decimal and Non-Decimal Numeration
Natural Numbers and Zero
Factoring and Special Products
Unsigned Rationals
Non-Metric Geometry
Informal Geometry
Approximation
Mathematics in Science
Mathematics in Social Science
Chance
Finite Mathematical Systems.[9]

The curriculum for grades 9–12 includes both the material now being taught as well as new topics in mathematics. In the ninth grade the course includes a study of the algebraic structure of the numbers of arithmetic, real numbers, coordinates and linear equations, functions and ordered fields. The eleventh grade includes material now commonly taught in the twelfth grade. The list of topics is as follows:[10]

The real number system
Coordinate geometry in a plane
Quadratic functions and their graphs
Quadratic equations
Complex numbers
Systems involving equations of the second degree
Exponents and logarithms
Mathematical induction
Permutations, selections, and the binomial theorem
Sequences and sines
Algebraic structures
Introduction to coordinate trigonometry
Equations and identities
Circular functions of composite angles
Trigonometric analysis
Systems of first degree equations in three variables.

The twelfth grade mathematics program contains:[11]

Sets, functions, and relations
Polynomial functions

---

[9] From *Studies in Mathematics Education.* Copyright © 1959 by Scott, Foresman and Company, Chicago, p. 10.
[10] *Ibid.,* p. 12.
[11] *Ibid.,* p. 13.

Exponential and logarithmic functions
The circular functions
Definition of matrix; vectors, identity and 0 matrix
Addition of matrices, multiplication by scalar, multiplication of matrices, inverse matrix
Algebraic properties
The matrix (2×2) as a transformation
Solution of equations by matrices
Distance preserving matrices in two dimensions
Matrices and determinants

ADVANCED PROGRAMS IN THE HIGH SCHOOL

For any kind of an advanced program to take place in the twelfth grade the student must have completed the necessary background work by the end of the junior year. If the curriculum planner insists that the traditional sequence be followed, then the gifted student must have finished algebra, geometry, solid geometry, and trigonometry before the senior year. This can be accomplished in several ways. Two common approaches to the problem are: (1) start algebra in the eighth grade, and (2) start algebra in the ninth grade and accelerate the program. In either case the mathematics offered to the gifted student during grades 9, 10, and 11 is an "enriched" type of mathematics.

In September, 1958, for example, Seattle began a mathematics program for the able student in which the student begins algebra in the eighth grade and completes intermediate algebra by the end of the tenth grade. During the eleventh grade the course is divided into two semesters: the first semester's offering includes modern mathematics, such as probability and statistical inference; the second semester's, trigonometry. The twelfth grade is for advanced mathematical analysis.

The Advanced Placement Program. The Advanced Placement Program is sponsored by the College Entrance Examination Board (CEEB). The program was known at one time as the Kenyon Plan and once received financial support from the Fund for the Advancement of Education. Since 1955 the College Entrance Examination Board has administered the program on a nationwide basis. In 1956 there were 386 students enrolled in the program in mathematics; just two years later the number had zoomed to 1200 and is still increasing. Very simply the program is a plan whereby students in high school may take college subjects and receive college credits for them just as if the students were taking the subjects in college. At the end of the year the pupils take the Advanced Placement Test in mathematics, a thorough test lasting about three hours. The scores on the test are reported on a five-point scale: 1–fail; 2–pass; 3–creditable; 4–honors; 5–high honors. In several colleges advanced standing with college credit for the high school work is given only if the student receives a 4 or a 5.

As with all other curriculum innovations, the Advanced Placement Program in mathematics has been subjected to adverse criticism. Some of the criticisms come from the students themselves and therefore must be considered quite carefully. Many students seem to resent the emphasis upon the examination. They object to the need to hurry through the topics in order to be sure that the materials have all been covered for the examination in May. They would prefer to learn mathematics for the sake of the knowledge itself, they say, and to be able to take time to ponder upon some of the mathematical concepts and to exchange ideas with their classmates in class discussions.

Parents and teachers also find cause for complaint in the program. Some parents complain that the students spend too much time at their books, although the students themselves do not all seem to mind the pressure. In the minds of the teachers the most serious charge is that in practice the main objective of the course is to pass the examination and not to gain a full comprehension of the beauty of the science of mathematics.

On the other hand, the Advanced Placement Program has yielded some very fine by-products. It has increased interest in mathematics for the college-bound students as well as increased opportunities in mathematics for the gifted students. It has also been instrumental in causing the present mathematics curriculum to be scrutinized as it never has been scrutinized before. For this purpose the College Entrance Examination Board itself appointed a Commission on Mathematics which has done fine work, and the National Council of Teachers of Mathematics has set up a Committee on Secondary-School Curriculum. More important than anything else in the opinion of the writer, however, has been the change in attitude on the part of the teachers and the college professors. Out of the advanced placement program has come a mutual respect and understanding for each other's problems. College professors have taken a leading role in organizing institutes and workshops for mathematics teachers for advanced study.

College and University Programs for Gifted Students. In addition to the Advanced Placement Program some colleges and universities have been quite active in providing programs for high school pupils during the regular school year or during the summer. The programs held during the school year are pretty much a permissive type of thing. In them highly selected students have been allowed to attend college classes while still enrolled in high school. One college has permitted a student to attend regular classes at the end of his junior year. Another university allows a high school student to take the course in differential equations. During the school year 1956–57 the Ohio State University allowed four high school seniors from the University High School to attend classes in college mathematics. On the basis of scores obtained from the Ohio

State Psychological Examination and the proficiency and placement test in mathematics, one high school senior was enrolled in sophomore calculus and three other students in college algebra. All concerned seemed enthusiastic about the experiment.

In 1958 Florida State University explored the hypothesis that gifted high school students can easily learn much of modern mathematics by organizing a six-week summer mathematics camp for a very select group of high school students to study high-powered mathematics. In this camp students did work in fundamental concepts of set theory, fundamental concepts of group theory, fundamental concepts of matrix theory, n–dimensional geometry of squares, cubes, edges, faces, hyperfaces; the statement calculus (by means of truth tables); quantifiers. They also studied the statement calculus as a deductive system using the Hilbert–Ackerman system, programed an IBM 650, executed the programs, and studied congruences.

This summer camp was reported to be quite successful. Students learned many new mathematical concepts and gained insights into mathematics that they never thought possible.

CORRESPONDENCE COURSES IN MATHEMATICS

Many high schools in the United States have small enrollments. In fact in some Midwestern and Western states more than half of the schools have fewer than 100 pupils enrolled. Although many offer intermediate algebra, few schools of this size can support any advanced mathematics programs beyond the second-year algebra course. One economical way to supplement such a limited offering in mathematics is to encourage the students to enroll in correspondence courses.

An immediate question that arises about correspondence courses is how well do the students who take them do in college. The answer seems to be, very well indeed. G. B. Childs made a study of students with and without correspondence courses in their background.[12] Students who had had high school correspondence courses achieved a higher grade-point average than did students who had not taken such courses. The difference in scores is significant at the 4-per-cent level of confidence. Although Childs' study did not attempt to establish the reason for the indicated superiority of the correspondence study group, the findings clearly indicate that correspondence study can be a valid way of broadening the curriculum of the small high school and thus provide for the needs of all students.

[12] G. B. Childs, "Success in Initial Mathematics Course and of Students with Correspondence and Non-Correspondence Backgrounds in High School Mathematics," *Journal of Educational Research*, 4: 607, April, 1956.

SUMMARY

Mathematics, the queen of the sciences, is usually an elective in the upper grades of the high school. Still, a large number of pupils choose it. This is good because, in addition to being attractive to some pupils, mathematics is important vocationally and in the very defense of our country.

In the junior high school most pupils study arithmetic in grades 7 and 8. In grade 9 many schools divide the mathematics curriculum into two tracks: one for the college-bound, the other for the rest. In this double track the college-bound course is algebra, and the noncollege-bound course general mathematics—usually a course containing review arithmetic and frequently exploratory work in geometry, arithmetic, and algebra. On occasion general mathematics is offered as a true disciplinary course in all three junior high school grades. Sometimes junior high school mathematics is divided into three or four tracks, particularly at the ninth grade level.

Critics have found much fault with junior high school mathematics courses. Arithmetic courses in grades 7 and 8 are often repetitious and dull. As a consequence several experiments have been started to improve the junior high school curriculum and upgrade its standards, particularly insofar as bright pupils are concerned.

Senior high school mathematics too has been the butt of much adverse criticism. Some of this criticism has resulted from a misunderstanding concerning enrollment figures, but much of it has been pointed at inexcusably archaic courses of study. Not only has mathematics often been taught from an indefensible point of view, and by undesirable methods, but the courses of study have contained much deadwood while leaving out many important new concepts. Consequently several new plans have been proposed to break away from the routine pattern of ninth grade Algebra I, tenth grade Algebra II, eleventh grade Geometry, twelfth grade Trigonometry and Solid Geometry in favor of new programs placing greater emphasis on modern mathematics and "discovery" techniques. Especially important have been the plans for the gifted, which indicate beyond a shadow of a doubt that advanced mathematics courses for brilliant students can be made interesting and challenging. A particularly interesting program points up that qualified boys and girls can derive great benefit from taking advanced mathematics courses by correspondence.

SUGGESTED READINGS

ASSOCIATION FOR SUPERVISION AND CURRICULUM DEVELOPMENT. *Using Current Curriculum Developments*. Washington, D.C.: The Association, 1963.

Chapter 6 discusses the school mathematics study groups and extensive materials developed by such groups.

Biennial Survey of Education in the United States, 1948–50, Chapter 5, *Offerings and Enrollments in High School Subjects*. Washington, D.C.: Government Printing Office, 1951.

Contains material for comparative studies.

BUTLER, CHARLES H., and F. LYNWOOD WREN. *The Teaching of Secondary Mathematics*. Third edition. New York: McGraw-Hill Book Company, Inc., 1960.

Part I deals with the mathematics programs.

BROWN, KENNETH, and ELLSWORTH OBOURN. *Offerings and Enrollments in Science and Mathematics in Public High Schools, 1958*. Bulletin 1961, Number 5. Washington, D.C.: Government Printing Office, 1961.

Contains the latest statistics available.

BRUECKNER, LEO J., FOSTER E. GROSSNICKLE, and JOHN RECKZEH. *Developing Mathematical Understanding in the Upper Grades*. New York: Holt, Rinehart and Winston, Inc., 1957.

Chapter 2 is an excellent presentation of the development and organization of the junior high school mathematics program.

FEHR, HOWARD. "The Goal is Mathematics for All," *School Science and Mathematics*, Volume 56, February, 1956.

A good statement of what can be done in selecting content.

JOHNSON, LARRY K. "The Mathematics Laboratory in Today's Schools," *School Science and Mathematics*, Volume 62, Number 8, November, 1962.

Explains a new approach to mathematics.

KEMENY, JOHN, et al. *Introduction to Finite Mathematics*. Englewood Cliffs, New Jersey: Prentice-Hall, Inc., 1957.

An introduction to modern mathematics that includes application in biological and social sciences.

MALLINSON, GEORGE G., et al. "Final Report to the Central Association of Science and Mathematics Teachers of Its Committee on the Significance of Mathematics and Science in Education," *School Science and Mathematics*, Volume 54, February, 1954.

Includes good recommendations for improving mathematics programs.

NATIONAL ASSOCIATION OF SECONDARY-SCHOOL PRINCIPALS. *The Bulletin*, Volume 43. Washington, D.C.: The Association, May, 1959.

The entire issue has good material on mathematics.

NATIONAL COUNCIL OF TEACHERS OF MATHEMATICS. Twenty-fourth Yearbook. *The Growth of Mathematical Ideas, Grades K–12*. Washington, D.C.: The Council, 1958.

Good for an articulation study.

NEWMAN, JAMES R. (ed.). *The World of Mathematics*. New York: Simon and Schuster, 1956.

A good reference source composed of several volumes totaling 2,535 pages.

Chapter 13

The Fine Arts

Although art and music have long been considered necessary parts of a liberal education, in the secondary school this principle has been more honored in the breach than in the practice. In more than one school system, programs in these fields live a precarious existence. Yet few content fields can offer more to the individuals' self-fulfillment than do art and music. Each of them has an essential contribution to the general education of all youth and a special contribution to the artistically talented. Curriculum workers must not sell them short; they are essentials, not frills, despite attacks by "basic educators."

MUSIC

JUSTIFICATION OF THE MUSIC CURRICULUM

As the reader becomes familiar with the material in the curriculum area, he soon realizes that the various disciplines must compete for place in the secondary-school curriculum. The advocates of any subject or activity must be able to justify their recommendations for new additions or to defend a continued place for their courses in the program of studies. This is particularly true of the music curriculum, because some of its activities have been under attack as educational frills. As the cost of education continues to rise, one can expect these attacks to increase. Unless a case can be made for music, unless it can be said truthfully that music offers something worth-while educationally that no other activity offers, school districts cannot justify the expenditure. Let us then examine in a critical manner some of the values that music educators have said accrue from studying and participating in music.

General Aims of Music Curricula. Leonhard and House[1] have stated that since the beginning of the history of man the justification for music has been directed toward nonmusical objectives and further point out that some of the claims border on the ridiculous. Let us look at their list of typical claims made for music.

> Music education includes activities and learning which develop the social aspects of life.
> Music education develops the health of the students.
> Music education aids in the development of sound work habits.
> Music education instills wholesome ideals of conduct.
> Music education aims to develop good citizenship.
> Music education improves home life.[2]

Music, as thus conceived, is only a means to an end—an instrument to achieve something that is nonmusical. Moreover, these instrumental values themselves do not stand up when examined. Certainly musicians are not in better health than the rest of the populace. The claims for the wholesome conduct ideal apparently assume that music will still the adolescent spirit in some magical way. Yet music groups are notably discipline problem groups, especially to student teachers and beginning teachers.

Neither can the vague aim of good citizenship be used to justify music in the secondary schools. Certainly the area of social studies is more directly concerned with teaching aspects of citizenship. True, it may be argued that proficiency in music will contribute to the well-balanced personality, but are not highly skilled musicians sometimes emotionally unstable and exceptionally poor citizens? As a matter of fact, any subject in school can contribute indirectly to the very general objectives stated as the "Cardinal Principles" or the "Ten Imperative Needs of Youth."[3] If music does not have a particular contribution of its own in addition to the outcome gained from other required subjects, then the critics are right; it is a frill and should be eliminated.

Aims Unique to Music. Fortunately the music curriculum has valid unique values of its own.

1. Music is an aesthetic component in the world of experience.
2. Aesthetic experience contributes to man's greatest satisfaction in living.
3. Music is a part of every person's environment.

[1] Charles Leonhard and Robert W. House, *Foundations and Principles of Music Education* (New York: McGraw-Hill Book Company, Inc., 1959), p. 97.

[2] *Ibid.* (Used by permission.)

[3] See Chapter 7.

4. Music literature has been accumulating for centuries and is part of the cultures of the world.
5. Music develops the natural responsiveness that all pupils possess.
6. Music is a universal means of communication.

One reason why music should be a significant part in everyone's education is that aesthetically arranged patterns of sound are part of everybody's world. When any person experiences the aesthetic quality of music, he has a feeling that he cannot find elsewhere. Of course, a particular pattern of sound may be beautiful to one person and not to another, for music is a personal experience. Thus for beautiful music to contribute to the effectiveness of organized religion, the individual must be able to transform the symbolic experience into something that is meaningful to him. Through music education an individual can develop the power to control what happens to him musically, so that aesthetic quality of church music or other music then becomes less a matter of mere chance and more a matter of significant experience within the control of the individual. Such power can be a direct outcome of music education, and should be one of its principal objectives.

That we live in a world of tension is a worn-out cliché which, unfortunately, contains much truth today and for long into the foreseeable future. Music can offset this life of tension by providing experiences that balance the coldly objective aspects of living, the ennui of daily routine, and the ugly, drab appearance of a metropolis, and so help the individual attain emotional balance and satisfy his emotional needs. To do so is another valid aim for musical education.

Every day we are surrounded with music. Some is good, much is not. The great mass of secondary-school pupils needs to develop a positive aesthetic response to great music and a negative reaction to poor music. Another valid objective of the music education then is to develop music values that can provide individuals with the opportunity to better pursue the good life.

One of the functions of education is to transmit the cultural heritage. Graduates who do not have an understanding of music literature are ignorant of a major part of their heritage and so are restricted in their attempts to achieve the good life. Everyone ought to be familiar with the best operatic, orchestral, choral, and chamber music because he needs knowledge of music in order to operate as a thinking person in a well-developed civilization. Still another objective of music education is to pass on the music literature portion of our heritage. This goal gains particular significance when one remembers that music also affords a means of communication across the barriers of language. A skilled concert performer can convey the aesthetic content that the composer intended whether or not the composer or the audience is German,

Italian, Russian, or English. Once the learner masters the language of music he is in communication with centuries of musical meanings.

If a music curriculum is built upon the purposes or objectives stated above, the emphasis will be upon the direct values of music instead of the indirect or instrumental values (*instrumental* used here in the metaphorical sense of the word). In the past, educators have justified teaching music in the secondary school on the basis of its indirect values. Because the emphasis was not upon direct music values but rather on learning to adjust, some of the music taught degenerated to an appallingly low standard. Any school that justifies music instruction for its indirect values only weakens the case for it. Music should be taught primarily for its direct values or not at all.

Performing and Educational Objectives. Much of the time and energy devoted to music education in the secondary school is given over to public performances. All too often the continued employment of the band director or choral director depends upon how well the respective musical groups perform. In the case of the marching band, moreover, it is not always the quality of the music that counts in his favor, but rather the quality of the pageantry. In the following paragraphs the importance of learning performing skills will be analyzed in relation to the direct values of music education.

Music educators state that some instruction in performance skills should be included in *everyone's* formal education for essentially two reasons: one is to discover whether or not an individual has a liking or talent for musical performance, and the other is that making of music will help one to hear musical nuances better than if one did not have such experiences.

Let us examine the first of these reasons more carefully. In general music classes, instruction commonly begins with the recorder. Then if the pupil indicates an interest and talent, perhaps he may begin private or group lessons on some other instrument. Whether or not the student has any real talent can only be determined by going on to more advanced study. Yet even years of study and practice will not determine how far the student should go in music. Each new level presents itself with new challenges and new skill requirements. It is not unusual for students to spend hundreds of hours on practice and study only to stop short of the concert level of performance. Undoubtedly one should be able to provide simple performing experiences for pupils who might not otherwise have an opportunity to be exposed to them, but logically it would seem most unlikely that simple exercises on a recorder, for example, will indicate the full talent of all the pupils.

The second reason can also be questioned quantitatively—how much skill is necessary to get the full meaning from a musical selection? To consider the second reason one must first consider what it is that makes a concert artist. He is an artist by virtue of the fact that he has spent many years preparing himself for performances by developing ideas of the mood and effect that the composer intended and learning how to create the composer's intended effect through his own playing.

Obviously very few of the secondary-school students will ever approach the skill and artistry of the concert player. Yet according to the thesis of some music educators, to fully understand music requires just such a high level of performance. So to achieve the aesthetic aims of music in the secondary school other techniques must be used. Learning to play can yield many values, of course, but it should not be used as a primary method of developing music aesthetics.

Values of Performances. Theoretically the performing groups in the secondary school should provide opportunities for boys and girls to become acquainted with the great music literature of mankind and to experience the spiritual uplift associated with giving a good performance of great music. Unfortunately, when one examines the programs and curricula of our secondary schools, some of the music in them seems to be rather shallow. For instance, although the greatest music of all has been written for the symphony orchestra, in our secondary schools throughout the country there are relatively few orchestras—compared to the number of marching bands. Many times the writer, both as a student and as a visiting educationist, has attended orchestra and chorus rehearsals where no music fundamentals were being taught; nor was there any spiritual uplifting going on either, for that requires excellent, meaningful performance.

One of the great contemporary composers and an authority in the field of music has sharply criticized the marching band for its often misguided emphases.[4]

> Is Music one of the "frills" in education? The answer seems to me to be comparatively simple. If the highest ambition of the music department of the high school is to develop a marching band with slick formations, magnificently garbed in brilliant uniforms, and assisted by a champion group of baton twirlers, perhaps it is a frill—albeit a very attractive one.
>
> What I am trying to say, of course, is that important as the marching band may be in the matter of public relations, community spirit, and the like, we hardly can consider it as an end goal, particularly in a time when we are questioning frankly the matter of depth in American education.

On the other hand, large performing units can bring great benefits. Because of the large number of pupils in our modern schools, education

[4] Howard Hanson, "Music Education Faces the Scientific Age," *Music Educators Journal* (a publication of Music Educators National Conference), 45: 18, June–July, 1959, p. 18. Used by permission.

must of necessity be a mass effort. Music is unique in that pupils can gain much through large group instruction and participation in large group activities. If anything, at the secondary level, large choral groups, orchestras, and bands sound better than small ones do. Also large group experiences can give pupils aesthetic feelings from playing or singing fine selections and the exhilaration associated with participating in a well-disciplined group producing great music.

It would seem that performing groups are part of music education in the secondary school for the following reasons:

1. The music program gives opportunity for pleasure. Some music educators state that unless pupils derive pleasure from participation, the activity should not be allowed to continue.
2. Participation in a marching band, chorus, ensemble, or in the audience helps develop a fine school spirit, good morale, and gives individuals a sense of belonging.
3. Public relations are improved through publicity for a school that wins musical contests, plays for concerts, and provides small group ensembles for entertainment for civic groups.
4. The individual develops social interests, skills, and habits by participating in a performing group.
5. Performances are an outgrowth of the music program. After studying music for a number of years, individuals need an opportunity to make music.
6. Performances provide an opportunity for all musical organizations to take part. Operetta, for example, provides many opportunities for a chorus, solos, ensembles, and orchestra work.
7. Performances provide an opportunity to integrate and correlate music and other departments, such as art, English, dramatics, and physical education.
8. Secondary-school music develops ability and interest in music for future participation. In the community, performers are needed for civic opera groups, church choirs, civic choruses, civic orchestras, and so on.

Casual examination of the above statements will show that again some of them are concerned with nonmusical objectives of education. The pressures in any one community may be exceedingly great to emphasize the nonmusical objective, that is, entertainment. In such a situation the secondary-school student does not learn music, but instead spends much valuable time in endless rehearsals. It is up to the board of education to decide which values are more important to the student. Hanson would place the importance upon education.[5]

5 *Ibid.*, p. 19.

We must remember that the greatest contribution of the musician is music. Music for fun, music for recreation, is important. Music for dancing is important. Music for football games is important. But all of these vary greatly in importance. Let us never forget that the greatest importance of the art is as a communication of the most magnificent, the most inspiring of spiritual messages—messages which so transcend the power of the written or spoken word that their translation into speech would be utterly futile. Music at this level, like philosophy and like religion in their noblest moments, offers spiritual sustenance which the world greatly needs in this era of automation. For although living in an age of automation, man is not an automaton. He is a living breathing, spiritual being, and the nourishment of that spirit can be neglected only at our very great peril.

GENERAL MUSIC COURSES

The general music course has been in the curriculum for many years and in all probability will continue to be offered by secondary schools for many more. As with most of the offerings of the secondary school, opinions differ about the worth of the general music program. On the one hand, a group of educators sees the general music program as a way of realizing the objectives put forth for music education; other educators, on the other, question its value in the curriculum.

General music has been under a cloud because in some cases its emphasis has been upon nonmusical objectives. In such courses little music was really taught; rather students assumed a passive role with the frequent result that both teachers and students merely tolerated each other for the class period. Often the teacher played records *he* enjoyed and insisted that the students be evaluated in terms of his enthusiasm. This practice seems unfair. From the pragmatic point of view, even though he utilizes every technique and teaching aid possible to develop aesthetic sensitivity, all the teacher can do, in the final analysis, is to present the music to the pupils who either accept or reject each selection according to their likes or dislikes—*de gustibus non disputandum est.*

Aims of General Music Courses. In most schools general music is available to all pupils in the junior high school and to most pupils in the senior high schools. In theory, at least, it is not a replacement for the performing groups, but rather a course that offers exploratory and fundamental music activities. As such it can be conceived to be part of basic education, because general music is the base upon which other musical activities in the school are built. It is also a general education course to the extent that it seems fundamental that all pupils need to develop musical taste and appreciation. As the pupils progress from the first grade up through the primary and intermediate grades, and then the junior and senior high school, their discriminating abilities should be continuously developing. Because discrimination of musical qualities is largely intellectual, this means that the music program must develop musical skills and knowledge. For this reason, general music programs are now organized to develop the intellectual powers of the pupil as well as the emotional impact of the music.

In order to carry out its objectives, the general music course must include good music of all sorts. Some courses of study for general music courses exclude jazz; to do so is a mistake. Because the primary objective of the program is the development of aesthetic discrimination, jazz and other contemporary music are necessary parts of the course of study, so that pupils can learn to evaluate contemporary music as well as that of the past.

General music courses are taught both on the junior and senior high school levels. In systems organized on plans other than the 6–3–3 organization, general music may be offered in seventh or eighth grades and as a multigrade course in grades 9–12. Usually junior high school general music classes meet fewer than five days a week; sometimes only two or three. Senior high school general music classes, on the other hand, ordinarily meet 45 or 60 minutes per day five days a week. Such courses should carry full academic credit if the homework load is the same as in other academic courses; if no homework is involved, they merit only half a Carnegie unit.

Activities in General Music. Activities found in general music courses can be grouped into nine categories:

1. Listening. Listening activities are varied and include listening to tape recordings, phonograph records, and performances by individual artists and groups in out-of-school concert halls or parks or by means of television or radio.
2. Singing. Judging from the quality and quantity of singing of patriotic songs at school affairs, more attention needs to be given to this activity. In general music classes pupils have experiences in both unison and part singing, thereby receiving an opportunity to improve tone quality and diction and to learn to use their voices with some degree of confidence in singing and speaking.
3. Class concerts. Pupils present either vocal or instrumental concerts to the class.
4. Playing instruments. Pupils play such instruments as the recorder, bell block, and autoharp as exploratory experiences. Much of the work on these instruments is group work.
5. Resource persons. Visiting artists and guest speakers may speak on music and/or give illustrated lectures about some phases of music.

6. Discussion and reports. Pupils report on concerts and other musical programs that they have heard and seen. Discussion is pertinent to the reports.
7. Field trips. General music classes may visit instrument factories, pipe organ studios, churches, rehearsals of musical organizations, the state university musical organizations' concerts, and the like.
8. Reading. Students can read about the history of music in the United States and other countries, the theory of music, biographical material, church music, literature of music, opera, and the orchestra. Other miscellaneous readings might be concerned with the joy of listening and playing music, how to listen to music, careers in music, and other topics of interest to the adolescent.
9. View films. Many excellent films that give insights into music are available; among them are pictures of actual concerts by the great artists of our times. Other films present illustrated explanations of some of the aspects of music, such as basic facts of composition, harmonics, and the physics of sound.

Junior High School and General Music Courses. In the junior high school teachers tend to organize general music courses along the following guidelines:

1. Course emphasis is on providing exploratory experiences in music. Opportunities are also provided for the pupil to discover latent music skill and to determine whether he should continue lessons or change instruments.
2. Continuity is provided for those pupils that have experienced good elementary music programs. Here good articulation is necessary between the elementary and junior high schools to achieve sustained musical growth of the junior high school pupils. Quite often junior high school general music is the last formal musical experience a pupil has.
3. The activities offered in the course are varied but within the range and ability of the junior high school adolescent. Unfortunately, at present, there is a shortage of suitable instrumental and vocal music for junior high school boys and girls, but a few composers and arrangers are beginning to provide such materials.

The general junior high school music course can be a worth-while educational experience for the adolescent. It does not have to be a dumping ground course or an insipid "keep-'em-busy" course. General music can be challenging, interesting, and inspiring under the right teacher using the right course of study with the right materials. One course of study that illustrates the challenging nature of the modern course in general music includes works of more than 59 composers ranging from

Hugo Alfven through Bach, Beethoven, and Verdi to Jaromir Weinberger.[6]

Senior High School General Music Courses. On the senior high school level, general music courses are likely to provide experiences in depth. Although the exploratory function becomes of lesser importance than in the junior high school, senior high school courses may well contain exploratory experiences. Also, like the junior high school courses, the senior high school general music courses emphasize the aesthetic quality of music and provide a variety of music activities, the difference, of course, being that the materials selected are based on the more mature ability and interest of the high school pupils.

INSTRUMENTAL MUSIC

Performing groups are popular in the secondary school and for a number of years have enjoyed increased enrollments. Yet there is considerable difference of opinion among music educators about the value of the great emphasis on performing groups. No one would deny that certainly there is much value in playing in an organization under an inspired conductor. Certainly the spiritual uplift obtained from playing great compositions is more than worth the time and cost. Again the educationist is faced with a quantitative question, "How much skill is necessary before the spiritual uplift can be realized?" To have good performing groups it is necessary to rehearse and rehearse and rehearse. Students who begin their string instruction in the fifth grade, for instance,

---

[6] Los Angeles City Schools, *General Music I, General Music in the Seventh Grade.* Los Angeles City School, Los Angeles, California, 1958, p. 104.

The complete list is:

Hugo Alfven	Manuel de Falla	Ottorino Respighi
Leroy Anderson	Robert Franz	Nikolai Rimsky-Korsakov
Johann Sebastian Bach	Charles Gounod	Camille Saint-Saëns
Ludwig van Beethoven	Edvard Grieg	Franz Schubert
Hector Berlioz	George Frederick Handel	Robert Schumann
Ernest Bloch	Franz Josef Haydn	Jan Sibelius
Luigi Boccherini	Jacques Ibert	Bedřich Smetana
Alexander Borodin	Vincent d'Indy	Leo Sowerby
Johannes Brahms	Michael Ippolitov-Ivanov	Johann Strauss, Sr.
Max Bruch	Dimitri Kabalevsky	Johann Strauss, Jr.
John Alden Carpenter	Zoltan Kodaly	Igor Stravinsky
Emmanuel Chabrier	Edouard Lalo	Domenico Scarlatti
Carlos Chavez	Franz Liszt	Peter Ilich Tchaikovsky
Frederic Chopin	Robert McBride	Giuseppe Torelli
Eric Coates	Felix Mendelssohn	Ralph Vaughan Williams
Arcangelo Corelli	Wolfgang Amadeus	Giuseppe Verdi
Claude Debussy	Mozart	Heitor Villa-Lobos
Frederick Delius	Modest Moussorgsky	Antonio Vivaldi
Anton Dvořák	Sergei Prokofiev	William Walton
Georges Enesco	Maurice Ravel	Jaromir Weinberger

seldom attain enough skill to play Beethoven's *Ninth* by the time they arrive in high school.

Band and Orchestra. Although musicians pretty well agree that the ideal medium for experiencing musical ideas is a combination of orchestra and chorus, it takes many years of practice, study, and experience in orchestra to develop good string musicians. "Great" music is not easy and is beyond the scope of most high school orchestras. However, if society is to have symphony orchestras to enrich the lives of members of society, there must be some place that encourages and develops orchestral skills. The public schools have this charge.

Even so, recent years have seen a decline in both the number and quality of high school orchestras. Musicians and educators attribute this decline to the following reasons.

1. Cultural interests of the parents have changed. Seemingly the general public is more willing to support a school band than a school orchestra.
2. School administrators are less interested in orchestras than in bands. In this respect the administrators seem to reflect public opinion.
3. It takes less time for pupils to learn to play wind instruments reasonably well than it does to become even reasonably proficient on stringed instruments.
4. There are not enough performance opportunities for an orchestra, whereas a band can perform at every football and basketball game.
5. Emphasis upon academic subjects coupled with the limited school day and a wide choice of electives has caused the student to make choices that exclude the orchestra.
6. In many cases, present orchestras are being directed by persons not interested in procuring the necessary background in orchestra work. Such persons may be band men or vocal, theory, or piano majors.
7. The "flash," color, and sound of the marching band appeal to adolescents.

As we have seen, generally speaking, school bands are more popular than school orchestras. Many high schools with enrollments as small as 140 pupils in grades 9–12 support uniformed bands. Although properly organized band activities can do much to teach pupils aesthetic discrimination, all too often in practice the band activities actually used do not yield the aesthetic, moral, and spiritual values that they should. Instead they emphasize entertainment, noise, movement. Band activities of this sort cannot be justified.

On the other hand, band men throughout the country are now planning three- or four-year educational sequences for their bands. Such programs can provide developmental music experiences for band members, plus a variety of good, interesting music material, both classic and contemporary, in all sorts of musical styles.

Small Instrumental Groups. Small instrumental groups are a potential source of rich experience for high school pupils, for the small instrumental group is a means whereby the musically gifted may develop a degree of musicianship not possible in a band or orchestra. Also a small string ensemble can be a means for providing string experiences that otherwise might not be available to pupils, particularly in small schools. In addition, although as a rule small groups require a standard of performance greater than that necessary in large groups, because the ensemble literature available has a great range of difficulty, small groups can be organized so as to provide for a wide variety of skills. Small group work also helps to produce amateur and professional adult musicianship. If the objectives of music education are ever to be fully realized, small group work needs to be included. Ideally each school should have several first quality string quartets and small brass or woodwind ensembles.

VOCAL MUSIC

Chorus and Glee Clubs. The choruses and glee clubs provide an opportunity for all pupils to participate in a musical activity. Here again, the emphasis should be on the music objectives, not secondary values. In these activities pupils can experience the joy and satisfaction of direct music experience with a minimum amount of training and practice. Properly organized, they can also provide worth-while experiences that will cause pupils to continue their musical development. As conceived here, choral work is a means to an end—a way whereby the pupil is brought to realize that music has a place in his life.

Of course, choral programs have come in for their share of adverse criticism—sometimes justifiably so, for in some choral organizations the teacher is so busy preparing for public performances that he has no time to develop the aesthetic quality of the musical experiences. Instead he emphasizes showmanship, which, though important, is not consistent with the objectives of music education as a primary objective. Although it must be stressed that there is nothing wrong with public performances providing they are not overemphasized, sound choral programs are planned to meet the needs of all the pupils instead of yielding to public pressures and exploiting the talented. In the better programs, choral directors plan to develop musical skills and understanding over a period of years. To this end many choral directors provide instruction in tone quality, diction, music history, and the lives of the composers.

Small Vocal Groups. Of all the ensembles the small vocal ensemble is probably most exploited by the community and school, for it is a very mobile organization, and professional appearances of adult groups in night clubs, motion pictures, and on television have made such entertainment seem very desirable. Frequently this demand leads to an undue emphasis on popular music. As a result music educators feel that much practice and training needed to produce polished performances is wasted insofar as attaining the objectives set for education is concerned. Small choral ensembles have a place in the music curriculum, of course, just as small instrumental groups do, but it must be stressed here again that only those activities that are consistent with the objectives of education, and in particular music education, should be allowed to take place. After all, the purpose of the school's existence is to educate, not to entertain.

MUSIC FOR THE ACADEMICALLY TALENTED

In music there are two kinds of gifted pupils, and there should be two kinds of programs for them. One kind consists of the musically talented youths who have the potential to become first-class performers. For such pupils the school should emphasize activities that will develop high-level performance. The other kind consists of the academically able pupils whose musical skills and potentials are only average. For these pupils the curriculum should consist of high-level general music activities that emphasize the intellectual and creative aspects of music, for example, classroom work and listening activities that require greater discrimination, analysis, research, and more independent study than in most music courses. Types of music activities well suited to the able students are illustrated by the following examples:

1. Work in seminars, honor groups, small study groups, small performing groups.
2. Write reviews of concerts that were attended.
3. Interview people active in music in various capacities.
4. Compare recordings of the same selection.
5. Compare musical renderings with those in other media, for example, Edward Arlington Robinson's poem "Tristram" with Wagner's *Tristan and Isolde*.
6. Detailed studies of specific selections, such as *Ein Heldenleben*, the *Eroica Symphony*, *The Ring of the Nibelungen*, and *Tosca*.

Advanced Courses in Music. To date few specific courses in music for the academically talented student have been constructed, but several plans for improved courses for the able are being contemplated in various school systems. One of them is an advanced seminar in literature that includes music literature as well as the novel, poems, plays, and short stories to take the place of the twelfth grade English. Another plan is to broaden the scope of the advanced course in music theory so that it would include theory, composition, and music literature. Still another plan provides for able pupils to operate at relatively high levels as performers in small musical groups.

Presently advanced courses in music and music theory are being offered in only a minority of schools. According to a survey of 121 schools in 28 states, one third of the schools offered some course in music theory.[7] Interestingly the study found that music teachers believed such courses should be limited to able pupils only.[8] Because everybody "consumes" music, probably courses of this type are needed by the nontalented as well as the talented, and perhaps music teachers should reexamine their objectives.

Competing for Time. Providing music courses for the academically talented is complicated by the competition for time in the program. To find time for advanced music courses in the daily schedule will not be easy, nor will it be easy for the pupils to find time in their day for such courses. Chances are that the able pupil will be interested in the college-preparatory curriculum and attendant advanced courses in other academic areas. If the pupil combines performance with four or five solid one-unit courses, his time will be pretty well taken. The solution may be to substitute advanced music courses for other advanced college-preparatory electives. Advanced music can be just as intellectual and useful a study as advanced history, for instance, and the findings of the Eight-Year Study suggest the one course would be just as valuable for college success as the other. Before such substitutions become popular, however, it will be necessary to eliminate the prejudice against "nonacademic" courses on the part of collegiate and secondary-school administrators and teachers.

ART

Art should be pursued in the secondary school because it offers something unique to the individual. Few of the other subjects offer as much opportunity for developing creativeness and the powers of perception as the properly taught art course does. Also, through art courses individuals can develop aesthetic appreciation of the great products of art of the past as well as of the present. Therefore most educators agree that instruction in art is necessary for all.

For the most part, however, approval of art in the schools has been in theory only. Once the pupils have entered the secondary school, relatively few of them have extensive art experiences—if any at all. Some junior high schools require art of all pupils, but in many junior high schools and most high schools it is offered only as an elective, making

---

[7] Music Educators National Conference, *Music in the Senior High School* (Washington, D.C.: The Conference, 1959), p. 77.

[8] *Ibid.*, p. 79.

it quite possible for a pupil to complete six years in the secondary school without having any art experience at all.

Undoubtedly art should be part of the general education of every high school graduate, for it can make great contributions to the pupils' full personality development by encouraging sensory, muscular, and intellectual growth.

Sensory Aspects. In a narrow sense, aesthetic education in art is concerned with the use and enjoyment of works of art rather than with the production of visual fine arts. There are two schools of thought on the appreciation of art. One says that only through participation can there be appreciation; the other that to have an aesthetic experience one need not repeat the experience of the artist, but that the viewer can begin where the artist left off. Therefore they believe that to appreciate the works of Inca and Mayan artists one does not need to recapture the feelings and thoughts of the early Indian artisans, but rather that appreciation includes an understanding and admiration of the culture and the artist's skill. Through fully developing the power of perception in one's personality, one can understand and enjoy the finished work to a degree far beyond the inherent qualities of the art product itself. Moreover, just as time and native ability limit the skill of any individual pursuing music, so do they in visual arts. No one artist, much less a pupil, can paint with mastery the styles of Chinese, Persian, Impressionist, Renaissance, and other paintings. Yet pupils can perceive and understand all types and styles of art products for various art periods. The range of art appreciation possible for a secondary-school graduate to develop has no limits, even though he is not a maker of art.

Perhaps one should point out here that the purpose of the secondary-school art curriculum is not and should not be to develop an absolute standard of "good" art. Modern artists say that there is no such thing as "good" taste in art, but rather that taste in art is determined by the culture, the age of the viewer, and the artistic experience of both the viewer and the producer. Still there appears to be a delicate balance between what is art and what is not. The role of the art curriculum is to help each pupil develop his powers of perception to the point that he can decide whether an object is a thing of beauty or just a thing.

By thus developing the powers of perception and aesthetic response, the school can instill in the individual the knowledge and experience necessary to develop good taste as a discriminating activity—if nothing else. Ideally, though, the individual should also receive some kind of message from the work of art. Herein lies one of the many real challenges for both the secondary-school curriculum builder and the classroom teacher. Activities that develop knowledge and perceptual powers sometimes deaden enthusiasm, interest, and creative activity. The curriculum worker and teachers must somehow select and teach curriculum content in such a way that the vivacious, creative interest of youth is nurtured at the same time that perceptual powers are increased.

The pupil's attitude toward art is of course influenced by his own age, the attitude of his peers, tastes of children slightly older than he is, social pressures of various kinds, and the attitude of the community as a whole toward art. If the people of a community desire things of beauty in their homes, schools, and other buildings, the pupils' attitudes will be bent in that direction. Furthermore, the pupils' aesthetic values will also be shaped by the kind of art they hear praised or ridiculed in their community.

In art education aesthetic development implies a regular increase in perceptual ability—a steady growth from the naïve attitude of the elementary school pupil to a critical, analytical attitude in the secondary-school graduate toward works of art. These mature attitudes should reflect increased knowledge about style and types of art so that each individual has as part of his configuration of experience many visual experiences. Then he will be able to compare any new art products with the visual images of other works of art.

Muscular Aspects. In the elementary school children are interested in manipulative activities, and so the elementary school curriculum includes a rather extensive variety of such activities with little regard to sequential organization. Much of the elementary school work appears to the adult to be play, but to the child it is real work, albeit enjoyable work. At this stage interest and vitality are more important than the development of craftsmanship. This emphasis does not countenance laissez-faire teaching, however. Elementary school pupils should be led and guided to develop an understanding of aesthetic techniques and styles.

By the time the pupil reaches the junior high school he should be ready for more systematic art activities. Pupils should be encouraged to plan and complete art projects. Instruction should include help and guidance in selecting materials and equipment for the projects and in carrying them out. Projects, however, constitute just one step toward attaining the artistic objectives. As the sensory and manipulative experiences develop, the intellectual aspects of art appreciation begin to appear.

Intellectual Aspects. Developing and planning projects should be an integrative process that includes acquiring skills and developing critical attitudes. The pupils should explore the why of the artistic experience: "Why is this medium better?" "Has it been done before?" and so on. Every effort on the secondary-school level should be exerted to help the student think out relationships between his present artistic activities and other disciplines. Organizing one's own body of knowledge and experience is in itself one of the highest types of utilization of the intellect.

Some say that art is not an intellectual subject like history and the other academic subjects. But art, like history, can also be intellectually rewarding. Art is a discipline; it contains various forms of knowledge, for example, dance, music, painting, design, and sculpture. Even the joy of experiencing something in an artistic activity is a kind of intellectual activity even though largely nonverbal. Just as it takes training of the ear and intellect to hear complex musical forms, so does it require training of the eye and intellect to perceive complex and subtle relationships in art products. If properly organized, studies and experiences in art enable pupils to enjoy the arts through greater understanding and hence keener appreciation.

ENROLLMENT IN JUNIOR AND SENIOR HIGH SCHOOL

Reliable up-to-date statistics are not available to provide a picture of student enrollment in art in the secondary school. The United States Office of Education in Washington, D.C., has stated in a letter that these figures will probably not be available for some time. The last survey was the "Biennial Survey" of 1948–50, published by the United States Office of Education in 1951, which showed that 48 per cent of the junior high school pupils and 10 per cent of pupils in the senior high school were enrolled in art courses.[9] More recent studies seem to indicate that as far as art is concerned the situation has not changed greatly.[10] The higher figures for the junior high school are caused by the common practice of requiring art either as a constant or as a limited elective in these schools. On the senior high school level, it is a rare instance when art is required for graduation. Hence art must compete with more than 200 subjects, the selection of any one of which being influenced by social pressures of various kinds.

The senior high school level enrollment is such as to be of great concern. Art educators, curriculum specialists, school administrators, and boards of education need to take a good hard look at their curriculum organization to find ways to encourage more students to sign up for art courses. Art opportunities in the senior high school are greatly needed.

COURSES AND TOPICS

Junior High School Art. Theoretically a good art program in the junior high school should be all-inclusive to be consistent with the exploratory philosophy of the junior high school. Such a program should include

[9] "Offerings and Enrollments in High-School Subjects," Biennial Survey of Education in the United States 1948–50 (Washington, D.C.: Federal Security Agency, U.S. Office of Education, 1951), p. 25.

[10] Edith S. Greer and Richard M. Harbeck, *What High School Pupils Study*, OE–33025, U.S. Department of Health, Education, and Welfare (Washington, D.C.: Government Printing Office, 1962), p. 72.

two-dimensional and three-dimensional work with various media, such as clay, stone, wood, metal, cloth, and plastic. Courses that are too broad, however, may lead pupils to do superficial work with many media without providing sufficient opportunity for experience in depth. If the intellectual as well as the physical aspects of the personality are to be developed in art aesthetics, then depth as well as breadth is essential.

In practice the art programs offered in junior high schools vary considerably from school district to school district and from section of the country to section of the country. Two factors seem to be operating to cause this diversity: facilities and equipment available and the philosophy of the instructor. In the first instance, because of the great demand on the citizens' dollar, some districts starve their educational programs. When this happens, the art program is frequently the greatest sufferer and sometimes is completely hamstrung. In the second, teachers' philosophies seem to range between two extremes. At one extreme, the teacher sees art as an experience only for the elite, and therefore wishes to concentrate on the pupils talented in art to the exclusion of everyone else. On the other end of the scale, the teacher looks upon art as a necessary part of the personality of every pupil and consequently attempts to teach so that everyone can develop his abilities in creative learning to the utmost. Of course, in between these extremes lie various shades of gray.

Senior High School Art. The senior high school art program offers art for the consumer as well as for the producer. Both types of programs are taught, and should be taught, to develop aesthetic appreciation. Audiovisual methods and materials, such as slides, paintings, films, and field trips, to demonstrate and show space, line, form, color, and texture in different media, are shown. Properly instructed, the students can develop the value judgments necessary to become discriminating consumers and producers of art.

Art of this sort should be a part of the general education pattern of subjects that transmit our cultural heritage as part of the educational objectives of the public school. Yet very few senior high schools require art for graduation, and with the requirements in the so-called academic areas becoming increasingly greater, the possibility of high school pupils ever taking art is becoming smaller and smaller.

Art should be required for every pupil in the senior high school because:

1. All people need to develop aesthetic values for the "better life." The high school is the place to do this.
2. Art provides a satisfying, creative use of leisure time. (All the literature says that leisure time is increasing. See Chapter 5.)
3. A knowledge of art is necessary to understand the culture in which we live.

4. Experience with art in the senior high school provides a relatively fast way for a student to explore choices of art vocations.
5. Art is a part of everyday living—an understanding of the place of art is essential and can be developed in the senior high school.
6. The senior high school is supposed to meet all the needs and interests of the high school population. The need to express one's self is a definite need. Students *are* interested in architecture, sculpture, graphics, painting, design of appliances, textiles, layout, and community planning. All of these interests can be met through required art courses.
7. Whether the student terminates his formal education with high school graduation or goes on to higher institutions of learning is not pertinent when making the decision about an art requirement. For all concerned, the high school may be the last opportunity to develop critical art judgment. Most college students do not take any art courses.

Comparison of Junior and Senior High School Art Programs. The junior-senior high school art program is a broad one offering many experiences in two- and three-dimensional art. While some of the senior high schools offer a general course similar to the one at the junior high school level, more senior high school art courses are concerned with specific media or vocational opportunities.

In the junior high school the art curriculum might include any of the following activities: drawing; painting; carving; construction; graphics; modeling; craft carving; sculpture; craft graphics; craft construction; lettering. Among the media used in these activities are clay, stone, wood, glass, wire, metals, yarns, plastic, print, paper, inks, and interesting scrap materials. Design and appreciation are, of course, taught in relation to all of the media. In some of the electives history of art and consumer art are integrated into the activities.

All or some of the junior high school art activities may be included in core or block-of-time courses. In some schools art is one of two or three areas combined to form unified studies courses. In schools in which core units are organized about problems and interests of the pupil through teacher–pupil planning, art frequently becomes a part of the general education offering of the core curriculum. In such programs concepts of color and design may be taught as a part of the work in city planning or literature and art of a particular period taught in the history of man.

Senior High School Art Courses. In the senior high school art experiences are offered in courses such as the following:

Exploring Art. Offered four years.
As the name implies this is an exploratory course, covering all aspects of art. Emphasis is on developing appreciation and history of art. The course is also called *Art for All.*

Art I or *General Art.*   Offered four years.

The course is an introductory course and is a prerequisite for advanced art course. Such a course provides experiences with various media. Emphasis in the modern school is on creativity in the areas of drawing, painting, sculpture, design, and crafts.

Drawing.   Offered in grades 10, 11, 12.

Object and figure drawing are stressed.

Advanced Art.   Offered in grades 10, 11, 12. (Also called *Drawing, Painting, and Sculpture.*)

The areas of drawing, painting, and sculpture are included with advanced study in composition, emphasizing expression and development of abilities and appreciations. This course seems to be broader than the preceding course and offers experiences in depth.

Art Workshop.   Offered in grades 10, 11, 12.

Another name for this course might be *Art Service.* The course is designed for advanced students and offers them opportunities to do work for other departments of the school and work in the community. It provides an opportunity for practical experiences in lettering, layout, display, and illustration.

Commercial Design.   Offered four years. (Also called *Commercial Art.*)

Included in the course is the development of techniques, knowledge about materials and media for reproduction, for example, pen and ink, scratch board, Conté crayon, and lithograph pencil. The course is vocationally exploratory.

Graphic Design.   Offered in grades 10, 11, 12.

Emphasis in the course is on the printing process. Subject matter content includes lithography, silk screen, etching, linoleum, and wood cuts.

Interior Design.   Offered in grades 10, 11, 12.

Included in the course is an application of art principles to the planning of rooms and houses. Some of the content is similar to that included in the following subject.

Fashion, Textiles, and Interior Design.   Offered in grades 10, 11, 12.

The course deals with textiles, design of costumes, fashion, and interior designs. Activities include fashion drawing, construction of model rooms and furniture, printing textiles, and the study of color and texture and its relationship to the use of appropriate furniture and fabrics.

Dress Design.   Offered in grades 10, 11, 12.

Half- and full-size dresses are designed. The problem-solving method is used to provide intellectual experiences in the fashion field. Some of the activities of the course may be included in *Fashion, Textiles, and Interior Design.*

Design and Crafts.   Offered four years.

Emphasis is on creating designs and working in leather, ceramics, metals, fibers, and plastics.

Interior Design and Textiles.   Offered in grades 10, 11, 12.

Pupils create dimensional designs for drapery, table cloths, and scarves. Techniques of block printing, silk screening, weaving, and stencil are used. Experience is provided in the use of textiles and color in interior decoration; model making is also included. In many ways the course is similar to *Fashion, Textiles, and Interior Design*.

Jewelry Design. Offered in grades 10, 11, 12.

Work is usually confined to sterling silver. Soldering, sandcasting, and stone setting are the techniques used to complete the projects. Emphasis is on original creative designs.

Jewelry and Metal Work. Offered in grades 10, 11, 12.

The course is similar to the one above, with the addition of experience with metals. In addition the jewelry projects, bowls, trays, and so on, would be included.

Jewelry, Pottery, and Leather Design. Offered in grades 10, 11, 12.

Work is on an advanced level in jewelry, pottery, and leather. Considerable emphasis is on extensive creative planning. The course could be one in sequence to *Design and Crafts*.

Painting. Offered in grades 10, 11, 12.

The course includes techniques and media used by the contemporary artist in oil and watercolor painting.

Pottery-Sculpture. Offered in grades 10, 11, 12.

Pottery includes work with various clay processes and instruction in decorating and glazing techniques. Clay, wood, wire, metal, and plaster are used in sculpting.

Ceramics. Offered in grades 10, 11, 12.

The course includes work in pottery, such as building, throwing, and casting. Experiences in ceramic sculpture, tiles, and ceramic jewelry are provided.

Great Arts. Offered in grades 10, 11, 12.

Basically the course is a history of art course. Painting, sculpture, and architecture of past ages to contemporary society make up the course content.

Humanities. Offered in grade 11 or 12. (Also called *Fine Arts Seminar*.)

The course is offered jointly with the music department. Includes material in music, drama, literature, and historical art. The pupil is required to do extensive reading in these fields.

Art Honors. Offered in grades 11 and 12.

The course is for the student who is talented in art. An opportunity is provided for the student to plan and execute a minimum number of projects.

Needless to say, no one school offers all of the above courses. They are not presented here as a sample art curriculum nor as a complete list, but rather to show the wide variance. Whereas the field of mathematics has a limited number of offerings that at times differ only in instructional level, art courses are more likely to differ in the type of subject matter content. When schools offer three levels of algebra, it is still algebra. In art, however, art educators cannot agree on how to organize this very broad field of art into "bite-size" courses for purposes of instruction.

TRENDS IN CURRICULUM DEVELOPMENT IN ART

Several schools are trying new approaches to the problem of providing art experiences to all of the students. It is too early to say with any kind of accuracy how successful such efforts will be. Each school district needs to reorganize the curriculum to fit the needs and resources of its particular situation. Briefly some of the recent innovations are:

1. Visual fine arts and industrial arts are integrated. Team teaching is used so that each respective teacher is responsible for that part of the course of study that is his specialty.
2. Exploratory courses, for example, *Art for All* or *Exploring Art*, are being offered more and more. Audio-visual materials and techniques are used extensively to develop critical value judgments.
3. Humanities or fine arts seminars are offered to provide experiences in music, art, drama, and literature during the same course. The courses may be offered by individuals or by teams of teachers.
4. English and visual fine arts are correlated. Correlated activities include such activities as studying art products of the period of time being considered in the literature course; illustrating term papers, short stories, or poems that the students have written; writing reactions to pieces of sculpture, architecture, or painting; considering the interaction of art with other disciplines.
5. Social sciences and art are correlated. The pupils may apply principles of art to municipal planning, achieving mental health through pleasant home furnishings, comparing art products of the period being studied with contemporary art products.
6. A fine arts core is offered. Activities include small music group ensemble work, production of art products by individuals, and developing critical value judgments of fine art products. Students may meet as small groups for most of the time and then come together for activities lending themselves to mass presentation, as is a typical team teaching approach.
7. "Art for the Consumer" courses are being developed. The courses are designed to provide the students with a knowledge of art and its application to products and services associated with contemporary living: dress, housing, community planning, plays, theaters, movies, television, and so on.

Any one of the courses being offered in the secondary schools may have one or more of the features of the innovations listed above. In these courses teachers of music, drama, English, history, or science sometimes work with the art teacher and present some of the lessons.

CONCLUSIONS AND RECOMMENDATIONS

The general consensus of opinion is that every high school graduate should have at least some art experiences in his education. However, to justify including art in an already extremely crowded curriculum, art courses of study must offer benefits available in no other subject. To this end students need to experience both the joy of creating beautiful things and the discipline of developing value judgments in fine arts. In order to develop value judgments, the courses should contain activities in which a student can create art products as well as activities that provide experiences with art products; they should include both manipulative and vicarious experiences.

To give the needed art experiences, it would seem that some art must be required for every high school graduate. Whether the requirement should be a one-shot course or a continuing exposure to art principles and art products over several years has not been decided. Seemingly the practice that holds the greatest promise for achieving the objectives is to have a basic art course in the ninth or tenth grade required of all students, because some art principles and techniques are better taught as *art* than as a part of an integrated activity. Art for daily living, of course, would be one of the emphases in the course. As part of the work in developing value judgments, correlated work in art should be part of the English, industrial arts, music, and history courses of study. The art experiences then could be concluded in a fine arts seminar.

With this curriculum organization a student would be getting some type of art experience each year. The Ohio State University School has provided for fine arts experiences in grades K–12. In the secondary school the area is called *Related Arts*. Some of the *Related Arts* work is required, and some work comes in limited electives. The program is worth studying, because it provides basic information in the arts, yet it is flexible enough to provide experiences for the most talented students in art and music.[11]

SUMMARY

Nothing is more necessary for a liberal education than art and music. Yet their hold on a place in the secondary-school curriculum continues to be precarious.

In the case of music, perhaps one reason for its insecure status is that it has been taught for the wrong objectives. Music has distinct cultural and educational contributions of its own, and it should be taught for them—not for vague reasons of citizenship, health, happiness, and public

[11] The University School Faculty, *A Description of Curricular Experiences, Grades 7–12* (Columbus, Ohio: Ohio State University, 1956), p. 62.

relations. If it is not taught for its aesthetic values, then music should not be taught at all.

A similar misemphasis of values has sometimes placed the razzle-dazzle of musical performance, particularly band performance, above the musical objectives. Of course, pupils should learn to sing and play musical instruments, and it is good that they play and sing in public, but the music curriculum's purpose should be to develop musical taste, musical skill, and musical knowledge—not to please the crowd. When the spectator values of musical performances outstrip their musical values, the validity of the music curriculum is dubious indeed.

General music courses have been under a cloud largely as a result of their nonmusical objectives. This is too bad, because they contain fundamental and exploratory activities that make them basic education. Good general music courses can help pupils both to develop musical skills and knowledge and to discriminate between good and bad music of all sorts, both classical and popular, by means of a wide variety of music activities and experiences. These courses are offered in both the junior and senior high schools. The senior high school courses differ from those in the junior high school in that they are usually multigrade courses providing experiences in depth rather than exploration. Courses at both levels can be challenging and interesting and deserve a place in the general education of all youth.

Instrumental music is usually restricted to work in performing groups. Bands, particularly marching bands, are more popular than orchestras probably because of the glamor and pageantry associated with marching bands plus the fact that to build up a good string section in a school orchestra is very difficult and time-consuming. As far as stringed instruments are concerned, small ensembles are more suitable. They also have the advantage of making it easy to provide for individual differences, because to form small groups of fairly homogeneous ability levels is a relatively simple matter. In particular, small groups are especially suited for giving talented players a chance to play with other pupils of similar abilities.

The situation in vocal music is much like that in instrumental music. Again the emphasis is frequently on nonmusical performance values, rather than on developing in pupils the knowledge that good music has a place in one's life. Small groups have been particularly susceptible to exploitation and commercialization. Such practice is inexcusable and unforgivable. Vocal music programs should be directed toward developing musical skills, knowledges, and tastes.

The music curriculum should have two programs for the talented: one for the musically talented, the other for the academically brilliant but not especially talented musically. For the first type the school should make every effort to help the potentially gifted musician become a "star." For the others the program should contain high-level challenging general music activities emphasizing intellectual content, discriminatory activities, and musical analysis. For this reason, advanced courses in music, for example, music theory, should be available at the senior high school level. Such courses can be intellectually stimulating and inspiring. When well done they deserve a place in college preparatory curricula.

The story of the art curriculum closely parallels that of the music curriculum. Like music, it has aesthetic and cultural values that should have earned it a privileged place in the program of studies, but, so far, enrollments and number of offerings have been discouraging. In general, the junior high school art courses are exploratory and very broad—so broad that sometimes they become quite superficial. In the senior high school one is more likely to find a variety of distinct art courses of all sorts. At both levels, however, there seems to be a trend toward integrating art into other courses. At the junior high school levels art is occasionally included in core curricula and block-of-time courses. In the senior high school art experiences may be incorporated into humanities seminars, fine arts courses, and similar interdisciplinary endeavors. In these and other courses there seems to be an increasing stress on art for the consumer and in using good taste in everyday life.

In the opinion of the writers, art and music should be incorporated into the secondary-school program of every pupil. Some of the art experiences should come in separate courses aimed at teaching pupils how to use art in their daily lives, while other art experiences should be included in the pupils' study of literature, history, and other subjects.

SUGGESTED READINGS

CONANT, HOWARD, and ARNE RANDALL. *Art in Education.* Peoria, Illinois: Chas. A. Bennett Company, 1959.

Chapter 8 is of particular value.

DEFRANCESCO, ITALO L. *Art Education: Its Means and Ends.* New York: Harper and Row, Inc., 1958.

Written by one of the art education authorities. Students should read Chapters 8, 9, 10, and 13.

LOWENFELD, VIKTOR, and W. LAMBERT BRITTAIN. *Creative and Mental Growth.* Fourth edition. New York: The Macmillan Company, 1964.

Deals with the theoretical background for content selection.

LOWENFELD, VIKTOR (ed.). *The Junior High School Level.* Kutztown, Pennsylvania: Eastern Arts Association, Research Bulletin Number 4, April, 1953.

Sheds light on the choice of content for the junior high school.

MORGAN, RUSSELL VAN DYKE, and HAZEL NOHAVEC MORGAN. *Music Education in Action.* Chicago: Neil A. Kjos Music Company, 1954.

Chapter 15 presents material about the music curriculum.

MUNRO, THOMAS. *Art Education: Its Philosophy and Psychology*. New York: The Liberal Arts Press, 1956.

Chapters 1 and 9 are basic for curriculum development.

MUSIC EDUCATORS NATIONAL CONFERENCE. *Music in American Education*. Edited by Hazel N. Morgan. Chicago: The Conference, 1955.

A source book of data, opinions, and recommendations.

————. *Music in the Senior High School*. Washington, D.C.: The Conference, 1959.

Explains the four-year planned band programs.

————. *The Music Curriculum in Secondary Schools: Handbook for Junior-Senior High Schools*. Washington, D.C.: The Conference, 1959.

Has bibliography. The book was also printed as *The Bulletin* for March, 1959, of the National Association of Secondary-School Principals.

NATIONAL ASSOCIATION OF SECONDARY-SCHOOL PRINCIPALS. *The Bulletin*. Washington, D.C.: The Association, March, 1961.

The entire issue is devoted to art. Chapters 1 and 2 deal with curriculum specifically.

NATIONAL SOCIETY FOR THE STUDY OF EDUCATION. *Basic Concepts in Music Education*. Fifty-seventh Yearbook, Part I. Chicago: University of Chicago Press, 1958.

The first part of the book is concerned with the theory of music education. The second part, in particular Chapter 5, discusses the curriculum.

REED, CARL. *Early Adolescent Art Education*. Peoria, Illinois: Chas. A. Bennett Company, 1957.

Good bibliographies in this book.

SMITH, PAUL. *Creativity—An Examination of the Creative Process*. New York: Hastings House, 1960.

Explains the creative process and shows the relations of creativity to learning.

SUR, WILLIAM RAYMOND, and CHARLES FRANCIS SCHULLER. *Music Education for Teen-Agers*. New York: Harper and Row, Inc., 1958.

Presents educational and social significance of music.

TAYLOR, HAROLD. *Art and the Intellect*. New York: The Museum of Modern Art, 1960.

Emphasizes moral values and art experiences.

Chapter 14
Business Education

Authorities estimate that there are some 50,000 to 55,000 different occupations in the United States today. Yet of all these occupations only a relatively few have training programs in the public secondary schools. Why, with all these possibilities, has education in the business subjects come to play such a large part of the secondary-school curriculum? As with most curriculum matters not one reason seems to be solely responsible. Rather the present role of business education in the secondary schools seems to be the result of a combination of historical events, most of which are interrelated.

A BRIEF HISTORY OF BUSINESS EDUCATION

When, in the latter part of the nineteenth century, the typewriter was developed to the point that it had become a real aid to the office worker, office workers were largely male. Until that time middle-class women had been restricted to employment in the home or as schoolteachers. Only women from the poorer classes worked at other occupations. But the development of the typewriter and the correlated use of shorthand helped to change all that. By the beginning of the twentieth century women occupied many positions in offices and business schools as the demand for their skills grew.

The demand for bookkeepers also increased during and after the Civil War. As the business structure of the country became more and more complex, bookkeepers were needed to account for monies received and expended and to operate numerical control systems. At the same time, accounting systems and procedures also became more difficult and complex so that learning the "trade" on the job became less and less feasible. Consequently in the latter half of the nineteenth century enterprising citizens established independent "private-venture" business schools to meet the demand. As the expansion of industry and government caused the need for such workers to grow at an ever-increasing pace, public necessity favored the introducing of business courses into the high school curricula. So eventually typewriting, shorthand, and bookkeeping became established as part of the secondary-school curriculum.

Continuous Growth of Clerical Occupations. Today the expansion continues. In the early years of the century only one in twenty workers was engaged in any kind of clerical occupation. Today the estimate is that one in seven is involved in clerical work. About one fourth of these are secretaries, clerk typists, or stenographers; approximately 10 per cent, bookkeepers; and about 6 or 7 per cent, operators of the newer type of electronic machines. And so, instead of confining itself to stenography, typing, and bookkeeping, the business education curriculum now provides preparation for all sorts of clerical and distributive staff—among them secretaries, stenographers, business executives, typists, bookkeepers, office machine operators, file clerks, general office clerks, sales clerks, receptionists, telephone operators, mail carriers, ticket agents, and bank clerks.

Demand for Business Education. To sum up, various forces are working to create a great demand for products of business education, a demand that can be met only in part by the private schools of commerce. A large portion of the working force consists of clerical personnel, a major share of whom are women who permanently or temporarily leave their jobs to raise families. At the moment the clerical force is so large, that just to replace persons who die necessitates a relatively large labor pool. In addition both government and industry are expanding operations that demand ever-increasing record keeping and paperwork. Even the use of data processing machines has enabled industrial and governmental operations only to keep even. All factors taken into consideration seem to indicate that the demand for the schools to go on offering business education will continue to be the same at the very least. If predictions of statisticians and business educators come true, the demand for white-collar workers will *increase*, with a resulting increased need for business education courses in the public secondary schools.

BUSINESS EDUCATION AND THE CURRICULUM

THE DUAL ROLE

Like some other secondary-school subjects, business education courses can be either vocational education or general education. In fact, some business education courses may be offered as part of the general education effort of the department, and yet, at the same time, be part of one of the vocational curricula.

In the literature considerable emphasis is given to this dual role of the business education curriculum. In all probability this double purpose results from the changed demands upon individuals stemming from the development of our modern technological society. Today everyone engages in some kind of business activitiy. Each day of the year, the citizen is the consumer of one or more products or services of business and must use business techniques in operating his personal and household affairs, if for no other reason than because he must make a financial accounting each year to the Bureau of Internal Revenue.

His personal activities aside, each individual also needs a knowledge of business in order to cope with his civic responsibilities. Intelligent voting, for instance, frequently requires business knowledge. Obviously some instruction in business principles and practices has become a necessary part of the general education of all youth. And so the business education curriculum has had to add the new role of general education to its traditional responsibilities of vocational education.

OBJECTIVES IN BUSINESS EDUCATION

All the many statements of objectives for business education include both vocational and general aspects, as the following list illustrates.[1]

1. To impart knowledge and develop skills which will equip pupils for handling their own personal business affairs and prove useful in the everyday practical activities of personal, social, and civil life.
2. To equip pupils with occupational knowledge, skills, and understanding necessary for securing, and functioning competently in, initial employment in business.
3. To contribute to pupils' better understanding of our business and economic system with a truth-seeking, scientific attitude toward business and economic problems.
4. To acquaint pupils with vocational opportunities in the field of commerce, affording them opportunity for measuring their interests and abilities, and guiding them in the choice of work in which they evidence interest and may reasonably expect to succeed.
5. To teach high standards of business conduct, developing proper business and social attitudes and a sense of social responsibility.
6. To develop desirable personal habits, traits, qualities, and pleasing personality.
7. To prepare pupils for possible promotional opportunities in business.

[1] Robert A. Lowry, "The Status of Professional Thought Regarding Aims and Objectives of Business Education in Public Secondary Schools of the United States," *Research Studies in Business Education* (Stillwater, Oklahoma: Delta Pi Epsilon, Beta Chapter, 1950), p. 43.

8. To give training which will assist pupils in making subsequent occupational readjustments.
9. To assist in laying a foundation for continued study in institutions of higher learning.

NONVOCATIONAL BUSINESS SUBJECTS

The subjects concerned with nonvocational aspects of the curriculum have been termed *basic business education* and constitute the business education offerings that contribute to the general education of all pupils. In addition various business education concepts may be taught in subjects other than business education. For example, study of the nature of social security may properly be part of the courses of study in social studies, business law, general business, and homemaking.

In the past, business educators included a relatively large number of basic education courses in the curriculum. Among them were economic geography, general business education, business English, business arithmetic, business law, business organization and management, junior business training, personal record keeping, and consumer economics. Recently some school systems have tried to reduce this proliferation by combining the subject matter of several different courses into single integrated general business courses.[2] Thus in one instance, two courses, Basic Business for Everyday Living and Consumer Business Education, were established to replace several fractionated courses. In a similar manner mathematics and English departments have absorbed subject matter ordinarily covered in business arithmetic and business English into their own offerings. By eliminating extraneous subject matter and by utilizing effective teaching techniques teachers in these integrated courses should be able to achieve adequately the general education objectives set forth for business education courses in a relatively short time.

Some educators do not consider typewriting to be part of the basic education offerings in business education, yet it is certainly essential for many high school graduates if they are to operate efficiently both in the home and on the job. Other educators would have those students who are planning to attend college take typewriting as one of their electives; a few would require it. In any case typing is certainly a popular subject. Evidently pupils and parents are enough convinced of its value so that pupils enroll in typewriting to develop this skill for personal use. Undoubtedly a strong case can be made for making it part of each pupil's general education.

VOCATIONAL BUSINESS EDUCATION

In general, high school pupils are being prepared for four types of work: stenography, general office work (including typewriting), book-

---

[2] *Cf.* Lloyd V. Douglas, *Business Education* (Washington, D.C.: The Center for Applied Research in Education, 1963), pp. 93 ff.

keeping, and selling. To carry out preparation for these vocations adequately business educators must know the competencies that are required by businessmen for successful business performance. Employers are looking to the high school to prepare graduates so that they can step into an office and begin work with a relatively small amount of additional training. Regretfully some of the high schools have such low standards that their graduates are not well enough prepared to assume full job responsibilities upon graduation. Before they can perform the work for which they were supposedly prepared, it is sometimes necessary for them to take additional training either on the job or from a private commercial business college. When this sort of thing happens often, the validity of the vocational business education curriculum is indeed questionable, for vocational business education curriculum is satisfactory only if it prepares boys and girls for jobs that they can get and hold. Too often, curricula prepare pupils for jobs that no longer exist in business or teach them techniques that business has long since discarded. This brings us to a discussion of automation and business education.

AUTOMATION AND BUSINESS EDUCATION

Automation is a relatively new word, so new in fact that some of the dictionaries used in schools at present do not list it. In business education automation involves machines that handle computing, communicating, and data gathering functions. Such machines may perform just one function or combine several functions to form an automated data system. For example, a machine file of inventory data can be integrated with accounting and delivery data to provide for reordering, payment, cataloging, production scheduling, and other tasks. Moreover, the machine will do the job over and over again and again without fatigue, boredom, or error once the programer has given it the proper instructions. Thus automatic electronic data processing (EDP) provides a means whereby the dull routine jobs formerly performed by clerks of various kinds can be done by machine and so free human workers for higher level work involving initial thinking of various kinds.

Impact on Employment. In a study of the adjustments in offices that had introduced EDP systems a year before,[3] the United States Bureau of Labor Statistics showed that although automation affected only 5 per cent of the total office force, the particular units using EDP cut their personnel about 25 per cent within the first year after its installation. Most of these individuals concerned were clerks whose jobs involved tabulating, calculating, filing, checking records, and posting. Only a

[3] Helen Wood, "Trends in Clerical Employment," *Business Education World*, 42: 19, November, 1961. NOTE: Helen Wood is Chief, Occupational Outlook and Specialized Personnel Bureau of Labor Statistics, U.S. Department of Labor.

small proportion of them were in stenographic and secretarial jobs. Interestingly enough, the study showed that the total office employment for a four-year period increased an average of 7 per cent. Evidently once the routine types of jobs are handled by machines, personnel are freed to function in new areas not possible without electronic data processing equipment.

Recommendations for Curriculum Workers. In view of the statements above, specific recommendations can be made for curriculum workers.

1. Schools need to recognize that automation is here to stay. The business education department needs to recognize the vital role it is playing in modern business techniques.
2. No machine that will convert speech into a typewritten manuscript appears to be even "almost ready" for production. The need for stenographers and secretaries is still the same. With the expanding business complex and the large turnover, schools need to encourage more students to enroll in the stenographic or secretarial curriculum.
3. Numerous reproduction devices have reduced the demand for typists' services. Within the next ten years, however, all that the machines will do, it seems, is to keep the demand constant.
4. "Able" students need to be encouraged to enter business education. There is great demand for team leaders to handle programing that involves skills in mathematics, accounting, and engineering.
5. New emphasis on mathematics is necessary. It has been suggested in some literature that an integrated course called "management science" be offered. Such a course would include elements of business, mathematics, and engineering.
6. As has been stated a number of times in this book, emphasis in all subjects should be on critical thinking, that is, problem solving and creativity.
7. Key punch operations for IBM card or magnetic tape should be studied.
8. Small offices will probably continue to need bookkeepers. The subject should be offered for personal use and vocationally to meet the local demand.
9. While specific business skills should be developed, the curriculum should be so organized that business education graduates acquire a general knowledge of the business functions. High school graduates need to have a flexibility built in so they can adapt themselves to changing business conditions. Office positions associated with EDP are usually at the top of the office pay scale. High school graduates need to have knowledge of such positions and the education and ability necessary to qualify for them.

ENROLLMENTS

Enrollments by Subject. Because the latest enrollment figures in business education as in other fields are based on the 1948–49 survey[4] the statistical picture today is somewhat difficult to ascertain. However, the evidence available indicates that enrollments in business education are extensive and that most popular business education subjects are typewriting, bookkeeping, and shorthand.

The Graduate's Program. A recent study provides us with information[5] concerning the subjects pupils study for graduation from high school. In this study business education was classified as a nonacademic subject. Of all nonacademic areas business education was the most popular with the typical high school graduate having 10 per cent of his credits in that area. The graduate must be convinced of the value of the subject, because schools commonly do not require business education courses of all students for graduation. On the other hand, science is commonly required, yet the typical high school graduate devotes only 12 per cent of the total credits to science.

In a large measure, the apparent popularity of business education is due to the enrollment in typing. Many students in so-called college-preparatory curricula take typing for personal use. Another factor is that pupils in the business curriculum usually have to take typing as a requirement for that curriculum. Furthermore, many pupils in the general curriculum have as a goal the vague one of "working in an office." To them typing is a step in the right direction. Relatively few pupils take business education courses other than the "big three" of typewriting, bookkeeping, and shorthand.

Despite the favorable statistics for business education, many educators are convinced that the business education needs of society and the individual are not being met. Throughout the nation the white-collar group is becoming ever larger; merchandising and selling provide opportunities that pay more than many professions, and governmental operations on the local, state, and federal level are ever expanding with the population. Thus there appears to be an ever-increasing built-in demand for persons with a background in business education. Yet the number of high school graduates who are prepared to participate in the world of business is relatively small. More pupils are enrolled in curricula that provide no business background. A typical example is the college-preparatory cur-

[4] "Statistical Summary of Education, 1949–50," Chapter 1, *Biennial Survey of Education in the United States 1948–50* (Washington, D.C.: Government Printing Office, 1951).

[5] Edith S. Greer and Richard M. Harbeck, *What High School Pupils Study*, OE–33025, U.S. Department of Health, Education, and Welfare (Washington, D.C.: Government Printing Office, 1962), p. 116.

riculum, which allows no business education electives even though many pupils enrolled do not plan to attend college at all. Counselors need to explain the values of business subjects so that pupils will make intelligent choices.

JUNIOR HIGH SCHOOL SUBJECTS

The two most popular junior high school courses are typewriting and general business. Typewriting has been offered in grades 7 and 8 as well as in earlier elementary grades. Wherever such experiments have been tried they have met with considerable success. One explanation is that typing requires simpler muscle movements than does writing in either the cursive or manuscript style. Another is that motivation comes with learning something that can be used at once.

In the junior high school typewriting serves a threefold purpose: two of these purposes are to develop skills that the pupil can use both in (1) his schoolwork and, (2) his personal life. The third purpose is to explore the pupil's capabilities and interests in the field of business. For instance, because success in typewriting requires a certain amount of coordination through typing courses, a junior high school pupil can at an early age learn if he has the capabilities needed to become a typist.

The other course that occurs most frequently at the junior high school level is general business, which most junior high schools offer in the ninth grade. The course has developed into a multipurpose offering, having both a general education role and a specialized education role. In both capacities the course can fulfill the exploratory function of the junior high school. As a general education course the general business course provides basic business principles, facts of the business world and simple business skills of use to most every adult living in a technological society. As a specialized course general business is the "first" course in business education on which the advanced subjects are based.

HIGH SCHOOL SUBJECTS

In the field of business education there are thirty or more subjects offered by small and large high schools. Many of these are vocational. A partial list of subjects might include:

Typewriting I, II, III	Consumer Education
Shorthand I, II	Keypunch I, II
Introduction to Business—	Machine Accounting I, II
General Business	Bookkeeping I, II, III
Filing	Record Keeping
Secretarial Bookkeeping	Accounting
Retailing	Secretarial Practice
Business Law	Office Practice

Retail Selling	Clerical Practice
Business Arithmetic	Business English
Store Management	Marketing
Salesmanship	Cooperative Store and Office
Advertising	Training
Economics	Economic Geography
Selling and Advertising	Transcription

Most of the subjects listed above are offered in the four-year high school or the senior high school and are not offered at the junior high school level. Let us examine some of them more carefully in the following paragraphs.

Typewriting. Typewriting may be offered in almost any grade of the junior or senior high school. Because many students may not have had typewriting before they arrive at the senior high school, beginning typewriting should be open to pupils at all grade levels. Advanced placement can be given to those students who complete one or more semesters of typewriting prior to entering the senior high school. Business educators generally agree that typewriting and shorthand need not be taken concurrently.

Bookkeeping. This subject has the second highest enrollment in business education. First-year bookkeeping should be taught to achieve the objectives of general education as well as the vocational objectives. The subject should be restricted to senior high school students. It is commonly offered at the tenth, eleventh, or twelfth grade level.

Shorthand. On the face of it shorthand appears to be a very simple skill. Yet mastery of the subject demands competency in a number of specific skills: word mastery, excellent memory of symbols, good muscular coordination, keen hearing, and an excellent knowledge of the English language as a whole. In spite of the fact that numerous dictating machines are on the market, the demand for stenographers appears to continue. If a high school graduate is to have the skill required by business, two things are necessary: high standards and a relatively late introduction of the course.

General Business. Few three-year senior high schools offer a general business course, evidently on the theory that it is a ninth grade course. Yet provision should be made in any school district for senior high school students to take so-called ninth grade courses. What this means is that subjects should not have grade labels—if a student needs a course he should be able to take it. If the emphasis of general business is on developing understanding and appreciation of our business and economic system, the course can be justified for all students. Then the course could be part of basic education and also the first course in the vocational business education sequence. In the opinion of the writers there should be two courses: Introduction to General Business for all students and

Advanced General Business for juniors and seniors. To be justified both courses should be intellectually stimulating.

Business Arithmetic. Business arithmetic is offered at the junior high school level in the ninth grade and also in the senior high school. In senior high schools it is placed in tenth and twelfth grades more often than in the eleventh grade. The argument for placing it in the twelfth grade is that preview of the fundamentals and study of the advanced phases of arithmetic in the business arithmetic course at the twelfth grade level should eliminate deficiencies in pupils' arithmetic skills just before they go out into the business world.

The arguments are valid in all probability. Curriculum workers need to consider the over-all needs of the students, however. Many of the advanced business education courses in high school require the knowledge of arithmetic. Arithmetic skills are essential to selling and retailing, business law, bookkeeping, economic geography, and economics. For these courses, then, business arithmetic should be taken earlier in the school program of the pupil, probably in the ninth grade. If instruction has been for mastery and the subject matter has been presented in a meaningful way, graduates should retain the necessary arithmetic skills without the senior course.

Business Law. Business law, the subject that is sixth largest in enrollment, is concerned with credit, drafts, promissory notes, collateral notes, and acceptances. It was one of the first business education subjects to be offered by the high school. Although it is primarily a personal use subject it is listed in a few vocational business education curricula. Frequently it is offered during the first semester of the twelfth grade, to be followed in the second semester by a course in salesmanship.

Office Practice. Evidently opinion differs markedly about what the subject matter content of Office Practice courses should be. As a matter of fact, business educators cannot seem even to agree on the name; courses that differ very slightly in content may be called clerical practice, general clerical practice, secretarial office practice or office machines. Office practice may be a half-year course with the prerequisite of at least one semester of shorthand, or it may be a year course requiring the completion of a two-semester shorthand prerequisite. In any case the course is usually a twelfth grade vocational course in which the pupil gets a practical application of business principles combined with the development of machine skills.

Economic Geography. Once upon a time economic geography was called commercial geography. Nowadays examination of courses of study indicates that today the more appropriate name is economic geography, although a few high schools refer to it as business geography. Whatever its name, the course stresses understanding of the effects that geographic factors have upon the business of this country and other countries. Thus economic geography might just as well be a general education course as a vocational business education course. It is offered in the tenth grade more often than in any other grade, although many schools offer it for their twelfth grade pupils. Conceivably it should be offered at all senior high school grade levels.

Business English. Next largest in enrollment is business English. For a time the number of schools offering business English seemed to be declining. This decline appeared fortunate, because the course duplicated much of the standard English offering. However, business educators have been unhappy with the course content in the regular English courses. In many cases, they complain, the letter forms taught there are out of date and English teachers lack knowledge of the language of business. No known research has been done to ascertain the why, but recently there seems to have been an increase in the number of schools that offer business English as a separate course.

Salesmanship. Another name for salesmanship is Principles of Selling. In it general principles are presented, so that the course is useful to people engaged in all kinds of saleswork. Usually it precedes such courses as advertising and retailing in the twelfth grade.

Consumer Economics. The consumer economics course is sometimes called Consumer Education. Its course of study includes some attention to the relative merits of different brands of goods, principles of buying, financial problems of the consumer, such as budgeting and credit buying, pricing policies, and some study of the agencies that protect the consumer. There is ample material to warrant spending a whole year on the subject. The most popular time for offering it is the twelfth grade, although a few schools allow eleventh graders to take the course.

Retailing. Retailing is sometimes listed as Retail Merchandising. The course is concerned with various phases of merchandising, including store operation, organization, and store management. It is usually offered in the twelfth grade for pupils who have already completed a course in salesmanship.

Record Keeping. In some schools Record Keeping is nothing more than first year bookkeeping under another name. The name changers seem to think that Record Keeping sounds less dull than Bookkeeping and therefore will attract a greater enrollment. In other schools Record Keeping is a nontechnical, often low-level course in personal record keeping from which vocational bookkeeping material has been eliminated. In this form it is usually listed as a one-semester course for the ninth and tenth grades.

Transcription. Advanced shorthand and advanced typewriting courses have been integrated into the course called Transcription, although some schools have integrated transcription of shorthand with office practice. No clear trend for the transcription course is evident at this time. The course may be one semester long or a full year, and it is usually given in the twelfth grade.

Cooperative Office and Store Training. The part-time cooperative plan has been used more in distributive businesses than in any other type. It is usually a twelfth grade subject and is one semester in length. Students spend about half a day in part-time cooperative work in stores and other distributive businesses and the other part of the day in school studying retailing and related studies. The program is supported with federal aid to education.

Key Punch Operation. This course includes parts of the machine, knowledge and use of the program panel, the development of skills on numeral and alphabetical material, alternative program key punch, and sorting. The course is a one-semester course offered at the twelfth grade level.

Machine Accounting. Material of the course includes wiring, principles of machines, the use of sorters, collators and interpreters, summary and reproducing punches, and programing. The course can be a one-semester or a year course at the twelfth grade level.

SPECIFIC BUSINESS CURRICULA

The sequence of courses required for graduation from business education curricula varies considerably from state to state and city to city and school to school, one of the most critical factors influencing the business subjects being the size of the school itself. Therefore it is difficult to present typical curricula that fit every situation. The curricula listed below are merely illustrative curriculum patterns. Although based on curricula offered in schools in Arizona, Connecticut, Florida, Pennsylvania, Ohio, North Carolina, West Virginia, Wisconsin, and Washington, they are not intended to describe the pattern offered in any particular school district.

General Business Education Curriculum

7th and 8th Grades:	One year of introduction to business and one year of typing.
9th Grade:	No business education courses.
	Pupils take general mathematics in the mathematics department; *or* enter the Illinois mathematics program.
10th grade:	Economic geography.
	Salesmanship.
11th Grade:	Bookkeeping (for personal use—nonvocational).
12th Grade:	Business organization.
	Business law.
	Choice of key punch, machine accounting, management science, consumer economics, salesmanship.

Stenographic Curriculum

8th Grade:	Typewriting.
9th Grade:	Illinois Mathematics Program or general mathematics.
	General business.
10th Grade:	Typewriting.
	Economic geography.
11th Grade:	Shorthand.
	Bookkeeping.
	Typewriting, if needed.
12th Grade:	Transcription.
	Choice of office practice, business law, consumer economics, advertising, salesmanship.

Bookkeeping Curriculum

8th Grade:	Typewriting.
9th Grade:	General business.
	Illinois Program of Mathematics.
10th Grade:	Economic geography.
11th Grade:	Bookkeeping—vocational and personal.
	Office practice.
12th Grade:	Business law.
	Key punch and machine accounting (large schools).
	Bookkeeping II.

Clerical Curriculum

8th Grade:	Typewriting.
9th Grade:	General business.
	Illinois Program of Mathematics.
10th Grade:	Bookkeeping for personal use (record keeping).
	Economic geography.
11th Grade:	Business law.
	Typewriting II.
12th Grade:	Clerical practice and office machines.
	Electives: Key punch, consumer economics, salesmanship, management science.

Retail Selling Curriculum

8th Grade:	Typewriting.
9th Grade:	Illinois Program of Mathematics or general mathematics.
	General business.
10th Grade:	Economic geography.
	Bookkeeping.
11th Grade:	Merchandising and store organization (retailing).
	Business law, one semester.
12th Grade:	Salesmanship, one semester.
	Advertising, one semester.
	Distributive education, one semester.

The sequences in the curricula listed above supplement the courses required of all students for graduation or admission to college. As we have stated elsewhere, local requirements often are greater than are the college entrance requirements. Still, all the curricula listed above will fit into most of the locally required lists of general education subjects that usually permit six to eight units of electives. (Some of the courses above are for a one-half unit.) It is obvious, therefore, that a student could follow one of the above patterns of subjects and still be able to attend college. Such a course of action would provide a pupil with a salable skill that can be used while attending college, the educational background for college admission, and the educational background for further business courses on the college level.

DISTRIBUTIVE EDUCATION

Distributive education is concerned with providing vocational training for pupils planning to engage in distribution and services to the public. Of all the programs offered in the field of business education it is the only one supported, even in part, by federal funds. Other business education programs, although truly vocational, have never been covered by the provisions for federal support of vocational education. Why this discrimination should exist is somewhat difficult to understand.

SUGGESTED COURSE SEQUENCE

The occupations involved in distributive education are classified into three areas: retailing, wholesaling, and services. On the secondary level more emphasis is placed upon retailing than on the other two areas. In an ideal retailing curriculum pupils should study all the major functions of the retail store, namely, merchandising, sales promotion, control, store operation, and personnel. In grades 8, 9, and 10 this curriculum would follow in the normal pattern of the business education curricula. Beginning in grade 11 the following sequence is suggested.

11th Grade: Merchandising and store organization. Some schools also offer Beginning Sales at this level. In addition to these courses one semester of business law might also be included.

12th Grade: One semester each of salesmanship and advertising and another course in distributive education, in which pupils would study any of the five major functions of retailing not included in the courses listed above. In addition, speech and human relations work should be given where there is a need. An additional Carnegie unit is given for completion of work experience under the supervision of both a business education coordinator and an employer.

This suggested curriculum represents excellent practice. The more usual practice is to allow pupils who enroll in distributive education to earn one credit for course work specifically in distributive education and one credit for on-the-job training. Although some schools may begin course work for distributive education in the eleventh grade, most schools restrict the distributive work program to twelfth graders. In this aspect of the distributive education curriculum pupils are placed in the business establishment of a cooperating merchant, where they usually work as paid employees for about 15 hours a week, often afternoons and Saturdays.

ENROLLMENT IN DISTRIBUTIVE EDUCATION

Approximately two fifths of the nation's work force is engaged in the distributive occupations, and all trends indicate that these numbers will increase. Yet only a relatively small percentage of high school pupils enroll in distributive education courses. This lack of popularity is unfortunate, for distributive education curricula have had considerable success in preparing pupils for rewarding careers after graduation. With the great need for the distribution of the vast amount of goods industry is capable of producing, perhaps more attention should be given to directing qualified students into distributive education in the secondary school.

SUMMARY

Because of the great changes in American industry and business the need for clerical and business workers continues to increase. Consequently business education curricula, including the distributive trades curricula, seem to have a rosy future. Because these curricula are predominantly vocational curricula they should be based on the realities of the business world they serve. For this reason the curricula need to be continually brought up to date. In this connection the growth of automation must be seriously considered and planned for in business education curricula.

The junior high school offers nonvocational business education courses that also serve as bases for further business education courses. Most frequently these courses are typewriting and general business. In the senior high school several differentiated business curricula are open to pupils. Among them are general business, stenography, bookkeeping, clerical, and retail selling. It should be noted that in spite of the general opinion, the requirements in these curricula frequently allow for adequate preparation for college entrance.

Strangely enough, the only business education curriculum supported by federal funds is the distributive education curriculum. This curriculum is, in practice, largely concerned with preparing pupils to work in the retail trades although other types of distributive trades, for example, wholesaling, may be included. In general this program is arranged similarly to programs in other vocational courses. Boys and girls combine practical work in business concerns, usually retail stores, with academic work in the school. As a rule distinct distributive education courses are limited to the upper high school years and the cooperative work program to grade 12.

SUGGESTED READINGS

AMERICAN BUSINESS EDUCATION YEARBOOK. *Educating Youth for Economic Competence.* Volume 15–16. New York University Bookstore: Eastern Business Teachers Association and the National Business Teachers Association, 1958–59.

Approaches business education from pragmatic point of view.

——. *General Business Education.* Volume 6. New York University Bookstore: Eastern Business Teachers Association and the National Business Teachers Association, 1949.

Chapter 2 presents philosophy of business education for secondary schools.

——. *Curriculum Patterns in Business Education.* Volume 13–14. New York University Bookstore: Eastern Business Teachers Association and the National Business Teachers Association, 1956–57.

Presents "patterns for clerical, stenographic, bookkeeping, DE, and basic business."

DELTA PI EPSILON. *Research Studies in Business Education.* Monograph Number 1. Stillwater, Oklahoma: Beta Chapter of Delta Pi Epsilon, Agricultural and Mechanical College, 1940.

Provides foundation material for curriculum study.

DOUGLAS, LLOYD V., JAMES T. BLANFORD, and RUTH I. ANDERSON. *Teaching Business Subjects.* Englewood Cliffs, New Jersey: Prentice-Hall, Inc., 1958.

Chapter 2, "The Business Education Curriculum," is pertinent.

DVORAK, EARL A. (ed.). *Informal Research by the Classroom Teacher.* New York: New York University Bookstore, 1961.

Procedures for the selection and evaluation of curricular materials in various business education subjects are included—as well as results of classroom research.

FORKNER, HAMDEN L. *Curriculum Planning in Business Education.* Eighth Annual Delta Pi Epsilon Lecture, Chicago, Illinois, December 29, 1949. Cincinnati, Ohio: South-Western Publishing Company, 1950.

A detailed presentation of current problems by subjects.

NATIONAL ASSOCIATION OF SECONDARY-SCHOOL PRINCIPALS. "The Business Education Program in the Secondary School," *The Bulletin.* Washington, D.C.: The Association, November, 1949.

Updated, revised, and republished as a book: The Association, 1957.

PERRY, ENOS C. "Looking Ahead in Business Education," *Journal of Business Education,* 38: 85–86.

Explains the changes necessary for business education to be up to date with industrial procedure.

TONNE, HERBERT A. *Principles of Business Education.* Third edition. New York: McGraw-Hill Publishing Company, 1961.

Chapters 17, 23, and 24 are pertinent.

TURILLE, STEPHEN J. *Principles and Methods in Business Education.* Staunton, Virginia: McClure Printing Company, 1958.

Considered to be a basic textbook for understanding the business education curriculum.

WALTERS, R. G. *The Business Curriculum.* Monograph 76. Cincinnati, Ohio: South-Western Publishing Company, 1951.

Patterns of business subjects are presented.

WALTERS, R. G., and C. A. NOLAN. *Principles and Problems of Business Education.* Chicago: South-Western Publishing Company, 1950.

Chapter 3 is a good summarizing presentation. Chapters 5, 6, 7, and 8 present material about specific business education areas.

Chapter 15

The Vocational
and
Practical Arts

Some Definitions. In this chapter the term *vocational education* refers to formal instruction at the high school level that prepares pupils to work in specific vocations. In this context it differs from *technical education* and *professional education,* terms that are used to designate post-high-school courses and curricula requiring higher skills and longer periods of training.

In some writings the term *vocational* is used to designate the manner in which a course is supported. Thus an auto mechanics offering that receives federal aid is called vocational auto mechanics as opposed to the simple designation of a nonfederally supported course as auto mechanics. In home economics, vocational home economics receives federal funds, whereas nonvocational home economics receives no federal aid. This distinction is not followed in this chapter.

TRADES AND INDUSTRIAL CURRICULA

The field of trade and industrial education offers a great variety of programs. The following list illustrates the types of programs offered for full- or part-time trade and industrial instruction in the secondary schools of the country:

Air Conditioning and Refrigeration	Acetylene Welding
Appliance Repairing	Airplane Maintenance
	Arc Welding

Auto Body Repairing	Landscape Gardening
Automotive Maintenance	Machine Shop
Building Trades	Needle Trades
Cabinetmaking	Painting and Paper Hanging
Carpentry	Patternmaking
Commercial Art	Photography
Cosmetology	Plastics Fabrication
Drafting	Plumbing and Pipefitting
Dry Cleaning	Practical Nursing
Electrical Communication	Printing
Electrical Maintenance	Radio and Television Repairing
Electrical Wiring	Sheet Metal Fabrication
Electronics	Shoe Repairing
Food Trades	Tool and Die Making
Foundry Work	Upholstering

ENROLLMENT

During the past fifteen years new developments in the American way of life have given trade and industrial education a new importance. Partly because of the increased use of labor-saving devices on the farm, where nowadays such new machines and processes as cotton pickers and chemical weeding do the work formerly done by many men, the American economy has become more industrial than agricultural. At the same time the population explosion and the increased standard of living have caused unprecedented demands for goods and services, which in turn have caused more job opportunities in trade and industry. Consequently large numbers of pupils seeking vocational education are turning to trade and industrial education.

In addition a relatively new worker, the technician, has appeared on the scene to swell the need for trade and industrial education. More than a simple craftsman, but less than an engineer, the technician implements the plans and ideas created by the engineers. Thus, although the technician does not need the creative skills and high training of the engineer, he must be able to communicate with both engineers and craftsmen. Therefore his educational needs fall midway between those of the engineer and the craftsman. As yet the role of the technician has not been clearly enough defined for educators to determine at what academic level he shall receive his technical education. Presumably there will be various levels of technicians, some of whom would be best trained in junior colleges while others should receive their training in the last two years of the senior high school. In any case technicians are now being trained at both levels, thereby increasing the enrollments in trade and industrial education in the high schools as well as the junior colleges and technical institutes.

Recent enrollment statistics for vocational education are not available.

The last complete survey was done in 1948.[1] However, it is possible to make some general statements concerning vocational education enrollments. By far the greatest number of pupils are not enrolled in vocational education of any kind. As far as trades and industrial education courses are concerned, the enrollment in grades 9–12 seems to be well under 10 per cent, and of this number not all are enrolled in shop courses. About one fourth are enrolled in shop mathematics, trade science, and other vocationally related subjects and about a fifth in mechanical drafting (drawing). Of the number enrolled in the preparatory trades, the largest enrollments seem to be in machine shop, auto mechanics, electrical work, carpentry, and printing. Yet as varied as the offerings in trade and industrial education are, they barely make a dent in the vast number of occupations in which pupils may find work. This abundance of potential occupations and vocational education curricula makes the problem of determining the trades and industrial offerings in the school a crucial one. Probably the one criterion most essential in determining what to offer in trades and industrial education is the demand for workers in that locality. When there is a need for a certain type of worker in a community the secondary school should consider well the advisability of providing a curriculum by which to train workers to meet the need.

Subject Apportionment. Federally supported vocational curricula are affected largely by stipulations of the Smith–Hughes Act. Ordinarily instruction time in academic areas amounts to 25 clock hours, or thirty 50–minute periods per week, but because vocational classes seldom require extra preparation at home in addition to classwork, the norm for the total weekly instruction time in vocational high schools is set at 80 clock hours, or in terms of class periods, thirty-six 50–minute periods. This time must be divided up among three areas: shopwork, related subjects, and general education subjects. In accordance with the provisions of the federal law, 50 per cent of the instruction time, 15 clock hours, is devoted to shopwork in vocational high schools. One half of the remaining time, 7½ clock hours, or 25 per cent of the total, is given to related subjects, whereas the remaining 7½ clock hours are given to general education subjects.

Related Subjects. In vocational education programs science, mathematics, and technical subjects that supposedly give pupils the background necessary for good understanding and appreciation of their vocational studies are called related subjects. Frequently their content is very similar to that of traditional academic courses in the field. For instance, vocational mathematics course content is quite similar to that of general mathematics in the general education program. Arithmetic, algebra,

---

[1] "Offerings and Enrollment in High-School Subjects," *Biennial Survey of Education in the United States, 1948–1950* (Washington, D.C.: Federal Security Agency, U.S. Office of Education, 1951), Chapter 5.

geometry, and trigonometry are included in the courses of study for both programs, but in the vocational program the courses emphasize applying mathematical skills and knowledge to occupational and shop problems.

As far as time and quality of instruction are concerned, standards for vocational education programs are controversial. Timewise, pupils devote as many years to mathematics and science in vocational curricula as in the typical traditional high school program. Because applied mathematics or science courses are usually more closely related to the needs of the pupils than academic courses are, it may well be that pupils learn more and retain more from them than from traditional mathematics and science courses. At any rate one point of view holds that the applied science and mathematics courses are more meaningful than the academic courses and hence develop greater comprehension in the field of study. In the final analysis, however, each individual course will have to stand, not on whether it is applied or academic, but on whether or not the instruction in the course develops the ability to solve problems, think critically and analytically, and arrive at logical conclusions. Courses in related subjects can be intellectually stimulating and at the same time give pupils pursuing vocational goals meaningful experiences.

Types of High School Programs. In some parts of the country at least part of the responsibility for trades and industrial education has been turned over to technical high schools, which are an important aspect of the educational organization of the city or state. In most cases the technical high schools are operated with local, federal, and state funds, although in Connecticut technical high schools are primarily supported by state funds. In general, technical high schools have more freedom to vary the proportion of a pupil's time devoted to shopwork, related subjects, and general education. Table VII shows the average number of periods of instruction devoted to the various subjects in different types of high schools.[2]

College Entrance and Vocational Study. It is interesting to note that careful study of Table VII will show that it is possible for pupils to have vocational training in specific occupations and still accumulate enough units for college entrance. Because most colleges require only 8 to 10 Carnegie units in specific subjects for admission, the 50 per cent of the time spent on general education will satisfy all, or most all, of the entrance requirements. When the related subjects, such as mathematics and laboratory applied science, are added to the general education subtotal, the total will satisfy most colleges as far as the number of units are concerned. With proper curriculum organization there seems to be little reason why pupils in the secondary schools cannot carry on vocational

---

[2] Alfred Kahler and Ernest Hamburger, *Education for an Industrial Age* (Ithaca, N.Y.: Cornell University Press, 1948), p. 96.

TABLE VII. AVERAGE NUMBER OF PERIODS DEVOTED TO VARIOUS SUBJECTS IN DIFFERENT TYPES OF HIGH SCHOOLS

SUBJECT	GENERAL HIGH SCHOOL COLLEGE PREP.	TECHNICAL COLLEGE PREP.	HIGH SCHOOL TERMINAL	VOCATIONAL HIGH SCHOOL TERMINAL
English	5	5	6⅔	4
Social Studies	3	2½	2⅔	3
Health Education; Hygiene	2	2⅔	2⅓	2⅔
Foreign Languages	5–6⅔	3⅓	—	—
Mathematics	5	—	—	—
Mathematics (Technical, applied)	—	5	4⅔	4
Science	3⅓	—	—	—
Science (Applied)	—	5	3	2⅔
Drawing, Art	1⅓	3⅓	—	—
Mechanical or Applied Drafting	—	—	5⅓	1⅓
Applied Technical Subjects	—	—	2	2⅓
Shopwork	2	6⅔	13⅔	20
Commercial Subjects	1⅔–3⅓	—	—	—
TOTAL:	28⅓–31⅔	33½	40	40

Periods last 50 minutes in academic high schools, 45 minutes in other schools; average school year is 38 weeks.

activities during their last two years of high school and still prepare for admission to a junior college, state college, or state university.

VOCATIONAL AGRICULTURE

Many urban dwellers have never heard of vocational agriculture, yet it is offered in over 9800 schools in the United States.[3] The Biennial Survey of Education mentioned earlier in this chapter showed that at that time there were some 364,185 students enrolled in agriculture. The number constituted about 6.7 per cent of the total enrollment of the schools.[4] At the end of the fiscal year of June, 1960, there were 463,960 pupils enrolled in agriculture in day classes, according to the Digest of Annual Reports of State Boards for Vocational Education.[5] It is not known how many of these were in federally reimbursed programs.

[3] *Digest of Annual Reports of State Boards for Vocational Education,* Fiscal Year Ending June 30, 1960 (Washington, D.C.: U.S. Department of Health, Education, and Welfare, U.S. Office of Education, 1960), p. 10.

[4] *Ibid.*

[5] *Ibid.,* p. 8.

COURSES OFFERED IN VOCATIONAL AGRICULTURE

At the ninth grade level the subject matter in vocational agricultural courses is general in nature. Usually it is not until the eleventh and twelfth grades that the pupils have any opportunity to specialize in agriculture and procure adequate vocational preparation in agriculture.

In general, work in agriculture is in two areas: farm mechanics and agricultural science. Farm mechanics, which constitutes about 40 to 50 per cent of the work in vocational agriculture, includes a study of farm machinery, farm power, and farm shop skills. Agricultural science, on the other hand, emphasizes the intellectual aspect of farming. Among the topics used to make *units* for agricultural science courses are crops, livestock, soils and water, fertilizers and their control, and farm management.

Although the purposes of vocational agriculture are concerned mainly with productive agriculture, in the last few years the offerings have been expanded to include the guidance function. To this end, in some vocational agriculture courses, information about professions and occupations in agriculture is presented. Subject matter pertinent to agriculturally related occupations has also been introduced into some course outlines.

FUTURE OF VOCATIONAL AGRICULTURE

Educators disagree about whether offerings in agriculture should be increased or decreased. One argument is that the trend toward increasing urbanization is causing less need for courses in vocational agriculture. Other educators and farmers state that both courses in vocational agriculture and courses in general agriculture education should be taught in a greater number of schools. Certainly in a world so dependent on agriculture a strong case could be made for including instruction in general agriculture education, particularly agriculture science, in the curriculum of every high school.

HOME ECONOMICS

Home economics is concerned with activities associated with the home and all aspects of living in the home. Its subject matter includes many disciplines, for home economics draws upon psychology, art, biology, biochemistry, sociology, chemistry, physics, and economics to provide the subject matter for the course of study.

OBJECTIVES OF HOME ECONOMICS

The objectives of home economics should be stated as the understandings, appreciations, and skills that a student might possibly develop from taking a home economics program. The list below is not complete; the reader will undoubtedly be able to add some that would adapt the home economics program to the needs of his local district.

Understandings

1. Family goals and patterns vary—there are differences in traditions, customs, and family patterns.
2. Each person in the family must assume a fair share of the responsibility of maintaining a good home and family life.
3. Good relations among family members are important. Each member of the family has status and worth as an individual.
4. The family's decision concerning the use of its resources must be accepted by all its members.
5. All families have difficulties and problems. The ability to overcome problems strengthens relationships.
6. Happiness may be attained through wholesome family activity.

Appreciations

1. A good home is important to the family, the city, the country, the world.
2. Utilization of the fine arts makes the home environment a more pleasant and satisfying one.
3. The family member who appreciates his home and family shows it in love, gratitude, loyalty, pride, respect, and cooperation.

Skills. Some of the skills listed below fall in the areas of guidance and leadership. The objectives as stated below imply that the homemaker will both acquire the knowledge and develop the mental and manipulative skills necessary to achieve the goals as stated.

1. The family member can establish moral and spiritual values that give meaning to the personal, family, and community living.
2. The consumption of the goods is done in ways that reflect the goals and value system of the family members.
3. The home is maintained in such a way that the goals of the family are realized; it should be comfortable and convenient and have attractive physical environment.
4. The home is conducive to the healthy growth and development of all members of the family at all stages.
5. The young receive the proper education during the formative years.
6. The personal life of members of the family is enriched through proper use of leisure time by enjoying the arts, humanities, and wholesome motor activities.
7. Good interpersonal relationships are maintained within the home and within the community.
8. Proper, nutritious, tasteful, eye-appealing meals are planned, prepared, and served.

9. Existing materials of clothing and household equipment are conserved through proper use and maintenance.
10. The family is well groomed, tastefully dressed, and well mannered.
11. The family establishes long-range goals for financial security and works toward their achievement.
12. Intelligent decisions regarding the use of personal, family, and community resources are properly executed.
13. Members of the family purchase those consumer goods and services that are appropriate to an over-all consumption plan and wise use of economic resources.
14. Family members participate intelligently in legal-social programs that directly affect the welfare of individuals and families.
15. Mutual understanding and appreciation of other cultures and ways of life are present in the family.

JUNIOR HIGH SCHOOL HOME ECONOMICS

Trends and Problems. Why should home economics be part of the junior high school curriculum? What can be taught in the home economics class that is not included in the courses of study of other academic subjects that are required in the junior high school?

Most everyone would accept the statement that the family is essential to the democratic way of life. It is in the family that the first education of the child occurs and the basic needs of the individual personality are met. In addition to operating as a family member, every person should also be an effective member of the various groups in which he operates. He should maintain his mental and physical health; he should think critically, act responsibly, understand the world he lives in, develop moral and spiritual values, and accept the responsibilities, duties, and privileges of citizenship. Home economics courses have much to contribute toward helping pupils achieve these goals.

The most common areas covered in homemaking courses—clothing, foods, family relations, child development, health, home nursing, management, consumer education, housing, and careers—lend themselves strongly to developing in young people the skills, attitudes, and knowledges necessary for good family relationships and family living. If family life is as important as we say, then boys and girls need opportunities to learn the skills for family living early in adolescence. For this reason home economics classes should be a must in the general education of all youth—boys and girls—for at least one of the junior high school years.

Junior High School Enrollments. Enrollment figures indicate that home economics courses do play a large share in the education of girls in most junior high schools. In Beulah Coon's study (Table VIII) she found that from three fifths to three fourths of all the girls in each junior high school grade were enrolled in home economics courses during the 1958–59 school year.[6] But for boys the report shows quite a different story. Only 2 per cent of the seventh grade and none of the eighth and ninth grade boys were taking home economics courses. It seems self-evident that as a partner in the family enterprise the human male as well as the female needs to have knowledge of family living. The local boards of education will have to formulate the policy enabling the professional educator and qualified lay persons to decide how much "family knowledge" should be included in boys' curricula. But certainly *some* instruction in homemaking and family living should be required for boys in the junior high school years.

TABLE VIII. PERCENT OF STUDENTS ENROLLED IN HOME ECONOMICS DURING THE 1958–59 SCHOOL YEAR IN THE JUNIOR HIGH SCHOOL

GRADE	BOYS	GIRLS
7	2	63
8	0	73
9	0	60

SUBJECT MATTER IN THE JUNIOR HIGH SCHOOL

There are two kinds of home economics: vocational homemaking courses that are subsidized by the federal government; nonvocational homemaking courses that receive no federal aid. Evidently all seventh and eighth grade homemaking courses are considered nonvocational, for federal subsidies do not begin until grade 9. As far as subject matter is concerned, the junior high school vocational homemaking courses do not seem to differ a great deal from the nonvocational courses. Table IX gives

TABLE IX. PERCENT OF TIME SPENT ON DIFFERENT AREAS IN JUNIOR HIGH SCHOOL GRADES 7–9 IN VOCATIONAL AND NONVOCATIONAL COURSES

AREA	VOCATIONAL 9TH GRADE	NONVOCATIONAL 7TH	NONVOCATIONAL 8TH	NONVOCATIONAL 9TH
Clothing	35	42	41	40
Foods	31	34	34	36
Family Relations	9	7	6	6
Child Development	7	6	6	4
Health and Home Nursing	5	3	3	4
Management	3	2	2	3
Consumer Education	1	1	1	2
Housing	8	4	6	5
Other	1	1	1	—

[6] Beulah T. Coon, "Home Economics in the Secondary Schools," speech given at the American Vocational Association Convention, Home Economics Section, in Los Angeles, December 9, 1959. The speech is a report of a very reliable study of home economics programs in 3800 schools of the United States.

an idea of the degree of difference in content emphasis between the programs.[7]

From this table one can see that in both vocational and nonvocational homemaking courses 66 per cent or more of the time is given over to foods and clothing in the junior high school grades. This relatively high percentage of class time for food and clothing disturbs some educators—and with reason. When judged by the role these areas play in the work week of the typical homemaker, the amount of time spent on them in the junior high school curriculum does seem disproportionate. Upon close examination of the clothing units the lack of proportion seems still greater, for then we find that over 60 per cent of that time is spent in clothing construction—an activity that occupies a relatively small amount of time in the lives of most modern housewives. Undoubtedly the emphasis in junior high school homemaking courses needs reexamination.

Deemphasizing clothing construction would permit other understandings and skills to be developed and make way for more time for the areas of child development, family relations, consumer education, management, and nutrition. Because both the nonvocational and vocational courses of study are heavily weighted toward foods and clothing, it appears that both types of home economics programs need to be reorganized.

Units in Homemaking Courses. A survey of homemaking programs of studies would show that some schools have already changed some of their emphases. New courses called Family Living tend to differ from older courses called Foods or Clothing both in scope of content and emphasis. This change of direction is also evident in unit approaches suggested in guides published by various states and school districts. For instance, the homemaking program recommended by the state of New York includes a general homemaking course in grade 9, and in grades 7 and 8, courses including such units as Playing with and Caring for Small Children, Helping with My Clothes, Looking My Best, Selecting and Preparing Foods for Health, Helping at Home, Living Happily with Family and Friends.[8]

Another sequence of units that provides the bases for excellent courses in grades 7 and 8 is contained in the following course outlines:

7th Grade:　The Girl and Her Home
　　　　　　Care of Clothing
　　　　　　The Girl and Her Money
　　　　　　Safety in the Home and School
　　　　　　Food Study

---

[7] *Ibid.*

[8] Bureau of Home Economics Education, *Planning Guide Homemaking Education* (Albany: The University of the State of New York, The State Education Department, 1950), p. 14.

8th Grade: The Girl and Her Family
              Helping with the Family's Food
              Helping to Care for Younger Children
              The Attractive Girl
              The Girl and Her Friends

In one school, as part of the Child Care Unit, the pupils participate in baby-sitting experiences that are both a service to the community and a worth-while educational experience for the early adolescent. A unit of this type could be quite practical, because junior high school girls are often asked to do baby-sitting chores. Additionally it has been found that as the young girls study the behavioral traits of their young charges they examine their own habits and actions. Some homemaking classes include actual taking care of children in class. (Parents leave small children at the nursery while shopping or attending meetings.) In these classes junior high school girls gain the experience of handling young children under guidance of the home economics teacher. Experiences of this sort are far removed from the narrow confines of Foods and Clothing.

Core Approaches. Courses such as the ones mentioned above illustrate that it is quite possible to organize junior high school courses so that all girls in the school can have some kind of suitable home economics training. Some schools do exceptionally well in this respect. One school offers girls who plan to major in home economics a core program in which their home economics studies are coordinated with mathematics, English, social studies, and science classes. In this school average girls are placed in an "activity" program that emphasizes laboratory experiences commonly encountered in the home and in which they can work with various types of activities. Here they receive instruction in such household activities as mending, home nursing, clothing construction, washing, ironing, and the like, at the proper level. Other girls in the school who do not take either the core or the activity homemaking course must take the family living program, which meets 90 minutes each week.[9]

SENIOR HIGH SCHOOL HOME ECONOMICS

Enrollment. One thing certain about home economics education is that most senior high school boys are not in the program. Senior high school enrollments in home economics for boys are even smaller than those in the junior high school. Because for the country as a whole only about 1 per cent of the boys in grades 7–12 are enrolled in home economics courses,[10] obviously senior high school enrollments are almost nil. Senior

[9] *Home Economics for Boys and Girls in 7th, 8th, and 9th Grades.* Some Description of Promising Practices (Washington, D.C.: U.S. Department of Health, Education, and Welfare, Office of Education, Division of Vocational Education, 1956), p. 17.

[10] Coon, *op. cit.*

high school enrollments for girls' home economics courses are also lower than in the junior high schools. According to Coon's survey only 40 per cent of the girls took home economics in the tenth grade; 28 per cent in the eleventh grade, and 34 per cent in the twelfth grade, as compared to the nationwide average of 49 per cent for girls in grades 7–12. Of all the girls 42 per cent were enrolled in schools having vocational programs and 51 per cent in schools having nonvocational programs.

An explanation for the fact that more girls do not take home economics in the senior high school must include several factors. One is that after the junior high school level home economics is an elective and so must compete with the prestige of the college-preparatory pattern of subjects. (It is significant that in grades 7 and 8 home economics is often required for girls, causing high enrollments for those grades.) Another factor is the trend to increase the units required for graduation in the fields of science, mathematics, and social studies. In addition many schools limit pupils to approximately four units of solid subjects per year. When these factors are combined, the desire and opportunity to take home economics naturally decrease as the student progresses from the ninth grade upward.

Justification. Recently there has been a tendency to question the validity of offering home economics courses in the high school curriculum. But certainly home economics subject matter warrants a larger space in the senior high school than it now has.

By the time students arrive in the senior high school some of them are thinking seriously about the future prospects of marriage. Regretfully many of them, when they graduate, are still not prepared for marriage. This lack of preparation becomes even more alarming when one considers that teenage marriages seem to be on the increase.

Since the beginning of time families have always had problems. Among today's family problems are:

1. In the case of early marriages the relative immaturity of the persons involved.
2. Limited help available to the homemaker to care for the family.
3. The changing role of men and women.
4. Competition for the time and interest of the husband, wife, and children, which takes them out of the home.
5. Insatiable demand for mechanical appliances and other material things.
6. Family mobility.
7. Pressures and tensions of the technological age.
8. Barrage of new products, new practices, new ideas.
9. Advancing cost of living coupled with ever-present danger of inflation.
10. Employment of the wife outside of the home.

For a family to operate efficiently, happily, and securely some agency must teach the family members to be flexible and adaptable in their behavior and how to think critically about family problems so that they can make wise choices and decisions. The school is the logical agency for this teaching, and within the school it is the teacher of home economics who is responsible for developing understandings, skills, and attitudes necessary for successful family living.

Casual examination of the problems of family life shows that much home economics content is related to and appears in other subjects in the high school curriculum. Social studies courses, particularly *Problems of American Democracy*, are concerned with many of the same family problems ordinarily covered in family relations blocks in home economics programs. Health is frequently taught in physical education and biology classes. But home economics differs from other subjects in that it is primarily concerned with strengthening family life by educating the individual for family living and giving him all the concomitant knowledge, skills, and attitudes. Home economics is the only subject in the high school curriculum that deals with all aspects of living in the dynamic problem-begetting culture of today. It is the only subject that has concerned itself with the practical ever-present pattern of daily living. Because the family is most important to all concerned, and because home economics is the only subject concerned with all aspects of family life, syllogistical reasoning would seem to state that home economics should be studied by all students.

Curriculum in Home Economics. In the senior high school, as in the junior high school, the home economics curriculum seems to be lagging behind the times. Again, at each grade level foods and clothing receive the greatest portion of time. Although Table X shows an increased proportion of time devoted to family relations in the twelfth grade for both vocational and nonvocational courses, with a small increase for the eleventh-grade vocational program, it must be noted that 44 to 74 per cent of the time is devoted to only two areas. One would have difficulty justifying that kind of proportionment. Again the disparity becomes even greater when the Clothing subject matter is analyzed.[11] In senior high school Clothing, from three fifths to two thirds of the time, is spent on the making of clothes. Obviously relatively more time needs to be allocated for child development, family relationships, consumer education, management, and nutrition in the senior high school as well as in the junior high school.

Units in Senior High School Homemaking. In spite of the overemphasis on clothing and foods, school systems and state departments of education have devised sequences of units that over a period of five or six years cover all aspects of homemaking.

[11] *Ibid.*

TABLE X. PERCENT OF TIME SPENT IN DIFFERENT
AREAS IN EACH GRADE OF THE SENIOR HIGH SCHOOL

	VOCATIONAL			NONVOCATIONAL		
	10TH	11TH	12TH	10TH	11TH	12TH
Clothing	31	28	23	39	36	26
Foods	30	26	21	35	29	22
Family Relations	7	10	16	4	5	17
Child Development	7	8	8	4	6	8
Health and Home Nursing	6	4	4	4	4	4
Management	4	5	7	3	3	6
Consumer Education	2	4	3	2	3	4
Housing	11	14	14	8	10	12
Other	1	1	2	1	1	1

The New York State Bureau of Home Economics Education would include units in the following areas: relationships—personal, social, and family; child care and development; foods, clothing; housing; health and home care of the sick; consumer problems and management.[12] In the junior high school grades, as we have seen, each of these areas is well covered in their recommended course of study. In the courses of study for the high school level, units in these areas appear again—Homemaking III alone having units in every one of the areas.

The Connecticut guide for home economics education, which bases the content for homemaking courses on the recommendations of a United States Office of Education publication,[13] recommends that local districts include the following aspects of homemaking in their high school programs:

1. Selection and purchase of goods and services for the home.
2. Maintenance of satisfactory personal and family relationships.
3. Selection, preparation, serving, conservation, and storage of food for the family.
4. Selection, care, renovation, and construction of clothing.
5. Care and guidance of children.
6. Selection and care of the house and its furnishings.
7. Maintenance of health and home safety.
8. Home care of the sick and first aid.
9. Consumer responsibility and relationships.
10. Selection and provision of educational and recreational experiences for family members.
11. The interrelation of the family and the community.

[12] Bureau of Home Economics Education, *op. cit.*, p. 40.
[13] Home Economics Education Service, *Connecticut's Curriculum Guide—Home Economics Education* (Hartford: Connecticut State Department of Education, 1955), p. 2.

Still another list of areas for senior high school home economics courses is provided by a curriculum of the Cincinnati Public Schools.[14] The areas are as follows: "Managing family resources, housing for the family, safe family living, personal development and the family, family members as consumers, family and community living, health and family living, food for the family, children in the family, family relationships, clothing for the family."

These three lists are markedly similar. Curricula of home economics of other states include all or almost all of these same areas.

To summarize them briefly, the lists of home economics areas might resolve into the following:

1. Consumer problems and management.
2. Social, family, and personal relationships.
3. Selection, preservation, preparation, serving, and conservation of food.
4. Clothing.
5. Selection and maintenance of the house and its equipment and furnishings.
6. Child care and development.
7. Health, care of the sick, and home safety.
8. Selection of educational and recreational experiences.

This list is a rather ambitious one. Only a few of the high school graduates who complete home economics courses will be proficient in all eight of the areas. Nevertheless its completion would be desirable for all pupils.

Although it is probably not necessary for homemaking courses to be a general education requirement for all pupils in the senior high school, and although there is undoubtedly some danger that the spiral curriculum design of home economics curricula may lead to duplication, instruction in these homemaking areas is both practical and desirable. Possibly it is time to seriously consider introducing homemaking content into the general education of all senior high school pupils by means of general education or core courses such as those suggested by Billett and described in Chapter 7.

INDUSTRIAL ARTS

For purposes of clarity the industrial arts curriculum is defined as that part of general education that includes a study of the materials, processes, and products of manufacturing.

In recent history a great wave of enthusiasm has swept the nation for

[14] Cincinnati Public Schools, *Home Economics Education, Grades 10, 11, 12* (Cincinnati, Ohio: 1957), p. 27.

the do-it-yourself project. One might jump to the conclusion that because the do-it-yourselfer is very much a part of our culture we must provide industrial arts instruction so that the individual citizen can make repairs, construct various projects, and perform simple maintenance tasks without killing or maiming himself. If this were the only reason for including instruction in industrial arts in the curriculum, then it would have to be eliminated. Luckily a much better case can be made for the subject on the junior and senior high school levels.

An important function of the industrial arts curricula is that of providing exploratory activities. The industrial arts program can help the pupil gain information about various industrial occupations. In its courses the pupil can become acquainted with the products of industry and undertake projects that will familiarize him with various types of industrial operations.

"The happy person is the creative person." If this slogan is carried to the extreme, the push for creativeness could become just as deadly as the lack of creative activity that is now common to some classes in the secondary school, but today the danger is slight. There is a crying need for teachers to make specific provisions for creativeness both in his teaching and in the student's products. The industrial arts program can do much in this area. In it the pupil can design and then produce practical things of beauty. To develop creativeness is one of the principal functions of industrial arts courses.

Another goal of industrial arts is to develop an appreciation of good craftsmanship. Good craftsmanship goes along with good design. Some lists of objectives attempt to justify the inclusion of industrial arts in the secondary-school curriculum by just asking for an *appreciation* of good craftsmanship. That is not enough. For a product to be a thing of beauty there must be good craftsmanship, and craftsmanship is dependent upon well-planned, diligent work—not on a few lessons. In the secondary schools it can be produced only through intelligent practice accompanied by diagnostic teaching. In the past there have been too many of the "turn 'em loose and let 'em saw" kind of activities in the shop. Of course not every pupil can become a superior craftsman, just as not every pupil can do A or 1 work in Latin. The point here is that the goal should be high enough so that it will challenge all pupils—the mechanically adept as well as the mechanically inept—and give each the opportunity to savor the taste of work well done and to know what good workmanship means.

One of "the Cardinal Principles of Secondary Education" is that the schools should somehow provide experiences that enable the high school graduate to use his leisure time wisely. That is asking quite a bit when even a casual observer can see that entire industries in the United States are devoted to enticing citizens to use their leisure time unwisely. Yet every subject now being taught in the secondary school can somehow be used to develop a leisure time activity. Industrial arts is not an exception. Its subject matter can be a source of a whole multitude of hobbies and projects. Some of the more popular are photography, boating, fishing, hunting, mosaics, metal sculpting, amateur radio, hi-fi, furniture making, and textile printing. Needless to say, these leisure time activities would be termed a wholesome and wise use of leisure. Providing skills, attitudes, and appreciations conducive to worthy use of leisure time is not the least of the functions of the industrial arts curriculum.

Considering the Cost. In evaluating the scope and role of the industrial arts curriculum one must consider carefully the cost of the program. Industrial arts is second only to physical education in capital outlay for plant and equipment. It is not unusual for an industrial arts shop to cost as much as a quarter of a million dollars. Therefore, before including industrial arts in the secondary-school curriculum, the board of education, the professional personnel, and the informed lay public should take a good close look at their community. They need to obtain all pertinent information and then decide whether or not it is worth the expense to provide practical arts for the youth of the community in view of the technological needs of the nation and of their own particular city or town and the resources of the school district and state. In almost every case, a well-conceived and executed program is well worth the cost.

Types of Shops. To a large extent, the curriculum is influenced by the manner in which the classroom is organized. And so it is that the industrial arts shop organization determines how the objectives of general education are realized. In the United States there are three types of shop organization. These are the comprehensive or composite general shop, the limited general or general unit shop, and the unit shop.

The largest enrollment is in the comprehensive general shop. It is the kind of organization that provides equipment and facilities for educational experiences in two or more industrial areas. Some schools can offer as many as 10 to 15 types of industrial operations in the same shop. For example, general shop facilities may provide for woodworking, drawing, metal work, electricity, electronics, welding, arts, ceramics, textiles, leatherwork, transportation, and photography. This fact is important, for it is only by having equipment and facilities for many activities that the exploratory function can be realized.

The limited general shop has equipment and facilities for working with a particular material, such as wood or metal, or for activities confined to a related group of industries, that is, electrical industries or manipulation of wood. A general woodshop, for example, might include such activities as cabinetmaking, carpentry, woodfinishing, upholstery, wood carving, wood turning, modelmaking, furniture making, and patternmaking. In this type of shop pupils can have exploratory experiences in depth.

The unit shop is organized for activities pertinent to a single industrial occupation. Examples of the unit shop include machine shop, welding, printing, sheet metal, auto mechanics, mason shop, and electronics. The unit shop is usually found at the senior high school level to provide the specialization that is required.

Instructional Areas. Industrial arts has been divided into several general instructional areas. All industrial arts programs include one or more of the areas listed below:

1. Drawing and Planning
2. Woodworking
3. Metal Working
4. Electricity and Electronics
5. Graphic Arts
6. Transportation and Power
7. Plastics
8. Leatherwork
9. Ceramics
10. Textiles
11. Home Mechanics

Home mechanics is not a true area, because it includes skills and knowledge in the areas of woods, metals, electricity, and textiles. When the course of study is formulated for home mechanics, the curriculum maker will be faced with the usual problem of deciding what to include and how much time should be spent on each of these areas.

JUNIOR HIGH SCHOOL INDUSTRIAL ARTS

Curriculum Content. The industrial arts offerings in the junior high schools vary little from district to district and from state to state. To illustrate this point let us examine the placement of various areas of industrial arts for two school districts and the recommendation of some state departments of education.

	7th Grade	8th Grade
School District A	Woodwork	Graphic Arts
	Crafts	Metal Work
School District B	Drafting	General Shop
(Areas for 7th	Electricity	Graphic Arts
and 8th grades)	Leatherworking	Metalworking
	Plastics	Woodworking
State Department A	General Drawing	Metals
	Graphic Arts	Crafts
	Woodwork	
State Department B	Drawing	Electricity
	Wood	Metal

State Department C	Wood	Handicrafts
(May be taken either	Metal	Graphic Arts
grade or both grades)	Electricity	Comprehensive
		General Shop

The lists are taken from actual course outlines in the West and Midwest. As can be seen above school districts A and B and the state departments A and C have included the same areas in the seventh and eighth grades. The areas are not identical as far as the lists are concerned, but in fact the courses include similar subject matter content. For instance, crafts would include leatherworking and plastics and comprehensive general shop would include metal work, woodwork, and electrical work among the activities. So we see that the differences in the offerings are not very great.

In the field of "related information" opinions differ more sharply. *Related information* is an all-inclusive term that embraces all concomitant learnings that are *not* as manipulative as the projects undertaken by the pupils. The items studied as related information are legion and could embody names of tools and materials, manufacturing processes, qualities of products, preparation of working sketches, the study of occupations, the work of the loom tender, and many others. Some instructors feel that such topics should be dropped from the curriculum and that industrial arts courses should include only those activities that produce craftsmen. Instructors of this sort state that industrial arts courses should revert to their narrow role of the days when the industrial arts was manual training. Such a return to the past seems very unlikely, however, for, to attain the objectives as set forth by the writers in the field of industrial arts, by the teachers of industrial arts, and by the supervisors of industrial arts programs, one must include related information in the curriculum.

Coeducational Industrial Arts. For years industrial arts courses were strictly masculine pursuits, but today coeducational industrial arts courses and courses for girls are not at all uncommon. The required course, called Home Mechanics Laboratory, recommended for Chicago schools having fewer than 250 boys and girls in grades 7 and 8 provide an excellent example of a coeducational approach. This course includes instructional units in home maintenance, electricity, metals, house and garden, and homemaking I, II, III. It is a practical kind of course and among other things presents material on landscaping the grounds, caring for lawns, testing soil for acidity or alkalinity, germinating seeds, working with finishing materials, replacing hardware of various kinds, using metals in the home, keeping tools sharp, making simple electrical repairs, and other tasks common about the house.

Another proposal, quite similar to the Chicago recommendation, suggests that a course made up of a 12-week block of time devoted to art, homemaking, and home workshop education respectively be required for all boys and girls for at least one year in the junior high school. The industrial arts areas represented in a home workshop block might include electricity, woods, drawing, blueprint reading, design, and metals. Although such a course has merit the curriculum maker is again faced with the ever-present enigma of deciding whether to cover many areas in one year or to cover fewer areas but study them in depth. Much more research and experimentation is necessary before detailed recommendations can be made. The courses discussed above appear, however, to be the type of courses that would be quite useful to a home owner.

Coeducational industrial arts education may also be approached by way of the core curriculum. In a three-hour block of time, for instance, manipulative industrial arts and mathematical skills could be developed in science problem-solving activities requiring the construction of test equipment.

INDUSTRIAL ARTS IN THE SENIOR HIGH SCHOOLS

Industrial arts courses are designed to fulfill the general education function. If a pupil has taken basic industrial arts courses and then continues to work in one area for two semesters or more, his work should ordinarily be in the vocational area. One state's course of study has designated the following as senior high school industrial courses: auto mechanics, third- and fourth-year drafting, electronics, graphic arts, handicrafts, photography, and metal working. One cannot tell from the names of the courses whether or not they are vocational, but seemingly any course that is taken after the exploratory industrial arts course could be a vocational course. It really depends upon the purposes established for the course. One school system distinguishes between the courses by the simple use of the adjective *vocational*. For example, aeronautics is offered as an exploratory course. It is followed by vocational aircraft powerplant mechanics. Similarly auto mechanics and advanced auto mechanics are considered to be industrial arts nonvocational, but another course is called vocational auto mechanics. The latter course has as prerequisites metals I and II, and auto mechanics I and II.

Courses Offerings and Placement. Some of the nonvocational industrial arts subjects offered in the senior high school are general shop, woodworking, mechanical drawing, metal work, printing, electrical work, handicrafts, and automobile mechanics. These courses are commonly offered at multigrade levels, although some of the more advanced courses that require a high degree of maturity are restricted to the eleventh and twelfth grades. Industrial arts offerings in the senior high schools include the following courses:

Electricity	Art Metals
Power Mechanics	General Crafts
Mechanical Drawing	General Metals

Machine Drawing	Electronics
Architectural Drawing	Home Mechanics
Graphic Arts	Plastics
Photography	Welding
Aeronautics	Sheet Metal
Auto Mechanics	Leatherworking
Woodworking	Jewelry
Printing	Ceramics

Unfortunately some of the senior high school industrial arts courses have become a dumping ground for pupils near failing or failing in academic subjects. Although it is true that often the industrial arts program can do something to provide guidance for the student who is doing poorly in academic subjects, it does contain facts and skills that would benefit the bright as well as the slow pupil. For example, the pupil who plans to be an engineer needs to develop his manual dexterity. Industrial arts needs to be made a challenging experience for all the students who enter the program.

SUMMARY

Vocational education is differentiated from practical arts education in general in that it deals with content that directly prepares pupils for a specific occupation. As used in this book it is differentiated from technical and professional education, which both imply education in an institution of higher learning.

Trade and industrial education offers a large variety of programs. Recent changes in the American social structure, population explosion, and the conversion from an agrarian to technical society throws a new importance on the field.

Despite the field's importance, relatively few pupils are enrolled in vocational subjects. Where they are enrolled, their programs are usually divided half and half between academic courses and shopwork. As a rule half the academic courses are "related subjects" and the other half general education. With such a curriculum it is quite possible to prepare for college entrance within the vocational curriculum. Frequently, because the academic courses are well tied in with meaningful shopwork, they are more effective than the ordinary academic courses.

Vocational agriculture is offered in approximately 10,000 American high schools. In general the course work is divided between farm mechanics and agricultural science. Because of the decreasing number of adults employed in agriculture, some doubt about the future of this curriculum has arisen. Still, the importance of agriculture in our economy is so great that there seems to be a need for at least some instruction in vocational agriculture.

Home economics is offered both as a vocational and nonvocational curriculum. Because of its content, which deals with home and family life, probably home economics should be part of every youth's general education. However, very few boys have any contact with home economics education.

In the junior high school, home economics education is strictly nonvocational. In the senior high school the curriculum is both vocational and nonvocational. Little difference between the two programs is evident, however, judging from an analysis of offerings in both curricula. At both senior and junior high school levels home economics courses seem to overemphasize food and clothing at the expense of other more important areas of home and family living. With better emphases home economics instruction could well be made part of the general education of all boys and girls. Much of its content lends itself well to the core curriculum approach.

Similarly industrial arts courses could well be made part of the general education of all pupils—boys and girls—particularly at the junior high school level. At present it is all too often a dumping ground for pupils lacking in academic ability. Because the industrial arts curriculum is expensive to maintain, school boards and school staffs must assess it carefully.

SUGGESTED READINGS

AMERICAN VOCATIONAL ASSOCIATION. *A Guide to Improve Instruction in Industrial Arts.* Washington, D.C.: The Association, June, 1953.

An anti-manual training approach.

ARNOLD, WALTER M. "Area Vocational Education Programs," *School Life*, 42: 16–21, January, 1960.

A geographic area approach to vocational offerings.

CALIFORNIA INDUSTRIAL ARTS COMMITTEE. *Suggested Courses of Instruction in Industrial Arts for the Senior High School Level.* Sacramento, California: California State Department of Education, 1955.

Contains several general ways of organizing the subject matter.

CHICAGO PUBLIC SCHOOLS. *Teaching Guide for Industrial Education.* Chicago: Board of Education, 1959.

Shows how an industrial arts program can be articulated for grades K–12.

CONNECTICUT STATE DEPARTMENT OF EDUCATION. *Connecticut's Curriculum Guide—Home Economics Education Including Resource Materials for Community Planning of Home and Family Life Instruction and the Home Making Sequence.* Hartford, Connecticut: Division of Vocational Services, 1955.

An excellent topical outline.

DEPARTMENT OF INDUSTRIAL ARTS, DENVER PUBLIC SCHOOLS. *Industrial Arts Education in the Denver Public Schools.* Denver, Colorado: Department of Instruction, Denver Public Schools, 1952.

All Denver publications provide excellent specific suggestions for the classroom teacher.

DENVER PUBLIC SCHOOLS. *Home Economics Education in the Denver Schools, An Instructional Guide for Junior High School.* Denver, Colorado: Denver Schools Division of Instructional Services, 1959.

————. *Home Economics Education in the Denver Public Schools, An Instructional Guide for the Senior High School.* Denver, Colorado: Denver Schools Division of Instructional Services, 1959.

DIGEST OF ANNUAL REPORTS OF STATE BOARDS FOR VOCATIONAL EDUCATION. OE–80008, U.S. Department of Health, Education, and Welfare, Office of Education. Washington, D.C.: Government Printing Office, 1960.

A statistical presentation.

DIGEST OF ANNUAL REPORTS OF STATE BOARDS FOR VOCATIONAL EDUCATION. OE–8008–60, U.S. Department of Health, Education, and Welfare, Office of Education. Washington, D.C.: Government Printing Office, 1961.

A statistical presentation.

FUTURE HOMEMAKERS OF AMERICA, INC. *Official Guide for Future Homemakers of America.* Fifth edition. Washington, D.C.: Future Homemakers of America, Inc., 1950.

A basic work.

IDAHO STATE CURRICULUM DEVELOPMENT AND TEXTBOOK COMMITTEE. *Industrial Arts Study Guide for Grades Seven Through Twelve.* Boise, Idaho: State Department of Education, 1955.

A well organized guide that outlines an excellent program.

KAHLER, ALFRED, and ERNEST HAMBURGER. *Education for an Industrial Age.* New York: Cornell University Press, 1948.

Evaluates vocational education. Chapter 5 treats of curriculum.

MC CARTHY, JOHN A. *Vocational Education: America's Greatest Resource.* Chicago: American Technical Society, 1950.

Provides background in vocational education for decision making.

MC CLURE, WILLIAM P. "The Challenge of Vocational and Technical Education," *Phi Delta Kappan,* 43: 212–217, February, 1962.

Explains an idea for reorganizing vocational education in the high school.

MC CLURE, WILLIAM P., *et al. Vocational and Technical Education in Illinois.* Urbana, Illinois: Bureau of Educational Research, College of Education, University of Illinois, 1960.

Presents offerings and enrollments for the state.

MAYS, ARTHUR BEVERLY. *Principles and Practices of Vocational Education.* New York: McGraw-Hill Book Company, Inc., 1948.

Organized by subjects.

NEWKIRK, LOUIS V., and W. H. JOHNSON. *The Industrial Arts Program.* New York: The Macmillan Company, 1948.

Most of the material is still current.

NEW YORK STATE EDUCATION DEPARTMENT. *Education of Youth for Personal and Family Living.* Albany, New York: The University of the State of New York, 1955.

This and other New York State publications furnish excellent aids for curriculum workers.

ROBERTS, ROY. *Vocational and Practical Arts Education.* New York: Harper and Row, Inc., 1957.

A detailed presentation of sections of this chapter. Has good bibliography.

UNITED STATES DEPARTMENT OF HEALTH, EDUCATION, AND WELFARE, OFFICE OF EDUCATION. *Home Economics for Boys and Girls in the Seventh, Eighth and Ninth Grades. Some Descriptions of Promising Practices.* Misc. 3422. Washington, D.C.: Division of Vocational Education, Home Economics Education Branch, 1952.

The title is self-explanatory.

———. *Homemaking Education in the Secondary Schools in the United States.* Washington, D.C.: Government Printing Office, 1947.

A status report.

UTAH COMMITTEE OF INDUSTRIAL ARTS TEACHERS. *Industrial Arts in Utah, Part One—A Handbook for Teachers and Administrators.* Salt Lake City, Utah: Utah State Department of Education, 1941.

This with Part II provides an example for courses of study development.

———. *Industrial Arts in Utah, Part Two—A Course of Study.* Third edition. Salt Lake City, Utah: State Department of Education, 1957.

WILLIAMSON, MAUDE, and MARY STEWART LYLE. *Homemaking Education in the High School.* Fourth edition. New York: Appleton-Century-Crofts, Inc., 1961.

The book on home economics education.

Chapter 16

Health,
Physical Education,
and Recreation

Physical educators are presently engaged in a great dispute about various aspects of their curriculum. As in so many other curriculum areas, the dispute arises partially from a problem of meanings. When, for instance, is a person physically fit?

The differences in the answers to that kind of question are reflected in major disagreements concerning what the role of physical education should be. Should it be limited solely to helping young people develop strong bodies, or should it be used to develop pupils' total personalities? Should it be concerned with the development of skills, knowledges, values, and attitudes? Should it be academic and include intellectual content similar to that in other courses? The answers to these questions have still not been settled.

Differences in beliefs notwithstanding, the scope of the physical education curriculum has been considerably expanded since its inception. Many modern physical education departments have built up their programs to the point where they are truly departments of health, physical education, and recreation. Therefore in the following sections we shall attempt to analyze programs in health education, physical education, and recreation, with the intent of pointing out strengths and weaknesses along with an indication of the direction that developments in these areas may take.

THE HEALTH EDUCATION CURRICULUM

Health education is, or should be, a part of the general education of all youth in the secondary school, for certainly if a person is to function properly in modern society he must be healthy. To accomplish its mission, which includes providing adequate instruction in health matters and school health services, the health education program must utilize both direct and indirect instruction and guidance services. In addition, if it is to successfully promote good health habits and attitudes, the health education curriculum needs the support of all the resources of the school and the community.

HISTORICAL GROWTH

A better understanding of health education may come from considering the developments of the program since 1900. At that time there were four distinct programs, medical inspection, physiology and hygiene classes, physical training, and temperance instruction, which have since merged to become Health, Physical Education, and Recreation. Between 1900 and 1930 social pressures of various kinds caused numerous changes in these offerings. Health facilities were improved, courses in physiology and hygiene were rearranged and expanded into health education, and physical training grew to become physical education, with a new consequent role in attaining health objectives.

WHAT ROLE FOR HEALTH EDUCATION?

This growth and change has been attended by considerable confusion partly because of a lack of agreement among those concerned with health of the pupils as to who should be responsible for the various areas of the health education program. Medical associations, for instance, have sometimes been critical of the scope and conduct of various activities that the school has assumed in the name of health education. And it may be that some school health activities would be more properly the responsibility of the department of public health than of the public schools. Further evidence of the lack of agreement about responsibilities is shown by controversies in communities about things like school immunization and dental examination programs and instruction in such topics as human reproduction, birth control, the phenomenon of birth, sex education, and emotional control in human life. At times controversy over such topics has become so hot that the boards of education have felt it necessary to eliminate them from the curriculum in the interest of peace and quiet.

WHOSE RESPONSIBILITY?

The confusion in health education is also evident in the fact that health education today is not the province of any one department. Instead instruction of various aspects of health education is shared by various secondary-school departments, for example, physical education, hygiene, social studies, the sciences (especially biology and general science), and home economics. Additional health education functions and responsibilities are carried out by other teachers, the maintenance crew, the janitorial staff, bus drivers, the guidance staff, medical services personnel, and school lunch workers. As a result of this sharing of responsibility, the health education curriculum is sometimes replete with duplication and repetition. A recent Master's thesis indicates[1] that topics such as personal health (physical and mental), disease, personality development, the adolescent, human reproduction, and heredity and environment may be included in the courses of three, or, in a few cases, four different departments.

A comparison of the following list of most common health education topics with the content of courses in science, home economics, and social science will demonstrate the scope of the problem of duplication.

The topics most often considered in health education instruction in the secondary grades are:

Body Mechanics	Boy and Girl Relationships
Exercise	Cleanliness
Family Living	Care of the Feet
Home Nursing	Relaxation
Mental Health	Human Relations
Excessive Indulgence	Essential Physiology
Harmful Effects of Alcohol,	Noncommunicable Diseases
Tobacco, Narcotics	Communicable Diseases
Nutrition	Essential Psychology, Sociology,
Personal Care	and Applied Physiology
Physiology and Diseases	Safety
Safety and First Aid	Human Reproduction
Dental Care	Sex Hygiene or Social Living
Eye Care	Heredity
Ear Care	

Divisions of Health Education. Much of the literature in the field of health education stresses that the health education program should be organized around the needs of youth. Similar statements have been made for all other fields. As in the other fields, whether to give priority to the immediate needs of youth or to their future needs is a problem that requires decision of the curriculum worker. In health education this problem is mitigated by the fact that providing for present and future health needs is not an either-or proposition, but rather requires a "both-and" decision. Therefore curriculum makers in health education can center their work around the pertinent health needs of youth, which have been documented in a number of studies.

---

[1] Linda Barter, *An Investigation of Duplication Between Home Economics and Certain Other Secondary School Curricula,* Unpublished Master thesis, University of Arizona, Tucson, 1961.

According to Harnett and Shaw these needs fall into eight major categories.[2]

1. Home and Family.
2. Opportunity for optimal physical growth and development.
3. Emotional adjustment.
4. Protection against disease and illness.
5. Development of physical skills and competence.
6. Reasonable protection from hazards and injury.
7. Sex adjustments.
8. Dental health.

Out of the needs has come the common division of health education into three areas: healthful school living, school health instruction, and school health services.

Healthful School Living. Healthful school living is most concerned with arranging the environment in such a way that the physical surroundings and emotional climate of the schoolhouse envelope are healthy and wholesome. Included in this category are healthy interpersonal relationships, high standards of safety, hygiene and sanitation in the building, transportation facilities, and equipment; provision for mental and physical health of all school personnel, provision for school lunches, and all the other necessities that make up what is termed the healthful school day.

School Health Services. School health services are an integral part of the health education program. They include the services of medical and nursing personnel, as well as the medical and dental examinations, and liaison with the home. A relatively new service, that of psychiatrists and clinical psychologists, illustrates the growing interest and concern about mental health in the schools.

School Health Instruction. Health instruction presents planned learning experiences that are related to healthy living. Ideally the instruction should be organized so as to be interesting as well as informative to young boys and girls. It should develop and reinforce desirable health attitudes. It includes instructional activities having to do with health integrated into other subject matter courses and extracurricular activities, as well as those distinct separate courses called health education. Health instruction is also included in such activities as auditorium programs and club demonstrations. Driver education and safety education classes may also be considered part of the health education curriculum.

CONTENT OF HEALTH EDUCATION COURSES

Instruction in health education courses follows no set pattern. In some districts a semester of health education is one of the senior high school requirements for graduation. In other schools a separate course is offered only in the junior high school. In still other schools health education is offered as a six- or eight-week concentrated effort as part of the semester of physical education. Some schools, unfortunately, make no real effort to teach health education at least in a formal way. Instead health education is relegated to incidental learning in such courses as biology and home economics.

The grade levels of the health education courses tend to determine the content of the courses. In the high schools, however, some of the instruction is intended to review and reinforce the knowledge and habits learned in earlier grades. This practice creates something of a problem because, as far as course organization is concerned, the difference between meaningful reinforcement and boring repetition can be pretty fine. The problem of meaningfulness is aggravated by the repetition of material included in other subjects and the broadness of the topic which precludes any depth study when many of the topics are included in a course.

DRIVER EDUCATION

Like many other aspects of the curriculum, driver education is a controversial subject. Tens of thousands of people are killed each year on our highways—in fact, more have been killed on highways than in all the wars in which the United States has been a participant. To stop this carnage, the people have turned to the schools for instruction in driver training and safety. To many critics and friends of public secondary education this new responsibility seems to impose an additional burden on schools, which already are finding it difficult to carry out all their responsibilities. And so the issue is whether or not the public schools should teach driver education or whether it should be left to private enterprise, another public agency, or the home. Reasons usually cited against including driver education in public secondary schools are:

1. Driver education is very expensive to conduct. In order to allow for time-behind-the-wheel teaching, classes must be kept small, thereby inflating per pupil costs. The use of mechanical or electronic training devices for large group instruction does not materially reduce the cost because of the expense of the necessary equipment.
2. It is difficult to work the six- or eight-week course into the "normal" schedule of classes.
3. If driver education is part of the physical education or any other curriculum, it takes part of the time needed for instruction in that subject.
4. Driver instruction represents just another invasion of the responsibilities and duties of home.

5. Driver education is not "basic education" and therefore should not be included in the offerings of the school.

On the other hand proponents of driver education put forth strong arguments in its favor. Their arguments are:

1. From the point of view of the state, the public school is to prepare the young for adulthood so that the state can continue to exist. Because the schools have been delegated to carry out the function of instruction, it is only natural, therefore, that instruction in driver education be given to the public schools.
2. Offering driver training is consistent with the general welfare principle that when the people are threatened with an unsafe condition the state needs to step in and make the proper provisions. Statistics have shown that teenagers who have successfully completed a driver education course have a significantly lower accident rate. Insurance companies have recognized this fact with lower premiums for the driver-educated teenager.
3. Safety education is considered to be a part of physical education. Driver education falls within the general classification of safety education.
4. The automobile is part of our culture. Teaching how to drive an automobile is one way to transmit our cultural heritage.
5. Basic education is that which is concerned with what is essential for a person to know. In many communities it is absolutely necessary that members of a family know how to drive so that they can operate efficiently as a family unit and lead a normal life.

Driver training usually includes both work in the classroom and time behind the wheel. Topics that may be covered in the classroom include:

History of the automobile
Psychology of the driver
Physical characteristics of the driver
Study of the automobile
Legislative and physical laws
Economics of owning and operating an automobile
Vocations of the automobile industry
Provisions for traffic and its control

Behind-the-wheel students are taught safety, simple ways to check the car, and control of the automobile. If actual automobiles are used, their use represents a limitation of driver training, for only three students can be taken with the driver at any one time. If several hundred pupils need the instruction, obviously other methods need to be devised if driver education is to become universal.

PHYSICAL EDUCATION

It seems that in every national emergency a magazine writer or two starts a clamor about the poor physical condition of our youth. Usually the basic conclusion that American youth are physically unfit is based upon statistics that have some relationship to the relative number of men rejected as unfit for military service. Actually most of these rejections result from other reasons, but the mere statement is enough to touch off explosive demands for more physical education in the public schools. Consequently more students are now enrolled in physical education than in any other subject with the exception of English. During the 1940's enrollment of physical education students increased more than other subjects. Of all secondary students, about 75 per cent were enrolled in physical education in 1950.[3] In the junior high school 91.4 per cent of the students were in physical education as compared with 69 per cent in the senior high school.[4] The high percentages may be still higher today, because the trend is toward a three- or four-year requirement of physical education for graduation from the high school. If the high school graduates are physically unfit it is not because they have not had the opportunity to take physical education courses. Research is necessary to determine if the length of the period, methods of teaching, or the curriculum being followed is responsible for any of the alleged deficiencies.

In curriculum construction the terms *athletics* and *sports* are often used incorrectly. Here *athletics* will refer to competitive games involving physical activity, accepted rules of play, and a system of scoring for determining winners from among two or more contesting individuals or teams. *School athletics* will refer to all such games in which students participate under school auspices. The term *athletics* as thus defined is to be distinguished from *sports*. The key defining words for athletics are *competitive*, *rules of play*, and *systems of scoring*. Whether or not competitive activities are engaged in by a team or by individuals is immaterial. Practically all of the school athletics are team activities.

The term *sports* is an all-inclusive one and it covers athletics, but all sports are not athletics. Some high schools and colleges have golf teams that compete with other schools. In this instance golf becomes athletics, but when an individual plays it for his own amusement, exercise, enjoyment, and so on, golf becomes a sport. Other sports include skin diving, parachuting, fresh-water fishing, deep-sea fishing, hiking, and mountain climbing.

There seems to be some difference of opinion about whether or not

[3] "Offerings and Enrollments in High-School Subjects," *Biennial Survey of Education in the United States, 1948–50* (Washington, D.C.: Federal Security Agency, U.S. Office of Education, 1951), p. 25.
[4] *Ibid.*

athletics should be considered a part of physical education. Physical education teachers and some coaches would like to divorce interscholastic athletics from physical education because of recent attacks on the overemphasis on athletics. Such action might be politic, but, in fact, physical education includes both athletics and sports—all separating efforts notwithstanding.

In the next few pages four aspects of physical education will be considered: the basic physical education program, intramural athletics, extramural athletics, and interscholastic athletics.

THE BASIC PHYSICAL EDUCATION PROGRAM

Generally speaking, in many schools the girls' physical education program is a better program than that for the boys. It has more activities, is better organized, and offers subject matter that is more nearly consistent with the stated objectives of physical education. In too many schools boys' physical education places far too much emphasis on baseball, basketball, and football. In terms of carry-over objectives, as well as others, such emphasis cannot be justified.

Objectives. Physical educators should have as a goal the development of individuals to be knowledgeable, participating members of society. High school graduates need to be prepared for a lifetime of activity. Although many programs emphasize the acquisition of physical skill, physical education must be something more than skill acquisition or a mere studying of rules and amenities. Learners need to develop a knowledge of the game, that is, the nuances, strategy, history, and problems of playing. Furthermore, such knowledge should be particularly extensive about games, sports, and activities in which pupils may participate after graduation.

Pupils also need to learn how to maintain physical fitness. Our technological developments seem to mean that more and more people will be doing less and less work of a physical nature. Pupils need instruction in developing healthy living practices in our age of automation.

General objectives for physical education can be set forth in five all-inclusive statements.

1. *Each physically educated person is physically fit.* The body should be free of physical defects and have proper muscle tonus to successfully perform physical activities, for good muscle tonus reduces fatigue, thus enabling one to perform his daily tasks with a high level of efficiency.
2. *A physically educated person has an optimum number of physical skills.* Such basic skills as walking, running, dodging, throwing, carrying, lifting, judging moving objects, and climbing are needed to operate efficiently and safely without strain. After having learned

basic skills an individual can then learn those skills associated with various team and individual sports and games.

3. *A physically educated person has healthy attitudes and habits.* Human relations are an important part of this objective. As stated the objective means that the student should experience those learning activities that cause him to develop attitudes of respect, tolerance, and friendliness for others. High on the list of attitudes to be learned in physical education is sportsmanship, which combines one or more of the attitudes noted above with a willingness to work for the best interests of the group and the ability to control one's emotions under stress.

4. *A physically educated person has adequate recreational skills.* For one to enjoy a recreational activity and to get from it the most recreational value, the participating person needs to have a reasonably high degree of skill in the activity. This fact suggests the desirability of physical educators including in their secondary-school programs not only the teaching of recreational skills immediately valuable to pupils, but also skills necessary for those activities that can be used for recreation in adulthood.

5. *A physically educated person has a wide knowledge of games and sports.* Physical education should go far beyond the mere development of highly skilled performers who can please the public and satisfy their own egos. To make physical education worthy of its place in the curriculum a new emphasis in physical education is needed. The physical education curriculum should be intellectualized. It should include units designed to develop powers of discrimination, greater appreciation of the fine points of play, and insight into the role of physical education in social organization.

Activities in Basic Physical Education. Activities included in basic physical education can be divided into the following categories.

1. Adaptive activities
2. Games, sports, athletics, play and aquatics
3. Self-testing, combat, and self-defense activities
4. Out-of-door activities

Adaptive activities are activities designed to correct physical defects. They make up what is called corrective physical education and include the use of mental health measures as well as physical exercises to correct physical deficiencies. In classes to which pupils are assigned in order to correct poor posture, for instance, exercises are given to the pupils to improve the balance of the weight in the pelvis, thorax, and head, the position of shoulders and sternum, and the position of segments of the spinal column.

Games, sports, athletics, play, and aquatics activities are multitudinous. A partial list includes:

Drill Team	Dance	Cheerleading
Kick-ball	Baseball	Golf
Wrestling	Field Hockey	Aerial Darts
Lifesaving	Softball	Badminton
Diving	Speedball	Deck Tennis
Canoeing	Volleyball	Handball
Sailing	Football–Touch	Horseshoes
Rowing	Soccer	Shuffleboard
Swimming	Field Ball	Table Tennis
Pom-ponning	Track and Field	Tetherball
Twirling–Rope	Archery	Tennis
and Baton	Hockey–Ice	Bowling
Fencing	Gymnastics	Skating

Dancing, field hockey, pom-ponning, twirling, and archery are more prevalent in the girls' physical education program than in that of the boys.

Such activities should include more than just skill development. Teachers can also include the history of the sport or activity and its present significance. In addition, in teaching these activities teachers should include such important learnings as the style of play, strategy, hygiene, consumer values, social values, personal values, and moral values.

Self-testing, combat, and self-defense activities are especially useful for meeting the physical fitness objective. Particularly desirable for this purpose would be a well-rounded program of gymnastics, including such activities as forward roll, head stand, hand stand, double tumbling, cartwheels, and backhand springs (to name just a few). For such a program one needs adequate apparatus, including parallel bars, high bars, trampolines, still rings, mats, ropes for climbing, side horses, and a balance beam.

Contact sports, such as judo, boxing, and wrestling, are also important conditioners, but unless judo and boxing are treated cautiously they may be dangerous. If proper equipment and supervision are not available, judo and boxing should be omitted from the physical education program of the high school.

Out-of-door activities are the last group of activities to be considered. A growing number of school districts provide summer camps for the pupils. In addition camping may be taught during the normal school year, with the pupils camping at a site nearby the school. Other popular out-of-door activities are hiking, the camera hunt, and hunter's safety. These activities are advantageous in that they possess a great amount of carry-over value and can also be tied in with science and such social studies topics as conservation, biology, and the study of wildlife.

The intellectual study of sports, games, leisure time activities, and other aspects of physical education has remained a largely neglected area. There seems to be no reason why this needs to be so. Physical education abounds with topics that would lend themselves to intellectual study and would help pupils satisfy their present needs and at the same time prepare for future problems. For example, a unit could be developed on Sportsmanship. Pupils might study behavior on the playing field in various athletic games to identify good, bad, and indifferent practices. The pupils' activities would be similar to those in academic classes: field trips to games; interviews of players, coaches, sports writers, and referees; discussion of social and personal values. Other topics that could be treated similarly are:

1. The Olympics
2. Sports for the Golden Years
3. American Dances
4. Sports Survey
5. Hosteling in the United States and Europe
6. Recreation for Busy People
7. Patio Activities
8. Back Yard Sports
9. Recreation in College

Carry-over. If the objectives of physical education are to be fully achieved, pupils must continue to participate in physical activities after they graduate from high school and enter adult life. Similarly the physical education activities should carry over into the leisure time activities of the adolescent prior to graduation, if pupils are to be physically and mentally healthy.

If the school's program were meeting the needs and interests of adolescents, there would be a high correlation between the curriculum and pupils' leisure time activities. This is not the case. In a doctoral study, Lynn Vendien discovered that the in-class program of physical education for girls had little relationship to girls' leisure time activities.[5] Leisure time activities with the largest degree of participation include swimming, ice skating, roller skating, social dancing, softball, boating, bowling, table tennis, tennis, and golf. Many of these activities are not included in the curriculum of the basic physical education program. If basic physical education programs are to contribute to the happier adult life, then revision of the physical education curriculum is necessary.

Coeducational Activities. Despite the fact that most physical education activities have been sex-segregated, many schools throughout the country

---

[5] Lynn Vendien, "Are You Teaching Leisure Time Skills?" *Journal of Health, Physical Education, and Recreation,* 31: 40–41, November, 1960.

have introduced physical education activities for "mixed" groups. These coeducational activities first began to appear in the high schools during the mid-1930's and by now have become well-established. The trend seems to be for an increase in the number of physical education programs that include coeducational activities.

Advocates claim several advantages for coeducational activities in physical education programs. One of the more important advantages is that in coeducational classes girls seem to learn faster than they do in segregated classes. Other advantages are:

1. Students like coeducational classes better.
2. Either a male or female teacher may conduct the activity.
3. Students develop skills in working with the opposite sex.
4. Students develop an understanding of the opposite sex.
5. Facilities are used more efficiently.

There are some factors that argue against the use of coeducational classes in physical education. Among them are:

1. Some religious groups oppose mixing sexes in physical education classes.
2. Boys may attain less skill in mixed classes.
3. Boys and girls may try to impress members of the opposite sex to the detriment of the physical values of the program.
4. Some pupils may develop feelings of inferiority more easily in mixed groups than in segregated groups.

Whether or not a school should have mixed classes seems to be dependent upon the objectives of the school's program. If the emphasis is on the development of physical skills, segregated classes give a better chance of developing them. If, however, social development is a goal, then some coeducational activities need to be included. In general, these should be activities that require agility and skill rather than strength, power, speed, and endurance.[6] Typical coeducational sports activities include volleyball, softball, handball, table tennis, bowling, swimming, camping, skating, and the like.[7]

INTRAMURAL PROGRAM

Intramural activities consist of participation in sports within the limits of the school site. Participation is voluntary and should be so. If properly organized, the intramural sports program provides opportunities for pupils

[6] A possible exception to this rule is tennis. Although mixed singles or doubles can be a valuable educational experience, proficiency in tennis is dependent upon strength, power, speed, and endurance.

[7] Hilda Clute Kozman, Rosalind Cassidy, and Chester O. Jackson, *Methods in Physical Education*, 3rd ed. (Philadelphia: W. B. Saunders Company, 1958), p. 461.

to develop skills in sports and games they learned in the basic physical education program. It follows logically, therefore, that the intramural curriculum should have more activities than the sports usually found in interscholastic athletics. In terms of the objectives stated for physical education, one cannot justify a limited interscholastic athletic kind of intramural offering. If students are to develop skills and attitudes that will provide for healthy recreation as adults, then provision should be made for those activities that are participated in by adults.

Participation in intramural athletics is at a low ebb in many school districts just now. School boards seem unwilling to allocate funds to provide facilities and personnel. When critical choices between providing for intramural or interscholastic athletics must be made, interscholastic athletics usually wins. For example, during the basketball season the school team too frequently has priority use of the gymnasium.

Another stumbling block to intramural athletics is the problem of providing time for the activities. In rural districts pupils must leave for home immediately after school is out. Other districts have problems of after-school work commitments. So that all students can participate, intramural sports need to be scheduled before school, during the activity period, during lunch hour, after school, and on Saturdays. The schedule needs to be flexible to meet the needs of individual school populations. To ensure the greatest amount of carry-over values, activities that require no more than four persons should be emphasized.

EXTRAMURAL ATHLETICS

A logical extension of the intramural program is to have the best team or all-star team play another school or school district. The program differs from that of interscholastics in that the competition is arranged informally —there is no set schedule of games that must be played during the season, and there are no leagues, league championships, district or divisional play-offs, or other highly competitive and highly organized types of arrangements.

Extramural sports usually take the form of festivals, play days, telegraphic meets, sports days, and invitational contests. Festivals and sports days are very similar in that the schools maintain their identity. In festivals, the participating teams are the various intramural champions. Sports days provide opportunities for pupils other than the champions to participate in various sports, although each pupil represents his school. Play days are organized so that the schools are not competitive with each other. Instead, "color" teams or play day teams are organized from the participants. Such an arrangement removes much of the emotionalism associated with interschool competition. Play day usually provides many activities in team and individual sports with a social activity following the competition. Telegraphic meets provide for a comparison of results by telephone, mail, or wire, while invitational contests may include symposiums, a single game, match, or jamboree.

Extramural athletics do have advantages that indicate that more activities of this nature should be encouraged. Much has been said in recent years about providing experiences for the high-ability student. Extramural athletics does just that, but in a breadth that is not offered in interscholastic athletics. Also, students who do not want to devote the great amount of time needed for interscholastic competition and yet want to compete with other schools can do it within the framework of the extramural program. Emphasis in the competition is not on the intense desire to win at all costs, but on the happiness that can be achieved by playing the game, and of course to win, but not at all cost. The extramural athletics activities provide ample opportunity for participation in competitive activities and the development of attitudes and skills necessary for cooperation. Most of the undesirable practices and pressures of interscholastic athletics are eliminated.

INTERSCHOLASTIC ATHLETICS

Interscholastic athletics are the most controversial activities of the curriculum. No matter what is said, there is always someone ready, willing, and eager to take the opposite point of view. It is expected therefore that the forthcoming statements about interscholastic athletics will not be accepted by all our readers. The ideas presented here are, however, accepted by many writers in the field of health, physical education, and recreation.

The theory behind interscholastic athletics is that the activities are necessary to provide opportunities for those youths who are highly skilled in athletics. It is justified on the same basis that advanced placement is provided for the relatively few students in academic subjects who have the high ability to handle advanced courses. Along with the theory goes the principle that special opportunities for the highly skilled players are supplemental to the physical education program and are not meant to replace opportunities for all students.

Weaknesses of Interscholastic Athletics. Although several critics of interscholastic athletics challenge the very existence of the activities, the point of view here is that athletics do have a place in the curriculum. It is not that interscholastic athletics as such are bad; rather it is the undue *emphasis* on the activities that has made it necessary to reexamine the entire program in relation to the objectives of physical education. When one does so the following weaknesses appear evident:

1. Values engendered by present practices in some schools are bad for the players and other pupils. Instead of the positive aspects of

good citizenship, winning is valued above all else. Players may be taught how to use fists and elbows in unsportsmanlike ways. Cheating, deceit, and ruthlessness may be condoned. Spectators may be permitted or encouraged to develop hysterical responses. By calling it school spirit, administrators and coaches may justify frenzied "preparation" of the student body through pep meetings and rehearsals. Visiting players and spectators may be regarded as enemies. Opposing players as well as game officials may be subjected to verbal and physical abuse to the extent that police escorts are needed to protect them. When actions like these are permitted, then the learning that occurs does not lead to the best development of the individual's personality.

2. Participation in interscholastic athletics holds the highest esteem of all the activities sponsored by the school. Pupils, teachers, members of the board of education, and administrators may all contribute toward this weakness. The star athlete may be singled out for attention by all concerned. Other athletes are rewarded with banquets and trips. Before a "tough" game, they may be permitted to stay at home from school or to attend a "relaxing" movie so that they will be "ready" for the big game. Condemnation of nonparticipants who could be good athletes but won't conform is permitted by the faculty. At present time the teenage boy or girl who is not interested in athletics still has a low status in spite of the new emphasis on science and mathematics and academic excellence.

3. Financial and personnel resources of a school district are provided for the benefit of the few with the neglect of the many. When schools overemphasize interscholastic athletics, priority is given to to the needs of the program. Instead of instructional equipment and supplies, football lights, bleachers, equipment, time and motion projectors, cameras, and so on, are purchased with the only money available. The physical education program also suffers, because the varsity equipment may come out of the physical education budget. Equipment that could be used by large numbers of students for the entire school year is sacrificed for equipment for the use of a few. Varsity football locker rooms may be left standing idle after the end of the football season while locker facilities for physical education classes are overcrowded. Girls' physical education needs are often ignored in favor of the boys' interscholastic program.

4. Partial or complete financing from non-tax sources causes educational objectives to be pushed aside in favor of attendance and gate receipts. Games are played at night in order to increase attendance. To prevent loss of income, games are played in almost any kind of weather, and safety provisions are violated or ignored.

5. Coaches are often relieved of their duties for having losing teams. This weakness is related to point number 4—losing teams draw poor

crowds. If interscholastic athletics are to be considered educational activities, winning games should be only one of the many reasons for having the sport.

6. In some "sport" cities, coaches receive bonuses from booster groups for a winning season—often an automobile. Booster groups that indulge in such practices sometimes feel that they have the right to influence the school athletic policy, thus by-passing the elected board of education.

7. At the junior high school level particularly, interscholastic athletics are a health hazard. Pediatricians, orthopedists, and professional educational organizations advise against the young adolescents' participating in athletic competition between schools. Their objections are based upon physical and emotional limitations of the junior high school student. Most school administrators and boards of education, however, pay little heed to such recommendations.

Value of Athletics. Whether we like it or not, athletics with all its high degree of competition is a part of our culture. Because one purpose of the schools is to transmit culture, then knowledge of athletics is a proper part of the curriculum. There are two ways one can get a knowledge of the game—by playing and by studying the game without playing. Interscholastic athletics at the high school level thus become a way in which the youth can learn another aspect of our culture.

Athletics is also said to be an activity much like Advanced Placement courses for able students. There is some question about the validity of such an argument. The very able football player can develop all the prowess and knowledge of the strategy of the game through intramurals with occasional telegraph meets. Football players engaged in interscholastic athletics do not seem to be in any better physical condition than athletes do who specialize in noninterscholastic athletics, such as tennis or swimming, for example.

As has been stated previously, but is mentioned here again for emphasis, intellectual consideration of athletics has been sadly neglected and wrongly so. Physical education can perform a great function in the transmission of culture, if the spectator sports are considered from an intellectual point of view. In the physical education classes time should be given to the study of strategy, rules, sportsmanship, and other pertinent topics by using all kinds of materials. Many high schools, for example, now imitate the colleges and film every game. The films could be used in physical education classes for the above purposes.

STANDARDS OF PHYSICAL EDUCATION

Standards for Sports. The Division for Girls' and Women's Sports of AAHPER has published standards for sports for girls and women. The standards, which have been widely endorsed and are equally as pertinent to boys' sports as girls', read as follows:

1. Sports activities for girls and women should be taught, coached and officiated by qualified women whenever and wherever possible.
2. Programs should provide every girl with a wide variety of activities.
3. The results of competition should be judged in terms of benefits to the participants rather than by the winning of championships, or the athletic or commercial advantage to schools or organizations.

Health and Safety Standards for Players

Careful supervision of the health of all players must be provided:
1. An examination by a qualified physician.
2. Written permission by a qualified physician after a serious illness or injury.
3. Removal of players when they are injured or overfatigued or show signs of emotional instability.
4. A healthful, safe, and sanitary environment for sports activity.
5. Limitation of competition to a geographical area which will permit players to return at reasonable hours; provision of safe transportation.

General Policies

1. Select the members of all teams so that they play against those of approximately the same ability and maturity.
2. Arrange the schedule of games so there will be no more than one highly competitive game a week for any one team or girl in any one sport.
3. Allow no player to participate in more than one full-length game or match in a vigorous activity, or its equivalent, in one day of organized competition.
4. Discourage any girl from practicing with, or playing with, a team for more than one group while competing in that sport during the same sport season.
5. Promote social events in connection with all forms of competition.[8]

Attainment of Standards. Nationally the physical education program falls far short of perfection. A national survey[9] has found that existing programs attain only 30 per cent of the generally accepted standards for physical education programs. From this study it is obvious that emphases in physical education are out of joint. The portion of the physical education curriculum most concerned with carry-over values receives little consideration. Schools ranked highest in the categories of organizational policies and athletic programs; at the other end of the scale were remedial work and swimming. Although "athletics programs" include both intramural and interscholastic athletics, it is the interscholastic athletics that

[8] Division for Girls' and Women's Sports, AAHPER, *Sports Library for Girls and Women* (Washington, D.C.: National Education Association, biannual), p. 7.

[9] Karl W. and Carolyn Bookwalter, *Purposes, Standards, and Results in Physical Education*, Bulletin of the School of Education, Indiana University, Volume 38, No. 5, September, 1962.

receives the emphases. Very important from the viewpoint of carry-over is the area, in the study, labeled Program of Activities. Logically this program should be the heart of any physical education curriculum. Yet despite its importance the program of activities was ranked close to the bottom in the 3000 schools evaluated. Evidently considerable reorganization in the physical education curriculum is needed before it can achieve the objectives stated for it in the literature.

RECOMMENDATIONS FOR THE IMPROVEMENT OF
PHYSICAL EDUCATION PROGRAMS

In view of the apparent need, the authors will venture the following suggestions for the improvement of physical education programs.

1. Qualified teachers should be assigned to teach physical education. The tendency for coaches to be assigned to teach academic subjects is not desirable. Coaches should have a physical education major and teach in the major.

2. For curriculum reorganization of the athletic program, use the checklist developed by the Educational Policies Commission. It can be reproduced for local use without infringement of copyright laws.[10]

3. The total physical education program should be part of the general instructional program. Activities of all kinds need to be articulated with those of other departments of the school.

4. The physical education curriculum should be for *all* students not for the select few. Allotment of resources should be equalized for boys and girls.

5. All activities in the curriculum should be evaluated in terms of the objectives approved by the school board, the superintendent, advisory councils, and the faculty of the school. Carry-over values should be emphasized.

6. Systems of evaluation should be improved.

7. Elements of professionalism and commercialism should be eliminated from the curriculum.

8. Any physical activity must be appropriate for the maturation level of the pupil. Thus age, physique, interests, ability, experience, and health need to be considered for boys and girls.

9. The physical education curriculum should include all sports and games previously stated. Progression of the teaching of water skills should be emphasized in grades 1–12.

10. Emphasis throughout the entire program should be on instruction. Play is important, but after the pupils obtain a general idea of a

---

[10] Educational Policies Commission, *School Athletics, Problems and Policies* (Washington, D.C.: National Education Association, 1954), p. 88.

game or sport, one purpose of instruction should be to develop the greatest degree of proficiency.

RECREATION

In spite of the fact that all subjects, and particularly the cocurriculum, provide knowledges and skills that pupils may use for recreation, both at present and in the future, recreation is frequently considered to be the province of the department of physical education. In fact, frequently the official name of the department is the Department of Health, Physical Education, and Recreation, just as the name of the physical educators' national professional organization is The American Association for Health, Physical Education, and Recreation.

Recreation should be distinguished from leisure time activities in general. Watching television, a football or basketball game, or any other kind of spectator activity is a leisure time activity, but is not true recreation. A leisure time activity becomes recreational when it satisfies the need of an individual to be active or when it offers an opportunity for the human spirit to regenerate itself. Very often after a period of tension-producing activity the individual appears to be drained of all energy. In actuality, it is the spirit that has been devitalized. To recreate an enthusiastic, energetic type of personality takes something more than just mere idleness. It takes the kind of activity that permits the human personality to achieve something and do it well. The person needs some kind of an activity that permits him to reestablish his drive and self-esteem.

Recreation and the Curriculum. Recreation may be expressing one's self in a hobby, an avocation, or some "fun" activity. Recreational activities may be for the young or old; they may take only a short period of time or require years to perfect; they may allow for creative expression or for simple motor action; but for the greatest value the activity should be entirely different from the type of daily "work." Typical recreation activities include the following: woodworking, woodcarving, ceramics, folk-song singing, singing, playing musical instruments, square dancing, hiking, studying pictures, sailing, golf, tennis and other sports of nonspectator type, digging for archeological finds like dinosaur eggs and tracks, high fidelity, photography, collecting of old furniture, refinishing old furniture, fishing, hunting, ham radio operator, and traveling.

Just using the activities listed above as a guide would require instruction in industrial arts, art, music, science, geography, and physical education. Possibly the physical education curriculum has more to offer in the area of recreation than any other subject matter area of the secondary-school curriculum. Nonetheless, to be effective, provisions must be made for teaching recreational skills and knowledges in every subject field of the curriculum.

Provision for recreation by the schools is deemed necessary in order to teach boys and girls how to use their leisure time in a worthy manner. Mental health experts agree that recreation is very necessary to good mental health. If the schools are to prepare the young citizen for living in these tense times, then one of the objectives is the developing of individual skills for effective participation in recreational activities.

Community Recreation. Because of the nature of recreation, many recreational activities are of the organized type that require community action of some kind. The question immediately arises, "Who is going to organize and lead it?" Some say that the schools ought to take the leadership, because education is not contained within the walls of the school ground. Others say that it is the responsibility of the city, county, or state to provide recreational leaders to handle the pertinent problems. If the schools assume the responsibility, then the designated school person must coordinate recreational activities in the community. In this manner the school would of course become a true community school. A well-coordinated activity of this kind could ultimately save the taxpayers money, because it would avoid the erection of duplicate facilities by the schools and community recreation commissions. A school-supported recreation coordinator could serve to make the public aware of the problem and to lead the way in working out an equitable arrangement for supporting recreation activities.

SUMMARY

The profession is at considerable difference of opinion concerning the scope and aims of the health, physical education, and recreation program. The opinions range from beliefs that physical education in the narrow sense of body building should be the total program, to beliefs that the program should deal with all aspects of the personality in the broader sense through activities, intellectual as well as physical, in all the areas of health, physical education, and recreation.

Health education consists of three areas: Healthful school living, school health instruction, and school health services. Topics in health instruction are somewhat controversial and frequently duplicate topics in other courses. Sometimes this material is taught in courses called health education, but frequently health education is parceled out by various other departments in dribs and drabs, helter-skelter without much, if any, planning.

Basically the physical education curriculum can be divided into four compartments: basic physical education; intramural athletics; extramural athletics; and interscholastic athletics. The basic physical education program consists of adaptive activities, games and sports, combat self-defense, and self-testing activities and out-of-door activities. Intellectual aspects of the program have been largely neglected. Although the literature makes much of the teaching for carry-over values, in practice relatively little is being done in this area. Still there seems to be a trend for schools to incorporate coeducational physical education activities that do have carry-over and socialization values into the basic physical education curriculum.

Many schools provide a wide variety of intramural athletics activities. Illogically enough, this program, which could well be the heart of the physical education curriculum, is frequently neglected in favor of interscholastic activities. Intramurals deserve better treatment. In some schools extramural athletics are used as a capstone of the intramural program. These activities consist of relatively informal competition between members of different schools. They have been most popular with girls and junior high schools.

Interscholastic athletics hold too prominent a place in boys physical education. Frequently the amount of time and effort spent on these interscholastic teams is way out of proportion to the number of pupils benefiting. Often interscholastic games are accompanied by unsocial behavior of many sorts and sometimes by downright immoral instruction in how to cheat effectively. Overemphasis is giving interscholastic athletics a very bad name, and it is time that the interscholastic athletics programs in our schools undergo an "agonizing reappraisal." As they stand they can seldom be justified.

Driver education is frequently associated with instruction in health and safety. Whether or not driver training should be part of the school program has been a cause of much debate. What the future place of driver training in the curriculum will be is still moot, but there is no doubt that someone must provide such instruction. Where adopted, the course of instruction, which includes both theoretical classroom work and behind the wheel training, seems to have paid off in reduced numbers of accidents.

Physical educators have included recreation as part of their title. Again, just what the role of the school should be in this area is undecided, particularly insofar as community recreation is concerned.

SUGGESTED READINGS

AMERICAN ASSOCIATION FOR HEALTH, PHYSICAL EDUCATION AND RECREATION. *Education for Leisure* (A Conference Report). Washington, D.C.: The Association, 1957.

An excellent presentation of the school's role in leisure activities.

ASSOCIATION FOR SUPERVISION AND CURRICULUM DEVELOPMENT. "Fitness and Health," *Educational Leadership*. Washington, D.C.: The Association, March, 1963.

This issue is particularly good for studying present problems. Bibliographies of various articles are current.

BROWNELL, CLIFFORD LEE. *Principles of Health Education Applied.* New York: McGraw-Hill Book Company, 1940.

A good basic book.

BROWNELL, CLIFFORD LEE, and E. PATRICIA HAGMAN. *Physical Education— Foundations and Principles.* New York: McGraw-Hill Book Company, Inc., 1951.

Chapter 9 is particularly good for curriculum development.

DUNCAN, RAYMOND O., and HELEN B. WATSON. *Introduction to Physical Education.* New York: The Ronald Press Company, 1960.

Chapter 7 gives a good general treatment of the subject.

EDUCATIONAL POLICIES COMMISSION. *School Athletics, Problems and Policies.* Washington, D.C.: National Education Association, 1954.

Contains criteria that can be used for the control of athletics.

HARNETT, ARTHUR L., and JOHN H. SHAW. *Effective School Health Education.* New York: Appleton-Century-Crofts, Inc., 1959.

Stresses cooperative action necessary for education for health.

KILANDER, H. FREDERICK. *School Health Education.* New York: The Macmillan Company, 1962.

A fairly complete treatment of the health curriculum at the secondary school level. Content and methods are presented in an integrated manner.

NATIONAL ASSOCIATION OF SECONDARY-SCHOOL PRINCIPALS. *The Bulletin.* Washington, D.C.: The Association, May, 1960.

The entire issue is devoted to presentations about physical education.

NIXON, EUGENE W., FREDERICK COZENS, and FLORENCE STUMPF FREDERICKSON. *An Introduction to Physical Education.* Fifth edition. Philadelphia: W. B. Saunders Company, 1959.

Chapter references are annotated. A 364-item bibliography is included at the end of the book.

OBERTEUFFER, DELBERT, and CELESTE ULRICH. *Physical Education.* Third edition. New York: Harper and Row, Inc., 1962.

Chapters 8 and 9 pertain to curriculum development. Both should be required reading.

WILLIAMS, JESSE FEIRING. *The Principles of Physical Education.* Seventh edition. Philadelphia: W. B. Saunders Company, 1959.

Written by one of the top authorities in HPER. Guiding principles are intensively examined and developed.

WILLIAMS, JESSE FEIRING, and RUTH ABERNATHY. *Health Education in Schools.* New York: The Ronald Press Company, 1949.

Chapter 8 should be read by students of curriculum development.

Chapter 17
Guidance and
The Cocurriculum

THE GUIDANCE PROGRAMS

This chapter consists of two distinct parts. The first major section deals with the guidance program; the second section deals with the cocurriculum.

THE NEED FOR GUIDANCE SERVICES

Many forces have increased the importance and need for guidance and guidance services in recent years. Among them are the tremendous growth in the secondary-school population and the resulting diversity in the make-up of the student body. High school teachers of a relatively few years ago taught only a small group of intellectually able youngsters from educated and economically secure homes. Today these teachers face the problem of providing suitable education for a vast heterogeneous mass of youths from all strata of society and all levels of mental maturity.

So far the American secondary school's record of serving the needs of individual pupils has not been impressive. Large numbers of youths get lost in the crowd and never realize their potentials. Others achieve success only after striving in blind alleys. About one third of American boys and girls drop out of school before completing high school. Evidently the curriculum has not been adequate for them.

Such waste seems inexcusable. To prevent it, Congress incorporated provisions for the support and improvement of guidance, counseling, and testing programs in the National Defense Education Act of 1958. By this law the Congress provided for federal support for the improvement in the

370

programs of guidance, counseling, and testing in the states and the creation of university and college institutes for the training of counselors. In passing this act the Congress has given long deserved recognition to "the deep significance of student personnel work in education as the great essential to make education work in a democracy in a world in which technology and defense are important."[1]

THE GUIDANCE PROGRAM

The first formal public school department of guidance was established in Boston, Massachusetts, in 1911.[2] This program, like other early programs, was concerned only with vocational guidance. Since that time the scope of the guidance program has grown to embrace three fields: vocational guidance, educational guidance, and personal-social guidance. The following list showing ways in which guidance programs directly serve individuals illustrates the extent of the expansion of the program.

Admission and School Placement
Orientation in Successive Educational Levels
Assisting in Self-Understanding
Understanding Environmental Opportunities and Demands
Making Life Plans and Adjustments
    Vocational Guidance
    Educational Guidance
    Planning Educational Programs
    Extracurricular Programs
    Students As Junior Citizens
    Housing
Achieving Physical and Mental Fitness
Guidance in Learning to Learn
Self-Direction of a Life Plan
Fostering a Value System and Self-Discipline
Identification and Treatment of the Exceptional
Placement and Follow-Up.[3]

Because of this growth the modern guidance program encompasses five guidance services: (a) the individual inventory service, (b) the information service, (c) the counseling service, (d) the placement service, and (e) the follow-up or evaluation service.[4] Although each service

[1] Arthur A. Hitchcock, "Milestones in the Development of Personnel Services in Education," *Personnel Services in Education* in Nelson B. Henry (ed.), Fifty-eighth Yearbook, National Society for the Study of Education, Part II (Chicago: University of Chicago Press, 1959), p. 297.

[2] John N. Brewer, *The Vocational-Guidance Movement* (New York: The Macmillan Company, 1926), pp. 20–26.

[3] Margaret E. Bennett, "Functions and Procedures in Personnel Services," in *Personnel Services in Education,* Nelson B. Henry (ed.), *op. cit.,* pp. 110–127.

[4] Walter F. Johnson, Buford Stefflre, and Roy A. Edelfelt, *Pupil Personnel and Guidance Services* (New York: McGraw-Hill Book Company, Inc., 1961), pp. 14–15.

has a distinctive role, in practice they overlap and intertwine so that one can hardly distinguish where one leaves off and another begins.

The Individual Inventory Service. The individual inventory is sometimes called the "analysis of the individual."[5] Together the two names adequately describe the purpose of the service. It is through this medium that essential information about the individual is collected, assessed, stored, and made available for use. Among the items of information essential for a successful individual analysis are personal information, home environment, preschool history, health information, school history, aptitudes, abilities, personality traits, nonacademic and out-of-school activities, and plans and interests.[6] This information is gathered from a myriad of sources. Among them are previous school records, school testing programs, case studies, interviews with the pupils and parents and others, questionnaires, autobiographies, and routine and extraordinary reports from teachers and other school personnel.

The Testing Program. In recent years much weight has been placed on the use of standardized tests and the development of adequate testing programs. This movement has been greatly strengthened by the provisions of the National Defense Education Act of 1958, which granted funds for testing programs "to identify students with outstanding aptitudes and abilities" so as to "insure trained manpower of sufficient quality and quantity to meet the national defense needs of the United States."

Just what a good testing program should be is debatable. The State Department of Public Instruction of South Dakota suggests the following as minimal.

1. Scholastic Aptitude Tests—minimum of three, two at elementary level (grades one through six) and one at secondary level (grades seven through twelve).
2. Achievement Tests—minimum of four, use in grades three through nine.
3. Vocational Abilities or Aptitude—minimum of one, use in grades eight through twelve (the earlier the better).
4. Interest Inventory—minimum of one, use in grades nine through twelve.[7]

Tests should not be the sole method of studying the individual, however. When used they should be used for a well-defined purpose, and the results should be interpreted to the pupil, his parents, and his teacher.[8] The New Jersey State Department of Education strongly warns

[5] Franklin R. Zeran and Anthony C. Riccio, *Organization and Administration of Guidance* (Chicago: Rand McNally and Company, 1962), p. 24.

[6] Herman J. Peters and Gail F. Farwell, *Guidance: A Developmental Approach* (Chicago: Rand McNally and Company, 1959), pp. 129–132.

[7] *Guidance Service Handbook for South Dakota Schools* (Pierre, S. Dak.: State Department of Public Instruction, 1959), pp. 46–47.

[8] Frederick M. Raubinger and Robert Withey, *Remember the Individual in New Jersey Secondary School Guidance* (Trenton, N.J.: Department of Secondary Education, 1962), p. 10.

against the misuse of test scores and other "impersonal solutions to the guidance problem."[9] This *caveat* is well taken. Signs seem to indicate that both parents and teachers have been overly impressed by test results.

The Cumulative Record. To be of any value, information about the pupils must be readily available to teachers and guidance specialists. Therefore the cumulative record is the heart of the individual inventory service. Too often, unfortunately, information placed into the cumulative record rests there undisturbed, either because teachers do not recognize its value to them or administrators have been afraid that teachers might misuse confidential pupil information if it were made available to them. As administrators, guidance specialists, and teachers become more sophisticated, we can look forward to a more intelligent use of the cumulative record and individual inventory service.

The Information Service. The information service provides pupils with information concerning vocational, educational, and personal social matters. Information is disseminated in many ways. Among these are group guidance classes, orientation programs, the counseling process, library and reference shelves, units in core or other courses, and so on. The following description of the Wichita, Kansas, program illustrates the type of information made available to pupils.

1. Information concerning educational requirements and opportunities beyond the secondary school.
    a. Current catalogues available for colleges, universities, and special training institutions.
    b. Current information regarding financial assistance as scholarships, loans, and other forms of student aid.
2. Information about local and national occupational opportunities, requirements, trends, and employment conditions.
3. Special programs to inform parents and students, such as "Career Days" and "College Nights."
4. Visual aids in the form of posters, graphs, charts, photographs, pamphlets and other materials to present information of guidance value.
5. Information concerning agencies and persons qualified to render assistance for physical, emotional, educational, vocational, or employment needs.[10]

The Counseling Service. Zeran and Riccio define counseling as "a learning process, warm and permissive in nature, by which one human being, properly trained, helps another to come to a closer realization of his total personality."[11] Its purpose is to help pupils to help themselves toward the fullest realization of their own potentials.

In spite of heated discussions concerning theories of counseling tech-

[9] *Ibid.*, p. 3.

[10] Robert H. McIsaac, "Guidance Services," in Lester D. and Alice Crow, *Readings in Guidance* (New York: David McKay Company, 1962), pp. 562–563.

[11] Zeran and Riccio, *op. cit.*, p. 103.

niques very few counselors operate out of any established theoretical system.[12] Rather most counseling is done from a frankly eclectic position, in which the counselor tries to vary his techniques to serve the client and the occasion. Most school guidance programs are combinations of directive and nondirective techniques, individual and group counseling, and teacher and specialist counselors. If Goldman[13] is right, this is all to the good, for the best type of counseling is one that combines process and content.

Group Techniques in Counseling. Although many guidance experts consider counseling to be a one-to-one proposition, several persons have been experimenting with group or multiple counseling. Whether or not such techniques will eventually prove desirable is still problematic, yet one advocate, E. Wayne Wright, believes that multiple counseling has values not found in individual counseling: (1) the lifelike setting for making decisions and choices, thus helping individuals to discover new ways of relating to others; (2) the influences of peers through group interaction and group norms; (3) the opportunity for free expression of opinion and emotions with less personal reference; and (4) the opportunity to give and receive support as a group member.[14]

The Placement Service. The placement service's function is to help boys and girls make and implement vocational, educational, and socio-personal decisions. Instead of being merely an "actuarial" process whereby data concerning boys and girls are matched with job opportunities, the placement service strives to develop understandings and attitudes in the young people so that they can make their own decisions properly. Increasingly attention is being placed on helping pupils select the proper curricula, courses, sections, and cocurricular activities within the secondary school itself, as well as helping them find the proper niche in their post-secondary-school careers.

Recently conditions have caused high school guidance counselors to put greater emphasis on providing placement services for prospective college students. These services sometimes start early in the secondary grades and include helping pupils to select suitable colleges, providing them with information concerning financing college careers, guiding them into proper preparatory courses, and aiding them in their applications.

For those pupils who are not going to college, or who drop out before their high school graduation, the placement service endeavors to find

[12] Harry Borow, "Modern Perspectives in Personnel Research," in Nelson B. Henry (ed.), *Personnel Services in Education, op. cit.,* p. 216.

[13] Leo Goldman, "Counseling: Content and Process," *Personnel and Guidance Journal,* 33: 82–85, October, 1954, contained in H. B. McDaniel, John E. Lallas, James A. Saum, and James L. Gilmore, *Readings in Guidance* (New York: Holt, Rinehart and Winston, Inc., 1961), pp. 163–167.

[14] E. Wayne Wright, "Multiple Counseling: Why? When? How?" *Personnel and Guidance Journal,* 37: 551–56, April, 1959, contained in Crow and Crow, *op. cit.,* pp. 216–224.

jobs. For this purpose the guidance specialists attempt to keep in close touch with the local labor market to help curriculum workers provide programs suitable to the market and to guide pupils into courses that will prepare them for the world of work. To these ends work experiences are frequently helpful. Many opportunities as apprentices are open to likely candidates. Under certain circumstances vocational rehabilitation opportunities are also available. In the successful placement service, guidance personnel are aware of these opportunities and help the pupils to be ready to take advantage of them. As in the other guidance services, placement is a developmental process.

The Research or Follow-up Service. One of the functions of the follow-up service is to help pupils after they have left school. It also gives the school data on which to evaluate the efficacy and suitability of its curriculum and instruction by finding out how well its pupils have fared in their postschool life. These data are chiefly obtained by follow-up studies in which the school sends inquiry forms to its graduates and dropouts, colleges or other institutions of higher learning, and places of employment, to find out whether the secondary-school work was beneficial and whether the curriculum and other activities were adequate. Junior high schools should seek similar information from senior high schools. In addition, the follow-up services should look for information from the pupils in the school. Such studies may well be the basis for curriculum revision and continuing guidance service for individual pupils or former pupils.

THE TEAM APPROACH

The contemporary point of view recognizes that effective guidance programs require a team of workers. In addition to teachers and counselors the guidance team includes administrators, librarians, nurses, coaches, and specialists in the field of psychobiological adjustments such as psychologists, physicians, psychiatrists, and psychometricians.

The Role of the Teacher. The key player in the guidance team is the classroom teacher who stands in a strategic position to see the multifarious problems with which pupils are plagued. Oftentimes these problems stand between pupils and academic achievement and must be solved, at least to some degree, before the pupils can adequately profit from academic instruction. Whatever the type of help needed by the students, the classroom teacher bears the responsibility of recognizing it early and either giving the indicated help or referring the student to the person or persons who can provide the guidance needed. To this end the classroom teacher is faced with the problem of assisting each of his pupils to recognize, examine, and understand his interests, aptitudes, strengths, limitations, opportunities, problems, and needs.

The Role of the Counselor. Although the teacher is the central figure in the guidance team, guidance specialists are also necessary. The principal guidance specialist is the guidance counselor. It is he who carries out the bulk of the specialized guidance services. Among his responsibilities are:

1. Obtain the cooperative participation of the staff.
2. Recommend areas for study and research.
3. Assist in the development of in-service programs.
4. Encourage teachers to identify students needing assistance and also those having special talents.
5. Identify potential dropouts and seek to salvage them.
6. Encourage pupils to accept the responsibility for full utilization of their potentials.
7. Provide help in developing and carrying on case conferences.
8. Stimulate teachers to provide materials for individual cumulative record folders and to use the cumulative record professionally.
9. Confer with parents.
10. Refer pupils needing additional assistance to the proper persons.
11. Maintain good public relations with the local and state agencies.
12. Assist the school librarian in obtaining and keeping current materials on occupational, educational, and personal-social information.
13. Help gather materials for information service.[15]

It is important to note that the guidance counselor's responsibility does not include disciplinary cases, slow learners, attendance, delinquency, and the handicapped. Although he can and should help with problem cases, the counselor who concentrates on them is violating his trust. His principal work should be with normal boys and girls.[16]

The Counseling Staff. Although some schools attempt it, to run a guidance program without an adequate staff of counselors is very difficult. Ideally, according to Conant's report, the counselor–pupil ratio should be one counselor for every 250 to 300 pupils.[17] Thus a school of 1000 pupils should have a professional guidance staff of one head counselor or director of guidance services, and at least three full-time counselor assistants. If the school is coeducational, both male and female counselors should be available. Unfortunately the ideal has not been reached in many schools, but as a result of the provisions of the National Defense Education Act, the ratio is being lowered rapidly.

Many counselors are teacher counselors who act as teachers part time and counselors part time. Probably the use of such teacher counselors enhances the chances of successful guidance team operation. The fact that the teacher-counselor is a teacher and not just another administrator helps keep the lines of communication and operation open. Also his

---

[15] Adapted from Zeran and Riccio, *op. cit.,* pp. 194–200.

[16] Peters and Farwell, *op. cit.,* p. 450.

[17] James B. Conant, *The American High School Today* (New York: McGraw-Hill Book Company, Inc., 1959), p. 44.

teaching helps him to become well acquainted with pupils and keeps him in touch with the realities of the classroom.

On the other hand, informed opinion seems to prefer the use of full-time guidance specialists insofar as possible. Because they do not have to split themselves between teaching and counseling, the full-time counselors can make themselves more readily available to pupils and become more fully competent than the part-time teachers. Furthermore they are not hampered by conflicting roles, for example, discipline, and thus should find it easier to establish rapport with counselees so that they will open up and speak freely. In practice many schools find that the only reasonable way to staff the guidance program is to use a team of both full-time counselors and teacher-counselors. Even when the staff of counselors is adequate, much of the face-to-face counseling and data gathering must still be done by homeroom and classroom teachers.

Counseling and Creativity. Counseling should not be a method for manipulating boys and girls. The current interest in research on creativity has uncovered many reasons to believe that "coercive strategies" for manipulating boys and girls stifle their creativity. Torrance believes that creativity can be encouraged only through relationships that are open, nonthreatening, and creative. In writing of his position he places emphasis on the counselors'

> experiencing genuine pleasure in the creative powers of the counselee; respecting creative ways of learning; being a helpful guide; engendering genuine empathy rather than stimulating identification processes; exploring the positive forces in personality rather than exploiting personality vulnerabilities; mutual searching for the truth rather than giving the "big lie"; following the lead of the counselee rather than maintaining a singleness of purpose; providing a friendly environment; making a stand for mutual understanding; and respecting the dignity and worth of the individual.[18]

Clearly to be such a counselor one must have a truly congruent personality free to be an authentic person without pretense or evasion.

GROUP GUIDANCE

Group guidance has an important place in the guidance program. In general, guidance experts feel that it should be used to supplement and complement, but in no way supplant the counseling process. Group guidance techniques are primarily important for both data gathering and information giving services. They lend themselves well to such guidance areas as orientation of new pupils, vocational planning, learning about

---

18 E. Paul Torrance, *Guiding Creative Talent* (Englewood Cliffs, N.J.: Prentice-Hall, Inc., 1962), p. 187.

occupations, problems of youth and personality development. Group guidance also has the advantages of occurring in a format with which the pupil is accustomed and of giving the individual pupil group support in facing and understanding his problems. The mere fact that in the group situation he learns that his problems are not his alone may be a great boon to a harried youngster.

In group guidance classes the tendency is to emphasize the pupils' own ideas and experiences and to utilize methods by which the learner uses his own resources to arrive at meanings useful and serviceable to him personally in the light of his own experiences. Although it is true that sometimes group guidance is concerned with content of courses in vocations or occupations, evidently the ideal in group guidance differs very little from that of the experience curriculum or what in Chapter 7 we have chosen to call the "true core."

Homeroom Program and Core Curriculum. In many schools the homeroom period is simply an administrative device by which the school administrators control activities of the pupils. Such homeroom programs are of little value as guidance vehicles, although frequently they are used as the medium through which pupils make their academic decisions. Other schools make use of homeroom periods for the furthering of guidance objectives. In such schools the homeroom can become the center of the guidance program for each individual pupil. It provides a useful medium for studying the pupils, for discussing pupil problems, for disseminating guidance information, for individual counseling and interviews, and for referrals. Homeroom classes should use a maximum of pupil participation and planning and a minimum of teacher directing and talking. The various techniques of group dynamics, such as informal discussion, role playing, and dramatics, can be utilized effectively. Portage High School (Indiana) utilizes a pupil council and pupil leadership teams to carry on the homeroom program. Among typical topics used are Choosing Your Career, Looking Toward High School, School Clubs, What Good Is High School?[19]

Guidance in Core and Block-of-Time Classes. Similarly block-of-time and core curriculum classes lend themselves admirably to the guidance role. Because block-of-time classes keep teachers and pupils together for two or more periods each day, the teacher has a good chance to learn his pupils well, to build up good rapport with them, and to deal with them individually.

In addition to these advantages the teacher of a true core class utilizes methods, techniques, and content that aid the guidance process. The Hazel Park Junior High School, St. Paul, Minnesota, offers a good example of a guidance-oriented core curriculum. To carry out the guidance

[19] Thomas Rood, "A High School Guidance Council," *Bulletin of the National Association of Secondary-School Principals* 46: 109–111, November, 1962.

function at Hazel Park a parent–teacher conference program has been set up. The guidance objective also figures prominently in the topics chosen for core program units. Among the typical topics listed are Orientation To Our School, What Is An American? The World Of Work, Vocations, and Home and Family Living.[20]

Guidance in Other Classes. Each of the courses in which a pupil enrolls is a potential guidance medium. It can serve as a source of information about the pupils and also as a vehicle for teacher counseling. The content itself can be made to serve guidance functions. Problem-solving techniques, differentiated assignments, individual work, group work, projects, and teacher–pupil planning can be used effectively to carry out guidance objectives in almost any class. Subjects like business education, industrial arts, and home economics have exploratory values that may help pupils make vocational and educational choices. Academic subjects also may uncover latent interests and abilities and lead the pupil to future adult vocations or avocation. Music, art, literature, and composition courses may give one an opportunity to release tensions and to foster creativity.

Guidance and the Cocurriculum. From the guidance point of view the cocurriculum is particularly important. Through its activities pupils are given opportunities to understand themselves better and to improve their social adjustment. Some of its organizations serve as effective media for group guidance and orientation activities. The variety and informality of the activities often make them excellent for exploring interests and talents. They also provide opportunities to learn important skills and attitudes not easily developed in the classroom and to bolster up faltering personalities, as Berg[21] points out. Certainly, when used in the manner Berg envisages, the cocurriculum can be one of a guidance worker's most effective allies.

> One student may need to learn to accept continuing responsibility, but he is not ready for it. For him, appropriate guidance will center in making it possible for him to achieve success, first, with shorter-term tasks, and, later, with longer-term responsibilities. In the case of another student the problem may be one of entry, that is, acceptance as an active rather than a passive member of a group. He is capable of doing a job for the group, but no one knows this, and he does not know how to make his talents visible. The guidance most likely to be profitable to him will involve an appreciation of entry tasks. The duties of a clean-up committee for a dance, for example, are prosaic in nature; yet volunteers are eagerly welcomed. Every student group has similar jobs which need doing but which are not eagerly sought after. Yet, they provide entering wedges for increased responsibilities for other tasks and, in consequence, for increased personal growth.

[20] See Chapter 7 for further description of the Hazel Park core program.
[21] Irwin A. Berg, "Internal and External Resources of the Personnel Staff," in Nelson B. Henry (ed.), *Personnel Services in Education, op. cit.*, p. 142.

The Guidance Program of the Future. What the future of the guidance program will be is difficult to say. In 1950 Traxler[22] identified twelve "emerging trends in guidance." They are:

1. The first trend is one toward more adequate training of guidance personnel.
2. The second trend is toward making guidance an all-faculty function and toward co-operation between specialists and classroom teachers.
3. The third trend is toward closer co-operation of the guidance services of the school with the home and other agencies in the community.
4. The fourth trend is toward the orderly accumulation and recording of a variety of information concerning each individual.
5. The fifth trend is toward increased use of objective measures in guidance programs.
6. The sixth trend is toward differential prediction of success on the basis of test batteries that yield comparable scores in broad areas.
7. The seventh trend is toward increased interest in the use of improved techniques in the appraisal of personal qualities of pupils and the treatment of maladjustment.
8. The eighth trend is toward a middle position between directive and nondirective guidance.
9. The ninth trend is toward recognition of relationship between remedial work and guidance.
10. The tenth trend is toward the use of improved case-study techniques, both for purposes of better understanding of individual pupils and for in-service training of teachers.
11. The eleventh trend in guidance is toward the availability and use of better sources of occupational information.
12. The twelfth trend in guidance programs is toward the use of follow-up studies.

There is every reason to believe that these trends are continuing at a more rapid rate today.

SUMMARY

In this chapter we are concerned only with the five services that make up the guidance program, the need for which has been recognized as national policy by the passing of the National Defense Education Act of 1958.

In spite of quarrels about theoretical positions most guidance programs are eclectic. They use directive and nondirective counseling techniques, individual and group methods, and full-time and part-time counselors. Not only is the usual guidance program a synthesis of many theoretical positions, it is also the result of the teamwork of many different workers, teachers, counselors, administrators, and specialists of various kinds who

---

[22] Arthur E. Traxler, "Emerging Trends in Guidance," *The School Review*, 58: 14–23, January, 1950, in Farwell and Peters, *op. cit.*, pp. 147–156.

combine their efforts to help boys and girls find and fulfill themselves. To this end the guidance program attempts to serve all pupils—not just problem pupils—throughout their entire stay in the secondary school and, if possible and desirable, after they have left school.

COCURRICULAR ACTIVITIES

Because the best learning is complex and interrelated with the whole life, classroom instruction must be enriched and extended by cocurricular activities in which students extend and test their beliefs and experiences.

The importance of out-of-class activities is evidenced by the attempts on part of curriculum workers to avoid the use of the term *extracurricular* with its implication that the activities concerned are extra or additional to the curriculum. In this book we shall use the terms *cocurriculum* and *cocurricular activities*. In the sense that we shall use it, cocurriculum can be defined as that part of the curriculum which is not included in pupils' regular courses and which does not carry credit for graduation.

COCURRICULAR TRENDS

The major trend in the cocurriculum is a gradual blurring of the lines of distinction between the cocurriculum and the regular curriculum. This major trend is caused by two subordinate trends. One is the trend of cocurricular activities to become curricular, as in the case of music, dramatics, speech, and similar activities. When the school newspaper is published by the journalism class, the activity is no longer cocurricular, but curricular. The other is the trend of curricular activities to spread into the cocurriculum. When a group of boys and girls form a club to meet with a teacher to study ancient Greek, or a group of pupils meets in the laboratory in the evening or on Saturday morning to carry out original scientific investigation not connected with any course, their activities are cocurricular.

The Description of Activities issued by Rehoboth High School, Rehoboth, Delaware, vividly illustrates the blurring of the lines between the curriculum and the cocurriculum (Figure 9).

FIGURE 9. DESCRIPTION OF ACTIVITIES (REHOBOTH HIGH SCHOOL)

1. *English Enrichment:* 11–12. Extra help for college-preparatory students in composition; assistance in preparing for college entrance examinations.
2. *Science Enrichment:* 10–11–12. Extra help for students having difficulties with physics, chemistry, and biology. Also for the student who would like to do extra work in the field of science.
3. *French Enrichment:* 9–10–11–12. Extra help for the student having difficulty in French. Also for the student who would like to do extra work in French.

4. *Adaptive Physical Education:* Extra help to students who have posture problems, who lack coordination, who need muscle-building exercises, and who need areas of physical education not available in a regular gym class. Boys' classes will be limited to ten (10), girls classes to twenty (20).
5. *Public Speaking:* Training students to speak before a group, to make a prepared speech. Practice with the tape recorder will be given.
6. *Dramatics and Speech:* Working on skits and small dramatic productions.
7. *Group Guidance:* Assisting the student in planning a career.
8. *Newspaper:* Training in all phases of getting out a school newspaper, such as news reporting, editorial writing, production, art, and so on.
9. *Service Club:* Making repairs to school equipment, building equipment needed in the school, work on individual projects.
10. *Equipment Service:* Servicing football equipment.

From a quick perusal of this list one cannot tell whether individual activities are curricular or cocurricular. The activities in French, English, and science deal with areas that have been traditionally curricular. On the other hand, physical education, public speaking, newspaper, dramatics, and speech represent areas that have traditionally been cocurricular, but are now commonly curricular.

Whether cocurricular activities should be made curricular is doubtful. Each instance should be decided on its own merits. Undoubtedly the granting of academic credit does give an activity status, but it also tends to formalize the activity. When an activity carries credit, academic pride requires that the activity justify the credit. As a consequence, willy-nilly, the activity tends to lose its spontaneity and its *joie de vivre*.

So it seems that although granting a cocurricular activity course credit may give the activity curricular status, it may also deprive the activity of qualities that make cocurricular activities most desirable.

AIMS AND FUNCTIONS

The aims of the cocurricular program are the same as those of the curriculum, and they contribute to these aims by (1) reinforcing classroom learning, (2) supplementing formal studies, (3) aiding total life adjustment, (4) integrating learning, and (5) democratizing school and American life.[23] Undoubtedly the reader can find numerous examples of these functions in his own experience with the cocurriculum. French club activities, for instance, undoubtedly both reinforce and supplement classroom learning by providing motivation, practice, and new opportunities for studying French and by providing pupils' social experiences. The French club, through its social activities and the use of French in social and practical situations, can also contribute to the pupils' adjustment to life, to the integration of his knowledge of French into his total experience, and to his learning how to conduct himself democratically. Regular

[23] Robert W. Frederick, *The Third Curriculum* (New York: Appleton-Century-Crofts, Inc., 1959), p. 55.

classes can also function in these ways, but when the formality of the regular classroom and the press of academic credit are removed seemingly these functions can be carried out more easily.

Although the cocurriculum does foster all the educational goals, certain goals seem to be particularly congenial to the cocurriculum. Anderson and Gruhn[24] list five of these:

1. To help pupils develop qualities of leadership, group cooperation, and other qualities essential to effective democratic living.
2. To help pupils acquire certain personal and character qualities, such as self-confidence, poise, initiative, resourcefulness, courtesy, and self-control.
3. To help pupils explore various interests, talents, and abilities, in a manner which would be difficult in the usual classroom program.
4. To assist pupils to be active and creative, and to gain the satisfaction that comes from accomplishing things that to them are interesting and worthwhile.
5. To give pupils an opportunity to apply many of the fundamental skills and much of the knowledge which they acquire in other ways in the classroom program.

COCURRICULUM ISSUES

Who Should Participate in the Cocurriculum? Cocurricular activities differ mainly from the so-called curricular activities in that the cocurricular activities are not required for graduation. Ideally it seems that each pupil should participate in the cocurricular activities best suited to him, but this goal is hardly ever achieved in practice. Instead we find that some boys and girls, when left to their own inclination, seem not to be engaged in any cocurricular activity while others are appropriating all the places of honor to themselves. To prevent such imbalances secondary-school administrators have resorted to various devices that artificially spread cocurricular participation among all pupils and limit the amount of participation permitted to any particular pupil. Among them are rules requiring every pupil to participate in the cocurriculum, using point systems to prevent overparticipation and setting up minimum academic standards for participation in cocurricular activities.

Presently there seems to be a turning away from the use of artificial controls to restrict and distribute pupil participation in secondary-school cocurricular activities. Instead administrators are increasingly turning to guidance and informal controls within the cocurricular activities for control of pupil participation. These procedures have the advantage of fitting the cocurriculum to the child rather than the child to the cocurriculum and of providing for flexibility.

Despite the definite tendency not to restrict participation by arbitrary

[24] Vernon E. Anderson and William T. Gruhn, *Principles and Practices of Secondary Education,* 2nd ed. (New York: The Ronald Press Company, 1962), p. 280.

controls, faith in controls still runs strong. Only about three fourths of the senior high schools permit participation in cocurricular activities on a voluntary basis, whereas about three fourths of the junior high schools require participation.

Scheduling the Cocurriculum. It used to be that all cocurricular activities were scheduled after school. With the modern concept of cocurricular activities it became customary to schedule some noncurricular activities during activity periods or club periods within the school day. Some schools have carried this trend a step farther and schedule cocurricular activities in regular class periods just as they would schedule curricular activities.

Critics of our secondary schools have been afraid that moving cocurricular activities into the daily schedule would lead to frivolity and watering down of the serious academic purposes of the school. As a consequence, several secondary-school administrators have instituted a movement toward moving cocurricular activities to out-of-school hours. Whether this movement will start a new trend is not yet clear.

In truth, *when* the cocurricular activity is scheduled really makes little difference as long as (a) the schedule does not prevent the participation of pupils who should participate, and (b) the schedule allocates to the activity blocks of time suitable to the nature of the activity.

Probably the only answer to the scheduling problem is to schedule cocurricular activities both during school and out-of-school hours. In Melbourne High School (Florida) cocurricular activities have been spread throughout the day and evening with considerable success.

MARKS OF GOOD COCURRICULA

Determining the most appropriate cocurricular activities for any given school is a very important phase of the planning stage of the program. Faculties should give attention to the interest and wishes of pupils, but pupil interest cannot be the sole criterion for setting up a cocurricular program. Rather the following principles should be held paramount.

1. The cocurricular program should be planned so as to assure its fullest contribution to the educational aims of the school.
2. Each activity should be guided by a competent and sympathetic member of the faculty.
3. Every pupil should have ample opportunity to participate in the program. The school should support enough different activities to permit each pupil to participate in congenial activities.
4. Cocurricular activities should be recognized by inclusion in the school schedule. Each activity should be selected at a time that would allow each interested pupil to participate.
5. Participation in cocurricular activities should be based on democratic principles. No pupil should be barred from any activity or office because of financial or social considerations.

6. Pupils should be given adequate opportunity to develop leadership qualities. These can best be developed by allowing pupils to hold offices of responsibility and trust under guidance.

7. Cocurricular activities should reinforce and supplement curricular activities by utilizing approaches and materials not possible in regular classroom and furthering learnings additional to those fostered in the regular curricular activities. They should not, however, repeat classroom activities.

8. The cocurricular activities should be so administered as to avoid the development of false ideas and attitudes and the setting up of false or inadequate value systems.

9. The activities should be pupil-centered and, as far as feasible, student-planned and -directed. All activities included in the cocurriculum should reflect pupil interests, purposes, and needs.

10. The cocurriculum should be flexible. It should be easy to add new activities when desirable and to drop old activities when they have outlived their usefulness.

11. The cocurriculum should be adequately financed. Because it is a real part of the curriculum, funds should be provided by the School Board. No matter where the funds come from, however, measures for adequate fiscal supervision and control should be maintained.

12. The cocurricular activities should be subjected to continuous evaluation and reevaluation. As a consequence of this evaluative process the best cocurricular programs will probably be in a continual state of revision.

THE PROGRAM OF COCURRICULAR ACTIVITIES

Today's secondary-school curriculum includes a wide variety of cocurricular activities. Frederick's list of activities (unannotated) covers six full pages of his text[25] and includes 281 special interest clubs alone. In the following paragraphs we shall consider the various types of activities that may make up the cocurricular program.

Pupil Participation in School Government. The secondary-school principal is responsible to his superintendent and his board of eductaion for the operation of his school. He cannot evade or delegate this responsibility. Yet over the centuries able secondary-school administrators have been delegating part of their authority to their pupils. Oftentimes this turning over of authority to students has resulted in great gains for the pupils and the schools. For the development of good citizenship, for instance, no activity seems to be more effective than pupil participation in school government.

If student participation in school government is to be worth while,

[25] Frederick, *op. cit.*, pp. 429–435.

however, it must be meaningful. Pupils must be given real responsibilities. Many so-called student councils and student governments are merely puppet parliaments in a totalitarian state. This practice is neither wise nor necessary. Under guidance within well-designated limits pupils can successfully carry out many functions of school government. In a tough Detroit vocational high school a school council effectively established a good educational climate in what had previously been an incorrigible situation.[26] In Plainview Senior High School (Long Island) the student council has the power to enact and enforce legislation governing all student activities that are neither curricular nor athletic, as the administration or the faculty of the school may otherwise determine.[27]

Large Technical Activities. Music activities, such as chorus and band, dramatics, school publications, and interscholastic athletics require special skills and knowledges beyond the repertory of the average teacher. For this reason and because such large technical activities are so much in the public eye, they present a peculiar problem for secondary-school curriculum workers and are usually entrusted to specialist teachers and coaches whose reputations may hang on their successes. Naturally these teachers tend to limit student participation to pupils they feel to be potential experts and to rule the activities with the hand of iron not always covered by the velvet glove. Although their efforts may yield excellent results they may vitiate the potential values of the cocurriculum. Boys and girls should have opportunities to try their own hands. An honest student-written editorial, even if mediocre, is preferable to a superior one written or rewritten by the teacher-sponsor.

In order to solve the problem of excellence versus opportunity for all, some authorities advocate two levels of productions—one at the varsity level, so to say, and one at the intramural level. Under this scheme membership in the varsity level productions is limited to pupils who can demonstrate their proficiency while membership in the intramural activities is open to anyone who wishes to try.

The School Clubs Program. There are four varieties of school clubs: service clubs, curricular clubs, special interest clubs, and social clubs. The different roles and functions of each of these types are quite well indicated by their names. Examples of service clubs are the audio-visual clubs, or school patrol club; of curricular clubs, the science, or Latin club; of special interest clubs, the photography, or international relations club; and of social clubs, the square dance groups, hiking clubs, skating clubs, and so on.

Basically the contribution of one club is much like that of another, no matter what the type. The important thing is that the club reflect pupils' interests and concerns. For that reason clubs—particularly social and

[26] See Earl C. Kelley's *In Defense of Youth* (Englewood Cliffs, N.J.: Prentice-Hall, Inc., 1962), pp. 68–89.

[27] *Student Handbook* (Plainview, N.Y.: Plainview Senior High School, 1960), p. 70.

special interest clubs—tend to be transitory and eclectic. That outmoded clubs can close down to be superseded with new vital ones, and that small clubs that serve only a few persons with specialized interests have a place in the cocurriculum, are among the virtues of the club program. Often it is through such clubs that the school can best provide for pupils having unusual interests, talents, and needs.

Social Activities. A good portion of the secondary-school cocurriculum consists of activities that are primarily social. Among them are such activities as parties, dances, socials, receptions, banquets, proms, and social clubs. Social activities can help boys and girls to learn social skills and amenities. In one instance, as part of the preparation for the tenth grade dance, the pupils under guidance of their sponsor conducted classes in dancing, the etiquette of the ballroom, and the care and treatment of chaperones. In addition the pupils selected the band, designed the decorations, distributed the tickets, and cleaned up the mess after the ball was over. Presumably this activity carried with it great benefits in character building, self-direction, self-discipline, and good citizenship training, as well as being fun.

Social activities can also lead to better human relationships and attitudes. Provisions should be made so that as far as possible no child is hurt or discriminated against by the activities. To this end costs should be held down to the point where they are not prohibitive for any student or burdensome on any family, and school social activities should be open to all pupils. Social activities should not be schools for snobbery for the haves and frustration for the have-nots. For this reason, because of their secret nature and because of their many cases of malpractice within them, secret societies, fraternities, sororities, and other "exclusive" clubs are not acceptable and should not be tolerated in any public secondary school.

The Semicurricular Activities. Homeroom, assembly, commencement, and similar activities are so closely tied to the central purpose of the school curriculum that they are called semicurricular. The common attributes of these activities as listed by Frederick are:

1. They are mandated. Participation is forced by absolute edict or by custom and tradition.
2. Participation is not rewarded by credit toward promotion or graduation.
3. They enjoy the approval of the faculty and administration; in fact, they are safeguarded and perpetuated by the institutional authorities.
4. They are sponsored, looked after, even at times directed by the faculty.
5. They have a long history as part of their deliberate education, with the possible exception of the homeroom idea.
6. They involve most of the students and the faculty.
7. They have no strong or conclusive identification with any subject or institutional department.
8. They are relatively immune from criticism or even attention by the general public.

9. They are markedly integrative. They represent diverse interests, both curricular and extracurricular.[28]

SUMMARY

Cocurricular activities have attained a place of high importance in American education. Many opportunities are provided for students to patricipate in such activities as student government, assembly programs, community betterment projects, and service, interest, hobby, and activity clubs. These usually evolve out of the ongoing activities of the total school program.

Participation in student government association, work as library and office assistants, or serving as members of the audio-visual aids crew, as members of the cafeteria aides, as members of the safety council, and other like clubs and organizations, give students valuable experiences, involve them in true-to-life situations, and give them status, a sense of worth and belonging. The activities and responsibilities provide opportunities for adjustment and growth in accord with student needs and interests and contribute as well to the proper functioning of the secondary school.

The cocurricular program furnishes excellent opportunities for learning experiences to fit the needs of all individuals. In the school they can provide encouragement and help to students interested in fields beyond the usual scope of the curriculum.

Cocurricular activities help satisfy the need that students have for independent thinking, for independent action, for belonging, and for achieving. They deserve the same careful planning and supervision as any other curricular activities.

SUGGESTED READINGS

COCURRICULUM

AMERICAN ASSOCIATION FOR HEALTH, PHYSICAL EDUCATION AND RECREATION. NEA *Outdoor Education.* Washington, D.C.: The Association, 1956.
    Justifies outdoor education in the total educational program.
BENERDD, GLADYS. "How Do Pupils Benefit by Participation in the Co-Curricular Program?" *The Bulletin of the National Association of Secondary-School Principals,* 37: 103–111, March, 1953.
    A description of pupil benefits from the co-curriculum.
BENT, RUDYARD K., and LLOYD E. MCCANN. *Administration of Secondary Schools.* New York: McGraw-Hill Book Company, Inc., 1960. Chapters 9–11.
    Chapter 9 deals with the student activity program. Chapters 10 and 11 deal with intraschool and interscholastic activities.
BURRUP, PERCY E. *Modern High School Administration.* New York: Harper and Row, Inc., 1962. Chapter 7.

[28] Frederick, *op. cit.*, p. 309.

A discussion of the role, functions, financing, and administration of the extracurricular activities from the principal's point of view contained in Chapter 7.

BUSH, ROBERT N. "The Proper Place of the Extracurriculum in High School," *California Journal of Secondary Education,* 34: 257–262, May, 1959.

An argument for balance between curriculum and the co-curriculum.

BUTLER, GEORGE D. *Playgrounds: Their Administration and Operation.* New York: The Ronald Press Company, 1960.

The content is described in the title.

DAVIS, PAUL, and JERRY J. GERICH. "What Is a Defensible Activities Program for the Senior High School?" *The Bulletin of the National Association of Secondary-School Principals,* 43: 167–171, April, 1959.

Secondary-school principals give the basic principles of a defensible activities program.

DOTY, RICHARD S. *The Character Dimensions of Camping.* New York: Association Press, 1960.

Gives an excellent justification for camping as an outdoor education activity.

"Extracurriculum," *The Bulletin of the National Association of Secondary-School Principals,* 46: 254–263, February, 1962.

Abstracts of five studies on extracurricular activities in the junior high school.

FAUNCE, ROLAND C. *Secondary-School Administration.* New York: Harper and Row, Inc., 1955. Chapters 9 and 10.

Chapters 9 and 10 of this book on administration deal with student activities and student participation in student government.

FREDERICK, ROBERT W. *The Third Curriculum: Student Activities in American Education.* New York: Appleton-Century-Crofts, Inc., 1959.

A textbook giving a fine overview of basic principles and problems concerning the co-curriculum and detailed account of problems and practices in the various activities.

GORDON, C. WAYNE. *The Social System in the High School.* New York: The Free Press, 1957.

Chapter 4 describes the role and importance of student organizations in student life as reported by an astute trained observer.

GRINNELL, J. E. "Our Most Dangerous Neglect," *Phi Delta Kappan,* 41: 213–216, February, 1960.

Discusses the role of student activities in developing character education.

GRUBER, FREDERICK C., and THOMAS BAYARD BEATTY. *Secondary-School Activities.* New York: McGraw-Hill Book Company, Inc., 1954.

A textbook detailing the role and practices of the many kinds of pupil activities.

HAMILTON, H. H. "Educational Value of the Extracurriculum," *The Bulletin of the National Association of Secondary-School Principals,* 43: 132–136, December, 1959.

A report of research concerning the value of co-curricular activities.

JOHNSTON, EDGAR G., and ROLAND C. FAUNCE. *Student Activities in Secondary Schools.* New York: The Ronald Press Company, 1952.

One of the few good textbooks on the subject.

KARNER, E. F. "Check Points for Improving School Activity Programs," *School Activities*, 32: 133–135, January, 1961.

Contains criteria for evaluating the co-curriculum.

KILZER, L. R., *et al. Allied Activities in the Secondary School*. New York: Harper and Row, Inc., 1956.

An excellent textbook on the co-curriculum.

MCKOWN, H. C. *Extracurricular Activities*. New York: The Macmillan Company, 1952.

A classic textbook in the field.

MCLEAN, R. C., JR. "The Extracurriculum in Some Steps Toward Integration," *The Bulletin of the National Association of Secondary-School Principals*, 40: 135–138, October, 1956.

A plan for giving curriculum activities educational purpose by making the club program the center of the curriculum.

MILLER, FRANKLIN A., JAMES A. MOYER, and ROBERT B. PATRICK. *Planning Student Activities*. Englewood Cliffs, New Jersey: Prentice-Hall, Inc., 1957.

A detailed description of extracurricular activities and their role as well as consideration of the purpose and organization of the co-curriculum in general.

MUELLER, PAT. *Intramural Sports*. New York: The Ronald Press Company, 1960.

Emphasizes the importance of intramural sports as opposed to interschool athletics.

NATIONAL ASSOCIATION OF SECONDARY-SCHOOL PRINCIPALS. *Student Council in the Secondary School*. Washington, D.C.: The Association, 1955.

A handbook of student council activities.

O'NEIL, H. R. "Let's Limit Participation in School Activities," *School Activity*, 31: 21–22, September, 1960.

A proposal for use of point system to prevent overparticipation.

SCHOLL, P. A. "Co-Curriculum Activities or Study Halls," *The Bulletin of the National Association of Secondary-School Principals*, 40: 129–141, October, 1956.

An argument for replacing at least some study halls with extra-curricular activities.

SHELLEY, G. N. "All This and the Three R's Too," *Illinois Education*, 48: 274–275, March, 1960.

A description of a junior high school co-curriculum program scheduled during the last period of the school day.

SHEPHERD, EVERETT M. *How to Sponsor Student Activities*. Wolfe City, Texas: Henington Publishing Company, 1960.

An excellent guide for sponsors of co-curricula activities.

TOMPKINS, ELLSWORTH, and ROBERT C. STORY. *The Activity Period in Public High Schools*. U.S. Office of Education, Bulletin Number 19, 1951. Washington, D.C.: Government Printing Office, 1951.

A report of high school activity period practices.

"What Extra Class Activities Should Be Included in the Program for Junior High School Students," *The Bulletin of the National Association of Secondary-School Principals*, 42: 12–16, April 1, 1958.

A summary of recommendations presented by speakers at a discussion group at the 1958 N.A.S.S.P. Convention.

WOOD, DONALD L. "Student Activities—A Hope or a Delusion," *The Bulletin of the National Association of Secondary-School Principals*, 46: 201–203, April, 1962.

A summary of the history and present status of the activity program and a plea that its potential be properly implemented and capitalized upon.

YON, J. F. "How May Extracurricular Acitivities Contribute Most Profitably to Education," *School Activities*, 32: 266–267, May, 1961.

A discussion of the relation of the co-curriculum to the major objectives of secondary education.

GUIDANCE

ANDREW, DEAN C., and ROY DE VERL WILLEY. *Administration and Organization of the Guidance Program.* New York: Harper and Row, Inc., 1958.

A standard text on the administration of guidance programs.

ARBUCKLE, DUGALD S. *Counseling: An Introduction.* Boston: Allyn and Bacon, 1961.

An excellent introductory text on the subject written by an advocate of the nondirective school.

ASSOCIATION FOR SUPERVISION AND CURRICULUM DEVELOPMENT. *Guidance in the Curriculum.* Washington, D.C.: The Association, 1955.

An overview of guidance and its relationship with teaching.

BEASIO, SPARTOCO. "Guidance Services for Suburban Junior High Schools," *The Bulletin of the National Association of Secondary-School Principals*, 46: 196–201, April, 1962.

A report of a study of the guidance services offered by thirty junior high schools located in suburban areas of six large cities.

CHASE, FRANCIS S., and HAROLD A. ANDERSON (eds.). *The High School in a New Era.* Part VI. Chicago: The University of Chicago Press, 1958.

A collection of papers presented at the Conference on the American High School, October, 1957. Part VI deals with problems in the guidance area.

COTTINGHAM, HAROLD F., and WILLIAM E. HOPKE. *Guidance in the Junior High School.* Bloomington, Illinois: McKnight and McKnight Publishing Company, 1961.

An excellent guide for planning and implementing a guidance program at the junior high level.

CROW, LESTER D., and ALICE CROW (eds.). *Readings in Guidance.* New York: David McKay Company, 1962.

An excellent collection of articles concerning guidance. Particularly useful are the descriptions of guidance programs in school systems.

EVRAIFF, WILLIAM. *Helping Counselors Grow Professionally.* Englewood Cliffs, New Jersey: Prentice-Hall, Inc., 1963.

This book contains materials gained by interviews with adolescents and is intended as a case book for educational counselors wishing to improve their professional competence.

FARWELL, GAIL F., and HERMAN J. PETERS (eds.). *Guidance Readings for Counselors.* Chicago: Rand McNally and Company, 1960.

An excellent book of readings in the guidance and personnel work.

FAUNCE, ROLAND C., and NELSON L. BOSSING. *Developing the Core Curriculum.* Englewood Cliffs, New Jersey: Prentice-Hall, Inc., 1958. Chapter 8.

Chapter 8 deals with guidance in the core curriculum and points up the contribution core curriculum can make to secondary-school guidance programs.

FINDLEY, WARREN G. "Student Personnel Work—Elementary and Secondary," *Encyclopedia of Educational Research.* Third edition. New York: The Macmillan Company, 1960. Pp. 1427–1433.

An authoritative summary of status and trends in the area of public school guidance.

"Guidance," *NEA Journal* (Special feature), Pp. 1–17, January, 1959. Reprint.

A series of popularized articles explaining the guidance point of view and its implementation.

"Guidance and Counseling in the Secondary School," *The Bulletin of the National Association of Secondary-School Principals,* 43: 1–122, October, 1959.

An issue of the bulletin consisting of a collection of articles on secondary-school guidance.

HOPPOCK, ROBERT. "Best Books of 1962 on Vocational Guidance," *The Bulletin of the National Association of Secondary-School Principals,* 47: 158–164, March, 1963.

A marvelous bibliography. Similar bibliographies have been published annually in the *Bulletin* for a number of years.

HUTSON, PERCIVAL W. "The Rationale of Guidance," *The Bulletin of the National Association of Secondary-School Principals,* 42: 121–128, March, 1958.

An analysis of the functions and purposes of the guidance program.

JOHNSON, MAURITZ, JR., WILLIAM E. BUSACKER, and FRED Q. BOSMAN, JR. *Junior High School Guidance.* New York: Harper and Row, Inc., 1961.

A good text for beginners in the field of guidance in the junior high school. Many excellent suggestions for teachers and principals.

JOHNSON, WALTER F., BUFORD STEFFLRE, and ROY A. EDELFELT. *Pupil Personnel and Guidance Services.* New York: McGraw-Hill Book Company, Inc., 1961.

A standard textbook describing personnel and guidance programs and techniques. Particularly good on how to do it.

JONES, ARTHUR J. *Principles of Guidance.* Fifth edition. New York: McGraw-Hill Book Company, Inc., 1963.

Latest edition of a pioneer work in guidance which gives a good overview of guidance. Although Chapter 8 deals with guidance in the secondary school, the reader will probably derive more understanding from earlier and later chapters.

"Junior High School Development, Practices, and Research," *The Bulletin of the National Association of Secondary-School Principals,* 46: 316–334, February, 1962.

A section of this bulletin is directed to research studies in junior high school guidance.

MILLER, CARROLL H. *Foundations of Guidance.* New York: Harper and Row, Inc., 1961.

A standard textbook which well portrays the role and tools of guidance in the school.

NATIONAL SOCIETY FOR THE STUDY OF EDUCATION. *Personnel Services in Educa-tion.* Fifty-eighth Yearbook, Part II. Chicago: University of Chicago Press, 1959.

Major yearbook which summarizes the history, philosophy, organization, function, and theory of the guidance and personnel services.

NORRIS, WILLA, FRANKLIN R. ZERAN, and RAYMOND N. HATCH. *The Information Service in Guidance: Occupational, Educational, Social.* Chicago: Rand McNally and Company, 1960.

A good reference on the information service.

PETERS, HERMAN J., and GAIL F. FARWELL. *Guidance: A Developmental Ap-proach.* Chicago: Rand McNally and Company, 1959.

An excellent basic text in guidance.

PETERS, HERMAN J., and BRUCE SHERTZER. *Guidance: Program Development and Management.* Columbus, Ohio: Charles E. Merrill Books, Inc., 1963.

This book presents principles, procedures, and plans necessary for ini-tiating, developing, and appraising a modern school guidance program. The book is based on recent research and literature.

"Phases of Guidance in the Secondary School," *The Bulletin of the National Association of Secondary-School Principals,* 45: 1–154, November, 1961.

The entire issue is made up of a collection of articles on secondary-school guidance.

RAUBINGER, FREDERICK M., and ROBERT WITHEY. *Remember the Individual in New Jersey Secondary School Guidance.* Trenton: Department of Secondary Education, 1962.

A reaffirmation of the guidance point of view and an analysis of the role of guidance programs and guidance workers.

SHARTLE, CARROLL L. *Occupational Information: Its Development and Appli-cation.* Third edition. Englewood Cliffs, New Jersey: Prentice-Hall, Inc., 1959.

A good reference on specialized field of guidance work.

TORRANCE, E. PAUL. *Guiding Creative Talent.* Englewood Cliffs, New Jersey: Prentice-Hall, Inc., 1962.

An authoritative discussion on recent research in creativity and its im-plication to guidance and counseling.

TRAXLER, ARTHUR E. *Techniques of Guidance.* New York: Harper and Row, Inc., 1957.

A classic general text.

WARTERS, JANE. *Group Guidance: Principles and Practices.* New York: McGraw-Hill Book Company, Inc., 1960.

A description of the method and techniques of guidance through groups in the curriculum and the extracurriculum.

WRENN, C. GILBERT. *The Counselor in a Changing World.* Washington, D.C.: American Personnel and Guidance Association, 1962.

A discussion of the future of counseling in public schools.

ZERAN, FRANKLIN R., and ANTHONY C. RICCIO. *Organization and Administration of Guidance Services.* Chicago: Rand McNally and Company, 1962.

A textbook which contains good description of the guidance services and the roles of guidance personnel.

Chapter 18

New Developments

Nowadays curriculum changes and movements for curriculum changes develop so rapidly that to keep up with all of them is quite impossible. Among recent developments affecting the curriculum are increased emphasis on content, an increased interest in creativity, greatly increased activity by the federal government, a great number of curriculum studies and projects by professional and quasi-professional groups, increased support of school experimentation by independent foundations, many new technological discoveries and inventions, and much experimenting with school organization.

B. Othaniel Smith says that "every 25 years we get excited about content." He points out that in the 1920's curriculum workers were busy trying to clear the deadwood out of the curriculum. Now, he says, we "are at the content again."[1] But this time the movement is directed not to clearing out dead content, but to refurbishing and restocking the academic content of secondary-school curriculum. As a result various individuals and groups have started an "almost bewildering" number of special projects and studies dealing with the academic subjects in the school curriculum. In a report written for the National Education Asso-

[1] *The Scholars Look at the Schools.* A report of a discipline seminar (Washington, D.C.: National Education Association, 1962), p. 5.

ciation project on instruction Dorothy Fraser lists 42 of them—all having to do with the teaching of the academic disciplines in the elementary and secondary schools.[2]

The scope and objectives of the various curriculum studies in the academic disciplines differ greatly. Some of them are limited to the study of certain subjects only (for example, physics or biology); others encompass an entire field (for example, science, foreign languages, or mathematics). Some of them have prepared scientific materials to teach by; others have produced broad recommendations to guide curriculum builders and textbook writers. The reader can find reference to some of the important ones in the chapters of the text having to do with the various subjects.

Some of these projects have been initiated by curriculum specialists; many others by academic professors. All too frequently, the college subject matter specialists, because of the reaction against the reforms of the twenties, have completely ignored the curriculum specialists and educationalists in formulating and proposing new methods and curricula in their disciplines. Sometimes this neglect has led to a tremendous amount of waste effort and the replowing of already well-harrowed ground.

THE GROWING CONCERN ABOUT CREATIVITY AND THE ABILITY TO THINK

Another movement that may have great significance to the secondary-school curriculum of the future is the growing demand that the curriculum foster creativity and the ability to think. In a sense this movement is complementary to the movement for strengthening the academic disciplines, which was described in the preceding section. In another sense the movements run contrary to each other. Although curriculum innovators feel the necessity for pupils to know essential academic background, their desire to develop pupils' rational powers has caused them to place their major efforts on teaching methods that encourage transfer from one context to another and the ability to think clearly.

The importance of method over content is evident in several of the studies of the disciplines themselves. In the University of Illinois Committee on School Mathematics program, for instance, "the materials and methods have been designed so as to stress discovery of generalizations by the pupils."[3] The same emphasis on thinking and originality is true of several other projects in the academic fields, particularly those having

[2] Dorothy M. Fraser, *Current Curriculum Studies in Academic Studies* (Washington, D.C.: National Education Association, 1962), Table of Contents.

[3] *Ibid.*, p. 32.

to do with the academically brilliant. Probably skill in thinking is being taught consciously more often today than in recently preceding years.

Information Gathering vs. Creative Thinking. Even so, not as much has been done to sponsor creativity and thinking power in the pupils as many educators would like. In spite of much lip service to the need for creative and original thinking, many of the emphases in the new secondary-school curricula and methods seem to be directed in the opposite direction—toward the thoughtless ingestion and repetition of facts. Instead of freeing the mind, these "rigorous" information-gathering courses may condemn the capable pupil to hidebound conformist mediocrity and forbid him freedom to think for himself originally and creatively.

Thoughtful teachers try to avoid this contingency by giving pupils many opportunities to use the information in their courses in problem-solving situations in which pupils can discover and create knowledge and skills by themselves. To this end, some teachers have made their classes into laboratories for learning in which pupils actively and diligently pursue learning rather than passively accept information given to them *ex cathedra* by the teacher or a textbook. This method has much to recommend it. Not until more teachers adopt this type of teaching will we succeed in teaching boys and girls to think originally and creatively.[4]

RETURNING CONCERN FOR INDIVIDUAL DIFFERENCES

Presently a renewed concern about provisions for individual differences is having considerable influence on the secondary-school curriculum. During the thirties and forties, because of their supposed deleterious effects on pupils' attitudes and mental health, many of the plans for individual differences initiated in the twenties were abandoned.

Today the exigencies of the cold war and the current reaction against the so-called progressive era have brought about a quite different point of view. Attempts to provide for individual differences by formal administrative schemes have become the rule rather than the exception.

Homogeneous grouping, in the form of ability grouping, has become common in our larger secondary schools. Frequently the school provides no special instruction for the different ability groups; the teachers just teach the same material at different rates. More and more, however, curriculum workers seem to be finding it advantageous to use different approaches for different groups.

In order to secure continuity of instruction for pupils of different abilities, many secondary schools have developed curriculum tracks. The tracks, which are sometimes called rails or streams, are simply curriculum

---

[4] E. Paul Torrance, *Guiding Creative Talent* (Englewood Cliffs, N.J.: Prentice-Hall, Inc., 1962), Chs. 8 and 9; Lawrence Kubie, *Neurotic Distortions of the Creative Process* (Lawrence: University of Kansas Press, 1958).

sequences for different ability groups. In some schools pupils placed in a track move together in all subjects of the curriculum, but the trend seems to be to place pupils into tracks subject by subject.[5]

Individualizing Instruction. Although the worth of individualizing instruction as a means for providing for individual differences seems obvious, progress toward individualizing instruction in the secondary school seems, on the whole, to be slow. So far most individualized instruction seems to consist only of special projects for the academically talented pupils. If the trend toward providing for individual differences continues, one can expect more individualized programs designed to serve pupils of all kinds. The increased adoption of teaching machines and programed instruction may completely individualize some aspects of the curriculum and eliminate the lock step required by current instructional methods and the new emphasis on large group instruction.

Older schemes for individualizing instruction are also being revived. In the Warrensburg, New York, Central School, ninth grade pupils study English according to the contract plan. In this plan, which was in vogue thirty and more years ago, as each pupil fulfills his contract, which he does individually, he is free to go on to the next one or to do additional extracredit work. Ungraded school plans such as the ones used in Melbourne, Florida, and in Middletown Project[6] of Middletown, Rhode Island, are also versions of old plans designed to let each pupil proceed at his proper pace.

However, the unit method, one of the most promising of the plans for individualizing instruction to be introduced before World War II,[7] does not seem to be gaining popularity. This plan and the classroom laboratory plan should be utilized more than they have been, for they hold great potential for providing both for the common needs and individual differences of boys and girls. With methods like these, teachers can actually provide for individual differences directly in the classroom by varying pupils' work in accordance with individual interests, abilities, and plans.

Curricula For Talented Pupils. Recently particular attention has been paid to identifying and educating the talented. Some of these projects have been partially described in earlier chapters. They include plans for enriching the curriculum and accelerating pupils and, not infrequently, a combination of the two.

---

[5] See Nelson B. Henry (ed.), *Individualizing Instruction,* The Sixty-first Yearbook of the National Society for the Study of Education, Part I (Chicago: University of Chicago Press, 1962), especially Chs. 10–14.

[6] B. Frank Brown, "Schools of Tomorrow—Today," *Bulletin of the National Association of Secondary-School Principals,* 46: 255–258, May, 1962; Sidney P. Rollins, *The Middletown Project* (Providence: Rhode Island College, 1962).

[7] Roy O. Billett, *Fundamentals of Secondary School Teaching* (Boston: Houghton Mifflin Company, 1940), Chs. 16–18.

Plans for accelerating academically talented youngsters include programs leading toward early admission to college and advanced placement in college, as well as programs that simply take the pupils more rapidly through their secondary-school courses without particular reference to collegiate curricula. Although programs leading to early admission to college are probably becoming slightly more popular, they are not finding such ready acceptance as programs leading to advanced collegiate standing do.

Principals and parents prefer advanced placement programs because they are more flexible. As administered by the College Entrance Examination Board, pupils in the Advanced Placement Programs may take advanced placement examinations in whichever subject they feel ready. Successful passing of the examination may excuse the student from the first year and sometimes the first two years of college study in the subject.

In other advanced placement plans, colleges make their courses available to high school students either by inviting them to campus to take certain courses or by sponsoring college courses in selected high schools to be taught either by college professors or picked high school teachers. Successful completion of such courses may entitle the student to full academic credit from the sponsoring college.

Not all of the programs for the talented have to do with early college admission or advanced placement. Many of them—for example, the outstanding program for the gifted in Portland, Oregon—simply try to enrich the curricula of able pupils. Remarkable because of the breadth of its program, which recognizes talent in art, music, writing, dramatics, mechanical ability, dance, and social leadership as well as academic aptitude, the Portland program includes accelerated sections in regular courses, seminars in specific subjects, interdepartmental seminars, and special talent classes.[8]

Curricula for Slow Learners. Of late, programs for slow learners have not received as much attention as have programs for the talented. Nevertheless, many secondary schools are providing excellent programs for them. In the program for slow terminal pupils at Haaren High School in New York City the following provisions are noteworthy.

1. The basic courses have been modified to fit the needs and capacities of the pupils.
2. Prevocational industrial arts shops are utilized to give the boys marketable skills and to provide motivation in other subjects.
3. Art electives are made available for nonverbal pupils who are skillful with their hands.

---

[8] Elizabeth Paschal, *Encouraging the Excellent* (New York: The Fund for the Advancement of Education, 1960), p. 36; see also *The Gifted Child in Portland* (Portland, Ore.: Portland Public Schools, 1959), Chs. 6 and 7.

4. Work experience in industry is provided.
5. Courses of importance to terminal pupils have been moved into the ninth and tenth grades so that pupils will surely have these experiences before dropping out.
6. Participation in the extracurriculum is encouraged. Interscholastic sports are particularly important, but at Haaren the school also sponsors assemblies geared to the interests of the pupils, civic programs that appeal to their pride, and dramatic and cultural programs that give them a lift.[9]

Being a large city high school, Haaren High School has many facilities at hand not available to other schools, but terminal programs of similar nature are offered in many schools throughout the nation. Presumably the interest in providing for the talented will make programs for the slow learner even more necessary. Certainly the present concern about the waste of American youth because of the great number of dropouts should amplify the need for suitable programs for nonacademically oriented boys and girls. Among these are programs, such as the Higher Horizons program, aimed at helping culturally disadvantaged youth.

EXTERNAL INFLUENCE

A most heartening development in secondary-school curriculum development is the new interest and activity of agencies and groups, some of which used to feel little, if any, responsibility for the improvement of secondary education in the United States. Among these groups making distinct contributions to curriculum development are scholarly organizations, philanthropic foundations, and agencies of the federal government. Some of the activities of these groups have been noted earlier in this chapter and in preceding chapters.

ACTIVITIES OF THE FEDERAL GOVERNMENT

Lately the federal government has been spending unprecedented millions of dollars for projects directly or indirectly involving the secondary-school curriculum.

Under the provisions of the National Defense Education Act of 1958 the United States Office of Education has sponsored curriculum research and innovations in secondary-school science, mathematics, foreign languages, technical education, and guidance. This program permits the government to finance training programs for teachers, purchase of equipment, information and research centers, research, supervisory services,

[9] Saul Israel, "Don't Forget the Slow Learner," *Bulletin of the National Association of Secondary-School Principals,* 46: 74–76, March, 1962.

and experimenting with new methods and techniques. In 1962 the Office of Education added a new program for supporting centers in English and Social Studies as a means of training teachers and improving the curriculum and instruction in these subjects. Through its Cooperative Research Program the Office of Education is gathering much new data based upon both basic and practical research, which should help curriculum workers to new insights in matters of curriculum and methodology.

Governmental influence on secondary education is not limited solely to the activities of the Office of Education. Frequently projects of the National Institute of Mental Health have a more or less direct bearing on secondary education. More directly the National Science Foundation contributes to curriculum research and teacher education in the sciences.

CONTRIBUTIONS OF PROFESSIONAL ORGANIZATIONS

The National Education Association. As one would naturally expect, the National Education Association and its departments have contributed much to curriculum research and development. Among the prominent National Education Association projects are its Project on the Academically Talented Student and its Project on the Instructional Program of the Public Schools.

The Project on the Academically Talented Student has published a number of important booklets descriptive of instructional and curricular practices suitable for use in identifying and teaching academically talented students in the various secondary-school subjects. Several of these reports have been quoted earlier in this book.

The Project on the Instructional Programs of the Public Schools has also published several reports. In general, these reports describe bases for curriculum decision, making curriculum decisions, and implementing curriculum decisions once made. Like the reports of the Project on the Academically Talented Student, these reports should make a significant contribution to the future of the secondary curriculum.

The National Association of Secondary School Principals. Undoubtedly the National Education Association's department most concerned with the secondary-school curriculum is the National Association of Secondary-School Principals. In recent years committees of this organization have studied the various secondary-school subjects and issued position papers describing the Association's view of what instruction in these subjects should be. Each of these statements was worked out by a committee of school administrators and experts in the subject field, and has been officially adopted as association policy. One of the association's most far-reaching projects, the Staff Utilization Project, will be described later.

The Association for Supervision and Curriculum Development. The Association for Supervision and Curriculum Development has been exerting a steadying influence, which is greatly needed during a period of almost frantic experimenting with the curriculum. During this period the Association has studied the bases and purposes of the curriculum. In its publications it has discussed the role of the secondary school, the nature of the learner, the nature of learning, the sources of the curriculum, and other problems of curriculum improvement. Its research institutes and subsequent reports have been greatly helpful in bringing to curriculum workers new understandings of the nature of the teaching-learning processes and their implications for revisions of curricula and methodology. Three reports especially significant to secondary-school curriculum builders are *The Junior High School We Need, The High School We Need,* and *What Shall the High Schools Teach?*

Other Professional Organizations. Other professional and scholarly groups have also been active in curriculum development. Many of the new developments in foreign language teaching are the result of the effort of the Modern Language Association. The National Science Teachers Association has issued a statement about science teaching, *Planning for Excellence in High School Science,*[10] which criticizes present science curricula and proposes guidelines for their improvement. Similar projects have been sponsored by teacher organizations in almost every subject field.

THE ROLE OF THE PHILANTHROPIC FOUNDATIONS

Most of the recent curriculum research and studies that have not been supported by the federal government have been financed by one or another of the philanthropic foundations.

The Fund for the Advancement of Education. The Fund for the Advancement of Education of the Ford Foundation has been particularly diligent in supporting curriculum study and innovation. By and large, the secondary-school curriculum projects supported by the Fund are projects designed to lead to more efficient staff utilization, to the strengthening of the teaching of academic subjects, and to other innovations meant to ensure that the schools get the most from each instructional dollar. This emphasis originally received its direction from a desire to fulfill the great need for better teaching during a teacher shortage. What the impact of the Fund on the secondary-school curriculum will be is difficult to tell, but all evidence indicates that it will be large.

The Conant Reports. Among the most influential of foundation studies are those conducted by James B. Conant with the support of the Carnegie Corporation. These studies have led to three particularly important reports, *The American High School Today, Education in the Junior High School Years,* and *Slums and Suburbs.* In brief, these reports generally

---

[10] National Science Teachers Association, *Planning for Excellence in High School Science* (Washington, D.C.: The Association, 1958).

support the curricula common to our comprehensive secondary schools but seek to refine them and make them more effective. Because of Dr. Conant's prestige as a scientist and ex-president of Harvard University, the Conant reports are having a great deal of influence. His recommendations are responsible for much of the current emphasis on strengthening the academic studies in secondary schools.

INFLUENCE OF NEW TECHNOLOGICAL DEVELOPMENTS

The past decade has seen the development of many new instructional machines and devices and their introduction to the school. Most startling of these are teaching machines and television. Great advances have been made and are being made in the development and use of other electronic and nonelectronic audio-visual aids and instructional apparatus. The impact of this new and improved technology upon the secondary-school curriculum may well be spectacular.

In general, machines are useful in imparting knowledge to boys and girls. They can make the presentation of subject matter stimulating and forceful. Some of them can actually teach boys and girls, and so can be used effectively in the individualizing of instruction. Because of their force and vividness they may be very useful in developing attitudes and ideals as well as establishing clearer concepts.

But the machines cannot do the whole job of teaching, at least not yet. So far none of them can do much more than present information and provide practice. They do not seem to be able to teach pupils the intellectual skills or develop powers of critical analysis, original thinking, or creativity. Presumably the role of the technological gadgets in the secondary school will always be auxiliary.

TELEVISION AND THE SECONDARY SCHOOL CURRICULUM

Television has proved greatly useful for bringing to the classroom experiences that are not available to the pupils in any other way. Properly used, it can open new vistas to the pupils and confront them with new challenges. Types of programs that have tremendous potential for widening the curriculum include programs that record unusual historical events, for example, a presidential inauguration or our first astronaut's trip into space; extraordinary cultural events, for example, a program of the New York Philharmonic Orchestra or the N.B.C. Opera Company; or to show the pupils distant, unusual, or hard-to-see things, for example, life in India or the making of steel. Television can also bring to the class lectures and demonstrations by master teachers and specialists who can present their subjects in a form and with an authority far beyond the capabilities of the classroom teacher.

After a slow start educational television now seems to be securing a firm place in the schools throughout the country. Both commercial and nonprofit television stations are telecasting educational programs of more or less merit. In addition communities and states have established either open- or closed-circuit telecasting systems for transmitting to the schools.

Usually in the television class the television teacher presents lectures and demonstrations supported by elaborate audio-visual effects, whereas the classroom teachers follow up the television classes with discussions, recitations, practice activities, and other classes conducted in the regular classroom. Sometimes courses are conducted entirely by television, but this practice seems to be exceptional. In some instances television has been used to bring courses to schools that do not have the faculty competent to teach them. In such cases the bulk of the teaching must necessarily be done by the television teacher with a minimum of follow-up by the classroom teacher. In this way, for instance, small schools that do not have any teachers on the staff trained in physics have been able to offer physics classes for the pupils.

Considerable objection has been raised to the use of television instruction, first, because of its supposedly dehumanizing effect, and second, because it tends to handcuff the school curriculum to the television schedule. The validity of the first argument is debatable, but that television teaching does tend to clamp the curriculum to the television schedule is undoubtedly true. In balance the evidence seems to indicate that television can best be utilized to augment classroom teaching.[11]

AUTOMATED INSTRUCTION AND THE CURRICULUM

Automated instruction or programed learning is just beginning to enter the secondary school. At this point just what effect it will have on secondary education is yet to be seen. So far, about the only programs to find any general acceptance are nonmachine-programed books in mathematics and English grammar.

The adoption and use of automated programs on a large scale could bring revolutionary curriculum changes. Automated instruction has immense potential for individualizing instruction. Conceivably its use could lead to complete individualization of instruction with the resultant elimination of courses, marks, and promotion as we now know them. Experimental evidence indicates that the use of programs might possibly lead to more thorough learning by all pupils than educators had felt possible. Undoubtedly schoolmen will find a place in the schools for automated instruction that will make at least some curricular adjustments necessary.

Despite their effectiveness teaching machines and automated programs

[11] Alexander Frazier and Harold Wigren, *Opportunities for Learning: Guidelines for Television* (Washington, D.C.: National Education Association, 1960).

do have serious drawbacks. They are completely mechanical and impersonal, and so far they have been most successful in teaching facts and skills only. Evidently the teaching machines and programs are more adapted to putting things into the mind than for teaching how to use the mind. Still, combined with discussion, problem-solving, and other techniques, their contribution to the curriculum of the future could be enormous.[12]

OTHER AUDIO-VISUAL DEVICES

Improvement in audio-visual aids and the introduction of new audio-visual devices has also altered the potential future of the secondary-school curriculum.

One of these new devices, the language laboratory, is really a teaching machine. In its most sophisticated form it asks the pupil a question, allows him to answer, and then corrects him. Its use promises a degree of excellence in foreign language instruction seldom achieved before in our schools. The language laboratory should also prove useful in the teaching of speech and other English language arts.

Other electronic devices that are sure to have considerable influence on the curriculum include the tape recorder, the improved motion-picture projector, the overhead projector, and slide viewers. Devices like the overhead projector are useful for pointing up classroom presentation. They lend themselves to traditional classes and to large group presentations. New motion-picture projectors, slides and filmstrip viewers, and tape recorders can also be used individually or in small groups without much skill needed in the use of the equipment. The addition of these devices to the teacher's armory should make possible much more flexible curricula. They should also make it possible for every school to bring to its pupils experiences far beyond the resources of the average faculty. Quite possibly the schools of the future will use these new instructional devices to become real laboratories of learning.[13]

INFLUENCE OF NEW DEVELOPMENTS IN SCHOOL ORGANIZATION

Perhaps even more influential in determining the future of the curriculum than the new technological developments will be the many new organizational changes. Experimental changes in school organization

[12] A. A. Lumsdaine and Robert Glazer, *Teaching Machines and Programmed Learning* (Washington, D.C.: National Education Association, 1960), pp. 570–572.

[13] *Planning Schools for New Media*, OE–21021, U.S. Department of Health, Education, and Welfare, Office of Education (Washington, D.C.: Government Printing Office, 1962), gives vivid illustrations of new and projected audio-visual devices and materials.

have been adopted by so many secondary-school systems as to be almost common. Among these changes are team teaching, large group instruction, use of teacher aides, flexible scheduling and promotion plans, the house or little school plan, and the plans for making secondary schools really community institutions.

THE NASSP STAFF UTILIZATION PROJECT

The National Association of Secondary-School Principals' Project on Staff Utilization has already had considerable influence on secondary education and bodes to be even more influential in the future. By and large, the greatest amount of its influence has been in the area of school organization.

This project was born in 1955 out of the great anxiety concerning the supply of secondary-school teachers. At that time "the history of preceding years and projection for the future offered little hope that the numbers of available certificated teachers would increase in sufficient numbers to cope with expanding student population and added educational responsibilities."[14] To stem the tide, the commission took as its goal the finding of ways to improve secondary education in spite of the teacher shortage. For this purpose the commission sponsored and helped finance research projects in a hundred or so schools. The commission did not restrict the type of project except to limit the aim to better staff utilization. Within this scope the commission welcomed study of students, teachers, curriculum, and facilities. Projects attempted included experiments in team teaching, large and small group instruction, independent study, use of clerical assistants, flexible scheduling, use of teaching labs, instructor assistants, material aids for a rural community, faculty summer study, use of machines for teaching, and the improvement of guidance services. Some of these projects are described in this and other chapters.

The National Association of Secondary-School Principals Staff Utilization Studies seem to be having an impact on secondary-school curricula. Basically their approach to curriculum content is a flexible one in which stress is given to "basic content" for all boys and girls and "depth content" for pupils with "the ability and interests that go beyond basic provisions." In its proposed school of the future the commission features independent study and research, small group discussion, increased library and laboratory supported by learning-resources centers, the increased use of staff specialists, increased emphasis on individual differences, and economical use of expert instructional talent in large classes. The commission hopes that the use of flexible curricula will make it possible to teach each boy and girl all the basic knowledge he can acquire, some

[14] J. Lloyd Trump and Dorsey Baynham, *Focus On Change—Guide to Better Schools* (Chicago: Rand McNally and Company, 1961), p. 18.

degree of competence in the use of intellectual skills, and deep knowledge and skills in the areas of his special interests. In the commission's proposed school of the future, pupils will be free from the compartmentalization of contemporary curricula. Instead each pupil will enter new areas of study as he becomes ready. Figure 10 shows how the pupils' time might be divided in such a school.

FIGURE 10. HOW AN AVERAGE 14-YEAR-OLD STUDENT MIGHT SPEND HIS SCHOOL TIME[15]

Average Minutes Per Week

Subject	Required Basic Education			As Selected By Personal and Professional Decision	
English	100	50	40		
Social Studies	100	50	40		
Foreign Language	60	40	40		
Mathematics	80	40	60	Choice Among The Subject Areas	
Science	80	40	70		
Fine and Practical Arts	80	40	30		
Health–Physical Education Recreation	40	40	80		
Total	540	300	360	240	360
	Large Group	Small Group	Independent Study	Group Activities	Independent Study
				Depth In His Own Area	

+

Extra hours available for independent study in educational facilities open and supervised additional hours, days and weeks

MAKING THE SCHOOL SCHEDULE FLEXIBLE

The Staff Utilization Commission's School of the Future is based upon the principle of flexibility. In the past this principle has not been greatly honored in American secondary schools. Slowly the pattern of fixed scheduling is being broken. Quite frequently secondary schools are scheduling classes for four long periods each week instead of five shorter ones. Rotating schedules, in which Monday's first-period class becomes Tuesday's second-period class and Wednesday's third-period class, and so on throughout the week, are becoming commonplace. So is the use

[15] *Ibid.,* p. 54.

of two schedules that can be interchanged to allow for assemblies and other special activities. Schools of the Catskill Area are experimenting with interchanging morning and afternoon schedules biweekly.

Recently some secondary-school administrators have introduced a plan for developing the schedule around short basic periods or modules of from 15 to 30 minutes each. Because the school administrator can schedule a class for a single module or for several of them, this type of scheduling gives the optimum in flexibility. Assuming a 20-minute module, the administrator can schedule classes for 20 minutes, 40 minutes, 60 minutes, or any other multiple of 20 as he thinks most desirable. Inasmuch as some classes are best taught in short periods (audio-lingual French practice) and other classes need long periods (120-minute laboratory period or 180-minute block-of-time period), this type of scheduling promises to meet the need for a much-desired versatility in daily schedules.

Another device to add flexibility to the schedule is to schedule activities, including some elective classes, after school or on Saturdays. At the Fox Lane School in Bedford, New York, pupils voluntarily attend classes on Saturday morning. The E. O. Smith school in Storrs, Connecticut, holds some elective classes and extraclass activities after school. Several schools keep their libraries and laboratories open evenings and Saturday mornings for pupil use. In some of these schools teacher aides supervise these extended activities. Obviously the use of long periods and flexible schedules permits the school to offer a more varied program of studies.

THE UNGRADED SCHOOL

In another attempt to introduce flexibility into the curriculum, curriculum innovators have turned to an old-fashioned idea—the ungraded school. In the ungraded high school the schoolwork is divided into levels, and the pupil moves from level to level as he becomes ready, much as used to be the custom in the one-room schoolhouse. Theoretically, then, in the ungraded secondary school the able pupils can move rapidly from elementary to advanced courses, whereas the less able progress more leisurely, seemingly without the pressures that sometimes accompany acceleration and grouping. This plan also allows pupils both to accelerate and to dig deeply into subjects of special interest or value to them. In every case progress depends upon readiness.

The ungraded school concept seems to be meritorious. Marking time, unnecessary repetition, and gaps in essential learning should be largely eliminated in the school organized in this fashion. Whether it will fulfill its promise has yet to be seen, but it does seem to offer bright prospects for enriching the curriculum.[16]

---

[16] Brown, *op. cit.*

SUMMER SESSIONS

Variety and flexibility have also been added to the secondary-school curriculum through the inauguration of summer school programs. Although summer schools are no novelty, until quite recently their offerings have been pretty much limited to remedial courses for pupils who have failed during the school year. Nowadays many schools have greatly expanded their summer programs. Practice varies greatly among the schools and may include summer schools and summer camps.

A number of secondary schools offer regular academic courses for which they may or may not give credit toward graduation. Enrichment programs for the talented are quite common. So are enrichment opportunities in art, music, outdoor education, and science education. Among the courses frequently available are driver education, art, music, crafts, sports, typing, industrial arts, and homemaking. By offering these classes the schools give pupils opportunities to expand their personal curricula by taking courses that ordinarily they could not get into their programs during the school year. Because of their evident value, there is every reason to believe that the trend toward increased summer offerings will continue.[17]

TEAM TEACHING

Largely because of the support received from the National Association of Secondary-School Principals Staff Utilization projects, team teaching has become increasingly more popular in the secondary schools. Basically team teaching is any plan whereby two or more teachers teach the same group of pupils cooperatively. It varies from the informal cooperation of two teachers who happen to be assigned to teach the same section in the courses to highly formalized teams of master teachers, classroom teachers, teacher assistants, and clerks.

In the more formal plan just mentioned, usually the master teacher, sometimes called the teacher-presenter, conducts large group classes of 60, 100, or more pupils by the large group method or sometimes by video presentation. Classroom teachers and teacher assistants follow up the large group presentations with class discussions and individual and other small group activities. In addition to aiding in the actual teaching, teacher assistants may also assist by proctoring tests, correcting papers, checking attendance, and performing routine tasks considered to be of less than fully professional nature. The clerks keep the records, maintain the files, prepare stencils, type up letters and reports, and perform other clerical tasks that teachers so often find onerous.

[17] Terrance Hatch, "Summer School—Stepchild of Public Education," *The Bulletin of the National Association of Secondary-School Principals,* 46: 199–203, September, 1962.

Usually when one refers to team teaching nowadays he has in mind some scheme like the above, although frequently teams based on this pattern do not have the services of clerks or assistant instructors. Theoretically the plan is supposed to advance better provisions for individual differences of pupils and teachers. It permits teachers to teach the content they know best and makes it possible for teachers to teach in the ways they are most effective, for some teachers are more at home with large groups, some with small groups; some are better at lecturing; some at leading discussion, and others at individualizing instruction.[18]

Despite this declared purpose, critics of this team teaching approach complain that it forces the curriculum into a rigid pattern. They claim that since the teacher-presenter must present his large group classes to every pupil all at the same time, it forces them all into lock step.

Another type of team teaching is practiced in Mountain Lakes, New Jersey, and elsewhere. In this plan teachers of four different subjects who all teach the same pupils meet at scheduled periods to discuss their pupils and to correlate and coordinate their activities. Similarly, in 1962, in the Ridgeley High School of Baltimore County, Maryland, an English teacher and a social studies teacher, who both taught the same class section, planned together to correlate their teaching.

This type of team teaching has much to commend it. It has been used for a long time with success. Through group planning teachers in the team can decide how best to meet the needs of individuals, how to coordinate their activities, and how to promote the integration of learning in their pupils.

LARGE CLASS INSTRUCTION

Frequently associated with team teaching, but not necessarily so, is a new trend toward large group instruction. According to its advocates large group instruction is advantageous because it gives pupils opportunity to sit in class under the best teachers and to learn from highly trained specialists. Advocates also point out that large group instruction reduces teachers' hourly loads so that they can have more time to prepare well. It has also been claimed that teaching large groups makes teachers more effective, for in occasional lectures to large classes teachers tend to rise to the occasion and do their very best.

Various techniques have been devised to make large group instruction more beneficial. Included among them are more effective use of audio-visual aids, particularly the overhead projector, and the use of teacher assistants. Of course, the many techniques for television teaching, which is a special type of large group instruction, are adaptable to large group class instruction and can be used quite profitably.[19]

[18] See Trump and Baynham, *op. cit.*, pp. 83–87.
[19] *Ibid.*, pp. 74–78.

USING TEACHER AIDES

Many of the jobs that the classroom teacher performs are not professional but only use up time that the teacher could use better in other ways. Among these are such clerical tasks as typing, filing, posting records, taking attendance, and running duplicating machines. To relieve teachers of these tedious, nonprofessional tasks, several school systems have given them teacher assistants or aides. Not only can teacher aides perform clerical tasks, they can also relieve teachers in many other ways. They can assume monitorial responsibilities, such as corridor, lunchroom, library, and study hall supervision. They can prepare audio-visual materials and equipment for showing and assist the teacher in class by running the machines and handling the equipment for them. They can score certain kinds of tests and assignments. In some cases they can read themes and papers. They can aid in conducting and supervising field trips, projects, and individualized or grouped classes.

When properly used, teacher aides should make it possible for classroom teachers to teach better, to spend more time with individual pupils, to prepare for classes more thoroughly, and to devise better courses. With teacher aides to help them teachers should have a better chance to free themselves from the necessity of drill, lecture, and recitation and permit them to help pupils develop their powers to think through the use of problem solving, independent research, discovery techniques, and group processes.

Of all the recent innovations the use of teacher aides seems to be the one that holds most promise of allowing teachers to do the sort of creative teaching that will provide for pupil differences in class and give pupils opportunities to realize themselves more completely.[20]

THE SCHOOL AS A COMMUNITY INSTITUTION

More and more the secondary school is tending to become a community institution. In addition to providing schooling for boys and girls in the classroom, the modern secondary school takes the pupils into the community and brings the community into the classroom. As part of their school experience in an increasing number of schools boys and girls may participate in work programs, civic activities, and recreational programs. In many communities much, if not most, of young people's social life is centered in the school. Moreover the schools' program is not limited to boys and girls. Many secondary schools are expanding their programs to give adults both cultural and social experiences. Anderson and Gruhn[21]

[20] *Ibid.*, pp. 80–83.

[21] Vernon E. Anderson and William T. Gruhn, *Principles and Practices of Secondary Education*, 2nd ed. (New York: The Ronald Press Company, 1962), p. 310.

list six practices by which secondary schools have been becoming community educational, cultural, and recreational centers. They are (1) cooperation between school and community agencies in developing activities for youth and adults; (2) increased parent participation in the program of the secondary schools; (3) recreational and enrichment programs during vacation and out of school hours for youth and adults; (4) upward extension of education for all youth beyond the twelfth grade; (5) the development of adult education programs; and (6) the development of the schools as a cultural center for the community.

THE RANDOM FALLS PLAN

In 1956 Archibald Shaw and John Lyons Reid proposed a revision of secondary education that carries the school as a community institution idea to the ultimate. The proposal encompasses three headings that in practice would be so interrelated that to identify each one separately would be difficult. The headings are:

1. Citizenship development through vocational and service contracts with local (and ultimately state and national) employers and agencies which are planned by the student and his advisors.
2. Development of the individual's resources through the body of common and specialized learnings pursued primarily within the confines of the school campus.
3. Community service, the utilization by the student of community resources (physical and human) as well as the use of school resources (again persons as well as things) by members of the community.[22]

The suggested program is intended to be completely flexible and to allow pupils to gain experience both in the classroom and in the community twelve months each year. Thus young Tom Turner, a fourteen-year-old boy whose program serves as an example, spends two weeks working in a factory shipping department, two weeks working as a packer in a store, and two weeks as an office boy. He also participates in a research project having to do with insect damage to building materials, in a civic project involving planting and transplanting trees and making trails in a park, and as den chief for a pack of Cub Scouts. For physical fitness he plays soccer and baseball, skates and does posture improvement exercises. His class studies in common and specialized learnings include social studies, number skills, science and mechanics, communications, myths, languages, botany, and ancient civilization. Truly Tom's program for the year is a broad one, taking him into several areas of academic and community life.

In later years his experiences become even broader and give him still

[22] Archibald B. Shaw, "The Random Falls Idea," *The School Executive*, 75: 47–86, March, 1956.

wider experiences to include such things as dramatics, workshop, advisory youth committee to the recreation council, a project on visual aids to learning, work as an aide in the audio-visual office of the state department of education, participation in a primary election, as well as a rigorous academic program.

The Random Falls idea has not caught on in its entirety and may be held off from fruition by the current emphasis on academic disciplines. Still, it is a plan that bears studying. If the American secondary school is ever to do the complete job that writers of educational goals hope for, quite possibly the Random Falls plan may be the way.

DESIGNS FOR SMALL SCHOOLS

Today the general assumption is that in order to give pupils a good secondary education with all its ramifications, the secondary school must be a relatively large institution. One thousand pupils is often considered to be a minimum. Conant in his report on the American High School suggests that schools whose graduating class numbers fewer than one hundred pupils should be eliminated.

But to eliminate small secondary schools is not always possible. In many areas rural geography and climate of opinion make school consolidation neither feasible nor desirable. The problem then is to adapt teaching in the small secondary schools so that their pupils can have the same advantages as pupils in large schools do.

For years teachers and administrators have been coping with this problem. Recently two fairly large-scale studies, the Rocky Mountain Project and the Catskill Area Project, have attacked the problem in force with results that forecast some success. Among the techniques they have found promising are the use of multiple classes, flexible schedules, correspondence courses, television, tape recordings, moving pictures, teacher aides, and shared instruction.

Multiple Classes. By using multiple classes, small rural secondary schools can bring courses to their pupils that they could not bring to them otherwise. Multiple classes are an old story in rural high schools. In such classes one teacher conducts several courses in the same room simultaneously—a practice not so very uncommon in small secondary schools over the years. Teachers who teach multiple classes use the same techniques used by elementary teachers who group within a class. With the advent of mimeograph machines, teaching machines, audio-visual devices, and teacher aides, to teach such classes should become progressively easier. That secondary-school teachers should consider multiple class teaching novel reflects the sterility of secondary-school methodology of the past. In spite of presenting the teacher with a complex methodological problem, multiple classes may possibly give boys and girls even greater opportunities to learn than they would have in a large **high** school. Not only do multiple classes bring the pupils opportunities for a fuller curriculum, but teaching a multiple class almost forces the teacher to permit pupils to study individually and creatively.

Ways to a Fuller Curriculum. Television, films, recordings, and correspondence courses also can bring to small schools experiences and courses that otherwise would be unavailable because of the lack of a competent instructor. True, these courses may not be as rewarding as those taught by really competent teachers, but on the other hand, many a person has learned to become quite expert in one field or another via correspondence or television courses. The small secondary school provides pupils opportunity to study such courses under supervision.

For two or more schools to share a teacher of specialized subjects is another way to bring fuller curricula to small secondary schools. Sharing teachers is not a new technique. Music and art teachers have traveled from school to school for years; Latin and physics teachers can travel too. So can pupils. In this day of school buses, to carry a group of pupils from one school to another to attend a class or to use equipment not available in their own building is hardly a major problem.

The Small School of the Future. The procedures described above and the experience of the Rocky Mountain and Catskill Area Projects indicate that the curricula of small secondary schools need not be thin ones. There seems to be no reason why rural youth should not be able to have curricular opportunities of the same caliber as their city or suburban cousins.

THE HOUSE PLAN

Although small schools are attempting to emulate large schools, the large schools find much to envy in the small school. So the House Plan, or School Within a School, has been invented to bring to large schools the advantages of intimacy and face-to-face relationships of the small school.

The detailed operations of the house plans differ, although fundamentally their patterns are alike. In the house plan at the Scarsdale, New York, Junior High School[23] the houses are physically separated from each other and each has a separate faculty, but all houses share common facilities, such as homemaking rooms, shops, library, auditorium, and gymnasium. Pupils are assigned to a house for their entire stay at the school so that they may become familiar with each other and their teachers. The Newton Senior High Schools[24] follow much the same plan

[23] Walter F. Fogg, "Scarsdale Plan is Flexible and Relaxed," *Nation's Schools,* 67: 65–69, June, 1961.

[24] See Gertrude C. Creedon, "A House Plan for Newton High School," *Educational Forum,* 24: 397–404, May, 1960, for a description of the house plan devised for the Newton High Schools.

except that the pupils do not all have classes with their own house faculty, although as far as possible pupils from the same house are scheduled together with teachers from their own house. The house plan in Evanston, Illinois, is similar, but there the houses do not have separate faculty assigned.

The house plan has much to recommend it, for it combines good features of both large and small schools. The more intimate relationships in this type of organization lend themselves to improved guidance services and to curricular provisions adapted to the needs of the individual pupils. The house plan represents another sign of the concern for individuals in the modern school program.

EXTENDING THE TEACHER YEAR

Curriculum improvement takes time and effort. Just to prepare oneself to teach one course is a difficult, time-consuming task for which few teachers really have time enough. To make up for the shortage of time for curriculum improvement several school systems employ teachers for the summer months to work in curriculum development, class preparation, and other professional duties. In some schools this extra employment consists of a week or two for all teachers, in others the period is longer, and in some only designated individuals are hired for the summer, usually to work on the preparation of plans, guides, bulletins, and other curriculum materials. For school systems to conduct summer workshops and courses in which teachers can study new methods, techniques, curricula, and developments in academic fields is no longer uncommon. If this trend for summer curriculum study continues, it should prove beneficial to both the school and to the teachers.

INFLUENCE OF THE TESTING BOOM

Partly because of the European secondary education with its baccalaureate, General Certificate of Education, and matriculation examinations, partly because of the growth of scholarships granting agencies, partly because of the growth of testing services and the availability of machine scoring, and partly because of the availability of National Defense Education Act funds for testing programs, the past decade has seen a phenomenal growth in the amount of standardized and external testing in the secondary schools.[25] According to the count of the Joint Committeee on Testing today there are more than 20 national testing

[25] External tests are defined by the Joint Committee on Testing as "tests which are initiated by or sponsored by one or more agencies outside the local school district." Joint Committee on Testing, *Testing Testing Testing* (Washington, D.C.: American Association of School Administrators, Council of State School Officers, National Association of Secondary-School Principals, 1962), p. 8.

programs and new ones are "hatching overnight."[26] Such massive outlays of time, talent, and money are bound to have great effect on the curriculum. And there is no doubt that they do. Brickell points out that in New York State "copies of previous Regents Examinations constitute at least 10 per cent of the curriculum of the typical high school academic course.[27] Nearly half of the administrators replying to a questionnaire prepared by the Joint Committee on Testing stated that they used test results to aid in "curriculum change and evaluation."[28] Truly the man who writes the tests determines the curriculum.

In the eyes of the public and of many educators the good curriculum is the one that prepares pupils for the test. Judging a school's worth by such tests is very dangerous, for they do not take into account the type of pupils enrolled in a school nor their goals and expectancies. As a rule tests can tell us about only part of a school's program. They can indicate fairly well how well pupils have learned and retained facts and skills, but they are not very good at measuring the more important school objectives—for example, changing of attitudes and inculcating democratic ideas. Besides, although tests can measure pupils' mastery of facts and skills, they do not guarantee that the facts and skills measured are the ones that should be measured. Not infrequently tests are gaited to out-of-date, second-rate curricula. In such instances an up-to-date, first-rate curriculum would show up badly according to the test scores.

One of the most frequent uses of tests is to determine whether or not to admit pupils to courses, curricula, or schools. The College Entrance Examination is an example of this type of use. This use of tests greatly influences the curriculum, because teachers and administrators tend to lay out their courses so as to ensure good test results. Because tests are best suited for measuring knowledge of information, this precaution is liable to lead to the teaching of facts, memory work, and manipulation rather than true understanding. In such situations teachers are often hesitant to try new methods and materials because of fear that they may hurt their records. For the same reason administrators are afraid to launch new curricula. The New York State Department of Education seems to be convinced that the Regent's Examination has held up curriculum progress in the state.[29]

Obviously the presence of external examinations tends to bring undue emphasis to that part of the school program subject to the testing. For this reason, quite frequently vocational studies, health education, and homemaking receive less attention than they should because faculty

[26] *Ibid.*, pp. 8, 12.
[27] Henry M. Brickell, *Organizing New York State for Educational Change* (Albany: University of the State of New York, State Department of Education, 1962), p. 40.
[28] Joint Committee on Testing, *op. cit.*, p. 22.
[29] Brickell, *op. cit.*, pp. 40–41.

attention is glued to the college preparatory curriculum which will be tested externally.

Because the recent emphasis on testing has been so great the American Association of School Administrators, The Council of Chief State School Officers, and The National Association of Secondary-School Principals[30] have collaborated on a study designed to create a sane attitude toward testing. By it they hope to create an attitude among school officials and lay people that will make testing a useful tool in the school rather than, as threatens to be the case, the school's becoming the pawn for the testing program.

SUMMARY AND CONCLUSIONS

This chapter is an attempt to summarize some of the trends and movements pertinent to the secondary-school curriculum. Most of the innovations in both curriculum and method that have been described seemed to be designed to cram information into pupils' heads. Comparatively little seems to be being done, in spite of much lip service, to foster better teaching of process, structural generalization, ideas, values, and intellectual skills.

These trends are running contrary to the increasing amount of evidence that good education is not information getting. New findings in educational research tend to reinforce the theory that pupils should learn creatively. Instead of learning mere facts and figures, boys and girls should learn to discover and think things through themselves and so gain the intellectual skills by which they can use content to fill their present and future needs. To reach the greater educational goals the curriculum must allow plenty of room for individual differences of all kinds and for the development of creativity. Some of the new methods, techniques, curriculum projects and trends are truly aimed at freeing each pupil's mind. Unfortunately more of them are not, even when designed to be so. In all too many instances contemporary methods seem to be moving toward enslaving the minds in old superficial patterns under the guise of rigorous study and the pursuit of excellence.

SUGGESTED READINGS

"Advanced Placement Programs in Secondary Schools," *The Bulletin of the National Association of Secondary-School Principals*, 42: 1–171, December, 1958.
    Almost the entire issue is devoted to articles about, and description of, advanced placement programs and their syllabi.

[30] Joint Committee on Testing, *op. cit.*

ASSOCIATION FOR SUPERVISION AND CURRICULUM DEVELOPMENT. *Using Current Curriculum Developments.* Washington, D.C.: The Association, 1963.

Exceedingly valuable listing and commentary on the many new projects, studies, and sources of curriculum materials.

BRAMELD, THEODORE. "Education in Conservative Key: The Proposals of Dr. Conant," *The Bulletin of the National Association of Secondary-School Principals,* 45: 23–33, October, 1961.

A critique of the Conant reports and proposals by the leading reconstructionist.

BRICKELL, HENRY M. *Commissioner's 1961 Catalog of Educational Change.* Albany, New York: State Education Department, 1961.

An annotated list of projects being conducted in the state of New York.

———. *Organizing New York State for Educational Change.* Albany, New York: State Education Department.

A description of methods and problems of educational change in New York State.

CONANT, JAMES B. *The American High School Today.* New York: McGraw-Hill Book Company, Inc., 1959.

A very influential study and defense of the comprehensive school which makes specific curriculum recommendations for the future.

EDWARDS, ROSALINE M. "A Slow Learner Program," *The Bulletin of the National Association of Secondary-School Principals,* 42: 130–132, February, 1958.

A description of a program for slow learners in Falls Church, Virginia.

EVERETT, SAMUEL (ed.). *Programs for the Gifted: A Case Book in Secondary Education.* Fifteenth Yearbook of the John Dewey Society. New York: Harper and Row, Inc., 1961.

A collection of articles describing programs for the talented both here and abroad.

FLIEGLER, LOUIS A. *Curriculum Planning for the Gifted.* Englewood Cliffs, New Jersey: Prentice-Hall, Inc., 1961.

A series of articles by specialists in the various fields, recommending approaches for teaching the gifted.

FRASER, DOROTHY M. *Current Curriculum Studies in Academic Subjects: A Working Paper Prepared for the Project on the Instructional Program of the Public Schools.* Washington, D. C.: National Education Association, 1962.

An attempt to summarize the contributions of all the major curriculum studies in process as of January, 1962.

FUND FOR THE ADVANCEMENT OF EDUCATION. *Decade of Experiment.* New York: The Fund, 1961.

A summary of experimental programs sponsored by the Fund.

The Gifted Child in Portland. Portland, Oregon: Portland Public Schools, 1959.

A description of one of the country's best programs for gifted children.

HATCH, TERRANCE E. "Summer School—Stepchild of Public Education," *The Bulletin of the National Association of Secondary-School Principals,* 46: 199–203, September, 1962.

A study of the state of summer school programs in American high schools.

JENKINS, L. L. "School-Within-a-School Concept," *The Bulletin of the National*

Association of Secondary-School Principals, 46: 192–193, September, 1962.
A description of the school-within-a-school program at Southwest DeKalb High School, Decatur, Georgia.

JOINT COMMITTEE ON TESTING. *Testing, Testing, Testing*. Washington, D.C.: National Education Association, 1962.
Criticism of the overuse of and misuse of external tests by a committee representing leading educational associations.

MICHAEL, L. S. "New Directions to Quality Education in Secondary Schools," *The Bulletin of the National Association of Secondary-School Principals*, 45: 11–18, January, 1961.
Reviews the contents of J. Lloyd Trump's *Images of the Future* and *New Directions to Quality Education*.

MORSE, ARTHUR D. *Schools of Tomorrow—Today*. Garden City, New York: Doubleday and Company, Inc., 1960.
A rather naïve uncritical report of new practices and developments in secondary schools.

NATIONAL EDUCATION ASSOCIATION. *The Principal Looks at the School: A Status Study of Selected Instructional Practices*. Washington, D.C.: The Association, 1962.
A status study concerning elementary and secondary-school practices in the pre-Sputnik and post-Sputnik years and projected practices for the future. A working paper prepared for the NEA Project on Instructional Programs.

———. *The Scholars Look at the Schools*. A Report of the Disciplines Seminar. Washington, D.C.: The Association, 1962.
A report of a seminar in which disinterested scholars from various disciplines discussed the contributions of the different disciplines to the curriculum. A working paper prepared for the Project on the Instructional Program of the Public Schools.

NATIONAL SOCIETY FOR THE STUDY OF EDUCATION. *Education for the Gifted*. Fifty-seventh Yearbook, Part II. Chicago: University of Chicago Press, 1958.
Places education for the gifted in proper perspective with reference to the total educational program.

New Teaching Aids for the American Classroom. A symposium on the state of research in instructional television and tutorial machines, OE–34020, U.S. Department of Health, Education, and Welfare, Office of Education. Washington, D.C.: Government Printing Office, 1962.
A concise catalog of the new educational technology.

OLDHAM, FRANCES H. "Length of the School Day and the School Year," *The Bulletin of the National Association of Secondary-School Principals*, 46: 194–198, September, 1962.
A suggestion that the ten-month school year be reexamined and a consideration of some of the implications of longer school days and school years.

PASCHAL, ELIZABETH. *Encouraging the Excellent*. New York: The Fund for the Advancement of Education, 1960.
A report concerning special programs for gifted and talented students supported by the Ford Foundation.

POLATNICK, SAMUEL. "Experimentation in the New York City High Schools,"

The Bulletin of the National Association of Secondary-School Principals, 45: 74–76, February, 1961.

A summary of several experimental programs in the New York school system, among them the High Horizon Project, enrichment programs, and innovations in guidance, methods, and materials.

PRICE, NELSON C. "An Evaluation of the School-Within-a-School Plan of Secondary-School Organizations," *The Bulletin of the National Association of Secondary-School Principals,* 46: 185–191, September, 1962.

An attempt to evaluate the unit plan used in Azusa high school. Concludes that the school-within-a-school has merit.

ROLLINS, SIDNEY P. *The Middletown Project: The Development of a Non-Graded Secondary School.* Providence: Division of Graduate Studies, Rhode Island College, 1962.

A report describing and evaluating the ungraded high school project at Middletown, Rhode Island.

"Schools of the Future—Now." *The Bulletin of the National Association of Secondary-School Principals,* 46: 241–272, May, 1962.

A report of a panel in which new innovations such as team teaching, ungraded schools, and flexible school scheduling are discussed by principals who are among their strongest advocates and practitioners.

SKINNER, B. F. "Teaching Machines," *Science,* 128: 969–977, October 24, 1958.

A basic reference on Skinnerian theory and Skinnerian programs.

"Student Differences and Secondary School Offerings," *The Bulletin of the National Association of Secondary-School Principals,* 47: Entire issue, March, 1963.

An issue of the *Bulletin* devoted to description of programs being used to provide for individual differences. Most articles are aimed at programs for the talented. Since the late 1950's many issues of the *Bulletin* have been devoted to new programs actually in the schools.

"Teaching Machines and Programmed Learning," *NEA Journal,* 5: 15–30, November, 1961.

A special feature comprised of a series of articles concerning the use of programing at a relatively simple semipopularized level.

TORRANCE, E. PAUL. *Talent and Education: Present Status and Future Directions.* Minneapolis: University of Minnesota Press, 1960.

An aid to teachers in measuring the adequacy of present practices in education; makes some predictions for the future.

TRUMP, J. LLOYD. *Images of the Future: A New Approach to the Secondary School.* Washington, D.C.: National Education Association, 1959.

Presents a plan for reorganizing the school to achieve quality education economically by better utilization of staff.

———. "The American High School in 1970," *Frontiers in Secondary Education IV.* Paul M. Halverson (ed.). Syracuse, New York: Syracuse University Press, 1960.

Describes the school of the future by contrasting it with the school of 1959.

———. "A Look Ahead in Secondary Education," *The Bulletin of the National Association of Secondary-School Principals,* 42: 5–15, January, 1958.

Predicts different categories of teachers, specially designed school plants, and the reorganization of the curriculum to identify and teach the basic elements of knowledge and understanding.

TRUMP, J. LLOYD, and DORSEY BAYNHAM. *Focus on Change, Guide to Better Schools*. Chicago: Rand McNally and Company, 1961.

The best description of the "Trump plan."

WILES, KIMBALL. *The Changing Curriculum of the American High School*. Englewood Cliffs, New Jersey: Prentice-Hall, Inc., 1963.

Chapter 15 deals with the high school of the future.

Chapter 19

Organization and Evaluation
for Curriculum Improvement

Basically there are two ways to organize the curriculum: one, the experience curriculum described in Chapter 6 as the true core curriculum, in which course content is built around experiences or problems and disregards the usual subject matter lines; the other, the familiar subject-centered curriculum, in which the courses are organized around fields of knowledge or disciplines.

Almost every, if not every, senior and four-year high school in the country is organized on a subject basis, even though it may offer a core program as part of its program of studies. In this sort of organization the pupils meet with their teachers on a regular schedule for periods of from 40 to 75 minutes duration to study specific subjects. The recent experimenting with large block-of-time and with module scheduling has seldom changed the basic subject scheduling concept. In this respect, subject-centered curricula differ from the experience curricula, in which time is allocated for the study of problems rather than subjects.

CRITICISM OF SUBJECT CURRICULUM

Faults of the Subject Curriculum. In spite of its secure hold on the secondary schools the subject-centered curriculum has been criticized severely. Among the criticisms have been:

1. It leads to courses becoming out of date and out of touch with contemporary life;

2. It encourages teaching by "regurgitation";
3. It leads to the proliferation of courses and emphasis on trivia;
4. It results in duplication of course content;
5. It emphasizes the logical at the expense of the psychological.

The validity of these criticisms has been investigated in an earlier chapter. Probably they are specious at best; it is the way one uses the organization, rather than the organization itself, that makes the difference.

Merits of the Subject-centered Organization. Subject-centered organization does have some merit. Organization by subject may permit a saving of time, for the teacher, because of his prior knowledge, can select the most significant subject matter from the mass of material available. Organization by subject matter also lends itself to organizing the content in an orderly fashion and so facilitates classroom presentation. Also well-developed subject matter organization allows for investigation in depth and for developing in the student an understanding of the structure and methodology of the various scholarly disciplines. In this way the teacher can utilize features of both psychological and logical course organization. The Illinois course in mathematics is an excellent example of the combining of psychological and logical course organization in a subject-centered curriculum pattern.[1]

ORGANIZATION OF THE SUBJECT CURRICULUM

Programs of studies in American secondary schools utilize one or the other of the following types of organization: (1) the single curriculum; (2) the constant-with-variables curriculum; (3) the multiple curriculum.

In the single curriculum all courses are constant; no provision is made for variable courses. It can best be seen in the self-contained classes of the elementary school. Except for very small high schools, some junior high schools, and private preparatory schools, few secondary schools today use the single-curriculum organization.

The Constant-with-Variables Plan. Most frequently secondary schools utilize the constant-with-variables or multiple-curriculum patterns. In the former type certain courses are required of all pupils. These subjects are constants, presumably basic to the general education of all youth in the district. In addition the pupils may select from elective variables to provide the necessary number of units for graduation and to prepare themselves for their particular goals. In this type of curriculum plan there are no tracks. Rather pupils select those courses that seem most suitable to their purposes, talents, and needs. In this way the constant-with-variables organization allows each pupil to plan his own individual curriculum.

[1] See Chapter 12.

The Multiple Curriculum Plan. In the multiple-curriculum organization different patterns of courses are set up for pupils with different goals. Examples of the curricula or "tracks" that may be found in a multiple-curriculum organization include general, vocational, technical, practical arts, business, college preparatory, special education, and fine arts. Sometimes these categories are further subdivided in accordance with the particular needs of the pupils. Boston, for example, has bookkeeping, merchandising, office practice, and stenography curricula within the business education division; Pittsburgh offers two or three tracks in the academic, general, and business curricula. Some school systems offer as many as sixteen separate curriculum tracks for their pupils.

Mobility from track to track varies according to the educational philosophy of the school's faculty, staff, and board of education. In some schools students may not elect any courses from another track. In other schools pupils are not limited in their choice of electives once they have selected the required curriculum constants.[2] Many schools use plans midway between the two extremes.

College-preparatory Curricula. Generally speaking, college-preparatory curricula are all quite similar. Usually the requirements include four years of English, two or three of social studies, two of mathematics, one or two of science, and two of foreign language—a pattern that differs only in minor details from the recommendations of the 1899 report of the Committee on College Entrance Requirements.[3] However, happenings in recent years indicate a general stiffening of these requirements as high school staffs revise their college preparatory courses and curricula to meet the requirements of the colleges.

Whether or not increasing college entrance requirements results in better college and university students is questionable. Studies such as the famous Eight-Year Study sponsored by The Progressive Education Association[4] show little correlation between specific patterns of subjects taken in high school and academic success in college. In the Eight-Year Study it was found that students from experimental programs differing from the conventional academic college-preparatory curricula did as well academically as their matchees from conventional schools. In fact, in some of the academic areas, the differences were somewhat in favor of

[2] A constant is a course required of all pupils for graduation. When multiple tracks are used the term *constant* does not cover the situation. A pupil must take the courses required in his tracks, but these are not required of all pupils in the school. Subjects required of pupils following a particular curriculum pattern are called curriculum constants. Subjects not required for graduation are called variables.

[3] Arthur E. Traxler and Agatha Townsend, *Improving Transition from School to College*, A Study of Admissions by the Committee on School and College Relations of the Educational Research Bureau (New York: Harper and Row, Inc., 1953), p. 66.

[4] Dean Chamberlin, Enid Chamberlin, Neal E. Drought, and William C. Scott, *Did They Succeed in College?* (New York: Harper and Row, Inc., 1942).

the graduates of nontraditional programs. But more important than the accumulation of facts was a slight superiority of graduates of nontraditional programs in work habits, intellectual curiosity, and ability to weigh evidence. Morever, the study indicated that graduates from schools considered to be very experimental seemed to do better college work than graduates from less experimental schools.

> . . . graduates from the most experimental schools are characterized not only by consistently higher academic averages and more academic honors, but also by a clear superiority in the intellectual intangibles of curiosity and drive, willingness and ability to think logically and objectively, and an active and vital interest in the world about them. . . . The students from the least experimental schools are, on the other hand, seldom indistinguishable from their matchees.[5]

Again it seems that it is not so much the content that matters as the attitudes, habits, and skills that are engendered by the methods used in teaching it.

General Curriculum. The general curriculum is a pattern of courses that is not designed to lead the pupil to college or to any particular vocation. As a rule it consists of a minimum number of required courses, plus a relatively large choice of electives. The electives may be either free electives or limited electives or a combination of the two.

A general curriculum program might be as follows (this is not typical, but just illustrative):

Language Arts–English	3–4 units
(Literature, Speech, Drama, Journalism)	
Social Studies	2–3 units
Mathematics	1 unit
Science	1 unit
Electives	9–13 units

In theory, the general curriculum is sound. Its limited number of specific requirements lets the pupil select under guidance those courses that seemingly are most likely to fulfill his needs. Some critics object to its flexibility and lack of specific requirements on the ground that they may lead to pupils' electing only "nonsolid" subjects. That this danger does exist is of course quite true, but good guidance programs can minimize it. There is no reason why a general curriculum should not be fully as "intellectual" as any other curriculum. In truth, the general curriculum could be the most effective route to a truly "liberal" education. Through it the pupils can become thinking individuals with more than a passing knowledge of art, music, literature, and the sciences.

Other Curricula. Other curricula, such as practical arts, business, and special education, usually are based on the same set of required subjects

---

[5] *Ibid.*, pp. 173–174.

given for the general curriculum, plus additional requirements suitable to the particular area of emphasis. Examples of business and practical arts curricula are described in earlier chapters. Special education curricula, for example, curricula for the mentally and physically handicapped, low achievers, and emotionally disturbed children, should differ from other curricula only in that emphasis on selecting materials and methods appropriate to the needs of the pupils is absolutely essential. In all curricula teachers should provide adequately for individual differences; in special education curricula they *must!*

PROBLEMS OF ORGANIZATION

Most problems of school curriculum organization stem from the conflicting needs to provide learnings common to all pupils and at the same time to adequately allow for their individual differences. Curriculum workers attempt to meet the first need by providing constant courses, and the second by elective courses, curriculum tracks, ability grouping plans, and similar devices.

THE CONSTANT COURSES

The constants are supposed to ensure that high school graduates acquire basic understandings in the subject matter areas. In the seventh and eighth grades most of the courses offered are constants. In the upper grades courses are much more likely to be specialized.

At the moment the trend seems to be to add more constants to the curriculum. In fact, if all the current demands for constant courses are met, little time will be left for electives in the curriculum.

Several dangers seem to be inherent in constant courses. Unless articulation is very good, constant courses may foster repetition and consequently waste pupils' time. In history, for instance, the Revolutionary War is covered many times, with resulting boredom.

Obviously, if the instruction were good, curriculum makers would have no need to worry about repetition, for pupils in constant courses would be studying different material according to their needs. Regretfully one must admit that the evidence indicates that contemporary secondary-school courses tend to be too inflexible to allow much differentiation within them. If the typical secondary-school teachers' methodology continues as it is now, the curriculum probably should include fewer constants so that pupils may be guided into courses commensurate with their needs, abilities, educational attainment, and goals.

ACHIEVING FLEXIBILITY

In the majority of cases, American educators have relied mainly on the elective system to meet the individual needs of their pupils. Yet no matter how many electives are offered, the needs of individual pupils can be met only in part through the elective system. If the pupil's time is to be well utilized, the teacher must organize each course so that there is an optimum opportunity for new learning for each pupil.

Tracks and Streams. As we have seen earlier, many schools have divided their curricula into tracks to help gain curriculum flexibility. By providing a different pattern of courses from other tracks, each track gives individuals both alternative courses from which to choose and a basic pattern to follow toward a specific goal. Because of the latter feature, multiple curricula programs have considerable guidance value. In using them, however, a few simple precautions seem to be necessary.

1. Care must be taken to avoid creating a caste system. Tracks must not be allowed to become marks of social or academic hierarchy; to do so would result in driving pupils into curricula in which they did not belong as well as branding pupils in certain curricula as inferior. One way to avoid this problem is to call all curricula college preparatory and to provide ways for pupils to meet entrance requirements in all tracks by requiring a basic pattern of constants common to all tracks.

2. A pupil should be allowed to take any course he wishes (free elective for him) as long as he meets the prerequisite for the course and takes the required courses necessary in his curriculum track. In practice this statement means that pupils enrolled in college-preparatory curricula should be allowed to take courses like typing or business practice as free electives, if it seems desirable.

3. The program of studies should include enough tracks to meet the present and future needs of all the pupils no matter what their life goals may be.

Ability Grouping. The majority of city schools use some form or other of ability or homogeneous grouping. The more than 30 plans in use include plans based on such factors as intelligence quotient, mental age, chronological age, interest, achievement scores, teacher grades, ungraded groups, track plans, sociometric grouping, social maturity grouping, and combinations thereof.

Grouping is nothing new—it has been used throughout this country for more than 100 years. Yet teachers and other educators are of diverse opinions about the value to the learner of any kind of grouping. The most common advantages and disadvantages attributed to grouping by its opponents and proponents seem to be:

Disadvantages:

1. It is undemocratic.
2. Any kind of grouping by one trait ignores the wide distribution of various traits and abilities within the same group.

3. Actual achievement does not always correlate with the capacity to comprehend.
4. Poor attitudes result, with some students developing inferiority and superiority complexes.
5. If the grouping is made on the basis of mental age, the range on the categories of the test for the same mental age will mean that true homogeneity has not even been made with the mental age itself.
6. No materials are available for different levels in various subjects.
7. Because studies do not support the advantages of grouping, it is more trouble than it is worth.

Advantages:

1. It is democratic to have students competing with their own kind.
2. Present-day intelligence tests have been so refined that the results may serve as a basis for behavior for the whole individual. Therefore intelligence test scores are a valid grouping means.
3. The range of personality traits is reduced through grouping.
4. More wholesome attitudes can be developed through grouping.
5. Better learning results are possible for both the slow and fast learners.
6. Methods of teaching that are most suitable for slow, fast, and average groups can be used best when pupils are grouped.
7. Acceleration of the able student is facilitated.

The controversy about grouping rages intensely enough in some areas to cause disastrous splits between various camps of teachers, administrators, and parents. Unfortunately, objective data by which to solve the disagreement are meager and contradictory. Research in the area has proved inconclusive. Moreover, in practice, grouping has not been accompanied by the changes in methodology and curriculum organization upon which the theory behind ability and homogeneous grouping is predicated.

Restrictions Causing Rigidity. Much of the rigidity in current secondary-school curricula comes from artificial restrictions placed on the curriculum. One of the most common of these is to limit the number of units a pupil may take during a year. Many schools limit the student to four so-called "solid subjects," a solid being a course that meets five days a week and requires preparation for classwork. The purpose of this annual limitation is to protect pupils from possible overloading. Nonetheless, there seems to be no reason why, under guidance, some youths should not be allowed to undertake a heavier load, whereas other pupils should limit themselves to fewer units. One should match the curriculum to the pupils. Artificial barriers, such as unit limitations, may hinder learning instead of promoting it.

Another frequent restriction compels pupils to take six years to complete grades 7–12. This restriction has been discussed somewhat in the preceding chapter. At this point it will suffice to point out that many pupils who have completed secondary school and entered college early have turned out very well. Perhaps a more permissive plan would be in order.

Another area in which permissiveness may be of advantage concerns systems that forbid pupils to take courses above or below their grade level. Many schools do not permit freshmen or sophomores to take junior or senior courses or for junior high school pupils to take senior high school courses, and vice versa. Wherever possible, it would seem desirable to avoid such restrictions. A fundamental principle of curriculum organization should be to make it possible for any pupil to take any course that he needs for his intellectual development when he needs it. The basis for selection should be need and ability rather than grade level. Unnecessary restrictions may make the administration problem simpler, but they interfere with this basic curricular goal.

EVALUATING THE CURRICULUM

The foregoing discussion should have convinced the reader that there is room for improvement in most secondary-school curricula. To keep secondary-school curricula current and valid in today's world of change requires continual review, reexamination, and reevaluation. From time to time each curriculum should be evaluated by an outside agency, such as the state department of education or a regional accrediting agency. Such evaluation may be salutary, but to be of most value, curriculum evaluation should be self-evaluation by the teachers and administrators most concerned in view of the stated goals and philosophy of the school. The goals themselves should also be reviewed from time to time in relation to the needs of both the local and larger society, the nature of the learners and learning, and the stated goals subscribed to by the teaching profession at large.

Evaluation of the secondary-school curriculum should be interpreted in the fullest sense of the meaning of the word evaluation. To evaluate the curriculum, then, it is necessary both to measure the development or status and also to determine the worth or value of the growth or status. For the qualitative measurements various psychometric devices may be used. To determine their value requires the use of judgment and standards. Therefore two basic ingredients are necessary in the evaluating of any educational program:

1. A statement of goals, purposes, or objectives.
2. A quantitative and qualitative determination of the social, physical, emotional, spiritual, and mental growth of the pupils.

EDUCATIONAL GOALS

Any criteria to be applied to an educational program or to the graduates of the program should be evolved and applied with reference to the intent of the program in the first place. Pedagogically speaking, this intent is more properly labeled objectives, goals, aims, or purposes. What these purposes should be, at least as far as the authors of this book are concerned, has been explained in Chapter 6, "The Role of the Secondary School." Further comment on them here would be superfluous except to note that in spite of widely different standards held by educators and laymen, educational purposes themselves are subject to evaluation in accordance with such broad principles as those set forth by representative educational groups in California.[6]

1. The American public school has many purposes.
2. The public school program must be developed to meet the needs of *all* children and youth.
3. There is no single standard of achievement which can be applied to *all* children in the public schools.
4. The *way* children learn is important as well as *what* they learn.
5. Education, as other fields, requires specific expertness.

The important point for us to remember here, however, is that one should evaluate the curriculum in relationship to the goals set for that curriculum. That this should be so seems obvious, yet many evaluators ignore the fact that any judge of a product must first have in mind the quality and/or quantity of products that one intended to produce. Thus if a breeder of chickens, for instance, has as his objective merely to produce a large number of chickens, then to see whether or not the breeding program is effective and efficient is merely a matter of counting. However, if his objective is to produce white hens that lay double-yolk eggs with white shells, the success of his program takes on an entirely different complexion.

Similarly in American education, if the goal is to stimulate quality of intellectual development, the evaluation cannot be measured by the number of isolated facts the pupils have learned in the program.

COMPONENTS OF QUANTITATIVE EVALUATION

To be valid any quantitative evaluation must have several component parts: (1) A means of assessing the outward behavioral change in the student; (2) a method of determining inner behavioral change; (3) a process for determining environmental and personal factors that influence, either detrimentally or beneficially, any behavioral change.

[6] Arthur H. Rice (ed.), an editorial, "Narrow and Reactionary," *The Nation's Schools*, 67: 36, January, 1961.

Education As Behavioral Change. Unless there is a behavioral change, there is no education going on. For the purpose of evaluation we are interested in the behavior per se, but more important we are interested in the *behavioral change* that has taken place. It is not enough to say that a student can speak well and in an informed manner about contemporary events, but also "how has his performance *now* changed from his performance the previous year." If there is no continual annual pattern of *behavioral growth* in each and every student, then something is wrong, and it is the function of the evaluator to find out what it is.

It is equally important to know whether the pupil's inner behavioral development is progressing satisfactorily. In addition to their effect on scholastic achievement, for instance, the development of healthy attitudes will affect his success in life long after graduation from high school. Although ultimately, of course, the measuring of any mental process can only be approximated from the outward behavior, modern psychological techniques make it possible to estimate inner behavior with some degree of confidence.

Many environmental factors affect pupils' behavioral changes. Among them are type of neighborhood, socioeconomic status of the family, mental status of parents, church affiliation, companions, recreational activities, and home atmosphere. Before one can say that a school activity or a course of study is the sole contributor to the success of a high school graduate, one must first ascertain whether or not his experiences outside the school produced the observed results. In actuality a typical high school teacher has a pupil under his direction a relatively small portion of the time during a fiscal year. The curriculum should neither be praised nor condemned for pupil behavior caused by other environmental factors.

Similarly any change or lack of change may be the result of personal factors. The personal characteristics of the learner himself may seriously retard any desired change. Thus it may not be the fault of the curriculum content if little or no annual growth occurs. Rather failure may result from poor physical condition, mental health, previous learnings, attitudes, and inadequate skills and habits of working, studying, and thinking. Admittedly most of the above factors are not immediately apparent to a casual observer. Nevertheless, they can be assessed by use of the proper devices. It is therefore emphasized that to properly determine whether or not it is the curriculum that is influencing change, *all* factors must be considered.

Appraising Pupil Progress. Each classroom teacher has a part in the evaluation of the curriculum. Each teacher is with the pupil every day the student spends in the school. The classroom teacher then is the best person to determine the progress of individual students. There are many ways in which he can do this—considerably more than just an occasional test of one kind or another. All measures must be applied in terms of the objectives, goals, or aims of the teacher as part of the total statement of philosophy of the school.

1. Objective and Essay Classroom Tests.

Such tests enable a teacher to appraise student progress in terms of some rather specific objectives. They also enable the teacher to determine quickly and inexpensively the relative strengths and weaknesses of individuals and groups in the classroom. Although such tests may be used solely for grading purposes, classroom tests do make it possible for the teacher to gather evidence for modification of the curriculum and methods of instruction.

2. Standardized Tests.

Standardized tests help teachers and administrators to compare the performance of pupils in their particular school to that of pupils in other districts. There is some danger in the fact that overuse of standardized tests will result in the all-important test being the determiner of the curriculum.

3. Checklists, Rating Scales, Inventories, and Questionnaires.

Tests can only provide a small part of the total information needed to assess adequately the performance of an individual. In addition one needs instruments that can elicit knowledge of a pupil's personal social behavior, performance of various skills, quality of work being done, interests, ideals, habits, and health. Such information can be gathered largely through the use of rating scales, inventories, and questionnaires.

4. Observation, Anecdotal Records, and Interviews.

For an act of "seeing" to be "observation" it must involve the following characteristics on the part of the observer: it must be done with a purpose in mind; it must be specific; it must involve perception; it must involve recording of what was seen; and it must supplement what is recorded by other measures of gathering information. Recording is probably best done in the form of anecdotal records or short statements for the pupils' permanent file. The informal interview can be used very effectively by the teacher, often to provide information that is impossible to gather in any other way. By using an interview, a teacher can check on the accuracy and validity of previously recorded data and also observe a pupil in a controlled situation for clues to the presence of disabilities, conflicts, frustrations, fears, hates, abnormalities, and prejudices.

5. Sociometrics, Sociodrama, Autobiography, and Other Similar Techniques.

The science of sociometry can be used to determine the structure of the class; it is also a very effective means of discovering the friendship patterns within the group. Like other measures, it should not be used alone. Sociodrama is a projective technique that enables the teacher to gather information about a pupil's home, family relationships, his beliefs, ideals, attitudes, and prejudices. The autobiography also provides a means of obtaining insight into the same areas listed above.

6. Case Studies and Case Conferences.

Although the formal case study is very time-consuming, the informal case study can be done as part of the regular teaching activities. If all the measures of evaluation are used, a teacher will have an informal case study, provided he does four things: (1) interprets the facts in terms of the pupil's over-all development; (2) summarizes and draws conclusions about which experiences provided the most learning for the pupil; (3) provides such experiences; (4) evaluates such experiences by using the data gathering measures. The case conference is used in many schools, although it is not always called by that name. Essentially a case conference is a meeting of all persons concerned with a pupil for the purpose of arriving at a course of action for improving the pupil's progress.

7. Miscellaneous Measures.

Miscellaneous measures include recordings (before and after), photographs, diaries, and logs kept by the pupils themselves.

Other Sources of Data. Other sources of data include these:

1. Opinion Polls.

The opinions of graduates, employers, colleges, or governmental officials are a good source of information, but their use is accompanied by several dangers: the returns may not be a true sample; responses may be on the basis of emotion instead of rational thinking; the thing being polled may have changed since the individual had the experience; the response of the person being polled may not be a true one. Consequently one should use results of polls carefully and only in conjunction with other measures of evaluation.

2. Interviews of Employers.

Because the employer is the one who has to be satisfied as to whether or not a person is vocationally efficient, he is the logical one to contact to determine the success of a vocational program. Through the use of employer interviews evaluators can gain insight into the performance of graduates on their jobs. Thus they can ascertain which of the traits are the result of the curriculum of the school.

3. Postgraduate Success.

In general, we judge the postsecondary academic success of our high school graduates by viewing their grades in the postsecondary institutions. To do so one may use either the grades themselves or the grade-point average. The use of grades is illustrated by a study comparing freshman grades of students in regular colleges, universities, business schools, and nursing schools with the grades the students received during their senior year in the same subject[7] as a basis for curriculum change. Robert Hill,

---

[7] Michael Morry, "The Importance of Curriculum Developments of Making Follow-Up Studies of Students in College," *The Bulletin of the National Association of Secondary-School Principals,* 44: 126–134, February, 1960.

on the other hand,[8] used the grade-point average of college freshmen to compare the scholastic achievements of parochial school graduates with those of the graduates of public high schools.

4. *Armed Forces.*

The rejection or acceptance of men and women by the armed forces is a subject in itself. Certainly a follow-up study of a school's graduates in the armed forces would give valuable information about the degree of attainment of objectives of the school in a military setting.

5. *Vital Statistics.*

The number of divorces, murders, mental patients, and so forth, among graduates would also give information about the success or failure of a school's program. Because the public schools are instruments of society to preserve itself, any evidence of societal breakdown should be of concern to educators.

Evaluating the Educational Program. In the opinion of the authors, one of the best means of evaluating a given program, plant, and school administration is the *Evaluative Criteria,*[9] which was first printed in 1940 by the Cooperative Study of Secondary-School Standards. The criteria were revised in 1950 and again in 1960. Ordinarily application of the *Evaluative Criteria* involves first a self-evaluation on the part of the staff of the school, followed by a visiting committee composed of principals, teachers, superintendents, and college professors who check the self-evaluation of the staff. Whether or not the evaluation is of any value depends upon the courage, integrity, and knowledge of the visiting committee and the school staff. If the *Evaluative Criteria* are truthfully applied and the staff and visiting committee go about their tasks with honor and diligence, then the *Evaluative Criteria* is a very fine means of determining the quality and quantity of the school's program. A side benefit is that after seeing a fine program the principals and superintendents tend to go to their own schools and improve their educational programs.

However, the instrument used is not so important as that the evaluation be thorough and honest, and that those best informed and most concerned, that is, the teachers themselves, have a major share in planning and carrying out the evaluation. In any case, the evaluation should concern itself with such considerations as the following criteria assembled by Harold Alberty.[10]

A. Does the curriculum make adequate provisions for all youth regardless of intelligence level, interests, race, creed, or socioeconomic background?

[8] Robert E. Hill, Jr., "Scholastic Success of College Freshmen from Parochial and Public Secondary Schools," *School Review,* 69: 60–66, Winter, 1962.

[9] National Study of Secondary-School Evaluation, *Evaluative Criteria* (Washington, D.C.: National Study of Secondary-School Evaluation, 1960).

[10] Harold B. Alberty and Elsie J. Alberty, *Reorganizing the High School Curriculum,* 3rd ed. (New York: The Macmillan Company, 1962), pp. 469–473.

B. Has our school developed and implemented a basic philosophy of education that rests squarely upon democratic values?

C. Is the curriculum based upon a dynamic conception of the learner and the learning process?

D. Is the curriculum based upon the immediate and predicated needs, problems, and interests of the learner?

E. Does the curriculum provide effectively for learning through direct firsthand experience in the school and the wider community?

F. Does the curriculum provide an effective program of general education, designed to develop the ideals, attitudes, understandings, and skills needed by all citizens in our democracy?

G. Does our school make effective provisions for all of the non-vocational and vocational special interests of the students?

H. Does our school utilize a modern plan of unit teaching and learning?

I. Does our school provide effectively for democratic student participation in the classroom?

J. Do classroom teachers carry on effective programs of group and individual guidance through the day-to-day learning activities of the classroom?

K. Does our school have a definite, well-understood policy toward including controversial issues in the curriculum, and are such issues consistently taught?

L. Has our school developed and made available adequate resource units, files, or guides to aid teachers in the cooperative planning of learning activities?

M. Does our school provide adequately for audio-visual materials as a regular part of classroom instruction?

N. Is the curriculum of our school evaluated in terms of the values of democratic living and the goals expressed in the statement of philosophy?

O. Does our school engage in a systematic, continuous, and democratically organized program of curriculum improvement?

EVALUATING THE PROCESS OF CURRICULUM EVALUATION

During the past decade or two there have been many curriculum innovations. Changes have been incorporated because somebody was of the opinion that the new practice was better than the old. Conversely changes have been opposed because someone believed that the old way was better than the new. Unfortunately, little evaluation, if any, accompanied some changes, and often changes were made simply for the sake of change or sometimes for publicity. Yet it seems self-evident that unless a practice or a bit of subject matter content has been properly assessed, one does not really know whether to adopt it or continue it or discard it. It follows, then, that each school system needs good evaluation procedures and that these procedures should be reviewed from time to time. The following criteria are recommended for use in evaluating the evaluating process itself.

I. Evaluation is a continuous process.

Curriculum change is an ongoing activity. If school personnel and school boards are to know what they are doing, it is absolutely essential that present, past, and future practices be rated. When a change is proposed, evaluation of the change should be an integral part of the proposal.

II. Sound research procedures are followed.

Although not all evaluation will be research, when it is, the research design should meet acceptable standards. Needless to say, the results of the research should be interpreted in an honest manner.

III. Evaluation should always accompany curriculum planning and organization.

It is not enough to change over to BSCS biology, or to PSSC physics, or team teaching, or programed instruction, for instance, and then rest upon one's laurels. It is necessary to determine whether or not the new course is meeting the needs of the individual pupils according to the philosophy of the school district.

IV. The evaluation process must be consistent with the goals, aims, or objectives of the school system, the state, and the nation as far as public education is concerned.

V. One person should have the responsibility for initiating, maintaining, and reviewing evaluative procedures.

Because one person has the responsibilities mentioned above, this does not mean that evaluation is to be a one-man show. On the contrary, many will be involved. Still, if evaluation is to be done, somebody has to be responsible. It therefore should be directed by a curriculum specialist, preferably an educationist, who has a broad background and who can objectively consider all proposals. It should probably be somebody with broad interests and study in many disciplines. Subject matter specialists are liable to be unsuitable because they tend to see the curriculum from the narrow point of view of their own interest or discipline.

VI. Committee assignments should be used only where necessary.

VII. Participants in the evaluation should be utilized in their own areas of competency.

People outside the school staff may be utilized. There is no objection to this procedure; however, leaders and others in the community should not be consulted about curricular matters of which they are ignorant. There has been too much pooling of ignorance just to say that everybody has been involved and that the procedure followed is democratic. It is anything but—the essence of democracy is that decisions are made by an informed citizenry.

VIII. The evaluators must make every effort to obtain all the pertinent information and materials, and administrators should make all information and materials available to the evaluators.

IX. Evaluation of the school's program should use the depth approach, for example, the units, outlines, tests, lecture notes, lesson plans, syllabi, and other records of teacher organization of the material should be part of an evaluative study of the content of a particular subject being taught.

X. Dissemination of information about the evaluation should be on a regular basis.

Because the evaluation is continuous, the faculty, administrators, and board of education should be informed of the progress and findings as they occur.

XI. Evaluation should be organized.

Through cooperative planning the director or other person responsible for the evaluation needs to develop a definite plan of action for evaluation. Each person needs to know his part in the over-all operation.

XII. Individuals and groups taking part in the evaluation should be encouraged and aided in participating to the full extent of their abilities. Anything or anyone inhibiting free expression probably should be eliminated or changed.

ORGANIZING FOR CHANGE

ROLES IN CURRICULUM DEVELOPMENT

The final responsibility and authority for curriculum development rests on the people through its official agent, the board of education. However, the wise school board does not presume to shape the curriculum nor to select textbooks or other materials of instruction. Rather, like any other effective group of trustees or board of directors, it limits itself to setting general policy and overseeing the professional personnel it has hired to implement its decisions. Any board, and there are many, that attempts to determine content and sequence of courses and select materials of instruction will not be well served, nor will it serve its community well.

The Role of the Public. The lay public's responsibility for curriculum development is also one of general policy formation and advisement of the board of education and its professional employees. Even though many school systems and schools maintain lay advisory committees, lay persons should leave the carrying out of their wishes to the professional staff members who, if competent, should be much better able to carry out the wishes of the people than the people themselves.

In spite of this *caveat,* lay participation in curriculum development can be justified from a very practical standpoint. First of all, the people of any community control the financing of public education, and public support based on public understanding is indispensable to the adequate financing of education. Second, wide public understanding, support, and acceptance of curricular practices are absolutely essential if the demands of pressure groups on both local and national levels are to be adequately dealt with. Inadequate evaluation of education, unjustified criticisms of education, and the demands of groups with vested interests can be adequately dealt with only if the educational leadership has developed public interest, understanding, and support of the curriculum program by sharing with the lay public the responsibility for policy decisions in curriculum development.

Role of Central Office Staff Personnel. As chief executive officer of the board of education, the superintendent of schools is charged with the implementation of curriculum development throughout the school system in accordance with the directives of the board of education. Usually the superintendent carries out this mission by creating a suitable staff organization for curriculum development and by delegating the actual curriculum development to subordinate officials. Chief among these are the curriculum directors, supervisors, and building principals.

Ordinarily the role of the supervisors, curriculum directors, and other central office personnel is to coordinate, consult, advise, and to provide materials for the teachers and principals. In some systems they give over-all leadership, but more often they are resource persons. The bulk of the actual leadership in curriculum revision usually falls on the principals. In small systems, of course, the superintendent may have to assume the functions of supervisor, curriculum director, and principal himself.

The Principal as Status Leader. Ordinarily the principal of the school is the active status leader in the field of curriculum development. He provides opportunity for teachers, parents, and students to plan together. He assists those involved in planning to identify problems and to find ways in which these problems can be solved. He facilitates work by providing time for planning and by making resources available. Most important of all, he provides the democratic leadership needed to help the teachers discover, diagnose, and solve curriculum problems.

If one examines leadership practices, he will find three general methods: the autocratic to the right, the democratic at midpoint, and laissez-faire or free rein to the left.

At times the leader must adopt and use the autocratic method, but if he veers too far to the right, he sets up a dictatorship. Often periods of organization and reorganization provide instances when autocratic methods are useful, as, for instance, certain basic decision making is needed to determine points of departure and to give security to the group. There are also times when the laissez-faire method of leadership is best. When groups have set goals, decided on ways of working, collected resource materials, and established good rapport, leadership as such does not have to be evident. If, however, the leader uses only this method, a chaotic situation results. For most activities, however, the group can and should operate at midpoint on the scale—in the democratic fashion. As status leader, the school principal must adopt leadership methods best suited to the occasion and his personnel.

The following guideposts show how good human relationships in group action to improve curriculum can be produced by the secondary-school principal:

1. Democratic leadership is most effective when it faces creative talents of all group members.
2. Leadership is most effective when shared among the group.
3. Leadership is best which establishes good rapport among group members.
4. Adequate leadership provides security for the group as well as for the individual members.
5. Good leadership helps to define specific goals within the larger framework of general goals.

Role of the Teacher. In the final analysis, the curriculum is determined by the teachers in the classroom. Because of this fact and because no one knows more about teaching specific subjects than the teachers themselves, most curriculum authorities hold that the bulk of the formal curriculum revision should be in the hands of the teachers. Consequently, as a rule, it is the teacher who forms the heart of curriculum development committees, who finds and develops curriculum materials, who builds curriculum guides, and who introduces and tries out innovations in the classroom. If the principal provides the leadership, the teacher provides the work.

The Pupils and Curricular Development. Pupils also participate in curriculum improvement projects and curriculum development. Normally this participation consists solely of pupil–teacher planning activities in the various courses. In some schools, however, the pupils actually participate directly in evaluating the program and supplying information about pupil and community needs and resources available. In this context the pupils act as consultants and lay advisors; it would seem difficult to find more qualified resource persons than the pupils.

STRATEGY FOR CURRICULUM CHANGE

Curriculum change may take place on four levels: first, the level of the individual teacher in the classroom; second, the school unit; third, the school system; and fourth, external agencies, such as state agencies, legislature, accrediting associations, curriculum-study groups (for example, PSSC), professional associations, and pressure groups. The first three of these actually build the curriculum in the schools; the fourth usually provides materials and exerts pressures upon school systems to provide the type of curricular experiences they desire.[11] In general, however, authorities seem to agree that the key unit in curriculum building is the individual school and that in typical schools a broken front rather than solid front attack on curricular problems is most advantageous. In general, then, most curriculum advances develop by individual teachers, or groups or departments, in a single school attacking problems that seem to be of particular importance to them.

System-wide Organization. Nevertheless, in order to avoid unnecessary duplication and to coordinate efforts and avoid waste of time and money, school systems find it necessary to set up some kind of system-wide organization for curriculum revision. Although no particular plan holds for every school district, the following description of the organization for curriculum development in Denver is representative of excellent practice.[12]

Although charged by law with the responsibility for all curriculum matters, the Denver Board of Education in fact limits itself primarily to broad policy matters and delegates the mechanics of curriculum development to the professional staff. For this purpose the board maintains a large and capable central office staff. Nevertheless, the building principal is the key person in curriculum matters and is responsible for all curriculum matters in his building.

Coordinating the Schools. In order to provide for coordination, central coordinating committees are provided at the elementary, junior high school, and senior high school levels and an over-all Executive Board of the Instruction Committee, which "authorizes committees' appointments, defines their responsibilities, and recommends dismissal when committees have completed their tasks." In addition to these committees there are curriculum committees consisting of classroom teachers elected by their departments in the high school or junior high school faculty who report to the Instruction Committee and their Executive Board. The principal concern of the curriculum committee consists of instructional matters, such as recommending textbooks and other materials and exchanging information on promising methods that have been developed in the various schools.

Other committees are formed upon authorization by the Executive Board by the central office for the primary purpose of curriculum building. These committees usually consist of teachers and administrators at

---

[11] J. Galen Saylor and William M. Alexander, *Curriculum Planning* (New York: Holt, Rinehart and Winston, 1960), pp. 538–539.

[12] The description is taken from Lloid B. Jones, "Curriculum Development in the Public Schools," in A. Harry Passow, *Improving the Quality of Public School Programs* (New York: Bureau of Publications, Teachers College, Columbia University, 1960), pp. 190–216. Mr. Jones was Director of Department of General Curriculum Services, Denver Public Schools, at the time of writing.

FIGURE 11. ORGANIZATION OF THE SCHOOL SYSTEM FOR CURRICULUM IMPROVEMENT

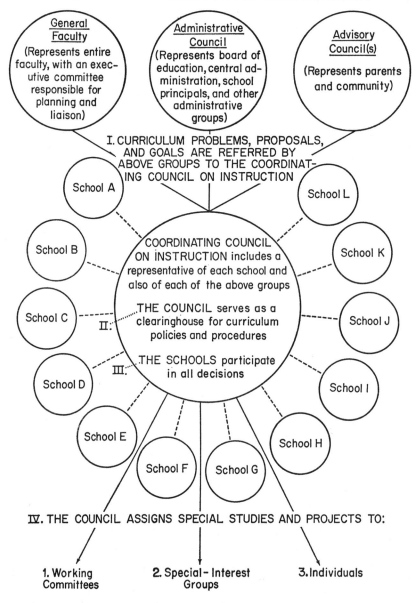

all levels from K through 12, except in cases in which the subject to be considered is offered only in the secondary school. Examples of curriculum committees are the K–12 committees or the English Program and the K–12 Study Committee for the Gifted.

In addition the district is divided into areas that consist of all the junior high schools and elementary schools that feed into a particular senior high school. To coordinate the work in each area there is an area council consisting of all the principals in the area. These councils are concerned primarily with such tasks as putting instructional programs into action, working with the lay citizens, gathering information concerning population and building needs, and budgeting matters.

In general, then, it can be seen that although the principals are the key people in the Denver program, all personnel are represented through a system-wide council or steering committee that seeks to coordinate efforts and various committees that work at specific tasks either on a building or system-wide basis. In general, this plan approximates common practice in many school systems. Saylor and Alexander have created an excellent diagram (Figure 11) to illustrate this type of organization for curriculum improvement. Each school system that actively tries to improve its curriculum must develop its own specific apparatus, but in general, school systems settle on an organization of the type illustrated.[13]

BUILDING RESOURCE UNITS AND CURRICULUM GUIDES

Implementation of curriculum change and improvement usually moves from the planning group to the classroom by means of curriculum guides, courses of study, resource units, and other curriculum bulletins and directives. Sometimes these documents are prepared by central office personnel, individual teachers, the state department of education, or commercial or philanthropic organizations. But the most useful ones are the ones prepared by groups of teachers who are teaching the courses concerned, for they know the problems and possibilities in their courses first hand. Besides, teachers who have had a share in the preparation of materials tend to be more willing to grow with the materials than are teachers who feel that the units and guides are imposed on them from above.

Curriculum Guides. Among the most useful tools for curriculum development one can furnish a teacher is the curriculum guide. In addition to providing the classroom teachers with suggested outlines for their courses, the curriculum guides should also contain information concerning resources, materials, methods, evaluating devices, and the like. To be most satisfactory, these guides should be suggestive rather than prescriptive. They are not supposed to be crutches for faltering incompetents, but rather vaulting poles for adventurous professionals. The scope of a good curriculum guide is well illustrated by the table of contents of the Martinsville, Virginia, Eighth Grade Science Guide,[14] which includes:

[13] Saylor and Alexander, *op. cit.*, p. 558.
[14] *Eighth Grade Science Guide*, Martinsville, Virginia, 1960.

Philosophy
General Science Purposes
Scope and Sequence
Prerequisites for Use of Multiple Texts
How To Use Teaching Materials
Evaluation
Using the Content Areas
Introducing General Science
Earth-Astronomy Units
Biology Units
Chemistry Units
Physics Units

The Resource Unit. More and more the resource unit is becoming a major tool in curriculum development. It performs the task of giving the classroom teacher aid, support, and inspiration, while at the same time encouraging him to freely develop his own approaches.

Each resource unit is a repository of information and ideas suitable for use in teaching a particular topic. Perhaps they should be more suitably called source units, for they are literally the source of teaching units and lesson plans actually used by the teachers in the classroom.

Although resource units may be written for use in particular courses, they are seldom designed for any particular group. Rather they present a collection of ideas and materials that any teacher might turn to for guidance and information. Frequently their contents would be equally helpful to teachers of different grade levels and courses. The contents of a typical resource unit might include such things as:

An overview
Suggested terminal learning products
Suggested learning activities
Important content
Bibliography for teachers
Bibliography for pupils
Audio-visual aids available
Sources of information and materials

Good resource units can do much for curriculum improvement. By bringing to the classroom in a compact form ideas for teaching—objectives, materials, and techniques—they can free the teacher from much gruelling hack work and give him the time and resources for teaching creatively.

RESEARCH, ACTION RESEARCH, AND EXPERIMENTATION

As far as possible classroom instruction should be based on the findings of sound research. Unfortunately, sound research in curriculum matters is hard to find, and perhaps always will be. Therefore much of the time, curriculum innovation must be based on empirical evidence and classroom experimentation that does not meet the rigid requirements of formal research. Sometimes this experimentation is action research, and at other times it is simply the trial-and-error method.

The truth of the matter seems to be that if we want to determine whether a curriculum procedure is good in a situation, the only way we can find out is to try it once, or more than once, and then evaluate the results as carefully as we can. Such experimentation is more valuable when it is controlled. However, if attempts to control the experimental situations begin to violate the normal classroom atmosphere, the findings may be more erroneous than they would have been without any controls at all. For this reason, in the long run most important educational advances have been made by applying the problem-solving approach to specific curriculum problems—not by formal educational research. It is the teachers who experiment in their classes who make the changes that really count. They should be encouraged to do so, for without this experimentation, curricula and courses soon become dreary. To require teachers to stick closely to any given course of study or method is the surest method known of killing the curriculum.

THE CURRICULUM OF THE FUTURE

And so it is that the curriculum moves forward. What the secondary school of the future will be like is too early to say. Undoubtedly it will be different from that of today and that of the past. If it is not, curriculum workers will have failed, for neither present nor past schools have been markedly successful.

If the new secondary-school curriculum is to succeed, it must be based squarely on sound scholarship in the subject matter it attempts to teach and careful study of the sociological, psychological, and philosophical considerations involved. Still, in spite of advances in curriculum theory and increasing knowledge concerning learning and teaching, the curriculum of the future will be the result largely of cutting and trying. Already energetic educators and scholars, supported sometimes by foundations or government grants, but often on their own, have by their experimentation upset the curriculum on both national and local levels. This is as it should be. Let us hope that curriculum workers will continue to have vision enough to experiment boldly and to evaluate severely.

SUGGESTED READINGS

ALBERTY, HAROLD, and ELSIE J. ALBERTY. *Reorganizing the High-School Curriculum.* Third edition. New York: The Macmillan Company, 1962. Part IV.

Part IV gives principles and procedures for curriculum development and construction of resource units.

ALEXANDER, WILLIAM M. "Assessing Curriculum Proposals," *Teachers College Record,* 63: 286–293, January, 1962.

This article proposes that a State Curriculum Evaluation Commission be established.

——. "Cooperative Action for Curriculum Improvement," *Educational Leadership,* 16: 268–270, February, 1959.

Emphasizes the need for closer cooperation among state, regional, and local educational units in promoting curriculum development.

ASSOCIATION FOR SUPERVISION AND CURRICULUM DEVELOPMENT. *Action for Curriculum Improvement.* 1951 Yearbook. Washington, D.C.: The Association, 1951.

An excellent yearbook devoted to the problems of initiating and carrying through curriculum change.

——. *Balance in the Curriculum.* 1961 Yearbook. Washington, D.C.: The Association, 1961.

A yearbook concerned with one of the most vital phases of curriculum development. Chapter 8 deals with the role of various people and agencies in making curriculum decisions.

——. *Leadership for Improving Instruction.* 1960 Yearbook. Washington, D.C.: The Association, 1960.

A yearbook discussing the role and strategies of educational leaders and others on the educational team in upgrading educational curricula.

CASWELL, HOLLIS L. *et al. Curriculum Improvement in Public School Systems.* New York: Teachers College, Columbia University, 1950.

Chapter 5 lists criteria for evaluating curriculum programs. Several programs are described.

CONANT, JAMES B. *Slums and Suburbs.* New York: McGraw-Hill Book Company, Inc., 1961.

Discusses the educational problems arising from two contrasting socio-economic areas of modern cities.

COREY, S. M. *Action Research to Improve School Practices.* New York: Bureau of Publications, Teachers College, Columbia University, 1953.

Basic presentation of action research as a tool for curriculum development.

EDUCATIONAL POLICIES COMMISSION. *Education and the Disadvantaged American.* Washington, D.C.: The Commission, N.E.A. and A.A.S.A., 1962.

Tells who the disadvantaged are and outlines programs to meet their needs.

GWYNN, J. MINOR. *Curriculum Principles and Social Trends.* New York: The Macmillan Company, 1960.

The last part of Chapter 15 considers evaluation of the curriculum. The annotated bibliography provides excellent sources for study in the area of evaluation.

HENRY, NELSON B. (ed.). *The Measurement of Understanding.* Forty-fifth Yearbook of the National Society for the Study of Education, Part I. Chicago: University of Chicago Press, 1946.

Various contributors describe measurement in high school subjects.

JACKSON, JAMES. "How Boardmen Can Evaluate the Curriculum," *American School Board Journal,* 142: 17, February, 1961.

The article gives a principal's approach to evaluation of the curriculum.

KENNEDY, R. H. "Teacher Readiness for Curriculum Improvement," *The Bulletin of the National Association of Secondary-School Principals,* 45: 70–74, September, 1961.

Discusses the relationships between teachers and administrators in promoting curriculum improvement.

KRUG, EDWARD A. *Curriculum Planning.* Revised edition. New York: Harper and Row, Inc., 1957.

An excellent textbook on curriculum development. Chapter 10 deals with curriculum development in local schools and school systems.

LEESE, JOSEPH, KENNETH FRASURE, and MAURITZ JOHNSON. *The Teacher in Curriculum Making.* New York: Harper and Row, Inc., 1961.

The text describes the way in which teachers can adapt the curriculum to the needs of pupils while observing individual differences.

MACKENZIE, GORDON N., and STEPHEN M. COREY. *Instructional Leadership.* New York: Bureau of Publications, Columbia University, 1954.

A report of a study in curriculum development in Denver secondary schools by the Horace Mann Institute of School Experimentation.

MC NALLY, HAROLD J., *et al. Improving the Quality of Public School Programs.* New York: Bureau of Publications, Teachers College, Columbia University, 1960.

An analysis of curriculum problems, principles, and procedures followed by an appraisal of the programs in seven school systems.

MITCHUM, PAUL M. *The High School Principal and Staff Plan for Program Improvement.* New York: Bureau of Publications, Columbia University, 1958.

A sort of handbook on how a principal can organize and promote curriculum change.

NATIONAL STUDY OF SECONDARY SCHOOL EVALUATION. *Evaluative Criteria.* Washington: The Study, 1960.

An excellent list of criteria to evaluate the present program of the secondary school.

PASSOW, A. HARRY (ed.). *Curriculum Crossroads.* New York: Bureau of Publications, Columbia University, 1962.

A report of a curriculum conference. Chapter 4 deals with curriculum change; Chapter 2, with the role of the teacher in decision making.

———. *Education in Depressed Areas.* New York: Bureau of Publications, Teachers College, Columbia University, 1963.

Fifteen specialists explore the question "Have the public schools a responsibility for educating culturally disadvantaged children in depressed areas?" Primary concern is given to problems of urban areas, but the authors consider conditions of cultural deprivation of rural and small town areas.

"The Principal's Role in Improving the Curriculum," *The Bulletin of the National Association of Secondary-School Principals,* 43: 1–119, February, 1959.

This issue of the bulletin is devoted entirely to curriculum organization. Contains several examples of successful practice in curriculum revision.

PRITZKAU, PHILO T. *Dynamics of Curriculum Improvement.* Englewood Cliffs, New Jersey: Prentice-Hall, Inc., 1959.

An attempt to determine the bases for curriculum improvement and to bring about curriculum improvement by means of creating better learning experiences.

SAYLOR, J. GALEN, and WILLIAM M. ALEXANDER. *Curriculum Planning.* New York: Holt, Rinehart and Winston, Inc., 1954.

One of the best textbooks in the field. Chapter 16 having to do with organizing for cooperative participation in curriculum planning is particularly pertinent.

————. *Curriculum Planning for Better Teaching and Learning.* New York: Holt, Rinehart and Winston, Inc., 1959.

An excellent guide for those planning curriculum reorganization or curriculum improvement programs.

School Programs for the Disadvantaged. Education Research Circular Number 2, February, 1963, American Association of School Administrators and Research Divison. Washington, D.C.: National Education Association, 1963.

A compilation of descriptive elementary and secondary programs for disadvantaged pupils.

SCHWARTZ, ALFRED, *et al. Evaluating Student Progress in the Secondary School.* New York: David McKay Company, Inc., 1962.

An excellent description of the instruments used to gather information about the pupils.

SPEARS, HAROLD. *Curriculum Planning Through In-Service Programs.* Englewood Cliffs, New Jersey: Prentice-Hall, Inc., 1957.

A presentation of various techniques and plans for curriculum improvement as practiced by various school systems.

STRATEMEYER, FLORENCE B., *et al. Developing a Curriculum for Modern Living.* Second edition. New York: Bureau of Publications, Teachers College, Columbia University, 1957.

An outstanding work on curriculum development. Part IV concerns curriculum development and the use of research as a base for curriculum improvement.

TABA, HILDA. *Curriculum Development: Theory and Practice.* New York: Harcourt, Brace and World, Inc., 1962.

A helpful guide for in-service study groups.

Index